"A DELICATE AFFAIR"
ON THE WESTERN FRONT

"A DELICATE AFFAIR"
ON THE WESTERN FRONT

AMERICA LEARNS HOW
TO FIGHT A MODERN WAR IN
THE WOËVRE TRENCHES

TERRENCE J. FINNEGAN

In loving loving memory of my parents, Theodore J. and
Elizabeth M. Finnegan, and Private First Class Cyril V.
Finnegan, a medic who served at Seicheprey.

"Everything in war is linked together, is mutually interdependent,
mutually interpenetrating."

Lieutenant Colonel Ferdinand Foch, *Principles of War*

First published 2015
by Spellmount, an imprint of

The History Press
The Mill, Brimscombe Port
Stroud, Gloucestershire, GL5 2QG
www.thehistorypress.co.uk

© Terrence J. Finnegan, 2015

The right of Terrence J. Finnegan to be identified as the Author
of this work has been asserted in accordance with the
Copyright, Designs and Patents Act 1988.

British Library Cataloguing in Publication Data.
A catalogue record for this book is available from the British Library.

ISBN 978 0 7509 5232 3

Typesetting and origination by The History Press
Printed in India

Contents

PREFACE

This book took a long time to compile – a decade in fact. I became interested in the 26th Division when I acquired letters my grandfather wrote to his mother and siblings providing a brief glimpse through a rigid censor of where he was during the twenty months that he served on the line and in occupation of Germany (he was reassigned to the 32nd Division as a medic and marched into the Rhineland). Research at the National Archives was continual, examining the entire set of 26th Division files and attempting to write a modern assessment of the Yankee Division, a task that was actually successfully accomplished by Mike Shay in 2010. Working on my book *Shooting the Front* took precedence in 2003, so I delayed researching the Yankee Division until that was completed. The battle of Seicheprey became my focus as I discovered the wealth of data in the National Archives offering both American records and German war diaries – an opportunity to describe in detail how all combatants perceived the ongoing struggle; and at the same time to draw wider conclusions about the US entry into the war. After this came an effort to delve deeper into a multitude of sources that addressed AEF command and their biases. Central to the story are files from Vincennes that provide insights into French command thinking, as well as the maps and documents that the 1st Division held in preparing their operations in the Woëvre. The end result is this work – telling the story of Americans going into the front line of the Woëvre region and assuming complete responsibility for the first time to defend the terrain of another nation.

The availability of primary source data made the research intoxicating. However, the story that is told is not a blended weave – it is more like a patchwork quilt – each episode integral to understanding the battle; echoing *Maréchal* (a *lieutenant colonel* at the time he wrote the lectures) Foch's apt description of what constituted the military art: "Everything in war is linked together, is mutually interdependent, mutually interpenetrating."

The key point on the Allied map of the American sector was the village of Seicheprey. The name has caused some confusion. The *Hartford Courant* specifically addressed the issue in 1922, when it covered the ceremony to memorialise the 20 April 1918 battle, fought mainly by Connecticut soldiers of the 102nd Infantry. Mayor Edmund Ferville of Hartford, Connecticut, visited Seicheprey to dedicate the 102nd Infantry memorial fountain. "For the benefit of soldiers and of French scholars in Hartford, it may be recorded that in the conversation the pronunciation of the village was sometimes 'Sesh-pray' and sometimes 'Sesh-uh-pray.' Hartford linguists are given to calling the name 'Seesh-pray'."[1]

What made the research so captivating was access to German plans, orders, and assessments. Thanks to a post-war agreement between the **Generalstab** and the US Army, the plans were transcribed and shared so that former enemies could gain an appreciation of how forces were applied in the battle. The Headquarters American Forces in Germany at Coblenz received copies of war diaries of many German divisions. Significant to my research was the **78. Reserve-Division** War Diary from the National Archives and Records Administration (NARA) Record Group 165. Divisional Order No. 3 was the final plan for **Kirschblüte** – at a time when the Germans required intellectual acuity and flexibility to stay the course as a totally fresh American enemy arrived.

I had to rely on two basic sources for establishing consistent nomenclature. Without them the reader is faced with thousands of different titles, spellings, word orders, and meanings. French unit titles such as *armée, corps, division,* and *régiment* follow *Les Armées Françaises dans La Grande Guerre, Tome X*, published in 1923. German unit designations were acquired from ***Grosser Generalstab: Die Schlachten und Gefechte des Grossen Krieges 1914–1918***, published in 1919. As for the American Expeditionary Forces, I followed *Order of Battle of the United States Land Forces in the World War*, published in 1931. I took the liberty of straying from that source and modified the unit titles of the 26th Division by adding the letter suffix 'nd' as opposed to 'd' to the ordinal number of that division's subordinate units.

Finally, a note on the fonts. The reader will note a different font used for German ranks, units, and technical terms. This was intentional to differentiate the combatants but also to try, via the language used at that time and place, to get into their thinking. In doing this, I found the discussion to be more fascinating because when I used the actual term it just made more sense in describing the moment. Even native German speakers may find some of the terms odd or archaic; but wherever practicable, these are the actual terms used. To aid the reader, unit and technical translations and rank equivalents to the US Army are provided in the body of the text and indexes.

ACKNOWLEDGEMENTS

It is easier to write a military history account on aviation than on ground troops – airframe, unit, description of sortie, and identification of aviators provide a consistent framework for author and reader alike. Describing ground operations is more challenging because of the different perspectives when describing all echelons. It gets more complicated when you attempt to include multiple-combatant viewpoints, such as the French and German units in this book. The fact that every account has its own axe to grind and none has 360° vision, it requires meticulous files to keep everything straight. I hope the work paid off. Not only did I have a better understanding of the operations in progress, I gained a tremendous respect for the combatants involved. This was especially true in recounting the German experience – one that has not been given as much coverage over the century. I am grateful that the National Archives at College Park still holds copies of the War Diaries and libraries across the country have copies of regimental histories. This story of Seicheprey attempts to pay tribute to all the combatants. In light of the centenary commemorations underway, it is long overdue to acknowledge their commitment, courage, and legacy.

My appreciation goes to many professionals that previously helped me with *Shooting the Front* and additional, exceptional people who helped in so many ways. Over the years the following have generously and unstintingly provided advice and information: Steve Maffeo, Jim Streckfuss, Steve Suddaby, Bob Doughty, Mike Shay, Peter Bogdan, Aaron Weaver, Alan Toelle, Jim Fahey, Jim Davilla, Mike Hanlon, John Abbateillo, Tom Wallace, Steve Thornber, Ted Hamady, David Zabecki, Mitch Yokelson, Kevin Ryan, Jon Viser, Monique Duvall, Jan Milles, Andrew Woods, Carl Bobrow, Susan Lintelmann, Jim Hallas, Tim Nenninger, Yves Fohlen, Chris Chatfield, Susan Mitchem, Tony Langley, Dana Lombardy, Bob Ellis, Bob Montgomery, Dennis Showalter, and Wells Ziegra. I want to thank the professionals at SHD, Daniel Hary, Marceillen Hodier, and their fellow archivists who came through with the data that had lain untouched for decades every time I showed up at Vincennes. German contacts who helped me with research include Gerhard Wiechmann, Markus Pöhlmann, Christian Stachelbeck, Sebastian Laudan and Fred Rump.

The author at IWM Duxford, Cambridgeshire, England; an airfield with a history that dates back to the Great War.

Special thanks go to three groups of close friends. Nicholas Thiele was enthusiastic in his search for relatives of German soldiers who might have had a journal or letter recounting the experience. Thanks to Nicholas we found several regimental histories. I had the pleasure of working with Helmut Jäger and Dieter Gröschel, both acknowledged experts on First World War aviation, who tirelessly helped me finalize the correct German (though any errors that remain are mine alone) and uncovered some amazing last-minute material on aerial units in the region. My dear friends from Massachusetts, Len Kondratiuk and Jim Controvich, consistently came through with superb data, reviews, and counsel. Finally, I thank Bob Ford and Frank Carrano, two native sons of Connecticut who carried the flame for the 102nd Infantry and the Seicheprey experience and provided everything their archives held.

My appreciation beyond family comes to three people in Great Britain who were instrumental in making *A Delicate Affair* possible: Nicholas Watkis (of 'Thackers' fame), whose tenacious drive to assist in any way resulted in

The History Press committing to the work; Steve Erskine (SDR) for his never-ending support in making the substance relevant to scholars, enthusiasts, and the public at large; and finally, my editor, Shaun 'b rgds' Barrington, for his years of patience taking emails and phone calls from afar and always focusing on the end result, a book that achieves the objective of telling a story long forgotten.

Susan and Teddy continue to provide the loving atmosphere to help make the best use of my time. My dedication for *A Delicate Affair* is to the two people who gave me the most inspiration in my passion for the study of history, my parents, Theodore J. and Elizabeth M. Finnegan.

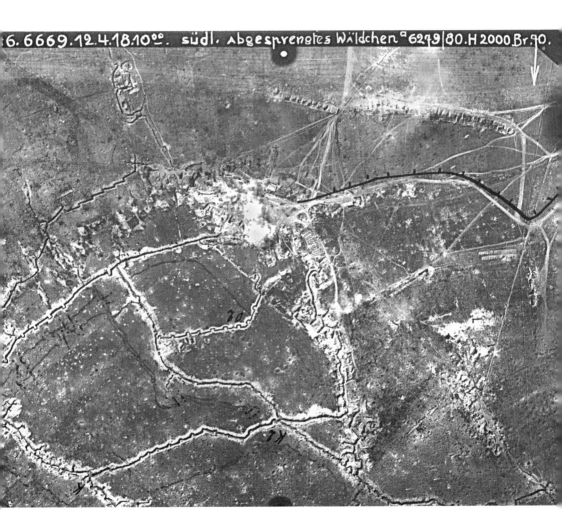

Aerial reconnaissance by *Bayerische Fliegerabteilung 46 Lichtbild* of the American trenches at the Gooseneck south of Apremont during the German *Abgesprengten Wäldchen* raid on April 12. (Bayerisches Hauptstaatsarchiv, Abt. IV Kriegsarchiv, Munich)

INTRODUCTION

When President Woodrow Wilson requested Congress to declare war on the German Empire in April 1917, the American military was experienced only in fighting guerrilla war. It now had to come to terms with global responsibilities – and was woefully unprepared. The transformation that took place in a short time after arrival in Europe demonstrated commitment to victory, but it was a goal made more difficult to achieve by bias, pettiness, and self-aggrandizement. Forgotten by most Americans in understanding their country's rise to military might in the modern era is the debt owed to the tutorial of French command; harsh lessons learned by the French in the first years of the war, when catastrophic losses saw ground lost.

A quiet sector on the Western Front was the obvious choice for the newly arriving American forces. They proceeded to the front line with the same enthusiasm as their Allies three years prior. The rush to battle rocked the foundations of the existing military art, using technology that ensured mass casualties. It was this environment that the US Army entered, independent from their close-at-hand French comrades-in-arms in their first acquaintance with positional war. Until the Saint-Mihiel offensive of September 1918, the level of conflict at the Woëvre did not involve many divisions on the line. At most, it was a clash between regimental-sized units. Americans entered the line at the Woëvre with the responsibility of defending French ground – ground that was scarred with three years of struggle, that had witnessed all of positional war's agonies. In the absence of a sustainable offensive capability, enemies settled for static destruction.

The first six chapters explore what made this conflict so challenging and in many ways horrendous for a new modern army. America's new enemy, of course, already had over three years' experience in positional war when the US Army and marines entered the line. French military tutelage governed American understanding of positional war, which included attention to sectors, prioritising operations, mastering a new generation of weapons, a decisive role for artillery (the king of battle), and making intelligence work effectively. All combatants at the front became conditioned to the hazards of attacking en masse, holding ground and counter-attacking. The cost in lives and capital was beyond imagination. What is truly astonishing is that the armies on the Western Front stayed in place and endured.

The second section describes the combatants in the Woëvre. There were three distinct military cultures – French, American and German – each with their own traditions and experience. There were also two subcultures within the newly arriving American forces – Regular and National Guard (commonly referred to at this time as militia). The 1st ("Fighting First") Division arrived in the Woëvre under the command of Major General Robert Lee Bullard. His division defined how Americans, particularly those that represented the Regular Army, went about holding ground on the Western Front. The 26th "Yankee" Division followed under the command of Major General Clarence Ransom Edwards. The 26th Division was National Guard from the north-east United States. They proudly saw themselves as in the warrior lineage that defended the first colonialists and subsequently served throughout the history of the nation. Both came for the first time in their history under a foreign command. What the early months at the Woëvre line illustrated was that American soldiers were individually tenacious but lacked a critical depth of command and the ability to liaise effectively – to communicate laterally within the military formation or with Allied counterparts. This was further exacerbated by inefficient communication with the newly established higher American Army Headquarters command and staff, known by their location at Chaumont. The headquarters had a monumental challenge in shaping a new American military with the largest divisional structure of any combatant.

The Germans saw Americans at the front as novices. They proceeded to unleash the war's most ghastly weapons – gas and high-explosive – in addition to making continual raids. The 1st Division successfully accomplished the first steps in acclimatising to the roles and responsibilities of positional war. The 26th Division expanded its area of responsibility at the front and within a week had fought two major engagements against two separate divisions. The irony was that the French commanders recognized the 26th Division's accomplishments. American military leadership only saw the mistakes.

The third part considers in detail an affair at the front that exemplified contemporary military thinking and its ability to effectively shape the battlefield. It was a learning game at the Woëvre. Thorough German planning of combined arms held Allied forces in check but gradual attrition achieved by fresh American combatants of equal fervour filling the lines meant time was running out for the Germans. Those Americans who fought at Seicheprey on 20 April 1918 were just the vanguard of the thousands who would arrive every week.

German planning for **Kirschblüte** (the codename "Cherry Blossom") thoroughly addressed combined-arms roles and missions involving a regimental force augmented by assault experts and neighbouring artillery. The combined arms involved, classified as an **Erstürmung** ("taking by assault"), successfully accomplished well-defined objectives. What made the affair even grimmer was the French practice of sacrifice positions – a procedure imposed on American military thinking by the French tactical command. Though the French did not use the term when addressing the men, for obvious reasons, preferring "principal line of resistance". What worked was the tenacity of the individual Americans, who demonstrated incredible courage, in many cases fighting to the death. This was what resonated with the German commanders. They now faced a fresh enemy with purpose. The main problem the Americans experienced was not the quality of their individual soldier. It was liaison. The Americans struggled for their entire time on the Western Front with effective organisation of liaison, culminating in the final major offensive of Meuse-Argonne. It was the hardest objective for the Americans – decision-making based on an accurate knowledge of where your men were and what they were doing. The culmination of the affair was the attempted counter-attack. It proved to be a life-changing moment for the officer in charge, one that, as we shall see, required moral courage.

The final section looks at how events in this quiet sector of the Western Front were interpreted. Deciding what was reality and shaping the public's attitude to modern war was principally done by the media. At the time of the Seicheprey affair, the British and French were locked in a desperate struggle with enormous German forces. Seicheprey was a minor piece in the Allied and German press. The American press sprang into action – a battle was fought and by all accounts (particularly from Major General Clarence Edwards – a well-known and trusted general officer) the Americans were victorious. Numbers ruled like a scorecard covering a ballgame – success was defined by casualty statistics. With the conclusion of battle came assessment: what went wrong – what went right. Pershing's command faced a conundrum. He wanted to make a change but was finding it hard to remove a commander closely associated with prior presidential offices, as well as having a strong regional following in the politically powerful north-east United States.

The term a "Delicate Affair" comes from an exchange of notes between two close friends, American military legends of the twentieth century. General John J. Pershing, commander of the US Army in the First World War, called the struggle at Seicheprey an "affair", a term liberally used by French military staffs (*l'affaire*). Prior to publication, Pershing corresponded with a select few to review and comment on his draft of *My Experiences in the World War*, one of the most significant works on America's role. One of his closest confidants in the later part of his life was General George Catlett Marshall, a monumental figure in America's military history. At the time, Lieutenant Colonel Marshall counseled Pershing not to unearth matters that would arouse strong emotions in the north-east United States. It was a "delicate" thing. His counsel was sound. Pershing's single paragraph tactfully summed up an affair that was well known by every American soldier that fought in 1918 but was left to fade away with the passage of time.

PART I

A NATIONAL BUSINESS

CHAPTER 1

The Future of France

The Woëvre region's frontier between France and Germany at the outbreak of hostilities in August 1914 became an active battleground until the Armistice four years later. Attention was drawn to the north where the advancing German armies swept through Belgium. The eventual Allied success at the First Marne was the focus. The first adversaries in the region were German cavalry from Metz entering the lowlands of the Woëvre north of the road between Pont-à-Mousson and Commercy. Small skirmishes took place between the advance units of both armies.[2] On 18 August, *Maréchal* Joseph Jacques Césaire Joffre created the *Armée de Lorraine* and placed it under the command of *Général* Maunoury. It was to be composed of reserve divisions originally assigned to the *IIIe armée*. The mission of the *Armée de Lorraine* was to cover the right flank of the *IIIe armée* against German forces from Metz.[3] The *Armée de Lorraine* held the ground from Etain (east of Verdun) to Pont-à-Mousson on the evening of 21 August.

The Woëvre region was traditionally defined by the three bishoprics (*Trois-Évêchés*) of Metz, Toul, and Verdun. When armies invaded west from central Europe they traversed the Lorraine plateau in north-east France, a succession of ridges rising out of the plains: the Argonne, the Meuse Heights, and the Moselle plateau. Continuous rolling hills covered Verdun in the north to Toul in the south. The higher lands

beckoned alluringly to the toiler in the clay lowland, and villages crowded each other along the slopes of the plateau scarp, while for the most part tiny hamlets dotted the surface of the more sparsely inhabited plain. The Woëvre's easterly edge dropped sharply, in some places precipitously, to the flat Woëvre plain, which became swamps and marshy ground starting north of Toul in the forest of La Reine. The Woëvre was an uninhabited wilderness of marsh and woodland; buttes and islands supported limited habitation.[4] The western side of the Woëvre comprised the Hauts de Meuse along the Meuse River and on the eastern side a series of buttes alongside the Moselle River. The wet clay soil restricted movements to the roads and made many unfit for travel.

Prior to 1914 French defence doctrine purposely left the Woëvre undefended – the premise was that invading German armies would be caught in a trap due to the impassability of the terrain. The French *Grand Quartier Général* (GQG) considered the Woëvre Plain impassable on account of the poor nature of its roads.[5] French doctrine accepted the necessity of a "*Bataille de la Trouée de Charmes*" (the Battle of the Charmes Gap) – an action that finally took place in September 1914 and resulted in defeat for the Germans. The *Trouée de Charmes* with Toul and Épinal as primary population centres offered a western entry into Lorraine and the means of flanking Metz-Thionville and Nancy-Massif de Haye.[6]

Along the Meuse River from Verdun to Toul the French established fortifications reminiscent of Louis XIV's Vauban network. Before the war they relied upon these hills as their main line of defence against an attack from the east.[7] The Germans had their own series of permanent fortifications from Thionville to Metz, and between the two adversaries the Woëvre plain itself was not fortified, since the prevailing strategies saw the region as defended from the adjoining ridges. The Germans planned early on to seize the heights and deny French ownership of the Woëvre. They saw ground gained in this region as isolating the fortified city of Verdun and reducing French ability to attack German territory. German artillery in place at Metz was capable of hitting French targets in the eastern Woëvre. The French army compensated for this by drawing their forces back almost to the Meuse heights. Planning on both sides did not envision a protracted war in the region. The *6e corps d'armée* defended southern Woëvre between the Verdun-Conflans line and the Saizerais plateau. An additional corps comprising two divisions, corps artillery, and the *6e brigade de cavalerie*, defended Toul to Verdun, and was held in readiness to support *20e corps d'armée* to the south and *2e corps d'armée* in the northern Woëvre. A third division, *12e division d'infanterie*, comprised a general reserve in the St. Mihiel-Commercy region.[8]

It was a traumatic time for France. Their initial battles were cataclysmic in scale and catastrophic in casualties. The ultimate horror (to date) came on 22 August 1914 when French forces to the north-west of Woëvre suffered 27,000 killed at the Ardennes and Charleroi.[9] The horrific losses prompted President Raymond Poincaré to write in his journal of 24 August 1914, "Now the future of France depends on her powers of resistance."[10]

Nine days after establishing the *Armée de Lorraine*, *Général* Joffre reorganized the forces as *VIe armée* under the command of *Général* Maunoury. German forces advanced towards the Woëvre while the Marne battle near Paris was in full fury. A principal intelligence source monitoring the German advance were radio intercepts, particularly when the German **Armeen** were given call signs that began with the same letter.[11] French aerial reconnaissance reported German units on 3 September 1914 east of the Woëvre in the region of Thézey-St-Martin and Alaincourt, approximately 50 kilometres from Toul. By the time the Battle of the Marne concluded, the Germans had advanced to just north of Thiaucourt.[12] German forces comprising the **V. Armee-Korps** and the **Armeeabteilung Strantz** were under the command of **General der Infanterie** Hermann Christian Wilhelm von Strantz. They advanced between the Maas and Mosel rivers, the area that became the Germans' southern Woëvre front for the entire war.[13]

BATTLE LINES ON THE WOËVRE

On 19 September, less than a week after the end of the Marne battles, the *VIIIe armée* advanced in the direction of Mars-la-Tour when the subordinate *8e corps d'armée* encountered **General der Infanterie** von Strantz's advanced guard – three army corps spread out on a curve 50 kilometres long. To the east, the Germans commenced an offensive on the left bank of the Moselle with Nancy and Toul as the objective. In the southern Woëvre area the **III. Bayerisch. Armeekorps** held 10 kilometres of ground north of Thiaucourt to Woel. The **V. Armeekorps** was to the Bavarians' right and **XIV. Armeekorps** to the left. Once the Bavarians commenced their operation, they simply kept on going – an advance measured in kilometres. It was a breakthrough of a sort – a rare experience in the war. Attacking the French where they least expected, the Bavarian offensive quickly achieved its objectives before the startled French could move up reinforcements to counter and regain territory. Advancing German cavalry from Metz now skirmished with French defenders in a region of small farming villages that included Seicheprey and Flirey. These villages and their surrounding woods were quickly captured. It was here in 1917 the

Executed at Flirey, *Soldat* François Fontanaud, the 17th soldier on Mesnieux's list. (*De Flirey à Apremont – Le bois de Mort-Mare*)

US Army first assumed independent responsibility for holding ground on the Western Front.

Général Joffre sent a telegram on 20 September to *Général* Dubail, commanding *Ire armée*, directing him to use *16e corps d'armée* "with a view to assailing the flank of the enemy troops which are moving to attack Hauts-de-Meuse or the Commercy gap". At the same time Joffre advised *Général* Sarrail, commanding *IIIe armée*, of the arrangements and ordered him to take measures to repulse any frontal attack the Germans might make on him. The *75e division d'infanterie* holding the Hauts-de-Meuse near Hattonchâtel was violently bombarded by German heavy artillery, and the next day fiercely attacked. *Général* Grand d'Esnon, *75e division d'infanterie reserve* commander, was killed at Vigneulles.[14] The defence of the two geographically strategic points gave way and German forces took possession of Hattonchâtel and Creue.[15] The French *75e division d'infanterie* simply disappeared, becoming one of the few French divisions never reconstituted after the fighting. The annihilation of this division meant that the French were unable to hold natural strongpoints such as *Côte 380*, the butte of Montsec.[16] The **10. Ersatz-Division** of the **Armeeabteilung Strantz** commenced fighting on Montsec from 1 October 1914 – a battle that continued until 27 April 1915.[17] Over a year later the French attempted one last major attack to dislodge the Germans from Montsec. They failed, leaving *Côte 380* in German hands – providing the best high-ground position in the region for continual observation – until a month prior to the Armistice.[18]

Général Joffre assessed his predicament in the east: "Our attacks continued during the following days; but while they halted the German advance, they failed to regain the lost ground. In this affair the commander of the *IIIe armée* was lacking in foresight and activity – in foresight, because he neglected the information which indicated that large concentrations were being effected in the Woëvre; in activity, because he did not make proper use of the *6e corps d'armée*, one of whose divisions had been garrisoned in time of peace at St. Mihiel and knew the ground admirably." (Joffre wanted to get rid of *Général* Sarrail and exploited every opportunity to criticize him.) On 22 September the German assault established the battle line Richecourt-Seicheprey-Lirouville.

St. Mihiel fell to the Germans on 24 September, the beginning of a four-year occupation. American commentary four years later assessing the front line stated, "The German possession of St-Mihiel cuts both canal and railroad at that place and greatly embarrasses the French transportation system."[19] The consequences of this German attack at St. Mihiel were serious. It placed the main rail, road, and canal supplying Verdun in enemy hands and brought the main lines of communication into Verdun within range of German guns. Verdun was supplied by a single railway – the *Petit Meusin*, a narro-gauge line running from Bar-le-Duc. The danger presented by such conditions became evident when the Battle of Verdun started in February 1916. Verdun was effectively neutralised as a base from which the French could conduct sustained and meaningful offensive operations in the region.[20] To France, the German occupation of St. Mihiel became a visible and lasting *hernie* (hernia).[21]

Greater movements of forces were also taking place 30 kilometres to the north as the German Crown Prince attacked Varennes and the Argonne in an attempt to capture Verdun. The Woëvre now witnessed major conflict to the east of St. Mihiel. Twenty-five kilometres to the east at St. Baussant, the *16e corps d'armée* attacked **Armeeabteilung Strantz**. When St. Mihiel fell, the battle line was Xivray-Loupmont-Apremont-St. Mihiel and the heights overlooking the Meuse and Spada-Maizey.[22] On 25 September, German forces withdrew to higher ground leaving Flirey, Seicheprey, and Xivray to the French. More French reinforcements arrived on 27 September. They encountered the Germans digging the first of many trenches into the soggy ground that became the hallmark of positional warfare. The German artillery now commenced barrages against French positions. Seicheprey and its neighbour to the south, Beaumont, were favoured targets. French counter-attacks at Flirey and Apremont were inconclusive and it appears they were inadequately equipped and without adequate artillery support. The *31e corps d'armée* under the command of *Général* Delétoile occupied the ground to the south.[23] On 28 September the **Garde Ersatz Division** of **Armeeabteilung Strantz** commenced operations against the French at Flirey.[24] The casualties in these battles accounted for half of all the deaths that the region saw in the entire war.[25]

By October the lines of resistance were established by both combatants. The newly created *Secteur Lahayville* now had trench networks 400 metres north of Seicheprey facing St. Baussant.[26] By 13 October, the *128e brigade d'infanterie* of

the *64e division d'infanterie* occupied the *Secteur Lahayville* that included the village of Seicheprey. The *339e régiment d'infanterie* now faced the left and centre of the ridge north of *Bois de Remières*. The right sector of the ridge occupied by the *128e brigade d'infanterie* moved a few kilometres to the north-east at *Bois de la Sonnard*. On 26 October, the *64e division d'infanterie* of the *31e corps d'armée* ordered the *128e brigade d'infanterie* to dig in opposite the Germans at Seicheprey on the ridge crest. The first line closest to the Germans was to be held by just enough infantry to monitor the German lines until reinforcements from the second line came forward.

Lieutenant Colonel C. Petitjean, *128e brigade d'infanterie* commander, stated that his mission was "progression" – a term that now meant to advance into the enemy's position, trench fighting.[27] French forces were now fixed around Seicheprey. A battalion held the area north of the village around the cemetery. Another battalion occupied *Bois de Remières*. The remainder of the regiment faced the enemy near *Bois de la Sonnard*.[28] Maps now showed the first and second trench lines. On 29 October, *Lieutenant Colonel* Petitjean reported to the *64e division d'infanterie* commander that his officers were able to provide a definitive assessment of the German forces in the lines facing his brigade. The German front lines were now continuous with a strengthened second line of trenches. Available ground and aerial reconnaissance pointed out that German front lines appeared to be abandoned during the day. French lines were now 70–200 metres from the German lines – defining what became known as "No Man's Land".

North of Beaumont the French established a second line of defence that became the foundation for tactical operations governing the remainder of the war in the Woëvre.[29] A ridge traversed the sector containing the St. Dizier-Metz highway. It was a kilometre to the south of Petitjean's front line and served as the central point for defence. During the three-and-a-half years of occupancy it had been strengthened by both sides with a series of trenches and wire entanglements, organized in great depth.[30]

"Progression" had ghastly consequences for all combatants at the front. The valley where *Lieutenant Colonel* Petitjean's brigade held ground soon became a killing field. Along the centre of the valley was a wide stretch of marshy land containing the remains of hundreds of French and German soldiers.[31] Numerous graves and bones came to the surface as artillery rounds slammed into the area. The dead decomposed and created a foul miasma. By 1918, when the Americans occupied these French lines, whenever a new trench was dug in the sector it was not uncommon to uncover a corpse. Looking out on No Man's Land, human remains were observed sticking out of the ground. A shoe at the surface would contain the foot and part of a leg.[32]

REDUCE THE SALIENT

Minor skirmishes became the norm for the most part. A French attack against St. Baussant on 12 December met with catastrophic losses, including several hundred prisoners taken by German forces. The **Armeeabteilung Strantz Guarde-Ersatz-Division** fought the battle mainly from *Bois de Remières*, which became the central focus for Woëvre operations until the end of the St. Mihiel offensive. On December 1914 *Général* Joffre placed the *32ᵉ corps d'armée* at the disposal of *Général* Sarrail. The simultaneous advance of the Germans on the heights of the Meuse and in the Argonne alerted Joffre to place more effective fighting units at the Woëvre. He personally considered the *32ᵉ corps d'armée* to be one of the best.[33] It was the *32ᵉ corps d'armée* that became the godfather of the US Army on the Western Front from January to August 1918.

The new year saw *Général* Joffre focusing on St. Mihiel. He issued a series of instructions on 21 January, ordering *Iʳᵉ armée* to attack **General der Infanterie** von Strantz's detachment presently holding St. Mihiel on the east bank of the Meuse.[34] The following months did not achieve the goal Joffre sought. On 18 March he informed *Général* Dubail that he wanted *IVᵉ armée* to undertake the operation to reduce the St. Mihiel

salient as soon as possible, employing all means at his disposal in this attack. *Général* Dubail had four *corps d'armée* and a *corps de cavalerie* to work with. GQG planned an offensive for 5 April on the southern Woëvre plain to relieve Verdun. The plan comprised two simultaneous attacks on either arm of the salient, one in the direction of Verdun-la-Chaussée and the other centred on Toul-Thiaucourt. On 30 March the French *73ᵉ division d'infanterie* attacked along the Moselle River capturing over 500 metres of enemy trenches west of *Bois-le-Prêtre* in the *Quart-en-Réserve*. The *1ʳᵉ corps d'armée* and *2ᵉ corps d'armée*, which were to operate east of Verdun and against the northern arm of the St. Mihiel salient, were moving up the line with the intent of establishing themselves within assaulting distance, where they were to remain until the artillery bombardment commenced. The *31ᵉ corps d'armée* established itself at several points only 100 metres from the edge of *Bois de Mort-Mare* (Death Pond). On 3 April, the French *12ᵉ corps d'armée* attacked on its left. Their attack took place on the road to Thiaucourt towards Regniéville. Surprise was essential but the most difficult element to bring about. Orders were issued for absolute secrecy but, in spite of this, it was disconcerting to *Général* Joffre how rapidly news spread. He discovered to his chagrin that the date and location of the attack were common knowledge in Paris. With surprise lost, the Germans responded by beefing up their forces, adding the **121. Infanterie-Division.** .[35]

Unfortunately for the French, the April weather turned to rain. At first sight, it seemed to *Général* Joffre that the weather supported the French thanks to the lack of effective German aerial reconnaissance. The Woëvre became a quagmire and the trenches within flooded. The artillery found it difficult to take up position, observation of fire was almost impossible, and the shells buried themselves in the spongy ground. A feeling of uneasiness spread to both troops and staffs. Joffre thought a postponement prudent but French soldiers could not be kept for long in the misery that came with flooded trenches. *Général* Dubail gave the order for the attack to commence.[36]

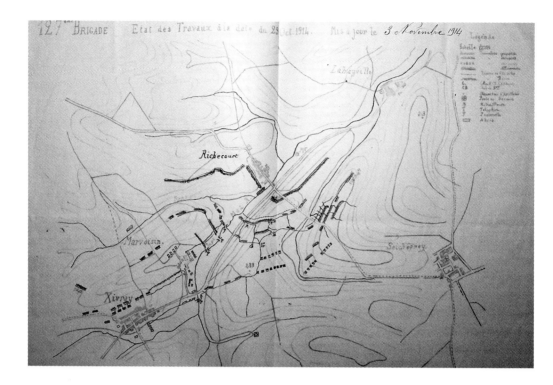

The main battleground west of Seicheprey became a maze of trenches in the autumn of 1914 that remained four years later. (SHD)

The *8ᵉ corps d'armée* and *31ᵉ corps d'armée* attacked on the left of *12ᵉ corps d'armée* applying pressure along the entire southern face of the "hernia", or bulge.[37] North of Flirey at *Bois de Mort-Mare* heavy fighting took place with significant losses. The French suffered 1,500 dead and a hundred prisoners taken. No Man's Land became a 50 metre area of abject misery for the next few years. Limited artillery did not achieve the destruction required and lack of adequate aerial reconnaissance handicapped the infantry advance. Woëvre mud completed the horror. French forces bogged down and German artillery annihilated those stuck in the clay. For four days, half of the existing stock of French heavy guns attempted to cut the wire obstacles in front of the French infantry. On 12 April 1915, the 4-kilometre front moved forward but Dubail's First Battle of Woëvre faltered at the German front line. The planned front for the attack was 80 kilometres, one of the largest of the war. *Général* Joffre intervened and pulled forces of the *1ʳᵉ corps d'armée* from *Général* Dubail's *1ʳᵉ armée* and left only *2ᵉ corps d'armée* and *12ᵉ corps d'armée*. Joffre learned that success was only possible "where attacks are

thoroughly and methodically organized; where … defences have been completely destroyed and after the first and second lines of the enemy's trenches have been demolished …The establishment of these conditions is a matter for the Commanding General."[38] The Germans applied their own lessons from positional war – adding more machine-gun firepower to each division and replacing several 77mm guns with larger howitzers to destroy trench works. Fighting continued through June 1915, but the St. Mihiel bulge remained.

METHODICAL PROGRESSION

In an attempt to salvage the failing offensive, *Général* Dubail ordered his *armée* to change its tactics of intense assault to "methodical progression". The new directive did not include the previous advantage of surprise. The result of the campaign was disastrous. From 26 March to

30 April 1915, the French lost 65,200 officers and men. In comparison, German losses suffered in the same period throughout the entire Western Front were slightly over 80,000.[39] The French Woëvre offensive shifted from Regniéville to the north of Flirey at *Bois de Mort-Mare* on 19 April. Dubail's failed offensive was the last major operation on the southern Woëvre front. Henceforth, names like Seicheprey and *Bois-Brûlé* indicated minor skirmishes until the Americans occupied the southern Woëvre front in February 1918.

The abortive effort by a single company of *poilus* (infantrymen), the *5ᵉ compagnie du 63ᵉ régiment d'infanterie*, on 19 April 1915, was the last act of a failed offensive. On that day they were ordered to recapture the last 200 metres of trenches at *Bois de Mort-Mare*. The battleground was covered with bodies from previous attacks. French artillery could not neutralise the effective German barrages. The *5ᵉ compagnie* collectively refused to assault the ridge. On 18 April, as the *5ᵉ compagnie* moved into battle on the front line, a *poilu* shouted out to a general officer, "We never refused to attack and we are always ready to do our duty, but if the artillery does not demolish the networks of barbed wire and defences in order to open the passage, we will not go up to get killed unnecessarily." Another shouted out, "It is not our turn to attack." On April 19 at 0600 only 40 of the 250 men in the *5ᵉ compagnie* left the trench and advanced towards the German lines. After a few metres they were devastated by German heavy artillery.

French commanders in the southern Woëvre front immediately took extreme measures. Delétoile ordered *Lieutenant Colonel* Paulmier, battalion commander, to make an example and have the entire *5ᵉ compagnie* executed. *Général* Delétoile's counterpart *Général* Castaing protested. Delétoile quibbled, deciding that five soldiers were to be shot on the spot for refusing orders to advance.[40] Adding to the misery, *Général* Joffre, just passing through the area, learned of what had transpired and refused to grant clemency to any of the convicted. In the same breath Joffre threatened the *63ᵉ régiment d'infanterie* with dishonour and loss of their battle flag.[41]

Lieutenant Mesnieux, *5ᵉ compagnie* officer in charge, was tasked to come up with the list of five to be executed. Mesnieux's counterpart in charge of the *4ᵉ Section*, *Sous-lieutenant* Boulant, refused to accuse any of his men. Mesnieux then came up with a cowardly methodology. Two men were chosen by lot, the other three were nominated by their superiors, arrested, and charged with the capital offence of cowardice under fire. *Lieutenant* Mesnieux turned to a nearby soldier and asked for a random number. The soldier responded "17." *Soldat* François Fontanaud, the 17th soldier on Mesnieux's list, was immediately arrested and charged. Mesnieux's enlisted senior sergeant Chaufriasse selected the name of *caporal* Antoine Morange randomly from a personnel roster. *Soldat* Félix François Louis Baudy was a stonemason working the roads in Lyon prior to enlisting in the *armée*. He belonged to *la Confédération Générale du travail* (CGT), a union organization that was believed to be socialist. The association was enough to condemn him. *Soldat* Henri-Jean Présbot was also a CGT member from Villeurbanne. A fifth soldier, *Caporal* Coulon, was also chosen by lot. He was spared execution for being labelled *simple d'esprit* (a simpleton) when in fact he was able to bribe his way out of the mess.[42] A *conseil de guerre* (court martial) was held with *Capitaine* Minot chosen to defend the accused. Minot was not a lawyer and only had five minutes to talk with the accused before the *conseil* commenced. The next day, on 20 April 1915, *Lieutenant Colonel* Paulmier carried out the execution order on the edge of *Bois de Manonville*. He did not order comrades in the *5ᵉ compagnie* to complete the task. New recruits to the unit that had just arrived and did not know the victims manned the firing squad. After the execution, Paulmier told *Capitaine* Minot that he had done everything he could to prevent this travesty.[43] Almost three years to the day in the same southern Woëvre front location, a decision was made in battle not to commit forces against the enemy, climaxing in a less tragic outcome. *Bois de Mort-Mare* would haunt the French military leadership for the remainder of the war.

"THE NATIONAL BUSINESS"

A summary of the war by an ambulance driver at Pont-à-Mousson, east of Seicheprey, after a year serving stated: "The fierce, invisible combats are limited to the first-line positions, averaging a mile each way behind No Man's Land. This stationary character has made the war a daily battle; it has robbed war of all its ancient panoply, its cavalry, its uniforms brilliant as the sun, and has turned it into the national business."[44] By 21 February 1916, when the Germans commenced the massive Verdun campaign, the St. Mihiel region had become known by the French as a convalescent home, a quiet sector for units recovering from other battle fronts.[45] The Germans likewise took advantage of the docility of the Woëvre and labelled it a **ruhige** (quiet) front. No matter how many offensives were planned, the French were unable to shift the line of the St. Mihiel hernia. The lines of September 1918 were exactly where they had been in September 1914. **General der Infanterie** von Strantz continued to lead German forces in the Woëvre until 2 February 1917 when **General der Artillerie** Max von Gallwitz took over German operations on the southern Woëvre front. **Armeeabteilung Strantz** became known as **Armeeabteilung C**.

It took the leadership of *Général* Pétain to save the *armée* by not following the draconian examples of his predecessors. He assumed command from *Général* Robert Nivelle after the April 1917 debacle at Chemin-des-Dâmes. Pétain's leadership and acute sense of the needs of the *poilu* kept the *armées* intact – avoiding dissent such as that of the *64ᵉ régiment d'infanterie* at Flirey two years prior. General John Pershing, AEF commander-in-chief, had the greatest respect for Pétain. In the years following the war at a private dinner honouring Pétain he stated, "I want it to be understood that this man is the greatest general of the war."[46]

Disgruntled *poilus* throughout the Western Front knew the *Internationale*, including those in the Woëvre region. (Louis Barthou in his memoir of the war recalls German and French soldiers singing it together in their opposing trenches.) The executions of members of the *5ᵉ compagnie du 63ᵉ régiment d'infanterie* on 20 April 1915 were not repeated in 1917. *Général* Pétain commenced a programme of relief for the forces, personally visiting ninety divisions and making substantial improvements. The French military operations that followed did suffer awful casualties; but they were only half those under Nivelle. Pétain's defence-in-depth meant markedly decreased French casualties.

By 1917, French and British divisions were depleted. They had been obliged to reduce the proportion of infantry in their divisions. So critical was their situation that in the spring of 1917 they found themselves unable to furnish replacements even for the infantry. The thought of an almost inexhaustible reservoir from which, without expense to themselves, they could draw men to keep up their depleted units, was naturally seen as almost miraculous. Such was the principle that underlay their dealings with the General Headquarters American Expeditionary Force (GHQ AEF) at Chaumont and the American government in Washington.[47]

The southern Woëvre front may have developed a reputation as a place for divisions to recuperate away from the horrors of Verdun and the Somme but it was no vacation. As one soldier from the 101st Engineers recalled, "We were in possession of a low range of rolling hills overlooking a little valley. Across the way were more hills, these in possession of Fritz. His front line was down in the flat country. Over among the hills, behind the front range and in positions well concealed, the enemy's big guns were stationed."[48] At the very end of 1917, GHQ AEF at Chaumont sent Major Hugh Aloysius Drum to the southern Woëvre front to acquire impressions of the area the 1st Division (the "Fighting First") would defend. Drum's diary entry was revealing: "Poor fellows! Their life of real hardship now begins."[49]

CHAPTER 2

"They Must Shed Blood"

In 1922, a German citizen walked into the American Headquarters of the Army of the Rhine at Coblenz and provided his assessment of the American fighting spirit. He had an issue that had resonated with him and many others for some years and he wanted to express his feelings to the representatives of the responsible nation. It was the gnawing fact that the "game" the Americans played eventually led to the defeat of the Germans.[50] They experienced victory in a manner that defied the well-established traditions of war that had served the German peoples for centuries. The Americans could still look upon the war as the "game." There was a spirit of competition invoked by youthful exuberance. Victory meant teamwork and the arriving American forces were rookies. The image of conflict being a "game" was pervasive – an attitude that prompted Germans at all levels to infer the Americans were not taking the war seriously. Such thinking was incomprehensible. "How could such an attitude have ever achieved victory?" was the man's complaint.

It was an attitude found at all levels. Sergeant (Master Engineer Junior Grade) William L. Langer, of Company E, First Gas Regiment, was a first-generation American whose parents came from Germany and settled in Boston, Massachusetts. Shortly after the Armistice, Langer wrote *With "E" of the First Gas*:

We and many thousands of others volunteered. Perhaps we were offended by the arrogance of the German U-boat campaign and convinced that Kaiserism must be smashed once and for all. Possibly we already felt that, in the American interest, Western democracy must not be allowed to go under. But I doubt it. I can hardly remember a single instance of serious discussion of American policy or of larger war issues. We men, most of us young, were simply fascinated by the prospect of adventure and heroism. Most of us, I think, had the feeling that life, if we survived, would run in the familiar, routine channels. Here was our one great chance for excitement and risk. We could not afford to pass it up.[51]

Prior to the 1st Division's entry into the Woëvre in January, a "hate campaign" was initiated involving posters throughout the training area and speakers reminding the soldiers of German atrocities.[52] Colonel George H. Shelton, commander of the 104th Infantry, 26th Division, employed a similar approach to instil the proper fighting spirit: "The Boche is a bully, and he is always yellow. He will fight, and he will go on fighting beyond where he can win. He will try every nasty trick to kill you and make you suffer. Don't forget that. When you meet him remember what he has done, and meet him with hatred in your hearts and venom on your bayonets. I shan't be satisfied with even 40 to 1 – and I don't want you to be."[53]

Sergeant Langer first saw action in June 1918 two months after the 1st Division had left the Woëvre and the 26th Division ("Yankee Division", YD) under the command of Major General Clarence Ransom Edwards was preparing to leave for Château-Thierry. The First Gas Regiment was to commence operations at Seicheprey with the 26th Division. Langer's comments reflected an amazing absence of malice and intensity: "What strikes me most, I think, is the eagerness of the men to get to France and above all to reach the front. One would think that, after almost four years of war, after the most detailed and realistic accounts of the murderous fighting on the Somme and around Verdun, to say nothing of the day-to-day agony of trench warfare, it would have been all but impossible to get anyone to serve without duress. But it was not so."[54]

A PRECARIOUS TIME

The year 1917 had witnessed setback after setback for French and British armies in disasters such as the French *armée* spring offensive on the Chemin-des-Dâmes and the recent British Army losses at Passchendaele. The *armée* occupied about 500 kilometres of the Western Front and their depth of reserves was diminishing. Adding to their pessimism were the military reverses in Russia and Italy – both with catastrophic losses. A Russian capitulation meant a one-theatre war in Europe with as many as forty German divisions redeploying west, reinforcing a well-established German army.[55] German leadership knew of the mutinies underway in the French *armée* but made the incorrect assumption that this was akin to the collapse of the Russian army – allowing the Germans to dictate terms without a major offensive.[56] *Général* Pétain had however drastically reduced the tempo of operations on the front lines and transitioned to a new phase in the war: *"J'attends les chars et les Américains"* ("I am waiting for the tanks and the Americans.")

For the Imperial German Government, 1918 was like stepping back in time to 1914 but with an exchange of dimension. Instead of facing two sets of enemies separated by space – France/Great Britain and Russia – Germany now faced two sets of enemies separated by time: France/Great Britain and the United States. German military assessment of American forces at this time recognized the American army needed to reorganise and strengthen to successfully enter into combat at the front. And according to German calculations, improvements to American army fighting quality were going to take a very long time. They were of course aware of America's depth of human resources. They also saw training to withstand the challenges of positional war as a massive challenge.[57]

The attempt to destroy troopships en route to France by a concerted U-boat campaign did not succeed. German prisoners spoke for their countrymen while confined at Camp Coëtquidan, the major American training facility in western France. Seeing more and more Americans arriving at the camp they decided that the Americans were in fact English in disguise, because the troopships "could never get by their submarines".[58] The highest echelon of the German military command saw that fresh forces in great numbers could prove the winning edge – something that experienced forces along the entire Western Front also realised. Timely decisions had to be made by the German leadership to neutralise enemy potential before the balance of power shifted. German success in 1918 lay in the best possible battle planning and its successful execution.

Emotions were running high, particularly American attitudes and expectations. General George C. Marshall, one of the greatest American soldiers of the twentieth century, recalled the words of the leading French statesman, Georges Clemenceau, meeting with soldiers of the American 1st Division early in August 1917: "He [Clemenceau] insisted that the Americans must get into action right away. They must shed blood."[59] Clemenceau was fearful of French units collapsing under

Brigadier General Malin Craig at the end of the war. His loyalty to his seniors at Chaumont was commendable, but his antagonism towards divisions on the line was not. (Ferrell, *In the Company of Generals*)

German pressure or widespread mutiny. Général Pétain personally briefed General Pershing on 25 November 1917 regarding the current French armée disposition – 108 divisions of competent troops on the immediate front and those held in reserve. As of that time, French losses had been approximately 2.6 million: comprising men killed, died of wounds, permanently incapacitated, and prisoners. The *poilu* was motivated to continue the struggle based on hatred alone – but it was a waning emotion.[60] Général Pétain then met with General Pershing several times from 23 December 1917 to 11 January 1918 concerning the employment of American troops. He wanted the Americans to accelerate their training so that if necessary they could serve as reinforcements. Common ground was achieved when Pétain advocated American infantry regiments under the supervision of American commanders become brigaded with French divisions at the front. American presence at the front better served what was necessary – improving French morale and public opinion.[61]

The initial expeditionary force comprised an evolving infantry division of regular troops with a totally different experience base – forty years of guerilla warfare fighting American Indians in the south-west United States; Philippine insurgents; and most recently Brigadier General Pershing's expedition into Mexico. Learning to work with allies was another serious challenge. General Pershing stated in his post-war assessment: "We were totally unprepared for war and our army was inexperienced in the conduct of joint operations in conjunction with the armies of allied powers. Practically our sole participation in such operations up until our war with Germany had been the minor one of the China Expedition of 1900."[62] One member of the initial cadre of the GHQ AEF staff that went to Europe with Pershing was Captain George S. Patton. Throughout his time in Europe, Patton was one for a direct and candid assessment of an individual or issue. He reflected on how Pershing weathered this time setting the course to make the American Army a separate and independent force. "No adulation could persuade him to countenance the placing of American men in French and British units. It is to his iron resolution to form an American Army that we owe the great heritage of a victorious America, victorious in her own right, and by her own means."[63] As it concerned his initial assessment of Pershing's French counterpart, Général Pétain, Patton wrote that the General "dresses with Napoleonic simplicity wearing no medals and just three little stars on his sleeve to show that he is a Major Gen … I think it is rather unfair as he has so much responsibility he ought to be paid for it at least."[64]

It was a learning experience for all the Allies. The French and British commanders had to come to terms with American attitudes and expectations. In turn, the Americans had to learn to compromise with veterans of three years of positional war. French liaison warned that in the 1st Division (equating to the American military in general), "the high command is not yet, in the area of directing operations, up to its responsibilities."[65]

General Pershing recalled in his post-war deliberations that ramping up the nation to successfully engage in war was a challenge throughout. Not only was getting troops to theatre difficult, extensive training was critical. The American factories now became fully committed to support the armies but their assembly lines were still being built. Pershing recognized the severity of the Allies' depletion of manpower, but held to the position that the French were not in sufficient touch with the political process, creating a feeling of disappointment that gradually deepened into depression that winter. Their depression became even blacker when they faced a German army no longer fighting the Russians. The 1918 forecasts showed a German army ready for new offensives. American military leadership did not want to get bogged down in positional war, preferring to train the army to break the stalemate that kept forces on both sides in check. Maintaining momentum of attack through sustained firepower was now a priority. The division was to be bulked up and reorganized to fight prolonged battles through sustained frontal attacks. Mobility was secondary to the firepower necessary to breach German defence and exploit the breakthrough. General Pershing advocated that the new army division "achieve a capacity for sustained battle which would ensure that American divisions would not falter short of their objectives as British and French divisions so often had done."[66]

For the Allies, the numbers were intoxicating. In late 1917, senior French military estimates showed forty-four American divisions were being generated for combat and heading to Europe. Each American division comprised 27,123 men, twice the strength of either a French or British division. The Allies saw four American divisions in training and heading to the front lines. Thirty divisions were expected to be in theatre by the end of 1918 – equivalent to seventy-three French divisions of 11,000 men each.[67] It was an astounding revelation. American manpower was to make the ultimate difference in the war. They couldn't come fast enough. Colonel John Henry Parker, a legend in US Army circles for his exploits in the Spanish-American War that earned him the nickname "Gatling Gun", was a member of Pershing's first wave of military experts helping to establish the AEF in theatre. When he arrived in France that June, Parker was asked by an anxious *poilu*, "Can your American soldiers, new as they will be, stand up against the Germans? Bring them quickly, for we are almost exhausted."[68]

EUROPEAN ASSESSMENTS

As Pershing struggled with European civilian and military leadership to maintain command of American forces and avoid the Allied demands for amalgamation into existing British and French divisions, assessments of American military ability surfaced through various senior staffs and liaisons. French assessment on quality and experience of American forces was sobering. American divisions belonged to Regular Army, National Guard, or the National Army. The French assessed the Regular Army strength at 300,000 men. Regular cadres were weakened by numerous transfers to the National Guard and National Army. The French did agree that the Regular units kept up their traditions of discipline and appeared capable of quickly acquiring the flexibility necessary to fight effectively within positional war. There was greater concern about the National Guard, assessed strength at 425,000 men: "This is the militia in time of peace." As militia, the military force was capable of bearing arms, but in practice it was reduced to about 125,000 men requiring periods of training. French concerns about the National Guard were stark: "They suffered from want of discipline due to political influences – recruitment chiefly covered men employed in banks or trade whose physique is only mediocre."

The French saw American objectives to push the National Guard into war as serving local political interests. They held out the greatest hope for the newly established National Army – vast sources of manpower derived from a nation-wide draft. The National Army provided a rich source of human capital that promised to keep the American army manned sufficiently to finally defeat the Germans.[69]

Even the German military assessed the National Guard's value as "small". Twenty-four drill days annually for three years did not match up to the experiences that the war had taught all combatants to date. The Germans labelled the newly established National Army as disorganized militia. What concerned the Germans were the numbers. National Army recruits, all men (citizens) capable of bearing arms between the ages of 18 and 45, for the present constituted untrained forces, but their eventual wartime strength equated to 15 million.[70] A post-war discussion by **General der Artillerie** von Gallwitz's Chief of Staff, **Oberst** Victor Keller, described a hope "that it would never be possible for a

nation unaccustomed to permanent military training to raise and properly to train fighting troops fit for the most difficult war in history." But Keller's assessment concluded with the historical lesson of 1918. Lessons learned by the first two divisions on the line, 1st Division and 26th Division, were applied to the many complete divisions that arrived, culminating in the July battle at Villers Cotterets near Soissons that preempted any further German efforts to conduct a major offensive for the remainder of the war. The American effort at Villers-Cotterêts was "the turning point of the war [and] showed the German Army that the training of the American fighting forces had made extraordinarily rapid progress and that the fighting value of these forces was high."[71]

The two leading Allied generals at the Woëvre pose with their staff, second and fourth from right. Major General Liggett served as administrative commander and *Général* Gérard was tactical commander. (Pépin Papers)

REORGANIZING AN AMERICAN ARMY

After the United States declared war on 6 April 1917, British and French officers convinced American Army seniors that their army lacked firepower and effective command and control. Their suggestions had an ulterior motive. Both the British and French tried to persuade American leadership that the quickest way to employ effectively untrained manpower was through amalgamation, incorporating American soldiers as individuals or in small units into existing French and British divisions. The Allies wanted American manpower to flesh out the formations drained by three long years of annihilation at the front. They were to hold to this idea up to the Armistice. The serving US Army Chief of Staff, Major General Hugh L. Scott, opposed American soldiers serving in Allied units – holding firm that Americans could be reorganized to meet the challenge. General Scott saw reorganization as a means of proving the quality of the American soldier. He directed a study of a divisional structure to comprise two infantry brigades, each with two large infantry regiments as well as light and heavy artillery, signal and engineer troops, and service units. Key to the thinking was that 13,000 infantrymen in the American-designed division could provide a force with greater mobility and enhance the ability to exchange units in the line and maintain battle momentum.[72]

General Pershing presented his views to the War Department as to the proper organization of his Army and all its parts, its supply, and the order in which the units designated were to reach France. Pershing's propositions to President Wilson's Secretary of War, Newton D. Baker, came in the form of "projects", such as general organization, service of the rear, tanks, and the schedule of shipping priorities.[73]

The first definite plan for the creation of an American Army was the General Organization Project directed by Secretary of War Baker. He wanted another look beyond what General Scott was directing for divisional requirements. General Pershing and his fellow West Point classmate Colonel Chauncy B. Baker came up with a larger "square" infantry division structure that fitted American objectives to conduct offensive operations on a large scale in France. This suited the reality of positional war with limited manoeuvrability.[74] Their goal was to field at least 20 combat divisions with the necessary proportion of depot and replacement divisions forming five corps.[75] The US Army's transformation to a "square" division consisting of two brigades and four regiments was deemed necessary to fight positional war and be ready for open war. Approximately 25,000 men made up two infantry brigades (both brigades held two infantry regiments and one three-company machine-gun battalion). Thanks to American employment of available French artillery pieces and organization, the artillery configuration was modified in favour of proven roles and missions at the front. The field artillery brigades supporting each infantry division came from available French artillery: one 155mm howitzer regiment, two 75mm field gun regiments, and one trench mortar battery. The division fielded enough soldiers to fight prolonged battles in a positional war environment.[76]

The National Guard in 1917 mobilized into the US Army as administrative divisions set up in 1913.[77] The construct of Regular Army and National Guard ceased in 1917. Thanks to the urgency of getting the US Army ready for war in Europe, a series of divisions at set strength and numbered according to source of manpower became the standard. Regular Army divisions were identified by division numbers 1–25; National Guard divisions were identified with the numbers 26–75; and National Army divisions followed sequence after 76. Brigades also fell into the numerical sequence. The 1st Division now consisted of 1st Infantry Brigade and 2nd Infantry Brigade but their regiments retained their original unit identification. The National Guard 26th Division comprised the 51st Infantry Brigade and 52nd Infantry Brigade.

Subordinate 26th Division regiment nomenclature commenced with the 101st

Infantry and continued in sequence for the remainder of the National Guard divisions.[78]

To meet the new challenges of positional war, the American infantry regiments increased in strength from 2,061 to 3,600 personnel. Machine-gun numbers were quadrupled from four to sixteen guns. The American division now included three battalions of machine guns. More firepower was added by the addition of light mortars, rifle and hand grenades, one-pound field pieces (37mm), and automatic rifles. The American logistical tail of supply, ammunition, and engineer trains was reinforced with countless trucks. French liaison voiced trepidation over the American division size, which in the view of their experienced officers was unmanageable. The dilemma was quintessentially American. "The automobile traffic is fantastic", and the "movement of trucks and wagons was triple that of any French sector. The division's appetite for scarce supplies was insatiable and supply discipline virtually nonexistent."[79]

THE WOËVRE FOR *LES AMÉRICAINS*

French senior military attention addressed the question as early as May 1917. *Général* Foch wrote to *Général* Marie-Eugène Debeney, *Général armée du Centre*, requesting Debeney recommend a good site for training American soldiers. *Général* Debeney knew the area intimately. He previously commanded Ire *armée* forces along the Woëvre from mobilization to early January 1915. Debeney subsequently returned to command Ire *armée* in the Woëvre on December 1917, providing tactical command to the American 1st Division occupying the Ansauville sector the following month. Debeney replied two days later on 22 May that the *armée* camp at Gondrecourt in the region Neufchâteau-Nancy-Épinal was a good place because it was in proximity to the southern Woëvre front that the Americans would in all likelihood cover. Gondrecourt was approximately an hour south of Seicheprey. It had been used as a training camp for two

French divisions, relevant in that a 27,000-man US division was planned for later that year. Gondrecourt serving as an initial training location pleased French seniors and, eventually, Pershing. American forces would be in a region that better served French rather than British forces. When Pershing received word that he was to go to France with four infantry regiments and an artillery regiment, he interpreted the order to mean that the troops were to form one division. On 16 June 1917, the "First Expeditionary Division" of four regiments headed to France. When the division arrived at the Gondrecourt Training Area on 5 July 1917, 1st Division, AEF, became the permanent designation.

General Pershing reflected on what direction the American Army should take once they arrived on the Continent. The French war plans addressing the role that Americans were to play naturally reflected French national interests. It is a reasonable assumption, though difficult to prove, that the French conception of military operations was largely territorial in scope, aimed at reconquest of French soil. If heavy fighting and subsequent destruction were to take place, it was best from the French view that this should happen in districts where the damage would be least. GHQ AEF felt the best way to serve the Allied cause was by the formation of American armies to be employed along sections of the front of the greatest strategic importance. That envisioned end governed American operations until they created the American First Army in September for the St. Mihiel offensive. It followed Pershing's desire to have the force necessary to conduct an independent action against the Germans.[80]

Pershing conferred with Pétain regarding a suitable location for an American front. Pershing's staff initially recommended Lorraine while en route to Europe on the S.S. *Baltic*. Pétain agreed to Pershing's request because Lorraine made sense as it did not interfere with British plans for defending the vital channel ports. The French were not to have Americans defend Paris in 1917 – a position that changed the following June when American troops

Major Bruns was the primary adversary of both 1st Division and 26th Division when they served on the Woëvre. He developed *Einladung* and was *Kampf-Truppen-Kommandeur* (KTK) for *Kirschblüte*. (Von Bornstedt, *Reserve.Infanterie. Regiment 259*)

rushed to defend Château-Thierry from the German offensive. Other benefits for Americans in Lorraine included supply lines placed well south of the front, away from any possible German advance and more billeting and training areas for green American troops arriving in great numbers, plus rail links. The strategic goal of cutting off vital German resupply lines westward of Sedan was highly attractive, as was carrying the war to German soil; and finally, they posed a threat to the important economic regions of the Saar and Longwy-Briey, which produced almost half of the raw materials used in making German munitions.[81]

In November 1917, Pershing's lead for operations at GHQ AEF, Colonel Fox Conner, submitted a staff memorandum that advocated the AEF "find its natural employment during 1918 on the front immediately west of Pont-à-Mousson", a town at a strategically important river crossing on the Moselle. Advanced planning estimates concerning a small offensive west of Pont-à-Mousson called for nearly four months to prepare. American planning required not only the identification and commitment of infantry but the organization of the extensive supply and transportation needed. Conner commented that the preparation to meet the present conditions required far more time than would a more "conventional" mobile form of war. Pershing agreed on 15 December 1917 to Conner's proposal that planning was to be finished by 1 February 1918.[82]

Pershing and Pétain continued to discuss American entry onto the Western Front, with an agreement reached on 11 January 1918. Pétain stated: "I understand perfectly that you cannot consider the idea of a final attachment of American units to French divisions … We are thus entirely in accord as to principles."[83]

On 24 January Pershing noted in his diary that he "made arrangements for the 26th Division to proceed to the quiet sector with the French near Soissons on February 5th."[84] Pershing saw establishment of a sector occupied by American forces as a way to avoid amalgamation. Allowing Americans to fight within their own divisional structure meant "a renunciation upon their part of all efforts to incorporate our forces in their own and in British divisions. I indicated my wishes to the French on February 6, 1918, that I had tentatively decided to adopt as an American sector the present front of the 1st Division extending the lines to the left and that I desired it to become purely American on June 1, at which time I would have 4 trained combatant divisions, together with the proper proportion of army and corps troops." The German offensive of 21 March 1918 upset all of his plans and deferred their eventual execution until September.[85]

FRENCH TACTICAL CONTROL

French interests and French views dominated the initial conduct of operations by the Americans. They argued that they possessed seasoned, smooth-working divisions, which had become depleted through serious losses, and urged Pershing and the American leadership to accept the idea that these divisions could absorb a large percentage of comparatively raw recruits and still be able to function creditably. Pershing's military policy was "merely the confirmation of the national policy and ... the constant efforts of our High Command [GHQ AEF] to meet the views of the French High Command [GQG] was the logical continuation of the attitude displayed by our sentiments and our people toward France at the moment when we entered the war." The Americans would readily support the appointment of *Général* Foch as the Generalissimo of the Allied Armies on 14 April 1918.[86]

The French GQG directed French military operations like a general staff. The "Army Group" arrangement was created after the first months of the war, when the disasters of the opening French campaigns clearly demonstrated the commander-in-chief had difficulty overseeing a large number of armies. The idea of army groups became reality; three were established – *Général armée de l'Est*, *Général armée du Centre*, and *Général armée du Nord*. Each had a commanding *général* and general staff. Complex service organizations were realigned to other commands. French military units found their identity through *corps d'armée* or *divisions d'infanterie* – assigned to an *armée* in a provisional fashion and passed from one *armée* to another following manoeuvre against the enemy. French command and control was not what the Americans or British had in place. For example, French aviation was managed through the GQG's Chief of Aeronautical Service at officer field grade level (*commandant* or *lieutenant colonel*) serving the French *armées* as counselor in the technical employment of aeronautics. This authority exercised direct command of

French air units assigned to *armée*. A second GQG group under the Director of Stations and Services maintained authority over a vast extent of territory along the entire *armée* front – freeing the *armée* commander from all other affairs to concentrate on the direction of operations in the battle sector.[87] French experience to date favoured a division staff composed of a *Chef d'État-Major* (chief of staff), chief of artillery and directorate seniors for intelligence, operations, and supply.

The first French *armée* that American forces served in the Woëvre was the *Ire armée* under the command of *Général* Debeney. The *Ire armée* mission was "to ensure the defence of the front of the Southern Woëvre and of both banks of the Moselle, in liaison to the North of Nancy with the *VIIIe armée*, which ensures the defence of the industrial region of the Meurthe [river]."[88] It was also entrusted with the defence of the Meuse valley to cover the bases of the *IIe armée*. *Général* Debeney and his *Ire armée* were subsequently replaced by *Général* Augustin Grégoire Arthur Henry Gérard and his *VIIIe armée*. Gérard had been a general in the Woëvre region since 1915. Gérard's reputation in the military was not good – he was known more as a militant freemason and an ardent republican than a master of the military arts.[89]

The most significant military unit in the French *armée* was the *corps d'armée* – the appropriate echelon to conduct planning and administration for active operations. *Corps d'armée* had an assigned commander, staff, troops, and services that could be transported and committed to all sectors on the Western Front as required. The experiences of the war changed French military thinking – increasing artillery firepower, applying a standard of three to four divisions per *corps d'armée*, and adding elements from *aviation militaire* to create a more mature and modern fighting force. The Battle of Verdun in 1916 was the turning point for rethinking the assignment of *corps d'armée*. The latter became "divisible" so that GQG could assign appropriate divisions to *corps d'armée* commanders to commit at the appropriate time and place in the evolving battle.

At Verdun, up to fifty *corps d'armée* assigned to the battle became an *armée*. This process extended to most of the *corps d'armée* occupying fronts in a stable condition such as the Woëvre.[90]

The French *général* who mentored the US Army's adaptation to positional war was the commander of the *32e corps d'armée*, *Général* Fénelon François Germain Passaga. In mid-January 1918, the *32e corps d'armée* comprised four *divisions d'infanterie* and the 1st Division. As tactical commander of American divisions serving on the Woëvre, Passaga groomed and guided the Americans to better understand how the war was fought and how the Americans could effectively contribute. Passaga's assessment of American military potential acknowledged the potentially disastrous ethos of the "game". "The American soldiers accustomed to action, across their wide spaces, impatient to show the vigour of the 'American fist,' used to go into the line with their sleeves up, ready to pounce upon the enemy. I was afraid to see these men, carried away by impulse, be mown down by the guns and the machine guns of an unseen enemy and pay as we had done for their War experience by a welter of blood."[91]

Général Passaga was a worthy mentor. His early successes with French *armée* overseas in South-east Asia (Cambodia), Senegal, and North Africa garnered his reputation and advancement. At the commencement of the war, Passaga commanded the *38e brigade d'infanterie* at the Marne. The next year he led a brigade of *Chasseurs Alpins* in the Vosges, fighting hard battles without benefit of sufficient artillery. At the end of 1915, Passaga's brigade fought a decisive battle at Hartmannswillerkopf (near the Swiss border) that stopped an important German advance. At the tumultuous Battle of Verdun in 1916 *Général* Passaga commanded the *division Gauloise*, which led to his promotion and command of the *32e corps d'armée*. In April 1917, Passaga commanded *32e corps d'armée* at Chemin-des-Dâmes. His manner was frank and open, tactful in command, and sympathetic to the challenges faced by the arriving American divisions. It was *Général* Passaga who shepherded the Americans through the realities of modern positional war.

While at Chemin-des-Dâmes, Passaga's command within the *32e corps d'armée* included the *69e division d'infanterie* under *Général* Monroe. Subordinate to the *69e division* was a special regiment that gained the deep affection of American forces fighting in the Woëvre region. The *162e régiment d'infanterie* commanded by *colonel de cavalerie* Jules-Alexandre Bertrand, a hero of Verdun, served as instructor, fellow combatant, and trusted friend. Bertrand was equally vital in nurturing both 1st Division and 26th Division through their adaptation to combat roles.

AMERICANS ARE COMMITTED TO THE LINE

General Pershing made it clear in his post-war writings that the delay in securing an American sector along the front caused "no little anxiety".[92] General George Marshall offered a few thoughts on General Pershing in his later years, considering him as a top commander, operating very largely through his operational staff – primarily through Colonel Conner, who eventually led the G-3 organization. When it came to Pershing's involvement with fighting, "He would make a temporary headquarters at the front. And, of course, for quite a long time he commanded the First Army before it was split into two armies and then he commanded the group of armies ... General Pershing as a leader always dominated any gathering where he was. He was a tremendous driver, if necessary; a very kindly, likeable man on off-duty status, but very stern on a duty basis."[93]

The French and British kept the pressure on to amalgamate Americans into their divisions. Pershing made it clear that American divisions such as the first four in theatre, the 1st, 2nd, 26th, and 42nd divisions, could not attain maximum efficiency and development until administered as a unit under exclusive American control. Having a sector occupied and controlled by Americans best answered Pershing's needs. This was not welcomed by the French as they assessed the American state of readiness as inadequate; and they had a legitimate, growing concern that the Germans were now preparing a major offensive that could prove catastrophic for the Allies.[94]

As agreed between General Pershing and *Général* Pétain, an American corps commander and staff were also to receive instruction from the French *32ᵉ corps d'armée* governing the sector. Leading this newly designated I Corps serving as administrative command for the American forces on the line was Major General Hunter Liggett. A West Point graduate from 1879, Liggett was well respected by both senior staffs at Chaumont, Washington, DC, and the commanders of the divisions that he worked with. He came to the war as commander of the 41st Division – a National Guard Division comprising of troops from Washington, Oregon, Montana, Idaho, and Wyoming. Liggett's 41st Division Chief of Staff was Lieutenant Colonel Malin Craig, who possessed extensive experience starting in China with the Boxer Rebellion, four different tours in the Philippines, and the Santiago Campaign in Cuba. Craig held every regimental staff position for which his rank made him eligible. As the 41st Division became assigned to serve as a depot division, Craig was transferred to Colonel Conner's office.[95]

The division that led the way into the Woëvre in January 1918 was the 1st Division (known at this time as the "Fighting First") under the command of General Robert Lee Bullard. The deployment of the 1st Division to the southern Woëvre front was unique in many ways. It was not configured like the French division, which only comprised the elements of combat and lacked services, which were mainly provided by the *corps d'armée*. It was to complete its period of training in the Ansauville sector of the Woëvre. The 1st Division was to enter the line one brigade at a time accompanied by part of the divisional artillery and the other services with a seasoned French division on either side. The brigade designated to be second to the line was to continue training in the rear areas and

give special attention to open warfare methods. In essence, the Americans had a division holding the front line with only half of its total force in place. To the west at Chemin-des-Dâmes the 26th Division was to be attached, by regiments, to a French corps for front-line duty; the 26th Division staff was to be attached at the same time to a similar staff of the French corps and function within the limits of its responsibilities. The front of one brigade allowed the 1st division to learn the role of positional war without having to risk soldiers to operations beyond the scope of their experience.[96]

Major General Bullard was an exceptional leader – immersed in the military arts, having a had very successful career serving around the world in the Philippines, Cuba, France, and south-west United States. He understood the evolving role of the US Army as well as any officer. Bullard was no nonsense with his troops and his manner reflected a professional standard maintained throughout 1918, culminating in his promotion to lieutenant general and command of the II Army during the final Meuse-Argonne campaign. When General Bullard assumed command, one of his first acts was to acquire Brigadier General Charles Pelot Summerall to lead the 1st Field Artillery Brigade. It proved to be a brilliant move.[97] Bullard was fluent in French and got along with *Général* Debeney, *Général* Passaga, and *Général* Monroe – accepting their tactical control of his Division.

Bullard continued to soothe the French generals in their own language and felt that he had their confidence. The French made it clear that the 1st Division was under the control of the more experienced French military commanders. Bullard briefed his administrative American commander, Major General Hunter Liggett, and the senior GHQ AEF staff contact at Chaumont starting with Colonel Conner (who was also fluent in French) on the challenges he was facing being under tactical French command. Key to Bullard's thinking was that French battle experience was significant and appreciated, but his purpose as the first American commander of a battle sector on the Western Front was to build the command and staff to take on the responsibility that would served the AEF best in their conduct of the war. Essentially, he wanted full control of the sector, which Liggett and Conner promised to press the French to give him. Bullard gained the confidence of *Général* Debeney and on 5 February successfully took command over the area designated for the 1st Division from *69ᵉ division d'infanterie* and subsequently established his *poste de commandant* (*PC*) at Ansauville.[98]

THE GERMAN FORCES OF THE WOËVRE REGION

The German **Generalstab** (General staff) set the pace of battle. The **Generalstab** officers were trained to display efficiency and common sense – taking the work of a fellow **Generalstab** member and applying the same body of basic ideas and principles of operational and tactical thought.[99] In the First World War it became necessary to appoint strong personalities as chiefs of the **Generalstab** to underpin commands under the direction of the nobility – whereby the chiefs effectively commanded the prince's armies. The "Chief System" established a culture where army commanders accepted orders from **Generalstab** officers holding considerably lower rank. Orders issued by junior **Generalstab** officers "for the commander" were to be executed.[100] The culture was unique. In German staffs, **Hauptmann** (captain) **im Generalstab** (**i.G.**) could act as if they were superiors of higher-ranking officers. Senior non-**Generalstab** officers had to accept working for **Generalstab** officers who were junior. **Erster Oberquartiermeister der Oberste Heeresleitung General der Infanterie** Erich Ludendorff directed military operations in the west, dealing with **Generalstab** for the most part.[101]

Managing the war was done mainly through **Oberste Heeresleitung [OHL]**, consisting of the **Generalstab des Feldheers**, an inner circle of selected staff officers. Kaiser Wilhelm II was Supreme Commander. Headquarters, **Grosser Hauptquartier OHL**, moved during the course of the war.[102] **Oberste Heeresleitung (OHL)** (German

High Command) was the senior command headquarters for German operations on the Western Front. **Generalstab** officers at unit staffs were **Truppengeneralstab** (Line General Staff Officers). The Prussian **Generalstab** system allowed for and positively encouraged the work of a powerful advisor to the responsible superior. Such was the relationship between **Feldmarschall** von Hindenburg and Ludendorff. Contributing to the deliberations of the **Generalstab** were the commanders along the Western Front that comprised the **Heeresgruppe** (Group of Armies). The standard German **Armee** varied with the sector they occupied at the front. Usually an **Armee** included three to six **Korps** totalling fifteen divisions. At the eastern end of the Western Front in the Lorraine and Alsace sectors the German forces were further organized into **Armeeabteilungen** (Army Detachments) of up to ten divisions.[103] The major German command opposite the French *Iʳᵉ armée* and *VIIIᵉ armée* in the Verdun region was **Heeresgruppe Gallwitz** (Army Group Gallwitz) under the command of **General der Artillerie** Max von Gallwitz. He served as the primary German commander facing the Americans on the Western Front in 1918, with the exception of Cantigny, Château-Thierry, and the Second Marne. The most important 1918 American offensives at St. Mihiel and Meuse-Argonne had to contend with the brilliance of von Gallwitz. He was a 44-year veteran by 1914, and as his rank title indicated, his career progressed through the artillery. Throughout the war he was integral to key operations, starting with the initial drive into Belgium, quickly followed by command on the Eastern Front, then supporting the **8. Armee** at the Masurian Lakes. He led German forces in several significant battles – most notably at Verdun and the Somme in 1916. Two weeks after the bloodiest day in the history of the British Army (1 July 1916) Gallwitz assumed command of the newly established **Heeresgruppe Gallwitz**, dissolved five weeks later. At the same time he commanded **2. Armee** and held that command until mid-December.[104] At that time Gallwitz returned to Verdun to command the **5. Armee**. He arrived in time to command

German forces against a surge of French counter-attacks, subsequently keeping the Verdun sector stable for the following year. On 21 December 1917 he received the **Schwarzen Adler** (Order of the Black Eagle), the highest order of chivalry in the Kingdom of Prussia.

Von Gallwitz had five divisions under his control as **5. Armee** commander at Verdun. On 11 March 1917, **Generalleutnant** Georg Fuchs was appointed **Oberbefehlshaber** (commander in chief) of nine divisions in the **Abschnitt zwischen Maas und Mosel** [sector between the Maas and Moselle rivers] known as **Armeeabteilung C** (Army Detachment C). Fuchs had a long career within the **Generalstab**. At the commencement of the war he served as commander of **16. Infanterie Division** based in Trier. His distinguished career featured battles mostly in the Champagne region and Verdun. In 1916 Fuchs served on the Eastern Front at Galicia, enduring the full thrust of the Brusilov offensive. For his accomplishments Fuchs was awarded the *Pour le Mérite*. Allied intelligence assessed the 61-year-old Fuchs a "specially clever and capable general".[105] Von Gallwitz now had Fuchs supporting his overall command **Heeresgruppe Gallwitz** at Verdun, covering western Verdun to the eastern edge of the Woëvre. **Gruppe Gorz** and **Gruppe Mihiel** were subordinate commands to **Armeeabteilung C,** controlling German forces in the southern Woëvre.[106]

One of the nine divisions of **Armeeabteilung C** holding the southern Woëvre front north of Seicheprey was the **78. Reserve Division** (**78. R. D.**) that had served on the Eastern Front for two years followed by a tour of duty to the west of Verdun. The commander was **Generalmajor** Paulus von Stolzmann, a very capable officer who developed a reputation in the German army as a dependable chief of staff. As an **Oberstleutnant**, he was assigned to **IX. Armeekorps** in the first Marne campaign. In January 1915 von Stolzmann was transferred to Hungary as **Generalstabchef der Süd-Armee**. His years on the Russian Front were exceptional, assisting in many victories that earned him the *Pour le Mérite* from the Kaiser. As **Generalmajor** he was **Generalstabchef** to **General der Infanterie** von Linsingen's newly formed **BugArmee**. He was

named by the Kaiser on 21 July 1916 to assume command of **78. R. D.** on the Russian Front. In April 1917 the **78. R. D.** was transferred to the Western Front on the Aisne. His ability to plan for success in battle was proven. The **78. R. D.** transferred to Verdun and eventually was assigned to **Armeeabteilung C** under the command of von Gallwitz and Fuchs.[107]

To the west of **78. R.D.** was the **5. Landwehr Division** (**5. Ldw. Div.**) under the command of **General der Infanterie** Karl Auler. **5. Ldw. Div.** was very familiar with the Woëvre region, having occupied the same ground since 1916. The average age of the soldiers was 30. Many came from nearby Metz.[108] The **78. R. D.** was subordinate to **Gruppe Gorz** located at Gorze, 20 kilometres to the north-east. Their divisional counterpart, **5. Ldw. Div.** was subordinate to **Gruppe Mihiel**, 9 kilometres to the west. Both Auler and von Stolzmann reported to Fuchs. The **78. R. D.** comprised three infantry regiments whose manpower was derived from three different German regions. **Reserve Infanterie Regiment. (Res. I. R.) 258** (Rhenish from the Rhineland-Palatinate) occupied Richecourt; **Res. I. R. 259** ("Oldenburger" from Lower Saxony) occupied St. Baussant, and **Res. I. R. 260** ("Hanoveraner" and "Braunschweiger", also from Lower Saxony) operated out of the St. Baussant-Flirey road. In 1915, the **78. R. D.** saw action on the Russian Front to the north of Grodno. The next year **78. R. D.** remained in the Illukst (region of Dvinsk) until April 1917. At that time the division transferred to the Western Front and went into line in the Burnhaupt sector to the north of the Rhône-Rhine Canal. In June 1917 the **78. R. D.** fought at the Chemin-des-Dâmes and was victorious at Vauxaillon. Two months later the division moved to the Verdun front as a reserve at the time of the French Offensive – conducting a counter-attack on 13 September and occupying the southern Woëvre front until the middle of October. Allied intelligence discovered that the **Res. I. R. 258** and **Res. I. R. 259** both experienced desertions at this time, which suggested a waning resolve to hold the sector. In the middle of December 1917 the **78. R. D.** was withdrawn from the Abaucourt sector and put at rest for instruction in the region of Chambley-Mars la Tour (18 December–11 January 1918), then proceeded to the front line north of Seicheprey around 12 January. While in the southern Woëvre front, the division acquired replacements from nearby Alsace-Lorraine. The **78. R. D.** were part of the **Abschnitt zwischen Maas und Mosel** region from 1 February to 27 May 1918 – assuming responsibility for **Abschnitt G** covering the southern area of Thiaucourt, which included Richecourt, Essen, Lahayville, and St. Baussant.[109]

What was unusual about the **78. R. D.** operation there was the assignment of an **Artillerie-Kommandeur (Art.Kdr.)** within **Generalmajor** von Stolzmann's division. **Generalleutnant** Wilhelm Hoffmann was a reactivated general officer who had retired prior to 1914 and was called back.[110] The German method of artillery command and control gave a great deal of freedom to the leaders of artillery units. The relationship of German artillery units to infantry units was one not of subordination but of cooperation. At the Woëvre, German battle planning took a unique course. They assigned **Generalleutnant** Hoffmann to orchestrate a division's limited number of artillery pieces at his own discretion. It was **Generalleutnant** Hoffmann who conceptualised the use of German firepower against American forces initially assigned to the front lines in 1918.

CULTURAL DIFFERENCES

French success in conditioning Americans for positional war was accomplished through military liaisons in place throughout the divisions and headquarters staffs. French liaison officers constantly interpreted their army's rules and methods and tried to reconcile them with American ideas and habits. Confidence between the two armies grew thanks to this liaison. George Marshall recalled the role of French liaison in the Ansauville sector later in life. In particular, he had a close relationship with *Capitaine* Germain Seligmann, for whom he had the greatest respect: "We had several big exercises there and we had some regimental demonstrations there, and the

French were there all over the place, rather super-critical. There was plenty to criticise …"[111]

French military mission members such as *Capitaine* Rouvier, a three-year combat veteran, came to the United States to educate the American military and public at large about the realities of the positional war being experienced. His *Present Day Warfare* helped convey to Americans how war was now fought. He reminded the American audience of one important piece of baggage each soldier should bring across the Atlantic: " a strong hate for the *Boche*, a strong desire to meet him, to fight him, and to beat him … all of the unit, from the leader to the private, will form one body, one soul, animated with one single, almighty desire, to kill the *Boche* and drive him back to his country."[112]

It wasn't all sweetness and light. When French liaison officers arrived, some of their American counterparts pretended not to understand them and accused them of lacking candour. It was termed "French politeness". One reaction to this cultural trait was a defensive tactic: concealment.[113] Some of the French had difficulty relating to the Americans, describing them as "often rather limited mentally; [they] have a strong tendency to draw upon their experiences on the Cuban expedition, the one to Manila, or in Mexico, which they think was waging war, and tend to reject advice as an insult to their national pride."[114] Another French liaison recalled with a certain amount of disdain that the Americans exulted in the constant evocation of Law and Liberty and called on the memory of the Crusades and Joan of Arc.[115]

Major George Patton reflected on the French in his own idiosyncratic way: "The French are certainly nice and do everything they can to help us. They are some soldiers too. Personally I like them much better than the British, possibly because they do not drink tea. Which to my mind is a most hellish and wasteful practice."[116]

Military intelligence assessments on America's relations with France showed ruffled feathers from the start. It was expected by the French that it would be well for Americans to follow their customs. The French, particularly the man in the street, expected great things from the Americans. In June 1917 when the first soldiers arrived in France there was

Colonel Bertrand, commander 162ᵉ régiment d'infanterie, was the most respected French commander serving with the Americans on the Woëvre. (Sibley Photo Album)

his Brigade with senior 26th Division staff, talked some sense:

> There should be made to cease the constant talk of getting away from the French which has filtered down from Chaumont to the Battalion and Company Commanders. What in the Name of Heaven could we have done without them? What would we do now without them. Outside of food and clothing, they either have furnished us or are furnishing us with everything that we have needed or are needing to enable us properly to do our work. In place of fault finding with their instruction and supervision, we should welcome it while we have it and make the greatest use of it while we can, as we in this Division have always done.[118]

a tendency among the officers – who should have known better – to tell the French, who had been fighting for their nation's survival for over three years, that the US had stepped into the breach to show the Allies how the war was to be won. The Americans were at first reluctant to take advice until it had been forced upon them by practical demonstration – by losses.[117] This partially explains Clemenceau's insistence, recalled by Marshall in 1957, "the Americans must get into action straight away." American officers and men were observed making fun of the Allies and implying that if they had been any good they would have finished the war long ago. Well-informed circles indicated that some American officers were not willing to mix with French officers of their own class. This proved irksome to the French, whose sophisticated courtesy is and was well known. They resented this disregard for their proffered hospitality.

Brigadier General Peter Edward Traub, 51st Infantry Brigade, while discussing training for

The Europeans did take notice of the wealth of Americans arriving in theatre. The soldier's purchasing power was impressive. The American military received a much higher wage than the Allies – twice as much as the British and four times as much as the average *poilu*. An American private earned $30 a month while stationed in the United States. Serving overseas in Europe entitled him to three more dollars for the same period and proportionally increased with each promotion.

Prices increased as more American soldiers arrived. It became hard for the French to buy articles in the villages back of the lines without spending considerably more than before for the same product and far more than the average Frenchman could afford. David Englander writes that the arrival of the American armies aggravated the relative deprivation experienced by the *poilu*. American servicemen were, however, considered less aloof than the British. As one *poilu* wrote, "*C'est un allié: l'Américain c'est un copain. Tu comprends?*"[119]

CHAPTER 3

War in the Woëvre Trenches

Lieutenant Colonel C. Petitjean's *128ᵉ brigade d'infanterie* had their first experience of trench warfare in the southern Woëvre front.[120] Two strongly fortified enemy emplacements faced each other and primarily engaged in operations described as *coup de main*, raids; the German terms were **Patrouillenangriff** (raid) or **Unternehmen** (operation or enterprise). Petitjean's battleground helped American units transition from training scenarios into actual war conditions. America's Army learned the art of modern warfare in the Woëvre in the first half of 1918, but Pershing's forces did not witness major operations at the army level until the St. Mihiel offensive commenced on 12 September 1918.[121]

When the 1914 war of manoeuvre stalemated at the rivers Aisne and Ypres, the military art of positional war commenced. October 1914 witnessed the first excavations of ground. Trenches of the American Civil War around Petersburg in 1864 provided the American military with some vague understanding of positional war. Future Allied and German military leaders, including General Pershing, witnessed one of the first applications of trench warfare in the 20th century in Manchuria, when they were on-scene during the 1905 Russo-Japanese War.

An in-depth knowledge of the battlefield's terrain was essential for all combatants. An understanding of relief, height, slopes, and identifying both natural and artificial objects on the surface became key to conducting the campaign.[122] For the most part, the invading Germans took the initiative and acquired readily defensible terrain and commenced earthworks. Such was the case in the southern Woëvre when **Armeeabteilung Strantz** reached the limit of their advance. Trenches in the Woëvre remained static for almost the entire war.[123]

Sectors defined positional war. The general scheme revolved around combat managed through the "sector" – from the front line to the depth of ground held by a division. Sectors were compared to a "human hand and arm, with the main arteries running down the arm and feeding the spread fingers through the smaller veins which lead to the finger tips and return."[124] They further divided into "sub-sectors", each normally held by a unit at regimental strength with their front line comprising several "centres of resistance" designed for a battalion-sized garrison. Centres of resistance were organized around several "strong points", the first line fortified with wire entanglements and other obstacles. Aerial reconnaissance provided photographic data to create a continually updated cartographic record. Sector planning required keeping the appropriate amount of weapons and personnel in place. To do it right transformed resources into numbers – a log book of calculations applied to a given grid square.[125]

Years of positional war created elaborate systems of firing trenches to the front, dugouts (*abris*) in the rear, communication trenches (*boyaux de communication* – referred simply as *boyaux*, literally "guts or tubes") from rear to front and connecting trenches to flanking groups. Sector strong points supported each other. The rule was to hold as many men as possible in *abris* with a company or two in reserve.[126] Sectors were linked by several *boyaux* – decreasing in number as the distance from the front line increased.[127] Combat in positional war meant pushing forward sector by sector, following waves of infantry, making use of the ground and naturally where possible avoiding the enemy's artillery and flanking fire. Maintaining the advance meant successful application of weapons such as machine guns and trench mortars.[128] Sustaining combat required effective distribution of supplies, requiring special narrow-gauge railroad lines to the sectors.

Sgt William Thorpe (formerly Douglas Fairbanks' cameraman) works in the flooded trenches. (*Pictorial History of the 26th Division*)

The *boyau* let the infantry manoeuvre safely within the trench labyrinth and provided a route for reinforcement. The initial line of rifle-pits became roomy trenches, allowing combatants to stand and move about without being shot. The forward firing trench was dug deep and narrow to provide the best protection. However, the combatants soon learned that this design limited the infantry's ability to circulate. To avoid having to enlarge the trench, a series of smaller circulation trenches were organized along the main firing trench. The design and building of trenches evolved throughout the war.

Boyau configuration varied with the terrain. One soldier described the pattern they occupied in the Woëvre: "Leading from our second line trench at the top of the hill down to the front line were various intercommunicating trenches (*boyaux*). They were constructed in zig-zag fashion. It would never do to run straight lines for this would expose the men passing up and down to the view of the enemy. It's harder to detect movement of traffic in a zig-zag trench built on an incline, besides it's not so easy to rake those trenches with shell or machine-gun fire."[129]

Natural divisions between sectors were sometimes provided by topographical features such as canals, rivers, main roads, or railway lines. It was generally assumed that three battalion sectors represented a regimental boundary.[130] Analysis of sector and unit echelon alignment commenced once a network of *boyaux* was identified – deployment activity, reinforcement routes, and centres of resistance. Both sides used aerial reconnaissance to identify and evaluate important lines of communication and focus on levels of activity and possible unit assignment.

Soldiers identified their sector by the most prominent feature. The sector in the Woëvre was called the Toul sector (largest city in the region), "*De la Reine*", (the largest forest), "Ansauville Sector" (location of 1st Division headquarters under the command of Major General Bullard) or a combination, "*La Reine et Boucq*" (the largest forest near the front lines and the village of the château occupied by Major General Edwards).

LIAISON

A key assumption of battle was that the infantry-man did not know where he was. In the noise and tumult it was not easy to see or know what was happening. The map governed every minute of positional war. Liaison provided the means to interpret and react to the map. Good liaison kept the commander appraised of the ongoing battle. Liaison entailed transmission of information and orders "necessary to accomplish a concerted effort".[131]

Liaison among adjacent units was a problem identified by Chaumont frequently at this time but not resolved. Liaison required telephone, wireless, ground telegraph lines, aeroplanes, and *ballons captif*. Communication in the front lines was primarily by telephone. Thousands of metres of telephone wire were fastened to the trench walls. The prevailing attitude was string new wire rather than repair old wire. The abundance of wire added to the congestion within the trench area, making evacuation of the wounded harder.[132]

Runners were the last resort in battle. They provided good results if they survived. A 102nd Machine Gun Battalion member paid his respects:

> The runners are game little lads. Seldom have I heard them mentioned, but let me tell you it takes some nerve to be a real runner. He makes his trips regularly each day, and at such other times as necessary, from one place to another. Over the Top or up through the communication trenches, it makes no difference – on they go. In the day many places are covered by machine gun indirect fire, yet they are not afraid … We had an attack of gas, which lasted almost twenty-four hours, yet these lads did their run through the thickest of it. You've got to hand it to them; a good one is a game lad.[133]

In many cases, including on the Woëvre front lines in 1918, the runner became the only way to conduct the battle.

POSITION 1

The French managed the war through three positions along the front lines. Position 1 created a zone of defensive terrain between the line and the hostile line where the enemy resided – No Man's Land. No Man's Land was only 50 to 100 metres in width in many locations along the 650-kilometre Western Front. After three years, changes on the front line meant Position 1 was sometimes marked by abandoned trenches running everywhere. The French gave Position 1 a strange, phenomenological description: "it is the expression of a fact".[134] For the ground now occupied by the Americans, the main Position 1 trench was Sibille Trench, which linked *Bois de Remières* to the north-west of Seicheprey across to *Lieutenant Colonel* Petitjean's *128e brigade d'infanterie* battleground of 1914. The primary function for troops in Position 1 was to maintain vigilance. Patrols became a constant feature for each unit embedded in the front lines.

They looked for the location of saps (trench construction into No Man's Land), bombing positions, and listening posts.[135] Each defensive point in Position 1 was to become a small salient against any enemy activity, but the front line could be destroyed by artillery fire.

When the 1st Division arrived, the three lines of trenches were to the front of the St. Dizier-Metz road. The most advanced of the three lines that comprised Position 1 was known as the "old front line" and was not in use.[136] Major Theodore Roosevelt Jr., a battalion commander with the 26th Regiment, mused on the changing dynamic of his sector. What had required a battalion-sized element to maintain a kilometre of ground on the front line now only took a company of soldiers.[137] Roosevelt's 1st Division commander, Major General Robert Bullard, had his own thoughts on Position 1. Bullard's counterpart to the east, *Général* Monroe, *69e division d'infanterie*, upheld the *a priori* assertion that the first lines of Position 1 of the Woëvre front line were were to be held at all costs. Bullard logically saw defence best maintained from the rear trenches. To make Position 1 fit Bullard's expectations required 1,500 men working up to three months to expand and improve the woefully neglected trench networks. Bullard's discussions with his American commander, General Liggett, reinforced his thinking. Liggett advised General Bullard that while he thought it was none of his business, he recommended he draw back to the rear position.[138]

POSITION 1–BIS

Position 1-Bis was the intermediate or second line, where the main defending force operated from more elaborate networks. Planning operations included a detailed assessment of Position 1-Bis and procedures to interdict the enemy.[139] Sector commanders worked out what was required to apply their forces on the line of resistance. The value of forces in place depended on their position. Following his discussions with General Liggett, Bullard's 1st Division operated mainly from the second line, something that the Germans did as well.[140]

The *32e corps d'armée* plan of defence governing 1st Division and 26th Division emplacement at the front did not contemplate reinforcing those troops in front of Position 1-Bis in case of a major German assault. For both divisions, if an assault was underway, troops in front of Position 1-Bis were to fight it out alone. The trench system existing in front of Position 1-Bis may have served the French in those years where both sides "lived and let live" in a "Quiet Sector", but those conditions had changed.[141]

Protected *abris* and more effective strong points became the solution to both holding ground and inflicting a heavy toll on the attackers. A few good *abris* existed in this sector, but there were not enough to house the majority of the men. Barbed wire lay in front of the defences but was poorly arranged. *Abris* constructed under ruined houses afforded good shelter during the daytime. In many places it was impossible to proceed any great distance in a trench without climbing onto the parapet above. 1-Bis position trenches were excavated, but the soil was rocky and hard making construction work difficult. Beaumont Quarry, down the slope from Beaumont, while serving the defenders as an ideal shelter, was almost uninhabitable. Water leaked from every crack in the stone roof and walls. When rain fell for even a short time, every part of the floor was waterlogged. There was a lack of ventilation, atrocious sanitary conditions with salvage and waste everywhere, and a foul stench that never went away. The soldiers in Position 1-Bis seeking refuge at Seicheprey, Marvoisin, Beaumont, and *Bois de Remières* had to contend with similar conditions. The *1re division marocaine*, predecessors to 1st Division, never established a latrine system. It was said *1re division marocaine* never did keep up a sector. When the 26th Division assumed the sector from the 1st Division, the condition of the *abris* had not improved.[142]

On the ridge that overlooked the Seicheprey valley, the Beaumont Ridge provided another layer of defence. A few hundred yards to the south the Remières Trench connected *Bois de Remières* to Seicheprey. *Boyaux* Jury-Remières looped from *Bois du Jury* where the *162e régiment d'infanterie* operated into the southern edge of *Bois de Remières*. Position 1 and Position 1-Bis line of trenches were managed by subsectors known as F-1, F-2 and H-1 defining the area of operations for the companies assigned.[143]

In Center A, soldiers lived in *abris* near the St. Dizier road – every night going to their posts along the forward edge of the ridge. Center B *abris* were in a narrow, deep ravine, sloping to the west from the road leading to Seicheprey. Center D was Beaumont Quarry occupied by the company assigned as well as the Machine Gun Company covering the area. Center E *abris* were under the ruined houses. South of the entire ridge of the St. Dizier-Metz road were battery positions. The 1-Bis occupied trench line ran from Marvoisin eastward, crossing the Rupt de Mad river, along the "Q" trench, *Boyau des Nanteis*, Sibille Trench (in front of Seicheprey), the *Boyau de Remières*, northern edge of the *Bois de Remières* and finally the *Bois Carré*. The front line was divided into four subsectors from east to west: F-1, F-2, H-1 and H-2. Each subsection was held by Company A. Platoons and squads manned the strong points, advantageously placed on slightly higher ground to cover the "draws" and the front between posts with flanking fire.

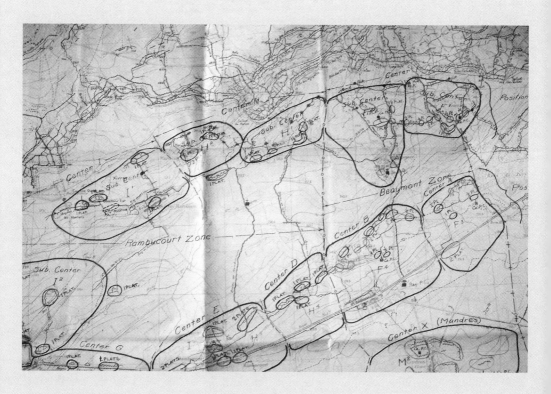

Centers A, B, C and D.

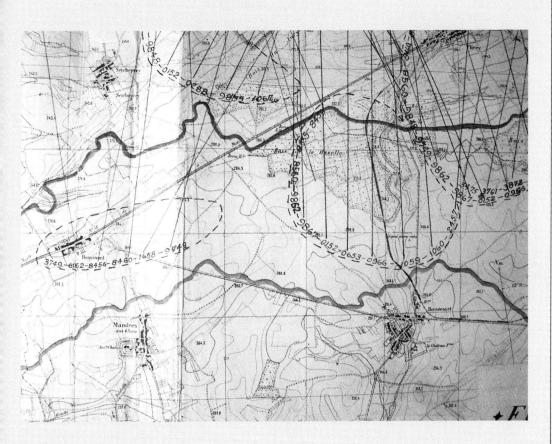

1-Bis map.

Outposts and listening posts were established in front of this line. Patrols linked up covering the unoccupied areas. The widest break was between H-1 and F-2 north-west of Seicheprey. In the *Bois de Remières* the stand-to positions were near the centre. The strong points for the Americans were in the corners of the woods.[144]

The Germans' view to the south showed a continuous rise of terrain constituting the Beaumont Ridge. Both 1st Division and 26th Division had their respective regiments establish their headquarters on that ridge, providing a central location for command and control between Position 1-Bis and Position 2. From Beaumont a road ran down to Seicheprey, through the village and straight on into the enemy lines. In front of Seicheprey and *Bois de Remières*, which lay to the right of the village, was a gentle slope, laced with a system of half-ruined trenches, unsuitable for effective defence.[145] A deep ravine and a quarry in front of Beaumont were of tactical importance in organising the defence of the principal line of resistance. The tactical advantage lay with the Germans. The Americans in their assigned sector had a number of awkward salients, difficult to defend. Their front was entered by several shallow ravines which could afford cover to an attacking force, aided by observation from *Côte 380*.[146]

POSITION 2

The third and most important French area for defence was Position 2 comprising the position of resistance and its advanced works south of Position 1-Bis. French military policy emphasised that forces were to secure Position 2 at all costs.[147] *Général* Passaga clearly stated Allied roles and missions for the southern Woëvre front in his 7 February memorandum, "Personal and Secret Instruction on the Conduct of Defence in the Sector of the *32e corps d'armée*":

> The troops in sector will be reinforced so as to allow the arrival of the large units destined to offer battle in the line of resistance. The aim of this reinforcement is not to increase the density of the first line [Position 1], but to strengthen the resistance by a more ample disposition in depth. *Corps d'armée* are to occupy Position 2 … divisions of reinforcement will be placed in second line and occupy the second position.

The 1st Division was to be echeloned in depth to allow for any breach to be thwarted or delayed so that reinforcements could successfully manoeuvre.[148] When *Général* Gérard, *VIIIe armée*, took command over the southern Woëvre in April 1918, the defence policy shifted from Position 2 to Position 1.

"WET AND SLOPPY"

When the Americans came to the Woëvre in 1918 they assumed responsibility for terrain that was appalling. The Rupt de Mad, a 62-kilometre south-western tributary to the Moselle River, ran along a part of No Man's Land with high banks covered by German trenches and machine-gun pillboxes.[149] The ground along the French front lines was so low that only shallow trenches could be dug and these were largely filled with water. Winters on the line were miserable experiences, especially in the marsh land to the west and north of Seicheprey village. Spring rains created additional misery thanks to clay capturing and

retaining the surface water and creating a swamp. The clay made combat nigh-on impossible and wretched to live with. When heavy rains came, streams and marshes flooded throughout the valley.[150] Private Raymond Wunderlich, 101st Engineers, recalled the Seicheprey setting: "The ground out in front in that little valley which formed No Man's Land, was wet and sloppy – almost marshy. The trenches and dugout walls oozed water all the time. In fact, by the side of the front trench near our dugout we had a little spring. We didn't even have to carry water to the place. But the whole region was badly shell torn. This was the country over which the French and the Germans had been fighting for four years. Up the line twenty-five miles to the north-west was Verdun."[151]

Lieutenant Colonel James L. Bevans, Chief Surgeon of the 26th Division, recalled after the war the horrible environment: "One typical camp of about a hundred men looked more like the hiding place of old time brigands than anything else. The men lived in little caves and dugouts … The cook-house was a half completed wooden building, the rain coming through in streams, and no attempt had been made at paving with duck-boards to prevent mud; the cooks waded about in rubber boots." Bevans' replacement recalled, "In many of the trenches the men were knee deep to waist deep in liquid mud most of the time … Many slept in the mud on the firing steps … Lice were becoming a nuisance."[152] Trenches in the southern Woëvre front averaged about 2 metres in depth and were wide enough to permit men to pass each other easily. There was a remarkable network of intercommunicating trenches that became so complex that a guide was assigned to escort support troops going north from Position 1-Bis to avoid them being lost in the labyrinth.[153] Walking the trench was a hazardous undertaking. The revetments were either broken or pushed inward by the pressure of the crumbling bank – making the trench more exposed to enemy fire. Shells of ordinary calibre could be heard approaching, and the promptings of self-preservation soon taught the soldier to gauge the probable point where the missile would strike by the sound of its flight. A faint, far away rustle announced the departure of the missile from the enemy's battery pit, and all ears instantly attuned to it. If it passed high overhead with a diminishing wail, all well and good, but if it suddenly swept upward in pitch and changed abruptly to a harsh, demonic scream, the danger was real. The only precaution was to throw oneself flat in the mud or dive headlong down an *abris* passageway. The flying steel fragments ranged in size from that of a tip of a ballpoint pen to ribbons of steel as large as a man's finger.[154] There were long stretches where the trenches contained water 30-60cm deep over soft mud. Over the years engineers tried to build drainage ditches but they became useless as the elements and explosions filled them with clay and soil. In turn, the rains transformed the diggings into rivers of soft mud, sometimes to a depth of almost 1 metre throughout the entire length of the trench network. Duck-boards laid in to allow transit became hidden in the mud or obscured by water. Gaps between the boards from incessant traffic and explosions created deeper pits that men descended to the waist in. Runners carrying emergency messages were delayed. It was telling that even Chaumont staff members relayed to headquarters that the condition of the trenches was extremely bad. What the Americans recalled of the Woëvre was mud and muck.[155]

Abris accommodations in the Seicheprey sector were spartan at best. It was hard to escape underground because the imperviousness of the clay created more basins to hold water. All of them had to be pumped out and in some instances all that was possible was to keep the water sufficiently low so as not to flood the bunks. Only when the late spring arrived did the Americans see improvement. The subsurface room measured on average 3 metres by 3 metres with a ceiling at 2 metres. Loose dirt and camouflage comprised the roof. As for the floor, it was rough lumber that provided minimal protection against the constant water seepage that came to the surface with every footstep. The *abris* was designed to accommodate a squad of eight men. Four tiers of bunks built of rough lumber filled the already cramped space. The soldiers slept on bunks with just enough room to turn over. The procedure for retiring was to pull off footwear but leave everything else on – allowing for a rapid response to an attack or call to stand to. The *abris* also served as cover against the threat from gas. At the *abris* door a gas curtain was hooked at the top with a wire loop over a nail and attached to a string. Whenever the gas guard gave the gas alarm while the squad was sleeping, all that was required to seal the *abris* was to pull the string to drop the curtain.[156] Rats were tolerated as canary equivalents – providing warning to sleeping soldiers when senseless squealing and running in all directions woke them to gas fumes infiltrating the area.[157] *Abris* supporting forces on Position 1-Bis were backed up against the Beaumont road. Their entrances connected to short trenches that were angled rather than proceeding straight in to prevent any illumination being detected when a match or candle was lit. Trench discipline prohibited smoking in the front line at night. The policy was not well enforced. One method to feed the habit was to pull a sack over one's head to shield the light from view when dragging on a cigarette or pipe.[158]

The terrain did not help concealment or provide much protection for artillery emplacements. The region's natural features forced artillery within Position 2 to divide into two groupings – west and east – proscribed by a series of lakes and extremely marshy ground.[159] Like the infantry in Position 1 and Position 1-Bis, the artillery operating out of Position 2 suffered from the water. The gun pits were miniature lakes, requiring crews to wear slickers when operating the guns. The daily routine when not firing was to determine what was the priority for the crew – deal with the water or improve the construction of the emplacement. Everything became flooded so pumps ran all the time. Inside the *abris* at night, the water rose almost to the level of the crew's bunks so slickers were worn continuously. When the priority was construction, all the building material of I-beams, sheet iron, and logs was carried under the net each day before sunrise or after sunset to

Generalmajor Paulus von Stolzmann, commander of 78.Reserve.Division, drawn by Oscar Bruch while he served on the Eastern Front.

a large tree. The gun-crew and officers were in similar dugouts – evil, damp holes under the ground, that would never dry out. Each dugout had several blankets always soaked with water as protection against gas. Our Infantry lines were not very far from this one-gun position. The support trenches for the Infantry were just a hundred and fifty yards in front of the gun.[161]

The combatants displayed an indomitable spirit while enduring the misery of that time. Lieutenant George Buchanan Redwood, Intelligence Officer for Company I, 28th Infantry, wrote to his mother describing the weather:

avoid detection. The path that led to the position was continued on to the woods beyond, and men approaching or leaving in the daytime had to do so one at a time.[160]

One description of an artillery emplacement in Position 1-Bis shows the artilleryman's kinship in suffering with his infantry comrades:

Our one gun was placed in a far from shell-proof gun pit on the edge of the road leading from the Beaumont to Metz (a section of the Paris-Metz Highway). Our dugouts were under the road with the entrances under the root of

I wish I could tell you more of our life here than the facts that we are well and weather (usually) is bad. We have had hardly anything but rain – that is, until it changed to snow, and today it has switched back to rain. It is amusing how savagely the enlisted men write home what they would do if they 'could only get that guy who called this country Sunny France.' Poor fellows! If they came expecting perennial blue skies and a semi-tropical atmosphere, they have been rudely enough undeceived by the last few months. They're always cheerful, however, and in the main are a fine steady lot of young fellows.[162]

CHAPTER 4

Assault over No Man's Land

Major Friedrich Bruns was an exemplary soldier, fighting in most of the worst battles the war had seen since the first shots of August 1914. He was a battalion commander in the opening days and was promoted to **Major** in October 1914 while assigned to the Verdun area. He was reassigned to the **21. Reserve Division (21. R. D.)** as battalion commander of **Res. I. R. 80**. The **21. R. D.** maintained a distinguished record throughout the war thanks to combat leadership by officers like Major Bruns. The **21. R. D** fought the French to the west in the Champagne sector during the opening salvos of the Verdun campaign. Four months later, **21. R. D.** returned to Verdun. Bruns led his battalion in battle after battle and was recognized for his abilities and leadership throughout. French counter-attacks against German positions at Verdun were extensive in August of 1916. **Res. I. R. 80** and Bruns' battalion held their ground, experiencing heavy losses, causing **Res. I. R. 80** to withdraw from the battle in September. **Res. I. R. 80** deployed back to the Champagne sector. After three months, the unit went back to Verdun and fought over the winter months until the 1917 French offensive at Chemin-des-Dâmes ramped up, requiring more German forces to repel the attack. **Major** Bruns fought with his battalion with great distinction, finally holding the ground near Reims at Ailette.[163] The year 1917 culminated in the great British tank offensive at Cambrai.

21. R. D. was ordered to the north to replace forces overwhelmed by the surge of tanks. **Major** Bruns and his battalion were part of the successful counter-attack that pushed the British forces back and as he had done in the years of combat, he held his ground.

After Cambrai, **Major** Bruns departed **Res. I. R. 80** for the Woëvre to assume regimental command on 27 January 1918 of the **78. R. D. Res. I. R. 259**. The regiment had just arrived in their assigned sector **zwischen Maas und Mosel**. **Major** Bruns choreographed most of the ground operations from his assigned **Abschnitt G** against the 1st Division and 26th Division at the southern Woëvre front. The **78. R. D.** was assessed as a third-rate division by Allied intelligence based on experiences and accomplishments to date including time spent at Verdun and subsequent deployment to the Woëvre. With Bruns, they assumed a character that demonstrated excellence on the battlefield – they mastered the ability to follow well-defined plans, striking hard and holding the ground.

THINKING THROUGH THE ASSAULT

The great offensives that marked the first years of positional war sought to annihilate the front lines, closely followed by attacking infantry that advanced into the pulverised trenches containing survivors that had not been killed or crazed. The advance proceeded against the trench works beyond the first line – enduring concentrated artillery fire from the retreating enemy as terrible as its own. Despite monumental efforts to break through, the great line of obstacles that defined the front lines was bent but never broken. Invariably in this holocaust at the front, both shells and men were pretty well used up. The infantry battle was not seen as a simple calculation of numerical strengths, assuming the more numerous prevailed. Rather it was a matter of comparative "fighting power" (which depended on rest, training and equipment), the care taken in preparation and the skill of officers and men, combined with rapid and determined action. Wherever possible, attacking infantry were assigned short distances to assault enemy lines. Attacks commenced from trenches, craters and *abris*, but "jumping off" positions were discreetly assigned so as not to alert the enemy and draw in lethal artillery barrages. Short distances reduced both casualties and the numbers required to achieve an objective. Infantry deployment was carefully planned since overcrowding led to additional losses from the wall of lead and explosives that came from the defenders.[164] The infantry battle between German and French forces broke down to the comparable 30-man combat group level of **Zug** [platoon strength] and *groupe de combat* (*GC*, French *armée* designation for infantry combat group). American soldiers learned *GC* tactics from the French upon arrival in Europe.

Treatises were soon prepared by veterans of positional war. One such work by *capitaine* Andre Laffargue, *153ᵉ regiment d'infanterie*, entitled *Etude sur l'attaque dans la periode actuelle de la guerre* (translated as "The Attack in Trench Warfare") made an important point about positional war. The American military acquired Laffargue's insight on attack thanks to the *Infantry Journal* publishing his work in July 1916. Laffargue's opening statement illustrated the frustration felt by the French and Allied forces after a year of conflict, culminating in stalemate. "The attack at the present period has become one of siege

warfare. We must accept it as it is, study it, tax our wits to find special means to prepare effectively for it and to orient the instruction of troops entirely with this in view."[165] For Laffargue the key problem was since the war had become a siege, it made very little difference in the overall scheme of things if a single trench or a few yards of ground were captured. The simple answer that he proposed was that a proper attack should not "nibble" at a defensive position, but, in the manner of "an immense and unlimited assault, delivered on all points of the attacking front, [should] swallow the whole of the enemy ground in a single gulp." To do this required "overwhelming superiority of fire" at all phases. Sadly for the Allies, Laffargue's novel concepts became rooted in the masterful thinking of the Germans – with consequences that governed the battlefield in the last year of the war.[166]

The German document *Proposals*, which slightly predated *Étude sur l'attaque dans la période actuelle de la guerre*, espoused immediate capitalization on success, breakthrough in one big attack (surprise as a "crushing blow"), huge barrages directed partly at enemy reserves and batteries, careful preparation, and novel features that Laffargue suggested, such as pushing forward "infantry guns". *Proposals* posited the first onslaught be "very strong" with companies coming on in four to six lines. Pivotal to successful assault across No Man's Land was avoiding wide stretches, shortening the time and distance by digging sap heads, or advancing by night and digging in close to the enemy. An important feature was that attacking waves would contain "special troops" detailed to clearing trenches and evacuating prisoners.[167]

The force arm that came with this thinking became one of the most illustrious of positional war – the **Sturmtruppen** (Stormtroopers) and **Stosstruppen** (assault force). Of the two, **Sturmtruppen** remained a fixture in the thinking of military doctrine for the remainder of the century, when the Nazis applied it to their own version of elite forces. The very notion of **Sturmtruppen** had a propaganda value: a power to raise uncertainty in the hearts of the enemy while

P.C. Ettighoffer and his colleagues in Res. 258. R.I.R. prior to deployment to *Maas und Mosel*.
(Ettighoffer, *Verdun*)

creating confidence in their fellow **Stosstruppen** fighting alongside. The celebrity of the few could, however, be a double-edged sword, as was recorded by Stefan Westmann, a medical officer serving in **Infanterie Regiment 119**: "The men of the storm battalions were treated like football stars. They lived in comfortable quarters, they travelled to the 'playing ground' in buses, they did their jobs and disappeared again, and left the poor foot sloggers to dig in, to deal with the counter-attacks and endure the avenging artillery fire of the enemy. They were so well trained and had developed such a high standard of team work ... They moved like snakes over the ground, camouflaged and making use of every bit of cover, so that they did not offer any targets for artillery fire. It has been said that Stormtroop units suffered disproportionately high casualties, due to the difficulty of the tasks they were given and the single-minded determination with which they were carried out. Conversely, it has been suggested that Stormtroop units actually suffered lower casualties because of their new tactics, and because they were specially chosen as fit men who were withdrawn between operations."[168]

Der Angriff im Stellungskrieg, or "The Attack in Positional Warfare", published on 1 January 1918, clarified the doctrine of **Stoss**, or shock, tactics, which ultimately affected the course of the 1918 offensives. *Der Angriff im Stellungskrieg* brought together the best ideas of what had been developed over the past three years into a single, universal instruction.[169] It emphasised thorough "education" of the assaulting troops, the role of command, the quality of inter-arm liaison and a "centre of gravity" to the attack. Naturally, troops were to be thoroughly trained and practised in attacking trenches, but they were also to be educated "in that spirit of bold attack and will to conquer, with which we entered the present war" and which was "the first guarantee of success." Command during the attack in positional warfare was not simply a matter of giving clear orders and ensuring co-operation between all arms and neighbouring sectors, but recognising and taking advantage of the fact that "every attack offers an opportunity for independent decision and action even down to the private soldier." Close liaison between all arms was not only seen as tactically important but as vital for informing the decisions of higher command, and preventing surprises from the flanks. The idea of a "centre of gravity," or focal point, a **Schwerpunkt**, was not new but ancient, and helped to ensure a superiority of force at a vital point where a modest success might produce results disproportionate to the effort. The man who personified this thinking in the Woëvre was **Major** Bruns.

Major Bruns' **Res. I. R. 259** commenced planning to assault American positions in the Woëvre two weeks after arrival.[170] His regiment's mission was to break through to the third line, destroy *abris* and trenches, and return with prisoners and booty. Bruns' first major operation against American forces in the Woëvre area employed a **Sturm-Kompagnie** (assault company) largely comprised of **Stosstruppen** from his own **Res. I. R. 259**. Adding to the punch were elite members of the Armée-level **Sturmbataillon 14**, one of fourteen that supported German infantry operations throughout the Western Front. Bruns saw any offensive strike against the enemy as requiring all resources. For his upcoming strike against the newly assigned 1st Division the **Sturmbataillon** had **Flammenwerfer** (flamethrower) weaponry. Finally, the **Pioniere** (engineers) would focus on destroying wire entanglements on the front lines followed by destruction of defences and *abris*. Bruns referred to his strike trio of **Stosstruppen, Sturmtruppen** and **Pioniere** as **Sturm-Kompagnie**.[171]

TRAINING

French *2e Bureau* intelligence from prisoners interrogated on 20 February 1918 showed battalion and regimental exercises covered an infantry advance. The battalion practised company advances in two waves of similarly equipped soldiers. In the front wave each squad of eight men deployed at intervals of two metres. The squad leader took his position in the middle of the squad. Men were armed with rifles and had gas masks. The second wave was 30 metres behind the first wave and in the same formation. Machine guns were placed between the two waves. The attack was made in three waves. The first wave comprised three companies arranged in double line formation. A fourth company deployed 100 metres behind the first three companies and filled up gaps in the line. Each company had three light machine guns and two heavy machine guns at the flanks of the formation. The third wave advanced in section columns – four infantry and three **Pioniere** placed alternately.[172] A **Gruppe** (section) was organized into two complementary **Truppen** (squads). One squad comprised riflemen to protect the other that carried the machine gun.[173]

Major Bruns' **Stosstrupp** training area was located 8 kilometres east of his regiment head-quarters at Bouillonville. Preparations for the assault were sanctioned at all echelons. **General der Artillerie** von Gallwitz institutionalised new attack patterns for his armies, with training areas for divisions, **Stosstruppen**, **Pioniere**, and his regional **Sturmbataillon** to better achieve coordination among all participants. **Stoss** preparation could take weeks or longer prior to the execution date. Clear guidance was provided to the assault force on what was required of each member who in turn made themselves entirely familiar with the ground to be traversed including the wire entanglements. Mornings were spent in practical drills, afternoons in theoretical instruction. All were trained to know the difference between French grenades, German **Handgranaten** and dummy grenades – mainly thrown by the attackers while on the run; practice included throwing from trenches in standing and lying positions. The **Sturm-Kompagnie** rehearsal took place several days before execution, reviewing what was necessary to achieve a very brief and violent artillery preparation using **Minenwerfer** (trench mortars).[174] Bruns chose the week prior to the assault for **Hauptmann** Seebohm, **Stosstrupp** commander, to conduct practice and coordination with the other elements of the assault.[175]

WEAPONS

German assault operations in the **zwischen Maas und Moselle** used most of the weapons that were integral to the Germans' "classical" plan of attack. Light machine-gun groups were assigned to the **Sturm-Kompagnie**. **Stosstruppen** were equipped for independent action, carrying rifles, pistols, **Handgranaten**, and entrenching tools. This element of the assault was very mobile and possessed concentrated firepower, the punch behind the infantry attack. Once set in motion the light machine-gun groups could carry on the fire fight and not rely on the groups of riflemen. The task of the machine guns was always the same – clear away obstacles in the way of the infantry's assault to bring offensive power to bear as far forward as possible.[176] Many **Stosstruppen** carried with them the first widely used sub-machine gun, the **MP-18**. The new sub-machine gun was light and easy to handle, and had much greater firepower than a rifle.

Heavy machine guns (**Model 08**) formed the connecting link with **Minenwerfer** and field guns. By virtue of their mobility, they supported the attack especially at points where the heavier weapons could not keep pace with the rapid advance. **Model 08** heavy machine guns assisted the progress of the attack of the light machine gun groups as well as attacking aeroplanes and tanks. The weapons provided additional security against enemy counter-thrusts during the forward movement. The machine gun also brought fire to bear against the flanks if necessary. The bulk of the **Model 08** machine guns were retained at the rear, firing through gaps in the German lines or firing over the German lines to support the attack underway or to deter enemy counter-attacks. **Model 08**s modified as anti-aircraft guns were considered a primary weapon against low-flying infantry contact aeroplanes.[177]

The **Flammenwerfer** helped break down resistance at isolated points such as blockhouses, machine-gun nests and centres of resistance.[178] The **Stosstruppen** employed **Flammenwerfer** specialists such as those from **Sturmbataillon.14** to destroy the enemy's will to fight.[179]

The 259 Reserve Infanterie Regiment was the first enemy regiment to confront the US Army in its own sector. (*Das Regiment*)

In some German assaults, **Pioniere** were the **Flammenwerfer** operators.[180] The **Flammenwerfer** device comprised a cylindrical casing with an outer tank containing 9 litres of liquid surrounding a centre globe that contained compressed air. The 11kg apparatus had a nozzle about 2.5 metres in length, the end of which contained an incendiary cartridge that ignited the ejected liquid in a stream of fire that had a range of 15 metres.[181]

Handgranaten, be it the **Stielhandgranate** (stick grenade, the most common type) or **Eierhandgranate** (egg grenade) were regarded as an indispensable weapon in trench warfare, both for offensive and defensive use. **Stielhandgranate** produced blast rather than splinters. **Eierhandgranaten** were ideal for defence creating a splinter effect against assault.[182] Hand grenades came into extensive use in trench fighting since their curved trajectories dislodged the enemy in trenches or shell holes. Four or five seconds elapsed between the release of the fuse and the explosion. In a war of position where the opposing forces lived and fought in underground chambers and semi-subterranean trench systems, the **Handgranate** was a most effective weapon.

Bruns included a **Granatwerfer** battery of six men in his planning to counter enemy rifle grenade elements. Deployed with German infantry companies, the **Granatwerfer** could throw a grenade a distance of 460 metres. It was portable, weighing slightly more than 38kgs, and extremely effective against trench positions, sentry posts, machine guns, and other infantry targets. The high rate of fire and accuracy made it an ideal weapon to use in support of infantry raiding parties. It was also useful in driving off enemy patrols that had been detected in No Man's Land.

MINENWERFER – THE PRIMARY WEAPON

Critical to German battle planning was the role of **Minenwerfer** (the abbreviation generally used by the Germans was **MW**). The common description for the weapon system was trench mortar – a weapon common on both sides. The Germans had better results. The **MW** gave the offensive more flexibility. A more apt description was "bomb thrower" – lobbing high explosive (HE) at a very fast rate and being an excellent weapon to annihilate front lines as well as counter machine guns. **Erster Oberquartiermeister General der Infanterie** Erich Ludendorff declared on 30 March 1918 that the **MW** was held in high esteem regarding German positional war strategies. The **MW** greatly aided offensive operations by breaking up points of resistance, repulsed hostile Allied operations, and reinforced points of resistance during withdrawal. The nine-day-old Operation *Michael* showed German commanders that the principal resistance offered by Allies was machine-gun nests distributed in depth. The aim of total destruction of machine-gun nests by the artillery bombardment prior to the assault was not achieved. Ludendorff sought neutralisation of machine-gun nests by means of heavy artillery fire and bombardment that included the use of gas shells. The **MW** was valued by German infantry thanks to the close proximity of the two. It could be quickly deployed into the lines as well as accompany infantry in the attack. When advancing troops came on machine guns, the weapon of choice was the light **MW**, firing up to 1,000 metres. Fire was decisive. Masses of troops were no longer the key to success. Advancing forces now had to employ medium **MW** whenever the attack came to a standstill, especially against villages and farms. The **MW** was to annihilate the enemy's infantry.[183]

The changing dynamic of the front line changed the role of artillery and **MW**. Artillery was moved further to the rear to ensure greater survivability from counter-battery fire. Trenches became more defensible so artillery had to be modified to drop projectiles at short range. **MW** became the weapon of choice providing more firepower at shorter distances.[184] The **MW** supplemented the artillery in many ways. **MW** and heavy gun fire was used against objectives that a planned rolling barrage could not reach. Light **MW** fire moved forward from line to line and from support point to support point in front of the rolling barrage. The medium and heavy **MW** did not fire during this phase. The heavy type cleared a space of more than 10 metres in diameter in a wire entanglement. Single fragments were scattered as far as 440 metres. With a delay action fuse the bomb could blow in mined dugouts with 10 metres of earth cover, while the medium type blew in covers with up to 4 metres of protection. Light **MW** were mainly used against personnel. All **MW** personnel were being trained to use all types of **MW** so that their equipment could be changed when desired. The organization of the battalion detachment was new – not more than two **MW** but with the same personnel strength of thirty. **Pioniere** normally crewed the **Minenwerfer** companies (an **MW** company attached to each division comprised two heavy, four medium, and six light pieces).

An independent **Minenwerfer Abteilung** was also formed for deployment at **Korps** level. The chief disadvantage was difficulty of concealment, with the position being normally so close to the enemy lines and the discharge easily visible from observation posts. Supplying ammunition for **MW** was a challenge because it meant moving heavy rounds through the trench networks to **MW** positions near the front lines. The process required attention to detail on several levels, including effective use of light rail networks to haul both **MW** carriages and ordnance forward.

The **MW** increased mobility on the battlefield. Assaults depended on them to keep pace with the advancing forces, especially once they breached the front lines. Policy made it clear that, "In attacks in which it is intended to break through to a considerable depth, every infantry battalion will usually be accompanied by two horse-drawn light **MW**. In addition, a horse-drawn **MW** company will be formed from the divisional **MW** company. It will consist of four to six medium **MW** with two or three ammunition wagons to each piece. The accompanying artillery and light **MW** will hold themselves in readiness, with caissons and guns limbered … The battalions concerned will see that these guns get under way in due time to support the attack."[185]

Trench mortars such as **MW** were not just maintained in German arsenals. *Capitaine* Rouvier from the French military mission explained to the American public what trench artillery contributed to battle in his book *Present Day Warfare*. Rouvier provided basic physics on the trajectory and described how the bomb once fired could be watched en route to the target. What proved vital in operations along the front line was rapid fire – seven projectiles could be fired from the same mortar and be seen simultaneously in flight.[186] Americans were primarily equipped with the British Stokes mortar – a simple tube-fired device. The French affectionately called their small trench mortar *le petit crapaud* (the little toad).

GERMAN *MINENWERFER* AND ALLIED TRENCH MORTARS

1916 Schwere Minenwerfer (1916 sMW)

The **1916 Schwere MW** comprised a 25-cm calibre steel-tube muzzle-loaded mortar that weighed 320 pounds. The **1916 Schwere MW** fired two types of projectiles: long projectile was 1.02 metres (40.15 inches) in length and weighed 94kg and the short projectile was .59 metres (23.20 inches) in length and weighed 63kg. The manning detail was one NCO and six cannoneers.[187]

Calibre: 25cm
Rate of fire: 20 bombs per hour.
Range: 500–1,000 metres.[188]

Schwere Minenwerfer (sMW)

The **Schwere MW** consisted of a gun, carriage, and wooden platform. The **sMW** was a smooth-bore 24cm steel tube that fired a heavy bomb fitted with four vanes similar to the French 240mm. The bomb weighed 100kg. The **Schwere MW** manning party consisted of one NCO and five cannoneers.

Calibre: 24cm
Rate of fire: 20 bombs per hour.
Range: 450–1,200 metres.[189]

1916 Medium Minenwerfer (mMW)

The **1916 Medium MW** was designed like the **1916 Schwere MW** except for a difference in the traversing gear. The bomb weighed 49.5kg. The **1916 mMW** manning party was one NCO and four cannoneers.

Calibre: 17cm
Rate of fire: 30–35 bombs per hour.
Range (medium explosive bomb): 150–900 metres.
Range (medium gas shell): 300–1,000 metres.[190]

THE CHOREOGRAPHY OF AN ATTACK

The holy grail was the breakthrough. Reserves were to be pushed in "where the attack is proceeding well." New divisions were not usually to relieve the old, but to be "interpolated between other divisions", so generating a fan-shaped extension of the attack, spreading into the rear of the enemy position.[194] German **Patrouillenangriff** in 1918 appeared to involve **Stosstruppen** tactics with the German **Armee**-level **Sturmbataillon** in support. The final objective for many German assaults was an enemy battalion command post, where important documents could be retrieved.[195] The **Stosstruppen-Bataillon** comprised 4 companies of infantry,

Neue Leichte Minenwerfer (LMW)
Neue Leichte MW consisted of three parts: barrel, jacket, and a circular plate platform with a total weight (including wheels) of 156kg. The **Neue Leichte MW** manning party was one NCO and four cannoneers. It also fired gas shells. The weapon had a new carriage which permitted direct fire, particularly for **Flachbahnlaffetten** (anti-tank defence).

Calibre: 7.6cm
Rate of fire: 20 bombs per minute
Range: 300–1,300 metres. [191]

ALLIED TRENCH MORTARS USED BY 1ST DIVISION AND 26TH DIVISION

3-inch Stokes
The 3-inch Stokes was a 21.7kg steel tube with breech piece mortar. Equipment assigned to Headquarters company of each infantry regiment. Typical crew was two personnel.

Rate of fire: 22 bombs per minute
Range: 1,100 metres. [192]

6-inch Newton
Equipment for division's trench mortar battery.

Rate of fire: 8 bombs per minute.
Range: 90–1,800 metres. [193]

1 company of light **MW** (16 pieces), 1 company of heavy machine guns (30 pieces) a battery of 77mm accompanying the infantry (4 pieces – dismountable) and 1 section of **Flammenwerfer** (5 medium and 5 of the smaller new model). The **Stosstruppen** attack was preceded by a short but heavy **MW** and artillery bombardment. Gas shellfire was sometimes directed against the batteries so that they were gassed out of action (**vergast**). **Stosstruppen** advanced in squad columns of six to ten men, followed by their accompanying batteries and light **MW**, machine gun and **Flammenwerfer Kompagnien**. The **Stosstruppen** were not to halt under any circumstances. Mopping up was accomplished by troops assigned to that task. [196]

Attack on a trench by **Stosstruppen** initially involved organising shell holes in front of their lines and establishing a departure trench or nest. Prior to executing the **Patrouillenangriff**, **Stosstruppen** patrols worked close to the enemy wire. **Ladungen** (elongated charges – the Allied version was known as the Bangalore torpedo) were placed under the wire and exploded later during the bombardment. If the pipe failed to explode, the **Stosstruppen** resorted to cutting through the wire by hand. Tape was laid to guide the main body.[197]

The **Sturm-Kompagnie** formed for the attack employing the first wave as a strike force with hand-picked grenadiers accompanied by experienced ammunition carriers with hand grenades, wire cutters, flares and signal equipment. They focused on reaching the Allied trench in a single rush across the open terrain. Hand grenades and individually carried machine guns, provided the main source of firepower.[198] As the wave advanced, machine guns opened fire at close range and "rolled up" the enemy trenches. Once at the designated objective, machine-gun groups dug in, fired against

Terror weapon: a flamethrower crew. (Ettighoffer, *Verdun*)

the enemy reorganization or counter-attack, or picked off the retreating enemy. Combat experience conclusively showed machine guns greatly aided **Stosstruppen** objectives. At first, machine guns served a defensive role. At Verdun, they accompanied the third wave of troops in most units. The **Bayerische Infanterie-Leib-Regiment** (Bavarian Life Guards Regiment) learned the value of machine guns accompanying the first wave. Assaulting troops were able to advance more effectively.[199] As the first wave penetrated enemy lines, machine guns were to cease fire and follow the first wave. As the wave advanced, the machine guns opened fire at close range. In this manner machine guns formed the main firepower for platoons pushing through as far as the initial objective. Upon reaching the objective the machine-gun groups dug in, covered the enemy reorganization, and harried retreating forces.[200]

Heavy machine guns in the attack covered first objectives of attacking infantry with a belt of fire, allowing for as few gaps as possible. Machine-gun groups pushed as far forward as they could as "offensive points" keeping the enemy down in their trenches and *boyaux* after the **MW** and artillery ceased fire. The distance between battle lines and the nature of the terrain determined whether machine-gun fire was directed against

the enemy front line or rear formations. Securing the infantry advance within the sectors allotted to them meant overcoming enemy front lines and annihilating any hostile machine guns that remained. Machine guns systematically swept enemy trenches and rear areas to nullify counter-attacks. **Stosstruppen** also used light machine guns to protect their flanks.[201]

French analysis showed German operations at this time were methodical in their infiltration, expanding across the front line. The infantry action started by small elements infiltrating through all the passages and approaches toward the flanks of the position to be taken. The frontal attack only occurred later, after the outflanking had been accomplished. In the face of such tactics, the French determined that flanking fire was not sufficient. The Allied solution lay in the Germans not finding holes in the lines. Those passages and approaches which were not swept by artillery or by machine guns were to be covered by the Chauchat automatic rifle. The field of fire there was very restricted so more automatic rifles were added to the attack.[202]

The second wave pushed towards the objective supporting the first wave, reaching a predetermined trench line, communicating with neighbouring assault elements, and occupied adjoining connecting trenches. The second wave included infantry who were good shots, men accustomed to bayonet fighting and carried an ample supply of **Handgranaten**.[203] After the assault, second-wave forces placed machine guns and **Granatwerfer** in position.[204] The first waves were not to stop until they reached their ultimate objective. Taking care of the enemy's shattered trench networks now became the work of the third wave.

The third wave carried **Handgranaten** and tools. It used **Flammenwerfer** to mop up trenches and *abris* shattered by the first and second waves. A telephone connection was established and maintained with the German front line following the initial assault. Runners between the liaison groups and the captured position were in this wave. Labour squads brought up material and consolidated the captured trenches. The support

section moved up and occupied the starting trench as soon as they were able. Ammunition carriers carried hand grenades, ammunition sacks, and ready-made entanglements furnished by the reserve companies.[205]

Though infantry and artillery were seen as the vital 'teeth' in *Der Angriff Im Stellungskrieg*, all parts of the army had their roles to play. **Pioniere** accomplished preparatory work including mining, helped move the artillery forward, and supported attacks on limited objectives. Signal troops set up networks in advance and, in the event of a major breakthrough, established communications with forward units as quickly as possible. Signallers were to be proactive and not assume that making a particular connection was the responsibility of others.[206]

BREAKTHROUGH

The breakthrough battle meant "penetration to the furthest possible objective" including capture of the enemy artillery on the first day, consolidation of gains, the bringing up of both fresh infantry and "the mass of artillery … devouring the series of hostile positions … rapidly and in depth". In this respect, the new German doctrine was reminiscent of *Capitaine* André Laffargue's urging, made in 1915, that

The primary artillery piece used by German forces throughout the war, the 77mm. (TAG Massachusetts)

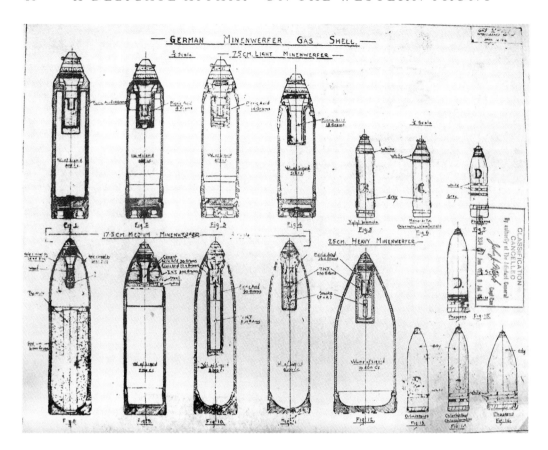

The variety of *Minenwerfer* bombs fired on the Americans was extensive. (NARA)

enemy positions should be "swallowed in a single gulp." Nevertheless, Laffargue had far more in common with what failed in 1916 than with what succeeded in 1918. *Der Angriff im Stellungskrieg* further postulated that though attacking in depth each assaulting division was best deployed on a fairly narrow front. The **Abschnitt** for a three-regiment division such as **78. R. D.** covered 2,000 metres. Amendments to *Der Angriff im Stellungskrieg* emphasised that more powerful and adequate artillery more likely stimulated further advance after the initial assault than fresh infantry.[207]

The concluding remarks of *Der Angriff im Stellungskrieg*, signed off by **Erster Generalquartiermeister General der Infanterie**

Ludendorff himself, were highly significant: "The great attack for a breakthrough requires that commanders and troops should free themselves from habits and customs of trench warfare. Methods of warfare and tactics have changed in detail. But the great military principles which formed the backbone of our military training in peace time and to which we owe all great successes in war, are still the old ones. Where they have been forgotten, they must be again aroused." Whilst the shock tactics of the infantry were undoubtedly a crucial element of the new doctrine, it is dubious whether they could have made much headway without co-ordination with the artillery, as was made clear by *Der Angriff im Stellungskrieg*.[208] The greatest challenge was moving the artillery forward. Knowledge based on combat experience served as the foundation for **78. R. D.** and the subordinate **Res. I. R. 259** under **Major** Bruns to commence battle planning against the arriving American army.

CHAPTER 5

1918: Kinetics and Chemicals

Death mainly came from a distance in the First World War. Artillery was the primary arbiter of fate for the entrenched combatants. Science added to the misery with the dispersal of chemical munitions. Artillery served as the primary delivery means and projection devices located at the front lines allowed poisonous vapours to drift across No Man's Land, creating agony and mayhem. Artillery remained the primary force arm and determined the limits of conventional lethality for the entire battle sector, including rear echelons. As one veteran remembered, "There is no way of adequately expressing on paper the sound a shell makes. It begins as a whine, and then, rising to a terrifying crescendo shriek it ends in a shattering crash."[209] The American novices at Plattsburg learning the military art were informed in the primary manual: "The amount of artillery on the Western front and the amount of ammunition consumed daily is appalling."[210]

As infantry advanced, artillery isolated the zone of attack from all means of access, to include trenches, *boyaux*, and lines of communication at the rear. It also destroyed areas where the enemy could assemble for attack and counter-attack. Once the infantry occupied new ground, the artillery sustained the position.[211]

A basic contemporary description of what constituted artillery's role was published in open sources by experienced veterans such as *Capitaine* Rouvier. Five types of artillery existed in the First World War – field artillery, heavy artillery, trench artillery, heavy artillery of great power, and railroad artillery. Field artillery comprised guns and cannon firing rounds with a very flat trajectory. Positional war weakened field artillery's effectiveness in striking an enemy protected in *abris* beneath the surface. Heavy artillery included traditional howitzers firing a more steeply curved trajectory. *Abris* were better protected on the lee side of a hill crest. Howitzers with lethal quantities of HE became the logical weapon to dislodge and destroy.[212]

American artillerymen heading to France had to learn their trade quickly to become effective and survive. The French employed the school at Coëtquidan, an artillery proving ground established by Napoleon, to train Americans. The US translated all the French artillery manuals. Artillery assumed a pre-eminent position among the entire combat arm, orchestrated by a broad range of information resources that provided near real-time targeting, linked by the twentieth-century communications of telephone and radio. Americans had to catch up to the standards set by French veterans and meet the critical expectations that came with assignment to an operational sector. The learning curve was precipitous – and as both the 1st Division and 26th Division would soon learn, there was no time to waste.

ARTILLERIEKOMMANDEUR GENERALLEUTNANT WILHELM HOFFMANN

Artilleriekommandeur (Art.Kdr.) Generalleutnant Wilhelm Hoffmann was tasked by the **Generalstab** and **General der Infanterie** Fuchs' **Gruppe Gorz** in mid-February to commence artillery planning for an **Unternehmen** against the US 1st Division. Hoffmann responded on 17 February stating his artillery's mission was to block off the final line to the front and flanks as well as dominate and neutralise the Allied artillery fire from areas south of the infantry's objective at *Bois du Jury*. Hoffmann initially calculated he needed twenty-four batteries to conduct the operation. He assigned three heavy batteries with counter-battery fire against any Allied barrage – the remaining twenty-one batteries were to conduct barrage fire in support of the **Stosstruppen** assault. The **MW** was to conduct preparation fire with gas rounds. To accomplish the assigned mission Hoffmann needed more artillery than **78. R. D.** possessed. In a quiet time such allotments could be easily accommodated from other divisional assets adjacent to the division tasked. However, this was at the height of planning and preparation for **Erster Generalquartiermeister General der Infanterie**

Ludendorff's Operation Michael offensive in the north. Hoffmann's seniority helped in acquiring additional artillery as well as the **Generalstab** recognising that an effective strike in the south helped divert possible reinforcements away from their upcoming offensive. Eleven reinforcing batteries were added, to include four more heavy field howitzer batteries. Almost a week to the day of the initial plan, Hoffmann's artillery was en route or already in place. A 40-minute barrage called for 10,380 rounds of HE and other rounds. Hoffmann's plan also called for 1,300 gas shells.[213]

Generalleutnant Hoffmann's strategy envisioned three artillery batteries in line augmented by other batteries to produce a box barrage of gas munitions on the Allied artillery. When the German infantry advanced, all the box barrage batteries were to switch to their box barrage areas. The German artillery fire was choreographed to have bursts of gas or HE fired against the Allied barrage batteries as the infantry crossed the barrage zone upon returning from the **Unternehmen**. Hoffmann envisioned strong fire against the flanking fire coming from Allied artillery emplacements in the area of *Bois du Jury*. German artillery also planned to target any artillery fire that originated west of *Bois de Remières*.[214]

Rekindling memories of *Leicht-Minenwerfer* for the readers of *Das Regiment*.

Specific guidance would come via coded telephone message. Key to the attack was **MW** fire. Artillery fire was to focus on the flanks that covered the west **Anschlussgraben** trench works and the north-west sector of *Bois du Jury*. **Abschnitt G.I** opposite Richecourt and **G.III** opposite *Bois du Jury* were to be prepared for attack. It was anticipated that obstacles such as wire entanglements and defensive works would be formidable – the solution was artillery.[215]

THE KING OF BATTLE

German artillery was to achieve **Niederhaltung** (domination) of enemy batteries. The **MW** paved the way for the **Sturmtruppen** by breaching the point of entry into the American lines.[216] German doctrine prioritized artillery firing against targets that were the most dangerous to the infantry – the first aim was to gain fire superiority over enemy artillery. A short but violent artillery preparation including **MW** preceded assaults for the purpose of cutting all wire and other communications, blocking the roads, and demoralising the garrisons. "The main object is to help the infantry break quickly through the enemy's strong points, to keep the attack going even in the face of strong enemy resistance, and to increase the element of surprise."[217]

Artillery was co-ordinated at **Division**, **Korps** and **Armee** level. Preparatory fire aimed at producing specific objectives in a short time span: "concentrated in time and space". As it concerned **Erstürmung**, the opening bombardment might be as short as a few minutes, some hours being required for major operations. Artillery fire was never to be allowed to become rigidly regular, thus allowing the enemy to take advantage of predictable lulls. Firing artillery of all calibres in a small area resulted in a concentration of fire that created **Trommel** ("drum") fire. Drum fire lowered the enemy's morale. In bombarding trenches, the common method was to allot target sectors to each battery, with a howitzer battery on every hundred metres of trench line. Where possible, trench bombardments were fired from a flank, thereby increasing the possibility of shells pitching directly into the trench. Heavy and super-heavy guns targeted deep dugouts, or important enemy locations containing machine guns. The **MW** concentrated on the nearest enemy positions. Lengthening range and pauses were calculated to make the enemy think attack was imminent. Perhaps the most problematic element in the breakthrough battle was to bring forward the artillery with enough ammunition over captured enemy ground. For this purpose, some of the batteries at least would remain unused in the first action, or rested for a period. They would then move over the battlefield as swiftly as possible, helped along by the **Pioniere** provision of bridging materials and other supplies. Horses would play a vital role.

Artillery employed a variety of tactics to support the battle: "creeping" barrages; pushing forward "infantry guns" and field artillery with the advancing troops; protective barrages to defend infantry on captured positions; and repelling counter-attacks.[218] The biggest problem in achieving surprise was the registration requirement to ensure accuracy of artillery fire. By 1918, artillery registration systems used combinations of direct ground and aerial observation, aerial photography, sound ranging and flash spotting, shell crater analysis, and information garnered from patrols, raids, and prisoners of war. However, the firing when registering the guns (**Einschiessen**) gave away battery positions and telegraphed the attack.

Planning Allied artillery operations meant attention to the smallest detail through a master map known as the *Plan Directeur*. Data was available almost on a continual basis thanks to the expansion of intelligence collection, analysis and dissemination. *Général* Pétain relied upon the *Plan Directeur* in developing his priorities for daily operations. The level of detail required was commensurate with the scale of the map. 1:5,000 maps served as infantry maps for planning attacks in the sector against German trenches; 1:10,000-scale maps enabled commanders to issue detailed orders to all elements. When a major offensive was planned, aerial reconaissance was constantly updated. Timely data was provided to batteries to effectively conduct counter-battery. *Plan Directeur* editions were issued as often as possible with changes as they occurred. The map was printed at the senior headquarters location or in Paris. In active sectors the topographical section of the army issued a map every day showing the enemy batteries seen in action during the preceding 24 hours, printed at night and distributed the next morning to appropriate units.[219] In the absence of a *Plan Directeur* artillery battery officers used a 1:80,000 map.[220]

Artillerymen had to know what direct fire, indirect fire, reverse slope, target and trajectory meant. Positional war called for variations of annihilating fire, rolling barrage, standing barrage, and harassing fire as well as definition of the area of responsibility for each artillery piece at the front. For the man in the battery it was a time of constant calculation. Guns were usually laid parallel to a given basic direction by means of a compass. This basic direction was used as the reference point for subsequent targets. In figuring the data, it was necessary to take into account the variation in muzzle velocity due to the different lots of powder, varying weights and types of shells, charge to be used and the atmospheric conditions. The objective became to outshoot the opponent. Batteries were assigned a zone within No Man's Land in case of sudden attack. At any moment of the day or night the battery was required to drop a standing barrage across the zone in response to a telephone call or signal rocket of various colours at the first sign of an enemy attack fired by the sentry in position. Batteries kept a man on constant rocket guard.[221] Being a member of the rocket guard meant each man stood watch for 2 hours and 5 minutes each night. The artillery battery maintained line of sight to the battalion headquarters. When the infantry launched a rocket and the rocket guard relayed the signal, the artillery battalion alerted the remaining batteries. The rocket guard was also responsible for alerting the batteries in his area. Communication was accomplished by two signal pistols. One artilleryman recalled having to stand in place the entire time on duty with eyes riveted to the battalion headquarters.[222]

The Allied term for preparing the battlefield for an infantry assault was counter preparation offensive (CPO). It covered destruction of the wire, destroying communications and annihilating machine-gun positions.[223] Maintaining an operational battery was not easy:

We had counter-preparation fires as well as barrages and indeed the blackboards kept in each battery position for the firing data of the guns were at all times covered with an array of figures and numbers which were bewildering and called for the execution of a great variety of fire. There was no denying that the personnel in the batteries did not like this brilliant galaxy of barrages. Aside from the extra data which had to be computed, the extra registrations which had to be fired, and the laborious moving of trails when these remote barrages were demanded, it was necessary in some of the positions to drag the guns onto platforms constructed in the open to the front or rear, because the field of fire possible from the casemates did not include part of the terrain where the barrage had to be placed.[224]

A standing barrage, known by the Germans as **Feuerblock** and the British as curtain fire, was a wall of falling shells placed to impact along the axis of the trench and force the defenders to take shelter in their dugouts. Barrage fire was adopted and perfected with the cessation of open warfare and commencement of positional war. It meant simply a rain of shells on a certain designated zone. It was a screen of fire through which the enemy could not pass without being annihilated. When the barrage moved from line to line at regulated intervals to protect advancing infantry in the big drives, it was called a creeping barrage. Standing barrages were fired in front of the trench under attack to stop the attack or at least catch enemy infantry moving into the open.[225] The barrage against the enemy in the trenches and dugouts prevented enemy fire against the advancing infantry. The Germans led all combatants in this tactic. In doing so they compiled the greatest number of heavy artillery pieces and highest proportion of howitzers.[226]

Rolling barrage (also known as creeping barrage) took place when the barrage moved from line to line at regulated intervals to protect advancing infantry in major attacks. After the CPO came the rolling barrage, which was dropped 50 metres in front of friendly troops, to be raised every 15 or 30 seconds as the case demanded. This barrage was timed and the infantry had to be careful not to pass it. It happened in some cases that they went ahead of the barrage, and the battery had to cease fire if it was aware they had. When their objective was known, a barrage line was laid in that vicinity, provided it was within range. As a rule artillery kept in touch with advancing infantry – but sometimes enthusiastic soldiers rushing forward too fast were caught in the curtain of fire.[227]

The Germans called the rolling barrage the **Feuerwalze** (fire roller). The rolling barrage was carried out by field artillery, batteries of light and heavy howitzers and light **MW**.[228] **Feuerwalze** sought to paralyse the enemy. German command planned **Feuerwalze** requirements within the infantry's attack zones to help curtail any enemy flanking manoeuvre.[229]

The **Feuerwalze** advance was painstakingly timed and watches were synchronized accordingly. The time of flight for projectiles was constantly considered. The distance of the first advance for light batteries (field guns and light howitzers) and for heavy batteries (heavy howitzers) was 300 metres. The distance of the subsequent advances of the light artillery batteries was 200 metres while heavy artillery was increased to 400 metres. After the first advance, the light artillery hammered one spot for 3 minutes. The heavy artillery struck their target for only 2 minutes. After the subsequent advances, the light artillery fired on one spot for four minutes, the heavy artillery eight minutes. In order that short bursts did not fall among advancing infantry, the heavy artillery advanced its barrage one minute sooner than the light

artillery. On some lines and in case of necessity on the terrain between them (e.g. on the rear lines of the first position, on the intermediary and secondary positions) the stationary period of the barrage lasted longer. This compelled the enemy stronghold to get well under cover before the arrival of the German infantry, and allowed **Stosstruppen** time to catch up with the barrage or to halt and recover their wind. **Stosstruppen** profited when they followed very closely behind the barrage. The Germans assessed that a single machine gun opening fire caused more losses than a few German shells might. Batteries not assigned to counter-battery fire, destruction of support points and rear lines, fire of interdiction, and support of infantry were assigned to help put down the **Feuerwalze**.[230]

Harassing fire worked on wearing down the enemy. Its chief effect was to compel the enemy to maintain a continuous watch by delivering infrequent bursts of fire and keeping him unaware of the duration and origin. Harassing fire assumed at some points the character of real prohibitive fire. It was in the majority of cases done by night at the usual hours of hostile traffic. Targets assigned to harassing fire depended upon miscellaneous information. The principal targets were communication and supply roads, trails, crossings, approaches to command posts, communicating trenches that could be enfiladed, narrow gauge tracks and depots, reverse slopes, and any points at which it was desirable to obstruct work.[231]

Rafale fire was a sudden scatter of shells, usually directed against a road or trench, and intended to catch the enemy unawares. *Rafale* was purposely fired at changing intervals. Sometimes it would be every 10 minutes throughout the day. The next day the fire came at alternate intervals of 10 and 12 minutes with a delay of, say, an hour, to lure the infantry out of the dugouts. A favourite ploy was to send over a second *rafale* about 2 minutes after the first, to catch the stretcher bearers or whoever might have run out to help any wounded men.[232]

Americans learned from the French how to harass and confuse the Germans with a single mobile gun. The Americans understood the Germans could easily pick up the flash from their network of flash spotters across the front. The French assured the Americans that being selected for this duty was quite an honour, hence the name, "sacrifice gun". One artilleryman recalled what the honour meant:

> Our duty consisted chiefly of drawing fire from the enemy, in other words, when the day was clear and German planes were in plain view, we would receive an order to open fire. The *Boche* planes would make note of the position of the flash and instruct the German Artillery to return fire on our position. They would direct the fire by wireless. As soon as the first few shells would land we would cease fire and if they were landing pretty close we would beat it to the dugouts. At other times the order would be to stand by the guns and await orders. This was a terrible ordeal, a nerve wracking experience, this openly flirting with death. When you are firing you do not notice it so much as you do not get time to see what is happening around you, but standing there in silence, waiting and listening to those shells coming in and exploding, the fragments flying through the air and falling around your gun-pit, is an ordeal which tries a man's nerve.[233]

One single-gun technique had the artillery piece move about a mile from the original battery location. During the night, the gun fired a 100 rounds to suggest a new battery had moved into the sector. After the firing, the gun quickly departed for another location. This roving or sniper gun went to a different place each night and came back to the original gun pit before dawn.[234] Besides the risk of counter-battery to the new position, the roving gun crew lost access to their kitchens at the battery and sometimes had to resort to eating berries found in the forest.[235]

Artillery in support of a trench raid usually followed a simple strategy. Short preliminary artillery and machine-gun fire for the destruction of the enemy's trenches, machine guns, and artillery. Then the fire would be shifted so that the bursting shells and bullets would fall on three sides of the trench area to be raided to prevent the occupants from escaping and the supporting troops from coming to their assistance. This enclosure of fire was called a "box barrage." Under its cover, the raiding party rushed forward in well-practised formations and if the artillery fire had not previously cut the enemy's wire, the German **Patrouillenangriff** had their **Pioniere** blow it open using **Ladungen** filled with explosives. After passing the enemy's wire, the raiding party proceeded in small

SRA report format for artillery. The role of artillery on a daily basis was reported to *Général* Gérard, 8. Armée. Both *Artillerie alliance* (Allied) and *ennemie* rounds were counted. (SHD)

The Schneider 155mm Field Howitzer at the ready. (NARA)

detachments to the portions of the enemy's trenches where it was expected that prisoners, machine guns or information could be obtained. When their mission was accomplished, the raiders would dash back to their own lines and the artillery and machine-gun fire would take the most appropriate steps to protect them.

Barrages were assisted by machine guns. The crossfire of machine guns covered the infantry from the lines of departure, at planned halts, or when the advancing party reached the objective. The machine-gun plan was drawn up by the division commander, assisted by the divisional machine-gun officer, in close coordination with the plan for artillery barrages. Every machine-gun battalion and company commander was provided with a fire organization order and every platoon commander and gun commander a fire chart. Battalion, company and platoon commanders prepared maps indicating their different positions, targets and schedule for each barrage. Barrages were put down on hostile entrenchments (most especially on shell crater fields between trenches) or on zones favourable for hostile counter-attacks (reverse slopes, folds, natural passages). If a sufficient number of machine guns was available, fire was directed along the whole front of attack. The machine-gun fire was maintained as long as the infantry halted at an intermediate objective and until the last objective was reached. Machine guns then resumed harassing fire.[236]

MEMORIES OF THE "88"

"Whiz-bang" was the term that described the momentary horror as an artillery shell slammed into the sector without warning. Lieutenant Colonel B. Walcot, General Staff, Second Army, addressed "whiz-bangs" in an intelligence pamphlet published for Allied combatants: "When sending back reports do not use fancy names, such as 'whiz-bangs.' The trouble is not that we do not know what a 'whiz-bang' is, but that different fancy names are used to describe the same article in different parts of the line. There are several popular terms for various German shells – a 'whiz-bang' in 999 cases out of 1,000 is a field gun shrapnel fired at close range."[250]

Several Americans serving in the southern Woëvre front described the experience and attributed it to Germans fielding the Austrian 8.8cm ("88") field artillery piece opposite their lines. It was said to be impossible to throw one's self on the ground before the shell burst, once it was on its way. The "88s" were known for their high velocity and were used exclusively at this time for anti-aircraft artillery. French *2ᵉ Bureau* intelligence never confirmed that weapon in the German artillery inventory facing the *VIIIᵉ armée* during the first four months of 1918.

The "88" seemed a deadlier weapon than the German "77" since the incoming shells gave little or no warning of their approach. One veteran recalled, "One hears a whiz in the air, and the explosion of the projectile follows almost immediately. The German guns, however, were more to our liking. One could, upon hearing the warning whistle of a '77' shell, seek a soft spot on the ground and flatten oneself in a leisurely manner. The Austrian guns are most effective, and no one who has been on the 'receiving end' is likely to forget them."[251]

GAS

Gas shells were fired by both sides in progressively increasing amounts until the Armistice. Of the total number of gas shells fired, 25 per cent were used by the British and over 50 per cent were used by the Germans.[252] Lieutenant Edward D. Sirois and Corporal William McGinnis of Battery C, 102nd Field Artillery, summed up most American infantry and artillerymen's views:

> Poisonous gas was the most fiendish invention of the whole war and every man had the fear of death by gas embedded in his heart. We had been told of its effect by our French comrades.

The most unforgettable location on the Beaumont Ridge was Dead Man's Curve, recalled in this post-war cartoon by the veterans who served on the line. (*History of the 101st United States Engineers*)

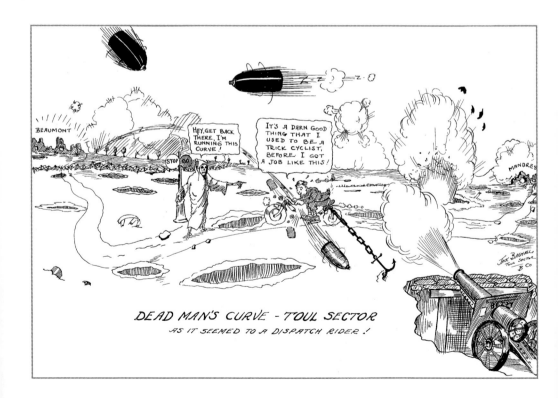

DEAD MAN'S CURVE - TOUL SECTOR
AS IT SEEMED TO A DISPATCH RIDER !

ARTILLERY COMPARISON[237]

ARTILLERIES ALLIÉS

Canon de 75 modèle 1897 Towed Field Gun
The ***Canon de 75 modèle 1897*** was the most celebrated field gun of the war – possessing the fastest rate of fire with 15 to 30 rounds per minute. The *soixante-quinze* established a new principle – the tube alone recoiled on a long sleeve without disturbing carriage, or aim, or cannoneers. The force of the recoil was used to bring the gun back again into firing position, when it could be fired immediately without reaiming.

Caliber: 75mm
Rate of fire: up to 15 to 40 rounds per minute.
Projectile: 6.8kg (HE, shrapnel)
Maximum range: 8,200 metres.[238]

De Bange 90mm cannon (Mle 1877)
Obsolete cannon that French had in stockpile to supplement the 75mm. Described by Americans in the 101st Field Artillery as "The Chinese Battery" because the guns were so antiquated, the powder for firing was contained in silk bags, the projectiles were like candlepins, and the inclined wooden runways for the guns to recoil against were not a match physically for the preferred 75mm. After the guns were elaborately loaded, the battery would stand clear while the gunner pulled the lanyard. There would come a crash, the muzzle would bang against the ground, the entire gun would slam backwards up the inclined runway for about 4.5 metres and then would come rattling back on rickety wheels and jolt into place in its gun pit to the cheers of the appreciative audience. Despite the drama associated with the firing of the 90mm the battery acknowledged that it was extraordinarily accurate in fire and possessed a longer range than the 75mm.[239]

Range: 6,900 metres.

Lahitolle 95mm Cannon (Mle 1888)
These were nearly obsolete cannon that the French had in stockpile to supplement the 75mm.[240] The 103rd Field Artillery's Battery A fired 95mm guns mounted on "great high wheels." There was no recoil mechanism to the gun. The piece had to be fastened to a steel plate in the floor of the emplacement to keep it from backing out of the gun pit. Two large blocks in the back of the wheels served to catch the piece, after it had been fired and rolled back into position. A large iron wheel on the floor, just fitting between the wheels of the piece, served to bring the gun back into the same position every time. Whenever the gun was fired the barrel rocked and tossed about for approximately 5 seconds – creating a very great danger to the gunner if he attempted to set the piece too quickly for the next fire. In spite of all this the gun was accurate. In setting the piece, the gunner placed himself directly before it,

set his quadrant at the proper deflection, rested it on a rail set in the ground in front of the piece, and then peered through the quadrant until the hair lines crossed in a mirror fastened to the front of the piece.[241]

Canon de 105 mle 1913 Schneider (L13S)

Projectile types were HE variety, intended to dislodge enemy elements or destroy fortifications.

Maximum range: 12 kilometres; 7.45 miles.

Modèle 1897 105mm

Rounds per minute: 6.
Maximum range: 12,250 metres.

French Modèle 1878

120mm gun.

Maximum range: 8,200 metres.

4.7-inch Field Gun M1906

60 produced and issued to the US Army. It fired French 120mm ammunition.

Modèle 1917 Schneider 155mm howitzer

The piece was designed to destroy enemy works such as batteries, shelters and trenches. It was not a weapon for firing barrages. Firing involved greasing the shell, placing it on the loading tray, screwing in a fuze, ramming the shell home, inserting the powder charge and primer, closing the breechblock, and pulling the lanyard. At the first shot the gun carriage would generally recoil a few metres until the trail spade seated in the earth and prevented further motion.

30 rounds per hour

Maximum range: 9,600–12,100 metres depending on shell.
Projectile: forged and semi-steel HE weight 43,5kg; gas shells.
Rate of fire: 2 rounds per minute average.
Maximum range: 10.8 kilometres; 6.7 miles.[242]

ARTILLERIE ENNEMIE

7.7cm Feldkanone 96 n.A.

The by far most numerous gun in the arsenal of the German Imperial Army in 1914 was the **7.7cm Feldkanone 96 n.A**; better known as the 77mm. Throughout the whole war, it stayed the workhorse of the German artillery, used on all fronts and in all battles. The gun in 1918 combined an inner tube rifled with 32 grooves, a recoil system, a new breech and a new carriage. The **FK 96 n.A.** was shorter-ranged, but lighter than the French *Canon de 75 modèle 1897*.

Calibre: 77mm (3 inches)
Rate of Fire: 10 rounds per minute. **Generalleutnant** Hoffmann's planning called for 6 rounds per minute.
Projectiles: Long HE shell with bursting charge of .9kg of amatol; Long gas shell (**Blaukreuz, Gelbkreuz, Grünkreuz**); 1896 pattern shrapnel containing 300 lead bullets or 220 steel bullets.
Maximum range: 8,400 metres.[243]

Feldkanone 16

A modified **7.7cm Feldkanone 96 n.A. with a 60cm longer tube.** The **F.K.16** was longer-ranged. It fired two types of high-explosive shells, which differed only in which fuzes they could accept. **Generalleutnant** Hoffmann's planning called for 5 rounds per minute.

Calibre: 77mm (3 inches)
Projectiles: Long HE shell with bursting charge of .9kg of amatol; Long gas shell (**Blaukreuz, Gelbkreuz, Grünkreuz**); 1896 pattern shrapnel containing 300 lead bullets or 220 steel bullets.
Maximum range: 10,700 metres (gas shell).[244]

10.5cm leichte Feldhaubitze 16 (10.5cm lFH 16) was a field howitzer mounted on a shielded recoil carriage. It was similar to the 98/09 howitzer but was a longer piece that fired projectiles a longer range.

Calibre: 105mm (4.1 inches)
Projectiles: Long HE shell with bursting charge of 1.8kg of amatol; Long gas shell (**Blaukreuz, Gelbkreuz, Grünkreuz**); 1916 pattern shrapnel containing 300 lead bullets or 450 steel bullets.
Rate of fire: 4–5 rounds per minute
Maximum range: 9,225 metres [245]

10cm Kanone 04 (10cm K 04) was a long range high-velocity field gun.

Calibre: 105mm (4.13 inches)
Projectiles: Long HE shell with bursting charge of .9kg of amatol, 1896 shrapnel containing 680 lead bullets.
Rate of fire: 1 round per 2 minutes
Range: 10,398 metres [246]

10.5cm Feldhaubitze 98/09 (**10.5cm FH 98/09**), a short barreled (1,625mm) 105mm howitzer also referred to as the **10.5cm leichte Feldhaubitze** (light field howitzer) **98/09**. The construction was similar to a field gun.

Calibre: 105mm (4.13 inches)
Projectiles: Long HE shell with bursting charge of 1.8kg of amatol; Long gas shell (**Blaukreuz, Gelbkreuz, Grünkreuz**); 1916 pattern shrapnel containing 300 laed bullets or 450 steel bullets.
Maximum range: 7,000 metres[247]

15cm schwere Feldhaubitze 13 (**15 cm sFH 13**)
One of the most important pieces in the arsenal of the German Artillery was the 150mm Heavy Howitzer. At the start of the war, most of them were of the type called **sFH 02** (i.e. **Schwere FeldHaubitze model 1902**). This piece was upgraded in several stages. The new gun fired some 1000 metres further than the old model 02. The gun was a development of the older 15 cm sFH 02 standard howitzer. Improvements included a longer barrel and a gun shield to protect the crew. The British referred to these and their shells as "5 point 9"s or "5 9"s as the bore was 5.9 inches (150 mm).

Calibre: 149.1mm (5.89 inches)
Projectiles: Long HE shell with bursting charge of 13.4 lbs of amatol; Long gas shell (**Blaukreuz, Gelbkreuz, Grünkreuz**).
Rate of fire: 3 rounds per minute. **Generalleutnant** Hoffmann's planning called for 2 rounds per minute.
Maximum range: 8,600 metres[248]

21cm Mörser 16 (**21cm Mrs 16**) or **langer 21cm Mörser** was a heavy howitzer introduced in 1910.

Calibre: 211mm (8.3 inches)
Projectiles: Long HE shell with bursting charge of 7.7kg of amatol; Long gas shell (mostly **gelb kreuz**).
Rate of fire: 1–2 rounds per minute
Maximum range: 9,400 metres[249]

The chlorine was inhaled and entering your lungs would form large blisters. In a matter of a few hours the blisters would burst, flooding the lungs with water and causing a horrible death from suffocation. Medical skill was unable to save you. Mustard gas however, was the most feared. When the fumes from this gas came in contact with any part of the body a red patch would develop. Shortly after, this would break and an intense burning of the flesh would be noticed and it would spread and spread, eating the flesh down to the bone. If the doctors received your case in time some relief was the result. If not, you had to lie still and allow this burning to go on until it had eaten up its strength. Mere description of the sufferings of gas victims cannot be portrayed in words. This was another method of teaching civilization, 'German Kultur.' It was a terrible sensation, sitting in a dugout with gas masks on, when you don't know whether the gas attack is going to last for an hour, a day or a week. All water is destroyed and all food not preserved in sealed cans has to be buried. [253]

Captain George Patton from Chaumont wrote to his wife that September, "The Germans shoot a gas which makes people vomit and when they take off the masks to spit they shoot the deadly gas at them. It is a smart idea is it not?"[254] Even General George Marshall recalled later in life, "Of course, the worst thing you can do with mustard gas is get in a wet dugout. That just permeates the whole business." [255]

The combatants experienced three distinct types of gas attacks. The first was the cloud gas attack that was dependent on wind direction and speed. The prevailing winds in Northern France from June to September were normally towards the German lines. The gas was carried to the trenches as a liquid in steel cylinders. The cylinders each contained 65 pounds of gas and had a pipe connected over the trench parapet. When the valves of the cylinders were opened the chemical mixed with the air formed a gas cloud of phosgene or phosgene mixed with chlorine. Gas attacks were usually made at night or in the early morning when meteorological estimates predicted wind velocities of 5–30 kilometres per hour towards the enemy lines.[256]

The second type of gas attack was through the projector, initially developed by the British in 1916 and known as the Liven's Projector. The device lobbed an American football-sized projectile using an electrical blasting mechanism 83cm long set at an angle of 45 degrees. When the British sector set up two thousand Liven's Projectors for the attack, it created the most amazing sight, illuminating the sky. The Liven's bombs toppled end over end like a football, crashing with a discharge and a bright flash. The British also used the Liven's Projector containing 30 pounds of oil for smoke and flame discharge.[257]

Gas shelling by **MW** was a particularly useful method of neutralising enemy batteries. The process did not achieve high levels of fatality or destroy enemy guns. It temporarily suppressed the gun crews while they struggled to don their masks or cleared the injured gas casualties from the battery positions.[258] Initially, the Germans used an 18cm (7.1-inch) smooth-bore **MW**, an

obsolete bronze muzzle-loading trench mortar. It was mounted on a non-recoil steel carriage. Gas bombs were launched through a large charge of black powder. In 1918, the Germans introduced the **Gaswerfer** (gas projector) – a steel tube about 1 metre in length – similar in design to the British Liven's Projector. **Gaswerfer** were set up side by side on wooden frames and placed so that the projectors were "laid" as required. A base plate was not used as the shock of the discharge was said to drive the projector into the ground. Like the Liven's, German **Gaswerfer** discharged simultaneously by electricity. The gas "bomb" employed by **Gaswerfer** was a thick-walled iron "rum jar" or "canister" about 17.5cm in diameter weighing 66 pounds and containing about 4 litres of liquid (phosgene) or a mixture of phosgene and chloropicrin. A similar **Blaukreuz** bomb was used in the same manner. The bomb had a solid filling – a mixture of HE and a substance that caused irritation along with pain in the nose and throat as well as constant sneezing. Visual effects from the German lines of a projector fire were dramatic, with a sheet of flame that appeared to run along the German trenches accompanied by a loud explosion. The bombs could be seen in flight making a perceptible whizzing noise along their flight path. On impact the bombs burst with a loud detonation producing a thick white smoke.[259]

Gas projectiles fired from artillery served as the third source of delivery. They had the advantage of not being dependent on wind direction. The best conditions for firing gas rounds from artillery was muggy weather or a very calm day. Artillery also had the advantage of firing concentrations of various gas projectiles against long-range targets that could be surprised and smothered. Artillery "special" shells contained lachrymatory (tear producing) or asphyxiating gases – particularly useful in counter-battery salvos. Gas shells exploded with a very slight report – the sound was the only warning to prepare for a gas attack and adjust the mask.

At the commencement of war, the US government appealed to the Bureau of Mines to provide 25,000 masks within three weeks.

Sadly, the quantity and quality of the first 20,000 produced two months later were not satisfactory. The rubberised fabric was easily penetrated by the chloropicrin vapour. General Pershing supposedly observed: "The only thing about them which is satisfactory is the strap around the neck." American can-do resolved the problem and mobilised the nation to acquire Brazil nuts, hickory nuts, walnuts, pits of peaches, and pits from prunes, apricots and cherries to fill filters. A single gas mask required charcoal from 7 pounds of pits and shells. Some 3,500 tons of charcoal were produced to service 1 million American masks sent overseas.[260]

The French emphasised gas discipline for all arriving Americans. Rules for gas masks were issued on 8 March to the 102nd Infantry while still assigned to the Chemin-des-Dâmes sector. Within 2 miles of the front line, both the French and English gas masks were to be kept on one's person, the English mask was to be worn at the ALERT position. Within the 5 mile limit both masks were worn slung, the French mask was to be taken up first and hung over the right hip, while the English mask was to be put on last and hung over the left hip. Beyond 5 miles and under 12 miles from the front line the French policy allowed either mask to be worn. Officers were ordered to watch all their soldiers to ensure the masks were available and ready to be worn. "Let us not bring discredit upon the Division or ourselves, and more especially when these precautions are necessary to beat the *Boche*."[261] The English-type gas mask had a mouthpiece, nose pincers and a can with a filter. The filter had a 5-hour life, then the soldier was ordered to seek protection within a shelter fixed with gas curtains. The soldiers determined that the filter could last as long as 12 hours.[262]

The German gas mask employed different materials to those of the Allies thanks to the ongoing naval blockade that limited access to rubber. Germans used specially treated leather as the material for the mask facepiece. Various oils and fats made the leather flexible and sealed up pores. The German mask was held firmly over the face by the means of retaining tapes that were elastic in nature. At the base of the facepiece was a metal projection into which a small metal canister containing absorbent chemicals was screwed. Once the canister was polluted by the gas, a new canister was screwed into place. The superior feature of the German mask was the eyepieces that maintained clarity for longer. British masks had to be wiped off every 5 minutes.[263] Wearing the mask became commonplace. The German command made it compulsory for officers and men to wear their masks for an hour every Wednesday and Saturday.[264]

INTEGRAL MEMBERS OF THE BATTERY

Throughout the entire war horses and mules were relied upon extensively. The standard heavy howitzer for French and Americans, the Modèle 1917 Schneider 155mm, required a ten-horse team. Eight million horses died in the First World War.[274] The artillery manual described the suitable kind of horse to be age 5–10 years, short, closely coupled, compactly built, plump, sensible and level headed. The horse should be quiet when mounted, with good straight gait, be able to jump, and stand without being held or hitched. Care for the animal was a routine part of the battery's duties. The carer observed eating habits, and looked out for sores, lumps, clean feet and normal droppings. Conditioning was acquired through regular exercise, regular feeding and good grooming.[275] At the front the motto "Horses First" was gospel to the drivers.

Dead Man's Curve, on the Beaumont-Mandres road, was a memorable place for man or beast heading into the combat sector of Beaumont, a mile from Seicheprey. The noise of the wagons was audible from great distances and on a still night the enemy systematically shelled this stretch of road with high-explosive and gas. Occasionally mules were killed and wagons smashed. Perhaps the driver was wounded or only "shaken up". The next night the same drivers went over the same road.[276] Drivers acquired horses from the French and took the time to learn appropriate commands. Once settled, horses were used every night to bring ammunition and supplies to the batteries. The horses were familiar with the most dangerous points in the southern Woëvre front such as Dead Man's Curve.

One battery lost five to an artillery round – the animals didn't know how to duck.[277] When the condition of the animal was without hope, it was necessary to put it down. Corporal Rogers, 101st FA recalled: "On a long hill many of the horses fell and lay in their harness, too spent to respond to any efforts of ours to get them on their feet. There was nothing to do but cut them free, drag them into the ditch and end their suffering with a bullet through the head."[278] Disease or exposure were major killers. It was heart wrenching for many a combatant to lose a four-legged team member.

An anti-gas horse respirator was developed by the British. The device consisted simply of a flannelette bag with a canvas mouthpiece. When tear gases were employed the artillerymen tied bandages around the horse's eyes.

Private Wunderlich of the 101st Engineers described one particular equine torment:

CHEMICAL WEAPONS USED IN THE WOËVRE, 1918

Phosgene
The most lethal common-use gas weapon creating 85 per cent of gas casualties in the First World War was phosgene. Phosgene was a colourless gas that was eighteen times more potent than chlorine. A particularly insidious poison – exposure to phosgene often had no initial symptoms but within 24 hours symptoms appeared. Phosgene combined with water in the tissues of the respiratory tract to form carbon dioxide and hydrochloric acid, which proceeded to dissolve the membranes and cause fluid to fill the lungs.[265] Phosgene was a favourite gas for German attacks. In strong doses it killed immediately.

French No. 5 Gas Shell – Phosgene
Grünkreuz 2 (Green Cross 2) – 60 per cent phosgene, 25–30 per cent diphosgene, 10–15 per cent diphenylchlorarsine. Caused sneezing in addition to its lethal effect.[266]

Diphosgene
Lung irritant and choking gas. A colourless, oily liquid – similar to phosgene – it had an added tear-gas effect. Diphosgene was developed because the vapours could destroy the gas mask filters in use at the time. It had greater persistence in the environment than phosgene, remaining at the point of release for over 10 minutes.[267] Diphosgene caused the victim to vomit and in the process of removing their gas mask he became exposed to more toxic gases (as described by Patton to his wife).

Grünkreuz (Green Cross) – Diphosgene – lethal.
Grünkreuz 1 (Green Cross 1) – Diphosgene with 30–66 per cent chloropicrin – lethal.[268]

Dichlorethyl Sulphide (Mustard Gas)
Mustard gas was not a true gas. Sulphur mustard (Dichlorethyl Sulphide) was used extensively causing more casualties than any other chemical in the war. Dispersed as an aerosol – mustard was not water soluble but contained high lipid solubility – which was rapidly absorbed into the skin.

The countermeasures against mustard gas were ineffective because gas masks did not afford protection against skin absorption. It remained in the environment for days and continued to cause casualties. This enabled mustard gas to be used as an area-denial weapon, forcing soldiers to abandon heavily contaminated positions. Contaminated clothing was weakened and after 24 hours rotted. Contaminated clothing could spread from one soldier to others. This was cruelly apparent in field hospitals when doctors were contaminated by mustard gas on patients.[269]

Gelbkreuz (Yellow Cross) – Dichlorethyl sulphide – lethal, attacked eyes and skin.[270]

Cyanogen Chloride

From the middle of 1916 cyanogen chloride (CK, "oxidised prussic acid") was used as a replacement for hydrogen cyanide. CK's potential advantage was it was more dense than hydrogen cyanide – less likely to be blown away by the wind and more likely to settle into trenches. Cyanogen chloride was a highly toxic "blood agent", a term used to describe poisonous chemicals distributed throughout the body by the blood. It caused immediate injury upon contact with the eyes or respiratory organs. It was especially dangerous because it was capable of penetrating gas mask filters. The French employed CK and called it Mauguinite – using No. 4 gas shells which tended to flash on impact and disintegrate.[271]

Diphenylchlorarsin

Called a "sneezing gas". It was in reality not a gas but a fine dust. It was a German shell-carried solid chemical; it dispersed in clouds of fine particles which could not be kept out of ordinary gas masks. It caused retching and vomiting. When concentrated it caused severe headaches.[272]

Blaukreuz (blue cross) – **Diphenylchlorarsin** and HE – caused sneezing plus HE effect.[273]

It was at Sanzey that the horses for the artillery, which was up front, were kept. Over on the other side of town they had the corrals and the tanks where they used to give the horses their sulphur baths … The cooties, which made life miserable for the soldiers, bothered the horses frightfully, adding their torment to that of other vermin. The poor equines would come in all mangy and that meant that they had to take a sulphur bath. They didn't like the smell of the sulphur and were often quite rebellious. But Uncle Sam had a way of handling the recalcitrant. The horses were driven up a runway, such as we have in our railroad yards for loading cattle at home, thence down a steep incline to a jumping-off place where the tank, just deep enough to force the horse to swim, was located. Tacked to the sides of the tank and stretching up several feet were strips of canvas to keep the water from slopping out. If the horse balked going down the incline, a bunch of husky Yanks helped him along with a rope. Many a vermin-infected artillery horse was thus shoved off unwillingly. In order to exterminate the cooties, it was necessary that every part of the animal be submerged. If the horse kept its head above water he was soused with the bucket.[279]

Members of Battery A, 103rd Field Artillery, paid tribute to their horses in their post-war memoir: "No fancy breed were you brave, old war horses, shaggy and strong! Not of the high-stepping, pedigreed kind were you, nor of the race blue-blooded ... Motley and mongrel, powerful of muscle and limb. Ever trying, willing, suff'ring. Ofttimes hours on hours in deep ooze 'neath heavy packs you waited and waited and shivered, while the cold night rain in miniature waterfalls streamed from your bellies and legs, mud encrusted and numb. You knew the bitter throes of steely war. Though you were without food and water, though loads were heavy, and though long the highway and up-hill, you kept the traces taut. Though you were weary and your backs were sore, and though your heads drooped low, you kept the traces taut. Though crossroads, turns, and hairpin curves were shelled and reshelled, though gas, as a veil, floated over the narrow, sunken lanes, you kept the traces taut. And when the men fell asleep in the saddle, drenched and exhausted, what of you? You kept the traces taut. You had no trappings, no gay ornaments, as had the chargers of warriors olden, no honors, no war-crosses, but you kept the traces taut. Brave old war horses! Long familiarity with you has bred in us the highest admiration."[280]

CHAPTER 6

Information on Enemy Movements

The Woëvre region, like all the rest of the Western Front, saw advances in intelligence collection, analysis, and dissemination. Every adversary had access to a variety of sources from the electromagnetic spectrum and from aeronautical engineering. *Capitaine* Jean de Bissy, an early French pioneer of aerial photographic interpretation, described his job as "to follow the destructive work of our Artillery and to register the victorious advance of our Infantry."[281]

For infantry at the front lines, survival meant observation.[282] Before an attack, the organization of the terrain and locations of the enemy's machine guns, trench configuration, wire entanglements and observation posts were to be committed to memory. By 1918, three years of trench warfare had taught combatants that economy of force was obtained through an arrangement in depth – described by the French as "obstinate defence." The German trenches were built to last and provide comfort. The French had no intention of establishing a permanent defensive network to keep the Germans eternally at bay. They had to retake their sovereign territory and drive the Germans out. On the Allied side, the underlying assumption of all construction was that one expected to move forward at any moment.[283]

The prototypical German trench network in the first year of positional warfare comprised a front-line firing trench reinforced by a second trench at a distance of 100 metres to as much as 1 or 2 kilometres. The first line held the initial defending troops, the second held both defence and counteroffensive troops, and the third line was primarily counteroffensive troops to reinforce against counter-attack. The first trench was the observation trench backed by a parallel trench to the north serving as a resistance trench. The second trench line paid particular attention to the terrain, frequently employing a rear slope for additional cover. Protection against artillery led to the final trench line having *abris* mostly on the opposite slope of a hill crest. The number of connecting trenches increased to accommodate the flow of infantry between the first trench and the second and third. Since trenches were configured to the terrain, they appeared irregular on the aerial photograph. Such irregularity also ensured protection from flanking enfilade fire. The distance between the lines depended on the topography or the situation at hand. It also reflected the German intention to offer prolonged and stubborn resistance. The lines held a succession of organized strong points. Reserve forces were set to ensure effective distribution of supplies. The artillery mainly operated from the reserve sector.[284]

Fundamental to trench warfare were traverses for defence. German traverses in sectors with reduced manning were usually spaced 15–20 metres apart. Photographic analysis determined that the typical traverse was 2–4 metres wide at the top, with a length of 8–10 metres. In very exposed positions, traverse length was reduced to 4–5 metres. In places exposed to flanking fire, special recesses for sharpshooters and machine gunners were included. German trench formation was defined by shadows from the earth and sandbags piled on facing front and rear.[285] The other feature of the trench included "dependencies", otherwise known as trench commodities, to promote sanitary living conditions. The aerial "signature" for cesspools and latrines was a small rectangular hole at the end of the small trench.

PRIORITIES

The top priority for Allied intelligence collection and analysis in 1918 was position of enemy units, be it army corps, divisions, or regiments, facing the Allied sector.[286] It was essential that the regimental intelligence officer kept his commander informed daily, "and make him take an interest in it."[287] A British intelligence officer described the best sources: "It may be stated that the most certain method of identifying the enemy's units is by obtaining prisoners or deserters. Next to this the best things are documents taken from dead or prisoners."[288] This was a well-established process for all combatants. The Americans were novices, but relied on more experienced French *2ᵉ Bureau* intelligence to hone their interrogation skills. As a senior British intelligence officer observed: "Most of the information which a prisoner has is information in detail regarding the enemy defensive works on his own immediate front. To extract this information from him requires time." What did not come with the new wave of intelligence and accessible information was an operational solution to break the deadlock.

When information was needed for refining operations, a trench raid was mounted either

Lieutenant Billy Schauffler and Lieutenant Monty Harmon proudly show off their Spad XI with the unique American flag insignia on the fuselage. (Aaron Weaver)

to capture prisoners for interrogation, or gather available evidence from the enemy trenches, or both. The raiding party had to make note of the trench construction, to include how the revetments were configured. Any article of equipment was a source for intelligence analysis: captured booty such as helmets, caps, rifles, shoulder straps and identity discs.[289] Sources of information from prisoners and raids on enemy territory included orders, personal letters and correspondence, providing unit identification.[290] Critical to Allied intelligence on German prisoners was the **Soldbuch**, or paybook. It served as identification and provided a starting point for discussion in the first interrogation.[291]

Prisoner interrogation became a science. German military intelligence was aware that the Allies had been told to expect beatings and other ordeals, and so "prisoners who, still feeling the violent emotions of battle, found themselves humanely treated … spoke more willingly even than the deserters." *VIIIe armée* interrogation centres took great care to ethnically separate prisoners. During the period that the 1st Division occupied their part of the southern Woëvre front, potentially anti-German Polish and Alsace-Lorraine prisoners were kept in separate locations and had better treatment and food, "which nearly always loosens their tongues."[292]

Foreseeing German intentions for an attack took everything into consideration. Intelligence operators in the Xivray area remembered that the German band played for the rotating German forces, to welcome fresh troops to the front as well as "playing out" the retiring battalions. When the German band played, intelligence could suggest the Germans were contemplating an attack, as fresh troops were brought in for that purpose.[293]

Priorities for American intelligence included the enemy order of battle. They wanted to know unit arrival, strength, habitual activities and distribution. The Americans knew, for example, that on the night of 13 January 1918 **78. R. D** with its newly established headquarters at Thiaucourt, relieved the **14. Infanterie Division**.[294] Two **Res. I. R. 258** companies occupied the first position lines on either side of Richecourt. They

also knew the soldiers' average age was between 20 and 35.[295]

At division level the intelligence officer's priority was knowing the enemy infantry's line of resistance, the number of effective troops in line constituting the order of battle, material and morale, ascertaining if reserves were being brought up, the strength of that support and when it could be brought into action.[296] For regiments assigned to the front line, the regimental intelligence officer's priority was to watch over the enemy defensive organizations and determine changes in observation posts, machine guns, shelters, and wire entanglements.[297] While the 1st Division was occupying the front lines opposite St. Baussant, the French interrogated a prisoner who explained the current assignment of **Res. I. R. 259**. He revealed that they held the line from the north-east corner of *Bois du Jury* to the *Nouveau Monde* trench. One battalion occupied the front line while the other two battalions supported at St. Baussant. A battalion was held in reserve at *Bois de la Sonnard* – a key part of German trench operations known as the **Bereitschaft** sector, where reserves formed to reinforce any sector under attack.[298] From prisoner interrogations the Allies knew about command posts and neighbouring kitchens in St. Baussant and *Bois de la Sonnard*, the regimental depot for supplies at the north-west corner of *Bois de la Sonnard*, and the ammunition dump maintained in barracks and shelters located in the southern ravine of the **Schlucht Lager** camp.[299] On the road towards Thiaucourt **Res. I. R. 259** maintained a battalion recuperating at Bouillonville. The usual relief period lasted eight days. Bouillonville also supported regiment training, including an **Unternehmen** practice area.[300]

Observation post (OP) stations were positioned along both sides of the front line (the French referred to OP's function as the *Service des renseignements de l'observation du terrain*, *SROT*).[301] Ground observation's incessant watch of the same enemy turf day after day offered fleeting opportunities that became valued intelligence. Telescopes, periscopes and field glasses combined with panoramic ground-level photographs, pasted together to form a horizon line mosaic, provided detail. The panoramic mosaics were annotated with degrees marked, so a consistent bearing to a recognized permanent point could be given for all observations. Ground observation intelligence collection was not done by all front-line personnel such as sentries and machine gunners. Their role required total concentration. Instead, the ground observer was a highly experienced infantryman who could piece together an evolving situation and report in a timely manner back to intelligence elements or artillery units.[302] Reflecting on this responsibility, Private Yeomans of the 101st Infantry recalled: "This was by no means a quiet sector. My first job here was on outpost duty. This is a hole in the ground with a tin roof where three men creep out every night and alternatively watch the German front line for any sign or attack. In the event of an attack, the outpost shoots up a signal flare, which warns the men in his own front line, but also exposes his position, and thus his goose is cooked."[303] A post-war memoir of Battery A, 103rd Field Artillery, concurred. "An observation post is a place of incarceration, situated as close to No Man's Land as the engineers could build it, and manned by artillery men, chosen for the work principally because if they should get bumped off, their organization would suffer little if any loss ... when the news gets out that you have been elected to the position, your friends all advance, look you in the eye, and shaking you by the hand, turn mournfully away."[304]

Observations for both intelligence and for fire-control were obtained from a chain of OPs along the St. Dizier-Metz national highway from Broussey-en-Woëvre to Beaumont, with another near Seicheprey. The first OP in the Toul sector set up by Battery A, 103rd Field Artillery, was OP12 and "like the overseas hat, was built not for beauty, but for utility. It was about six feet under ground, thirty feet long by five feet wide ... the Observation Room was handsomely outfitted with a map, a chair and aperture (at the height of the eyes) through which a binocular and a long light stick were thrust. The binocular, as is obvious, was to

increase the range of vision, and the stick was used to disperse the rats from in front of the aperture when the observer desired to cast his gaze on the enemy." Additional observation and information, particularly valuable in view of the large proportion of counter-battery missions, was supplied by the SROT 88 (a French flash-ranging section), where one field artillery officer was continually on duty with a private line to Regimental Headquarters; by the sound-ranging section (at first French, then American, engineers); and by aerial photographs, taken frequently. Additional help was provided by Balloon Company 2/B.[305]

Private Raymond Wunderlich of the 101st Engineers recalled:

It's hard for the man on the front line watch during the night time to tell what's going on out yonder in the shell-marked contested area. He's continually looking for something to develop. Every possible precaution must be taken against raids or surprise attacks. That's why each side sends out men on listening duty to crawl around on their stomachs and get as close as possible to the opposite line to pick up any little scrap of conversation that might happen to float over the enemy's parapet. It's a strict military order that there shall be no talking in the front line trenches, but soldiers under the long strain of the night will talk to each other now and then, generally in whispers or low overtone. Sometimes listeners have brought back valuable bits of information foolishly dropped on the wings of the night by a nervous soldier who couldn't restrain his tongue. That is why each side sends up flares. Always there is the hope of catching the other fellow in the act of spying.[306]

As for the new man on the OP12 job, the reward was "the graveyard shift at the telescope and you also rated the delectable job of carrying a five-gallon bidon of water and the day's supply of champagne from Beaumont, two kilometres away, through a winding trench, ankle-deep in mud and water."[307]

Captain Alban B. Butler's cartoons captured poignant moments of the 1st Division's time on the Western Front. Montsec's threatening silhouette clearly stayed with those who served in that sector. (Butler, *Happy Days*)

The most obvious features facing the Americans north of Seicheprey were the Rupt de Mad river, small villages, and the neighbouring forests. The first position of the southern Woëvre front directly facing the Americans included the villages of Lahayville and St Baussant and *Bois de la Sonnard*. French *2e Bureau* confirmed the Germans' primary command post occupied a dugout on the western edge of Lahayville. Many dilapidated trenches were described as full of barbed wire. Directly facing No Man's Land in the first position was a continuous double line of trenches. German trenches followed the Rupt de Mad to Lahayville and then proceeded east to the southern edge of *Bois de la Sonnard* 2 kilometres north-west of Flirey. West of Lahayville heading towards Richecourt the front line trench was occupied by observers every 50 metres.[308] Each German battalion on the first line had three companies in the first trench and supporting trench. Company A was held in reserve. Further to the south at Richecourt, one of the battalions had half of the personnel occupying a dugout at the Lahayville sawmill and the other half in Richecourt. The paucity of manning by the Germans was commented on by Lieutenant Richard A. Newhall from the 1st Division in February 1918: "I doubt if there were many (if any) Germans in the enemy front line. They usually went back quite a ways to sleep during the day. There are those in our battalion who advanced the theory that even at night the Germans held their first line with a wooden-legged flare shooter."[309]

The German intermediary position was parallel to the first at a distance of 300 to 500 metres between Richecourt and St. Baussant following the heights along the left bank of the Rupt de Mad. The trench network became a double line of trenches protected by barbed wire. The village of St. Baussant was surrounded by double and in some places, triple, lines of barbed wire. In the Position 1-Bis trench networks the machine gunners had concrete dugouts. Between Flirey and Essey to the north the Germans had constructed several good dugouts that could accommodate 16 to 20 men in the first and intermediate trench networks. Position 2 of the sector commenced two kilometres north of Richecourt at the Quart de Réserve. In intermediate and rear echelon lines the trenches were more established and occupied by most of the companies.

The Germans labelled their sector networks with alpha-numeric designations starting with A-1 in the west and moving through the alphabet as the trenches proceeded to the east. The reserve sector known as the third position was five kilometres north of Richecourt.[310]

German artillery operated primarily from this location. Trench names connecting the first and intermediate position gave the combatants a common identity. Four connecting trenches proceeded north-east out of Lahayville towards St Baussant. The names from west to east were **Stellung Laufgraben, Laufgraben 1, Laufgraben 2** and the **Zigzaggraben** (Zig zag trench). Zig Zag was a busy thoroughfare for German troop movement.[311] The French used titles on their maps covering the sector of *Boyau en Zig-Zag, Boyau den Bocks* (beer glass) and *Boyau des Teutons.*

SERVICE DES RENSEIGNEMENTS DE L'ARTILLERIE (SRA)

All Allied intelligence in the sector concerning artillery targets was worked by *Service des renseignements de l'artillerie (SRA)* for the respective *Armée*. *SRA* functioned like the *2e Bureau,* operating near the landing grounds of aerial observation *escadrilles*.[312] *SRA* further studied batteries, observation posts and associated target sets such as cantonments, bridges, stations, and depots of munitions. *SRA* officers were responsible for working out their own means of obtaining intelligence as well as those placed at their disposal such as *SROTs*, artillery spotting, sound ranging, flash spotting, and observation sections.[313] *SRA* assisted the French and American batteries in determining the accuracy of their fire. *SRA* personally ensured the rapid exchange of intelligence between the various artillery sections. It was a testament to how much American artillery valued their French *SRA* counterparts when the 1st Field Artillery Brigade commander, General Summerall, personally requested one officer be kept on station with the Brigade to better assist his artillerymen during their time at the southern Woëvre front.[314]

A sound-ranging observation post was located in *Bois du Jury* and along Metz-St. Dizier Highway. The site commanded the Seicheprey valley and covered portions of the German lines. Sound-ranging and observation sections were *armée*-level responsibilities, but they were authorized to support the *corps d'armée* with intelligence emanating from the assigned sector. Integral to the sound-ranging operation was a forward observer who could recognise the artillery piece being fired by the sound created. He phoned to headquarters any specifics regarding the weapon and location.[315] As the sonic wave travelled at the rate of 300 metres per second, it created an arc measured by several stations placed along the front. The time interval of the sound arc was plotted on a map. *Section de Repérage Par le Son (SRS)* used French milk cans about 1 metre high with the stoppers thrown away and platinum grid wires linked to microphones soldered into the top. The cans were placed on the arc tied by wire to a centre. The sound wave from the artillery projectile hit the various microphones. The microphones converted the sound into an electronic signal that was "photographed" onto tapes superimposed on the map of the region covered. The data was synthesised via a "computer" and the resulting information was passed on to the artillery via telephone. When the Allied artillery fired the SRS confirmed the rounds were on target, under target, left or right.[316]

Along the Beaumont Ridge to the south of the front lines the French established a flash spotting system of great efficiency for locating enemy batteries. Three observers were stationed some distance apart on the high ground, each with a telescope laid on the same point at zero and each connected by telephone with a central station at Petit Mandres. When an enemy battery opened fire, each observer laid his glass upon the flash and called his angle to the central station; these angles were laid off on the map and where the lines subtending the angle from each observer crossed, there was the battery.[317] The discharge of a high-velocity gun was distinguishable from a howitzer by the sharp, blade-like stab of flame emitted and the fact that little or no smoke was observed. The flash of a howitzer on the other hand had a distinct yellowish colour accompanied by a certain amount of smoke.[318] So accurate was the system that a report was made every time a

German battery fired and even of the number of rounds it fired, all the data being recorded on a chart showing active and inactive locations of German batteries. The absence of sound and light data prompted the artillery command posts to look elsewhere for targets.

Sound-ranging and flash-spotting observers employed a panoramic map and a map detailing location and range of the German artillery. Whenever the artillery fired the observer worked to form an estimate of the piece location, probable objective and calibre. Discerning the difference between the shell wave (*son de choc*) of enemy and friendly fire high-velocity guns was a challenge.[319]

German artillery units also employed sound-ranging and flash-spotting units. They set up artillery posts north of *Bois de Remières* and west of *Bois de la Sonnard*.[320] **Schall-Mess** (the German equivalent to *SRS*) employed a stop-watch, telephone, anemometer (wind-gauge), weather vane and thermometer. As each post heard a report from an artillery piece, they started their watch. Watches were stopped on the vibration from the warning post. The calculated difference in the course of the sound wave from its origin took into consideration measurements of atmospheric conditions, temperature, direction and velocity of the wind. The results were sent to a central post for final calculations and conclusion with the final data forwarded to the heavy artillery unit commander for counter-battery salvos.[321] **Licht-Messtellen** (German flash spotting) comprised a central station and eight observation stations distributed over a 20-kilometre front. Each post had eight men with four providing relief every two days. They employed optical measurements to determine the location of enemy artillery. The essential equipment for **Licht-Messtellen** control at headquarters was the Flash and Buzzer Board and the plotting board, which synchronized the observations. A telephone switchboard connected to the posts. The plotting board used a 1:10,000 map that traced each response from the posts. All calculations on identified artillery batteries were forwarded to artillery for counter-battery operations. Like sound ranging, the central station reported observations to the heavy artillery unit commander for subsequent targeting.[322]

AERIAL RECONNAISSANCE OVER THE WOËVRE

The Woëvre region was considered a quiet front where ground units recuperated from combat on more aggressive battlefronts at Ypres, the Somme, and Verdun. This included aviation operations. It was an ideal location for American forces to better understand the third dimension's role in warfare. As campaigns shifted to other locations that summer, American aerial operations become directly exposed to the German aviation elite – with increased losses of aviators and aeroplanes. While at the Woëvre, the Americans became more accustomed to the French *2ᵉ Bureau* process, which covered a myriad of sources and analyses. Aviation was an essential component of intelligence. One of the most important indicators for increased operations in a sector was sighting of Type **Ae Drachen-Ballon** ("kite-balloon") captive balloons, and additional aerial reconnaissance by aeroplanes. Captive balloons were ideal for monitoring operations close to the front lines especially with telephone connection to provide constant updates to ground commanders and artillery units. Aeroplanes extended the visual range for analysis by corps and army planners and operators. The two had similar missions of artillery direction, information gathering on enemy organization and enemy works, monitoring front and rear echelons, and assisting long-term analysis as it concerned combat sustainability through rail and road traffic.[323] Starting with the 1st Division, *32ᵉ corps d'armée* required the Americans to conform to the French *2ᵉ Bureau* intelligence process. This meant adding a topographic officer and draughtsman to the division's establishment to "make hasty drawings, sketches, and diagrams for the General Staff of the Division, study aeroplane photographs of enemy territory, to keep up to date the sector maps showing both Intelligence and Operations Information, to distribute maps,

Leutnant Forster and *Leutnant* Hirschler in their black DFW CV played a *Schlachtflieger* role in the Seicheprey battle. (Aaron Weaver)

and to collect and forward to the Corps at prescribed intervals the corrections in trenches and other military features for incorporation into new editions of the battle map at Army Headquarters."[324]

Fours years of warfare transformed aviation's role supporting operations at the front. Critical was the idea of **Zusammenwirkung**, everyone working together, or the "combining" of efforts for greater effect. Aviation resources focused on assisting ground operations leading up to an operation by providing intelligence and assisting in the cartographic updates. Only when the Germans became aware of the impending onslaught did German aviation become fully committed to mastering the enemy's air forces: clearing enemy observation balloons from the sky and shooting down aeroplanes.[325]

German aerial reconnaissance over the Woëvre was a sophisticated process; seasoned aviators worked with state-of-the-art aerial cameras and ground equipment for analysis and photograph distribution. Three German aerial reconnaissance units were assigned. **Armeeabteilung C's** specialized aerial reconnaissance was accomplished by the Bavarian **Fliegerabteilung 46b Lichtbild (Lb)** [Photo] [Bavarian FA 46b Lb]. Bavarian 46b Lb mainly supported **Armeeabteilung C** and was directly tasked by **Hauptmann** Friedrich Rutz, **Kommandeur der Flieger** of **Armeeabteilung C (Kofl C)**.

Additional reconnaissance was accomplished by another Bavarian unit, **Fliegerabteilung (Artillerie) 298b** [FA (A) 298b], and by the Prussian Flying Unit FAA 279. Aeroplanes flown in support of **Armeeabteilung C** included Rumpler C.IV (for high-altitude photo reconnaissance), DFW C.V or LVG C.V (for general purpose or infantry contact patrols) and Halberstadt Cl.II, Hannover Cl.II or IIIa flying **Schlachtflieger**/close battlefield air support missions that included low-altitude harassment of ground forces.[326] Hauptmann Rutz also controlled the **Stabsbild-Abteilung C** (Stabia C) located near Bavarian 46 Lb. Stabia C served as an intelligence collation centre that analysed aerial photographic coverage along with other intelligence relevant to the sector.[327]

French aerial reconnaissance over the southern Woëvre front in early 1918 involved four *escadrilles* subordinate to the *32ᵉ corps d'armée*. The lead aerial reconnaissance *escadrille* was Sal.122 operating out of Belrain, 20 kilometres west of St. Mihiel. As the *escadrille* designation showed, Sal.122 flew the Salmson 2 A2, the most impressive Allied aerial reconnaissance aeroplane of the war. It was sturdy, capable of carrying any one of the French aerial cameras of 120cm, 50cm and 26cm as well as the semi-automatic DeRam; and was still very manoeuvrable when fighting enemy aeroplanes.[328] Additional aerial reconnaissance was accomplished by *Escadrille* Sop.104 flying the Sopwith 1A2.[329]

Escadrilles AR 41 and AR 258 supported divisions assigned to *VIIIe armée* from the Toul area. The two *escadrilles* flew the most ungainly aeroplane in the French 1918 aviation inventory, the AR 1.[330] The *2e Groupe d'aviation* support to the Woëvre included Sop.277 flying Sopwith 1 A2s out of Belrain in support of *10e division d'infanterie colonial*.[331] A fourth *Escadrille* supporting *VIIIe armée* was Spa.34 flying Spad XI aerial reconnaissance to the south in Nancy. French Pursuit aviation comprised *escadrille* N 92 flying Nieuport 24's in support of *Ire armée* and *VIIIe armée* from Belrain west of St. Mihiel. Despite access to French aviation coverage, 1st Division commanders complained to Chaumont that lack of aerial support meant the Germans controlled the airspace over the Woëvre. This meant an inability to operate secretly in preparing raids and 1st Field Artillery Brigade's ability to conduct accurate counter-battery was limited.[332] Dedicated pursuit aeroplanes finally arrived but after the 1st Division had departed the sector. America's first operational pursuit squadron, the 94th Aero Squadron, set up operations near Toul flying the Nieuport 28.

America's first operational aerial reconnaissance squadron was the 1st Aero Squadron. The unit proceeded to Ourches on 4 April 1918 after five months training at Amanty. They had been fully equipped with Spad XI and AR 1 planes for aerial observation. Two other American squadrons in training, 12th Aero Squadron and 88th Aero Squadron, remained at Amanty and subsequently arrived at the front in May 1918. 1st Aero Squadron trained to work the following missions: command-directed assignments, long distance aerial photographic missions, adjustment of divisional heavy artillery fire and long-distance visual reconnaissance.[333] *32e corps d'armée* monitored 1st Aero Squadron's ability to successfully perform essential missions prior to their operational deployment to Ourches and let it be known while the 1st Division was in place that *escadrille américaine* needed to become more professional regarding their performance in the *avion réglage* mission: "To date their work was mediocre."[334]

When the 1st Corps Observation Group and the subordinate 1st Aero Squadron became operational on 11 April, their mission was primarily to keep Allied command informed of the general situation within enemy lines by means of visual and photographic reconnaissance. It was called upon to influence, whenever necessary, the adjustment of Allied artillery fire. 1st Aero Squadron was also required to be ready for contact patrols – which entailed training with the divisions in the responsibilities associated with aviation support. Aviation and divisions were to take part in terrain exercises and conduct panel exercises with the divisional artillery using wireless radio, since American aviation remained an apprentice. Post-war assessments by the 1st Corps Observation Group attested that the period in a quiet sector of the front best served the schooling of pilots and observers and rendered them more competent to undertake intensive operations elsewhere on a larger scale.[335]

American field artillery learned of the effectiveness of German aviators when they examined the wreckage of a downed aeroplane. They discovered a map showing all forward positioned artillery properly located, but the roving battery positions were not marked. The Americans were heartened by the latter.[336] 103rd Field Artillery's 155mm heavies provided a signature for aerial photography interpretation thanks to *abris* at the battery constructed above ground with earth, sand bags, I-beams, logs and reinforced concrete. Other signatures revealed quarters, storage areas and a first-aid station. A narrow-gauge track ran from the road to transport ammunition and supplies. All presented the Germans with an excellent target.

Communication between aeroplane and division was via wireless radio, visual signals, signal rockets from the aeroplane, and written messages dropped from the aeroplane. Ground communication to the aeroplane employed large panels, rockets, and Bengal flares. Radio liaison between the group and all points in the 26th Divisional area was established from the Group Radio Station. In addition, two pigeon lofts were set up at the aerodrome to provide additional communications networks.[337]

In American aero squadrons working the observation mission, intelligence was managed by the Branch Intelligence Officer (BIO). The BIO was assigned to the group by the G-2 Section of the General Staff. This officer was responsible for the collection, compilation, and distribution of all information on the enemy pertaining, directly or indirectly, to aerial operations. He was responsible for its collection, compilation and transmission to all higher commands. The assemblage, study, interpretation and distribution of aerial photographs was accomplished by the BIO assisted by the observer who had carried out the aerial photographic reconnaissance sortie. An equally important person in the observation unit was the Group Photographic Officer who commanded the aero squadron's Photographic Section. He was responsible for the photographic equipment of the group and was charged with supervising the installation of photographic apparatus aboard the aeroplanes of the squadrons. He supervised development and printing of all aerial photographs.[338]

BALLOON OBSERVATION

Captive balloons maintained continuous communication through the telephone to the ground. Covering the southern Woëvre area along the Beaumont Ridge was the French unit *Ballon 91*. In late February, the first operational American balloon unit, Balloon Company B/2, set up with *Ballon 91* and commenced operations. On 6 March the first American *Caquot* balloon ascension at the front was made by Captain Butler and Lieutenant Miller – surveying enemy territory and regulating artillery fire. The company was assigned for duty in support of the 1st Division.[339]

Divisional balloons supported division artillery fire with limited range. Balloons attached to heavy artillery devoted their time to counter-battery. During an attack the divisional balloon followed the advance of the infantry,

informing the commanders of the situation and disposition of the battle lines. Enemy disposition and movements were also monitored. During the battle *aérostiers* (balloon pilots) watched enemy batteries that commenced fire and informed artillery of their locations for counter-battery. Machine guns protected the balloons from enemy aviation. The cardinal rule was they never took their eyes off their sector.[340]

The *aérostiers* had to know the sector to the extent that any change in habits was quickly addressed. Essential battlefield knowledge was order of battle, units, train movements, and enemy defensive organizations within the first, second, and third lines. Battery emplacements and information about the activity of hostile batteries was key. In addition to offensive operations, the observer was required to know plans of defence to include destructive fire, harassing fire, counter preparation and barrage. Knowledge of the air service in the sector meant the observer was aware of what assets were available to fend off enemy aeroplanes. Liaison via telephone, visual signalling, wireless, panels, rockets, etc. passed the information to the commander in a timely manner. The observer served as the eyes of the battlefield commander once the attack commenced.[341] American *aérostiers* found working with French telephones and switchboards difficult. They were happier working with the US Signal Corps after they departed the Woëvre in support of the Château-Thierry and Second Marne operations.[342]

COLLECTION IN THE ELECTRO-MAGNETIC SPECTRUM

The French had the advantage initially when it came to communications since they operated with national networks already in place. The Germans had to import their own communication networks as they occupied territory. By 1915, communication networks at the front had been obliterated thanks to incessant artillery, requiring ground telegraphy to provide communications within the trenches.

Escadrille 122 flew the Salmson 2 A2. It was the leading allied aerial reconnaissance unit over the Woëvre subordinate to *32ᵉ corps*. (SHD B 78/1547)

Wire-tapping units intercepted ground telegraph lines (the French term for this telegraphy was *télégraphie par le sol,* TPS).[343] Three kilometres was the normal range for transmissions, enough to support the average front-line sector. Intercept stations working from the most forward trenches used the earth lines to listen in to the enemy telephone conversations. In an attempt to negate enemy radio intercept, patrols were told to look out for the antennae of the listening apparatus, usually consisting of two divergent wires coming over the parapet and being earthed at two points close to the adversary's forward trench.[344]

In 1916, the Germans established a cryptanalyst unit known as the **Abhorchdienst** (Intercept Service) that was considered comparable to that of the French.[345] All activity on the front lines was subjected to intense scrutiny through electronic means. One engineer recalled, "Fritz, listening through the rain and distant roar of the big guns, heard the sounds of our picks as they struck the rocks. Soon shells began dropping over on our side of the hill and then the machine guns opened up. All hell was soon popping, but we had to stay on the job."[346] Conversations were intercepted either by induction through TPS earth pickups or through actual wiretapping of the telephone lines. Many risked their lives to tap lines. Up and down the front line, conversations among all echelons became accessible to the enemy. Trench codes were established to counter this.[347]

Everything was put in code or cipher. The *32ᵉ corps d'armée* issued the Napoleon Code, written entirely in French – putting the 1st Division members at an immediate disadvantage because only a few could read French and work with the guide. Colonel John L. Hines, 16th Infantry, decided to make up his own code, which he called the Cauliflower Code: "Give me Brains. Brains, this is the King of Essex talking. Sunflower. No balloons, tomatoes, asparagus. No, No. I said no balloons! Oh, damn. My kitchens haven't come. Have them sent up." When they inadvertently mentioned someone's actual name, the line was cut. 1st Division telephone conversations eventually became plain English spoken quickly. Major Theodore Roosevelt, Jr. quoted one dismal effort with the source stating in the end, "If the message had been an important one, I would not have sent it in code."[350]

American soldiers employed their own vernacular to counter the eavesdropper. One artillery unit recalled a conversation:

At H hour and Q minutes put 10 beggars factotum [F.A. Shells – L.R. Fuse] on 6634. Can't be done. My horses [Piece] are out in the grass not in a stable [Guns not in position to fire]. Well, try one horse over this course then, starting him at the same time. Put him over the 6679 [German position or point of fire] course and load him with 50 bipeds falsetto [F.A. Shells – S.

Operational security policy travelled with the 26th Division from Chemin-des-Dâmes to the Seicheprey sector. Prior to arrival at the southern Woëvre front the Yankee Division set out their classified communication policy for the soldiers covering secure use of the telephone:

1. It is safe to assume that all telephone conversations within one thousand yards of the front line will be heard by the enemy. This necessitates great care in the use of the telephone. To prevent, as far as possible, the enemy gaining information through indiscreet use of our telephone, the following rules will be strictly observed:

    (a) REFERENCE TO LOCATION will never be telephoned.
    (b) From regimental P.C. forward, the telephone will be used for tactical purposes only; administrative matters will be transacted other than by telephone.
    (c) Messages referring to movements or operations of whatever size must be in cipher (except in attack, when secrecy will give way to urgency).
    (d) The designations of stations as used by the French will continue to be used; in all cases this represents a location and not an organization and does not change when new organizations occupy the locations.[348]

German warnings were acquired by the French and disseminated to Allied units.

Notice.

Beware of telephone conversations.

1. The enemy uses listening sets to intercept our conversations in the Zone of the Infantry and of the Artillery observation stations.

2. In consequence, take care:

    (a) Never to name a unit;
    (b) Never to mention the emplacement of our batteries, trench mortars, observation stations, P.C.'s, shelters, camps, convoy routes, kitchen emplacements, ammunition dumps, workshops, etc.
    (c) Never to mention in your conversations, contemplated actions, reliefs, losses, ammunition, effectives in the trenches, number of trench mortars, machine guns, etc.

The Notice concluded with:

4. Be just as careful, therefore, in your telephone conversations at the front as in your public conversations while on leave, where enemy spies and agents listen to your every word. Use Code exclusively. Never forget that your lack of forethought may cost not only your own life, but also the lives of several of your comrades.[349]

R. Fuse] and give him an hour to do it in. Here's something for you, Mac. About 100 wild women [German shells] just came into my house and drank up a lot of grape juice [incoming gas].[351]

There was an effort to eliminate grounded wires where possible. A constant programme of testing each line was established to determine the level of induction. Germans listened either through tapped lines or an induction apparatus. Whenever interference came – indicating that the enemy was listening in – it was as if the other receiver on a two-party line had been taken off the hook. When that occurred, one of the Americans using the line, by prearrangement, interpolated a word in the conversation that was a signal to talk gibberish. Employing deception techniques in telephone conversations via the lines became the norm. One intriguing outcome was ordering a rendezvous with a mythical general at a certain place and time and then watching the enemy artillery shoot up the emptiness.[352]

During the fighting and while the American commanders were arranging orders for a counter-attack upon the enemy north of Seicheprey, Brigadier General Traub, commander of the 51st Infantry Brigade, 26th Division, experienced the reach of intelligence through wire tapping while in telephone conversation with Major General Edwards. Suddenly they were interrupted by the voices of enemy "spies". The German operators brazenly announced their identity to the astonished generals and offered some facetious comment![353] When the 26th Division occupied their part of the southern Woëvre front, Lieutenant John Richardson, Balloon Company B/2, met with Brigadier General Traub concerning their operations. Richardson stood waiting and observed Traub talking on the phone when the conversation was suddenly interrupted by a German: "I know Brown Bear is you General Traub and Black Bear is General Edwards. I know you plan a raid upon our lines. You better not try it!" The 51st Brigade commander notified his Signal Corps men of the incident. They rushed to the location and tracked the

lines from the headquarters. Upon examination they found the place where the lines had been wiretapped.[354]

French command was not unaware of the problem. *Général* Gérard's *VIIIe armée* staff following the 26th Division's first major engagement at *Bois-Brûlé* made the observation that "The Americans seem to make use of the telephone habitually for liaison between the first parallels and the P.C.s of the Company commanders, a practice whose dangers, because of the numerous German listening posts, have many times been pointed out." French liaison officers were ordered to assure *VIIIe armée's* instructions were "well understood, and to see that they are carried out."[355]

"THE UNIFORM IS NOT A PASSPORT"

An interesting light on the German preparation and general spy system in the Seicheprey sector was shed by prisoners returning after the war. The Germans already knew everything about the 26th Division. Germans in American uniforms were living with troops of the 102nd Infantry in sector. Their cover was they came from a neighbouring regiment. New soldiers constantly arrived from replacement camps – their identity seldom came into question. Moreover, Germans chosen for this task spoke not only English but used the language with the added embellishments of American slang which they had learned in the United States before the war. The detection of such a person who was thoroughly familiar with American habits and customs could be very difficult, if not actually impossible. The Germans asked their American prisoners about the health of the cooks and kitchen force, by name and nickname, even narrated mess-line incidents, to prove their actual presence within the 102nd Infantry area. They jested about having shelled Brigadier General Traub at his Ansauville headquarters. Four years in the front lines had taught them a lot of tricks of the trade. The only error that was gleaned from post-war analysis was that the Germans did not correctly assess the number of automatic rifles in an infantry company. German espionage – always suspected but never really discovered – kept them informed of Allied movements and that the policy of the sector was not offensive.[356]

A 2 March 1918 memo from the **Generalstab** addressed an incident 16 kilometres north of Seicheprey at Charey, where a man dressed in a German officer uniform showed up at the telephone exchange and inquired about a contemplated offensive. The imposter even tried bribing the official with 100 Marks, who in turn brandished a pistol and chased him out of the office firing away. The "officer" escaped and warnings were sent out.[357] On the other side of the front line at the same time, Lieutenant Colonel George Marshall noted a suspicious discovery in a daily operations report in February: "A sack containing O.D. blouse without buttons, 1 pair O.D. breeches and 1 canteen without cover were found concealed in the Boy [sic] de Rambucourt."[358] Captain Strickland related in his postwar book *Connecticut Fights* a brazen but somewhat incompetent effort by a pair posing as Americans: "On one occasion two strangers, one uniformed as a colonel and the other as a major, passed up and down the front line trenches for an entire forenoon unchallenged, the troops believing them to be inspecting officers until an American officer, noticing that the colonel's eagles were pinned upside down, reported the pair to regimental headquarters and they were apprehended and passed back to higher authority for examination. No one ever learned what became of the case."[359]

Senior French commanders issued a warning through a memorandum dated 13 April 1918 from General Headquarters of the Armies of the North & North-east Staff, 3rd Bureau, No. 13685: "Absolutely reliable information proves that during the recent operations, detachments of German soldiers wore English uniforms or English helmets to get within our lines, under pretense of giving us aid, and then fired on us from the rear. The attention of the troops called to fight side by side with our English, Belgian, or American allies, is called to this new violation of the law of nations by our enemies. Whenever there is any possible change for doubt, small allied detachments fighting in liaison with our troops must establish their identity with certainty. Likewise, attention is called to the fact that the most careful identification of <u>every</u> allied soldier or officer circulating within the cantonments of the rear must be a universal principle; it is, indeed, certain that the Germans have succeeded recently in slipping into our lines agents dressed as Belgian, English or American officers. Reciprocally, every

Aerial photograph of Richecourt. (SHD)

French officer or soldier circulating in the zone of one of the allied Armies must always be provided by the French authorities with identity papers which will give rise to no doubt; furthermore he must submit to any investigation by the local authorities with the object of establishing his status. This memorandum was furnished to the American 26th Division on 20 April.[360]

On 16 April 1918, Private E.B. Rogers and Private N. L. Taylor of Company B, 102nd Infantry, reported that the previous night around midnight they saw "an American Soldier Flashing a light on our post near the dug out of Co. B's runners in full view of the Enemy's lines." Rogers and Taylor reported the soldier went past their post seven times and flashed his light at least three times. After he went by, German machine guns opened up in their direction. The two privates looked at the infiltrator and noticed he was wearing what they figured to be an officer's uniform. When challenged the unknown figure responded sarcastically. The mysterious "officer" then left a few minutes later. The report did not mention the two privates confronting the officer and demanding identification. Instead, they just reported the incident.[361]

Lieutenant Sirois and Corporal McGinnis of Battery C, 102nd Field Artillery, remembered extreme vigilance: "Treachery was in the air day and night. This sector was full of German agents and spies." Special orders were issued to those on guard, challenging everyone at night, both on crossroads and at points entering American lines. The countersign was changed every night and the procedure was as follows. Men repairing telephone wires wrecked from shellfire and runners carrying messages frequently had to pass through one or more points occupied by US troops. At 1600 each day one of these men would proceed to the Infantry PC with an order requesting the password to be used that night. Only an officer of the rank of major or higher could generate the password and countersign. Vigilance was maintained with a soldier on guard at each key location in the trench. The guard asked for the countersign, then the check-word. The same process was repeated through the trench network. No chances were taken. No matter what rank, everyone was suspect to the soldiers on security with a loaded rifle and shiny bayonet.[362] These precautions combined with the gradual stabilization of the American presence at the front soon made this form of enemy spy activity impossible.[363]

Major Doane of the 104th Infantry observed: "Spies inside our line evidently knew as much as we ourselves, for the relief was made under a very severe bombardment, all roads and trenches leading to the rear being heavily shelled practically all night long. All the towns in the rear of the lines were infested by German spies. Being so near the German frontier, and having for years intermarried, the natives who had been allowed to remain in their homes were in constant communication with the enemy."[364] Private Connell Albertine, 104th Infantry, echoed Major Doane's assessment of the people in the Woëvre and mentioned that on their arrival in the area a listening post reported a sign held up by the nearby German lines that read, "Welcome Yankee Division". The Apremont natives provided their German relatives with all the information they wanted.

Corporal Rogers, 101st Field Artillery, described a civilian ploughing a field behind the battery set up south-east of Beaumont. To the members of the battery the civilian was a spy who sent signals to observers at Montsec or the **Drachen** by the colour horse that he used to plough the field. One day it would be white, another day it would be black. The direction of the furrows suggested a code to aerial reconnaissance.[365] Trench gossip added to the distrust. One story had an old woman selling apples to soldiers in the town of Mandres, who had been watched and followed to her home. It was found that she was not a woman, but a man in disguise. A telephone with a line running to the German trenches was found in the cellar.[366] Another had a peasant woman communicating through the configuration of laundry hanging out to dry – providing the Germans with Morse code transmissions through the linen.[367]

Command guidance on this dangerous situation came from several sources. *32ᵉ corps d'armée* issued a memorandum to all divisions that enemy agents were procuring information from cantonments, stations, trains, and in cafes near the stations. *Général* Passaga emphasised the need for the greatest caution in conversations with strangers, civilians or soldiers. Such discretion was to be applied even among friends – avoiding talk of composition, command, and location of troops. Such operations security was defined as a strict duty. Within the 26th Division, Lieutenant Colonel Cassius M. Dowell, chief of staff to General Edwards, published a letter that reinforced the *32ᵉ corps d'armée* memorandum with further discussion on spies in French and American officers' uniforms being reported in the southern Woëvre front. He pointed out that "The uniform is not a passport." [368]

AN EYE OF MORDOR

Positional war required constant surveillance to maintain advantage. The Germans held the ace card in the southern Woëvre region. They captured the high ground in 1914 and made it into a fortress that withstood major French offensives for four years. *Côte 380* "Montsec", known as "The Key to Metz". was the advance sentinel facing the Allies in the southern Woëvre front – a geographical high point that became the subject of legendary press dispatches. [369] The Germans made Montsec one of the most valuable observation posts on the Western Front. Concrete underground observation stations overlooked every movement to the horizon. Six galleries were constructed within the mountain with entrances facing the opposite northern reverse slope for extra protection from Allied artillery fire. Montsec internal galleries were located on the highest part of the ridge, configured with massive timbers, and extended lighting and communication using speaking tubes that connected each observation post. The primary observation deck was configured to withstand any aerial or artillery attempts to blind the operation. [370] The **5. Ldw. Div.** of **Armeeabteilung Strantz** fought a continuous

battle over Montsec from 10 September 1916 to 23 February 1917. [371] The French and later the Americans learned that fighting positional war under the shadow of Montsec meant having to live with a significant disadvantage. [372]

From Montsec the battleground spread like a map. Every Allied move for miles south of Seicheprey, to include the Beaumont Ridge, Dead Man's Curve, and the towns to the south, was seen. A better vantage point could not be imagined. Soldiers in the Seicheprey area complained that they could not change a vermin-infested shirt without permission from the Germans. Slogging each day in the eternal muck that was the trenches, each soldier saw his adversary living high and dry. On clear days, American soldiers were forbidden to walk on the roads, as the olive-drab uniform was easily detected from Montsec against the white surface of the roads. The only time to reinforce ongoing operations was under cover of darkness or during inclement weather with a very low cloud ceiling. [373]

Allied offensive punch was also challenged by the terrain. Their artillery did not have the advantage of employing natural terrain. Establishing secure battery locations was a constant problem thanks to Montsec. The farmlands south of the front lines did not provide enough cover. Allied artillery was forced to set up within the spread-out villages in the area, relying on well-established (and well-known to the Germans) epaulements built from concrete slabs, logs, rocks, I-beams, and sand bags. [374]

Beaumont on the St. Dizier-Metz highway was important to the Allies. It was a crossroads on the only road taken by Allied traffic coming from Toul and heading north to the front line, particularly Seicheprey. Key towns on the route heading north to Beaumont were Ansauville, Hamonville and Mandres. Everyone in the sector knew the most significant road feature – one that combatants who survived the journey remembered as "Dead Man's Curve." The deep bow of Dead Man's Curve was highly visible, from the air or from Montsec. Not only was its distinct curve easily recognizable, it also traversed the steep grade of

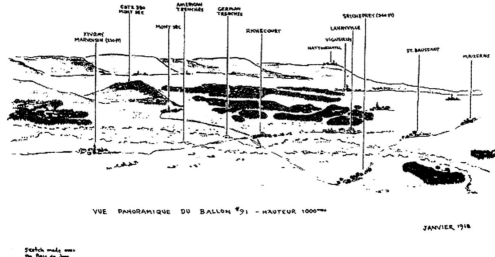

VUE PANORAMIQUE DU BALLON #91 - HAUTEUR 1000m

JANVIER 1918

Sketch made over
the Bois de Jury
Source: ADC 1st Ops, 17 Feb

The view of the Seicheprey sector drawn by *aérostiers* serving with Ballon 91. (Cochrane, *The 1st Division at Ansauville*)

Beaumont Ridge. Dead Man's Curve was a well registered target for German artillery. Behind the Beaumont Ridge were advance battery positions. The Germans were well acquainted with traffic patterns, having observed them for three straight years. A battery of guns targeted the curve at all times, shelling the location throughout the night at 10- to 15-minute intervals.[375] German artillery took a heavy toll among the water cart drivers and mules, supply and ammunition trains, and dispatch riders on motorcycles or mounted, as well as infantry units going in and out of the trenches.

The precision of fire made for high casualties as the Allies slowly wound their way towards Beaumont and Seicheprey. The dash across this junction meant revving engines, splashing mud, and – at the worst moments – screams of terror. Companies worked passage squad by squad. Along the road for some months of the year a dry irrigation ditch afforded some protection. It was the preferred route of those bound for Beaumont. Horse and mule carcasses littered the area. Any other shortcut to Beaumont was already targeted by the Germans. Any detectable movement resulted in well-placed rounds. Lieutenant Colonel George Marshall recalled

that increased activity on roads or in the lines triggered German artillery fire.

A fascinating rumour surfaced that a tunnel had been dug, at least 2 kilometres long and about 6 metres square. Its destination was the base of Montsec. Its purpose was to blow up *Côte 380* to make it a level plain in the Woëvre. Division engineers kept the rumour alive among the men in the sector – sometimes updates detailing progress were provided. The soldiers began to suspect the charade: "And Montsec still remains a part of topographical France."[376]

For the Germans, the southern Woëvre front, was an intelligence-rich environment. Attention to detail provided **78. R. D.** and adjacent divisions with the location of almost every machine gun, artillery piece, and PC, and the stronghold supporting each position. They knew more about the weak spots of the battleground than the new defenders.[377]

PART 2

COALESCENCE

CHAPTER 7

The Germans Prepare an Invitation

In January 1918 **40. Infanterie Division (40. I. D.)** left Richecourt on 15 January and was replaced by the **78. R. D.** under the command of **Generalmajor** Paulus von Stolzmann. The **78. R. D.** left their sector west of Verdun where they had held their position for almost a year, conducting a major regimental raid against the French that captured ground and took prisoners. The French *2ᵉ Bureau* assessed **78. R. D.** troop morale as in decline. **General der Artillerie** von Gallwitz and his **Generalstab** decided that **78. R. D.** should move to a quiet sector.

On the opposite side of the **78. R. D.** the French commenced preparations for the incoming Americans. *Général* Debeney, *Iʳᵉ armée*, *Général* Passaga, *32ᵉ corps d'armée*, and *Général* Monroe, *69ᵉ division d'infanterie*, were the senior French officers in the southern Woëvre front that guided the initial role of American forces. The French division in the southern Woëvre front, the *1ʳᵉ division marocaine* under *Général* Daugan had provided a spirited offence against the **40. I. D.** Bullard wrote post-war: "Of this division it seemed to me the French always made cannon fodder. Wherever the fighting was worst, where the sacrifices heaviest, they were sent." The division was initially Moroccan but after three years of intense fighting *1ʳᵉ division marocaine* comprised remnants of other organizations, notably the *Légion Étrangère*. It earned a reputation for conducting trench raids.[378] On 6 January 1918, *1ʳᵉ division marocaine* conducted

a major raid against Germans north of *Bois de Remières* that resulted in numerous casualties and prisoners taken. The success of this raid prompted German military leadership to plan a retaliatory operation. It was a parting shot from *1ʳᵉ division marocaine*. The inbound 1st Division relief was about to commence.[379] The following day *Général* de Castelnau, *commandant le groupe d'armées de l'est*, issued *Instruction Particulière N. 20* directing 1st Division and *69ᵉ division d'infanterie* to replace *1ʳᵉ division marocaine*.[380]

The 1st Division relief was conducted in the worst winter in living memory. The roads were clogged with deep snow and ice. Horses were put to a severe test trying to stay upright. On the night of 18 January 1918, the 1st Brigade entered the line and commenced relief of the *1ʳᵉ division marocaine,* completing the operation three days later. The initial headquarters for both 1st Division and 1st Field Artillery Brigade was Ménil-la-Tour and later moved to Ansauville. As Brigadier General George Brand Duncan's 1st Infantry Brigade first entered the sector, the Germans unleashed a **Gasschuss** barrage on the *1ʳᵉ division marocaine* artillery with mustard gas. Duncan's two regiments, the 18th Infantry under command of Colonel Frank Parker and Colonel John Leonard Hines' 16th Infantry set up operations from Beaumont and Mandres respectively. Frank Parker was familiar with the French *armée*, having attendedt he *École*

Supérieure de Guerre and served as an observer until America declared war. Parker became chief of the American Military Mission at *GQG*.

The 1st Division's 1st Brigade equalled the manpower of the *1ʳᵉ division marocaine* they were replacing. Colonel Parker's 18th Infantry overlooked the village of Seicheprey and *Bois de Remières* front lines. To Parker's left, 3rd Battalion, 16th Infantry set up their headquarters at Bouconville and defended Center H.[381] At Position 2, General Summerall's 1st Field Artillery Brigade was set in place. Major General Bullard immediately thinned the strong points in the trenches north of the Beaumont highway, leaving only two battalions (one from each regiment) to garrison the trenches and strongpoints. The other infantry battalion was drawn back to the main line of resistance. The frontline troops, however, were ordered to step up their raids and patrols. The 1st Division was to organise in depth, thinning out the front line closest to the Germans and dispersing the infantry through the sector in a series of successive echelons.[382]

The first three weeks saw the Americans totally subordinate to French control. When General Bullard's 1st Division took control of their sector on 5 February, he recorded his frustrations in his diary, noting he only had administrative and supply but not tactical command of his division. When the approval for tactical command was finalised he was in better spirits and recorded five days later his men "began harrying the enemy at once."[383] The Americans now were going to prove themselves. First, Bullard published Instruction No. 1 stating: "There are no orders which require us to wait for the enemy to fire on us before we fire on him; do not wait for him to fire first. Be active all over No Man's Land; do not leave its control to the enemy."[384] The 1st Division had been given a small daily allotment of No. 4 (cyanogen chloride) and No. 5 (phosgene) gas shells and immediately commenced firing them at the Germans.[385] Bullard recorded: "Well, we stirred him up and he came back at us. I am glad I can say that he was the one who came '<u>back</u>,' not we."[386]

German attention to American procedures had become fairly sophisticated as the 1st Division settled in. General Summerall observed that long sections of the artillery communications net disappeared during the night and communications were cut off with the batteries. The division responded with vigilant patrolling along the line. At that time an unknown signal corps officer "attached to brigade headquarters" was sent elsewhere and "the sabotage ceased." The officer had a German name and occupied a room next to the artillery brigade's staff mess. Summerall and his staff subsequently recalled that the officer with the German name was always in his room when they were eating. Summerall said his policy was never serve wine or talk operations at meals. However, in retrospect he stated: "I never doubted that this man was a spy, but nothing could be proved."[387]

The consummate master American military planner of the 20th century, General George Marshall, cut his teeth at Ansauville. Operation planning was poor – only when he intervened did it meet objectives. He was proactive and frequently toured the front-line Seicheprey area to understand what was in place and how to best defend against any potential German attack. Marshall knew maps as well as any American staff officer and reinforced his knowledge of the southern Woëvre front by personally validating defences annotated on *Plans Directeurs*. He discussed with General Bullard the fact that colourful displays on a map did not necessarily indicate that the boots were really on the ground to carry through plans in case of an emergency.[388]

Lieutenant Colonel Marshall noticed that Chaumont staff assumed a haughty demeanour while on the line. He recalled during a 1957 interview a "misunderstanding of our situation …These fellows at G.H.Q. were almost all my close friends and associates at Leavenworth, and most of them had been student officers under me … but we were wholly out of sympathy with each other, and I felt that they didn't understand what they were doing at all. They had become very severe and they didn't know what they were being severe about… General Pershing was severe, so they modeled their attitude on him. I was so outraged by this that I talked a great deal and I made a great mistake … I learned the lesson then I never forgot afterwards."[389]

Oversight of the 1st Division by GHQ AEF and liaisons created rancour. Their commitment to the front line was the only game in town and everyone wanted a part of it. Even though Ansauville was considered a quiet sector, it was the first time that an American staff had administered such a large and elaborate area. Marshall found the job demanding: "The work had generally to be carried on with four or five observers from G.H.Q. standing at one's elbow to watch how it was being done. This did not tend to quiet the nerves and promote the assurance of the division staff during their novitiate."[390] Marshall's lessons here shaped his future. General Summerall post-war observed: "No doubt but for General Bullard's courage and loyalty to his troops, GHQ would have crucified some innocent officer for not thinking … as throughout the war, there was an impassable gulf between GHQ and the troops. GHQ knew little of the real conditions or difficulties

and was always ready to sacrifice anyone who might be blamed."[391] The attitude of GHQ had ramifications not only for the 1st Division's role in the Woëvre but also subsequently for the 26th Division.

One of the first visits by GHQ AEF members from Chaumont was by Colonel Conner on 9 February, four days after General Bullard assumed tactical command. Conner spent time with the French *armée* in an artillery unit prior to the war. He was both respected and feared by divisional staffs. Conner had Pershing's attention and was quick to comment on battles fought. While observing the Seicheprey trenches with Lieutenant Colonel Marshall, an artillery round exploded nearby, wounding Conner. Captain

The 1st Division senior staff under Major General Robert Bullard (centre). Colonel Campbell King, Chief of Staff, stands to his left. Bullard's right-hand man is Lieutenant Colonel George Marshall. (Colonel Robert R. McCormick Research Center)

Patton wrote to his wife detailing the incident. "Col. Fox Conner got wounded last week. They were inspecting and came to a part of the trench full of water. They climed [sic] out on the top and ran along to avoid the water when just as they were jumping in again a shell blew up and cut Col C's nose and throat. He is all right again and will get a wound badge which is nice."[392] Conner was subsequently awarded the Purple Heart. He had been blooded at Seicheprey – and took a personal interest in the accomplishments of soldiers fighting in the southern Woëvre front for the rest of the war.

Bullard did not escape criticism while serving in the Ansauville sector. His Regular Army division did not demonstrate the staff work required to maintain an operational division at the front. Disorganization and poor communications plagued ongoing efforts. Bullard worked well with his French counterparts but had a tendency not to keep his staff informed of his decisions. Many of the older regular army officers did not grasp the tactical concepts of the Western Front and neglected detailed planning.

The cadre of French liaison officers had reservations about the division's commanders and internal management – knowing that combat at the front required more effective leadership. After 18 days in the Ansauville sector, Marshall reflected that *Général* Monroe's *69ᵉ division d'infanterie* staff officers were a bit overbearing in assisting their 1st Division staff counterparts – "too willing as a matter of fact". The French liaison's bias was entrenched from years of experience; and of course their view point was that of a Frenchman, " which is quite different from that of an American, particularly as to methods".[393]

Brigadier-General C.M. Wagstaff, British military liaison to GHQ AEF, described the sensitivities involved in sharing of information, particularly manpower statistics. He observed the French asking for information that was a "nuisance to work out". The Americans responded to the French that provision of such information came with a cost – they required identical information about the French *armée*.

Allied questions on manpower were potentially politically explosive. Wagstaff commented, "I cannot butt in too hard." After the 1st Division had been on the Woëvre line for a month, Wagstaff thought that "1st Division is quite happy in the line … They are still under the French for tactical command, but the Divisional Staff are getting more to do. Anyhow that Staff is quite all right. I am glad to say that (I believe on my suggestion) they have pulled nearly all their men out of the front line trench, and they hold their sector properly in depth now. The French wanted them to put the whole lot bang up in front."[394]

At the front line north of Seicheprey the soldiers were getting used to the harsh conditions. One of the novices was Lieutenant Sam J. Ervin of North Carolina. His company was positioned in the "deepest depression in the immediate area, filled with icy rainwater and could not be drained." It was exhausting. One night one of his soldiers got lost, stumbled back to the trench and was challenged by a sentry. The errant soldier, "a native of a European country, lapsed into his native language." The sentry shot and killed him. Ervin thought the shot signalled a German attack. He set off a signal rocket requesting a defensive barrage. Once he realised his mistake Ervin withdrew to an *abris* and fell asleep. The next day he was relieved of command and considered for court martial. Ervin requested an honourable discharge as a 2nd lieutenant and then proceeded to enlist as a private in his old company.[395]

FIRST FAMILY IN THE FIGHTING FIRST

General Pershing was inundated with requests to be part of the first wave of Americans heading to France. Former President Theodore Roosevelt made an impassioned plea for his sons to be included. General Pershing noted on 4 July 1917: "Two of the Roosevelt boys, Theodore, Jr., and Archie, reported yesterday. Unable himself to participate, their father's fine spirit is represented by his sons."[396] Both sons were assigned to the

26th Infantry. The oldest son Theodore Jr. was a former Major in the Connecticut National Guard and led a battalion in the 26th Infantry. His brother Archibald ("Archie") was company commander in the 26th Infantry. A third son, Kermit Roosevelt, proceeded to war as an appointed officer in the British Army serving in Mesopotamia. Kermit earned the respect of his British counterparts and was awarded the Distinguished Service Order and the Military Cross. In the summer of 1918, Kermit was assigned to command Battery C, 7th Field Artillery, and supported his brother Theodore at Meuse-Argonne.[397] The fourth son, Quentin, flew Nieuport 28s with the 95th Aero Squadron and was shot down and killed that summer.

"DOUGHNUT SISTERS"

In the early summer of 1917 Salvation Army Commissioner William McIntyre received letters from his two daughters, Irene and Gladys, asking his assistance in their request to be part of the Salvation Army war work in theatre. Irene was a Mt. Holyoke College graduate (class of 1913). Gladys was attending Pratt Institute. The sisters were not Salvation Army officers but thanks to William McIntyre's senior position, the two were able to acquire appointments. In January 1918 both proceeded to France and were initially assigned to the Gondrecourt training area with the 1st Division. When the division moved into the Ansauville sector, the McIntyre sisters moved with them, setting up a coffee and doughnut "factory" inside a ruined shed in Ansauville making pastries and pies for the soldiers coming back from the front lines. Their hard work made them celebrities. The media learned of Irene and Gladys and gave them the loving soubriquet "the Doughnut Sisters".[398]

The news picked up on one trip Irene and a Salvation Army colleague Cora Van Norden took to the Beaumont area in a truck to provide 1st Division soldiers with doughnuts and pies. The truck broke down and became an immediate target for German artillery – truck, doughnuts and pies became atomised with a few direct hits.[399] One correspondent recalled: "They didn't try to impress on any of us the fact that they were doing a wonderful job; in fact, they didn't talk about their work. And because of that spirit of self-effacement they 'sold' us on the Salvation Army, besides winning from all of us – soldiers and correspondents – all sorts of admiration for them personally."[400]

ARTILLERY ADVERSARIES

The first months of America's presence at the Woëvre was more a demonstration of "King of Battle" artillery operations than infantry. America's artillery leadership came from Brigadier General Summerall, 1st Field Artillery Brigade. His adversary **Generalleutnant** Wilhelm Hoffmann was a retired **Artillerie** officer called back at the outbreak of the war and now possessing three years of positional war experience. The two personified what artillery leadership required in modern combat. Summerall's counterpart in the 26th Division, Brigadier General John H. Sherburne, considered Summerall to be "generally rated as the number one military genius of the American Army."[401]

The earliest reported description involving **Gasschuss** on American forces occurred on the late afternoon of 1 February. The Germans fired 25 **Grünkreuz 2** (phosgene)/**Grünkreuz 1** (diphosgene) shells, recognized by their "peculiar swish and wobbly sound in passage" that fell harmlessly near the 6th Field Artillery in *Bois de la Hazelle*. The 1st Division's 7th Field Artillery replied with a long barrage of 6,750 (HE) and 80 No. 4 (cyanogen chloride) and No. 5 (phosgene) gas shells. The French disapproved of this tactic because the firing was fast and long-lasting. The next day Lieutenant Alban B. Butler, aide to General Summerall, wrote in his journal: "Our 155s fired 174 rounds – mostly gas shells on seven German batteries."[402] The principal **Gasschuss** and HE target the first month on the line was artillery, not infantry. Later, GHQ AEF weighed in and determined measures were to be implemented to shift the target to the infantry.[403]

The 1st Division arrived in France in 1917 without any gas training. Prior to occupying the sector at the southern Woëvre front the 1st Division received not only the most complete combat training of any AEF unit but also the most thorough gas training. Despite this, mistakes were made. The 1st Division suffered more gas casualties than small–arms or artillery shell casualties during this time. Major General Bullard commented that "A state of instruction adequate against the danger is extremely hard to obtain … Our gas officers were almost hysterical in their efforts to teach and impress our new troops; but knowledge and real efficient training came only after hard experience."[404] *Général* Passaga further directed that every 1st Division *abris* and shelter was to initiate proper procedures

Brigadier General Peter Traub stands before his soldiers from the 101st Infantry who fought valiantly on 23 February 1918 at Chemin-des-Dâmes. (*Pictorial History of the 26th Division United States Army*)

to effectively respond to mustard gas attack. His directive instructed that the British mask was to be put on first and kept on for four hours after the gas bombardment.[405]

Marshall was newly arrived at the front when he passed through a village as a gas alarm commenced. Marshall turned to a sentinel and asked if it was a real or practice alarm. The sentinel was busily putting on his mask and without taking a moment to recognise who was asking the question, sharply responded, "Put on your gas mask, you damn fool, and don't ask questions!"[406] Marshall made it a personal habit to don the mask whenever he walked along the highway to the trenches. Marshall had just slipped on the mask when a mule train of supplies proceeded down the same road. One "wizened old mule skinner sat huddled on the wagon seat" smoking his pipe. He glanced over and saw Marshall's figure with mask. The mule skinner shrieked out the alarm to the rest of the teams "Gaaazzzz!" The entire column turned around and proceeded as Marshall recalled "at a pace that threatened to carry them deep into Germany."

SRA reporting showed a violent bombardment took place on the first line south of Richecourt near Plantation Humbert. The French and Americans fired 12,555 artillery projectiles (of which 10,900 were 75mm) against 5,003 projectiles in a 24-hour period three days before the 1st Division took control of the sector. The report mentioned the Germans fired toxiques (gas).[407] Otherwise a few harassing shots occurred in the centre and left. The 7th Field Artillery fired a long-duration barrage of 6,750 HE shells. Lieutenant Butler reported happily that "the French are very much upset because we fired so long and fast."[408] Two days later on 5 February, two 7th Field Artillery 75mm batteries shelled the German gun positions as if it were a personal vendetta. Butler wrote the counter-battery was against Battery A that "we believe were responsible for [shelling #12 position on 16 January]," on the day the battery assumed the sector. SRA reported German artillery fired bursts against usual targets in Bois du Jury, Flirey, Bois de Remières and Bois de la Voisegne. The

Germans had a distinct advantage employing **Artillerie-Flieger** and **Drachen-Ballone** to work with the Montsec observation centre. German 77mm and 105mm were using toxic rounds against Beaumont, occupied by 18th Infantry.[409] "Gave them plenty of gas. 2nd Bn PC 7th Field Artillery at Rambucourt was shelled & gassed [in return]." Battery #12 was shelled again that day, and on 7 February Lieutenant Butler said that as a result "three men from Bty A, 6th FA went to the hospital this morning [with] faces and eyes burned."[410] The Germans had fired just one shell (**Gelbkreuz**) containing mustard gas along with numerous HE shells, marking the first time that mustard gas was used on American forces. On 8 February, a fourth casualty was evacuated with a burned buttock.[411]

Aeronautical support to the inbound 1st Division was provided by Ballon 91 at Camp de l'Hermitage and escadrille Sop. 104 at Toul flying Sopwith 1A2s.[412] The first dedicated American aerial support arrived on 24 February when Company A of American balloon aérostiers augmented the 91 Cie d'aérostiers two kilometres south of Ansauville.[413] The first American aérostiers demonstrated that Americans were quickly accepting their responsibilities at all echelons and in all areas of expertise. American aero squadrons supporting operations on the southern Woëvre front was a month away.

Under the prodding of 7th Field Artillery 75mm fire, **78. R. D.** artillery responded in kind, stepping up its fire from less than 100 rounds a day to more than 800 by the end of the February. During March **78. R. D.** artillery averaged 500 to 1,000 rounds a day – two bombardments that month totalled 2,000 or more HE rounds.[414] **Artilleriekommandeur Generalleutnant** Hoffmann was engaged in developing his strategy for **Niederhaltung** (dominance).

ANATOMY OF A GERMAN RAID

On the morning of 8 February, **General der Infanterie** Auler's **Ldw. I. R. 36** conducted operations to the east. To their surprise they encountered an American patrol from 16th Infantry and captured four soldiers. It was a new uniform and a new enemy. Even more surprising to the German staffs receiving a report of the engagement, one of the prisoners was a German-American. It was a significant discovery. Why did a German from America want to fight his fellow countrymen? The prisoner explained that it was not a war against the German "Volk" but was to liberate them from the rule of the Kaiser. The American melting pot that comprised the US Army created a something of a crisis in the German command.[415] More German-Americans were en route with each passing day and it made the command and staff wonder how the average German soldier was going to react to fighting this new enemy.

Von Gallwitz's **Generalstab** initiated the planning to engage the 1st Division through his chief of staff, **Oberstleutnant** von Bawelsz.[416] Planning commenced on 17 February and a coded telephone call was made. The call to **78. R. D.** termed the code word "**Einladung.**" Einladung was a grimly ironic name for the first planned German trench raid against the Americans in the Woëvre. It was now time to send an "invitation" to American forces to experience first-hand the realities of positional war.[417]

The 1st Division was no stranger to **Sturmtruppe** tactics. On the night of 3 November 1917, **7. Bayer. Landwehr. Infanterie. Regiment** executed the Jacobsbrunnen raid against the newly arrived 1st Division infantry elements brigaded with the French. Over 200 **Stosstruppen** and 17 artillery batteries conducted the assault and within 20 minutes three 1st Division soldiers were killed and eleven captured – the first American casualties and prisoners in the war.[418]

Von Gallwitz and Fuchs both recognized that a trench raid was an appropriate way to test the mettle of the American soldier. Discussions with von Stolzmann initiated **78. R. D.** planning for a sizeable raid. **Einladung** was to attack American positions in a well-contested battleground – the German sector of **Abschnitt G.II** – the area that constituted *Bois de Remières* and *Bois Carré* and No Man's Land. The attack objective

was the unimproved road just north of *Bois de Remières*, the south-western edge of *Bois Carré*, the dugout group just east of *Bois Carré*, and the eastern edge of the wood itself. **78. R. D.** was tasked with quickly breaking through the lines at dawn and penetrating as far as the northern edge of *Bois de Remières* to acquire prisoners and destroy *abris* and supporting trenches. Two **Res. I. R. 259 Kompagnien** augmented by members of **Sturmbataillon.14** armed with flamethrowers were to execute the raid. After 30 minutes, **Stosstruppen** were to return to the lines with **MW** and artillery ceasing fire 20 minutes later. The remaining battalions in the line were to serve as an emergency stronghold in position to be employed as required. The forces were to stage out of St. Baussant and within *Bois de la Sonnard*. Within 8 minutes of the opening rounds, **MW** fire was to shift to **Feuerblock** providing a rolling barrage for the **Stosstruppen** to advance as far as the final line planned for the raid. Von Stolzmann specifically emphasised "The strongest kind of **MW** fire on the point of entry of the raid, artillery box barrage especially strong on the west communication trenches and the north west of the **Jury Wald** [*Bois du Jury*], diverting artillery fire on the enemy position opposite **G I cd** [opposite Richecourt] and **G III cde.** [opposite *Bois de la Sonnard*]."[419]

Gasschuss was integral to the trench raid plan and **Gaswerfer** were added to the inventory. Long-range artillery was to fire gas rounds at the southern half of *Bois de Remières* using **Blaukreuz** projectiles "to effect gas alarms and reduce the combat efficiency of the enemy", while trench mortars put down a three-minute barrage. Artillery shelling was to employ 1,300 rounds of an unspecified gas in addition.[420]

FINAL PLANNING

The next day **Major** Bruns, **Res. I. R. 259** commander, issued his **Regimentsbefehl** [Regimental Order]. The operation was to occur on 1 March using **Stosstruppen** and patrols. The objective was to break through to the third line that bordered *Bois de Remières*. Bruns named **Hauptmann** Seebohm, a member of his **Res. I. R. 259**, not the elite **Sturmbataillon.14**, to be his **Kampf-Truppen-Kommandeur (KTK)** [assault commander] to lead the attack. The **KTK** could concentrate totally on fighting the battle, possessing command over battalions in the regiment and reinforcements. This allowed the **KTK** to respond to any Allied reaction. Bruns provided further details on roles and objectives.[421] Each **Kompagnie** was to consist of 5 **Stosstruppen**, 14 men, and 3 light machine-gun operators, **Sturmbataillon.14** with **Flammenwerfer** and supporting **Pioniere**. Bruns scheduled training for **Unternehmen Einladung** at Bouillonville, west of Thiaucourt, to commence 20 February.[422]

Generalmajor von Stolzmann defined the artillery tasks in his report on **Einladung**. They were closure of the break-in point for the front and flanks – especially the dangerous flanks of *Bois du Jury* and west of the break-in point. **5. Ldw. Div.** artillery would conduct distraction fire on American trenches in Marvoisin. **4. Bayerische I. D.** would fire on French positions north of Flirey and H2. **Generalleutnant** Hoffmann followed up with the **Divisionsbefehl** [Division Order] further defining the artillery plan. **X-Tag** and **Y-Zeit** were defined for the operation to raid *Bois de Remières*. The mission was restated – "attack the enemy creating losses" was added to the initial objectives of acquiring prisoners and booty and destroying enemy trenches and dugouts. **Einladung** was to be a daybreak trench raid with HE and **Gaswerfer** fire by the **35. Pionier Bataillon** under the command of **Major** Graf von Pfiel, synchronized with **MW** fire against the enemy trenches. **Generalleutnant** Hoffmann stated that artillery and **MW** were to conduct artillery registering to confirm range and accuracy of fire. He described the raid in detail for all forces to understand mission and purpose. **Major** von Pfiel's **Pionier Btl. 35** was integral to the raid's success, working with all forces in getting the right explosives in place to destroy portions of the wire entanglements as well as orchestrating gas rounds fired into the

abris and trenches. Security procedures were to be strictly followed.[423]

The next day Hoffmann published the **Artillerie Befehl** [Artillery Order] repeating key points in the planning for all participating artillery units. Annihilating fire was called for against the entrenched defenders. Again, Hoffmann made it clear that **Einschiessen** [registering fire by artillery] was to be planned and executed two days prior to **X-Tag** [day of the raid]. Artillery reinforcements were to proceed by rail to Bahnhof, train station Jaulny. Artillery units were to be in place seven hours prior to **Einladung**. Command and control of artillery was divided into two: **Nahkampfgruppe** [close range group] and **Fernkampfgruppe** [long range group]. 3000 rounds of artillery were to be fired within 30 minutes of the attack. When the attack was completed the **Nahkampfgruppe** was to take the lead and provide cover and defend against a possible enemy counter-attack. Munitions for the attack were to include high explosives to destroy the enemy trenches. Final planning was distributed to the artillery units and forces were committed to the attack.[424] **Generalleutnant** Hoffmann published the **Artillerie-Tagesbefehl** [Artillery Daily Order] the next day listing artillery units by commander, staff, and battle headquarters. The **Nahkampfgruppe** was commanded by **Oberstleutnant** Rochlietz working from **78. R. D.** headquarters at Thiaucourt. Rochlietz had three artillery groups under his control: **Gruppe "West"**, **"Mitte"** and **"Ost"**. The **Fernkampfgruppe** was under the control of **Major** von Funke, also headquartered at Thiaucourt. Funke's two subordinate **Gruppe "A"** and **"B"** were located in the strategic rear of the southern Woëvre front.[425]

Pionier commander **Hauptmann** Reinking assumed responsibility for outlining what was necessary for **Pioniere** to effectively complement the attacking **Stosstruppen** and artillery. What transpired was a carefully planned choreography of weapons available, type of rounds for each **Minenwerfer** piece, the augmentation to be acquired from other divisions and units in the sector, and the assignment of targets with each step of the **Stosstruppen**. Key targets were the wire entanglements in front. Where **MW** could not accurately destroy the obstacles, **Pioniere** were to set charges with the **Stosstruppen** using pipebombs. Reinking's planning took in the American trench layout, wire obstacles, and dugouts. **Einladung** preparation meant domination through barrage. Reinking listed 4 heavy, 40 medium, and 44 light **MW** for **Einladung**.[426]

Two days prior to **Einladung** Hoffmann published the **Artillerie Befehl** [Artillery Order] giving the **Y-Zeit** [zero hour]. Explosive shooting was to start at **Y-Zeit** and continue for three minutes. **MW** were to provide annihilating fire in advance of the **Sturmtruppen**. At **Y-3**, **MW** were to delay fire until the **Sturmtruppen** had broken through the wire entanglements. At **Y-8**, **Sturmtruppen** were to have captured the initial objectives of the front-line trenches. **MW** fire was to come down against targets south of the American front lines. At **Y-15**, four **Sturmbataillone** were to merge and continue south. The attack was to conclude at **Y-30** and the **Sturmtruppen** were to withdraw. At **Y-45**, the **Sturmtruppen** were to be safely back in German lines and the **Einladung** mission would be considered complete.[427]

Staff planning proceeded and initial drafts were forwarded up the chain to seniors at **78. R. D.** and Armeeabteilung C's **Gruppe Gorz**. Fuchs received approval from his superior command to proceed. **Oberst** Freiherr von Ledebur from **Generalkommando XXXVIII. Reservekorps** generated the **Armeebefehl** [Army Order] of 22.2.18. **Armeeabteilung** resources were now committed. A wireless detachment for increased command and control and a light field howitzer detachment from the neighbouring **14. Infanterie. Division** were now en route to **78. R. D.** Oberst von Ledebur's order also disclosed that ten more light **MW** were committed to the fight. **Sturmbataillon.14** was to augment the **Stosstruppen** with ten **Flammenwerfer**. Regarding artillery augmentation, **Fussa 25** (heavy artillery) was to provide two heavy field artillery pieces and ten 10cm field guns. **5. Armee** was providing transport

for the weapons to the sector. The additional artillery was to be in place on the evening of 24 February. **Oberst** von Ledebur also indicated that additional **MW** from **Sturmbataillon.14** and rear echelon supply were to assemble at Thiaucourt. Finally, **225.Infanterie.Division** near St. Mihiel was to contribute the augmented unit of **Sturmtruppen 14**. Three heavy **MW** from the **Armee** rear area park at Hattonchâtel were added to the overall firepower, as well as eight **1916 Medium MW**. All echelons had communicated their requirements and forces were in motion to areas designated for **Einladung**.[428]

78.R.I.B. and its **Generalstab** were to operate from their bunker at **Madine Lager** to the north. Bruns occupied his **Gefechtsstand** [battle headquarters] along with **KTK Hauptmann** Seebohm in their forward command in *Bois de la Sonnard*. **Art.Kdr. Generalleutnant** Hoffmann and **78. R. D.** commander **Generalmajor** von Stolzmann were in their headquarters at Thiaucourt. **Major** Graf von Pfiel, **35. Pionier Bataillon**, worked with **Hauptmann** Reinking at the St. Baussant front lines.[429]

The infantry rehearsed the raid five days in succession at the Bouillonville training ground. The **Pioniere** only rehearsed the raid twice. Shortly after midnight on 1 March the assault parties left Bouillonville and reached the first line via St. Baussant, along the communication trenches, which were in very bad condition.

GAS ATTACK

On the clear, cold night of 26 February at about 0140, **Res. I. R. 259** working with von Pfiel's **35. Pionier Bataillon** fired over 900 gas rounds at *Bois de Remières* where Colonel Frank Parker's 3rd Battalion under the command of Lieutenant Colonel R. H. Griffiths was holding ground. A second salvo was fired about 20 minutes later. 810 **Gaswerfer** loaded with flasks containing almost 14 tons of phosgene and 10 **Gaswerfer** containing the new diphenylchloroarsine gas were fired against the dugouts and supply rail lines in *Bois de Remières*. Observing the great white cloud that formed over the forest, **35. Pionier Bataillon** believed the attack a success. But the battalion never completed the elaborate raid that was immediately to follow the gas attack. The 3rd Battalion men plainly saw the flash from the discharge but the period between the flash and the release of the gas from the overhead explosion was so brief that many inhaled the gas before they could adjust their respirators.[430] Light signals and klaxons were heard by the Germans, but they did not see any response coming from the Americans. The remaining ninety-two bombs in the **Gaswerfer** were fired off 20 minutes later at 0212, landing in the reserve platoon area within *Bois de Remières*. At 0223 the American artillery responded and ceased at 0300.[431] Some projectiles exploded in the air, others on the ground. As one 18th Infantry soldier recalled, "The suddenness and the violence of the attack, coupled with the overwhelming fumes of the gas, were … horrifying." The commander of the trench mortar battery in the wood said the attack "was very sudden [and] we couldn't tell whether it was HE or gas. It all came down in one burst … The dugout door was blown in and the gas just rolled in."[432] Soldiers couldn't find their gas masks in time. Assessment after the battle stated the majority of the casualties were preventable through better discipline. Some soldiers removed their masks too quickly, only half an hour after the last shell fell. Others switched from the effective but uncomfortable small British respirator to the more comfortable but less effective French M2, receiving gas in the process. Some soldiers worked unmasked in the woods 48 hours after the attack despite the odour of phosgene in the air.[433]

Major Bruns' **Gasschuss** into *Bois de Remières* was effective. One third of Lieutenant Colonel Griffiths' company became gas casualties. The medical history of the 1st Division reported sixty-two gas cases admitted to the hospital, with 4 deaths accounted for. The final count of casualties reported by the Division Surgeon was that two men died in the field and eighty-three were evacuated. Of those evacuated, six died within 5–60 hours after reaching the hospital

at Ménil la Tour.[434] In a supplementary report, Griffiths described the panic that had seized some of his men following the initial salvo of bombs. Private Coleman panicked, screamed, and stampeded from the listening post down the trench and knocked down his two counterparts while they adjusted their masks. Coleman died shortly after reaching the dressing station. At another listening post, Private Earnest threw himself on the bottom of the trench and began to scream without adjusting his respirator. His colleagues tried to help but in the struggle they had their respirators impaired. They were gassed and Earnest subsequently died. In one *abris*, Private Wolozak from 6th Field Artillery was asleep when the bomb exploded nearby. At first he couldn't find his mask, became panic-stricken and inhaled the poisonous fumes. His colleagues found the mask and assisted him in getting it fitted. At that moment Wolozak panicked and said the mask was broken. A French gas mask was found. Unfortunately, while en route to the dressing station Wolozak panicked again, resulting in his breathing more gas and dying when he reached the dressing station. There was no doubt, Griffiths concluded, that a large number of the gas cases that developed some time after the attack were the result of failure to observe well-known precautions. It was also revealed that rice being consumed for breakfast that morning was allowed to stand exposed for several hours in the trench before being eaten. Griffiths ordered the report illustrating the failures of gas discipline read to all companies of the battalion.[435]

Colonel Campbell King, 1st Division Chief of Staff, further elaborated on what caused casualties in the 18th Infantry. The sudden attack caught men unprepared on sentry duty or in their *abris*; they did not have adequate warning to adjust their masks or lower the gas curtains. After the attack, men removed their masks on their own initiative, or changed to the M2, even though the gas continued to linger in the area at dangerous levels of concentration. Furthermore, the unmasked soldiers remained or worked in the *abris* and in low places in the woods, where gas lingered. The soldiers neglected to put out fires in the *abris*, thereby drawing gas from the trenches into the sealed shelters.[436]

On the morning after the attack, 1st Division G-2 reported that "about 70 bombs, 210-mm, chlorine and phosgene" had been launched between 0132 and 0145 from trench mortar and **Gaswerfer** sited west of *Bois de la Sonnard*. 1st Division G-3 agreed with the estimate of seventy bombs and suggested that they had been fired in retaliation, "as we have on two or three occasions fired gas at them and have unquestionably touched them up quite a bit more than they have been before in this sector for a long time." General Bullard reported that two volleys, each of 100 18cm **MW** shells, 80 per cent of them phosgene, crashed "with a loud explosion and bright flare of light" in and to the west of *Bois de Remières*.[437]

78. R. D. reporting on the operation stated the American artillery that day was more vigorous against battery positions. The German artillery continued registrations, harassed the usual targets and gassed two 1st Division batteries with **Gelbkreuz** (mustard). Three more were "very effectively gassed" the next morning, 27 February.[438] *SRA* followed up and reported that aerial photography of *Bois de la Sonnard* discovered **Gaswerfer**. The information was forwarded to American artillery and the located **Gaswerfer** were destroyed (flames were reported in the area) by 5th Field Artillery's firing around 700 rounds from 155mm howitzers. [439]

Henceforth, troops in the alert area were to wear the British mask at the alert position at all times, even while sleeping, and were to change to their French mask only when the British mask "became torn or punctured, and as a last

resort." [440] The French mask was not trusted by the Americans. Five weeks later, after the Battle of Apremont, *Général* Gérard's *VIIIᵉ armée* staff was looking for a way "of overcoming by every means (lectures, and above all trials in a gas chamber) the lack of confidence shown by the American troops in what they call the 'old French mask.'"[441]

Colonel Hines' 16th Infantry took measures following the **Gasschuss** on their 18th Infantry companions. The word got around that they might be next. French *2ᵉ Bureau* intelligence issued a warning that **Pioniere** remained in the area. **35. Pionier Bataillon** had planned a second **Gaswerfer** attack on Flirey – but American 155mm howitzers thwarted that. After they had dug out their **Gaswerfer**, **35. Pionier Bataillon** left *Bois de la Sonnard* to prepare for **Einladung**. After experiencing such a massive gas attack, the 1st Division made a concerted effort to spot and neutralise **Gaswerfer** installations.[442]

General Bullard and senior staff's immediate attention to the **Gasschuss** on *Bois de Remières* was disrupted when General Leonard Wood, former Chief of Staff of the US Army, paid a visit. Wood had lost the chance to command the AEF to Pershing and was incensed that he no longer held sway in an army at war. He had just completed a visit with the British Expeditionary Force (BEF) to the north and was bristling with criticism, based on what he learned from British approaches to positional war. Bullard was rebuked on several issues, such as having his artillery placed in too vulnerable a position, lacking *SRS* in the sector, and simply for not having the depth of tactical understanding of the British. General Wood did have a kind word for Lieutenant Colonel Marshall, "a good man

Lieutenant Colonel George Marshall in 1917. (Marshall, *Memoirs*)

and very much alive to the situation." Needless to say, Wood's timing and comments were not appreciated by the division's command.[443]

Général Debeney, *Ire armée,* sent General Pershing a letter expressing concern that the American press had published an article on the 1st Division and a gas attack on 26 February that resulted in 66 casualties. Debeney instructed General Pershing that publishing such information was forbidden by the *Général commandant en chef* as it gave the Germans valuable information on the effect of their actions. Another principle of modern war was introduced into American military thinking.[444]

SUSPICIONS OF GERMAN INTENTIONS

Lieutenant Colonel Marshall forwarded an instruction entitled "Defense of Ansauville Sector, Provisions for all alerts". Right up front he stated:

> The reason for all alerts is to prevent surprise by the enemy ... The enemy is conducting behind his lines maneuvers of rupture, which he intends to put into effect in a great offensive to be launched suddenly and without warning ... they include a sudden, violent, unexpected assault and the development of an assumed success by deep penetration through trench lines and a renewal of open warfare ... The notable feature of these maneuvers is the concealment of preliminary preparations, the power and above all the brevity of the preparations for rupture of the line, and the depth of penetration. In one maneuver the actual open preparation lasted a bare fifteen minutes, as opposed to previous preparations of at least several hours ... Harassing fire on trenches, communications, P.C.'s, O.P.'s and artillery emplacements, especially with gas shells, can be expected for days preceding as well as immediately before the assault.[445]

These conditions along the Woëvre reinforced Pershing's desire to avoid dissipating the manpower of the AEF to the small-scale local operations that came with positional war and strive for warfare of manoeuvre.

French officers assigned to the 1st Division counselled Marshall and his colleagues that a German raid on the sector was highly likely. He consulted with Major General Bullard on the increased risk. The best tactic was thinning down the front lines to teams of automatic riflemen and artillery liaison personnel. The remaining (18th) infantry rifle companies were to occupy counter-attack positions rather than the trenches at nightfall. Bullard understood the concern but held to the position that any retirement would injure troop morale. Marshall made it clear that morale would be the least of their concerns, should the Germans succeed in taking the ground occupied by a fully fleshed-out front line. All points along the front line were considered susceptible to raids, so at nightfall the men were pulled back. Bullard agreed and ordered the shift in forces.[446]

German artillery fire, which had been light and sporadic, was observed to be registering near Seicheprey. Captain Charles Coulter, regimental intelligence officer, was informed. Lieutenant Colonel Marshall was also aware of the change in German artillery concentration. He discussed this with his French liaison officer, *Capitaine* Germain Seligman, sitting on the hillside on a sunny afternoon after visiting a number of batteries and other positions at the front. Marshall noticed heavy explosions scattered about prompting him to ask Seligmann what that indiscriminate firing meant. Seligmann replied, "I tell you what I think they are doing. I think they are registering preparatory to shooting. They are registering." The two officers proceeded to chart every place that was struck and then discussed their observations with Colonel Parker.[447] The Germans were firing their artillery right on the edge of *Bois de Remières.* Marshall at once prepared a warning directive for General Bullard's signature. Colonel Parker pulled his 18th Infantry back from the forward trenches, leaving men only in the automatic rifle pits.[448] It was 28 February and **Einladung** was scheduled for the next day.

General Bullard stated that German intentions to raid some portion of Center F had been suspected for several days prior to the 1 March raid. Orders had been issued to the soldiers in the line to take special precautions and arrange for special artillery support of Center F, particularly in the *Bois Carré* sector. The strongholds supporting sub-centers F-1, F-2 and the eastern portion of F-3 were withdrawn from their trenches after nightfall on 28 February to positions in the open from 150 to 250 metres behind the first line.[449] Listening posts were placed in advance of each group.

The afternoon prior to **Einladung**, 18th Infantry reported heavy "Minnies" firing on F-1 near the regimental PC. This was the final alert. The F-1 commanding officer was told to note the registration, move his forces out of the area and be prepared to counter-attack. At 0130 on 1 March, Lieutenant George N. Walker, 6th Field Artillery liaison officer, witnessed fire from Battery F on targets near F-3. Noise was heard across the German lines including the dropping of pipes (**Ladungen**) just outside the wire. Battery F fired off 25 rounds and a sharp command was heard coming from the area followed by startled shouts and what appeared to be a hasty retreat by the Germans.

Meanwhile, **Hauptmann** Seebohm's assault **Kompagnien** (in the reports named **Sturmkompen)** left Bouillonville and proceeded to their jump-off positions in the assigned nests north of *Bois Carré*. As they reached the area they met up with their **Sturmtruppen** and **Pionier** counterparts. Coffee was served. They awaited **Einladung**.[450]

AMERICAN RAID PLANNING

In mentoring 1st Division on the realities of positional war, *Général* Passaga encouraged them to conduct their own raid against the **78. R. D.** Throughout February raid planning commenced between both staffs. *Général* Passaga

on 24 February requested the raid be executed either on 27 or 28 February. Brigadier General Summerall recommended a greater allocation of special shells and 155mm rounds. French staffs agreed and alerted the Americans that they were withdrawing some battery support after the raid was executed. A final critique was levied by *32e corps d'armée*. Telephone communication between front lines and artillery needed improvement. The signal corps officer with the German name did not come up.

Brigadier General Summerall choreographed his artillery to support an 18th Infantry raid opposite *Bois de Remières* and a 16th Infantry raid against Richecourt. The Allied estimate had one 75mm for every fifteen yards of front and one 155mm howitzer for every fifty yards.[451] The 6th Field Artillery (75mm) and attached units were tasked to support the 18th Infantry by conducting a box barrage, by neutralisation of enemy lines and diversions against batteries. Gas rounds were to be used if the weather permitted. The 7th Field Artillery (75mm) and attached units were tasked to support 16th Infantry with a box barrage, 3 minutes of fire on the first and second German lines and to conclude with another box barrage on enemy front lines. The 5th Field Artillery 155mm batteries were to execute neutralisation fire and counter-battery. Trench mortars were to support both raids.[452]

To the west at Chemin-des-Dâmes, elements of the 26th Division conducted a raid with their French counterparts against German positions. On 23 February, three columns of *64e regiment d'infanterie* and members of the 101st Infantry engaged the Germans. Brigadier-General C. M. Wagstaff mentioned the raid went well and the "26th Division (in line near Soissons) are very proud of their raiding feat … The 1st and 42nd Divisions are very jealous and are burning to do raids also. I think the French are going to let them have a go at it, and it will be a good thing."[453] The "game" the Americans were accused of playing included competition between divisions.

CHAPTER 8

Einladung

On 1 March at 0540, **Einladung** commenced with **Generalleutnant** Hoffmann and **Hauptmann** Reinking's planned **Gaswerfer**, artillery, and **MW** barrage blanketing Colonel Frank Parker's 18th Infantry holding F Sector, which included *Bois de Remières*. The barrage lasted half an hour, annihilating positions, demolishing *abris*, caving in trench networks and cutting off wire communications. American positions north of *Bois de Remières* at *Bois Carré* and the eastern portion of the 18th Infantry sub-center F-2 got hit hard by heavy howitzer shells and **MW** bombs. **35. Pionier Bataillon** blasted off a **Gasschuss** of 720 **Gaswerfer** shells on the trenches to be captured.[454] As planned, German 77mm and 150mm batteries located in *Mort-Mare*, Gargantua, *Bois d'Euvezin*, and Haie l'Évêque initiated their box barrage before the **Stosstruppen** departed, smashing the front with over 2500 rounds.[455]

As the **MW** fire commenced **Pionier 378. Bataillon's Pionier Kompagnie.79** under **Oberleutnant** Fritz detonated **Ladungen** charges on the wire entanglements creating 7 metre-wide lanes.[456] The **Stosstruppen** initial advance was slow. At 0543 four **Res.I.R. 259 Sturmkompen** supported by **Pioniere** from **Pionier Bataillon.378** and elements of **Sturmbataillon.14** uniformly moved forward in conjunction with the **MW** barrage through the wire entanglement to the American front lines under cover of the waning darkness. Bruns was pleased as he watched the attack from his command location. The light was just right. As planned, the **MW** supporting the initial breach of the wire lifted after three minutes to target further into *Bois de Remières*.[457] Two minutes after leaving their positions, the German assault force reached the American lines.

At 0548, **Leutnant** Deppen's **1.Sturmkomp**, **Leutnant** Knop's **2.Sturmkomp**, and **Leutnant** Kellner's **3.Sturmkomp** penetrated *Bois Carré*. The **Sturmkompen** slogged through a network of wire configured throughout the *Bois Carré* area north of *Bois de Remières*. Breech B had two **Sturm-Kompagnien** rush through into the north of *Bois Carré*. **Leutnant** Deppen's **1.Sturmkomp** had five **Stosstrupp** detachments and two **Sturmtrupp** detachments from **Sturmbataillon.14** with two **Flammenwerfer** and three light machine guns. **16 Pioniere** were also part of Deppen's assault. **1.Sturmkomp** went directly south into *Bois Carré* with two columns. As they came across trenches, detachments split into them, blowing up obstacles and destroying *abris*. One detachment moved west via the largest trench, Trench de Soutien, near the rendezvous point 279 and then proceeded directly south to the edge of *Bois de Remières*. The distance from jump-off point to turn-around was about 1 kilometre. Reserve **Leutnant** Knop's **2.Sturmkomp**, almost identical in strength to **Leutnant** Deppen's **2.Sturmkomp**, went into the eastern side of

Bois Carré. **Leutnant** Knop's **2.Sturmkomp [6./259 Knop]** breached one American trench without encountering resistance. Smoke was heavy and the ground was churned up from the barrage, making movement difficult. One detachment broke from the rest and linked up with Deppen's detachment at the edge of *Bois de Remières*. **Pioniere** blew up four small shelters. Knop's **Sturmkomp** discovered the mangled remains of several Americans killed by **MW** bombs and captured four American soldiers. Knop noted they were all wearing gas masks. An American machine-gun fired continually from a concrete emplacement located on the north-west corner of *Bois de Remières*, inflicting several casualties.[458]

The largest single assault unit was **Leutnant** Kellner's **3.Sturmkomp [3./259 Kellner]** with 6 **Stosstruppen**, 3 **Stosstruppen** from **Sturmtruppen.14** with 4 **Flammenwerfer** and 3 light machine guns and 32 **Pioniere** that included a **Pioniersprengtrupp**. Kellner's **Sturmkomp** entered American lines at Breach C, at the south-east corner of *Bois Carré*. As they traversed the wire entanglements, they came upon **Spanisschen Reiter** ("Spanish Cavalry", called Knife-Rests by the British, *Chevaux de frise* by the French) that plugged a gap. The formidable trench obstacle was destroyed by the **Pioniere** and the assault continued.[459] **3.Sturmkomp** went directly south along the eastern edge of *Bois Carré*, then turned west along the trenches that comprised the southern half of *Bois Carré* and moved west for about 200 metres. A portion of this raiding element reached Company F-1's PC before being repulsed. In this fast moving engagement, a telephone squad accompanied the **Sturmkomp** providing real-time communication back to **KTK Hauptmann** Seebohm. Runners were also employed to update the command element.[460] **Leutnant** Bartz from **Leutnant** Kellner's **Sturmkomp** ran to the west and proceeded to destroy a large *abris* that included a tunnel. As Bartz's **Stosstruppen** tried to advance farther they were hit by rifle fire from firmly entrenched Americans in *Bois de Remières*. **Leutnant** Bartz was killed and his **Stosstruppen** retreated with three captured Americans.

Lieutenant Colonel Griffiths had already complied with Lieutenant Colonel Marshall's order to note the points of registration and move his detachments out of the registered area before **Einladung** commenced. Despite the warning, a few *GC* patrols were out inspecting vacated trenches and *abris*. The soldiers were hit hard by the sudden barrage. The soldiers that complied with the Marshall order were the survivors.[461]

Company F, 18th Infantry, put up most of the resistance. The soldiers, in spite of the bombardment, remained outside their *abris* and immediately opened fire.[462] In one *abris*, Captain Stewart W. Hoover, Lieutenant John N. Greene, and several men were hit by a fusillade of HE. The ranking officer, Captain Hoover, was killed in the first rounds, requiring Lieutenant Greene, 6th Field Artillery liaison to the 18th Infantry, to assume command. Greene left the *abris* in an attempt to alert his 75mm batteries with a red signal rocket to commence barrage fire. The HE impact concussions were so strong that Greene could not get a match to light the rocket. It was such a chaotic moment with explosions all around that he could not remember if the rocket fired. An explosion came from the direction of the *abris* that he had just left. **Stosstruppen** had arrived throwing grenades. One shouted "Come out, Amerikaner!" Greene and another soldier fired back with their .45-calibre pistols. The Americans won that duel. Two **Stosstruppsoldaten** were shot dead. Greene's newly acquired squad set up for more attacks. When the Germans withdrew, Greene realised that he had been wounded by a grenade blast. He managed to limp back to an aid station where the medics removed fragments from his legs and shoulder.[463]

At 0555, **Stosstruppen** of **3.Sturmkomp** attacked the largest American shelter on the edge of *Bois Carré*. However, **MW** fire, possibly from **35. Pionier Bataillon** started falling among the German attackers. Another source of the devastating fire was postulated by the Germans to be American trench mortars firing from *Bois du Jury*. Whatever the source, the German attack was hindered by the unforeseen fire, preventing in part Bruns' objective of using the **Flammenwerfer** to shock the American defenders. The **Einladung Unternehmen** became bogged down in the barbed wire obstacles. It was at this moment that **KTK Hauptmann** Seebohm ordered the three **Sturmkompen** waves to withdraw. **Leutnant** Knop's wave did not reach their assigned objective due to **MW** fire. Bruns reported that the **Stosstrupp** plan to attack the large American *abris* fell apart because **MW** fire did not move to target *Bois de Remières*. He made it clear that he did not know if the **MW** troops were culpable or if the Americans had systematically sealed off *Bois de Remières* sector with their own trench mortar fire. Whatever the source of destruction, the **Stosstruppen** were not able to advance. At 0710 **Res. I.R. 259** reported that they had succeeded in part. The **Flammenwerfer** of **Sturmbataillon.14** ran out of oil so they also withdrew. Bruns' frustration was clearly evident in the report when he concluded at this point they were "**Unnötig zu früh verdrängt!**" [Unnecessarily displaced too early!][464]

Company I, 18th Infantry, fought several close combats with distinction. As the **Stosstruppen** advanced against Lieutenant Stephen C. Markoe's position near *Bois Carré*, he personally led the counter-attack that stopped them. Markoe was severely wounded in the struggle. Sergeant William N. Norton was surrounded by Germans but refused to surrender, making a bold dash outside his *abris* and killing a **Stosstruppsoldat** – the rest withdrew. Norton returned to his

abris and maintained defensive operations. When Sergeant Patrick Walsh's commander was killed, he assumed command and attacked the **Stosstruppen** in his area, inflicting heavy losses.[465]

4.Sturmkomp under **Leutnant** von Specht did not encounter any resistance. They entered 18th Infantry lines at Breach A, west of *Bois Carré*. **4.Sturmkomp** comprised 4 **Stosstruppen**, a **Stosstrupp** from **Sturmbataillon.14** armed with 1 **Flammenwerfer** and 3 light machine guns, and 12 **Pioniere** from **Pioniere Bataillon.378**. **4.Sturmkomp** turned right down minor tirenches and crossed over saps that led from the primary first line trench. In the process they blew up one *abris* and retired back to the German lines, leaving a number of unused charges.[466]

American infantry combat groups that had withdrawn earlier now regrouped and advanced, meeting the German **Stosstruppen** in the open in several places and driving the Germans back with rifle, revolver, and grenades. The 18th Infantry had already suffered heavy casualties from the artillery fire. The German raiders were surprised by the attack from this unexpected quarter and were badly cut up, their leader was

The battleground of *Einladung* north of *Bois de Remières*. Where "German raiders failed"? (Colonel Robert R. McCormick Research Center)

killed, **Flammenwerfer** abandoned on the ground, and a few of their number were captured. The German attackers quickly retired.

KTK Hauptmann Seebohm's **Stosstruppen** returned at 0630, 50 minutes after the first salvoes launched **Einladung**. At 0640, **FA (A) 298b** conducting artillery registration over the Woëvre reported that artillery strikes were not detectable in some areas. However, the **Artillerie-Flieger** commented that American artillery was more lively than the German.[467]

At 0655, 1st Sergeant Norton was able to leave the area where he distinguished himself in battle and went to Lieutenant Colonel Griffins' battalion PC in *Bois de Remières* with the log book that contained secret information concerning sub-center F-1. He reported verbally that F-1 had been raided by a large party – some of whom reached the company PC. Colonel Parker was notified and left his Beaumont headquarters and joined Griffins to ascertain the situation.[468]

"THE WHOLE BRIGADE OPENED FIRE"

Einladung was more noteworthy for the artillery exchange than the infantry close combat. In less than an hour **Generalleutnant** Hoffmann's four 75mm batteries fired 300 shells each. Shells hit several emplacements, nicking the barrels of guns, destroying log covers, and wounding several men. American artillery officers hit the Germans hard from the start of the raid. Major John W. Downer, 2nd Battalion, 6th Field Artillery, first heard the German **Ladungen** explode opposite F-3 followed by a forward observation post reporting **MW** fire in progress. After calling the PC, Downer decided a major attack was in progress and gave orders for a barrage at 0540 using a red signal rocket and telephone calls to alert the batteries to commence fire. The Americans expanded barrage fire in front of F-2 and F-1 five minutes after the first rounds struck F-3. Ten minutes after the Germans launched **Einladung**, the 5th Field Artillery 155mm commenced counter-battery against German

batteries in the *Mort-Mare* area. In this skirmish the "heavies" fired a total of 613 rounds.[469] **KTK Hauptmann** Seebohm noticed the 75mms were firing shrapnel rounds into the area they controlled. He assessed the 75mm was firing from *Bois du Jury*.[470]

Major Robert C. McCormick, commander of 1st Battalion, 5th Field Artillery, without waiting for the order, "knew it was an attack and opened fire. As soon as I opened fire everybody else thought the order had been given and the whole brigade opened fire."[471] The 155mm heavies were also assisted by French 90mm and 95mm. 6th Field Artillery and 7th Field Artillery 75mm fired over 5,000 rounds at **78. R. D.** targets north of *Bois de Remières* and other German batteries in the area.[472]

In the Position 2 area, Private Hugh Weatherman, Battery C, 5th Field Artillery, was mortally wounded while leaving the safety of his *abris* to save the battery's horses from artillery firing gas rounds. Weatherman refused medical treatment and urged the corpsmen to treat the other wounded men.[473] Captain John D. von Holtzendorf of Battery E, 6th Field Artillery, was directing his battery during the heavy barrage when he became seriously wounded. Private David Alvin Smiley, Battery C, 6th Field Artillery, served as a runner delivering messages. He left the safety of a trench and ran on open ground because it was quicker.[474]

SRA reported to *Iᵉ armée* that the American 1st Artillery Brigade response to **Einladung** totalled 2,302 75mm and 293 155mm rounds fired. An additional 102 75 mm rounds were fired in support by the adjacent *69ᵉ division d'infanterie*.[475] SRS reported a 210mm or possibly a naval gun 8 kilometres behind the front lines had fired rounds into Mandres.[476] Towards noon American batteries again shelled trenches, approaches and certain German battery positions with moderate harassing fire, which increased at times in intensity towards evening. Later that afternoon, German batteries shelled the trenches that comprised the **Einladung** battleground with two strong bursts of fire to disturb the American clear-up out of the trenches, as well as conducting counter-battery against two batteries and interdicting approaches and traffic points.[477] Later in the evening, German artillery fire was described by *SRA* as being quite keen against the American 1st Division sector, while artillery barrages against adjacent French units were nil. American and French batteries hammered German batteries in *Mort-Mare* with 75mm and 90mm.[478]

ASSESSMENTS BY THE GERMAN SOLDIERS

Leutnant Kiby, commander of **Stosstruppen** from **Sturmbataillon.14**, commented that they experienced weak resistance in their attack. Kiby reported that the American stronghold led by the second in command surrendered without fighting. He also observed an American surrendering but suddenly firing his pistol. Kiby said they "subdued" that American. **Leutnant** Henneboldt, **Sturmbataillon.14** commander of the **Flammenwerfertruppen**, thought that fighting the French was easier, since the Americans resisted the **Stosstruppen** advance with "cunning," using their pistols. The **Stosstruppen** noticed they were primarily rifle shooting. Crzonka noticed one American officer escaping to the rear with a leather case most likely containing classified maps. **Gefreiter** Schmidt reported that only a few Americans were armed and the defenders surrendered.[479] **Leutnant** Kühne reported at 0643 when his unit successfully returned to German lines that they encountered minimal resistance. **Oberleutnant** Fritz reported that Kühne's successful destruction of a large *abris* was a major accomplishment, which included three prisoners being captured.[480]

The newspapers stated that on 1 March at Seicheprey twelve Americans were captured. In general the Germans shared first impressions on the American soldiers as being poorly trained but that their material was considered good and could prove a problem in future operations. **Leutnant** Karl Hermann Solaro concluded that the American "revolver shooting is superior to ours."[481]

BULLARD REPORTS TO *GÉNÉRAL* PASSAGA

Major General Bullard forwarded "Enemy raid on Center F, March 1st" to *Général* Passaga on 2 March. It was a succinct précis of what his commanders provided. The enemy laid down a heavy barrage of artillery and **MW** on *Bois Carré* and the eastern portion of sub-center F/2. No mention was made of **Gaswerfer**. The times of the attack did not correspond with the German reports: "The enemy entered our lines about 20 minutes after the barrage started." A brief description of the attack followed. "About 50 men [**4.Sturmkomp**]entered at Breech A, blew up one dugout, searched the trenches nearby and retired … About 100 raiders [**1.Sturmkomp** and **2.Sturmkomp**] entered at Breech B, dividing into two parties. One party moved west through trenches until met and repulsed by a platoon of Co. F-2. The other party moved south until met and repulsed by a detachment of Co. F-1. About 50 raiders [**3.Sturmkomp**] entered at Breech C. A portion reached the P.C. of Co. F-1 before being repulsed. They blew up all dugouts en route with mobile charges … Practically all dugouts in subcenters F-1 were destroyed as well as a number in the eastern portion of subcenter F-2. The trenches were demolished."[482]

Bullard said enemy intentions to raid a portion of Center F had been suspected for several days and orders were issued for special precautions to be taken and arrangements for artillery support of Center F, particularly in the area of *Bois Carré*. He described for Passaga the garrisons of sub-centers F-1, F-2 and the eastern portion of F-3 being withdrawn from their trenches at nightfall to a position 150 to 250 metres behind the first line. As German artillery commenced registration fire, the 18th Infantry commander was ordered to move detachments out of the registered area. When the attack commenced, the infantry groups that had withdrawn advanced and met the raiders in the open. Rifle and revolver fire drove them back. Bullard concluded with a sobering observation: "If the garrisons of F-1 and F-2 had not been withdrawn as before explained, it is very probable that few would have survived the enemy's bombardment."[483]

GERMAN ASSESSMENT

Major Bruns reported that the immediate combination fire of artillery, **MW** and explosives from **Pionier Kompagnie.79** worked very well for the four attacking **Sturmkompen**.[484] He suspected that the Americans had an idea that the attack was to be executed and took appropriate steps. Bruns did not suspect the registration of artillery prior to **Einladung** was the culprit.[485] **Hauptmann** von Bulow from **Generalstab** considered that the dense artillery fire had prevented the Americans from escaping.[486] **Hauptmann** Seebohm reported shortly after his **Sturmkompen** returned that the fire plan was very punctual and had excellent results. **Einladung** struck American positions hard, and destroyed numerous *abris* and both American lines. The first battalion achieved their objective of destroying all known *abris* in their assigned sector. The third battalion penetrated into the northern edge of he *Bois de Remières*.[487] In his final report, Seebohm recommended seventy-three soldiers and support for the Iron Cross 2nd Class. Seven soldiers were recommended for battlefield promotion based on heroism and accomplishments demonstrated in the raid.[488]

On 3 March 1918 von Stolzmann forwarded to Fuchs at **Armeeabteilung C** his assessment. He emphasised that the Americans were totally surprised; they organized their position according to the principle of the outpost with the point of entry being thinly held and sentry posts withdrawing at first fire; coordination between American infantry and their artillery was perceived to be poor; and no enemy counter-attacks followed. **MW** fire was excellent. He made it clear that American close-in combat was very good, effectively using machine guns, rifle and hand grenades. He noted that **Stosstruppen** gained the impression the Americans resisted violently and surrendered less readily than the French in past raids.[489]

Von Stolzmann assessed American artillery to have started firing 7 minutes after the Germans commenced fire with **Gaswerfer**, artillery and **MW**. After the first barrage the Americans did not have a clear idea of what was transpiring at the front line and their artillery mainly struck the rear areas. At first, Allied artillery fire was intense against **G II** forward trenches opposite *Bois de Remières*, then changed to aimless harassing fire that ceased about 0800.[490]

MEASURES OF SUCCESS

General der Infanterie Max Hofmann, **General-kommando XXXVIII Reserve Korps,** presented to higher headquarters a summary for **Generalstab** consumption. He reported that a large number of Americans who opposed the attack from individual nests within their front lines were massacred.[491] The dramatic claim did not correspond with what Major General Bullard reported to *Général* Passaga, that the Americans killed were losses due to artillery. The Americans suffered three officers and sixteen men killed, two officers and twelve men wounded, and a total of sixteen additional men unaccounted for, either buried in the destroyed dugouts, or captured.[492] One of the officers killed was Lieutenant Harold F. Eadie, a graduate of Dartmouth College and Phillips Andover Academy. Eadie was the quarterback of the Dartmouth football team.[493]

Einladung Stosstruppen returned at the prescribed time to their own lines with twelve prisoners of the 1st Division's 18th Infantry and two light machine guns. The twelve prisoners were taken to the prisoner holding centre known as **Ortskommandantur Thiaucourt** under the command of **Major** Zwirnmann.[494] Later that morning Allied *aerostiers* observed troop movement north of the *Mort-Mare* area on the road from d'Essey to Bouillonville. It was conjectured it was a mix of prisoners and German soldiers.[495] **Generalmajor** von Stolzmann reported that preliminary interrogation of the prisoners highlighted the devastating effect on Americans of the **MW** fire. Interrogation revealed several

Around noontime, Major McCormick from 5th Field Artillery received a phone call from General Summerall's headquarters ordering him to report immediately to the 1st Field Artillery Brigade. McCormick left his battery on horseback and arrived when the general and his staff were being served lunch. General Summerall stood up, offered his hand to McCormick and stated aloud, "Thank God there is one man in this outfit who knows when to disobey an order."[505]

were shell shocked – repeating over and over that they felt they were immersed in a sea of flames. One prisoner went insane from the effects of the artillery fire.[496] Ten of the American prisoners were initially sent to Darmstadt in central Germany and were later transported to XVII District (Prussia) at Tuchel **Kriegsgefangenenlager**.[497]

German casualty reports listed **Leutnant** Naumburg and **Leutnant** Barz killed in the raid. **Pioniere.79** lost two non-commissioned officers and 7 **Pioniere**.[498] German totals listed seven men dead, two severely wounded, twenty-two wounded, eight missing, feared dead. Dead and missing correlated with Major General Bullard's assessment of two German officers and thirteen men killed within American lines. **Pionier Btl. 378** casualties included five wounded, one severely wounded. **Minenwerfer Komp. 262** had one severely wounded. **Minenwerfer Komp. 4** had one wounded. **Sturmbataillon.14** had one dead, thirteen wounded, one severely wounded, and two missing either dead or wounded.[499]

The Americans captured four prisoners during **Einladung** – two from **Res. I. R. 259** and two from **Pionier Komp. 79**. All four were wounded. Three of the four prisoners were taken by Artillery Liaison officers and men. One wounded **Stosstrupp** prisoner was interrogated at 1st Division headquarters that afternoon. He stated 180 volunteers comprised the force and that they had practised several days prior to execution. The prisoner mentioned another attack from **Gaswerfer** was expected. The prisoner was asked how he received the head wound. He replied that he was in a trench when an American ordered him to come out. He was slow in responding, resulting in the American

striking him over the head with the butt of a rifle. One final thought came from the prisoner. The interrogators asked him what the Germans thought of the Americans. He replied that the Germans thought the Americans were "very nervous because we shot so much."[500]

Based on French *2e Bureau* intelligence interrogations of deserters and prisoners, the Allied assessment of German losses from **Einladung** came to eighty-three.[501] Colonel Frank Parker reported that two of his soldiers ventured into No Man's Land that night and counted "over fifty" dead Germans and two dead Americans.[502] Captured equipment included an abandoned machine gun and quantities of grenades and explosives. When patrols went out that night they reported four bodies in No Man's Land with **Flammenwerfer** strapped to their backs. A description of the operation was found on the body of one of the dead officers, with a map displaying 1st Division positions.[503] GHQ AEF's G-2 discussed the raid in their Summary of Information, deferring to French analysis that the raid was a reprisal for the Moroccan Division raid prior to 1st Division arrival in the sector. French interrogation suggested that **78. R. D.** had fairly good morale. However, none of the prisoners believed that Germany would win the war. All prisoners did speak of the upcoming "great offensive" but did not know when or where.[504]

"YOU WERE NOT LATE YESTERDAY"

General Marshall recalled **Einladung** twice. In an interview in 1947 he remarked, "Well, it was too bad that one platoon commander was so uncomfortable outside (it was cold), that he took his platoon back in and met the raiders head on. And he lost, I think it was, ten prisoners. The other platoon commanders carried out their orders absolutely. They just shot up these raiders and we captured German prisoners … except for the loss of these few men by this platoon commander disobeying his orders and coming back into position at dawn, which is exactly the time the raid is carried out. Of course, he was killed, so you couldn't say very much about it."[506] Marshall remembered **Einladung** as an American victory: "And here the Americans had met the first raid and won really a victory. We had captured their flame fighters. We had captured – I think they had brought up even a gun – 47-mm gun or something like that. We captured a lot of them. We took a number of prisoners. We killed a great many, and it was altogether an American victory."[507] Marshall's post-war written reminiscence had more lustre.: "Our men fought beautifully and viciously, and covered themselves with glory. The result was apparently tremendously reassuring to the higher French officials."[508]

Général Passaga published General Order No. 119 the next day praising the accomplishments of the Americans with stirring words: "The Boche felt the weight and vigour of the American fist: repulsed, he withdrew to his position, leaving 13 dead (of whom 2 were officers) and 4 prisoners. The troops of the *32e corps d'armée* are proud to fight by the side of the noble sons of the Great Republic, who have so generously come to assist France and support her in upholding the liberty of the world, and will understand by this example of superb energy and coolness the extent of what may be expected from the joining in the struggle of our new comrades."[509]

However, the most memorable recognition came from Clemenceau himself. Leaving Paris the next night he arrived at the American sector at Ansauville on 3 March accompanied by *Général* Debeney, commander *I re armée*. A narrow road in a neighbouring forest was selected for the ceremony. A light snow was falling. Lieutenant John N. Greene, Lieutenant

John L. Canby, First Sergeant William Norton, Sergeant Patrick Walsh, Private David Alvan Smiley, and Private Budie Pitman, of the 18th Infantry arrived covered in mud and residue from the battle. General Marshall recalled:

… it was altogether an American victory. Well, that was so unexpected and quite contrary to French assumptions about our troops – they had seen so many untrained troops – that Clemenceau himself came from Paris and came right up there and I escorted him. He came up and he was giving *Croix de Guerre*. He was a very old man and in doubtful health, but fortunately he had on rubber overshoes. He gave these *Croix de Guerre*, but there was one fellow he didn't get. And as we were coming out … this fellow [Private David Alvan Smiley] came loping down the road and he was yelling, "Wait for me, wait for me!" He caught up. He was about six feet two and gangling and, of course, covered with mud. He had been through the raid and had done a very good stunt. He had taken several prisoners and Clemenceau had the medal for him. We had the name, and he was just yelling and yelling. Clemenceau understood a little English. When the fellow came up, we stood there beside the trucks, having a very hard time finding any place to stand. And Clemenceau put this on him and shook his hand and said, "You were called and you were late this morning. But yesterday was what counted and you weren't late yesterday," and congratulated him.[510]

"THE FINEST SOLDIER WHO EVER WORE SHOE LEATHER"

General Pershing noted in his diary on 6 March from Chaumont: "Heavy German raid repulsed by 1st Division on Friday [1 March] morning. The enemy also raided the 26th Division lines and were driven off."[511] Two hundred kilometres to the west along the Chemin-des-Dâmes front line, the 102nd Infantry of the 26th Division was brigaded with the experienced combat

Colonel Frank Parker commanded 18th Infantry during *Einladung*. (Colonel Robert R. McCormick Research Center)

veterans of *137ᵉ Régiment d'infanterie*. *Général* de Maud'Huy, *commandant le 11ᵉ corps d'armée*, was very positive about the contributions of the Americans. General Pershing commented after the war that *Général* de Maud'Huy "spoke with considerable enthusiasm of the men and of the officers of the 26th Division below regimental commanders, and especially praised their conduct of trench raids." Pershing mentioned that de Maud'Huy "complimented Traub, one of the brigade commanders, but was of the opinion that the higher officers, generally needed more experience to make them efficient."[512] The fact that the 26th Division was not regular US Army did not bother *Général* de Maud'Huy. They were soldiers who served in the harsh conditions along with his *poilus*. The evening before **Einladung** the 102nd Infantry was conducting relief of the 1st Battalion by the 2nd Battalion. Company A was relieving Company E in the centre of resistance sector at Mont des Tombes. Two platoons of Company A were in position. The third was entering the sector trenches. Company F had been scheduled to work in front of the wire in small groups along a 150-metre area north of the Chavignon–Pont Oger Road. The major feature of the front line, the canal, was 150 metres away.

At 2100 the Germans launched a violent rolling barrage with troops moving against the Allied lines. The barrage included a **Gasschuss** of **gelb kreuz** on the French and American trenches and supporting battery locations. The Allied artillery commenced fire 40 seconds after the German bombardment had started, with the exchange of fire lasting for an hour.[513] German attack objectives had two assault elements of approximately 500 **Stosstruppen** converging towards Chavignon, crushing Allied resistance and taking prisoners. Returning. **Stosstruppen** coming from Écluse were stopped and turned back at Chavignon. The other force was deflected eastward by the American resistance, failed to unite with the first group from Écluse and returned. The German raid did not penetrate the first line of defence.[514] Lieutenant Ralph Bishop, Company F, was commanding a working party in No Man's Land when the raid commenced. Under fire he placed his men in shell holes and led the fight. Bishop twice went through the barrages to recover bodies and collect his men from the battle zone. Sergeant Eric Olsen, Corporal Ralph Sanderson, and Private 1st Class Harold A. Brown of Company F came forward and helped Bishop save more men.[515] Commendations were received from *Général* de Maud'Huy and several *Croix de Guerre* were awarded for gallantry. Private William Darling, Company B, and Charles Sutter, Company F, killed by shell-fire, were the first casualties of the 102nd Infantry. The Germans also took eleven men prisoners.[516] Colonel John H. Parker, newly assigned commander of the 102nd Infantry, wrote two weeks later to Major General James G. Harbord, Pershing's Chief of Staff at Chaumont, regarding his troops' accomplishments that night: "The American militiaman, when he is properly led, is the finest soldier who ever wore shoe leather."[517]

CHAPTER 9

Post-*Einladung* – The Americans Attack

Private Raymond Wunderlich, 101st Engineers, described his experience serving as a combat engineer after the war: "Don't get the idea that your soldier boy goes over the top with head up, chest out and perfect martial stride. Not a bit of it. That's only the way the artists draw it. We went over with heads down and bodies bent. We had no desire to dispute the passage of a shell by obtruding our bodies in its path. Our attitude was always one most conducive to safety under conditions as we faced them. We wanted to be in position, if need be, to spread ourselves on the landscape with the greatest possible speed – and all in one piece."[518]

Now that they had been blooded by **Einladung**, it was time for the Americans to launch their own raid. For the first time an American combat unit was to plan and strike without French participation. Two raids were planned for 3 March. The 16th Infantry was to hit the eastern flank of the Richecourt salient. The 18th Infantry was to strike the north-western corner of *Bois de Remières*. Company F, 16th Infantry, was chosen to execute the first raid. This was the same company that had been hit by the **Bayerisch. Ldw. I. R. 7** in the 3 November 1917 **Jacobsbrunnen** raid. The war's first American battle casualties and prisoners were from Company F.[519]

Two weeks prior, Lieutenant Thomas W. Ryan, Jr., Company F, 1st Engineers, was told to report to Major Farrell, battalion commander. Farrell asked Ryan, "Would you like to lead the first raid on the German trenches?" Ryan replied, "Yes!" Ryan's assignment was to form two parties of Engineer troops to blow two holes in the German barbed wire. Ryan acquired two parties of eight men each to accomplish the task. Two gaps were to be created, allowing the raiding parties to enter into the first-line trench, go to the German communication trench and proceed to the second-line trench. Both raiding parties were to empty all German dugouts and capture prisoners. At the second line the two parties were to link up and return to American lines.

Ryan had to procure Bangalore tubes from supply centres – none of the Americans knew what they were. Undaunted, Ryan found Bangalore tubes from a French supply dump. Assembling the explosive devices was not an easy task. The British and French technique was to load the tube sections in the rear positions and carry them forward via a *boyau*. The Bangalore torpedo was 50 feet long and had seven joints – each one susceptible to breaking. Twisting trench revetments made such a task virtually impossible. Adding to the difficulty was the requirement to demonstrate their carriage to visiting French officers and American staff.

On 2 March the Americans conducted a dress rehearsal for the raid. It was snowing. First attempts at marshalling forces for the raid was a comedy of errors. Stealth no longer meant black jerkins, face and hands blackened. Traversing No Man's Land in dark apparel added to the risk. Major Wilson, 1st Division's Chief of Supply, was ordered to procure white clothes for forty men as quickly as possible. Wilson proceeded south to the city of Nancy, returning the next morning with what he assumed was the answer. A complete set of women's nightgowns of various patterns and degrees of frilliness was acquired. The quartermaster issued the white wear to the soldiers. Soldiers looking to win glory and honour for country and regiment did not want to be seen in drag. A soldier of great stature remarked that he was willing to sacrifice his life, but he'd be damned if the Germans would find his body in a woman's nightgown. Nature solved the problem: the snow melted.[520]

Lieutenant Ryan and Captain Sidney Carroll Graves, 18th Infantry raid commander, reconnoitred the German barbed wire to be destroyed. They were almost taken out by a Very flare over the area. They made it back to American lines unscathed. Later Ryan tried to examine the area personally but almost got hit by a sniper's bullet.[521]

On 3 March, Ryan's Engineer Pioneer detachment left Rambucourt around 1900 with two 16-metre long Bangalore torpedoes. The two teams tried their best to avoid any sharp movements that could weaken the joints on the tubes. After passing the PC at Center H, movement was very slow. The engineer officer found it hard to keep to the right route to Boyau Montais. Sometimes they had to slide the Bangalores across reserve trenches and shell holes. En route one Bangalore torpedo broke in two and had to be discarded. The engineer party reached the jumping off point at 0020. The connections to the torpedo were not completed until 15 minutes later – the time the raiding party was in position to proceed with the attack. Ryan heard a German Very light pop and ordered his men to hit the dirt. Everyone did so until darkness returned. The team shoved the Bangalore ahead until they heard another Very light pop. It was 0050, 10 minutes to the designated time of attack.

The American barrage commenced. Captain Graves ordered Lieutenant Ryan and his team back – the Engineer Pioneer detachment was now at great peril from friendly fire. The raid had been called off. The Bangalore was destroyed and the team withdrew, despondent.[522]

The Engineer Pioneer detachment supporting the 18th Infantry raid was under Lieutenant McClure of Company E, 1st Engineers. His unit left Beaumont at 2040 with the long and ungainly torpedoes. They reached Seicheprey at 2130. As with Ryan's, McClure's detachment struggled with manhandling the torpedoes through the mud and wire and over the freshly made shell holes. The last torpedo did not get to the jumping-off point until 0025. The raid patrols had not time to make the necessary investigation of the German wire to permit the torpedoes to be in place before 0100. The operation to the east was also called off.

General Bullard explained the situation to *Général* Passaga. Both raiding parties were not able to execute. The Engineer Pioneer detachments were not able to arrive at the designated place in time to apply the bangalore torpedo charges against the German wire. Failure was due to the extreme darkness and difficulties experienced in carrying long Bangalore torpedo charges from Position 1-Bis to the jumping off trenches. So they now knew torpedo charges had to be joined during the afternoon at points in advance of Position 1-Bis, Seicheprey, and the PC serving Center H.

Bullard wrote to *Général* Passaga: "The failure of this enterprise to be carried out is a matter of much regret and was due to our inexperience in foreseeing all the difficulties which were liable to arise. In this last respect it has been a very instructive and valuable lesson which should insure the successful avoidance of such eventualities in the carrying out of future operations."[523]

What General Bullard did not reveal to *Général* Passaga was the measure of the man. On the evening of 6 March Lieutenant Ryan was ordered along with Lieutenant McClure into General Bullard's car by Captain Shery, aide to the General. They arrived at his headquarters at Ansauville. Both lieutenants saluted with "knees probably shaking!" Bullard put them at ease at once, asked them to sit down and requested a first-hand report. Lieutenant Ryan talked about the French and British instructions regarding transporting Bangalore torpedoes, the orders prior to the raid and the sad results. After both explained what happened, General Bullard told them General Pershing had arrived that night from Chaumont to witness the AEF's first offensive strike into German-held territory. Pershing wanted to interview the first German prisoners captured by the Americans. Since the raids did not take place, Pershing turned to Bullard and asked for a full report. General Bullard turned to the two lieutenants and said: "I have already made up the report, I have written General Pershing that 'the failure of the two raids was due to the inexperience of all concerned – beginning with myself!!!'" Lieutenant Ryan concluded, "He was the greatest man I had ever met."[524]

General Summerall echoed Ryan's sentiments. His artillery had acquired a large reinforcement of guns from the French and fired an intense box barrage with 250 guns for both raids. The 1st Field Artillery Brigade did not receive an explanation for the cancellations. GHQ's query as to who was responsible was met by Major General Bullard's reply: "I am in command of the 1st Division, and I am responsible for everything that takes place in it. If you want to fix responsibility for the failure of the raids, I am responsible." Summerall stated the effect was "electric" within the 1st Division. Almost every officer and soldier in the division realised they were not to be made a scapegoat if they did their duty. From that moment, there was a mutual confidence in all ranks and a resolution that in the 1st Division no one should ever fail. Summerall observed the "Spirit of the First Division" was born right there and "grew to perfection."[525]

Harassment fire served both sides for the week following the 1 March **Einladung** raid. At one point the Americans fired 700 75mm rounds against German battery positions in Gargantua and *Mort-Mare*. Richecourt was hit

especially hard during this time.[526] **Generalmajor** von Stolzmann reported to **General der Artillerie** Gallwitz, **Generalleutnant** Fuchs, and **Generalstab** that an incident on 3 March with the **Pionier Btl. 35** resulted in twelve men killed and twenty-six wounded. The "lamentable misfortune" occurred during the removal of the **Gaswerfer**. A safety pin could not be reinserted in a projectile which had not fired during the earlier bombardment. As the **Gaswerfer** projectile was being removed it exploded.[527]

On 4 March the 7th Field Artillery batteries unleashed a major barrage on **G.II** opposite *Bois de Remières* and **G.III** south of *Bois de la Sonnard*. Both HE and chemical rounds were fired. Germans took note that over 6,000 rounds were fired by the Americans in an hour. Three hours later the Germans fired against the trenches north of *Bois de Remières* and *Bois du Jury*. It then became a barrage duel. Americans fired against Richecourt and **G.II** with the damage to German positions described as considerable.[528] German batteries continued to register American artillery positions and harass enemy vehicular traffic for several days. **FA (A) 298b** aerial reconnaissance was active that day conducting three missions over Allied lines.[529]

At the end of the week, **Res. I. R. 258** sent a night patrol to penetrate American lines south of Lahayville. They cut through several barbed-wire obstacles and engaged in a firefight that ended with the patrol returning unscathed. German artillery conducted harassment fire on American batteries including firing **Gelbkreuz** rounds.[530] The Germans detected one of the American patrols of approximately thirty soldiers in front of and within **Abschnitt G I** south of Richecourt and **G.II** outposts. This activity had been preceded by heavy artillery fire and gas munitions in high concentrations, particularly in the St. Baussant and Lahayville area. The Germans responded with artillery fire. Subsequent German analysis of the sector detected a surveyor's tape leading from the American trenches into a gap in the German wire south of Richecourt. This confirmed the American attempt to carry out a raid during the violent bombardment, thwarted by the Germans' effective fire. The Americans' initial attempt to test the front failed. They also left behind a rifle as well as a number of hand grenades and torpedoes in the German outpost. American artillery fire opened up strongly on the left of **G I**, the right of **G II**, a series of battery positions and approaches. It continued undiminished in strength for almost an hour. American artillery fired approximately 6,000 rounds, including gas. German casualties were only two killed and fifteen slightly wounded. The Germans also experienced twenty-two casualties from gas. A German transport park column between Essey and Maizerais received a direct hit from a gas shell, which resulted in one very ill horse.[531]

On the evening of 7 March, **78. R. D.** conducted two **Wirkungsschiessen** [fires for effect] totalling 684 77mm and 105mm **Gelbkreuz** [mustard] shells against batteries in *Bois de la Hazelle* and on the Rambucourt-Beaumont road. The gas officers of the 5th Field Artillery and 7th Field Artillery recorded a total of 280 mustard gas shells in the two bombardments.[532] The next day a raid was planned by a patrol against an American sentry post. **MW** and **Granatwerfer** were used. The German **MW** fired too soon, alerting the American sentries to withdraw from their outpost.[533] The Germans fired gas rounds into Beaumont and Rambucourt and south of *Bois de la Hazelle* on the morning of 8 March. The only loss to the Americans was that all the rations for the 8 March noon meal had to be thrown away. The only gas casualty recorded that day was a man who fell into a contaminated shell-hole.[534]

The German **Gasschuss** against American batteries resulted in an order that rubber boots, anti-gas gloves, and anti-gas suits for each man were henceforth to be kept at all battery and machine-gun positions and at artillery command posts, and were to be provided for all stretcher bearers and signal linemen in the division. This became standard equipment also for French artillerymen with the division, who were equipped with the M-2 and ARS masks, American rubber boots, oilskin jumpers, and mittens, and chloride of lime, soapy water, and bicarbonate of soda.[535] Such attention to protection was notable. It was not known if this

became policy for other divisions and if protected gear was provided for the remainder of the war.

That evening, **Stosstruppen** from **Res. I. R. 259** advanced against American positions occupying a forward sap where German observers detected sentry posts. Their raid was covered by **MW** and **Granatwerfer** to "box" in the area. **Stosstruppen** found the sap unoccupied and returned to their own lines with casualties. The Americans responded with a barrage in front of **Abschnitt G.II** and **G.I.**[536]

"A HIGHLY SCIENTIFIC AFFAIR"

Marshall recalled that during his time at Seicheprey a number of suggestions came from an assortment of experts on how best to fight this modern war.: "So imbued was everyone with the idea that modern warfare was a highly scientific affair that they attempted to inflict on us, en masse, a weird variety of appliances and schemes, many of which were excellent, but which we lacked time to assimilate."[537] One such expert was *capitaine* Tuczkiewicz, *Groupe Z, 34ᵉ Bataillon du Genie* (Engineer Battalion), *Iʳᵉ armée*. The day before the 1st Division was to launch their two raids against **Res. I. R. 259**, Lieutenant Colonel Marshall received a visit from Tuczkiewicz. Marshall showed him recent aerial photographs of German positions at Lahayville, *Bois de la Sonnard*, and St. Baussant. At the junction of the German Beer Trench and Zig-Zag *boyau* Marshall pointed out artillery and newly discovered **Gaswerfer** aligned in the direction of *Bois de Remières*. Recently fallen snow was missing from three battery locations, suggesting increased activity.[538]

Setting up *Groupe Z* projectors remained a dangerous task. It took *Groupe Z* at least six hours to ready the projectors for fire. It was a covert business moving projectors into the battle zone with silence the rule, no lights and no cigarettes allowed. Transporting projector tubes and support plates in the dark was especially difficult because the components were not robust. At the launch site the troops were told to bind the bottom of the plate with cloth to avoid noise and any digging required to set the projector in place had to be camouflaged to avoid detection. Electricians equipped with wirecutters and electrical tape set up the wires on the cartridge bag just prior to firing. The gas bombs were then placed in the tubes. If wind direction and conditions were not favourable then the mission was cancelled. Precautions prior to firing included having the gas mask in the waiting position and out of the case as well as all non-projector personnel kept 100 metres or more away from the battery positions. Once the projector was ready, the pins had to be removed before the crew could proceed to waiting shelters. [539]

Lieutenant Colonel Marshall introduced *capitaine* Tuczkiewicz to Colonel King. King made it clear that 1st Division wanted to use projectors as a reprisal weapon supporting their operations. He asked Tuczkiewicz if they had pinpointed favourable firing locations for the projectors. *Capitaine* Tuczkiewicz suggested firing from *Bois de Remières*, *Bois Carré* or a point midway between Seicheprey and the first line of the Sibille Trench. The discussion's wrap-up was not reported. *Groupe Z* proceeded immediately to work with the Americans and set up two projector firing sites west of Seicheprey. [540]

AERIAL CONFIRMATION

By this time the Germans suspected the Americans were planning a raid on the front trenches. German artillery started harassing fire on registered dugout groups, traffic points, and the trenches west of Xivray. The unusual behaviour of the Americans at this time prompted the Germans to withdraw their outpost zones in **G.I** and **G.II**, vacate the barrage fire posts for the night and "stand to" the sector and artillery. [541] Adding to the intrigue was the relief that took place within the 1st Division and completed on 6 March. The 1st Brigade under Brigadier General Duncan with the veteran 16th Infantry and 18th Infantry departed from the front lines. Brigadier General Beaumont B. Buck's 2nd Brigade arrived at Ansauville with 26th Infantry under the command of

Colonel Hamilton Allen Smith and moved into Rambucourt and Colonel Hanson Edward Ely's 28th Infantry occupied Beaumont.

Major General Bullard chose Lieutenant Colonel Marshall to lead the planning for 1st Division's first raids into enemy territory. Marshall was the recognized expert, familiarising himself with the entire 1st Division sector and determining roles for each unit in the area. Wherever possible he went beyond the map that portrayed forces in place. He wanted to see for himself. Effective planning meant knowing who was manning a particular point on the map and knowing to what depth effective defence could be accomplished in times of emergency. [542]

On 10 March two **78. R. D.** batteries were shelled with gas. The Germans fired back **Gelbkreuz** projectiles against 7th Field Artillery batteries. Then 75mm batteries from 6th Field Artillery and 7th Field Artillery cut several gaps in the **78. R. D.** wire, each about 15 metres wide, at various places to disguise the launch points. The Germans were prevented from repairing any gaps since artillery and machine guns covered the area until H Hour. **78. R. D.** fired 1,800-2,000 rounds that included 421 **Gelbkreuz** and **Grünkreuz** on the battery in *Bois de la Hazelle*. [543] The 6th Field Artillery gas officer said that almost 600 **Grünkreuz 2** (phosgene) and **Gelbkreuz** fell around the battery in *Bois de la Hazelle*. Two officers and eighteen men were evacuated – most of them with acute conjunctivitis from taking their masks off too soon. There were to be many more casualties for the officers and men who remained in the gassed area, oblivious to the mustard gas that had been fired with the phosgene. [544]

1st Division intelligence reported five German aeroplanes flew over the lines apparently taking aerial photographs and making observations the morning and early afternoon of 10 March. [545] Aerial reconnaissance, **Artillerie-Flieger**, and **Schlachtflieger** spent the day acquiring information that helped infantry and artillery leadership discern enemy intentions and develop appropriate counter-attack strategies. A more mature battle ground was in the making.

Three Americans chew the fat at the front: BG Frank Parker, LTC Theodore Roosevelt, and wife Eleanor Butler Roosevelt. (Colonel Robert R. McCormick Research Center)

The next day at 0425 a **Schlachtflugzeug** (either a **DFW C.V, LVG C.V** or **Halberstadt C.II**) from **FA (A) 298b** started the day's activity when it flew over the front line near *Bois du Jury*.[546] German aerial photographs of the southern Woëvre front showed Allied artillery and trench camouflage. Some dugouts were not effectively covered, or footpaths leading to the entrance clearly showed the location. American trench mortars were also located. Aerial photographs confirmed that the American trenches east of Marvoisin were under water.[547]

NOBODY HOME

At 0440, the 1st Artillery Brigade commenced their barrage with 75mm and machine guns towards Richecourt, St. Baussant, and Lahayville. Then St. Baussant experienced a very dense cloud of gas – an unusual occurrence for this sector. Despite being in the area the **Schlachtflieger** did not report this activity. The barrage lasted for about 15 minutes. At 0505 the German artillery returned fire and kept it up for almost an hour. The German response to the American barrage included neutralising fire as well as extensive harassment fire directed against *Bois de Remières*, *Bois du Jury* and *Bois de le Hazelle*. German artillery in the Gargantua and

Mort-Mare area fired at Seicheprey, Flirey, and south of Richecourt. German reports considered the Americans' initial barrage impressive but their own counter-barrage even more so. Only one German from **Res. I. R. 259** was reported affected by the gas.[548]

At 0550 Captain Joseph Quesenberry, Company K, led a detachment of four officers and eighty-seven men of the 18th Infantry and 1st Engineers, in a *coup de main* on the salient north of the western edge of *Bois de Remières*. The 1st Division had learned their lesson from the aborted 3 March raid attempt. Now twelve engineers carried additional Bangalore torpedoes to clear the path against the wire entanglements if the artillery was insufficient. Both 1st Artillery Brigade and auxiliary French batteries fired over 32,000 shells prior to the raid wreaking significant damage on the wire entanglements.[549] The artillery's work was satisfactory so the Bangalores were not used. The G-2 report stated,"All firing on the enemy's batteries was executed with gas shell, and three of the light batteries fired gas shell on the positions at St. Baussant and Lahayville throughout both raids."[550] The 1st Field Artillery Brigade also fired around 2,066 "special" shells of No. 4 (cyanogen chloride) and No. 5 (phosgene) in support of Quesenberry's morning raid. A total of 850 smoke shells were fired towards

Richecourt for the box barrage.[551] For the newly arrived American members of the Sound Ranging Section (SRS) south of Montsec, it was an impressive display of firepower. They recalled that the barrage continued for two hours. They learned that the artillery had obliterated the first German line.[552]

Quesenberry's raiders discovered the Germans had withdrawn their front-line soldiers as soon as the breaches on the wire were blown. His raiding party remained in the enemy's position for 20 minutes without suffering any casualties. Two men were wounded by machine-gun fire during the return across No Man's Land and one man was wounded and subsequently died by shellfire within the American lines.[553] The Americans swarmed through the wire and explored the enemy's lines to his third trench, which lay at a distance of about 300 metres from No Man's Land. No resistance was met and none of the enemy was found. The raiding party returned, according to its schedule, without suffering any casualties. So effective was the American counter-battery that there was practically no enemy artillery fire.[554] The raiding party carried out their operation as planned. A total of eleven Germans were found – one was killed by shellfire and three were killed by revolver or rifle fire. The remaining seven were seen retreating into the box fire while being pursued by members of the raiding party. Any further estimate of casualties was hindered by the abysmal trench and dugout conditions. All dugouts were caved in and the trenches were practically demolished and holding a great deal of water.[555]

The **78. R.D.** sent a message six hours later at 1105 that the American artillery appeared to be bombarding in support of an attack. The attack location appeared to be St. Baussant along the Rupt de Mad. Three Americans were discovered by **Leutnant** Prolsdorff in the German trenches.[556] The Germans subsequently reported that a 30-man American patrol was spotted wearing **Stahlhelme und khakifarbene Uniformen** [flat helmets and khaki uniforms].[557] Losses from both **Res. I. R. 259** and **Res. I. R. 260**

were two soldiers due to artillery. Despite the major barrage of gas including the projector bombs, only five men from **Res. I. R. 259** were gas casualties.[558] It wasn't until Quesenberry's detachment was safely behind the front lines that an artillery round struck and killed one of the Americans.[559]

Colonel King telephoned Colonel Eltinge, GHQ AEF, shortly after the Quesenberry raid returned:

> We made a trench raid this morning with the assistance of French artillery. It was participated in by 3 officers and 63 men (Americans), and penetrated 300 yards into enemy line. Entire raid was executed as per plan in every detail. Although no prisoners were taken, effect of raid on men taking part was excellent and they are in the highest spirits. Our losses were 3 wounded. 1 seriously and the other 2 slightly. We found upon reaching enemy trenches that they had evacuated them. Our raiding party went right on until they reached the edge of barrage, after making thorough investigation of vacant trenches. The work of our artillery was splendid. Literally smothering the enemy batteries. Our fire was so effective that the Germans were unable to get Battery A into action until 20 or 30 minutes after we had started. The enemy evidently had expected the raid for they had evidenced extreme nervousness up to the time it occurred.[560]

THE EVENING RAID

The raid on Richecourt that evening at 1940 shortly after dark was under the command of Captain Sidney Carroll Graves, three officers and seventy men of the 16th Infantry and one Engineer officer. The gap in the wire was effectively cut by artillery fire the day before. The raiding party carried out the operations as planned. About ten Germans were seen in a shell hole. It didn't offer them protection from rounds from a Stokes Mortar bomb followed by grenades. Graves' men found no deep dugouts

– only light shelters that were badly damaged. The caved-in trenches were in a miserable state of repair and filled with water. Two officers and three men of the raiding party were lightly wounded by grenade fragments and no other casualties were reported.[561]

The Special Operations Report stated both raiding party's carried out the operations as planned. Marshall recalled in his post-war memoir that the Americans being so new and keen did not expect any Germans to surrender and did not offer any quarter. As he stated, they "did not give the other fellow an opportunity to declare his intentions."[562]

In support of Captain Graves' raid, the 1st Field Artillery Brigade fired 4,345 "special" shells of No. 4 (cyanogen chloride) and No. 5 (phosgene). As in the morning they also fired 850 smoke shells. That evening Battery A, 7th Field Artillery, received 50 mustard gas shells in the rear of their position. Even while wearing masks, 1st Field Artillery Brigade personnel were affected by the fumes from the phosgene for two and a half hours. They dealt with the exposure by washing with soap suds and bathing their eyes with salt water. No casualties were reported and the men held their positions.[563]

Brigadier General Summerall made a point of praising Battery D, 6th Field Artillery, to Major General Bullard. Early on the evening of 10 March the battery had been hit with large quantities of mustard gas and many men were removed from the position. They were told to reassign their mission to another battery. However, the officers and men insisted on returning to their guns and backed both raids. Seven officers and fifty men were sent to the hospital to recover from the effects of the mustard gas.[564] Major John W. Downer, 6th Field Artillery, the first to commence fire on the Germans in **Einladung**, was recognized for additional heroism ten days later. While commanding his battalion supporting the raid he was severely gassed. Downer remained at his post and continued to direct his battalion while artillery shells slammed into his location.[565] Lieutenant Butler wrote in his journal on 11 March: "Although #15

[Battery D] was gassed heavily last night & the personnel withdrawn, they returned for the *coup de main* [in the morning] & served their guns with their gas masks & gas clothes on … [In the evening] gas was still pretty thick around #15 … After the evening raid everyone in #15 [was] withdrawn [to Ansauville] except a sentinel at each gun."[566] At the end of the evening raid, all officers and men were overcome by the gas and were evacuated. New personnel took over, dressed in rubber clothing and gas masks, and moved the guns during the night to new positions. In the same gas attack the position of Battery A, 7th Field Artillery, was also "so heavily and continuously shelled and gassed that … it was necessary to move that battery." One casualty from the bombardment was Captain Archie Roosevelt. Archie was with his 28th Infantry company when the shells rained in. One blast severely damaged his left kneecap and fractured his left arm. His follow-up actions won him the *Crois de Guerre* and Silver Star citation.[567]

Marshall was pleased that his attack plans covered two raids on one day. Quesenberry's morning raid was more or less a morale builder and also deceived the Germans into thinking that the raid was the only offensive that day. Captain Quesenberry was killed two months later at Villiers-Tournelles in Picardy by shellfire. Captain Graves remained with the 1st Division until after Cantigny, and was then returned to the United States and sent to Siberia with the 17th Infantry. The American Siberian Expedition was commanded by his father, Major General William S. Graves. Graves earned two Distinguished Service Crosses – the first while serving in the 1st Division, the second at Vladivostok.

"GREAT CONFIDENCES"

The **78. R. D** reported on the night of 11 March that the total German casualties from both raids and the artillery barrages came to two killed, fifteen wounded and twenty-two gassed.[568] **Hauptmann** von Bülow, issued the

Tagesbericht über den Verlauf des 11.III.1918 to Generalstab describing the day's events from the German point of view. Lively harassing fire was experienced in **Abschnitt G.I** and **G.II**. German soldiers in **G.I** trenches encountered enemy fire. Twenty minutes after the Americans attacked a very strong gas attack was suffered at St. Baussant, Lahayville and almost all battery positions in those sectors. The gas was lachrymatory – so heavy that one could only see up to 3 metres. A yellow signal ball from a rocket was observed. The Germans estimated the allies shot 10,000 to 12,000 rounds during this attack and 5,000 to 6,000 gas rounds.[569]

General Bullard in his report to *Général* Passaga praised the work of the French and American artillery, citing "the enemy's reaction in each raid being practically negligible. The fact that our infantry was able to penetrate from 150 to 250 yards within the enemy lines twice in one day without the loss of a man has served to inspire them with great confidences in our artillery. Their observation of the German trenches has also served to give them greater confidence in the strength of their own positions as well as a poorer opinion of the strength of the enemy's. Both raiding parties went into action in high spirits and came out with increased morale, though much disappointed in not taking any prisoners." General Bullard concluded his assessment of the day thanking *Général* Passaga for the outstanding support the French divisions had provided: "This division is greatly indebted to the *69ᵉ division d'infanterie* on our right and the *10ᵉ division d'infanterie colonial* on our left for the strong support given during these two operations."[570]

A QUIET SECTOR – YET NOT WITHOUT INCIDENT

Artillery fire from both sides was relegated to harassment fire for the next four days.[571] The day after the raids German artillery fired more **Gelbkreuz** rounds against American artillery batteries. Lieutenant Butler, recorded on 12 March: "The guns in D Bty were moved from #15, which is still full of gas, to position #87. Seven officers and 50 men are in the hospital with burned eyes, all from D Bty."[572]

On the evening of 14 March, 1st Division artillery fired a barrage at a location assessed by intelligence to be **Gaswerfer** trenches east of St. Baussant. A large flash was seen from the area being bombarded followed by two fires observed behind the town. Then they observed fires in the vicinity of Montsec 5 kilometres to the west. Two tiers of light, the first a straight line with 116 separate fires observed, followed by another 180 metres to the rear of the first, with thirty-four distinct fires. A powerful blast with a tinge of yellow, then red and then green appeared, suggesting the heat of the explosion was diminishing. Dense smoke rolled towards the south-west and the lines of the *10ᵉ division d'infanterie colonial*. A **Drachen-Ballon** at Hattonchâtel was observed signalling as it proceeded. When the artillery fired into that area the flames increased in intensity. As midnight approached both sets of flames ceased. A few days later German prisoners were interrogated and were not able to effectively explain the fires and stated that they did not know of a **Gaswerfer** attack for that time.[573] **Generalmajor** von Stolzmann did not mention any unusual activity to **Gruppe Gorz**. The observations will always remain something of a mystery.

On 16 March three **Stosstrupp** elements from **Res. I. R. 260** supported by artillery and **MW** fire and augmented by **Pioniere** and **Flammenwerfer** from **Sturmbataillon.14** penetrated French positions on the northern edge of *Bois du Jury* and blew up two *abris*. Combat was short and intense with many French casualties reported and two prisoners from the *162ᵉ regiment d'infanterie* returned to German lines. French and American artillery opened up four minutes after the attack had commenced against German positions on the east of **G.II** and west of **G.III** as well as directing harassment fire against German artillery. Within an hour artillery ceased fire and the sector became quiet.[574]

The 18 March was a memorable day for Lieutenant Van Vechtan's Sound Ranging squad.

After leaving their billets at Mandres they proceeded to Xivray on the north-west part of the 1st Division's sector to construct a forward observation post. At Rambucourt they started for the front line via the *boyau*, linking up with a courier who had just come from Xivray and had volunteered to guide them.

The squad entered the trench network in deep mud, carrying heavy packs. A rather tall private gave everyone the jitters by being too visible to the prying eyes at Montsec. Shortly into their hike artillery rounds burst around them causing Van Vechtan's men to flop into the trench mud. Moving forward in the muck took all the strength they had. After a few hours they emerged at what appeared to be their destination. It wasn't Xivray at all but Beaumont on the ridge. The volunteer had taken the wrong turn. The next day Lieutenant Van Vechtan took a guide who knew the trench network and he and his men eventually made it to Xivray.[575]

On 19 March, members of the 26th Infantry at Seicheprey noticed a German aeroplane dropping a new weapon – a gas balloon 45cm in diameter filled with liquid mustard gas. Two days later a second aeroplane dropped a device that exploded in the air creating a reddish-blue cloud. Neither caused casualties.[576]

Captain Butler noted on 20 March that the Germans had wiretapped the telephone line into Position No. 15. Two signalmen were called in to test the wire. All of a sudden German artillery fire commenced on the exact location with gas rounds poisoning the signalmen. Two days later Butler recorded: "Position #15 is still unoccupied & the enemy seems to know because he doesn't shell it any more."[577]

On 17 March US Secretary of War Newton Baker met with officers at Chaumont, among them Major George Patton. Patton recorded in his diary: "Met Secretary Baker and went around with him for a while. Seemed interested and intelligent." He wrote to his wife Beatrice: "He is a little rat but very smart." [578] On March 20, Baker talked briefly with the officers of the 1st Brigade, telling them that the nation was behind them and that they should work with the French in the common cause of democracy and liberty. The war, Baker said, must be fought through to victory, "as this is the last time in world affairs it will have to be done."[579]

CHAPTER 10

The Consequences of Operation *Michael*

Two months at the Seicheprey sector showed both sides what their job was. **78. R. D**. under the capable command of **Generalmajor** von Stolzmann and **Artilleriekommandeur Generalleutnant** Hoffmann knew how forces were to be employed in an environment not slated for a major operation. Three hundred kilometres to the north-west their colleagues were in the final stages of preparation for one of the greatest offensives of the war. The general intention of Operation Michael was to separate the British from the French – with the main effort directed against the British. The operation was intended to be the ultimate breakout, breaching an immense fortified front with enormous holes that entire divisions could pass though and allow for a war of movement. The public referred to this momentous event as **Die Kaiserschlacht** (the Kaiser's Battle) when the *Kölnische Zietung* announced that the battle was under the personal leadership of Kaiser Wilhelm himself. What endured was the name, not Wilhelm's impact on the battle.

The brilliant German artillery tactician **Oberstleutnant** Georg Bruchmüller, turned a 80-kilometre front into the epitome of **Niederhaltung** (dominance). His plan called for artillery batteries moving into position with stealth, undetected by aerial reconnaissance and the entire spectrum of intelligence collection. The majority of the batteries taking part in the operation were to move up into their firing positions only hours before the opening fusillade. These positions were prepared well in advance of occupation – camouflaged, stocked with ammunition, and hooked into the telephone nets. Battery commanders and fire-direction personnel moved into the positions well ahead of the guns to prepare firing charts. Despite the unlikelihood of such huge columns of trucks and horses moving entirely undetected, the process worked; for each of their major offensives in 1918, the Germans moved thousands of guns into their firing positions within a matter of hours.[580] Once Operation *Michael* commenced, the artillery struck with amazing violence. Bruchmüller advocated "neutralisation" through demoralising the enemy. Instead of using artillery to target obstacles and troops in trenches, his strategy called for a preliminary bombardment that decapitated the enemy's command and control networks of PCs, telephone exchanges and observation posts. The whole plan contemplated a preliminary assault, "short and brutal," which overwhelmed forward positions. Large numbers of gas shells of the non-persistent type were to be fired into certain areas through which the German infantry was later to pass, and gas shells of the persistent type were to be fired into those areas it was intended to isolate, without directly attacking. The final artillery barrage comprised an intense fire on the front lines for ten minutes followed by a "creeping penetration of the German infantry through the weak points in the line, thus cutting off those who held out." Light horse-drawn artillery and **MW** closely accompanied **Stosstruppen**. Forward movement meant there was to be no halt to consolidate captured positions. Battalion and regimental commanders, for the first time in several years, rode horses into battle. It was calculated that the leading assault divisions made an advance of 12 kilometres during the first 24 hours.[581]

Oberstleutnant Bruchmüller was masterful in applying deception. Camouflage was erected before any artillery positions were built. Deception included bogus orders, dummy wagon and caisson tracks, and construction of dummy positions along the front. Bruchmüller even misled some subordinate artillery commanders into thinking their artillery units were to support the main attack – spurring these elements to be more committed. As a finishing touch Bruchmüller used dedicated aerial reconnaissance to check on the preparations.[582]

Major General Tasker Bliss, America's representative to the Supreme War Council, was a recognized expert in military operations. His succinct assessment on 23 March to Washington highlighted the seriousness of the ongoing offensive. The German 37-division attack covered a front of 65 kilometres. Fifteen divisions were on a 16-kilometre front between the Sensée and Canal du Nord; twenty-two divisions between Gouzeaucourt and La Fère covering a frontline of about 50 kilometres. Of the thirty-seven German divisions, nine were already in the line and twenty-eight came from the reserve. On 23 March the enemy was reported to have broken through the reserve line in the British Fifth Army area at Vaux, Beauvois, and Poeuilly. The British called on French commanders to extend their line north of Péronne – twelve divisions were moved in to support this effort. The intelligence assessment to the Supreme War Council estimated that at least sixty-four enemy divisions were engaged in the attack. The assessment figured the German objective was Amiens, to be taken through breaking the line of the Somme south of Péronne.[583]

On 23 March *Général* Pétain decided to request that Pershing provide his best-trained American divisions for service in a quiet sector

to help alleviate the demands on the French in their support of the British at the Somme. Pétain wanted to integrate American divisions within French *corps d'armée* and *armée* in the southern Woëvre front. This was vigorously opposed by Pershing.[584] The irony was the 1st Division *was* for all intents and purposes an integral member of *Général* Debeney's *Ire armée* and *32e corps d'armée*.

Chaumont staff, following General Pershing's 24 March meeting with *Général* Petain, alerted Major General Bullard to the fact that the 1st Division was to be relieved from the Ansauville sector by Major General Clarence Edwards' 26th Division. The 1st Division was to pull back and concentrate near Toul, board trains and proceed to the assembly area near Gisors, north-west of Paris. The 1st Division officers read the signs: Debeney's troops moving north, the reports of the British Fifth Army's demise, the lines on the intelligence maps marking the German **18. Armee** moving past Montdidier and Noyon, towns that had been well within Allied lines for the entire war up to that moment.[585]

Bullard demonstrated leadership at this moment when he recognized that his soldiers were seasoned but required more experience to face the major German offensive underway. Bullard stated to Liggett on 24 March that French officers should be put into his subordinate units as commanders, so that the Americans might have men in command possessing war experience. He cited the fact that Americans who had fought with the British to date were particularly effective.[586] Major General Bullard accepted what was necessary to best serve what appeared, at the time, to be an alliance in collapse. However, a week later, in discussion with General Liggett's aide, Major Pierpont L. Stackpole, Bullard expressed his wish for American divisions to take over sectors independent of French command.[587]

Général Petain, through *Général* Camille Marie Ragueneau, *Chef de la Mission Militaire Française* at Chaumont, declared two days into Operation Michael that large French units from parts of the Western Front such as the Woëvre were to be made available to support operations in the north. In realigning French divisions *GQG* requested the 1st Division extend their front from two regiments to three regiments, freeing the adjacent *40ᵉ division d'infanterie*. In turn, American divisions in waiting, the 26th Division and 42nd Division, were to move under control of the French *groupe d'armées de l'Est* (Eastern Group). Ragueneau suggested the 42nd Division move east to Baccarat near Nancy and the 26th Division proceed to Lafauche near Neufchâteau.[588] *Général* Passaga followed suit on 28 March and ordered the American 1st Division to relieve the western part of the *10ᵉ division d'infanterie colonial* sector, covering Apremont, St. Agnant, Boncourt and St. Julien.[589]

Chaumont took decisive action, ordering Major General Liggett to place the 26th Division at the disposal of Passaga, *32ᵉ corps d'armée*. The 26th Division was to be ready to march within two days. Major General Liggett and *Général* Passaga were tasked to work the relief together. The 26th Division was to enter the southern Woëvre front by brigades. One 26th Division brigade was to proceed east of the 1st Division and be separated by a French unit in the middle. At a date to be set by *Général* Passaga and Major General Edwards, the 26th Division was to be united to the east of the 1st Division and Edwards was to assume command of the southern Woëvre front.[590]

Général Foch, soon to be Supreme Allied Commander, issued his order to hold the ground at all costs on 27 March. He addressed this to the *groupe d'armées de l'Est* and *du Nord*: "1. Not one more foot of French soil must be lost. 2. It is imperative that the enemy be stopped just where he now is; for this reason it is necessary quickly to organise a sound defensive front and prepare powerful reserves in the rear for manoeuvre, determinedly collecting troops for this purpose all along the front. 3. Only then can one dream of relieving the troops actually engaged."[591]

BUSINESS AS USUAL ON THE WOËVRE

Such massive preparations were never witnessed at the Woëvre. Efforts by the Germans to achieve annihilation and neutralisation at this end of the Western Front were measured in regimental sectors, not entire armies. Only when the Americans commenced the St. Mihiel offensive in September did the Woëvre see anything resembling what the Germans did in Operation Michael. The Ansauville sector and subsequent Boucq sector remained a location of raids.

On 19 March the first prisoner was taken by the 26th Infantry. Lieutenant Christian R. Holmes and Sergeant James A. Murphy led a squad of four and cut through twelve strands of wire entanglements before descending into a listening post holding two Germans. One was killed trying to bayonet Lieutenant Holmes. The other was taken prisoner screaming "Kamerad" at the top of his lungs. Their boss, Major Roosevelt, remembered being "pleased as Punch." They wanted to keep their newly acquired prisoner as a trophy. He did provide information on **Res. I. R. 258** opposite their location.[592]

The day after Operation Michael commenced started quietly for the troops at or near the front line. Excitement came when a German **Drachen** broke loose from its mooring and landed in No Man's Land. Colonel Ely, 28th Infantry, reported to 1st Division seniors that on the evening of 22 March a **Gasschuss** of mustard gas and chlorine caused seventeen serious casualties. Approximately 600 mustard gas shells were fired at the Seicheprey PC within an hour. When the gas projectiles struck, Ely called for retaliation fire but the HE or gas projectiles fired at the German artillery did nothing to stifle the barrage. Ely wanted more gas shells to be fired – putting the 1st Division "on a par with the French and English for protection against such gas shell bombardments." Major General Bullard took up the issue with Brigadier General Summerall. Summerall pointed out that it was difficult to neutralise the German artillery. For one thing, they had fifty-six batteries compared to the twenty-one batteries that the 1st Field Artillery Brigade had on line. Finally, the weather did not favour gas fire by the Americans.[593]

The latter half of March saw both sides experiencing violent barrages of HE and gas. It became an interesting time for Captain Louis

Captain Alban Butler commemorates General Pershing's talk to the 1st Division. (Butler, *Happy Days*)

"THE EYES OF THE WORLD ARE UPON YOU"

A WEEK at Chaumont-en-Vexin was spent in brushing up on open warfare tactics. General Pershing, as well as the staff of the First French Army to which the First Division had been assigned, watched its training with great interest, for these were the first American troops to go into the great battle. At the close of the week, General Pershing called together the officers and, to the accompaniment of the rumble of heavy artillery, told them of their mission, of their responsibilities and of his confidence in them.   *April 1918.*

{ 30 }

S. Davis, who replaced Lieutenant Wright as the 1st Division Gas Officer on 20 March. On that day, the Germans experienced a vigorous American and French trench mortar attack east of **Abschnitt G I** and west of **G II**. Throughout the day moderate artillery harassing fire landed on trenches, parts of the rear area and batteries. **78. R. D.** responded with their artillery harassing trenches and traffic points. The next day 7th Field Artillery fired on **Abschnitt G I** and **G II**. The next night an American raid against the eastern sector resulted in a captured prisoner. Such activity was of little significance. What was transpiring to the north-east of the Western Front on the Somme held everyone's attention.

At noon the next day artillery exchanges comprised both HE and gas. The Germans responded with the usual firing pattern hitting dugouts at Seicheprey with mustard gas.[594] Fuch's **Gruppe Gorz** made a decision that did not sit well with von Stolzmann. An additional division was ordered into the Woëvre. The Germans conducted a realignment of the sector, assigning **40. Infanterie. Division (40. I. D.)** between **78. R. D.** and **4. Bavarian I. D.** The three-day augmentation commenced the same day as Operation Michael. **40. I. D.** was a Saxon division rated third class by Allied intelligence. Now they were replacing **78. R. D.** in **G III** sector opposite Flirey, which had been held by **Res. I. R. 260**. The

4. Bavarian I. D. was ordered to the north to join the offensive underway. **40. I. D.** became operational **zwischen Maas und Mosel** on 14 April.[595]

The 1st Division appeared to be thinking ahead of Debeney's *I*re *armée* and *32*e *corps d'armée* commanders regarding the need to fully implement a system of defence-in-depth, or elastic defence. After receiving full reports of the German attack methods used at Caporetto in Italy and then later against the British, officers in the 1st Division pressed *Général* Passaga to allow the division to place "only a screen of men" in the most forward line of trenches; and have ready behind that line designated groups of reserves "held for reinforcement or counter-attack." Supporting artillery was to be withdrawn out of enemy gun range and ranged on No Man's Land and the front German trenches.[596] The discussions continued under Major General Edwards. However, *Général* Gérard, *VIII*e *armée,* arrived, taking Debeney's place. The result was that forces remained in place, putting American soldiers at the Woëvre at great risk for the next six months.

The **78. R. D.** conducted six patrols during the night of 25 March against American lines. They learned that the front lines were unoccupied by 1st Division troops. Only when they were heading south to the third line did they encounter fire. The Germans then conducted a small raid opposite **Abschnitt G I** and **G II** at midday. Artillery exchanges occurred. That afternoon the fire abated. The Americans conducted harassment fire throughout 27 March. One German battery position identified as No. 179 received over 400 rounds of incoming artillery shells. The **78. R. D.** batteries harassed the usual targets, especially a camp in *Bois de la Hazelle* and engaged a 155mm battery of the 5th Field Artillery.[597]

With **40. I. D.** coming into the Woëvre, **Res. I. R. 260** in late March commenced probes into the French lines opposite *Bois du Jury*. Throughout 28 March, artillery on both sides was active with harassing fire. That night around 2100, **Res. I. R. 260** made a major **Erstürmung** of the first and second lines at *Bois du Jury*'s north side. **Res. I. R. 260 Stosstruppen** reinforced by **Pioniere** and **Flammenwerfer** and supported by artillery and **MW**

fire, penetrated the trench system. The Germans advanced beyond the second line without encountering any Americans. Their forward movement ceased when **Res. I. R. 260 Stosstruppen** lost orientation in the darkness. American artillery fire, which did not open up until seven minutes after the start of the raid, targeted **Abschnitt G II** and **G III** and conducted counter-battery against the German artillery. German batteries fired a box barrage to cover the ongoing **Erstürmung** by diverting fire from **Res. I. R. 260**. Additional cover was provided by **Gasschuss** against American artillery batteries. A follow-on **Gasschuss**, originally planned for the early hours of the 29 March, was cancelled due to the weather. That night Major General Bullard told Stackpole that the standing French directive to counter-attack after every attack was not limited to infantry in a counteroffensive, but could be accomplished through retaliation by artillery.[598]

The **78. R. D.** did not let up on the 1st Division in their last days on the Woëvre. Between the hours of 2130 and 0030 on 28–29 March, G-2 reported that 1,000 HE, gas and incendiary shells were fired on Rambucourt in an attempt to neutralise four batteries there. The 6th Field Artillery said that 400 to 600 **Grünkreuz 2** (phosgene). **Grünkreuz 1** (diphosgene) and **Gelbkreuz** struck six of its batteries in the surprise gas bombardment. Three officers and eleven men were evacuated. These may have been from the squad reported by Lieutenant Butler to have taken off their masks because they were too warm. One sergeant who was "mentioned before for coolness under fire, will be tried as soon as he gets out of the hospital."[599] The 7th Field Artillery reported 350 gas shells on four of its batteries, with six casualties from a single 150mm mustard gas shell exploding in a gun pit. The 26th Infantry reported two casualties. Altogether, 2nd Infantry Brigade reported approximately 1,650 gas shells and 22 casualties.

When better weather came on 28 March, the Germans commenced a major artillery barrage with HE, shrapnel, and gas on Seicheprey and trenches to the north, Beaumont, Mandres, and Rambucourt. Two men were killed, two wounded, and eight gassed. In little wind and high humidity, said the 6th Field Artillery, "phosgene, mustard and tear gas swept the roads and batteries for five hours." All batteries of the regiment were subjected to the gas and HE bombardment, resulting in 29 eye cases, 21 of them in one battery where the men, in the absence of their officers, removed their masks. The 7th Field Artillery estimated 3,500 gas shells, most of them phosgene but some mustard gas, mixed with many more HE shells, that resulted in three gas casualties among five battery positions. The attack came at a time when "the roads were full of our division marching out and the 26th Division marching in … One man [at Mandres] from the 26th Division was gassed. He had no gas mask." Davis estimated that a total of 3,500 **Gelbkreuz**, **Blaukreuz**, and **Grünkreuz** of 77, 105, and 150 calibre had been fired on the batteries. He reported only thirty-two casualties, a tribute to good gas discipline. The 1st Division did not recognise the bombardment as a continuation of the earlier one. "We think," Colonel King wrote to Colonel Conner, "it was due to nervousness on the part of the Boche; that the movement [i.e., the relief then in progress] on this side made him afraid that something was going to happen." There were probably more than fifty-seven gas casualties as a result of this major gas attack, but not enough to make it an enemy success. Small consolation for the fifty-seven. The 1st Division would never know what, except for bad weather, it had escaped.[600]

Casualty counts were a normal part of business at the front. At the end of March 1918, **78. R. D.** reported 30 men killed, 10 officers and 165 men wounded and 2 officers and 21 men missing during the month that their enemy was the 1st Division.[601]

THE EXPLOITS OF LIEUTENANT GEORGE REDWOOD

The 1st Division conducted their last reconnaissance patrol with a patrol of fifteen men early in the morning against a sentry post in **Abschnitt G II b**. Five Germans were made prisoners at the point of the pistol. Under the command of Lieutenant George Redwood the patrol raided an observation post on the front line. Departing at 0200, initial progress was poor as the squad got lost and ended back in American lines. They reentered No Man's Land and eventually found the observation post. The aroma of coffee and fresh baked bread filled the air. After Redwood shouted, "**Ergebet euch**," five surrendered. Two others were shot reaching for their weapons. The situation became more precarious as more Germans rushed to the observation post. Redwood turned to his squad and said, "Come on boys, let's go." The patrol and prisoners worked their way to American lines. One of the German prisoners tried to run away and was killed. Redwood then fired at Germans rushing into the sector. The four remaining German prisoners (one NCO and three privates) from **Res. I. R. 259** were the first captured by the Americans: "Outwardly they were well clad but underneath they wore the thinnest and dirtiest underwear their captors had ever seen." In the interrogation the Germans were relieved that they were not to be shot. They had been told the worst of American treatment: "Woe to you if the Americans ever take you. We thought you were all going to be Indians."[602] Lieutenant Redwood summed up **Res. I. R. 259** soldiers he captured with, "En masse, of course, they are formidable, but individually they don't seem to be so eager for a scrap from all that I have heard and seen."[603] Redwood was killed 50 days later at Cantigny.[604]

The prisoner interrogation was accomplished by the newly arrived *VIIIe armée*, releasing their report on 2 April. Information from the four prisoners included time in service and assignments. Martin Rueland was with the **Res. I. R. 160** in 1914. He was wounded and assigned to the **Res. I. R. 259** in August 1915. Karl Engel was initially stationed on the Russian Front and subsequently assigned to the **Res. I. R. 259** in August 1917. Ernst Schmalkuche had been with the **Res. I. R. 259** since June 1915 and Heinrich Strater since May 1916. On 15 January they occupied their assigned part of the southern Woëvre front and replaced **14. R. D.**

The interrogation confirmed that **Generalmajor** Stolzmann was **78 R. D.** commander and stationed at Thiaucourt, as well as confirming **Res. I. R. 259** was commanded by **Major** Bruns. Their battalion had had only eight days rest since occupying the sector on 15 January. After **Einladung** the Germans expected a major American attack in the sector south of Thiaucourt. However, the prisoners had not seen more heavy artillery being deployed to the southern Woëvre front. If the Allies were to attack the **Res. I. R. 259**, German plans were to leave the first line immediately and proceed to the third position and organise the main defence. The prisoners reported that the intermediate position was in too poor a condition. Three **Schützennester** [Shooting Nests] were assigned between St. Baussant and the sector facing Seicheprey. **Res. I. R. 259** maintained a command post near Essey on the road to Bouillonville. The prisoners complained that rations were insufficient, consisting of 700g of bread per day. The interrogation took an interesting turn when they claimed that neither the regiment nor division had assault troops assigned. A specialised detachment called the **Streifkommando** had thirty men, but had subsequently been dissolved. The prisoners also revealed that **78. R. D.** was not large enough to conduct a division-level attack, but **78 R. D.** did conduct an exercise in mid-January with two regiments in attack, with the third regiment serving as reserve and executing a counter-attack. All four confirmed **78. R. D.** was going to remain in the Woëvre. Finally, the prisoners revealed a large tunnel was in place along the banks of the Moselle – suggesting a command centre for the region – and a *VIIIe armée* aerial reconnaissance sortie was launched to confirm the interrogation.[605]

AN ADMINISTRATIVE COMMAND

Major General Hunter Liggett, I Corps commander, was in a bind. He was General Pershing's number one commander in the AEF. Unfortunately, his command had only administrative control over the four divisions that were presently in theatre. Liggett had supervisory authority over the division commanders but did not hold tactical command. That was the responsibility of the French. Liggett shared his frustration frequently with his aide, Major Stackpole, who kept a diary that described Liggett's interaction with senior AEF commanders and staffs. He described Liggett's situation as "anomalous." Liggett stated that he wanted to call on brigade and regimental commanders because he knew them personally, though he would otherwise restrict his activities to division commanders. He felt no duty to relieve any of the present division commanders on basis of performance. Altogether Liggett was disappointed by the extraordinarily indefinite character of his authority and the limitations of his command, "which appears to extend to nothing but corps troops, practically nonexistent."[606]

The 26th Division was ordered to replace the 1st Division and became part of *Général* Gérard's *VIIIe armée*. Major General Edwards now came under tactical command of *Général* Passaga's *32e corps d'armée* with two French divisions, *10e division d'infanterie colonial* and *69e division d'infanterie*, on the flanks.[607] Relations with French command were complicated enough. It didn't help to have GHQ AEF staff under Pershing constantly on the offensive against what they perceived to be an incompetent 26th Division. GHQ AEF oversight of the 1st Division tested everyone's patience. General Summerall's memoir indicated an impassable gulf between GHQ and the troops. Now the troops had a commander who clearly relished the opportunity to ensure his men were cared for, and put GHQ in its place.

Major General Edwards by his nature was controversial and his primary antagonists resided in senior command at Chaumont and I Corps. Colonel Malin Craig was a superb staff officer but, unfortunately for the divisions on the line, insensitive to the realities facing soldiers after four years of positional war. A product of Georgetown University prior to attending West Point, Malin Craig exhibited a disciplined Jesuit and military training – aggressively resolute in his loyalty to higher authority such as Pershing and Liggett.[608]

In many ways he appeared as a grand inquisitor to the "heretics" that populated 26th Division staffs. Craig's post-war letter to General Hugh Drum spelled out his resolute attitude. Early in January 1918, he saw Edwards ridicule several senior officers in front of junior officers. He kept track of Edwards' activities and stated that the 26th Division commander never visited his troops at the front while they served at Chemin-des-Dâmes.[609] Stackpole's impressions of Edwards were also negative – recording on 27 January 1918 that the division botched a demonstration of firepower by 168 machine guns. Major General Edwards showed up hours later armed with excuses. Stackpole recorded: "General Liggett quietly said those things happen and that he would like to go home at once, which we did." That evening Liggett and Stackpole had dinner with Colonel Craig and Colonel Heintzelman from Chaumont. Stackpole and Craig discussed the issue and the man. Stackpole continued to update Craig on any mishaps involving Edwards.[610] Meanwhile, Craig contributed to the intrigue two weeks later by seeking out the chief surgeon for the division, Lieutenant Colonel Bevans, in Soissons. Craig requested Bevans elaborate on 26th Division assignments coming from GHQ AEF not being obeyed by the division. Just as the conversation was ending General Liggett walked up and advised Bevans to take Craig's discussion as a personal conversation. Bevans proceeded to report to General Edwards and was advised to file a memorandum for record with the 26th Division Inspector General.[611] A month later Stackpole related that General Pershing and General Liggett discussed Edwards at some length. Liggett informed Pershing that Edwards had not obeyed any of his orders in Chemin-des-Dâmes and had not visited his troops at the front. Liggett's assessment was Edwards was in poor health. Both Pershing and Liggett both agreed that the spirit and discipline of the 26th Division was excellent. Pershing told Liggett that he knew what Liggett was saying and he credited the 26th Division's spirit to Edwards' two brigade commanders (Brigadier General Traub, Brigadier General Charles H. Cole). Pershing now considered Edwards' ill health gave him grounds for dismissal and retirement.[612]

General Liggett was not blind to Edwards' shortcomings but he let it be known to Stackpole that Craig and his staff colleague, Colonel Heintzelmann, were prejudiced against him. Stackpole upped the ante by noting that "Colonel Craig was particularly concerned because he felt that acquiescence in the situation was not only a reflection on Liggett, Corps Commander, and his staff, but it endangered the lives of twenty-seven thousand men and it was too great a hazard to take the chance of some calamity in order to give Edwards a further chance."[613] General Liggett later told Stackpole that Edwards' removal was not his decision to make.

Central to both Chaumont's and Liggett's staff was Major Edward "Peter" Bowditch, G-3, I Corps. On 9 March, Colonel Craig directed Bowditch to serve as liaison with the French *10ᵉ corps d'armée* headquarters. The division was to report "all events connected with the service of their units in the trenches. By events is to be understood all casualties, patrol encounters, raids, etc., and, in general, operation events that are of importance or interest to higher authority." Bowditch was responsible for forwarding or submitting the reports to I Army Corps and for sending an exact duplicate of the reports to the French commander at the *10ᵉ corps d'armée* headquarters.[614] Bowditch left *10ᵉ corps d'armée* headquarters for Beaumont to serve as Liggett's primary liaison while the 26th Division was at the southern Woëvre front. His comments helped General Pershing in his tracking of Major General Edwards, the division, and supporting elements such as the newly assigned 1st and 94th Aero Squadrons. His official correspondence with Craig had a personal touch, addressing him as "Dear Colonel." Bowditch came from the upper echelons of American society, earning distinction two years in a row as an All-American football player, with a degree in law from Harvard. Bowditch established himself

The celebrated 155mm field howitzer, Betsy the Sniper, fires away to the north. (*History of the 103rd Field Artillery*)

in military circles through his professional and sports associations. As secretary to Consul E. Morgan, Bowditch was able to observe the Russo-Japanese War in Manchuria, meeting General Pershing and establishing a close personal and professional association. He served in the Philippines as Secretary to the Governor General and filled leading roles in Moro Province. Bowditch was an accomplished polo player with an impressive network of friends, including Pershing, Craig, and Liggett. In addition to his time in France working for Colonel Conner, Bowditch served in the latter half of 1918 as Pershing's personal aide-de-camp. He received the Distinguished Service Medal, always showing himself able in time of emergency, aggressive in action, and possessed of tact and sound judgement.[615] Major Bowditch was tolerated by 26th Division staffs. His constant reporting to Liggett and Craig was a new and better liaison but did not rectify the animosity between Division and headquarters.

One 26th Division staff member's post-war recollection of Chaumont is revealing: "Officers of the Corps or from General Headquarters, present with the Division, desirous of asserting a proper authority, zealous to hasten the Division's efficiency, perhaps made caustic comments on what they believed was a lack of discipline should one of their impeccable plans miscarry; whereupon the Division tended, outraged that its excellence should be even lightly called in question, to request that actual conditions be ascertained before conclusions were drawn and comments made. At no time, probably, did any American staff enjoy the authority of the French – perhaps did not deserve to; certainly, in the earlier stages of development of the Twenty-Sixth and all other American divisions, the Staffs were made to demonstrate their practical efficiency before being accepted as either guides or managers. But it equally is the case that, with time, fuller knowledge, and a more perfectly defined interdependence, the Staff and line, of the Twenty-Sixth at least, came to work effectively together for the common good."[616]

THE YANKEE DIVISION RELIEVES THE FIGHTING FIRST

Général Foch telegrammed the French Mission at Mirecourt HQ in the afternoon of 29 March: "By mutual agreement of the Commanders-in-Chief, it has been decided that the American 1st Division shall participate in battle." Foch's direction was to the point – prepare for the earliest possible relief of the 1st Division by the American 26th Division. That evening *Général* Passaga ordered the 26th Division to relieve the 1st Division in the *De la Reine* sector and the units of the *10ᵉ division d'infanterie colonial* east of the boundary set in order No. 344. The relief was complicated. Two divisions totalling almost 50,000 men exchanged positions in record time. The 1st Division was ordered to regroup to the Toul area and establish their headquarters at Gondreville with the 51st Infantry Brigade and 52ᵈ Infantry Brigade.[617]

Colonel King confirmed takeover at 0800 on 3 April 1918. Brigadier General Traub's 51st Infantry Brigade assumed command of their part of the southern Woëvre front on 3 April at 0800. Colonel John H. Parker's 102nd Infantry was confirmed to assume command of the regimental zone from both Colonel Hanson Ely's 28th Infantry and Colonel Hamilton Smith's 26th Infantry at 0800 on 2 April; Colonel Edward Logan's 101st Infantry followed suit next day with sub-sectors to the west of Seicheprey.[618] Now an American division assumed responsibility for an entire divisional sector. General Edwards noted later that his sector, after several changes and reorganizations, went from 7 kilometres held by the 1st Division to 18 kilometres of front. The 26th Division soldiers felt a tinge of pride because "the French felt we were qulaified to assume the responsibilities."[619]

When John J. Pershing graduated from West Point in 1886, the next cadet in the long grey line to assume his commission was Peter Edward Traub. He served as a cavalry officer in the West early in his career with subsequent tours as an instructor and assistant professor at West Point's Foreign Languages Department. His expertise in languages allowed him special assignments including confidential missions overseas while he was at the Army Staff College. Prior to the outbreak of war in Europe, Traub served in the Phillippines. He was assigned to the 20th Division in August 1917 and promoted to Brigadier General. Chaumont's Inspector

General on 21 March wrote Traub prior to his arrival in the Woëvre: "One cannot visit this Division without being impressed by the work of this officer, both with respect to the availing himself to the utmost of the opportunities of learning from his association with the French Army, and for his untiring work in visiting all points of his line, including advance combat posts day and night. In fact, any criticism must be that he has exposed himself too much.[620] He was a steady commander but at his time at the southern Woëvre front illustrated, Brigadier General Peter Traub controlled more than he led.

The 26th Division commenced a three-day withdrawal from Chemin-des-Dâmes front and marched toward the training area west of Neufchateau. Forty-eight hours after arriving in the rest area, 26th Division proceeded north to "La Reine" (based on *Bois de la Reine*) or Boucq Sector (the location of Major General Edwards' headquarters), north-west of Toul. The 18-kilometre line extended from the vicinity of Apremont to the west, in front of Xivray-Marvoisin, Seicheprey, and *Bois de Remières*, and finally terminating at the eastern end with *Bois du Jury*.[621] Secretary of War Baker made a brief visit with 26th Division seniors followed by a legislative commission from Massachusetts, charged with the duty of establishing a club-room and information office for troops from Massachusetts in Paris. Just as the legislative commission departed the 1st Division relief commenced.[622]

The departure of both divisions prompted accolades from their *corps d'armée* commanders. Major General Bullard's 1st Division was acclaimed by *Général* Passaga: "At this time when the First American Division is going into combat, the officers, non-commissioned officers and privates of the 32ᵈ Army Corps salute their brothers in arms whose bravery they have admired."[623] The 26th Division received a similar accolade from *11ᵉ corps d'armée*, *Général* de Maud'huy. "We have been able to appreciate their bravery, their sense of duty and discipline, also their frank comradeship … General Edwards has been pleased to consider the Eleventh Corps as Godfather to the

Twenty-sixth Division. The Eleventh Corps feels proud of the awarded honour, being sure that whatever they may be sent, the Godson will do credit to the Godfather."[624]

A CASE FOR STAFF COLLEGE CONSIDERATION

An absolute principle governing the French *armée* relief at the line was that relieving troops were to keep exactly the same organization as the relieved units. If alterations were to be made they were to be accomplished only after the relief had been completed.[625] As the 1st Division withdrew from the Ansauville sector, Major General Bullard assigned Brigadier General Summerall and his staff the responsibility of handling the relief. Although the 1st Division performed a considerable feat in clearing the area in three days (3-5 April), the transfer was not best managed. As 26th Division regiments proceeded north towards the Woëvre front, 1st Division guides had not been assigned, so confusion reigned. Liggett's staff was dissatisfied with the sector's state. Just who made the original complaints about the sector is unclear, but I Corps pursued the matter, ordering Edwards' staff to make a thorough investigation of the 1st Division's sloppiness. The inspector general's investigation found a score of dead horses and mules left unburied, others blinded and suffering with the mange, many more lame and sick left wandering aimlessly in need of veterinary attention. The billets, kitchens, and picket lines were "left in a shocking condition." The inspector general said the state of the facilities gave the impression it was an abandoned battlefield rather than a quiet sector. The 1st Division left an excessive amount of clothing, ordnance, and other paraphernalia, enough to equip a full division, that was not properly turned over to the incoming 26th Division supply authorities. The 26th Division's inspector general observed that having just left Chemin-des-Dâmes where they received the barest sort of replenishment of clothing and ordnance and replacing 1st Division accustomed

to such abundance reinforced the feeling that "there was willful discrimination against National Guard troops." Two other allegations were made by the 26th Division inspector: the usurping of hip boots, trench equipment necessary for operating in the deplorable conditions, and actual theft of artillery horses when they were tied up to the 1st Division echelons.[626] The report from I Corp's inspector general included concerns over disciplinary prisoners awaiting disposition, one straggler, and a stack of unburned classified documents in one infantry battalion's PC. On the basis of the investigations, Colonel Craig told Pershing's Chief of Staff, Major General Harbord, that the 1st Division was guilty of "demoralization, lack of discipline, and failure to obey orders that is utterly unexplained and beyond the experiences of regular officers at these headquarters."[627] Craig personally recommended general courts-martial for Brigadier General Summerall, the 6th Field Artillery commander, the 6th Field Artillery supply officer, Lieutenant Colonel George K. Wilson of Bullard's administrative section, and the officers of the 26th Infantry who were remiss in destroying classified papers. Acting on the report, Major General Harbord informed Major General Bullard of Craig's charges, but told him that GHQ AEF was going to straighten the matter out. Harbord did pass on to Bullard that there were to be more investigations and that the 1st Division had better not repeat its errors. Eventually, Pershing's investigators absolved the 1st Division of negligence.[628]

It is important to note that General Summerall, a distinguished leader in the US Army who made Chief of Staff, commented on these charges in his post-war memoirs with remarkable candour: "Later, when we were intensely engaged in Picardy, the inspector general of the First Corps investigated a malicious report against General Bullard and me charging negligence in the relief and found it to be entirely false. The investigation was inspired by the chief of staff of the First Corps [Colonel Malin Craig], who had a sadistic mind for injuring others. I had been a close friend of his parents and had known him since he was a boy.

Afterward, he had General Edwards relieved from command of the Twenty-sixth Division on false charges and blighted the career of an able officer. General Bullard remarked that while we were fighting desperately with our faces to the enemy, our own command was stabbing us in the back. We never felt safe from spying and false accusations, inspired by jealousy on the part of the men we were serving. Later, the First Division and I were to drink the dregs of this bitter cup when the division obeyed the order to capture Sedan."[629]

Major General Edwards did not maintain discretion at this time, complaining with his fellow flag officers and staff about the move. In addition to *Général* Passaga, General Edwards now worked for *Général* Augustin Gérard, commander of *VIIIᵉ armée,* instead of *Général* Debeny, *Iʳᵉ armée,* who was now supporting French operations against Operation Michael. As the relief progressed General Edwards spent a morning with General Bullard complaining that nine conflicting orders were sent in just one day to the 26th Division — something Bullard told Edwards that he had better get used to. Apparently, the discussion between the two became so acrimonious that Liggett's staff urged General Liggett to remove Edwards. Liggett did not — defending Edwards and ordering the relief to continue as planned. Edwards then followed up his conversation with Liggett expressing the same frustrations about the French staff making the relief a problem. General Liggett took the high ground, not sharing in the frustration but focusing on just one example: on the whole, the relief was proceeding but there was some confusion about Edwards'101st Trench Mortar Battery's billets and supplies.[630]

Orders, counter-orders, and additional sets of instructions, both written and verbal, poured into 26th Division headquarters from *VIIIᵉ armée* and *32ᵉ corps d'armée* headquarters. In his post-war letter to General Hugh Drum, Brigadier General Craig later recalled: "This relief was the most disgraceful case of mismanagement and inefficiency that I have ever seen in the Army. Units proceeded without any information as to where they were going and without supplies. This

was straightened out by my sending two officers of the I Corps staff to report to General Edwards to take hold and issue necessary orders."[631] The 1st Division was told where it should proceed and by what means. The rest of the relief was up to the staffs of 1st and 26th Division to determine. The 1st Division did not get their orders until after the 26th Division had started their movement — as directed by *32ᵉ corps d'armée* — the primary authority for the relief. The experience confirmed the AEF was in need of trained staffs covering all echelons. The 1st Division and 26th Division were critcized. Both felt the *VIIIᵉ armée* and *32ᵉ corps d'armée* were principally at fault.[632]

The 26th Division senior staff were now located at Toul near the *32ᵉ corps d'armée* headquarters. They accomplished very little as they processed orders delayed for various reasons tried to follow changes in the plan made by *VIIIᵉ armée* and *32ᵉ corps d'armée*. Guides for the inbound forces did not know the way. One regiment commander had his forces delivered to a location that had no further direction other than to disembark from the *camions*. Another regiment completed their relief and took position on the front line without any orders received. I Corps sent observers to monitor the relief. Events broached the absurd when the observing Chaumont staff officer made a major issue of rolling kitchens. The condition of the roads resulted in many being broken beyond repair resulting in several units resorting to improvised meal preparation, but this was hardly a strategic calamity.[633] General Edwards personally signed off a 25 March memorandum that explicitly ordered his brigade commanders to "personally inspect all units of their respective commands while on the march, and especially observe the tail of these columns to see that adequate measures are being taken to prevent straggling … all officers and non-commissioned officers of organizations will be instructed to assist in improving the conditions above mentioned, by correcting derelictions on the spot."[634] Issues were being addressed before they arose. Confusion in the ranks reflected the state of the army as a whole, trying to adjust successfully to the dynamics of modern warfare and to the effects of a massive mobilization.

Major Emerson Gifford Taylor, Adjutant for 102nd Infantry, succinctly summarised the flurry underway: "When staff work was still to be perfected, when everybody was anxious to do the correct thing, yet a bit in doubt as to how to set about it; when the French politely prodded, and commanding generals worried; when lesser commanders felt that they only knew what could and should be done; when everybody felt that somebody higher up was taking notes – though possessing not a whit more practical experience – of course there was a misunderstanding."[635] After-action reports were later analysed by the Army Staff College illustrating mistakes to be avoided in accomplishing a relief. Nevertheless, the objective was met. A total of 50,000 soldiers comprising two divisions of the line switched out on the southern Woëvre front.

"I DID NOT REALIZE THERE COULD BE SO MANY AMERICANS IN ALL FRANCE"

For Corporal Charles Leo Boucher of Company C, 102nd Infantry, the transition to the southern Woëvre front had its surprises: "We relieved soldiers from The First Division and, although this sector was supposed to be a quiet one, it wasn't long till it was turned into a 'Hell on Wheels' for us."[636]

Colonel Parker's 102nd Infantry completed their 42-day tour of duty at the Chemin-des-Dâmes on 20 March 1918. The original intention was to proceed to the 4th Training Area to await further instruction and prepare for new duties on the front line, but this was subsequently modified to use rail to allow the forces to assemble and conduct manoeuvres. The regiment proceeded to Brienne-le-Château, 60 kilometres north-west of Chaumont, in an impressive time of less than 24 hours. From there the 102nd Infantry marched east to Thonnance. Many men from the 3rd Battalion still suffering from a gas attack while serving at Chemin-des-Dâmes dropped out and required

hospitalization. On 27 March the majority of the 102nd Infantry was about 80 kilometres to the south of Seicheprey. On 30 March, French *camions* arrived to transport the regiment to the north. The remaining 3rd Battalion was assigned as reserve and billeted to the south at Ansauville and Mandres. The rest of the regiment assumed the territory they were to hold for the coming month at Beaumont and Seicheprey.

The 102nd Infantry commenced coordination with the 26th Infantry upon arrival. At the end of March, Major George J. Rau's 1st Battalion proceeded to link up with his 26th Infantry counterpart, Major Theodore Roosevelt. Roosevelt was in his Seicheprey PC working when Major Rau and officers found him standing in water up to his ankles, oblivious to the elements. It was a congenial meeting, issues were discussed, and details agreed regarding the final moments for 26th Infantry in Seicheprey.[637]

For Captain Dorst Patch, post-war memories of the relief were not positive: "We of the 2nd Battalion will never forget that relief. They came up to the front lines, yelling, singing, and waving flashlights, which could be seen from the German lines, in order to see their way around. We warned them that they were begging for trouble, but they told us they had come from the Chemin de Dames, a live and not a dead sector. They got the trouble they were seeking, for a short time later the Germans gave them an awful beating at Seicheprey."[638]

The next day in the afternoon, the 102nd Machine Gun Battalion arrived in Ménil-la-Tour. Once darkness came, they marched 7 kilometres to Ansauville: "By truck from Brechainville to Menil-le-Tour, going then to Liffel-le-Grand, Neufchâteau and Toul. Some trip. Truck crowded, rough gang, headache from gas. *Pas bon!* Hiked to Ansauville. Bunked in shack left in state of horrible filth by 28 Infantry machine company, 'Regulars.'"[639]

Dawn had hardly broken when Private Enoch Hall Doble, a medic from the 102nd Machine Gun Battalion's Sanitary Detachment was rudely awakened by his sergeant: "Pack your barracks bags up and get your backpacks ready …

In one hour you are leaving to go back into the trenches. The Germans have mounted another drive to reach Paris and are running over the English at Saint-Quentin. The First Division of the American Regular Army is being pulled out to back up the English. Our American Yankee Division of the National Guard and all of the 26th Division will go up to replace the First Division above Nancy and Toul." In less than an hour Doble and his colleagues from the battalion were in large buses and on the move again: "All day we passed walking soldiers and horse-drawn artillery … We, the 102nd Machine-Gun Battalion, Sanitary Detachment, would be out in front of everyone, even our own infantry. I did not realize there could be so many Americans in all France. We passed them all day and were still passing them when the sun went down. As darkness fell, we descended and marched with our mules pulling the carriages that carried our machine guns." The 102nd Machine Gun Battalion was one of the first units to enter Seicheprey. Doble described the final relief: "The men were quiet and sober as they marched. Once we heard an officer very quietly speak, 'You are going right where the real activity is, not like the quiet front where we were first.' We marched all night and then were told to say not one word since the Germans were on both sides of us, very close. At last we came into some kind of a village with smashed, broken-down houses [Seicheprey]. We quickly installed ourselves in one remaining corner of a house that had been shelled. It was well after midnight before we crawled into our bunks, such as they were."[640] That night they went into the trenches, relieving the Machine Gun Company of the 28th Infantry. They were "welcomed by shells."[641]

LOST EN ROUTE

French *camions* arrived on 30 March to transport the 102nd Infantry's troops and baggage to the Woëvre. The move was put under command of Major John James Gallant, a recent arrival in theatre from the Philippines. In his early enlisted years Gallant was wounded fighting in the Boxer

Rebellion in China. He then was assigned to the Philippines where he received a commission and honourably served seventeen years in the Philippine Constabulary. His boss the last year was Colonel Peter Traub. Gallant had many opportunities to show Traub he was competent, followed orders and "had the right stuff in him."[642] Pershing's future chief of staff, Colonel Harbord, commented on Captain Gallant's performance in 1905, "In the province of Misamis political agitators have, during the past year, succeeded in causing a spirit of rebellion in localities where the masses are unusually ignorant. The suppression of this required active field work of the constabulary for nearly eight months. During this campaign 270 outlaws, including the leaders, were killed, captured, or surrendered, due largely to the brilliant work of the senior inspector, Captain Gallant."[643] Gallant was an accomplished linguist, speaking eight languages and dialects. When the United States entered into the war, the 42-year-old Lieutenant Colonel departed the Philippines and travelled to France at his own expense to become part of the AEF. He was reinstated into the US Army Reserves as a major. Now in his first role as a field grade officer for the 102nd Infantry, he was challenged with a problem out of his control. The baggage and transport got lost en route to Beaumont, arriving on 3 April, three days after the 102nd Infantry troops arrived at the front. It was an inauspicious beginning for one of the most interesting characters assigned to the regiment.[644]

It wasn't just infantry that faced problems getting to the southern Woëvre front. Colonel Robert Sherburne's 101st Field Artillery senior staff reported to *Colonel* Carteron, *10ᵉ division d'infanterie colonial* artillery commander, making arrangements for the whole relief of the West Grouping to proceed the night of 3 April. They visited the positions to be occupied, assuming that Sherburne's 101st Field Artillery was north of Toul that night, ready to assume 1st Artillery Brigade positions the next night. Colonel Sherburne reconnoitred every likely road that 101st Field Artillery might have taken, looking for a 5-kilometre column that comprised his unit. No one seem to know the 101st Field

Robert Sherburne, commander of the 101st Field Artillery. (101st Field Artillery)

from a company clerk operating out of the 26th Division's temporary headquarters near the *32ᵉ corps d'armée* headquarters at Toul. They were now to proceed east towards the Moselle and marched in that direction but the weather had turned the road into a bog. Late that night the 103rd Field Artillery made camp. As the dawn arrived they were ordered to continue the march towards Toul. Fortunately the 26th Division staff made contact through *32ᵉ corps d'armée,* this time providing constant contact and nurturing the regiment to the north. At 0800 on 4 April the artillery command passed to Colonel Sherburne. Since leaving Brienne-le-Château, Sherburne's brigade had marched for nine days covering a distance, including detours, of 216 kilometres.[646]

Artillery's location or destination, including the *32ᵉ corps d'armée* staff at Toul. A telephone inquiry to General Edwards's newly established headquarters at Boucq also brought no satisfaction. Meanwhile, Sherburne's 101st Field Artillery continued heading north towards the southern Woëvre front.[645]

Colonel Sherburne went back to Boucq to find out what march orders the Division had issued to the artillery. There he learned that the staff had completely forgotten all about the artillery that day and had issued no march orders to them. Sherburne made full use of his vocabulary in sharing with the 26th Division staff how this information was perceived. They all proceeded to find the 101st Field Artillery – which had arrived safely on a cold and drizzly Easter morning at Colombey south of St. Mihiel and were spending the rest of the day catching a bit of rest. No orders for 101st Field Artillery arrived the next day so they remained in place. At noon a 103rd Field Artillery advance party arrived saying the rest of the 103rd Infantry was approaching. The march plan had the artillery arriving in the southern Woëvre front a day ahead of the infantry. The 103rd Field Artillery received confused orders

ARTILLERY IS SWAPPED OUT

At 0800 on April 5 Brigadier General Summerall passed the command of the artillery within the southern Woëvre front to his good friend, Brigadier General William L. Lassiter, commander of the 26th Division's 51st Artillery Brigade. Terrain governed the way artillery operated at the southern Woëvre front. Ponds, marshes, and acres of impassable muddy ground forced the artillery into two groups – east and west. The deep mud prevented 1st Division's artillery from moving the 155mm howitzers out of the sector or moving 26th Division's howitzers, so an exchange took place where the 5th Field Artillery and 103rd Field Artillery linked up south of the sector.[647]

Brigadier General Cole, 52nd Infantry Brigade, made a point of not interfering with Sherburne's control of fire within West Grouping, which now supported 101st Infantry and 104th Infantry. Brigadier General Traub's East Grouping covered most of the 26th Division sector. It included the 102nd Field Artillery under Colonel Morris E. Locke, 1st Battalion of the 101st Field Artillery, and most of the battalions from 103rd Field Artillery.[648] After dark the Germans, probably warned by their spy system that something was going on, fired a **Gasschuss** on Mandres that lasted until early morning. With shells falling fairly close and gas hanging like a fog, billeting became perilous.

The 101st Field Artillery proceeded to occupy ground in the western sector that had been French for the entire war. Three 75mm batteries from the 101st Field Artillery's Battery D, E, and F supported the *10ᵉ division d'infanterie colonial* as well as the newly deployed 104th Infantry. The 101st also inherited from the French a few De Bange 90mm cannon *(Mle 1877)*. Their front line targets included not only **78. R. D.** to the north and north-east, but also the **5. Landwehr. Division (5. Ldwr. D.)** to the west. Heavy artillery from 103rd Field Artillery's Battery F and one trench mortar battery rounded out the American artillery presence in the West Grouping.[649] 101st Field Artillery, Battery D, occupied an old French position in the low ground to the east of St Julien – one that enabled them to maintain a field of fire almost at right angles to the axis of the sector and to enfilade the front line. This served them well in the coming days.[650] They got settled, establishing the necessary communications to PCs, placing new camouflage over the 75mm artillery, improving existing shelters, and building gun-pit walls and roofs.[651] Battery C arrived at St. Julien to a welcome by **5. Ldwr. Div.** artillery firing HE and gas. Battery C men soon experienced German artillery firing rounds just as their meals were being prepared. Owing to the danger of observation from **Drachen** and Montsec to the immediate north-east, the Battery C kitchen was sequestered away in woods south of battery positions. Members of the battery learned to be deceptive, adding diversity to their routine by changing their lunch schedule. It unfortunately proved in vain because soon after implementing a new schedule, a **Gasschuss** struck the area at the very moment they commenced a meal. Consistently cold meals became the standard.[652]

"GOD-SPEED"

Battery C, 102 Field Artillery, got a dose of what awaited them as their convoy of *camions* worked its way towards Beaumont to relieve Battery E,

6th Field Artillery, after midnight. This particular crossroads was one of the most dangerous spots along the southern Woëvre front – under direct observation from Montsec. The road was one of the most important arteries of communication along the whole front.[653] Out of the black of night, a voice called out, "For God's sake men, get that truck the hell off this crossroad – don't you guys know where you are?" Battery C responded "no" – the voice then replied in a serious tone, "This is Dead Man's Curve." Battery C lost no time scrambling back into the trucks, quickly departing. It was the only road leading to the front and the Germans, knowing this, had a battery of guns trained on the curve at all times. At 10- or 15-minute intervals they would shell this spot all night. Immediately after leaving Dead Man's Curve, the dreadful whiz and screech of incoming shells was heard. Nine impacted at the crossroads with a blinding flash, shrapnel flying everywhere. Battery C ran their 75mm gun out of the *camion* and placed it in a vacant emplacement before running into the *abris*. The exchange between Battery C and Battery E personnel went well. The National Guard artillery crew was accepted as equals by the veteran Battery E: "A fine bunch of fellows," since Battery C came directly from Chemin-des-Dâmes. Shared combat experience eliminated any bias that the regulars had against the guardsmen: "They had heard of us and we of them; and so, while there was good natured repartee as to our divisional accomplishments, they left us the following night with hand-shakes and we wished them God-speed."[654]

Fourth section cannoneers of Battery A, 103rd Field Artillery, arrived on the Beaumont Ridge the night of 3 April and proceeded to the 5th Field Artillery's single howitzer position known as No. 413, or "Jones I." Jones I served as a "sniper gun" simulating a complete and active battery. Jones I's most notorious artillery piece was 155mm howitzer No. 1,312, better known as "Betsy the Sniper." Betsy served as the most forward howitzer in the sector – distinctly audible to the infantry to the north – a sound beloved by them as they proceeded down the *boyau* into Seicheprey. Betsy's close proximity to German lines made it a natural for harassing **Stosstrupp** movement north of No Man's Land. The crew for Jones I established their *abris* on the lee side of the Beaumont Ridge, modifying a stone-vaulted culvert dated 1808, which cut under the road next to the Jones I position. **Generalleutnant** Hoffmann's artillery fired more shells at Jones I's position than any other artillery position, earning it the sobriquet "Hell's Half Acre."[655] South of the ridge on the Flirey-Hamonville road, a second 155mm howitzer battery nestled within a grove of firs, known as "Jones II."

To the left of Betsy near Dead Man's Curve was a battery of 7th Field Artillery 95mm guns. The Davis Battery (Battery A, 103rd Field Artillery), under the command of Lieutenant Joseph Carlton Davis with Sergeant Joshua Broadhead as the senior ranking sergeant, assumed control on 4 April. It was also a popular target for **Generalleutnant** Hoffmann's artillery. Davis' men became very efficient despite the hazards – first to respond to infantry requests for artillery support.

West of Beaumont on the ridge was Bryan I, the former 5th Field Artillery 155mm howitzer battery. Battery B, 103rd Field Artillery, replaced the "regulars". A second platoon from Battery B proceeded south of the ridge to *Bois de Charnot* and occupied another 155mm howitzer battery known as Bryan II. This battery had its own notoriety since it included "Big Ben," the first artillery piece fired by the Americans in the war. Battery B took pride in knowing they held the ground with this historic piece.[656]

Battery F, 7th Field Artillery, had endured a rough night waiting for the 101st Artillery batteries to relieve them. For six hours German artillery pounded their positions with HE and **Gasschuss**. On 3 April, the batteries arrived and the relieved 7th Field Artillery departed – happy to quit the place. The newly arrived men of Battery C found the *abris* anything but shell-proof, putting on a brave face and saying they were glad to be "on the line" again.[657] The battery attempted to repair what was there but soon were ordered to move out 3 kilometres

east. Unfortunately, the new emplacement was nothing but a mud hole with the three *abris* built to provide billets for the crews waterlogged. Twelve men spent their first night moving one 75mm artillery piece about 6 metres into the gun pit. The mud was waist-deep in some places, and when dawn broke at last, the entire battery fell in and marched to the mess. The entourage appeared more "like a conglomeration of mud-balls than soldiers in the American Army."[658]

SWORD OF DAMOCLES

The 103rd Field Artillery was all over the sector with a mixed collection of 120mm rifles, 155mm Schneider howitzers, and 95mm guns. At times, when the Allies conducted small offensive movements, additional French guns to include 120s and 155s were temporarily brought in. During this period considerable use was made of roving sniper guns, which changed position daily.[659] Two batteries from different regiments set up at Rangeval on 3 April. Rangeval consisted of four houses, a monastery, and a dilapidated brick-factory entirely surrounded by mud. Adjoining the factory were small buildings that formed a courtyard. In these buildings and on the ground floor of the factory, 103rd Field Artillery men were billeted throughout. A long shed at one side of the building served as a stable. The most imposing feature of the dilapidated brick factory was a brick chimney some 25 metres high, which stood out for miles around. The 75mm gun crews of Battery A recalled: "The chimney had been tilted by some wanton Boche shell so that it shamed the Tower of Pisa and it was regarded by the drivers who slept beneath as a sort of Sword of Damocles. For the first few days, its temperament was carefully and prayerfully studied when it seemed to win from the drivers a degree of grudging confidence. The Monastery was sometimes called the 'Port of Missing Men' because it sheltered the only wine shop in the neighborhood."[660]

Near the very front of the Position 1 line set amid the debris and litter of the Seicheprey ruins were the anti-tank gun batteries of Battery B, 103rd Field Artillery. One member of the battery, Private Walter Wolf, recalled entering the area north of Seicheprey for the first time: "After a long and tedious journey we arrived at the training area, which was to prove quite different from what I had anticipated. Night had fallen, pitch black. At irregular and frequent intervals, I was startled by flares immediately in front of us. At this point the truck came to a dead halt, and we were told to dismount. The gang lined up in single file, each one putting his right hand on the shoulder of the man in front of him. Then 'forward, ho,' came in low indistinct tones. The rest of the journey was just a bewildering maze, a jutting, drifting communication trench, with duckboards here and there; most of them trodden deep in the mud, offering no protection whatever from the slime that was everywhere. Halting at the whistle and glare of every star shell, shuddering at the ping of every machine gun bullet, and the whine of every shell, we at last made our way into Seicheprey."[661]

Major Everitte S. Chaffee, 1st Battalion, 103rd Field Artillery, commenced orientation of his new sector by choosing to ride on horseback. "Up we go around 'Dead Man's Bend' [Dead Man's Curve] *à cheval*. On Beaumont Ridge my friend is advised by a brother officer that we have no business there on horses. At 'Jones 1' being on the crest we seem to draw a reluctant sort of shellfire. One of his lieutenants commanding – a former sergeant of the regular service – suggests that the major need not 'hurry away.' 'Jones 2' is an exhibition position to show visitors but with emplacements too broad for protection in conflict. Its captain called it a very good bit of eyewash."[662]

Major General Bullard bitterly remembered this time in his memoirs. He assumed erroneously that Clarence Edwards had pushed for the charges to be levied against Bullard's division. Ironically, the 26th Division was also censured for botching its liaison with 1st Division. Bullard mused: "It was altogether the most irritating experience of my life. It was a vicious blow from behind. It may, of course,

be said that observers from corps or higher headquarters made the reports, but it is a curious fact that the 1st Division had twice before been, and was many times afterward, relieved under like observation without any such reports. Almost at the end of the affair General Pershing passed my way, and apparently coming or having come to a just understanding of the matter, showed, for him, much impatience. 'Drop it,' he said, 'drop it; don't spend your time on it.' This satisfies me. Eventually there were signs that the reports 'boomeranged.'"[663]

1ST DIVISION PROCEEDS WEST

The first half of April 1918 was a busy time at Chaumont, tracking the location of the 1st Division en route west to assist the French forces and monitoring the 26th Division settling into the southern Woëvre front. General Tasker Bliss, American Representative to the Supreme War Council, communicated *Général* Foch's demands for information on the 1st Division to Colonel Conner at Chaumont. Was the 1st Division ready to go? Was the 1st Division under *Général* Foch's disposition? Did Pershing have another commander in mind since General Bullard was ill at the time? The response from Conner assured General Bliss that Bullard remained in command, the 1st Division was the most experienced combat division in the AEF and ready to fight, and that included war of movement. They could be applied anywhere Foch deemed necessary to help at this critical time. Pershing acknowledged receipt.[664] Under the best of circumstances moving AEF divisions in and out of a constricted sector under harassing shellfire would have been trying, and the 1st Division was in a hurry. To complicate matters, Edwards was already under suspicion at GHQ AEF for permitting casual discipline in his National Guard division and for criticising Pershing's staff.[665]

His experience of the movement of a 27,000-man division moved en masse from one sector to another proved invaluable to Marshall because in the coming months he would orchestrate two major offensives for the American Army – the St. Mihiel offensive in September followed by the largest American battle of the war at Meuse-Argonne in October. On 3 April the 1st Division was officially relieved by the 26th Division and the 2nd Infantry Brigade and divisional units moved south to the Gondrecourt training area. Commencing on the evening of 4 April and finishing by noon the next day fifty-seven trains were loaded and the 1st Division moved on. Motor transportation left in the direction of north-west Paris.[666] The 1st Division now transferred to the tactical command of the V^e armée. On 17 April the 1st Division moved north in stages where they resumed under the control of Ire armée and a new corps, 6e corps d'armée. The division assembled near Froissy and commenced preparation for Cantigny.[667]

On the morning of 16 April, General Pershing had a chance to meet with the 900 officers of the 1st Division two weeks after they had departed Seicheprey and the Ansauville sector. At a château courtyard north-west of Paris at Chaumont-en-Vexin, Pershing shared a few words about their mission. Bullard mentioned in his post-war writing that General Pershing's talk, "… was not oratory. He is not or at least was not then, an orator. He halted in his speech, after every few words saying 'eh, eh, eh.' But he had a message and he gave it."[668] Pershing post-war mused: "It was a source of real regret to me not to command the division in person and this coupled with the fact that its entry into the battle was of considerable moment led me to speak a word of confidence and encouragement … These splendid looking men, hardened by the strenuous work of the fall and by two months in winter trenches, fairly radiated the spirit of courage and gave promise that America's effort would prove her sons the equal of their forefathers."[669] His comments praised the American effort at assimilation: "You have now been on French soil ten months, and you have carried out a progressive system of instruction under varied circumstances. You have lived in billets according to the custom of European

armies; you have served in different sections of the trenches as a part of your training and have taken on a military complexion akin to that of our Allies. Officers of the Allies, in passing judgement upon your work, have expressed themselves as completely satisfied."[670]

Pershing then touched on leadership roles and responsibilities, addressing the officers: "I have every confidence in the 1st Division. You are about to enter this great battle of the greatest war in history, and in that battle you will represent the mightiest nation engaged … Centuries of military tradition and of military and civil history are now looking toward this first contingent of the American Army as it enters this great battle. You have behind you your own national traditions that should make you the finest soldiers in Europe to-day … We come from a nation that for one hundred and fifty years has stood before the world as the champion of the sacred principles of human liberty. We now return to Europe, the home of our ancestors, to help defend those same principles upon European soil … you are going to make a record of which your country will be proud."[671] He knew that the 1st Division was ready and that its morale was high. He was sure it would not fail him. When General Pershing finished, Major General Bullard said a few words, and the crowd of 900 officers dispersed.[672]

German observation noted increased traffic of American trucks and vehicles throughout the approaches to the sector, suggesting the rotation of units was underway. On 30 March, the day before Easter, **Res. I. R. 259** sent a patrol to the northern edge of *Bois de Remières* during the night and found both of the first American trenches unoccupied. From the American lines they brought out the bodies of two German soldiers, several rifles and a chest of rifle grenades.[673] As the relief was nearing completion the Germans shelled Beaumont on the ridge every 1½ hours from midnight on 3 April to 0700.[674] On 6 April 1918, the United States had been at war with the German Empire for exactly one year.

CHAPTER 11

Militia

Pershing's herculean efforts to establish a modern American army were made in the face of demands from his increasingly desperate European Allies for more manpower to flesh out divisions decimated by Operation Michael. Fresh manpower was indeed arriving, despite the U-boat menace, and heading to training areas. Pershing's Chaumont staff set standards they had established over their own careers, that American soldiers arriving in theatre were to conform to the discipline best exemplified by the proud traditions of West Point. Pershing nurtured his cadre of commanders to be in step with his goal of an American Army that would prove an equal to its battle-hardened Allies. When commanders did not meet his standards, Pershing had them dismissed. Such was the case when the first commander of the 1st Division, Major General Sibert, was replaced by Major General Robert Bullard. Bullard proved his worth throughout the war, successfully leading the 1st Division through the arduous first months in the line culminating in the first major battle between the Germans and Americans at Cantigny in May 1918. The relationship between Chaumont and Major General Edwards' 26th Division was not the same. The drama between the two consumed the attentions of many for the duration of the war.

At the time the 1st Division was experiencing their first major gas attack, on 26 February 1918 at *Bois de Remières*, the 26th Division brigaded with the 11ᵉ *corps d'armée* received a thorough inspection by Lieutenant Colonel M.A.W. Shockley of the Medical Corps. Shockley's report to Chaumont was supposed to review sanitation. Instead, he covered all aspects of operations at the front line. Shockley observed: "The first line fire trenches and support trenches were unsatisfactory as to position, protection, police and facilities for firing" – certainly not a medical assessment. Shockley expressed a serious concern that the Yankee Division militia were not up to the task – suggesting this was a contagion caught from the attitude of the French *armée* of 1917. He warned: "In general personnel of the 26th Division may receive some instruction as individuals while in the sector of the 11ᵉ *corps d'armée*, but they are receiving no training in the sense of teamwork and coordination. That the time spent in this sector as a divided organization is lost insofar as systematic training is concerned. That the command is losing considerably in the way of absorbing habits of sanitary regularity and carelessness as to military activity and morale: and in the suppression of the initiative and organization of positions and their desire for quiet along the front."[675]

Despite Shockley's assessment, the 102nd Infantry got along well with the French at Chemin-des-Dâmes and was developing a fighting spirit that made Colonel Parker feel very proud. The February German raid on Chavignon, where his men fought hand-to-hand and captured their first prisoner, put the fighting spirit of his regiment and division as a whole in a good light. There was a major German **Gasschuss** in the Chemin-des-Dâmes front on 16-17 March where over 30,000 gas shells were endured over a period of 24 hours. Parker thought that gas attack was particularly significant because it was the "new phosgene gas for which we had no mask that would give protection; steadiness in time of stress – that was the most marked quality of the outfit." Parker was proud to conclude that his Regiment had what it took. In fact he relished the French nickname for his 102nd Infantry: "*Le Régiment au Sourire*" (The Smiling Regiment).[676]

REPLACEMENTS

Many replacements had not received in-depth training. Military training back in the United States had tried to balance a successful introduction to the realities of positional war with the pressing need to replace losses. The US Army's Inspector General's Department decided that "the enlisted man can be trained for combat in 6 months."[677] Within the American Army General Staff, the Director of Operations Division and subordinate Operations Branch were responsible for "Recruitment, Mobilization, Overseas Priorities and Movement of Troops." The Personnel Branch handled officer issues (appointments, transfer and assignments) and conscientious objectors.[678]

Marshall recalled in 1957 that many of the American recruits received their rifles just before boarding the ship. As for in-depth and thorough training for the Western Front, some on board ship had had a look at a copy of a recently published booklet on trench warfare, borrowed from a British officer.[679]

The 26th Division started to see a sprinkling of Americans from the rest of the country enter their ranks. The senior National Guard officer billets had mostly been filled by GHQ

AEF assignments. Vacancies at the lower ranks now were being filled with volunteers and drafted men. In April 1918 the majority of new faces showing up at the 26th Division sector were from the Midwest. None of the soldiers reporting to the 104th Infantry had ever served at the front. Some replacements had been in service less than a month – knowing nothing about soldiery, not to mention the realities of trench warfare. Many were assigned to artillery but were reassigned to infantry when they arrived to quickly fill gaps. Guns, gas masks and operations were totally foreign. A sergeant in the 104th Infantry remembered one replacement staring at his rifle and cartridges in a puzzled and depressed manner. Four weeks prior to showing up at the front line he was a clerk back home and now was learning to defend himself and kill the enemy. Most soldiers had little time for a novice, even if it meant he could be of some value should combat commence. Teamwork came with training and experience.

GERMAN LEADERSHIP ATTENDS TO THE QUIET SECTOR

General der Artillerie von Gallwitz recalled that in the weeks after Operation Michael had commenced, the conflict in the West smouldered on without particular success. In certain positions there was heavy fighting, most particularly south-east of Amiens. German divisions were suffering great losses. Von Gallwitz let his concerns on the situation be known to **OHL** through **General der Infanterie** Ludendorff's assistant **Major** Wetzel; that the offensive should not become a stalemate at Amiens, putting at risk strength elsewhere on the Western Front. **OHL** proceeded to brief the commanders on 3 April that forty-one English and eighteen French divisions were used up. **OHL** lessons learned from Operation Michael reflected von Gallwitz's opinion. The prevailing intention was to mass forces for the attack with devastating artillery. Annihilation of main points of the line as opposed to rolling barrages was the preferred strategy. **General der Artillerie** von Gallwitz also advocated that divisional commanders exercise more leadership in their sectors. He made it clear that they were to spend more time at the front with their troops.[680]

General der Infanterie Max Paul Otto Hofmann, **XXXVIII. Reservekorps** commander, working from **Gruppe Gorz** called von Stolzmann with the order to prepare a major operation against the Americans in front of its right wing and centre (Seicheprey and *Bois de Remières*) as quickly as possible. German military leadership at **Gruppe Gorz** desired captured sections to be held for the purpose of "keeping enemy forces effectively in check." **78. R. D.** was to report its plans as soon as possible, providing an estimate of at what level **78. R. D.** could engage the Americans with an appropriate mix of artillery, **Minenwerfer,** and other weapons and set a date for the operation. Planning for a two regiment **Erstürmung** under the codename **Kirschblüte** [Cherry Blossom] was underway.[681]

RES. I. R. 258 CONDUCTS A RAID

Obertsleutnant Elsner, **Res. I. R. 258** commander, was restless. His **Res. I. R. 259** counterparts had clearly demonstrated the proper spirit with **Einladung** and it was time **Res. I. R. 258** was cast in the same light. Aggressive operations meant keeping the Allies in the Woëvre occupied and uncertain while the ongoing major offensives to the north continued. Raids were viewed as effective and the **78. R. B.** requested each regiment to look at opportunities to execute more across the sector. Elsner's battalion commander in Lahayville, **Hauptman** d. L. Menzel, requested approval to execute a raid against the Americans at **Alpha Wäldchen**, which was given by **Obertsleutnant** Elsner. **Res. I. R. 258** commenced planning the raid codenamed **Schnepfenstrich** [Snipe flight] for 14 April at dawn. **Leutnant** Obermüller's **III. Bataillon** and **Leutnant** Keun's **I.** and **II. Bataillons** were to comprise the strike force. A reserve unit under the command of **Leutnant** Wagner was to remain at Pannes to the north. **Schnepfenstrich** planning continued until

the day before execution, when von Stolzmann arrived to view the training and advised Elsner to delay the raid so as to combine it with the **Kirschblüte Erstürmung**.[682]

1.Kompagnie, (1./258) and **MG Komp. 1**, reported that two officers and twenty-eight volunteers went on patrol at 0100 of 5 April south of Richecourt. A back-up sixteen-man unit led by **Leutnant** Gunther and **Leutnant** Schmitgen proceeded into the position 1 area through a sap. They found a tunnel with kitchen rations containing a case of corned beef and rifle ammunition scattered about. The patrol could hear Americans nearby talking and coughing. Just then eight Americans rounded a traverse, apparently heading out on patrol. Close combat ensued. **Leutnant** Gunther, **Leutnant** Schmitgen, and **Vizefeldwebel** Dalheim sprang into the trench and finished off several Americans. Shots rang out and German and American hand grenades were thrown. Now the remaining Americans in the trench area came into the fight. More grenades were thrown over the parapet and parados. **Leutnant** Gunther was wounded in both knees and hands with splinters from grenade explosions. **Leutnant** Schmitgen was severely wounded in the abdomen and chest and was carried out of the trench by his soldiers, despite heavy fire from the Americans. **Vizefeldwebel** Dalheim was last seen chasing an American around a traverse. He did not return, suggesting he was either killed or captured. **Unteroffizier** Stieglitz fought bravely hand-to-hand and was wounded by a shot to the chest. The Germans were not able to retrieve him. Another three men were wounded. By 0230, the raiding party had withdrawn back to German lines. It was a reminder that venturing into enemy territory was not without cost.[683] German artillery during this raid fired eighty-two 77mm rounds, 100 105mm rounds, and twenty-four 150mm rounds.[684]

That same night Private 1st Class Leslie M. Lane, Company C, 102nd Infantry, happened to be carrying rations to the men in the front trenches near *Bois de Remières* when he encountered another German patrol. They quickly demanded his surrender but Lane refused, drew his pistol, and shot the patrol's leader. **Handgranaten** then flew and Lane was severely wounded. The German patrol returned to their lines. Lane was soon rescued by his colleagues and the mission of the advanced listening post continued.[685]

NEGLIGIBLE HOMICIDE

The bombardment had consequences concerning the infantry's trust of the artillery. In sector H west of Seicheprey shells rained in for an hour falling at the rate of 6 per minute early that morning. Major Rau recalled the front line wire being "blown to Hell". What angered Rau was that no one in the sector had called for artillery support. No six-star red

rockets were fired. However, several six-star white rockets were fired to get the artillery to increase their range. Telephone and blinker were used to urge range extension or ceasefire. Rau forwarded the report with pieces of shell found in the *abris*, including a piece taken from the body of one of three men killed by the round. Major Rau's assessment was the shell fragment was from a 155mm and the size of the shell holes created were 2 metres across and 1 metre deep, suggesting a howitzer. In addition to the three dead, Rau listed the remaining casualties as five wounded (one seriously) and three shell shocked. Rau's memo was passionate :

> The action of the artillery is inexplanable [sic] and cannot be understood by me or by any of my officers. This has done more to injur[e] the morale and fighting spirit of this Battalion than any other thing imaginable could have done. The men have the bitterest animosity against the artillery and since the affair of the Chemin des Dames and this affair, have lost all confidence in it and it will require a great deal of training and discipline before this particular company can be used in an attack against the

The Sallies of Ansauville serving the soldiers with a smile: Gladys and Irene McIntyre, Stella Young and Myrtle Turkington. (*Pictorial History of the 26th Division United States Army*)

Boche under our own artillery fire ... My feelings in this matter at the present time are beyond description. The matter of investigation and punishment suggested, I am leaving entirely to the Commanding Officer. In my mind this is negligible hom[i]cide.

Any response to this was not included in the files. Ten days later Rau's men went through a similar "Hell". [686]

A TON OF BRICKS

On 10 April German harassment fire hit both regimental and 51st Infantry Brigade PCs at Ansauville. [687] The shots shocked the prevailing calm in the area. The 102nd Infantry PC was located just behind the church. No one had considered operating there from below ground. Ansauville was considered quiet – not having been shelled for twenty months – even when the 1st Division PC was installed there in March. When the 26th Division occupied their portion of the southern Woëvre front, the Germans commenced registering on the Ménil-la-Tour road fork just outside the town. That evening, Colonel Locke, 102nd Field Artillery commander, was talking by telephone with Brigadier General Lassiter when a dull boom was quickly followed by the shriek of the shell and the explosion. "A ton of bricks must have fallen on Locke," General Lassiter is said to have remarked. The shell bounced off the reverse slope of the PC roof blowing tiles and plaster upon him. A second shell struck in the yard adjoining the 102nd Infantry's PC. The third round hit General Traub's room, spurring his move to a château known as l'Hermitage. [688] Memories of l'Hermitage were not favourable. It was surrounded by swamps, particularly in the winter months and early spring when the rains were incessant. Duckboards covered the ground but Salvation Army visitors recalled, "a single misstep might send one prone in the ooze up to the elbows. It was a very dangerous place." [689]

SALLIES

Ansauville was a well-remembered entry or departure point at the Woëvre. Troops could get a welcome cup of coffee or cocoa from the Salvation Army sisters Irene and Gladys and their helpers. Soon the soldiers were able to grab a doughnut or pie. Having marched for hours and without a warm meal it was a joy for the soldiers to come across the "Sallies." Private 1st Class Cyril Finnegan, a medic with the 102nd Field Hospital, wrote home on 24 April: "Remember when the Salvation Army use to play throw a nickel on the Drum in the square at Dover. How we used to laugh at them and how all the drunks would join and when they got sober drop out. Well when I go up to their hut I think differently of them. They are trying mighty hard to do all they can to make it pleasant for the Boys. Pies & doughnuts and cocoa are sold there each night and the place is crowded." [690] Private Chamberlin, 102nd Machine Gun Battalion, noted: "Saw two Ladies in Y.M.C.A., and more in Salvation Army. Real Americans, and the first seen in France!" [691]

General Edwards did everything he could to ensure the Sallies' safety and comfort. Military authorities recognized Ansauville was not a safe sector – subject to HE artillery fire and **Gasschuss**. The idea of American Sallies taking such unnecessary risks did not seem justifiable, so a wooden hut was set up at Mandres. The initial accommodation was spartan, but lumber was hauled from 100 kilometres away, and with the help of the soldiers the hut was made comfortable for all. The Sallies, as well as the men who frequented the hut, were still at risk. Once a barrage in the area partially destroyed the hut, scattering the supplies within and ruining the Victrola. The Salvation Army found an old wine cellar under a partially destroyed building. Everyone lent a hand and tables and benches were put in place and a range was placed within. [692] L'Hermitage became the final location for the Salvation Army during this time at the Toul sector. It was also risky because ammunition dumps were nearby. One salvo struck one site and set off 14 hours of exploding shells. The Sallies were ordered to the safety of their billets while the munitions exploded.[693]

Private Wunderlich spoke for the rest of the division: "I want to stop and say a word about the splendid work of the Salvation Army overseas. 'Oh, we don't say much about what we do – we do it.' The Salvationists have made a hit with the Yanks who have been up and in action. If there's any place in these United States where the Salvation Army needs assistance, the Yanks will help put them on their feet. The Salvationists gave to us and gave freely. If there was a charge for anything, it was always reasonable. If we had the money we got it; if we didn't, we got it just the same. 'The money you give us, boys, we simply put into other things for you,' was the way the Salvation Army man explained it. If they were passing around smokes, they didn't say 'Have a cigarette,' it was, 'Here's A PACK of cigarettes for you, Buddy.'"[694]

STUBBY

Stubby, a bull terrier, was one of the few celebrities of the Seicheprey affair. In 1917, Corporal J. Robert Conroy found a young pit bull terrier near his National Guard training post at New Haven, Connecticut and named him "Stubby". It was the start of an amazing relationship. Conroy, through adept manoeuvres, was able to smuggle Stubby onboard the troop transport heading to France. Prior to Seicheprey the Stubby legend commenced with the dog being credited with capturing a German soldier near the American trenches at Chemin-des-Dâmes. Conroy was assigned to Headquarters Company, 102nd Regiment, at Beaumont, where Stubby had the run of the place. He tended to become excitable, running, barking, and howling in an ill-fitting gas mask while artillery barrages hit Beaumont. Stubby became adept at providing advance warning to the troops in the shelter as gas rounds struck nearby. His legend grew every day while he was at the front despite the fact that in the entire war record of the 26th Division and the 102nd Infantry there was never one mention of Stubby. Through the astute manipulation of the media and subsequent senior contacts post-Armistice, Robert Conroy created a legend that generated an unparalleled affection.

Stubby. (Smithsonian Institution)

"NOTHING BUT WATER AND RATS"

26th Division continued the operations tempo of the 1st Division. The 102nd Infantry patrols north of Seicheprey and *Bois de Remières* were able to penetrate as far as the German second line. *Res. I. R 259* soldiers were found to be always busy at night on construction work, especially near Lahayville and St. Baussant. Heavy metal work in progress was always heard from narrow-gauge trains, trucks, and wagons. Talking, singings and music also drifted south from the German lines. Toward the latter part of the 102nd Infantry's time near Seicheprey and *Bois de Remières* a few soldiers ventured into the old trench networks, crawling about even in daytime without being spotted. These excursions into the front did not yield a prisoner. The Germans were in the second and third lines. When they did venture forth, it was on a definite mission – thoroughly planned and usually well executed.

Even in comparison with their torrid experience at Chemin-des-Dâmes, the 102nd Infantry occupying Seicheprey discovered the German artillery was far more active. The combination of HE and **Gasgranaten** struck like "a volley of thunderbolts" throughout the time they spent in the sector. Discipline and vigilance was required at all times in Position 1. Smoke from a cooking fire drew the attention of observers from the front lines and Montsec, drawing immediate artillery fire. "It sure is hell at times with the artillery banging away all day long and night the same way."[695]

For soldiers heading into Seicheprey, one stop made was at the *abris* supporting Betsy the Sniper. They took a moment to relax, drink coffee, eat meals, and talk about artillery support. The 102nd Infantry was grateful for what that howitzer meant, heard firing through the night. The 94th Aero Squadron frequently flew over and performed aerobatics in recognition of Betsy's silencing of German anti-aircraft guns.[696] In forward areas soldiers ran to the kitchen for each meal and ran back dodging shellfire each way. Enoch Doble of the Sanitary unit supporting the 102nd Machine Gun Battalion recalled leaving with his Red Cross colleagues carrying mess kits and cups to a large, broken-down building in Seicheprey where a kitchen operated behind high walls. Doble's kitchen in Seicheprey offered more protection than *Bois du Jury* where simple shelters provided the mess. German **Drachen** were in a circle to the north of Seicheprey salient. Doble remembered: "We were eating our breakfast in relaxation after the all-day drive and night marching when a shell tore through a corner wall above our heads and out the other side wall across the room. We were ordered back to our own dugout. There was stray firing all day long; it never let up." The Germans were registering their fire with every salvo. To the discomfort of the troops settling for the night, the artillery increased in intensity. In the dugouts, "The walls shook with each explosion and dirt and dust would drop down on our heads and shoulders. We were allowed no lights at all at night."[697]

On 2 April a battalion of the 102nd Infantry relieved a battalion of the 18th Infantry and inherited a 1st Division problem. They now acquired twenty-four "general prisoners" on front-line duties as labourers filling new shell holes and taking food rations for every meal to the soldiers in the forward machine-gun positions.[698] The men were convicted of various offences in summary and special courts. What disgusted the inbound 26th Division staff was that the prisoner service records and trial papers were missing. They were lacking appropriate clothing for duty on the front line and other suitable equipment. No provision had been made for their custody, transfer, or other care.[699]

Private Enoch Doble remembered Major Rau's headquarters in the village being a target for snipers, trying to "ping" the guard outside. The kitchen was a favourite place until one day at lunchtime three shells crashed the walls in. The dugouts were nothing but heaps of stones providing little protection and little comfort. Doble left his bunker near the Seine cemetery on the north-east side of Seicheprey and found three 28th Infantry disciplinary prisoners under guard, digging a new grave. Doble learned that the detail had been distributing food to the various machine-gun positions before daylight when, turning a corner, they came upon a patrol of three Germans. The 1st Division corporal guarding the prisoners pushed his group into a large shell hole. While climbing up to peek out, the guard came face to face with a German corporal crawling on his hands and knees to the edge of the hole. Each pulled a gun but the American's automatic was quicker. Doble saw the German's body was on the stretcher. The guard tasked Doble to search the remains – the corpse had a line of bullet holes in his face and neck. Doble noticed the dead man was young and handsome. He removed the helmet and searched the pockets, finding pictures of a young pretty wife holding a blonde curly haired baby in her arms. A lock of blonde hair was stuffed behind the picture. As Doble helped the prisoners lower the German soldier into the newly dug grave, he struggled to keep from breaking down.[700]

Major Chaffee from the 1st Battalion, 103rd Field Artillery, was billeted in a large house at Mandres. "On a quiet Sunday morning the blessed Brigadier [Lassiter] comes out and takes a Battalion Commander up into the luxury of his limousine and drives about. He stresses the importance and extent of the additional front assigned. And the Commander says, 'Yes sir, you ask results and then have ordered one of my best battery commanders to General Staff.' And the loyal Brigadier says he'll see – and Barker stays."[701]

Private Washburn, 101st Field Artillery, recalled the weather for the first ten days in the Seicheprey area was cloudy and rainy. Most of his spare time was spent indoors as opposed to being forced to contend with the elements. A French battery of 75s was about a hundred metres west of Washburn's position. He remembered a typical example of French *sang froid* as shells hit the area: "It was a constant source of amusement to watch these Frenchmen playing soccer within four thousand yards of the lines, as unconcernedly as if they were in Paris. One day the *Boches* started shelling their battery at a critical point in the game. As the first shell landed, the game ceased and the men disappeared, leaving the ball alone upon the field. In about twenty minutes, when the shelling had stopped, they returned, resuming the game as if nothing more serious than a thunderstorm had caused the delay."[702] Private Wunderlich, 101st Engineers, described his life on the Beaumont Ridge:

While we were living like rats down in these holes, the boys used to sneak up into Beaumont to shoot craps. The fellows seemed to be extremely fond of this game. It offered a little excitement during the leisure hours. The stakes were never very high, but at that, sometimes some of the boys would lose all they had left

right after payday. That wasn't very much, of course, after insurance and allotments had been taken out. Up on the front a fellow didn't have much use for money, anyway, and no soldier would let a comrade suffer needlessly. General Edwards was a good sport in so far as our little games were concerned. He used to say: 'Let the boys gamble among themselves if they want to. The money stays in the company, and it is a whole lot better for them to amuse themselves shooting the craps than to booze. The fellow who loses gambling may win fighting, but the fellow who boozes doesn't stand much chance.'[703]

In the early morning of April 6 the batteries laid down a barrage called in by the infantry, which resulted in the repulse of a small raiding party; this time the signals and telephone worked perfectly.[704] Telephone communication was critical for effective operations and required constant attention. Those that served the lines were given respect. One soldier remembered: "I have seen telephone men out working on the lines under the heaviest possible shell-fire. They go right ahead splicing their wires and reestablishing communication with the other units, regardless of personal danger. If a man is hit, another comes out and finishes the job. They don't fight; they make it possible for others to fire the guns. They just stand and 'take it,' with no chance to get back at the enemy. A telephone man at the front is 'game' clean through."[705]

For Corporal Rogers of the 101st Field Artillery heading north to the Beaumont Ridge from Mandres, the devastation at Dead Man's Curve was in evidence. On one side of the road he saw a dead horse still attached to a cart. On the other side an ambulance was turned over on its side. As he proceeded, incoming artillery rounds recommenced. Two infantrymen came running up the road and stopped by him. "Got a cigarette, Buddy?" one asked. "Sure. Where you from?" Rogers inquired. "Seicheprey, and it is one nasty little place. Nothing but water and rats."[706]

CHAPTER 12

"Daddy" and "Machine Gun"

Seicheprey was the defining moment for two American soldiers who were major influences on the US Army prior to the American declaration of war on Germany.

Clarence Ransom Edwards was the 3,020th graduate of West Point in 1883, the 52nd graduate in a class of fifty-two cadets. As Major General Harbord stated in his eulogy on General Edwards, "He was tall, slender and erect, a splendid horseman, handy with his fists, a good shot, a good dancer, a handsome and soldierly young officer."[707] He had a remarkable career, from the Philippines where he earned three Silver Star citations, then joining William Howard Taft as an advisor. It was his association with Taft that shaped his later career as a general officer. He made rank ahead of peers and became Chief of the Office of Insular Affairs. Returning to the United States, Edwards worked in Washington DC as military advisor to President Taft – a position that suggested he was on track to assume the sought-after position of chief of staff of the US Army. Edwards acquired military command along the Mexican border, Hawaii and the Panama Canal Zone. When the US entered the war, Clarence Edwards became a Major General and assumed command of the department of the North-East, responsible for military development in New England. In 1917 Edwards reconstituted the New England National Guard into the 26th Division. It was

a major challenge, for New England boasted the greatest legacy of any militia in the nation – the longest serving force anywhere in the United States.

Edwards' relations with French leadership were attentive to military decorum. He was deferential to *Général* Passaga throughout the entire time they were at the southern Woëvre front. His manner of communication was distinctive: "If I may be so bold, in view of what I understood was our common mind on the general principles, this is not the kind of a plan that appeals to me to meet the general principle of defense or the present emergency." He tagged reinforcing subordinate clauses to every utterance.[708]

Despite such circumlocutions, Edwards was remembered as a blunt, matter-of-fact soldier with no tact. He spoke his mind immediately – a trait that endeared him to his soldiers but quickly alienated him from the seniors at Chaumont. As if to counter Malin Craig's assertions of neglect, Edwards constantly visited the front lines, speaking to his men, getting to know them, getting to like them. He was called the "Old Man" by some, "Daddy" by others – but never to his face. A real affection developed over the time he commanded the Yankee Division.[709] Edwards was determined to put an *esprit de corps*, a "soul" into his Division. General Edwards was a strict disciplinarian who looked after his men

A rare photo of President Taft and family with his military advisor Brigadier General Edwards. The man on the left is unidentfied. (Tom and Joanne Wallace Collection)

and those who supported his division. He used to come by Balloon Company 2 when the men were eating chow. Edwards told the soldiers, "At ease, don't get up men! Are you getting enough to eat?" and leave without requiring the standing to attention or the salute. One private remembered, "Our Lieutenants could have taken lessons from him."[710] When the sweetheart of the AEF, Elsie Janis, arrived with her mother to provide song and dance performances, Edwards and his staff played the perfect hosts, providing tours and allowing Elsie to meet as many soldiers near the front as possible, and letting her fire an artillery round at the Germans. At one concert at Boucq, Edwards came and stood with his men, never once taking his chair.[711] As one private exclaimed, "Medals of honor? We didn't need them. Who could yearn for decorations knowing that his general held such an opinion of his men and had told the world about it?"[712]

Edwards made his men the priority when dealing with other seniors. *Commandant* Alain du Boisrouvray, French Military Mission's liaison to the 26th Division, recalled a conversation with Edwards while the Division was at the Chemin-des-Dâmes. "My men are tired having spent five weeks in the trenches. They have patrolled, they have been subjected to bombardment, they had experienced gas. It is time to have them sent to the rear. You helped us get to the front line. Help us leave." Du Boisrouvray went to *Général* de Maud'huy with Edwards' request: "My general, the Americans want rest." De Maud'huy was smoking furiously and answered, "Are they in the war or are they not?" *Commandant* du Boisrouvray replied: "If the German offensive occurs here, the state that the Americans are in will not allow the enemy to be stopped. They will not fail in America to accuse the French of having sacrificed their allies!" *Général* de Maud'huy thoughtfully puffed on his pipe and assumed a pensive air. The 26th Division was allowed to depart the front line on 18 February.[713]

Major General Edwards' care for his soldiers was exemplified by a "Confidential and Personal Talk" letter to all commanders, particularly aimed at the company commanders. He started off with:

Our conditions of service and occupation of this sector in view of what we have gone through, have given me much concern. It goes without saying that my sympathies are with the soldier, especially those in the mud. On account of the excellent spirit of this division and the battle conditions that we have faced, men in the advanced positions keep themselves on the alert, even sometimes when it is not necessary, during the night. They do not get enough rest.

After a while body and soul must succumb. These same conditions obtained with our Allies at the commencement of the war, and we are going through this practical experience. Officers and men must get rest, and conditions are bettering and settling down … My desire is to get these men deloused, cleaned up, and let them sleep and restore nature … The principle to have in mind is that of the tired housewife who under no condition can let the house become filthy or the dishes go unwashed. Some captains and battalion commanders do let such conditions obtain … The duty, therefore, of the organization commanders is by example and effort to keep up this sanitation and spirit, being jealous as they should to give the recuperative rest that is necessary for this command.

Major General Clarence Ransom Edwards. (USMA Archives)

His soldiers believed in him and appreciated what he did for them. He put the burden of responsibility on his junior officers. "Their constant and daily duty should be that of a kind and earnest father of a family in the protection and care of that family, at the same time insisting upon every member of it performing his proper function to do his part for the whole. As I have so often said, all that is necessary for an officer with the soldier is to show him and prove to him that you are absolutely interested in him and that you are trying to be fair, make your demands, and he will forgive you even your errors. I demand this and I demand cleanliness of person, equipment, billet, trench, and cantonment … Don't let me ever hear again from a soldier that he has asked his supply sergeant many times for clothes and cannot get them. If the fault is the company commander's after this talk I will hold him accountable."[714] Daddy had spoken.

Edwards' enemies in the service petrified his image for the remainder of the 20th century. Brigadier General Craig's last comments to General Drum regarding Edwards summed up General Liggett's apprehension when dealing with the man: "General Edwards was recommended to General Liggett for relief from duty with his division. General Liggett was in accord with the views of those making

the recommendation but invariably refused to take action because he considered his position as temporary and he further believed that the action should be taken by higher authority. He also laid great stress on the fact that the 26th Division, almost to a man, was intensely loyal to the Division Commander."[715]

Samuel Johnson Woolf, the American portraitist serving as a special correspondent with the AEF, recalled meeting with General Edwards in his retirement home in Dedham, Massachusetts. Woolf observed that it was Edwards' fatherly solicitude for his "boys" that endeared him to 26th Division veterans. Edwards talked of his time with Calvin Coolidge while campaigning for governor of Massachusetts. Coolidge recognized Edwards' popularity in the New England region was a plus for his campaign. Edwards liked to call the famously reserved politician who eventually became the thirtieth president of the United States "chatterbox." At the end of one trip Edwards noticed Coolidge's wife looking bored. Edwards said, "What's the matter, has the Governor been talking you to death?" Governor Coolidge coolly replied, 'Well, General, the things I don't say never get me into trouble."[716] Brigadier General Sherburne remembered General Edwards telling him "when he graduated from West Point he rated 80% of his class as of the finest type of men and only 20% as S.O.B.'s … after forty-five years of active service he had exactly reversed his percentages."[717]

General Pershing summed up his view of Major General Edwards in a post-war pencilled note, one that reflected Pershing's true feelings without the restraint of potential political backlash:

> A thoroughly conceited man with little ability to base it on. In no sense a loyal subordinate, and hence does not inspire that quality in others. Ambitious, but not willing to obtain advancement by merit. A politician on principle; was so as a cadet. Opposes every order and undertakes to win popularity by assuming to know more than those above him and sides with his subordinates in any attitude they display of being imposed upon. Never should have been given a division. Spoiled one of the best ones we had.[718]

Despite Pershing's statement, the soldiers of the 26th Division cherished Edwards for the remainder of his life. A more accurate assessment came from Major General Harbord: "It was perhaps because Edwards loved his men so well that they loved him; he knew thousands of them personally; commanded them in a very human way; was approachable at all times; was solicitous for their welfare and for their rights. He knew human nature and he knew soldiers."[719]

MACHINE GUN

Brigadier General (rank awarded upon retirement) John Henry "Machine Gun" Parker was born on a farm near Tipton, Missouri and graduated as the 3,498th cadet from West Point, class of 1892. His initial fame during the Spanish-American War earned him the tag "Gatling Gun Parker."[720] In the advance on Santiago Parker proposed to take one of the two Gatling guns which the Americans had with them and fire over the heads of the front line to check the Spanish reserves. It was an amazingly innovative application of an evolving weapon system. Parker's idea was executed – a stream of bullets went over the heads and far beyond the advancing American line and successfully kept back the enemy from reinforcing their front line.[721] Years later, Bullard reflected on Parker's accomplishment: "In the Spanish-American War at the Battle of Santiago, Parker demonstrated to the military world, for the first time, the value of the machine gun which, although existent long before that war, had never been understood or demonstrated as a valuable weapon. You know how the World War proved it. Parker's mind and conception had run far ahead of the advanced military minds of the world."[722]

In 1903 Captain John H. Parker was assigned to Fort Leavenworth, Kansas and organized a "model unit of machine guns," the precursor of the machine-gun company – further demonstrating what machine guns could do. Parker wrote several books that caught the public's attention on this and other military subjects that reflected a broad and deep intellectual capacity. His first book, *The Gatlings at Santiago*, put Parker in the limelight both within the US Army and the public at large. His next works, *Tactical Organization and Uses of Machine Guns in the Field* and *Citizen Soldiers* both addressed significant applications of modern weapons as well as innovative roles for the evolving modern US Army. Parker reflected later in life that his *Tactical Organization and Uses of Machine Guns*, met the test of time at Château-Thierry: "Never in all the history of the military art has any text been so perfectly vindicated as that little book, though it was 20 years before its vindication came."[723] Parker knew he had a good idea and kept badgering seniors

General John Henry Parker, D.S.C.

[10]

Yankee Doings commemorates the beloved 102nd Regimental Commander, Brigadier General John Henry Parker. (*Yankee Doings*)

initial crew of experts that arrived in France with Pershing providing guidance on how machine guns were to be employed by follow-on US Army forces through the automatic weapons schools that established and ran at Gondrecourt and Langres.[725] As the director, Lieutenant Colonel Parker conducted a tour of a French training centre for automatic weapons that summer. In his report Parker announced, "We are both convinced … the day of the rifleman is done. He was a good horse while he lasted, but his day is over … The rifleman is passing out and the bayonet is fast becoming as obsolete as the crossbow." The report was not well received at Chaumont. Lieutenant Colonel Paul B. Malone, heading GHQ AEF's training section, scribbled on his copy of Parker's note, "speak for yourself, John."[726] Parker mused, "Personally, I prefer the use of machine guns which gives them a chance to come out alive to the one that practically insures the death of more than 50 per cent and loss of one-half the guns. I believe in first line machine gun work when it is necessary, and use it when it is necessary. It was necessary at Seicheprey. It was used at Seicheprey. It was necessary at *Bois de Remières*, and was used at *Bois de Remières*."[727]

and superiors, including President Theodore Roosevelt, with recommendations to create a machine-gun corps with himself as its brigadier general. His manner and self-promotion infuriated Major General J. Franklin Bell. "He's a pestiferous, immodest ass," Bell wrote to the assistant secretary of war, "but has much ability notwithstanding and his disagreeable qualities must simply be tolerated for the sake of his usefulness." Bell did allow Parker to continue work, this time with Company A, 20th Infantry, to experiment further with the role of machine guns. Parker's work continued to be valued, but his recommendations for a separate branch beyond infantry and cavalry was dismissed.[724]

Pershing knew Parker. Parker served Pershing during the Mexican expedition against Pancho Villa. The two were talking one evening in January 1917 when Parker predicted Pershing was to become either chief of staff or commander of an expedition to France. Pershing was taken aback, as if he hadn't seen it coming. Four months later, Pershing was organising his command and soldiers for France. Parker became part of the

Parker knew almost all of the Chaumont staff. Once Captain George Patton drove him north to observe British operations. When they were returning from the visit, Patton accidently drove into a railroad gate and received a serious gash to the head. Parker bandaged Patton and took him to a nearby hospital. Later that month the two linked up again when the newly promoted Major Patton was visiting Parker's machine-gun school. Patton recalled Parker "insisted on calling me major."[728]

Colonel Parker had a remarkable family. His wife served with him in the Philippines and was instrumental in establishing schools for the natives in areas that were considered hostile. His son, Captain Henry Burr Parker, a non-graduating member of West Point, class of 1914, was in theatre at the same time but assigned to the 3rd Field Artillery.[729] The two managed to link up when Parker ran the automatic weapons school. Henry Burr Parker also served as an aerial observer while assigned as an artilleryman flying with four different *escadrilles* and two Aero Squadrons. On two occasions he was shot down and survived.[730]

On 13 January 1918, Parker received a phone call directing him to report to General Harbord, Chief of Staff. Parker was teaching the "Suicide Club," members learning to become machine-gun operators. He opined that the school was the first for training machine-gun operators in the world and it made the success of American arms possible. On that day Parker became an adopted son of the "Old Nutmeg State." Harbord told Parker that the 102nd Infantry was in bad shape.

Edwards post-war on parade.

The 26th Division was going into the front line and something had to be done quickly. All the 102nd field officers had been relieved and sent to other duties. "Someone must put a soul into that outfit, and General Pershing has personally selected you as the man he believes best fitted to do it."[731] Parker replied, "Say to General Pershing that no officer trained as I have could possibly refuse such an assignment. I will do my best to make good on the new job." Harbord concluded the discussion with, "That is exactly what General Pershing expected you to say. Now I shall try to repeat his exact words … Tell Colonel Parker there will be a pair of stars hung up on the Chemin des Dames for him. Tell him to go and get them!"[732]

Two weeks after Parker talked with Harbord, he met General Edwards. An air of paranoia hung over the meeting. Edwards was reserved. "I understand you are sent by General Pershing?" "Yes, General, I was so informed." "Great friend of yours?" "I have served on his staff twice, General; but do not claim to be at all intimate with him. On the contrary, our relations have usually been strictly formal and official. Of course I admire him greatly." "Know Chaumont pretty well, I suppose?" "No General; never was stationed there." "But you know all that group at Chaumont, of course. Did you hear any comment about me there, any indication that I might be relieved of command of the 26th Division?" "My assignment is to take command of a regiment in your Division, General. I have heard no gossip, and would not listen to it if I did. I expect to give you all the loyalty due to my Division Commander, just as I was loyal to Pershing while I served on his staff, and to do the very best I can for the regiment." The exchange assuaged Edwards' fears, who responded with, "I know you John Henry, and am glad to have you in my command. I shall remember what you have said. Can you, in addition to your other duties, help train the machine guns of the Division?"[733]

Colonel Parker loved to banter with *commandant* du Boisrouvray, who later described the man as "unusually tall, shoulders too wide for his size with a small round head … with a short nose and a round chin. He looked like a gigantic Buffalo Bill. He claimed to speak fluent French, Spanish and English – a fact that was somewhat true because he would consistently mix the three languages into one sentence."[734] One evening at Chemin-des-Dâmes Colonel Parker called du Boisrouvray to his headquarters: "Boar-Rouvray, my friend, I found a way to end the war." Du Boisrouvray was puzzled. "Yes," Parker continued, "simply change the spirit, take the offensive spirit of the Crusades … the spirit of Joan of Arc!" In a quiet voice he stated, "Do you know Mademoiselle St. Paul?" Du Boisrouvray replied that he had "heard about her. Parker trumpeted, "Well, here is the new Joan of Arc! It is mademoiselle St. Paul!" Parker met her at Soissons wearing a nurse's uniform that prominently displayed a red cross. Du Boisrouvray said John Henry Parker always saw the big picture![735]

Parker commanded the 102nd Infantry, the regiment he fondly called his "Nutmegs." Parker was in his element at Beaumont. He was very energetic. In every phone call he received, he proudly answered "Headquarters Division." Parker was quick to explain the array of machine gun deployments on the map. "Machine guns everywhere! More Germans nowhere!"[736]

Parker's regimental commander counterparts serving in the 1st Division mostly achieved what Major General Harbord predicted. Colonel John Hines was promoted to Major General and served as 4th Division commander that August, eventually commanding III Corps at the time of the Armistice. Colonel Frank Parker, 18th Infantry, was also promoted to Major General and became the 1st Division commander that led the division's final move towards Sedan during the last days of the war. Colonel Hanson Ely, 28th Infantry, later commanded 5th Division at Meuse-Argonne. Colonel Hamilton Smith from the 26th Infantry led his troops in battle at Soissons that summer and was killed by machine-gun fire. Parker's potential to achieve higher command was not hampered by lack of courage. General Edwards cited Parker twelve times in division orders for distinguished conduct in battle.[737] John Henry Parker was the recipient of no fewer than four Distinguished Service Crosses while serving as 102nd Infantry commander – more than any soldier in the history of the US Army – a measure of the man.

Two General Officer comrades-in-arms reunite after the war. (Boston Public Library)

CHAPTER 13

"Appendicitis" at Apremont and the *Bois-Brûlé* Sector

The *Bois-Brûlé* ridge was the cornerstone of the entire German defence in the sector and was held at all costs.[738] Colonel George Shelton's 104th Infantry relieved the *33ᵉ régiment d'infanterie coloniale* to allow the French to reinforce ongoing Allied efforts against Operation Michael. The 104th Infantry extended American responsibility for the front line to 18 kilometres with the 3rd Battalion occupying the front lines at the high ground of *Bois-Brûlé* facing the German-held village of Apremont. The *poilus* told the Americans that *Bois-Brûlé* and Apremont sector was known as "The Post of Honour" and had to be held.[739] Fighting over this portion of the southern Woëvre front over the years was intense. No Man's Land covered only 100 metres. One trench led directly into German lines and was only separated by sand bags.[740]

General der Infanterie Auler's **5. Ldw.Div.** knew the ground the 104th Infantry occupied intimately. On 20 March they conducted a major operation entitled "**Ruhekopf** [sleepy head] against the *52ᵉ régiment d'infanterie coloniale* and *53ᵉ régiment d'infanterie coloniale* opposite Apremont. Both the French and Germans claimed success and said their adversaries suffered major losses. The Germans had photographic proof. One officer and seventy-seven *poilus* were prisoners.[741] At Thiaucourt they assembled the prisoners to record the moment. Exactly a month later in the same location Americans were captured in battle.

It was also a time of change for **5. Ldw. Div.** occupying *Bois-Brûlé*. They had been fighting *10ᵉ division d'infanterie coloniale* for over a year. The **5. Ldw. Div.** brigade commander **Generalleutnant** von Waldow, commander of the **30. Ldw. I. B.**, was replaced by **Generalmajor** von Griesheim; von Waldow had commanded units in the area since 1915. **Generalleutnant** Fuchs, **Armeeabteilung C**, felt it was time to put new leadership to the test, especially now that American troops were entering the area. **Oberbefehlshaber** Fuchs ordered von Griesheim to commence planning for operations against the Americans, to include the possibility of **Erstürmung**.[742] Despite the fact that **5. Ldw. Div.** was adjacent to **78. R. D.**, their command element was **Gruppe Mihiel** to the west, not **Gruppe Gorz** to the north-east. Common operations between the two divisions required coordination through **Armeeabteilung C**.

A few nights after the 104th Infantry relieved French troops, the German artillery effort increased until it became a continuous bombardment from 6 to 9 April. On 5 April the 3rd Battalion captured a prisoner from a patrol of ten Germans attempting to raid one of the forward posts. Another German soldier was captured by a 1st Battalion outpost in front of *Bois sans Nom* while straying from his wiring party. The prisoner revealed that his officers were puzzled over the source of the newly observed olive drab uniforms: British, American, or French

Colonial? Identification was certain to be sought. In the early morning of 7 April, **5. Ldw. Div.** sent a small contingent against a 101st Infantry outpost east of Xivray. The patrol managed to capture three Americans. The next day another small unit from **5. Ldw. Div.** went over from the subsector at St Agnant opposite the 104th Infantry but suffered casualties after they blew up the wire entanglement in front. American artillery and rifle fire killed two Germans.[743]

PLANNING *ERSTÜRMUNG* IN THE *BOIS-BRÛLÉ*

Generalleutant Fuchs wanted **5. Ldw. Div.** to plan and execute a major **Erstürmung** in *Bois-Brûlé*. **General der Infanterie** Auler and **Generalmajor** von Griesheim directed the operation. **5. Ldw. Div.** planners made the decision to replicate the 20 March **Ruhekopf** operation against the newly arrived Americans. **Ruhekopf** had worked well against the experienced *poilus* so they didn't expect the inexperienced Americans to be any different. The force was to comprise three **Stosstruppkompagnien** manned from **5. Ldw. Div.** regiments: **Landwehr. Infanterie. Regiment (Ldw. I. R.). 25, Ldw. I. R. 36**, and **Ldw. I. R. 65**, and supporting elements. Each battalion was to include nine **Sturmtruppen** and forty **Pioniere**. Each **Stosstruppkompagnie** was to be made up of eight or nine narrow columns with each column

carrying six light machine guns. Following the **Stosstruppen** were assigned runners and supply men, with ammunition and tools for reversing the captured trenches to hold against the anticipated enemy counter-attack. Attention to holding the ground, unusually, was central to the plan. Each **Stosstruppsoldat** was to carry a greatcoat, ten days' rations and one or two bags of grenades.[744] **5. Ldw. Div. Stosstruppen** objectives were to capture the three enemy lines in the Louvire (eastern part of Apremont), *Bois-Brûlé* and *Côte 322*, and to hold the conquered position at all costs. During the day reinforcements were to assist in repelling counter-attacks and would relieve the **Stosstruppen** that same evening.[745]

French *2ᵉ Bureau* reported on 8 April that a battalion of **Sturmtruppen** had de-trained at Vigneulles, 13 kilometres behind the line. They assessed the **Sturmtruppen** were either to attack *Bois-Brûlé* in the west of the American sector opposite the 104th Infantry or *Mort-Mare* to the east, opposite the *69ᵉ division d'infanterie*. That night Colonel Shelton alerted his companies that the **Sturmbataillon.14** was at Hattonville rail station (the same place) and possibly heading to *Bois-Brûlé* opposite the 3rd Battalion. **Sturmbataillon.14** troops proceeded to Houdicourt [**Ostlager Kamp**] to conduct training for a powerful raid, either **Schnepfenstrich** [Snipe flight] opposite H-1 or **Kirschblüte** opposite Seicheprey and *Bois de Remières*. French *2ᵉ Bureau* analysis of the evening of 9 April showed German artillery was

The most commemorated moment in 26th Division history – the award of the *Croix de Guerre* by Général Passaga to the 104th Infantry for heroic action at Apremont. (NARA)

also being reinforced. Aerial photography from *Escadrille Sal. 122* at Belrain, *Escadrille AR 41* from Gondreville, and *Escadrille AR 258* from Toul confirmed a number of German battery positions opposite the 104th Infantry appeared to be modified to hold additional artillery.[746]

The first week that 104th Infantry occupied positions opposite *Bois-Brûlé*, German artillery and **MW** heavily shelled the area – it lived up to the French name for the sector, "kingdom of Minenwerfers." Destruction to trenches, entanglements and telephone lines meant runners were the primary means of communication, making effective liaison almost an impossibility. Colonel Shelton and his 104th Regiment discovered that the *10e division d'infanterie coloniale* was suffering from a shortage of ammunition, compromising their ability to hold their part of the front.[747]

German artillery fire mainly harassed American positions prior to the **Erstürmung**. The 101st Field Artillery 75mm batteries conducted counter-battery while the 101st Trench Mortar Battery, the sole American trench mortar unit deployed to this part of the southern Woëvre front fired into German lines. French *SRS 28* and *35* sound-ranging and flash-spotting units reported on April 9 that a considerable number of new German 105mm batteries and a 150mm battery had come into the sector and were firing for registration – further evidence that an attack was being readied against 104th Infantry positions opposite *Bois-Brûlé* and *Côte 322*. The 101st Field Artillery received the intelligence and followed appropriate readiness procedures. At 0415 on the morning of 10 April they were at their guns.

"BIG DOINGS AROUND APREMONT"

At 0445 the entire front of the 3rd Battalion and the right of the French lines were subjected to a heavy HE bombardment and **Gasschuss** lasting nearly an hour, followed by an attack in force on French positions. Colonel Sherburne at the 101st Field Artillery's PC near Vignot was startled by a heavy cannonade and sensed the situation in

an instant. Finding that it was too foggy to see signal rockets and that a brisk fire was falling on front lines and batteries, Colonel Sherburne observed the German artillery changing their fire pattern from counter-battery to barrage on the American front lines. It was well known among the veterans of the southern Woëvre front that German artillery always put down heavy fire on battery positions before beginning a raid. Sherburne sensed that an infantry attack was in progress and immediately ordered a barrage. Alert 101st Field Artillery and 103rd Field Artillery batteries opened fire across the American front line. The initial heavy German artillery fire managed to cut all the wires from battalion to the batteries. Major Perkins ordered Lieutenant Furber outside to fire the Very pistol signal. Instantaneously, Sanders and O'Keefe, whose respective batteries, E and F, were directly in the rear of Major Perkin's PC, started firing. Seeing the signal, Mitton's Battery D, out in the swamp, saw the flashes of the other guns, and also went into action. The French batteries joined in targeting the area west of the Roman road. Bullivant's 155mm howitzers fired on the second and third line of German trenches. The barrage was on its way before the infantry could get to the telephone to ask for it and continued for an hour and a half. **5. Ldw. Div. Stosstruppen** (estimated at 800 soldiers) were literally caught in the wire by the accurate American barrage and severely mauled. They were forced to retire – their mission to reach the American third line a complete failure.[748]

After talking with *colonel* Carteron, *10e division d'infanterie coloniale* artillery commander, Colonel Shelton, agreed to fire a second barrage and then modify the firing rate to prevent any efforts by the **Stosstruppen** to reorganise. Wires to Batteries E and F were temporarily repaired, and a second barrage was called for. Suddenly the lines were cut again – lines to battalion, Battery E and Battery F went out. After 15 minutes the mist blew away, and word came from the front line that the attack had been broken up. Ceasefire was called and an hour later the two batteries got the word and stopped.[749]

Catching **5. Ldw. Div. Stosstruppen** in the wire, the American and French barrage was decisive that first day. A few **Stosstruppen** did reach and occupy abandoned parts of the first line. Against *33ᵉ régiment d'infanterie coloniale* forces **Stosstruppen** advanced to the third line. Soon more **Stosstruppen** appeared, but despite their evident courage and determination they met a withering fusillade of shell and lead from the Americans. As **Stosstrupp** reinforcements arrived the combined attack force stopped and returned to German lines. From prisoners taken the Americans learned that the attack was by no means over and that the Germans planned further assaults. 3rd Battalion patrols went out immediately and discovered many hand grenades, explosives, materials for blowing up dugouts, fuses, insulated wire, and many yards of white tape. Many items were covered with blood.[750]

The Germans had anticipated the Americans were going to abandon the first line. Instead, the 104th Infantry stayed in place assisted by their artillery unleashing that effective barrage. The tactic followed the French doctrine of the sacrifice position. Those **Stosstruppen** that arrived in the first line were met with bullets and bayonets. Three medics displayed incredible bravery that day. Lieutenant Charlie M. Dodge, Private 1st Class Kenneth B. Page, and Private 1st Class Walter J. McCann all ran through a heavily shelled area to rescue wounded out in the battle zone and carried them back to the dressing station.[751]

Relief of the 104th Infantry's 3rd Battalion by the 2nd Battalion was scheduled that night and by daylight it was completed. It was arduous, with the Germans laying on a major barrage as the soldiers passed through smashed trenches and shell holes. Lieutenant Phillips' Company E relieved Lieutenant Galvin's Company L opposite *Bois-Brûlé*. Lieutenant Stiles' Company F replaced Company M at the Gooseneck, Captain Connelly's Company G became left support and Company H right support in the ruins of St. Agnant. The Stokes Mortar and 37mm platoons remained in the line. German intelligence from wiretapping gave them an idea that reinforcement and relief was in progress, prompting artillery barrage of all

roads and approaches that continued throughout the night. What remained of trench works in the battle area was of limited value to both defender and attacker.[752]

Gironville now served as the artillery PC. The 101st Field Artillery's Battery F had played the role of signal battery by opening fire and communicating with the other batteries in the area using rockets. Battery E saw their signal and commenced fire. Battery D followed suit when it heard the other batteries firing and joined in. The barrage sector of the three batteries was approximately 900 metres – five times the normal sector for planning. Each 75mm battery covered their piece of the sector firing twenty-four shots per minute. The teamwork between the three batteries saw even more rounds per minute fired on average during certain periods.[753] The 101st Field Artillery also fired their antiquated though accurate heavy permanent French 90mm and 120mm from batteries at Liouville Hill.

Nothing further happened on April 10 except the continuation of heavy enemy artillery fire. Information obtained from prisoners confirmed the presence of the **Sturmtruppen** augmenting the **Stosstruppen**. It was heartening for the Allies that American artillery had broken up what appeared to have been a carefully planned attack in force. The American infantry, from Colonel Shelton on down through the ranks, were fulsome in their praise for the artillery that day.[754]

SRA updated *VIIIᵉ armée* and *32ᵉ corps d'armée* on the extent of artillery fire during the struggle. A violent bombardment took place at two areas to the west in the 26th Division sector. Approximately 5,000 75mm rounds were fired at German targets north of St Agnant. The Germans responded with almost 1,000 rounds against French targets in the southern Woëvre front and 600 rounds against the Americans. Increased **MW** fire was observed in the area – a suggestion that more was in store for the men on the front line. To the east Seicheprey and Flirey also received heavy fire during the reporting period.

Corporal Ernest LaBranche, Battery E, 102nd Field Artillery, concluded his journal that night with a few comments that resonated both for the 104th as well as his artillery battery: "Terrific barrage from 5.45 to 7.30 this morning. Big doings around Apremont. We are successful. Bully for the 104th! Four mules of the supply company killed last night. Driver has arm blown off. All on 'Dead Man's Curve.' Motorcycle dispatch rider gets jipped. Runs into shell on curve. The Germans shell this curve every 15 minutes. Our caissons have been lucky so far, but we must not brag. We'll have our turn yet."[755]

BLINDDARM AND ABGESPRENGTEN WÄLDCHEN

The 10 April failure of **5. Ldw. Div. Stosstruppen** to capture prisoners resulted in Fuchs' **Gruppe Mihiel** ordering a new attack for 12 April, with one day to rehearse.[756] Under the codenames **Blinddarm** and **Abgesprengten Wäldchen** ["appendicitis" or literally "appendix"and "cut-off small woods blast"] two thrusts were planned. **Blinddarm** was to strike to the right at *Bois-Brûlé* and **Abgesprengten Wäldchen** was to proceed from Apremont. It was a question of occupying the advanced French position as far as, and including, the third line at the Louvière in the eastern part of the *Forêt d'Apremont*, at *Bois-Brûlé* and *Côte 322*, then to defend and to organise so as to hold indefinitely. The remaining **Stosstruppen** were experiencing problems with manning. The leading **Vizefeldwebel** [acting first sergeant] of **Ldw. I. R. 36** was taken prisoner. **Ldw. I. R. 65 Stosstruppkompagnie** remained intact but its reported strength for the next day was reduced by around forty men from the initial 10 April struggle. **Ldw. I. R. 25 Stosstruppkompagnie** was now reconstituted but had fewer men.[757]

5. Ldw. Div. Stosstruppen, as gleaned from prisoner interrogations, intended to widen their advanced combat zone to be able to make better use of **5. Ldw. Div.** first position. That afternoon recuperating **Stosstruppen** deliberated on what had gone wrong and how to put it right. They knew that French and American wire was partially destroyed at the time of the preceding day's raid, as well as cut by hand that night. They

sensed the allies occupied the forward line only sparsely. The best tactic, they surmised, was to attack the same area without artillery preparation to reduce enemy reaction time. The operation now was planned by the **Stosstruppen** themselves. Each **Stosstruppkompagnie** reviewed the maps and worked out details for the following day's operation. Better communication among the **Kompagnien** was a priority. Reinforcements played a greater role – aiding the **Stosstruppen** to drive back counter-attacks. That same evening they were to be relieved. In total the **Erstürmung** did not comprise more than 150 to 180 men, augmented by squads of carriers supplying ammunition and tools once their objective was reached. It was a plan doomed to failure.

The Americans did not idle in preparing for follow-on operations. There was serious damage to telephone lines to the 2nd Battalion Headquarters at PC Rabière. The only communication to 104th Infantry PC 21 kilometres away via Vignot was by motorcycle/side car. Six days of bombardment, with no opportunity for repairs, had left the trenches and wire in a wretched condition. So cut telephone wires were repaired and restrung. Captain Smith, Lieutenant Needham and the whole telephone detail worked night and day, often under shellfire, to perfect the system, stretching multiple wires in the exposed places in order to decrease the chance of destruction. Thereafter, no matter what happened, communication with artillery and infantry existed.

At 1330 on 11 April the Germans shelled Seicheprey and followed up the next day between 0745 and 0820 with heavy **Gasschuss**.[758] Corporal LaBranche recalled that day, "Rumors are that as the 1st Division could not take Montsec, the 26th must take it at any cost. It's only talk, of course; but I hope the Regulars hear of it. It will make them sore. Naval guns are being brought up. There ought to be something doing soon."[759]

DOOMED TO FAILURE – 12 APRIL

At dawn on 12 April a thick mantle of fog covered the land, and nothing of the front line, not even signal rockets, could be seen. There was no German artillery fire to give warning and barrage rockets were not observed.[760] The fog masked the Very light signals for the Allied artillery. The first time they became aware that Germans were on the attack was when the PC communicated at 0500 that **Stosstruppen** were occupying the front Chauvin and Dauer trenches. It was too late to lay down a barrage in front of the first wave. The only unit to see indications of an attack in progress was Sergeant Marty Joyce's 101st Trench Mortar Battery (TMB) who laid down an effective barrage with 6-inch Newton trench artillery, holding off the main body of the attacking forces until the American artillery commenced ten minutes later. One 104th Infantry soldier later acknowledged that "The 101st T.M.B. saved our necks – we will lug bombs for them forever."[761] Sergeant John A. Dickerman of Headquarters Company, 104th Infantry, had two 3-inch Stokes mortars cleverly camouflaged, providing supporting fire as a preliminary to any countercharge coming from the Americans' second line. After three minutes of Stokes mortar fire, Dickerman was supposed to move to a safer position to allow field artillery to commence with a rolling barrage. Dickerman remained in his position firing trench mortar bombs at the **Stosstruppen**. His squad was firing bombs so fast that the mortar tubes became red hot. Then the Germans located the trench mortar location and bombarded the area with high-explosive. Three men next to Dickerman were killed immediately – Sergeant Dickerman received forty-five separate wounds losing his right leg and left eye.[762]

The German attack extended across the entire front of the 2nd Battalion into the adjacent French lines. French forces were being driven back. The absence of accurate observation meant the artillery commenced fire on the Germans' front line where reinforcements and resupply were assumed to be concentrating. The barrage continued until the fog cleared, then fire was adjusted to observed portions of the American front-line trenches. The barrage lasted for an hour.[763] There was extensive German artillery activity bombarding the western side of the 26th Division sector in *Bois-Brûlé* and Louvière at this time. Additional artillery barrages commenced along the other 26th Division positions at Regniéville, la Hazelle, and Beaumont. The Germans fired a total of over 7,000 rounds against *VIIIᵉ armée's* divisions that day.[764]

The French artillery observation post at Liouville proved its worth. *Général* Gérard personally approved 101st Field Artillery personnel to control the battle from Liouville, which overlooked the whole front line facing Apremont and the adjoining *Bois-Brûlé*. This opportunity of a lifetime for a field artilleryman fell to Lieutenant Furber. He now had the catbird seat for the entire battle. He could clearly see **Stosstruppen** running across into what had been the American trenches by twos and threes. Furber worked with Battery F and held it ready for the next **Stosstruppen** coming across the line. No luck! Two more appeared. Furber yelled into the phone but something was wrong with the line. By the time he got the phone to function, the **Stosstruppen** had slid into the American trench. Furber watched while American infantry built up a sandbag barricade in the trench line known as the Gooseneck while the **Stosstruppen** moved closer. Suddenly he saw German helmets appear all along the American trench. The Germans were strongly reinforced and occupying American lines. Simultaneously, American barrage rockets went up from several points and the heads of the Germans dropped below the trench line.

Lieutenant Furber worked with one battery after another directing fire towards trenches where he saw **Stosstruppen**. Battery D, from their excellent positions firing enfilade did particularly effective work. **Stosstruppen** could be seen occasionally running across from their trenches by twos and threes, but whenever they gathered in their own line, indicating a mass effort to reinforce, barrages and concentrations broke them up. No reinforcing wave came across No Man's Land that day. Eleven barrages were called for and fired, along with a great many concentrations of one battery or more. The German trenches and communication lines received constant attention, and from 0500 until midnight the batteries were in almost continuous action.[765]

The **Stosstruppkompagnien** divided themselves into eight squads called **Trupps**. Each **Trupp** was provided with light machine guns. They reached the French position without being confronted but in the dark the squads became scattered; the men seemed to have had a bad feeling about carrying out an operation unaccompanied by artillery and which would expose them for a whole day to the enemy in front of their own position. **Trupps** which were to have reached the third line remained in the first or second with the supporting squads. Some of the supporting **Trupps** were said to have drifted back toward the starting trench before having reached the first trench line.[766] One **Stosstrupp** commander, however, **Leutnant** d. R. Verendes from **Ldw. I. R. 65**, personally stormed a machine-gun nest and overcame the unit in the trench. Verendes was awarded the **Ritterkreuz mit Schwertern des Hohenzollernschen Hausordens** (Knight's Cross with Sword of the House Order of Hohenzollern).[767]

Company F, 2nd Battalion, held the right front. Company E was to the left. Company H and Company G were in support. As the Germans hit the French positions they also struck Company E from the front, flank, and rear – driving in on the centre. Their attack reached the American trenches but they were forced back to an old deserted trench. Near the centre Lieutenant Knight of Company H led a successful counter-attack but was killed in the ensuing struggle. More ground was recaptured when Lieutenant Wilcox and members of Company E, combined with Lieutenant Edmunds of Company F, attacked troops in the deserted trench, driving back the Germans and taking twenty-four prisoners and three machine guns. Five were identified as members of the **2. Eskadron Ulanen. Regiment. Nr. 16**, part of **5. Ldw. Div.**[768]

Several German squads were missing or remained isolated. **Ldw. I. R. 25** and **Ldw. I. R. 65** units never communicated effectively. Communication back to the German lines became impossible in the zone of *Côte 322* where the open terrain was covered by artillery

fire. American artillery pounded the area forcing the Germans to seek shelter in shell holes. Meanwhile the infantry poured rifle and machine-gun bullets into the German positions.

The 103rd Field Artillery's 155mm battery targeted German communication trenches and counter-battery. An ominous development that plagued the 103rd Field Artillery for the remainder of April was short fire. The infantry were frantically calling the battery to lengthen the barrages. It was found that it was coming from one gun which on examination showed a bulge that reduced its range and accuracy.[769] A certain percentage of "shorts" were to be expected from supporting artillery, especially where the opposing front lines were so close. All the company commanders in the front line complained repeatedly that although the normal barrages invariably opened with remarkable accuracy, they shortened after a few minutes of firing, with friendly trenches being frequently hit. The artillery liaison officer worked hard all day to increase the range, and during 12 April the 75mm increased their range 175 metres. The guns were firing at extreme range and many of them were badly "shot out" and could not maintain the range upon becoming heated. There was no human error in this, or even ignorance; in fact, the gunners tried to compensate for the mechanical defects by ordering an increase in range of 50 metres after every 3 minutes of firing. The progressive range distortion had serious consequences a week later at Seicheprey.

Général Passaga arrived at PC Rabière at this moment to get an immediate update on the battle. Passaga was worried at first. However, as the battle proceeded he left greatly reassured having seen first-hand the Americans fighting.

At noon **Stosstruppen** remained in the American front lines at St. Agnant. An hour later they attacked Company F and failed to take the trench. To the east at *Bois-Brûlé*, German reinforcements advanced but were driven back. The Americans noticed that French liaison between strongly held locations was lacking. Liaison among *GC* was not effective.[770]

Later that afternoon the French battalion commander asked Major Harry L. Doane, 2nd Battalion, to assist in their counter-attack to regain the lost positions. Doane tasked Captain Edward J. Connelly, Company G, to lead the American attack. Connelly was a born leader, always at the front of his men He made a point of stripping his captain's bars from his tunic and going over the top. Connelly was a strict disciplinarian who expected the best from his soldiers.[771]

The Germans arriving in the trenches at 1700 were almost immediately discovered and attacked in the front line east of *Bois-Brûlé* by the Americans who at certain points penetrated the unoccupied intervals of the third line and mopped it up from the inside. Further west in the woods, the French attack also met isolated groups, who withdrew, were destroyed or surrendered. No German reinforcements arrived; at least those who were subsequently captured did not see any.[772]

Captain Connelly received a message by runner from Major Doane at 1705: "If at 1800 the French have not taken the point marked on the sketch, and you are not in liaison with them, the following will take place at 1900. Two platoons of the French will counter-attack on the plain both sides of *Boyau de Cannon Revolver*. You with two platoons will assist by counter-attack on the plain astride of *Frontil* trench and *Boyau Messemer*. This must be done at a rush. The number of the enemy is not known. After attack, return to trench *Frontil* and hold. Will let you know details as soon as possible. Doane." The combined counter-attack was launched at 1900 and its result was reported: "4/12 – 1930, to C.O. 2nd Battalion. Two platoons Company G went over the top at 1900. Cleaned up two boyaus. No Germans there but dead ones. Only one casualty known so far – Private Perdnea, Company G. Connelly."[773] Company G returned to trench *Frontil* and held the line.

Lieutenant Stiles told Major Doane that with the arrival of ammunition they were going to counter-attack and clear the front line. "Have killed many and stopped them. Need stretchers at once. Everything going O.K. Stiles." At 2130

the following was received from Stiles while at the Gooseneck position: "Major Doane: Artillery has stove up all our front line in bad shape. Several men killed. Wire also destroyed. Shall have to withdraw if it continues and save what men I can. Where shall I withdraw to? Stiles." Lieutenant Stiles was ordered to hold the position awaiting reinforcement by a platoon from Company H.

Lieutenant E.E. Phillips commanding Company E was a sergeant at the beginning of the war and was promoted shortly before the 104th Infantry left for France.[774] That afternoon Phillips alerted Major Doane that he needed ammo and barrage signals. The Germans now occupied Chauvin trench but Phillips' *GC* was fighting to keep them out of the next trench. Then Allied artillery started bombarding his area – Phillips called for help getting the word to them and requested that an artillery observer come forward. He also mentioned **MW** was making their situation more precarious. "They are getting my men. Phillips." Doane replied that evening via runner with questions. How many enemy were in the Chauvin trench? If Phillips were to attack, how many of his men could become casualties if friendly artillery were to strike Chauvin trench? Doane warned Phillips: "You may have to do it. Keep your tail up." Phillips responded that the Chauvin trench was destroyed by artillery and the German registration on the target was perfect. He cautioned Doane that taking the trench could be easy but casualties could mount – maybe the effort to hold that ground was not worth the price. The attack came, "leaning on the barrage." As in previous attacks in force on this front, the French right was driven back to the support line, leaving *GC* Messemer and Carcupine trench under German control and putting at risk Company E's left flank. The 104th Infantry's 2nd Battalion used all weapons at their disposal including the bayonet to stop the attack. At the Gooseneck the assault was more easily broken up; the terrain was more open and the trenches in better shape for defending. Many **Stosstruppen** remained in the abandoned trenches and continued to attack but they ended up withdrawing. On one part of the advance they almost encircled Company E's 4th Platoon. Just as they were tightening their grip, Company G arrived and helped drive them back. Major Doane received another Phillips message from Company E's runner that confirmed they still held the ground: "Am holding on same line as French. Send, if possible, artillery observer. Hope we will stay. Phillips." That night Major Doane and Lieutenant Phillips exchanged heartfelt messages: "Have made arrangements for Chauvin trench to be swept by MG fire all night. Think that will hold them down. Buck up!" Phillips replied, "I thank you. It will be a good idea. It will keep them busy. Men are tired but when I was down for the counter-attack they were smiling."

Corporal LaBranche made the observation on 12 April: "Guns are booming all the time. This harassing fire gets our goat. And they call this a quiet sector … Much shelling and gas on the Curve. *C'est la guerre!*"[775]

13 APRIL

As promised by Major Doane, machine guns from 101st Machine Gun Battalion arrived and swept the forward trenches throughout the night. German artillery fired another barrage that lasted nearly an hour. The **Stosstruppen** then attacked driving the French back from their forward positions, prompting the French to request a second counter-attack. Complying with the French request, the following order was dispatched from Major Doane to Captain Connelly. First he addressed the fratricide experienced the previous day: "Have fixed artillery. Are you sure it is our guns? Doesn't seem possible." Doane ordered Connelly to support the French request: "You will repeat counter-attack with the French. Repeat the same job as you did before on the plain both sides of *Frontil* trench and Boyau Messemer. Objective – G. C. Messemer at 0205. The French will have a full company this time. Acknowledge understanding and time. Doane." Captain Connelly reported that Company G suffered one officer and

fourteen men wounded. Connelly confirmed that the attack went well: "The enemy was prepared for this counter-attack. As soon as our barrage lifted and the attack was under way, his barrage fell on both attacking parties, in response to a strange yellow signal light. Neither party reached its objective, yet the enemy was forced out and the lost G.C. and trench reoccupied by the French, although complete liaison was not established until after daylight."[776]

Most of the supporting troops of the battalion had been in the line for nearly 24 hours and a request for withdrawal was made. Lieutenant Phillips urgently replied, "For God's sake don't pull them out [Company G]. There are not enough men to hold it if you do." Company E was holding a front of over 1,200 metres, most of it in the woods. The Americans were losing men. The absence of effective liaison with the French now became an issue. They did not know that the **Stosstruppen** had been driven out by the second counter-attack, so they called for a third counter-attack at 0830. Fortunately, this order was rescinded. Major Doane notified Captain Connelly that morning that concern over fratricide still remained: "Each gun will fire one test shot at 0830. Watch these on your front and report how far from you." Connelly replied with the news Doane was hoping for: "Have no map here of sector, but Company G has covered Frontil [trench] as far as part taken yesterday. Company E has had about thirty men mixed in. They are now on our right, but there has been quite a gap that I have filled with the balance of Lt. Heiser's platoon, and connection established. I and my officers were on the line all night. Men are tired. Condition of trenches very bad in many places, owing to shelling. Wounded and dead should be taken out at once. Litters needed. French patrols just came through and now in liaison with us. Germans evacuated GC Messemer and GC Carcupine after our last attack. All clear now. Connelly."

Three 103rd Field Artillery 155mm batteries fired a total of 7,468 rounds. By evening the ammunition supply was almost exhausted, and more was rushed up to the nearest possible point to the guns and resupplied as soon as darkness fell.

The road to the batteries was in full view of the Germans for 2 kilometres and at one time it appeared probable that the resupply would have to be made in daylight, but by registering shrapnel and using it in the last two barrages, the battery could fire until dark. During the evening the American artillery joined with the French in barrage and preparation for the counter-attack, which cleared all but a few points in the trenches and restored the lines. The light batteries alone fired more than fifty-six tons of projectiles during the day. The heavy battery, although not firing many rounds, added about fifteen tons more.[777]

Instructions were given to hold *Côte 322* come what may. During the night Company I and Company K of 3rd Battalion were sent to occupy the support line, a platoon from each being sent to Company G and Company E respectively during the morning to allow their worn-out men some rest. At noon Lieutenant Phillips updated Doane and confirmed the Allies were linked: "Capt Connelly has got through to the French and are now connected up. Have received 1 platoon Company K and four squads of MGs. Company E men must be relieved. They are falling asleep on sides of trenches and can hardly be awakened. Phillips."[778]

One replacement, Private Glenn Hill of Michigan, decided for himself to join Lieutenant Phillips' Company E. The replacement unit had assigned Hill to another company, who declared that he was missing. Despite the confusion (and having in effect not followed orders) Hill learned fast. He participated in one counter-attack and killed two enemy with the bayonet – later apologising to Lieutenant Phillips for not having handled the bayonet correctly in the struggle.[779]

Capitaine LeMeitour, French liaison to 104th Infantry, and Lieutenant Colonel Foote, 104th Infantry, arrived at CP Rabière to get an immediate update on the battle in progress. Around noon another lieutenant colonel arrived and reported as observer for GHQ AEF but by then the Battle of Apremont was virtually over.

The Apremont affair exemplified the best of individual soldiery. Chaplain 1st Lieutenant John B. DeValles, a native of St. Michael in the Azores, recognized that there was a serious shortage of stretcher bearers and departed immediately for Vignot. DeValles assembled the 104th Regimental Band under the command of Band Leader Ralph M. Dawes, gave them a pep talk and requested their help. Dawes's entire band volunteered to assist the medical corps as stretcher bearers and departed immediately to the front lines in a *camion* that was under constant shellfire.[780] One of the regiment's medical officers, Captain Hardwick recalled:

> During the latter part of the battle, I visited the line and while there the bandsmen came in bringing their litters loaded with wounded. They had toiled all day without respite amid shell fire and had stopped neither for rest nor food. ... Their hands had given out under the strain but rather than give up the work, these plucky fellows had wound their wrists with wire [acquired from the signal corps] and the litter hung from loops into which its ends were twisted. This wire had worn away the bandage that for a time had protected the flesh beneath so that now the blood dripped down from the cuts it had made in the skin.[781]

Late on the night of 13 April the Germans fired an intense barrage of over 6,000 rounds for an hour against both Allied divisions.[782] At midnight the lines were as they had been at 0500 – which meant the Allies felt justified in concluding the Germans had been thoroughly beaten in the Battle of Apremont.

Sixteen kilometres to the east, Corporal LaBranche of the 102nd Field Artillery was having an equally chaotic day:

> Stopped and took refuge in a barn when the gas horns started to blow. Put on our masks for a half hour. Dead Man's Curve was a hundred yards ahead and was being banged to hell. Infantry companies were going into the line. Shells were whizzing pretty thick. They stopped in the barn. The officers and sergeants came and encouraged them to come along. Our Infantry remarked that the G__ D__ed Boches

always knew when a relief was going in. Left Mandres and galloped to 420. The road was full of shell holes. We were shaken to pieces. Great activity all around. Night had now set in. Star shells pierced the thick darkness. Galloped back after stop at 420, going very fast and could not stop. Cart made as much noise as the shells.[783]

When the relief occurred after the battle, both French and American *aérostiers* observed the Germans put a major bombardment on the roads all night, proving they knew about the movement. The Germans had an outstanding spy system. The trenches in the area were pulverised and were about one metre in height when the reinforcements arrived.[784]

Action against American units also occurred to the north of St. Mihiel near Verdun at Marie-Louise. On the night of 13 April about 400 **Sturmtruppen**, **Stosstruppen**, and **Pioniere** following a 6-hour heavy barrage, struck the AEF's 2nd Division's 9th Infantry positions and advanced 700 metres. They captured seven medical staff, including a medical officer. In the attack the Germans attempted to pass themselves off as French *poilus* crying out "gas", which prompted the 9th Infantry soldiers to put on their masks. The Americans discovered the deception and then "the fight started." The Americans suffered fourteen dead, 102 wounded and gas casualties and twenty-eight men missing. Forty German dead were initially counted and eleven prisoners taken.[785]

THE FIRST VICTORIOUS AMERICAN BATTLE

That evening Major Doane departed for 104th Infantry headquarters to make a personal report. Major General Edwards' praise was passed to the troops by Lieutenant Colonel Foote: "Message from Division Commander says he appreciates highly the gallantry of this battalion. Notify all. Hold on tight. One company supports coming in tonight. Relief tomorrow night." The 104th Infantry suffered 200 casualties, 60 killed and

140 wounded. It lost two prisoners, one each from the 2nd and 3rd Battalions – one private, Pat Mean, wounded in the battle, got lost, went down the wrong *boyau* and was captured.[786] Forty-two German prisoners were taken, the largest number taken by the Americans to date. The 104th Infantry held the ground and at no time did they lose a single foot of trench. French recognition of the impressive accomplishment by the 104th Infantry resulted in 117 being awarded the *Croix de Guerre*. For the first time in the history of the United States Army an American regiment was decorated *en masse* by an appreciative foreign government. The three-day battle in the trenches south of Apremont was the first victory of American arms in the war. A letter of congratulations from Colonel Malin Craig was sent to Major General Edwards on 15 April. "The Corps Commander directs me to extend his warmest congratulations to the Commanding Officer and soldiers of the 104th Infantry and the Machine Gun Units associated with them in their recent series of encounters with the enemy."[787]

Général Gérard's *VIIIᵉ armée* staff were the first to prepare an assessment on what transpired at *Bois-Brûlé* on 15 April: "Lateral liaison between first line French and American units seems not to be carried out always in the most satisfactory manner," was the first statement of Gérard's memorandum. The American battalion commander "did not seem to know the exact boundaries of his sector." The subsequent lack of coordination between French and Americans culminated in major problems on 12 April. The lack of liaison made the counter-attacks attempted by the *10ᵉ division d'infanterie colonial* more difficult. *Général* Gérard ordered Passaga to investigate the shortfalls experienced at *Bois-Brûlé* and report back. Gérard also made clear that Passaga's task was to ensure liaison was "absolute between all the echelons of the Command and all the elements along the different occupied parallels."[788]

Colonel Conner at Chaumont conducted a review of the engagement for General Pershing on 16 April. The location of the attacks were 2 kilometres due west and 1 kilometre north-west of Apremont. The battle location was 8 kilometres south-east of St. Mihiel. At 0500 the Germans commenced their bombardment of the trenches on both sides of the *10ᵉ division d'infanterie coloniale* and the 104th Infantry line. The German attack was estimated to comprise up to 300 soldiers. Only outposts on the front line had troops. Both French and American troops had withdrawn from the first line. After the Germans occupied the first line the French called for a counter-attack, which was accomplished. The counter-attack was successful except for a short segment of the French front line being occupied by a German section called **Gruppe Messner**. When American artillery aided the French counter-attack the **Messner** group withdrew. It was reported that the Germans suffered heavily from the American artillery barrage, counter-battery firing with 95mm and 155mm.[789] On 12 April at 1100 the Germans conducted a separate attack in the direction of Apremont towards St. Agnant. It was directed towards a battalion of the 104th Infantry occupying St. Agnant. Between 1100 and 1500 the Americans withdrew from the St. Agnant front-line trenches. At this time Colonel Shelton, 104th Infantry commander, organized a counter-attack using bayonets and

drove the Germans out of the occupied front lines there. Major A.A. Maybach reported that Company F of the 104th Infantry conducted a bayonet charge through the communication trench at 1631. From the initial interrogation of prisoners it was determined that the Germans wanted to make certain that the French still held their troops on the line near Apremont. The raid was intended to draw French troops away from the Somme battle in progress to the north.[790] **General der Infanterie** Auler and his **5. Ldw. Div.** maintained their sector until eventually overrun during the St. Mihiel Offensive of 12 September 1918[791]

The second half of Colonel Conner's report to Pershing was a critique of the fighting ability of the 104th Infantry, implying the 26th Division as a whole. His comments were acquired from Major Bowditch, G-3, I Corps, observing 26th Division operations for General Pershing, General Liggett, Colonel Conner and Colonel Craig. Bowditch focused on the defective American system of liaison between front-line officers and the battalion commander

An unimpressive *Bois-Brûlé* trench. (History of the 103rd Infantry)

at the CP. The majority of messages were requests for reinforcements or ammunition. He pointed out that one important message to the battalion commander did not have the hour of the signature. His assessment showed liaison between the companies and the artillery failed during the 12 April action. Bowditch reported that the French counter-attack did not include the Americans since there was a linguistic communication breakdown – a sore point with Colonel Conner, fluent in French. The Americans did not counter-attack but just extended their lines so as to connect with the French lines. The bottom line from Conner's report to Pershing was that the discipline of the 104th Infantry battalion was not great: "… the action seemed to depend more upon individuality of the men than on organization."[792]

Americans from other 26th Division regiments had their own assessment. At *Bois-Brûlé* the French admitted that the Germans could come over and take prisoners at will – in fact, they always considered the outposts as "sacrifice men."

This was not acceptable to the Americans. The 104th Infantry withstood specially trained enemy troops for four days and captured prisoners themselves, instead of surrendering when the going got tough.[793]

German prisoner interrogations clearly indicated that **Erstürmung der feindlichen Stellungen im Bois-Brûlé** was deemed unsuccessful since not one American prisoner was captured (they did not know of the two mentioned). **Erstürmung** at *Bois-Brûlé* showed the Germans that the American front lines were sparsely manned. After the raid, **Stosstruppkompagnien** withdrew to their respective rest camps north at *Bois de la Montagne*.

The **Stosstruppen** were then reassigned to their original companies within the **5. Ldw. Div.**[794] The Germans who were taken prisoner agreed that this operation as conceived and carried out was doomed to failure.

JAPANESE PRAISE AND THE *COUR DE GUERRE*

A most unlikely testament to the 104th Infantry's gallantry at *Bois-Brûlé* and Apremont was published by the former Lieutenant Charles L. Furber, who served in the 101st Field Artillery in the Apremont battle as observer for the PC. On a post-war visit to Japan he attended a forum where a Japanese army officer assessed American forces in the war:

> Personally I do not agree with other military critics who have picked various events as the turning point of the war, such as the second battle of the Marne, etc. I myself consider of the utmost importance an obscure and comparatively unknown engagement at Apremont in the Toul sector. To explain: the military world, and particularly the *Boche*, freely asserted the belief that the American soldier would amount to very little in the war; first, because he wouldn't arrive soon enough or in sufficient numbers, and second, because he'd be inadequately trained. Especially he would never grasp the technical intricacies of modern artillery. At Apremont the Hun attempted to prove this to the world; to show up the inexperienced American troops, then for the first time holding a complete sector without close French supervision. The result was a complete boomerang, the American artillery showing not only great accuracy and speed in firing, but an unexpected ability to outguess the opposition. Thus, what was intended to be a heavy blow to the American morale, and therefore to the Allied cause, turned out to be the strongest of notices that the troops from the United States must be reckoned with as a powerful factor.[795]

The assessment is beyond irony in the light of events 20 years later.

Media coverage of the battle was overshadowed by the critical campaigns underway to the north. Operation Georgette had pushed British forces back, prompting Field-Marshal Haig to utter the famous phrase "Backs to the

Wall." The American soldier's paper, *Stars and Stripes*, did publish an account on 3 May, "When the Colors were Decorated." *Général* Passaga's 14 April 1918 citation honoured the 104th Infantry:

On April 12th, just past, the enemy supported by powerful artillery, made an attack in force on the lines held by the left of the Twenty-sixth American Division and the right of the *10ᵉ division d'infanterie coloniale* … In the course of the engagement, thanks to the vigorous and repeated counter-attacks of the Americans and of our Colonials, the enemy, in spite of his superiority in numbers, was thrown back from several trench positions where he had gained a foothold, and left in our hands more than forty prisoners and a large number of dead. During the fight, carried on under a severe bombardment, the American troops gave proof not only of their splendid courage, which we know, but also of a brotherhood in arms which was absolutely and ever present. With such defenders as these the cause of liberty is sure to triumph.[796]

Général Passaga years later in his memoirs reflected on the action:

The enemy was not slow in giving them the chance to measure sword with him. He was eager to recognise his new foe, and to make an impression on him, by severe lessons.

The **Stosstruppen** (shock troops), appeared at once between the Moselle and Saint-Mihiel. Their luck was out, every time, they left corpses upon the ground, and prisoners in the hands of the Americans. One of these attacks prepared and supported by much artillery was particularly fierce. It fell upon the 104th Massachusetts Infantry Regiment. This unit, during three days of battle, April 10th, 12th and 13th, fought gallantly, and inflicted upon the enemy a bitter defeat. I was especially pleased to be able to mention the regiment officially in the XXXII Corps orders. Thenceforward, American soldiers, whether they belong originally to the Regular army, the National guard, or the National army, gave me always proofs of admirable valour.[797]

For its gallantry in this action *Général* Passaga decorated the regimental colours of the 104th Infantry at the parade field near Boucq with the *Cour de Guerre,* a red and green ribbon with a bronze cross. This was the first time in history that a foreign power had decorated the flag of an American regiment.

"I am proud to decorate the flag of a regiment which has shown such fortitude and courage; I am proud to decorate the flag of a nation that has come to our aid in the fight for liberty."[798] Passaga then personally decorated 117 members for outstanding heroism and valour with the words, "*Je vous remets la Croix de Guerre, avec la citation du corps de l'armée.*"[799]

PART 3

THE CONSUMMATE PLAN IS EXECUTED AT SEICHEPREY

CHAPTER 14

Adjusting to New Enemies

Armeeabteilung C at **Gruppe Gorz** saw an opportunity to demonstrate annihilation. The assault codenamed **Kirschblüte** [Cherry Blossom] was to be with a 1½-regiment force employing more artillery than **Einladung** and a larger **Sturmtruppen 14** force doing more than solely operating **Flammenwerfer**. **Kirschblüte** was to prove how effective combined arms worked on the modern battlefield. **Generalmajor** von Stolzmann notified **Gruppe Gorz** in early April that **78. R. D** was deep into planning the attack on American positions north of Seicheprey from Lahayville in the west to *Bois de la Sonnard* in the east. Estimated time for the attack was between 24 and 30 April. Hedging his bets, von Stolzmann made it clear in his memorandum to Fuchs that the primary objective was to proceed as far as the southern egress of Seicheprey. Mission objectives were to destroy dugouts and return to the German lines. Critical to **Generalmajor** von Stolzmann's thinking was to get his attacking force to return on time and successfully defend against an American counter-attack. Holding ground at Seicheprey was never the purpose of **Kirschblüte**.[800]

Generalleutnant Wilhelm Hoffmann's 10 April memorandum expressed his overriding concern for the role that artillery would play in **Kirschblüte**. He made it clear that preparing artillery was more difficult than infantry. The first phase of any artillery preparation involved establishing positions as rapidly and secretly as possible. Augmenting **78. R. D** artillery with neighbouring divisional resources, **Gruppe Gorz** and **Gruppe Mihiel** artillery, was tricky owing to the unfavourable terrain between Montsec in the west and Maizerais to the east. Lessons learned from Brüchmuller's artillery planning in Operation Michael were being shared by German commands throughout the Western Front and Hoffmann did not view with optimism the task of manoeuvring additional resources to the rear areas of the southern Woëvre front without being discovered. Camouflage was essential in 1918, as was successfully demonstrated by Operation Michael. The rear echelon he regarded as almost impassable, with insufficient road networks and tramways to support **Kirschblüte**. No upgrades were in place since **zwischen Maas und Mosel** was considered **ruhige front** [a quiet front]. There was a dearth of labour to move the artillery. Marshy ground, as the French found out in the Woëvre of 1915, did not lend itself to successful artillery employment. Prepared positions were necessary in the swampy forests of Gargantua and *Mort-Mare*. In his memorandum to **Gruppe Gorz**, Hoffmann expressed his belief as **Artillerykommandeur** that **Kirschblüte** required more time: "I feel obligated to state that the preparations can hardly be completed in less than 12 days and that I therefore cannot take any responsibility in this respect."[801]

The **78. R. D.** was to report its plans as soon as possible, providing an estimate of the level at which **78. R. D.** could engage the Americans with an appropriate mix of artillery, **Minenwerfer**, and other weapons, as well as set a date for the operation.

General der Infanterie Max Hofmann, **XXXVIII. Reservekorps** commander, followed up on 14 April just two days after the end of Apremont by forwarding his assessment to **Generalmajor** von Stolzmann from **Gruppe Gorz**. Hoffmann predicted heavy losses for the Germans should they consider holding ground in conducting the **Erstürmung**. Territory held of course meant greater investment of resources in comparison with what had been the norm since 1915. Hoffmann feared Allied defences within *Bois du Jury*. He estimated that American and French artillery could provide a continuous bombardment of the German lines. Whatever the objectives of **Kirschblüte**, the **78. R. D.**'s artillery required considerable reinforcement. He thought such reinforcement was unrealistic and should not be anticipated. The lack of additional artillery meant that the attack could not count on permanent possession of the line. Considering the need for withdrawal posed not a tactical but a strategic question. A counter-attack against entrenched Germans resulting in their withdrawal only gave the enemy a sense of victory – something that the **OHL** and **General der Artillerie** von Gallwitz wanted to avoid under any circumstances. The best way to retreat would be at night. **78. R. D.** artillery was to control the battle throughout. By the time the Allies responded effectively with more artillery, the withdrawal was to be an accomplished fact. A retreat shortly after reaching the objective and by day increased the possibility of heavy losses. On the other hand, Hoffmann reasoned that it was possible to hold the captured position on the day of attack itself and any losses could be "diminished if the assault troops be distributed skilfully ... I therefore order that the line designated by the Division as the objective be held on the day of attack and evacuated the following night."[802]

German forces only had five days to finalise training, apply resources to the front line, manoeuvre artillery and adequately stock

both HE and gas projectiles. This placed great demands on both men and horses. The most difficult part was moving artillery and **MW** into final position without being detected. As with Operation Michael, the Germans successfully manoeuvred without being observed by all resources – ground, aerial, and electronic – during this critical time.

Generalmajor von Stolzmann's coordinated final plan with **Generalleutnant** Hoffmann and **Major** Bruns was clear and meticulous. Every major facet of an operation in positional war was clearly addressed. Elements of the **78. R. D.** were to attack American positions from the western **Alfa-Wäldchen** to *Bois de Remières* on the east, as well as the village of Seicheprey, in the early morning of **Y-Tag** (20 April) from the region of Lahayville to the western edge of *Bois de la Sonnard*. They were to hold the position gained, except the village of Seicheprey, until further orders. The objectives were damage to the Americans through losses, capture of prisoners and booty, as well as destruction of operational positions and Seicheprey itself before evacuation. **Generalmajor** von Stolzmann was commander of operations. The infantry attack was to be commanded by **Oberst** von Blankensee, von Stolzmann's commander of the **78. R. I.** Brigade. Like the previous major **Einladung** operation conducted on 1 March, Hoffmann remained the **Artilleriekommandeur**. **Major** Bruns, the man who planned **Einladung** and the 26 February chemical assault on *Bois de Remières*, was named **KTK**, an assignment for which he was well suited.[803]

Res. I. R. 259 Stosstruppen withdrew from the front lines on 13 April and commenced training near Thiaucourt. Battalions from **Res. I. R. 260** and **Res. I. R. 258** took their place. **Sturmbataillon.14** now assumed a prominent role, arriving in **Abschnitt Maas und Mosel** and finalising attack roles and responsibilities. Some **Sturmbataillon.14** personnel had been at the southern Woëvre front since 8 April.[804] French *aérostiers* observed from their balloon observation posts activity near Vigneulles suggesting rehearsal movements.[805]

The feeling in most units was that the boys from the other side of the pond would now learn about war. The best and most experienced soldiers were selected from the three regiments of the **78. R. D.** At their training ground in Essey, the **Stosstruppen** were told they were to conduct the first large attack against the Americans, the first **Sturm** against a new enemy. They all knew there was a major offensive to the north, which was being talked of as the decisive battle of the war.

FRENCH COMMANDERS RESHAPE THE FRONT LINE

As the German leadership finalised planning for Seicheprey, French military leadership had to come to terms with what best constituted defence of the first position in view of the surge in German offensive success. French command issued guidance in April that was disseminated to all generals in command of *armées*. *Général* Gérard's *VIIIe armée* with the 26th Division made changes to the existing forward defence. *Bois-Brûlé* showed Gérard that Americans fighting in the forward line made the ultimate difference. It was time to apply that knowledge throughout his *VIIIe armée* sector. "Sacrifice positions" became the watch word at the front. Such terminology resonated with the spirit of Verdun – they shall not pass. Colonel John Parker in his memoirs discussed the concept being introduced to him by *Général* Dogan, commander of *1re division marocaine,* in August 1917. The theory of tactical defence was based on "Centres of Resistance," staggered in depth, designed to break up German attack formations before they could reach the principal "Line of Resistance." The centres of resistance became "simple little islands of deliberate sacrifice where men fought to the end, in place." Parker observed that the "Americans talked less about it but managed to put the plan into everyday practice; they always intended to fight to the last man, if they were Regulars … if they were not, sometimes they were shamed into it."[806]

Général Pétain's views were a work in progress that was articulated to *armée* commanders in the field. On 24 January GQG issued directive No. 4 describing defensive positions on the front lines. The policy underwent scrutiny as Operation Michael exposed Allied weaknesses against well-orchestrated offensives such as that planned by Bruchmüller. Pétain's April policy advocated each component standing firm without looking to retreat. GC duty was to continue to hold even if it required fighting hand-to-hand. In his words, a machine gun taken out of action is not lost in vain if it is lost at the last moment. Pétain encouraged discretion in the conduct of counter-attack. Infantry were to compensate for inferior numbers by giving the adversary the unmistakable impression that battlefield gains came with a cost. Front lines had to be sufficient to enable the defending unit to hold the ground at any cost. *Général* Gérard echoed *Général* Pétain's feelings and made it a requirement for all echelons under his command.[807]

Général Gérard's new direction to Major General Edwards modified the *32e corps d'armée* 7 February 1918 terms of the 1st Division's role at the southern Woëvre front: "The troops in sector will be reinforced so as to allow the arrival of the large units destined to offer battle in the line of resistance. The aim of this reinforcement is not to increase the density of the first line, but to strengthen the resistance by a more ample disposition in depth."[808] General Edwards protested against the system in use of keeping a large number of men so far forward in sacrifice positions. As has already been explained, there were definite and rigid orders against sending reinforcements to these posts in case of attack; the line of resistance was along the national highway that ran on a ridge parallel to the front and 1.6 kilometres behind it. Edwards believed that if the system of keeping only sacrifice posts in the front line were to be kept to, far fewer men should be left out there.[809]

When Colonel Parker assumed command of his Seicheprey sector, he followed orders to hold the ground in accordance with the coinciding views of *Général* Gérard and *Général* Passaga and echoed by Brigadier General Traub as they pertained to a new concept of "islands of resistance." Parker determined that Passaga's direction was different from the nominal plan of defence that had been established and maintained by the French since August 1917. As the orders trickled down to the regiments, Colonel Parker in his capacity as 102nd Infantry commander saw the policy's impact on his regiment. Traub endorsed the new French policy without comment and forwarded it to both 101st Infantry and 102nd Infantry and directed the commanders to obey orders. Parker was strictly responsible for full compliance in every respect. From that moment on, Parker feared that if the Germans were to attack in force, it meant heavy losses for his regiment.[810] (Supporting Colonel Parker in the sector was Lieutenant Colonel Dowell, Major General Edwards' former chief of staff, a former enlisted man in the regular army who rose through the ranks and became a judge advocate assigned to the 26th Division. Dowell did not garner the approval of Liggett's staff and was ordered relieved. His work was thorough and he provided Colonel Parker with professional review of the work in progress. They made a good partnership in managing the 102nd Infantry.)[811]

On 15 April Parker exercised one of his greatest talents at this crucial time: he authored a response entitled "Strength of Outposts" to General Traub's 13 April prescription of a strength of not less than twenty-five men, or half a platoon, for posts. Parker told Traub that his men held a front line that he had personally reconnoitred. One company of his 3rd Battalion, Company L, was almost half-strength. *Bois de Remières* held posts for six half-platoons and a full platoon. Published unit numbers were illusory when kitchen, liaison and other duties were considered. Sentries posted in *Bois de Remières* were stretched out beyond the 10-metre policy to the edge of the woods. Parker dropped the hint that the "iron-clad instructions" of *Général* Gérard's policy were causing problems. At Seicheprey, Parker argued, his situation was equally precarious. He had to hold Seicheprey but manning for the forward lines north of Seicheprey thinned out his forces:

The sector to be held is so wide and the 3rd Battalion now holding the right half is so greatly reduced in effectives that literal compliance with the 1st endorsement is not possible without either the increase in the number of effectives in the present company, or the addition of another company. The spaces between groups are so great and the number of old boyaus which cut around through the sector is so great, that with the reduced effectives available it is utterly impossible to place a Fighting Group of 25 men to guard each of these old boyaus or even maintain adequate observation over them. Nothing that we can do can prevent an enterprising enemy from creeping through between posts and penetrating some distance without being discovered.

Parker was willing to be "held strictly to account" for all dispositions made by the regiment, but General Traub's orders were so rigid that Parker felt he had to state the situation as plainly as he could.[812] Colonel Parker recalled that for his troops occupying "'Centers of Resistance,' the orders were 'FIGHT TO THE DEATH IN PLACE' ... Send no reinforcements forward without permission. Fight it out on your main line of resistance, the 1-Bis position. These orders came from the French Corps Commander under whom General Edwards was serving, and they were sound orders. Tactically they were absolutely correct."[813] Parker further elaborated in post-war writings that the development of proper, elastic defence in-depth was an advancement for the French. He assessed their manpower as of doubtful quality. The German army was nearly at peak efficiency heading into 1918 and preparing for Operation Michael. Some means was needed to counteract the growing German capability, even if it meant just bolstering morale. Parker concluded that "one thing Americans never understood about the French was the manner in which they issued a complicated battle order insisting that a certain position must be held 'to the last man'... and then made provision in orders for a retirement to a second line of defense!"[814]

Ironically, Parker concluded his assessment on sacrifice positions with: "France was bled white and the coming aid from America was slow in arriving. Something new had to be publicized and this new defense system was as good as anything. The strangest thing about this new system was, it worked! The German Army was too slow-witted to realize what the plan was until they had bumped their noses into it, and even then their higher command was too far in the rear to fully appreciate what was happening to the badly whipped Frenchmen to enable them to inflict such terrific losses on German attacking troops."[815] However, it should be remembered that the Germans had moved beyond the range of their direct support artillery.

Général Gérard further defined the forward sector on 17 April. He made it clear that the only way for observation posts to escape previous destruction, then capture, was mobility, that is to say, the daily transfer of night observation posts (generally to a point well to the rear and to the flank of a day observation post). Gérard wanted his divisions, to include the 26th Division, to follow this to the letter. Gérard now required the observation half-platoon or platoon to be grouped together, on guard all night long with their arms in hand, and the commander in the midst of his troops, formed in a square. It was 24-hour duty in the zone of observation. Gérard ordered traps made with explosives to be set in the positions abandoned at night. Every precaution was to be taken to prevent Allied soldiers becoming the first victims. He ordered *corps d'armée* and division generals immediately to issue strict orders to maintain this posture – no exceptions were to be made: "Every violation will be very severely punished."[816]

On 17 April, an alert based on available intelligence was sent by Colonel Parker to his commanding officer holding *Bois de Remières*. An attack by the enemy was expected that night against *Bois de Remières* and the *162ᵉ régiment d'infanterie* to the east. He passed on General Traub's directive to move back one platoon from *Bois de Remières* to *Boyau Jury-Remières* to reinforce that defensive position. Parker then directed Captain Charles C. Stanchfield of Company B, 102nd Machine Gun Battalion, that two machine guns were to be moved from positions north of Seicheprey to the *Boyau Jury-Remières* to increase resistance at that point. Stanchfield duly realigned two machine guns from their position in north-east *Bois de Remières*. Parker specified that Company L's key defensive positions were now Sibille Trench, *Bois de Remières*, and the new one being set up at *Boyau Jury-Remières*. His last words to Company L were: "The fighting positions of the remainder of your company are not changed and you are to hold to the last."[817] At Seicheprey the 102nd Machine Gun Battalion positions comprised Company A and Company B.

General Traub responded to Parker's dramatic 15 April statement three days later with his policy memorandum: "Changes in location of troops and new construction." He directed Parker to withdraw one platoon occupying Sub-center F-1 to the 1-Bis position on the Beaumont Ridge at once. One platoon of the company occupying Sub-center F-1 was to be in place from dusk to dawn in the *Boyau Jury-Remières* with two machine guns providing additional firepower. Sibille Trench, the main trench between Seicheprey and *Bois de Remières*, was to be manned so that connecting *Boyau Savourey* and *Boyau Jury-Remières* were both effectively in connection with *colonel* Bertrand's *162ᵉRégiment d'infanterie*. It was obvious to Parker his assignment of 102nd Infantry was to be closely monitored by his commander to ensure compliance with French command policy.[818] Late on the night of 18 April Parker directed his adjutant, Captain Taylor, to publish Field Order No. 24.[819]

The 102nd Infantry and neighbouring *162ᵉ régiment d'infanterie* expected a raid by the Germans – the prevailing opinion based on available intelligence was the attack was being planned against the *162ᵉ régiment d'infanterie*. Company L platoons now maintained smaller groups throughout their assigned points in the southern Woëvre front. Stanchfield placed his machine guns to assist the new alignment on the night of 19 April, to ensure compliance with General Traub's directive. *GC* comprising twenty to twenty-eight men were positioned a short distance from the front line. Traub's directive that no sentinels were to be stationed beyond 10 metres at the front line was closely followed. The defensive posture in place was being spread dangerously thin.[820]

Major George J. Rau, 1st Battalion, 102nd Infantry, proceeded to Seicheprey with his men to commence relief of Captain Clarence Thomas' 2nd Battalion. Shortly after Rau was born in nearby Alsace, his parents emigrated to the United States and settled in Connecticut. At the first opportunity, Rau enlisted and successfully served as a Connecticut National Guard and was subsequently commissioned. Rau was competent, knew what it took to command men in combat and was a superb addition to the 102nd Infantry. His *GC* of twenty-eight men was assigned to forward positions.[821] Rau's Company C and Company D received orders that in case of attack, the front-line trench was to be held at all costs. Rau was fully aware there was to be no falling back – and he maintained that position in the coming hours.

Corporal LaBranche, watching the evolving situation from his 75mm battery position, saw that the new alignment was adding stress to the infantry's already perilous situation: "Unusual activities. Infantry Companies from home badly jipped … They looked all in. Still there is no sign of any relief."[822]

"One of the bravest …" Private Louis Ziegra battled single-handedly an entire thirty-man German patrol on 15 April 1918. (Courtesy of the Ziegra family)

"ONE OF THE BRAVEST MEN THEY HAD EVER SEEN"

Général Gérard's "sacrifice positions" order was followed to the letter by a lone private whose actions were communicated up to the highest German **Armee** echelons, but never recognized by the Allies. A single incident to the north-east of Apremont merited equal praise as the success of the 104th Infantry at *Bois-Brûlé*. At the regimental line dividing the 101st Infantry and 102nd Infantry, two men dressed in American uniform speaking perfect English arrived at the 102nd Infantry's Marvoisin company PC purporting to be on a liaison mission from the 101st Infantry, requiring sketches of the adjoining sector and the latest password. The officer at the PC declined to accede to the request, but his suspicions were not sufficiently aroused to hold the men. The men departed, passed a company runner, and proceeded north in the direction of the German lines.[823] Something was in the works for that sector.

Later that night, a thirty-man **Zug** from **7. Kompagnie, Res. I. R. 258 (7./258)**, under command of **Leutnant** Frederich, conducted a patrol 1 kilometre into American lines near Xivray on the regimental sector line separating 102nd Infantry to the east and 101st Infantry to the west. Frederich's **Zug** also included several **Husaren** [cavalrymen] that had just been sent to the front as infantry. **7./258** intercepted the

Company H rations and mail wagon heading towards Marvoisin. After passing Xivray, the wagon was moving eastward, passing over a stone bridge across the Rupt de Mad. It was a still night with the wagon making the only noise. Three men were on the wagon: the driver, the acting company mess-sergeant (actually Private) Louis R. Ziegra, and a rifleman serving as the guide sitting inside the wagon. They were heading to the front lines to Company H. Private Harry Marvin was looking forward to seeing his best friend Louis, as well as receiving rations and mail. As the wagon approached the bridge, bullets killed both mules. Private Ziegra fired back, killing one of the **Husaren** with a shot to the head. **Stosstruppen** jumped on the wagon and grabbed the driver. The driver was hit over the head with a rifle and fell backward into the wagon. The guide in the back took a bullet to the wrist and fell to the floor. Both proceeded to play dead. Then the fight began. Private Ziegra was shot at close range with a Becker-Hollander small-calibre pistol. The bullet entered his chin, missed the jaw bone, and exited near the right nostril. Despite the blood spurting from his head, Ziegra didn't stop

pummeling the German **Stosstruppsoldaten** that jumped him. He was eventually overpowered and taken away as a prisoner. **Vizefeldwebel** Ettighoffer remembered the American violently lashing out with his fists, flooring a German with each blow. Several assailants had bloody noses, a few broken teeth and black eyes. With the struggle over, the Germans robbed the wagon of mail and rations and went back to their lines with Private Ziegra. Private Marvin recalled: "They had to fight to carry him off and had there been four or five instead of 20 or 30 they never in this world would have taken him." At the opportune moment both driver and guide sprang up and ran north into the Company H kitchen area, where they decribed the fracas. A patrol quickly went out looking for Louis but found instead rubber waders, a sack of second-class mail, tins of corned beef, and an American and German helmet at a break point through the barbed wire.[824] Iron crosses from the scuffle were awarded to nine **Stosstruppsoldatenen**. **Gefreiter** Stollenwerk was promoted to **Unteroffizier** and the rest of the raiding party were given leave.[825]

Private Louis Ziegra became a legend among the Germans. He was a 25–year-old

Lieutenant Colonel George Marshall addresses the officers of 1st Division, an early example of the exemplary leadership he demonstrated for the rest of his career. (Marshall, *Memoirs of My Services in the World War, 1917–18*)

second-generation German-American whose father, Richard, bitterly opposed the German militarism of the time. Lieutenant Joseph P. Burke, an American officer captured that Saturday at Seicheprey, reported after returning from Germany in late 1918 that a German officer commented on Private Ziegra, stating that he was considered one of the bravest men they had ever seen. It was said that he had killed or knocked unconscious several of his captors while fighting with bare hands. It became necessary to knock him out with a rifle butt and carry him back to German lines.[826] Not only did Ettighoffer write about the incident, **General der Artillerie** von Gallwitz mentioned Ziegra's fighting spirit in his post-war memoirs: "An American of the 26th Division, captured at the southern front by Xivray had defended himself mightily and refused all testimony."[827]

VIIIe armée and *32e corps d'armée* staffs commented two days later on 17 April. The raid demonstrated the enterprise of the enemy. They expressed concern over German ability to penetrate Position 1 with ease and lie in ambush. The French command reminded units along the Woëvre that a more vigorous attitude was essential: "All that is necessary is a desire on the part of the Command to undertake them. 'WE ARE IN THE BATTLE'". *Esprit de corps* needed revitalization. New reporting criteria for colonels serving under *VIIIe armée* now required

a morning report detailing activity by their troops, to include listing weapons required for night operations: knife, automatic pistol, grenade, and automatic rifle. Those in command and second-in-command would carry a compass in all night operations.[828] Private Ziegra's capture made the western village of Marvoisin off-limits to all vehicles bringing rations. Two weeks later orders were generated stating that Marvoisin was to be abandoned during the evening hours. A stand-to position was established across the Rupt de Mad and along the "Q" trench. In his lifetime, Private Ziegra never received recognition for his valour that night.[829]

AMERICAN AVIATION CROSSES THE FRONT LINE

Aviation operations over the Woëvre were limited, since major campaigns to the north consumed most of the available aerial resources. Missions were sporadic and actual contact between adversaries was rare. General Summerall expressed frustration: "Enemy planes directed the fire of their batteries and also strafed our positions. Our air effort was feeble, and little help came from the French. I at once realized that all field artillery should be able to attack planes in order to carry out the mission of artillery to

Lieutenant Winslow looks closely at his kill that day, the first enemy aeroplane shot down by a member of the US Air Service in the war. (Aaron Weaver)

'destroy that element of the enemy which at the moment is most dangerous to the infantry.'"[830] Despite General Summerall's misgivings, it was an ideal start for American aviation. The 1st Corps Observation Group working with *32ᵉ corps d'armée* and 26th Division established a routine for aviators and ground support to better understand the tempo of operations. American post-war assessments of German aviation over the southern Woëvre front hardly mentioned aerial combat. Isolated observation planes were reported from time to time. No pursuit formations of more than five planes were operating and the presence of pursuit planes even in small numbers over the sector was rare. The Germans had in place an unusually strong concentration of mobile anti-aircraft artillery.[831]

1st Aero Squadron proceeded to Toul on 26 March 1918 after several months in training at Amanty. They acquired Spad XI and AR 1 for aerial observation. Counterparts at the 88th Aero Squadron later assessed the ARs as "large, cumbersome, depperdussin controlled ships … a great joke."[832] The 1st Aero Squadron was the first active squadron of the 1st Corps Observation Group at Toul flying under *32ᵉ corps d'armée* tactical control and 1st American Army Corps administrative control. Later in May, the 12th Aero Squadron and 88th Aero Squadron arrived in the Toul sector to flesh out the 1st Corps Observation Group in supporting the 26th Division. Missions were keeping the 26th Division informed of the general situation within enemy lines by means of visual and photographic reconnaissance, adjusting friendly artillery fire, and when possible conducting contact patrols with the infantry. For the latter, both infantry and aviation required training in communication with contact panels as well as radio to keep in contact with the 51st Field Artillery Brigade. As a novice to aerial operations in the southern Woëvre front, the 1st Aero Squadron was not expected to produce any important tactical results or render any great assistance to the conduct of operations. The pilots, with one or two exceptions, had never operated at the front. Most of the observers, after a course of intensive tactical and technical training in observation schools, had spent one or two months on duty as active aircrew with French *escadrilles* at the front. Observers brought exceedingly valuable practical knowledge. The reduced activity proved a blessing in readying American aviation to undertake intensive operations later that summer.

One of the first 1st Aero Squadron pilots was a former member of the 101st Engineers, Lieutenant William "Billy" Schauffler. Schauffler flew one of the first Spad XIs received by the squadron. Lieutenant Thomas J. Griffin, from the 1st Division's 28th Infantry, applied his infantry combat experience in supporting his aviator colleagues. As the first photographic officer for the US Air Service, Griffin held a special status. He had flown with French *escadrilles* prior to the arrival of the 1st Aero Squadron and had survived being shot down in No Man's Land. On 6 April, Major Ralph Royce, 1st Aero Squadron commander, took Griffin with him and conducted the first official sortie over the German front line and took aerial photographs. The prints were subsequently developed upon landing in the photo car along the side of the road, since the support buildings and barracks were still under construction.[833]

PURSUIT

The second aviation unit supporting the 26th Division was the 94th Aero Squadron under the command of Major Jean (John) W.F.M Huffer, flying Nieuport 28 fighters from their landing ground near Toul. The 94th Aero Squadron was considered competent to provide pursuit support to the 26th Division's sector.[834] The 94th Aero Squadron faced one primary adversary, **Jagdstaffel (Jasta) 64** under the command of **Leutnant** Hanke, a former infantryman. His **Jasta 64** comprised fourteen **Albatros D.Va** and **Pfalz D.IIIa** flown by seven pilots – three officers and four NCOs. **Jasta 64** unit strength included 100 enlisted personnel with three mechanics assigned to each machine. Their mission was to cover the **zwischen Maas und Mosel** airspace chasing enemy aeroplanes and attacking *Caquot* balloons. As of April, **Jasta 64** had not scored any aerial victories. **Leutnant** Hanke reported to **Hauptmann** Rutz, **Kofl C**, for the **Kirschblüte** operation. **Leutnant** Hanke designated three or four of his pursuit fighters to standby on alert throughout the day. When **Drachen** observers discovered hostile enemy aeroplanes the call went to Joppecourt and the **Jasta 64** pilots scrambled. **Jasta 64** pilots considered their **Pfalz D.IIIa** to be inferior to the **Albatros D.Va** in manoeuvrability; however, the **Pfalz D.IIIa** did possess a better climb.[835] Unit markings were large alternating parallel red and black bands on the fixed plane and the depth rudder. German aeroplanes were now identified by rectangular "Grecian" crosses. The previous Maltese cross was being phased out at this time.

America's first pursuit aerial victories were won on 14 April near Toul by Lieutenants Alan Winslow and Douglas Campbell, 94th Aero Squadron pilots. Pursuit pilots awaited calls confirming sightings of enemy aeroplanes from the Woëvre anti-aircraft sector control centres at Commercy, Lironville, and Dieulouard. Lieutenant Eddie Rickenbacker, still awaiting his first victory, flew patrols at this time. At 0840, Lironville called 94th Aero Squadron confirming a sighting of two German aeroplanes flying south toward the St. Gongoult aerodrome. Winslow and Campbell scrambled to their Nieuport 28s via motorcycle sidecars. A **Jasta 64 Albatros D.Va** and a **Pfalz D.IIIa** arrived over the St. Gongoult aerodrome, providing 94th Aero Squadron ground crew their first sight of aerial combat. Winslow outmanoeuvred **Vizefeldwebel** Antoni Wroniecki flying the **Albatros D.Va**, fired twenty to thirty rounds and watched him go straight down into an uncontrolled dive and crash.[836] Meanwhile, **Unteroffizier** Heinrich Simon flying the **Pfalz D.IIIa** engaged Campbell. Campbell outmanoeuvred Simon, got behind his tail, aimed and pulled the trigger. After fifty rounds, flames came out of the **Pfalz** fuselage and the plane crashed in a mass of flame. Simon was thrown clear and escaped with a broken leg and serious burns to the face, hands, feet, and lungs.[837]

Both American victors arrived at the crash sites to find jubilant French and American soldiers as well as a sizeable crowd of ecstatic citizens of Toul. Winslow met Wroniecki, "a scrawny, poorly clad little devil, dressed in a rotten German uniform" and identified himself as an American. Wroniecki replied to Winslow, "*Alors, la guerre est finie pour moi*" (So the war is over for me).[838] **Vizefeldwebel** Antoni Wroniecki later provided valuable information on **Jagdstaffel 64** that was published in the Summary of Air Information: Air Intelligence Bulletin. The remains of the German aeroplanes were put on display at Toul. Two days later, *Général* Gérard's aide decorated Campbell and Winslow with the *Croix de Guerre* with palm.

The aerial victories helped pave the way for subsequent visits by US commanders. Five days after Winslow and Campbell's victories, General Liggett visited Huffer's 94th Pursuit Squadron, equipped with new-type "baby" Nieuports. He shook hands with America's leading ace at the time, Major Raul Lufbery.[839] Two weeks later, Liggett visited 1st Aero Squadron and commented on their "commendable esprit."

BALLONS CAPTIF

Balloon Company B/2 continued operations when 26th Division took control of their portion of the southern Woëvre front. French commanders held authority over both French and American *aérostiers* on all matters that concerned technical and tactical employment. The French commander ordered Balloon Company B/2 to fly the *Caquot ballon* during every hour of visibility, resulting in an average 18 hours of daily operations.[840] The *aérostiers* noticed German aerial activity was high as the relief continued, seeing more **Drachen** to the north at Georges-en-Haye, Jaulny, Sagenau, Vigneulles, and Thiaucourt. Balloon Company B/2 took note that the Germans had at least twelve **Drachen** to their two *Caquot ballons*.[841] The biggest challenge Balloon Company B/2 faced in their first two months on the line was the

Major John Gallant paid his own way from the Philippines to Europe to fight. His passport application records the commitment. (Boston Public Library) weather. Poor visibility and no ascensions meant no liaison with the 26th Division. This was the case during the week of 18 April.[842] Whatever artillery observations were made on 18 April were from other sources. *SRA* determined that the German artillery fire was normal with the exception of 100 rounds fired at *Bois du Jury*.[843] The week prior to **Kirschblüte** was inconclusive for Balloon Company B/2. Operations were limited thanks to three straight days of miserable weather. They did manage once to conduct liaison with 103rd Field Artillery. On 17 April a night ascension was made by Lieutenants Koenig and Patterson but nothing of significance was observed – again, the weather was the culprit.

Anti-aircraft was well established, employing Hotchkiss machine guns and modified 75mm. The 75mm firing twenty-five shots a minute without recoil made it ideal for the role.[844] One French anti-aircraft location near the American artillery battery on Beaumont Ridge gave the Americans their first lessons in the art of air defence. A veteran *poilu* of three years at the same battery admitted his unit had never shot down an enemy plane. Despite the lack of success, the anti-aircraft battery men seemed in good spirits. The system employed by this battery in "spotting" an enemy plane entailed a man from the battery always serving in the front-line trenches. Whenever a hostile aeroplane flew over the sector, the battery was immediately contacted. Anti-aircraft men rushed to their posts at the guns and searched the sky for the hostile. After dark the battery kept fire to a minimum to avoid German counter-battery.[845]

"RUMORS ARE CIRCULATING"

Corporal LaBranche remembered some levity from Battery E: "Little gas. Thrills are becoming common. Jakie fell in the latrine. Men won't speak to him. Wait till Cav. [Lieutenant Cavanaugh] sees him. He'll smell him anyway. That dog knows there's a war going on. He knows when to drag when it isn't safe."[846]

Over the weeks that the 102nd Infantry was forward, they repaired trenches, drained as much of the water that they could, removed broken wood and replaced the wire. Hundreds of new duckboards were positioned. Old and damaged telephone wire was removed. The regiment did little to repair dugouts since this was a job for drier weather. Besides, there were more pressing needs. The occupied villages including Seicheprey were cleaned and policed daily. The men constructed covered French latrines wherever possible as well as introducing bucket latrines that served the needs of the troops just as well.

German artillery commenced registering 102nd Infantry's sector crossroads, PCs and avenues of communication and stopped their routine of harassing fire five days prior to **Kirschblüte**. 77mm was aimed at Beaumont and Seicheprey from Gargantua and *Mort-Mare*, 105mm directed fire on *Bois du Jury* and 150mm targeted Beaumont. OP and *SROT* reports suggested the possibility that additional artillery was arriving. Rear-area sightings of more trains arriving suggested supplies for a sustained operation were being delivered. Scuttlebutt offered the possibility that the Woëvre was being readied for a break in the Allied line in the east, encircling Verdun, and taking critical resources from the ongoing struggle on the Somme. Such speculation proved far-fetched as the Germans were fully committed to the north and what resources were left were to hold the ground.

Corporal LaBranche captured the mood: "Rumors that they are going to blow Mont Sec up and that the Pioneers are already digging the saps. Well, I wish they would blow something up or start something."[847]

Le saillant de Saint Mihiel 25 September 1914

The advance of *General der Artillerie* Strantz's *Armeeabteilung Strantz* over the Woëvre assumed the final position on 25 September 1914. The disposition of French and German forces is superimposed on a contemporary French map showing the topography. (SHD)

Lieutenant General Robert Lee Bullard, Commander of 2nd Army at the end of the war, who led the 1st Division while at the Ansauville Sector. (Joseph Cummings Chase, *Soldiers All, Portraits and Sketches of the Men of the AEF*, courtesy of Colonel Robert R. McCormick Research Center First Division Museum at Cantigny)

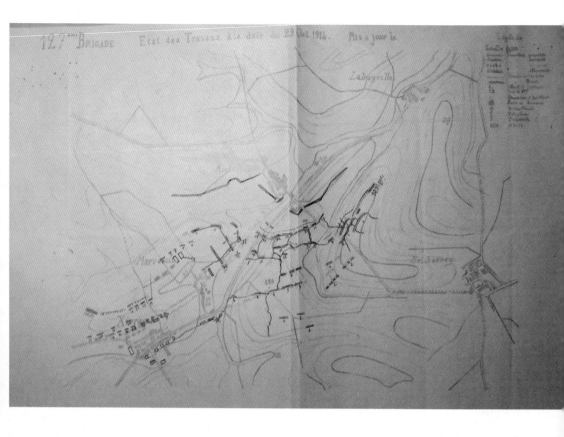

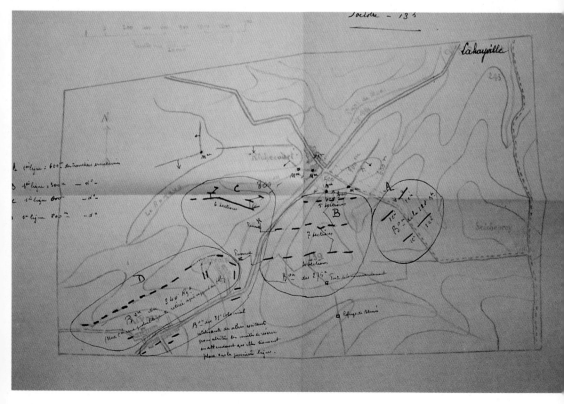

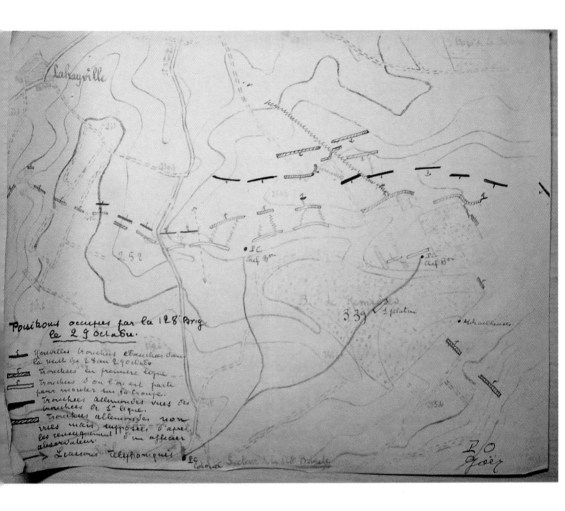

Above: To the northwest of Seichprey at *Bois de Carré* and north of *Bois de Remières* the French 128ᵉ *brigade d'infanterie* assume positions on 29 October 1914 that were maintained until September 1918. (SHD)

Opposite top: The trench networks assume the look that governed the battle ground in the sector by the end of October. Note the first employment of *boyaux* (communication trenches) connecting the front line to trenches to the rear. (SHD).

Opposite bottom: Positional War becomes the norm at the Woëvre in October. The initial trenches are established west of Seicheprey. (SHD)

Above: *Général* Augustin Gérard, commander of *8ᵉ Armee* and tactical commander of American forces until the St. Mihiel offensive. (Courtesy of Tony Langley)

Opposite top: The German trenches in blue cover the battle ground of *Bois de Mort Mare*, the location of *5ᵉ compagnie du 63ᵉ régiment d'infanterie's* aborted 19 April 1915 attack and the jumping off points for *Einladung* and *Kirschblüte*. (SHD)

Opposite bottom: The first battleground now seen from the assigned sector map of 1918. Trenches first built in 1914 became part of Position 1 Center H defence. Assigned platoon strength within the trench strong points is marked.

German aerial reconnaissance was well established both in technology and process by the time the Americans occupied the sector. FA (A) 298b executed aerial reconnaissance in support of 78. Reserve Division using two standard types of aerial cameras: *Fliegerkamera* (FK) Type I, a hand-held 25-cm camera, and FK Type II, a 50-cm aerial camera that was mounted in the observer seat. When *Stabia C* worked on *Armeeabteilung C* reconnaissance requirements, they had *FA 46b Lb* use longer focal length cameras, such as FK III, 70 cm, or FK IV, 120 cm. (Alan Toelle)

As well as having the best aerial cameras, the Germans employed an optical photographic rectifier built by Zeiss that merged coverage from the photographic plates to create a scaled mosaic image such as the *Stabia* shot assembled two days prior to *Kirschblüte*. (Helmut Jäger).

The McIntyre Sally Army sisters. Irene (right) spent 256 days at or near the front. (LOC)

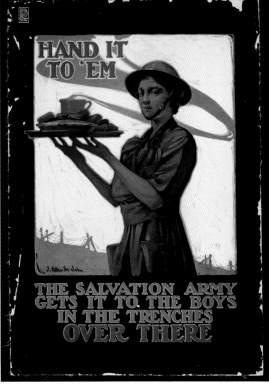

The military-style uniform of the Salvation Army was criticized in some quarters but not at home. (LOC)

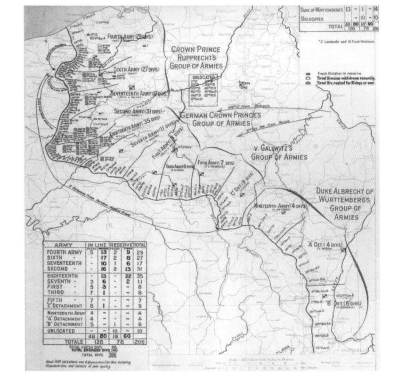

German Order of Battle, Western Front, 1 May 1918; *Armeeabteilung C* is shown in the centre of the Front. The divisions shown were in place in April 1918 when the Seicheprey affair took place. (National Archives)

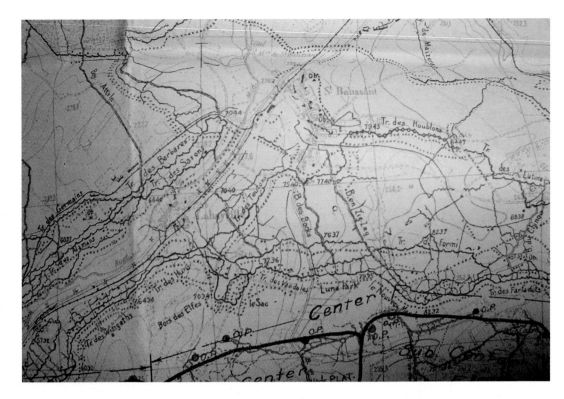

An incredibly detailed map view showing lines of trenches and critical communication trenches such as Boyau de Zig Zag and Boyau de Teutons directly north of Seicheprey in 1918. (SHD)

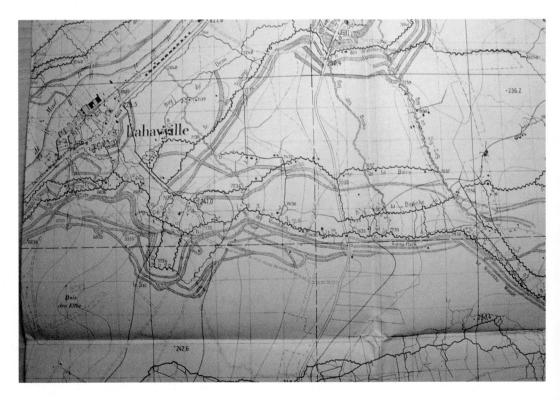

German trenches and barbed wire formations south of Lahayville to the west of St Baussant. (SHD)

Legend of a French 1:80,000 scale map of Toul sector, 1918, showing French defensive networks in place with 1ʳᵉ Position, Position 1bis, and 2ᵉᵐᵉ Position marked. (SHD).

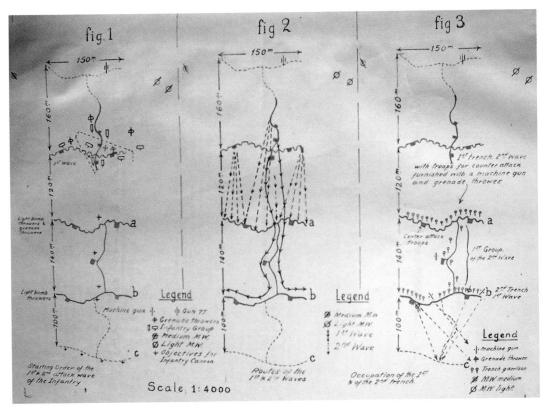

One of the most comprehensive descriptions of how a German assault was choreographed; this is an Allied intelligence assessment. (SHD)

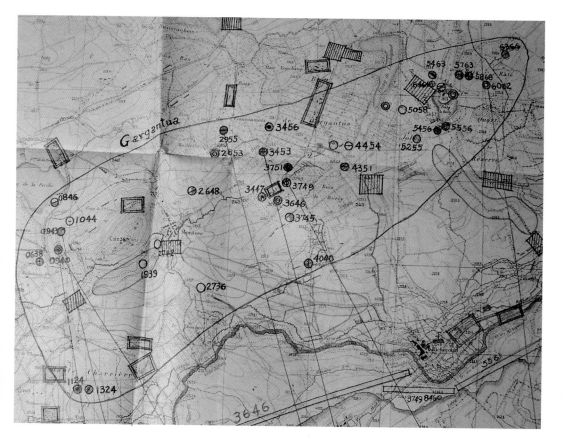

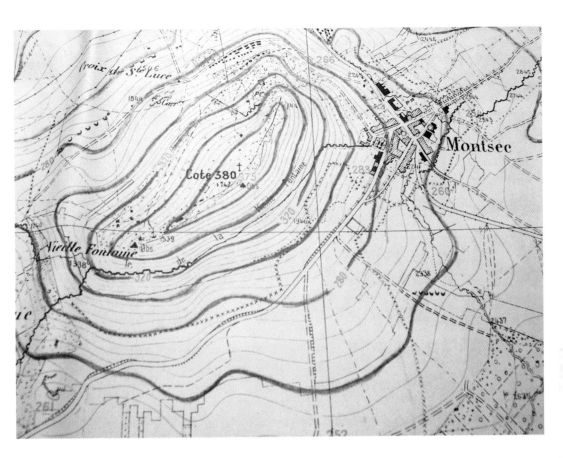

Above: Cote 380, better known as Montsec, was one of the most impressive geographic features along the entire Western Front. The Germans held this high ground until the St Mihiel offensive in September 1918 and governed all operations thanks to the ability to see any activity from this vantage point. (Archives – Museum Branch, Historical Services, The Adjutant General's Office, Massachusetts)

Opposite top: The surviving 75mm French gun used by the Connecticut National Guard at Yale University for understanding fundamentals of modern artillery prior to deployment to Europe. (West Haven CT Veteran's Museum/Jos Brunjes)

Opposite bottom: Detailed map used by both 1st Division and 26th Division on location of German artillery at Gargantua, northwest of Seicheprey. (Archives – Museum Branch, Historical Services, The Adjutant General's Office, Massachusetts)

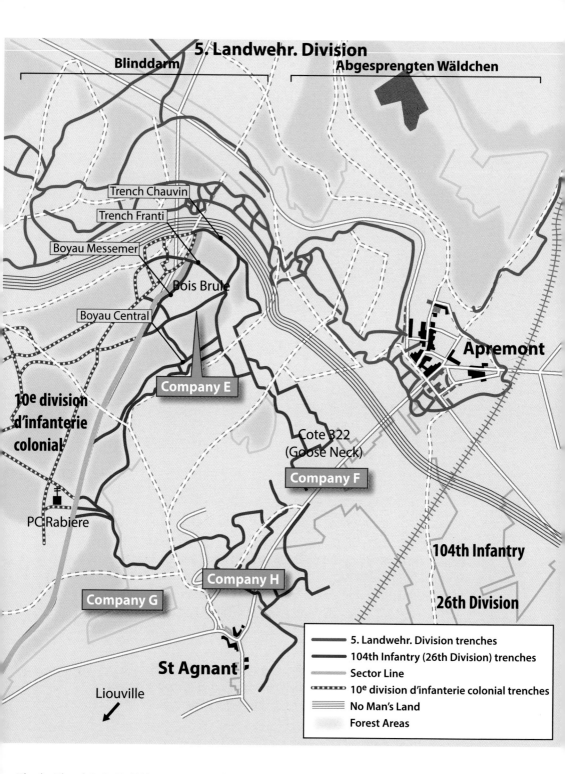

The battle of *Bois-Brûlé*/Apremont took place 10–13 April 1918. The German *5.Landwehr.Division* executed two operations (*Blinddarm* "Appendicitis" or more literally "Appendix", and *Abgesprengten Wäldchen*, "Cut-off Small Woods Blast") against the 104th Infantry, 26th Division, and the *10e division d'infanterie colonial*. They were successfully repulsed by the Allies. (Spellmount)

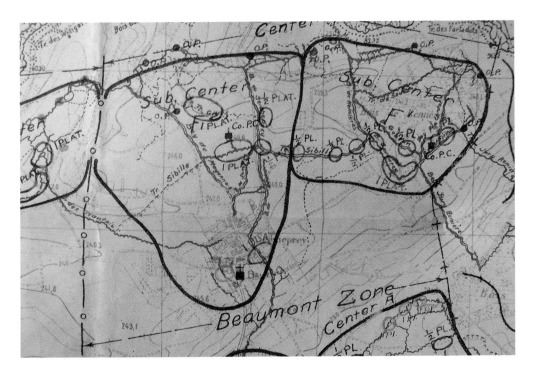

The Position 1 Beaumont Zone with Subcenter F1 (*Bois de Remières*) and Subcenter F2 (Seicheprey) defended by American forces throughout the last year of the war. Platoon assignments are indicated. (SHD)

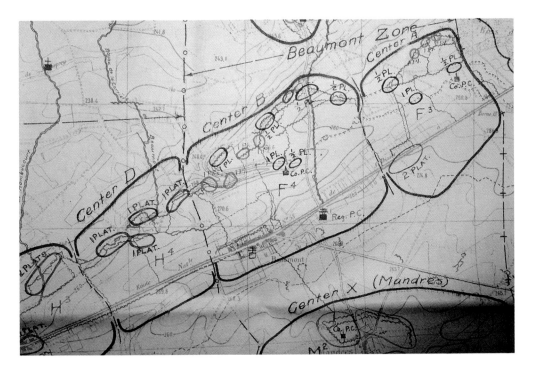

The critical Position 1 Bis sectors along the Beaumont Ridge; Beaumont was the regimental headquarters for both the 18th Infantry and follow-on 102nd. (SHD)

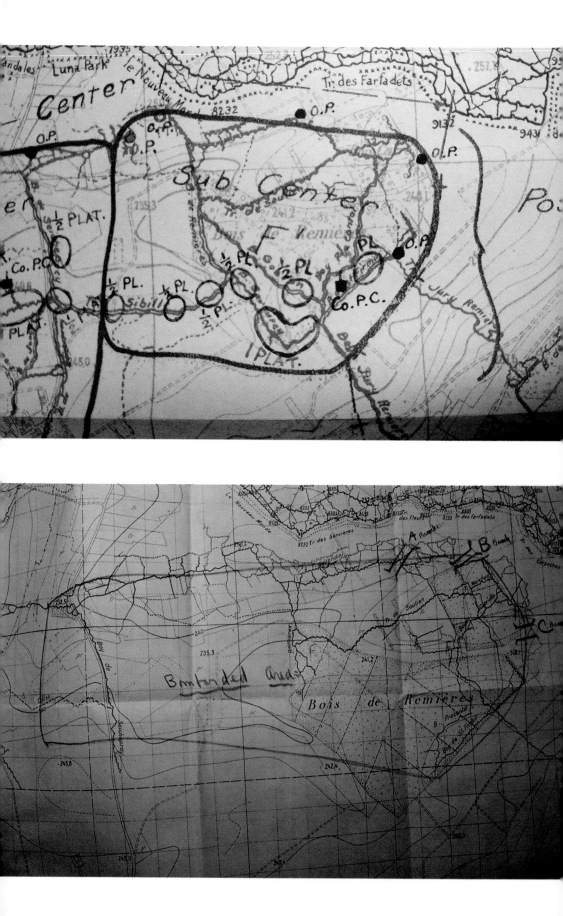

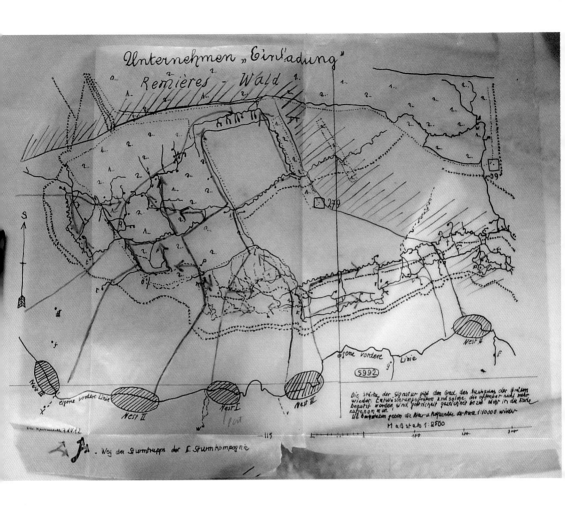

Above: The German account of the *Einladung* raid portraying the exact route of the assault units from their jump-off "nests" into *Bois de Carré* to the left and the American trenches north of *Bois de Remières* to the right. (NARA)

Opposite top: A detail of American positions at *Bois de Remières* where the *Einladung* and *Kirschblüte* assaults took place. (SHD)

Opposite bottom: A fascinating glimpse into Major General Bullard's simple narration for General Passaga of what transpired during *Einladung*; his sketch showing the three breaches in the lines. (SHD)

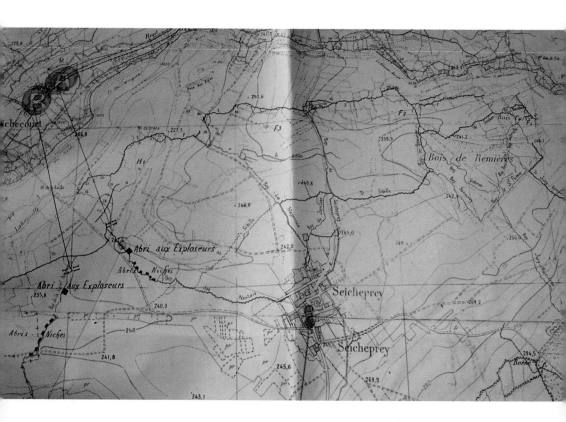

Above: State-of-the-art gas projectors as described to Lieutenant Colonel C Marshall by *Groupe Z, 34e Bataillon du Genie*; the two launch locations and direction of flight to the German lines outside of Lahayville are mapped. (SHD)

Opposite, top and bottom: Two maps from Major General Bullard's report on the first American assaults into the German lines north of Seicheprey and *Bois de Remières* on 12 March. Captain Quesenberry's morning raid took place north of *Bois de Remières* (above) and Captain Graves' evening raid breached the lines southeast of Richecourt (below). (SHD)

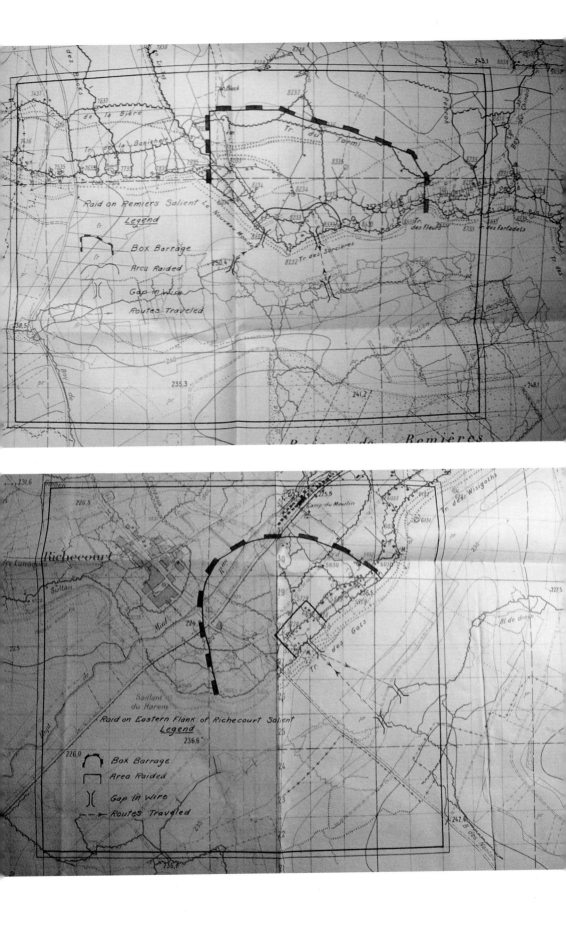

Raid on Remiers Salient

Legend

☐ Box Barrage

Area Raided

Ⅱ Gap in Wire

Routes Traveled

Raid on Eastern Flank of Richecourt Salient
Legend

⊓ Box Barrage

Area Raided

Ⅱ Gap in Wire

- → Routes Traveled

An amazing mosaic of German aerial coverage taken two days before the *Erstürmung* at Seicheprey. Details include defences along the 1-Bis line, the artillery emplacements for Bryan I and the Davis Battery, as well as anti-aircraft artillery locations in the sector to be attacked. (NASM)

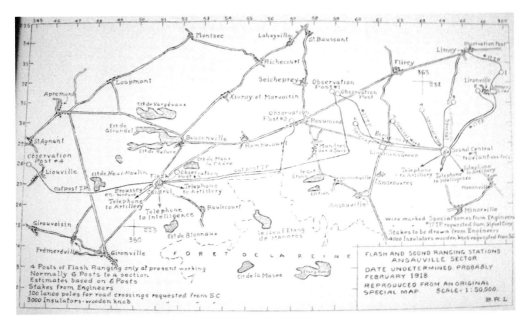

Flash and sound ranging, Ansauville. (World War Records, First Division A.E.F. Regular, Vol. 25)

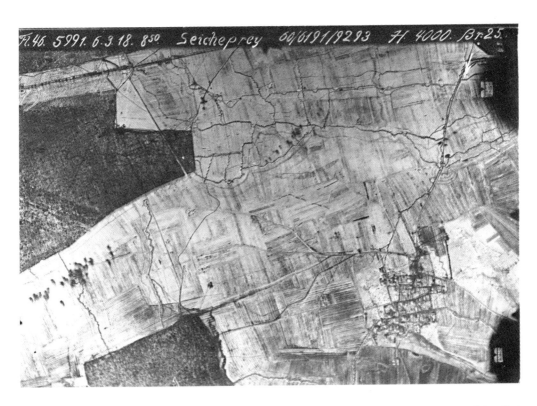

FA 46b Lb followed up on 18th Infantry prisoner interrogation from *Einladung* and acquired detailed coverage of Seicheprey on 6 March 1918 using a FK I 25cm aerial camera at 4000 metres. *Bois du Jury* is top left and Seicheprey village is at the bottom right. The battalion headquarters at the southern end of the village was identified and accuracy of artillery fire on key targets (shown by black smudge marks) analysed. (Bayerisches Hauptstaatsarchiv)

Above and opposite: Detailed map of the German attack with red overlay showing the entire artillery barrage plan in concert with the attack on Seicheprey, *Bois de Remières*. At the critical Position 1-Bis, German artillery neutralized any attempt to reinforce the Americans in the forward positions. (NARA and 102nd Field Artillery)

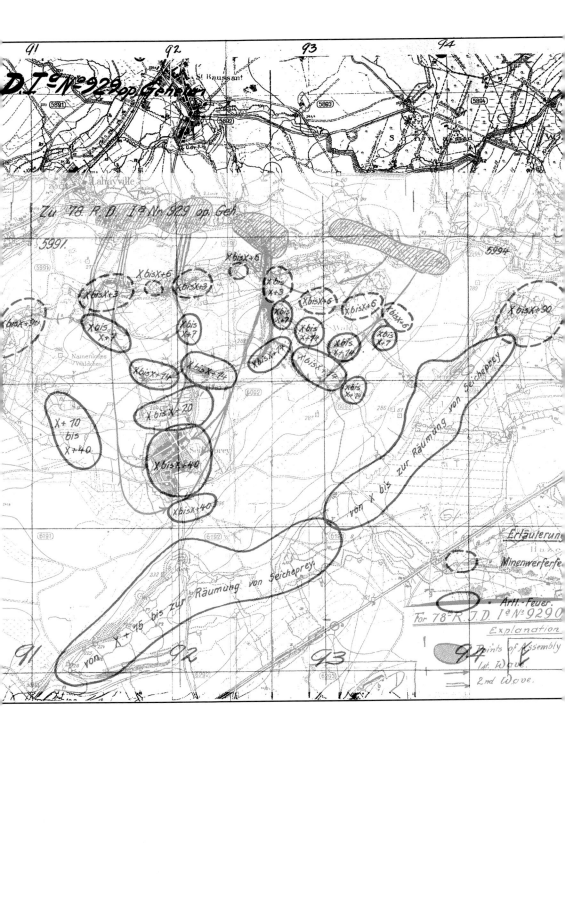

American prisoners; 117 survivors of *Kirschblüte* are photographed (below) prior to transit to Chalons for ongoing interrogation and incarceration in German POW camps. These photos were reproduced by the thousands and distributed via *Drachen* captive balloons along the Western Front. Americans at Seicheprey were able to identify their friends and confirm they were still alive thanks to this propaganda effort. (USAFA McDermott Library Special Collections, SMS 4, above, Yves Fohlen, below)

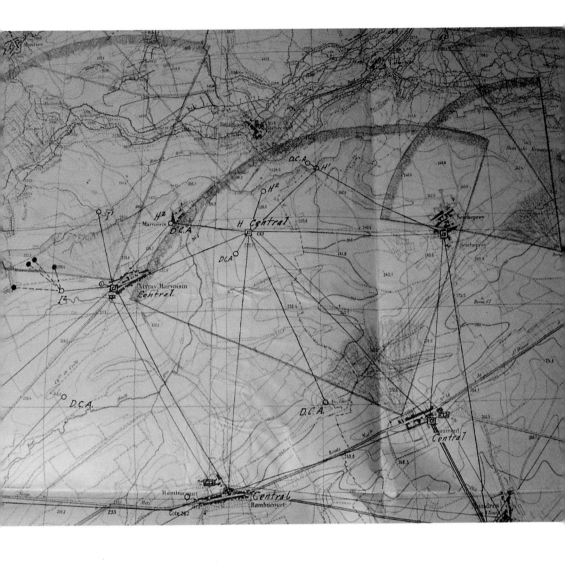

Liaison posed one of the greatest challenges to American forces. This was especially true during the *Einladung* and *Kirschblüte* assaults. Communications are portrayed in this 26th Division map. (Archives – Museum Branch, Historical Services, The Adjutant General's Office, Massachusetts)

Yankee Doings portrays Jury Wood.
(Yankee Division Veteran's Association)

The 103rd Field Artillery Regiment had to endure the tragic consequences of fratricide on forward deployed infantry while serving at the Woëvre. The unit's service was distinguished despite the shortfalls of the 155mm field howitzers. (103rd Field Artillery)

Above: Major Rau's grave at Aisne-Marne marks his last battle, the Second Marne. He was killed by an artillery round on 17 July 1918. (Finnegan)

Opposite: One of several German graves at Bouillonville of men who died during the *Kirschblüte* assault. *Leutnant* Tabke and *Vizefeldwebel* Winkelmann share their final resting place. (Finnegan)

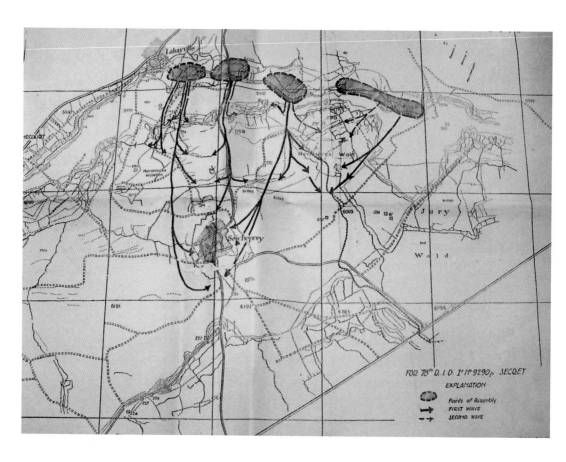

Above: General Passaga's visit to the United States was a celebrated event. Major General Edwards' personal copy includes an inscription. (Thomas and JoAnn Wallace Collection)

Opposite top: American forces continued to study *Kirschblüte* after the war. The cartography department at the US Army Headquarters of the Rhine at Koblenz drew up this detailed look at the attack. (NARA)

Opposite bottom: *Tanks at Seichprey* (sic) by Harvey T. Dunn, September 1918. Lt Col Patton's Renault tanks advance north. (Cornebise, *Art from the Trenches*)

On July 1922, the state of Connecticut memorialized the 102nd Infantry at Seicheprey with a fountain. (Finnegan)

On 3 August 1937 the St Mihiel Memorial of Montsec was dedicated on top of the rise, a fitting tribute to the American forces who defended the Woëvre from January to November 1918, longer than any other American sector of the front. (Finnegan)

Brigadier General John Henry Parker's final resting place at the Presidio in San Francisco; four Distinguished Service Crosses, a Distinguished Service Medal and a Silver Star. (Finnegan)

Stubby on the cover of *Parade* magazine, the most famous survivor of Seicheprey. Stubby died on 4 April 1926. Ten months later the *Herald* reported his falling in "at his last post … Stubby is stuffed. He was first enrolled as a stray dog in the Yale bowl. He went overseas with the 102d and was wounded at Toul. Back in America he led all the Legion parades he could. He met President Coolidge. He was decorated by Gen. Pershing." (Courtesy *Parade*)

General der Artillerie Max von Gallwitz commanded *5. Armee* from December 1916 to September 1918 and proved a formidable opponent to *Général* Gérard and General Pershing.

CHAPTER 15

Relief at Midnight

The midnight hour of 19 April was as clear and quiet a night as one could ask for on the Toul front. Just so quiet, however, as to be ominous; one of those clear, dreamy moonlit nights when the war seemed far away. An anonymous diarist described the environment at *Bois de Remières*:

> When I came up to the front line that night I could see no shelter for the men but a little piece of elephant iron, or rather sheet iron stuck in the trench side. Mud and water up to my middle. There is a hole in the trench side under this iron, under which the men can crawl to keep dry and to get a little sleep when not on guard. The stench around this trench is awful. Mud, stagnant water, broken pieces of rotten duckboard, refuse of all kinds, overflow from latrines four years or more old, parts of old clothing, and numerous other things that the boys in the S.O.S. [Sources of Supply] don't have use for.[848]

Battalion reliefs were scheduled every twelfth day by the battalion in reserve in Mandres and Ansauville, relieving one battalion in the front lines. The relieved battalion rested for six days and then relieved the battalion in the other part of the zone. On the sixth day at the front the battalion not scheduled for relief conducted an inter-battalion relief, the two companies in the 1-Bis position changing places with the two in the advance line.[849] Commanding officers remained to acquaint the new troops with operations. Captain George C. Freeland was Rau's Company D commander, having just relieved Captain Arthur F. Locke of Company M 12 hours prior in the sector known as F-2. Company L with Lieutenant Tyler had been relieved in *Bois de Remières* (F-1) by Company C under Captain Alfred H. Griswold. On the 1-Bis line, Company A went to Center A and Company B occupied Center B. By 0200 on 20 April Company M and Company L were back in regimental reserve in Ansauville for their week's "rest" while Company C checked out Sub-center F-1 with the three platoons occupying Sibille Trench. Company D checked out Sibille Trench with the two platoons they had. One platoon in Seicheprey prepared for duty that night. In front of Seicheprey two companies occupied two sub-sectors that were over half a kilometre in length. Each company had three platoons in the firing trench, while one platoon was kept in support for each company.[850]

Captain Harry Bissell commanded Sub-sector H-1 at the Beaumont "Q" Trench and Pont-Marvoisin. One of Bissell's platoon commanders of Company E was Lieutenant Charles "Butch" Lockhart, a spirited officer with a penchant for excitement. Unfortunately, his record was blemished since arrival in the Toul sector.

Lockhart was awaiting court martial, having been caught drinking brandy in the trenches with his men.[851] Lockhart's sector comprised 600 metres of *Boyau Nantais*, north-west of Seicheprey – difficult to manage at any time – incredibly challenging when casualties mounted.

The night was quiet, and the moon was bright enough to permit visibility of a mile. Despite this, the 1st Battalion of the 102nd Infantry was able to complete its relief of the 3rd battalion without enemy interference. By 0130, Company C was in position in *Bois de Remières* and Company D was in front of Seicheprey. Certain machine-gun squads and the 18th Infantry disciplinary prisoners were also occupying Seicheprey forward ground.

1ST PLATOON, COMPANY C

Corporal Leo Boucher's 1st Platoon, Company C, moved north as the day wore on and darkness fell. He formed his men in a single file alongside the church at Mandres. The usual orders were passed along the line: no smoking, no lights, no talking. Boucher also ordered them to remove and sheath bayonets so as to avoid any accidents. They moved along a well-camouflaged and torn-up road until they came to a garden gate that was still standing, where they dropped into a *boyau*. His men closed ranks and marched so as not to lose contact with their buddy ahead. As they proceeded into *Bois de Remières*, the platoon was aided by the moonlight. When German flares lit the sky, 1st Platoon froze in their positions "resembling trees or posts" until the light faded. Boucher proudly recalled his platoon made record time relieving the 3rd Battalion. Aligned with the map he placed a machine gunner at either end of his platoon's position. Then he assigned a bayonet man to either side to challenge anyone coming near their position. The rest of his men were allowed to rest up as best they could in the bottom of the trench.[852]

Corporal Boucher was a senior enlisted man so he assumed some platoon responsibilities. That night a runner arrived at Boucher's dugout

with orders to report immediately to Captain Griswold's CP. Boucher sat there at a hastily improvised table made from long planks on trestles that ran the length of the *abris*. Maps were laid out, with candles providing the only light. Lieutenant Albert Johnson, Company C headquarters staff, Lieutenant Harold B. Carruth, commander of 3rd Platoon, and a few sergeants were present. Captain Griswold, the company "Skipper," stood at the head of the table and began to explain the plans. He told his Company C leadership that the *2e Bureau* had tapped the enemy's wires and found out that an attack of "German Shock Troops" was in the making. (Though the information was more likely to have come from French civilian "spies" behind the German lines.) The consensus was it was to take place sometime that night.[853] He instructed Boucher not to advance beyond the point within the forest assigned as a defensive position.

Griswold told Boucher everyone was expected to hold their ground until the very last man. He asked Boucher if he had anything to say before they returned to their units. Boucher replied he needed additional men since his platoon had suffered recent casualties. Company leaders began looking at each other but no one volunteered to give up any men. Finally, Lieutenant Carruth volunteered to transfer a squad from 3rd Platoon to Boucher. Corporal Boucher chose Corporal George "Dodi" Gritzback and his men. By the following night Gritzback had earned the Silver Star for gallantry, but died in the struggle.[854]

Corporal Boucher and another soldier returned to their post at the north-east sector of *Bois de Remières* and crawled out into No Man's Land to reconnoitre the barbed-wire emplacements. They discovered the wire had been cut in zig-zag style. Looking at it directly gave the impression that the wire was solid but in fact the **Pioniere** had prepared for **Kirschblüte**. No sooner had Boucher regained his position than the moon clouded over – creating such darkness that he couldn't see his hand in front of his face. Boucher decided that his men should know what they all were in for: "I ordered bayonets fixed and hit the parapet."[855]

MACHINE GUNS IN PLACE

For several days the "alert" was maintained, but morning followed morning without any confrontation. Men grew more anxious, experiencing the exhaustion that came with constant readiness.[856] Captain Stanchfield, Company B, 102nd Machine Gun Battalion, placed his six machine guns around Seicheprey and six machine guns along *Boyau Jury-Remières* between *Bois de Remières* and *Bois du Jury*. All machine guns occupied open positions and most were set for indirect fire. When the enemy was sighted, the machine gunners were to fire direct. As midnight drew near, Stanchfield set up his headquarters in Seicheprey. To the rear of Seicheprey and *Bois de Remières*, Lieutenant Sanbarn's Company A defended the 1-Bis position of the Beaumont zone's Center A and Center B with twelve occupied positions.[857] Sanbarn's gun positions covered the German-occupied village of Richecourt to the north-east corner of *Bois du Jury*. Lieutenant Sanbarn also set his machine guns for indirect fire.[858] Machine guns on the north-east side of Seicheprey occupied outpost positions that had been taken twice before by the Germans in previous small raids. The outposts occupied low, swampy land requiring the water to be quietly pumped out by hand.

One position that 102nd Machine Gun Battalion occupied was a source of intense pride for Colonel "Machine Gun" Parker. In the Beaumont Quarry location known as Center D just south of his headquarters on the Beaumont Ridge, four machine guns were set up under camouflage the size of a table cloth. For 25 days and nights the guns operated without being detected by German observation posts, spies, or aerial reconnaissance. Parker's covert battery poured a continuous long-range indirect barrage across sectors F-1 and F-2 for 30 hours. German artillery searched all the area with shrapnel but failed to find these four guns, which continued

their work until the battle concluded. Colonel Parker, the US Army's number one expert on machine-gun employment, exalted in Center D unit's performance and the fact that the guns would later be "still on the job ready to repeat the operation."[859]

POSITION 1–BIS

French command's and General Traub's policy to have each company provide a platoon to reinforce the 1-Bis position weakened the forward sector's defence. Reconnaissance parties were sent forward before the relief but the battalion as a whole was not thoroughly acquainted with the trenches and the terrain they occupied.[860] The 102nd Infantry's principal line of resistance, where the major strong points were put in place, covered the 1-Bis position. The sectors comprised center A practically due south of Center F-1, center B south of F-2, Center D south of H-1, and Center E south of H-2.

At Grant Trench just north of Beaumont, Lieutenant Smith's 4th Platoon, Company M, was relieved by Lieutenant McGlasson's 3rd Platoon from Company D. Smith's platoon then proceeded to Ansauville by way of Beaumont, Mandres and Hamonville, arriving there at 0200. Lieutenant Fuessenich's Company M, 1st Platoon left the front-line Sibille Trench at 0030, proceeded south to Ansauville via Beaumont, Mandres and Hamonville. Lieutenant Boyd's 3rd Platoon, Company M, safely arrived in Ansauville at 0200. Sergeant Albin Backiel's 3rd Platoon of Company I was relieved in Center A position by Company A late at night and marched to Mandres. Lieutenant Edward Larned's Company I was relieved by Company A in Center A and proceeded to Mandres arriving at midnight. Company D, 102nd Infantry, had completed their relief of *Boyau Mayonnaise* (spelt variously as *Mayennaise, Mayennais*) by 0030.[861] 2nd Lieutenant C. R. Middaugh's 2nd Platoon, Company B, arrived in the cave that supported operations in Center B at 0200 and the troops dispersed to their bunks.[862]

Brigadier General George H. Shelton, commander of 104th Infantry at Bois-Brulé/Apremont, at the end of the war. He died shortly after the Armistice. (West Point)

line of support and machine guns echeloned in depth in *Bois de Remières*, near Seicheprey, and in the 2nd Battalion sector."[865]

Battery C, 102nd Field Artillery, operated in Hell's Half Acre. The battery painted a sign and hung it over the telephone detail's dugout, announcing to the world that their new residence was "Hell's Doorstep." About 250 metres to the right of the gun position was a small French canteen, concealed in the nearby woods, where champagne could be purchased for four francs a bottle. The Americans suspected the champagne was actually cider. While holding this position Battery C acquired a mascot, a little black and white fox terrier, named "Bumb."[866]

Colonel Parker observed that night to General Traub: "He [the enemy] was registering his guns for the extraordinary barrage ... the next morning."[863] All day Germans employed harassing fire by the batteries, systematically searching every *boyau* and every trench. Front-line preparations commenced as intelligence indicators suggested something was in progress across No Man's Land. During the day, two prisoners of war reported that a German **Sturmbataillon** was moving up through Montsec and it seemed likely that the enemy would attack the right of the Division the next day. 103rd Field Artillery batteries commanded by Major Chaffee received the intelligence and moved reserves of ammunition to battery locations, registered the 155mm guns, and prepared the units for action.[864]

Throughout 19 April the Germans harassed every *boyau* in the Beaumont Zone. This fire was *tire de réglage*, registering for the barrage unleashed the next morning. Major Bowditch reported to Colonel Craig: "Situation, afternoon of April 19, generally quiet, registering fire of some 20 to 40 heavy shells on Beaumont ... machine gun company between 5 and 6 in the

AVIATION OPERATIONS AT THE ELEVENTH HOUR

VIIIe armée aviation was busy flying aerial reconnaissance, *avion réglage*, and *liaison d'infanterie. Escadrille* AR.41 flew eight sorties, *Escadrille* AR.258 flew seven sorties and four reconnaissance. It was an uneventful day for American aviation along the Woëvre. 1st Aero Squadron reported that fourteen aeroplanes were available for duty but only three made it to the front lines and were unsuccessful working artillery adjustments. A fourth suffered engine trouble resulting in a forced landing, injuring the aircrew. Pursuit aviation by *Escadrille* N.92 flew five sorties. The 94th Aero Squadron also flew limited patrols that day along the southern front line of the Woëvre from Pont-à-Mousson to St. Mihiel. An hour later the second patrol flew west to east with no aerial combat to report. An alert was sounded when a German plane was spotted over Moncel and *Bois de Faux* east of Nancy and three Nieuport 28s scrambled, to no avail. Four Nieuport 28s flew a final evening patrol covering the same route the others had flown earlier.[867]

German **Drachen** operations were honed by years of experience on the front lines. Members of 101st Field Artillery, Battery B, recalled nine **drachen** were always up on clear days. Planning for **Kirschblüte** directed **Ballonzug 214** operating from their **Aufstiegplatz** [balloon bed] near Beney 11 kilometres to the north of Seicheprey to be the **Infanterieballon** [infantry balloon] in support of **Oberst** von Blankensee, commander of the infantry attack. The **Infanterieballon** ascended once that afternoon. Hoffmann as **artilleriekommandeur** had at his immediate disposal **Ballonzug 123**, with its **Aufstiegplatz** 12 kilometres north of Seicheprey near Jaulny, and **Ballonzug 215**, operating near Xammes 1 kilometre to the east of **Ballonzug 123**. Xammes was active with ascensions all afternoon. Jaulny **Drachen** ascended early that morning and later that evening. In the days before **Kirschblüte** all three **Drachen** were reported on station.[868]

Despite poor weather Lieutenants Taylor and Sedgwick from Balloon Company B/2 ascended that morning and returned within 45 minutes. A *Caquot* went up later at 1210 for the purpose of dropping a parachute to entertain Major General Liggett, I Corps commander, making his first visit to a balloon unit. Captain Butler ordered Master Sergeant Maricle to serve as the *aérostier* and simulate a parachute jump for General Liggett. Maricle ascended with sandbags weighing about 60kg affixed to the side of the basket. At 150 metres, Maricle became nervous with such a distinguished visitor observing his actions and cut the wrong rope, sending the sandbags plummeting to earth to crash 4.5 metres from General Liggett. Liggett reflected on the close call after the war: "I have no doubt that there were plenty of American soldiers who would have been most happy to have seen me dead."[869]

That evening Lieutenants McFarland and Taylor ascended and managed to acquire limited visibility up to 12 kilometres beyond the front lines, observing a **Drachen** descending from Beney. Unbeknownst to McFarland and Taylor, the **Drachen** was **Ballonzug 214**, the **Infanterieballon** providing observations for **Oberst** von Blankensee. The highlight of McFarland and Taylor's ascension was an artillery adjustment supporting the 90mm guns from Battery 406. Thirty-three shots were fired, of which twenty-seven shots were observed by McFarland and Taylor. They descended shortly after the incident at 1900.[870]

A PERVASIVE PROBLEM

Uncertainty prevailed with ongoing wireless intercepts, wire taps, and spies. Colonel Parker recalled: "For weeks our very Divisional Headquarters back at Bouck [Boucq] had housed a German pigeon loft just across the street from where General Clarence Edwards held his conferences, within microphone hearing distance of every unguarded voice, from which daily reports of all that happened at our division headquarters were regularly transmitted to German Headquarters by pigeon. For days the Germans had been cut in on the telephone wire of our own brigade headquarters, listening in on every conversation, sometimes sending false telephone messages to the various elements of the division. But we knew nothing of all that at the time, alert as we were for spies and tricks. Germans in American uniforms had penetrated into the Divisional lines, passed themselves off as members of some other seeking to find their way, seeing, hearing asking discreet questions, learning our every disposition. And none of us knew it."[871] It is impossible to ascertain the truth of this; there are no reliable reports of veterans coming forward after the war and admitting to such activity.

THE GERMANS TAKE UP ASSAULT POSITIONS

That day **Generalmajor** von Stolzmann issued a final warning on **Kirschblüte**. Should unfavourable meteorological conditions (storms or heavy rain) prevent the gassing of the enemy batteries during that night he planned to postpone the operation.[872] **Generalleutnant** Hoffmann reported that his newly acquired artillery was in place and camouflaged. He said the enemy had no knowledge of the operation, proven by the fact that the American relief took place two hours before the attack.[873] The veteran of **Einladung, Oberleutnant** Fritz, commander of **Pionier Komp.79**, reported that his **Pioniere** left Bouillonville at 0100 and reached their positions in the outpost area at **Abschnitt** G II opposite *Bois de Remières* at 0300. Their weapons and munitions had been assembled and readied for the **Pioniere** and **Stosstruppen** the previous night in the assigned nests. Fritz's men were prepared to blow up the obstacles and open up the passages through the wire entanglements and assist the **Stosstruppen** in the destruction of dugouts. He assigned a corporal and eight **Pioniere** to each **Kompagnie**. Additional **Pioniere** were allocated to the reserve **Kompagnien** in the third wave to carry more concentrated charges.[874]

Vizefeldwebel Ettighoffer's **7./258** left the rest area at Pannes at midnight for their **Kirschblüte** attack position. At his location the full moon was visible and the air was cold. He observed that Montsec to the south-west looked like an enormous monument. **7./258** arrived at the shelters within Lahayville on the bank of the Rupt de Mad. The **Stosstruppen** were provided with a mug of hot tea and rum. It was strangely quiet. Ettighoffer commented, **"Die Front schläft"** [the Front sleeps]. No flares were launched to disturb the night. **Stosstruppen** sat on the banks of the river and smoked. **7./258** were almost all Verdun veterans.[875]

That night to the west, 104th Infantry received harassing fire on positions near St. Agnant. About 70 **MW** shells dropped near *Boyau Central* and Trench Burchart and a good many other **MW** shells along with gas struck *Côte 322*. *SRA* reported eight hours of intermittent

The detailed coverage of the battery positions around Dead Man's Curve on the lee side of Beaumont Ridge. Lieutenant Davis Battery (a, b), Battery F (f, c), Battery D and Battery E (d) are marked for German artillery targets. Bhf (a railway station symbol) was used by Stabia to highlight Dead Man's Curve. (NASM)

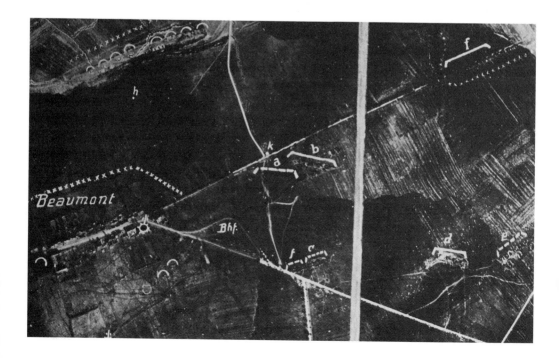

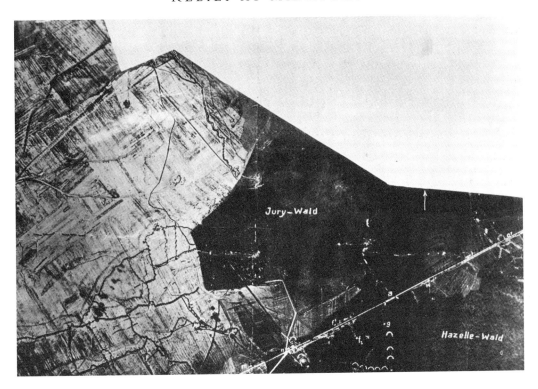

Bois du Jury, Bois de la Hazelle and *Bois de Remières* in a German aerial photograph. (NASM)

severe shelling of Ft. Liouville totalling 247 77mm rounds.[876] At 0250 the 101st Infantry PC to the west of Seicheprey at Rambucourt experienced a violent HE bombardment breaking all the telephone wires and with gas complicating the situation. The barrage was so heavy that Colonel Edward Logan, commander of the 101st Regiment serving to the west at Xivray, was unable to send runners in any direction. At Joinville, Lieutenant Ray Smith sent a coded message: "Left sector field, Boston; Minor struck out; Boston base on balls, Minors beginning knock a home run" – "Right company in first line location. One enlisted man killed and enlisted man seriously wounded. We were under heavy bombardment."[877] Captain Stanchfield from his PC in Seicheprey observed the barrage to the west hitting the 101st Infantry. Then he noticed a heavy barrage from the east moving his way.[878]

One artilleryman remembered an observation made by an old French sergeant: "*Quand les choses sont les plus calmes au front, gardez-vous contre l'attaque*" (When things are the most peaceful at the front, watch for an attack.)[879]

CHAPTER 16

"All Hell Was Let Loose!"

At the precise moment of 0400 (German war time, 0300 Allied time) planned for **Erstürmung**, **Generalleutnant** Hoffmann's artillery commenced a major artillery barrage. Initially, the Germans commenced a barrage opposite Colonel Edward Logan's 101st Regiment. It was a feint. The rest of the divisional line met the full fury, with Lieutenant Strickland at his position north of Seicheprey recalling, "All hell was let loose!" An artillery officer stationed beyond the Beaumont Ridge called it a murderous barrage.[880] A third recalled: "The Boche batteries now began to sweep the rear areas as well as the front line positions, with a deadly fire. Only a moment after signal rockets had sent out their warning, our Batteries opened up and the Battle of Seicheprey was on in full blast. Thousands of gas shells were falling all around the place and the air was poisoned from the deadly odor."[881] The intensity of the barrage was such as Americans had not yet experienced, hitting American front-line trenches within F-1 and F-2 for 30 minutes. The point of attack determined by the observation posts was between Richecourt and *Bois de Remières*. Lieutenant Sanbarn reported that the enemy barrage fire commenced at 0300 in the vicinity of *Bois du Jury*.[882] Initial observations were reported via telephone to Headquarters 51st Field Artillery Brigade shortly after 0300.

Within Seicheprey at this ghastly moment the situation was everyday. Major Rau was aware

of the heavy barrage all around but he was not receiving any messages from his front line.[883] At 0310, he heard machine-gun fire in the French sector to his right, assuming at that moment that the enemy was conducting a raid against the *162ᵉ régiment d'infanterie*. At 0318, Major Rau reported by telephone from Seicheprey, "All clear on our front."[884] Two minutes later Major Rau experienced a heavy barrage falling all over Seicheprey, "to our right, left, and rear, and also an intense bombardment on our front, and apparently a large number of shells were going directly over at some targets quite a distance to our rear."[885] At the 102nd Infantry PC on Beaumont Ridge, a kilometre south of Seicheprey Parker scrambled to make sense of the situation. Having been awakened by the noise from nearby batteries commencing fire, he had immediately dressed and arrived at his office at 0315. Just as he arrived at his PC, the area became smothered in artillery fire. Besides the constant flash from artillery fire, there was a kaleidoscope of colours from liaison rockets fired from the front-line positions: "There were red rockets with three white stars, the barrage signal for the day, and green rockets signifying that a gas attack was under way and many others meaning different things to the men who were on rocket guard. The relay stations along the Paris-Metz highway and farther back repeated the signals."[886] During the initial barrage, Private Robert Cassie of the 102nd Field Artillery manned his unprotected rocket-guard observation post throughout the violent bombardment, successfully signalling to his battery comrades to commence fire.[887]

At the forward artillery post to the east of Seicheprey, Private Walter Wolf also woke up to the explosions. He and his colleagues left their bunker for the surface to see what was going on. They looked to the north to see rocket signals from the front line outposts being fired. They became hypnotised by the horror of it all: "We were rapidly snapped out of it by a rain of shells, falling thick and fast and all about us. There was nothing to do but take cover, so away we went, but one 77 beat me to it, bursting just in front of me, and I found myself with a stinging wrist. The barrage lifted again cutting off all retreat."[888]

Immediately on commencement of the American barrage, the Germans responded with gas and explosive shells of all calibres, including 210mm, on Beaumont and positions near the front lines. Colonel Parker had just begun telephone communication with the commander of the right battalion when his lines were cut.[889] The next band of German artillery fire swept the lateral road along Beaumont Ridge to prevent reserves from coming to the assistance of Seicheprey. Still other bands of enemy fire were directed between the frontline units to prevent communication. The trenches around Seicheprey and *Bois de Remières* were prime targets. Battery positions, communication trenches, the 1-Bis position laying along the forward slope of Beaumont Ridge, and Beaumont itself, were subjected to such a terrific concentration of fire that after 8 minutes there was only one serviceable wire running out of Beaumont, a single slender thread of communication back to the artillery.[890]

At 0400 a gas alert was received at 102nd Infantry PC. Within the next 30 minutes all units in the area received and acknowledged the alert. The gas was being delivered from artillery rounds and not by **Gaswerfer**. The combined barrage lasted until 0430, when the Germans held fire for a few minutes, then proceeded to fire a heavy barrage on F-1, F-2, F-3 and H-1,

H-2 and Xivray – spreading into the American rear area of key road networks and the villages of Beaumont, Seicheprey, and Flirey. Allied firing continued all morning with the old front line in sector F-1 and F-2 kept targeted until 1200.[891] Captain Stanchfield and Lieutenant Karl M. Brouse visited their machine-gun positions to the right of Seicheprey and found them firing and covering their sector. Stanchfield remembered the fog being very dense with a visibility that did not exceed 50 metres. He found that certain guns to the west remained stood-down, not having received the signal to fire. He contacted those crews personally and returned into the village half an hour later, when the barrage fell on Seicheprey.[892]

It was a diabolical scene for all the senses. The early morning mist and fog settling along the bottom lands of the Woëvre was stirring with each blast from the devastating barrage. The suspense was over. Across the southern Woëvre front the rain of artillery fire came in such a volume that no one could have imagined such hellfire was possible. On Beaumont Ridge, the steady barrage of shells repeated a pattern of terror. The whistle of the incoming salvo was heard. At impact the concussions varied depending on proximity to gun crew and artillery piece. The patter of flying mud and shell splinters followed. Just as this seemed to dissipate another salvo arrived. For the men in the battery the explosion from their own piece firing punctuated the incoming symphony.

On the western side of the attack, **7./258** completed final preparations as the first rounds were fired. The soldiers that had tried to catch a few minutes of sleep were suddenly wide awake. German howitzers were the first heard, sounding like a deep bass drum. Looking to the north, they saw German barrage fire from Maizerais, Baussant, Euvezin, and Essey. The music now included light field guns, firing high-angle projectiles sounding like an express train on smooth rails. For **Vizefeldwebel** Ettighoffer, the desire to head back north to the safety of *Bois de Gargantua* was very tempting. Now the **Stosstruppen** saw Allied artillery around Flirey,

Limay, and Trommler firing back. Incoming rounds created tree-high columns of dirt against a darkened sky. The intensity of the German barrage was so great that windows rattled in Metz, Trier, Mainz and Koblenz.[893]

To the south-west of **Vizefeldwebel** Ettighoffer's unit, Yankee Division members of the 101st Field Artillery were at Gironville watching on, themselves incapable of effectively responding due to their location to the far west. The two-hour performance of German artillery lit up the entire landscape with flashes. Drum fire was the phrase that the barrage evoked.[894] Private Wunderlich remembered from his trench line west of Beaumont: "From where we were, we couldn't see the proceedings, but we could hear it, you bet. The hills rang with the roar of battle."[895]

Major Chaffee, 103rd Field Artillery, was sleeping at his quarters at Mandres late that night. He made the mistake of taking off his boots: "I can still hear that damned adjutant's hoarse whisper, 'Major, Major, wake up, they are machine gunning the street.'" He was up and running for the next 28 hours.[896]

78 R. D. PRIMARY OBJECTIVES

Hoffmann, von Stolzmann, and Bruns intended **Kirschblüte** to commence with an artillery barrage at 0300 and lasting until 0430, preparatory fire designed not to give away the point of **Stosstrupp** penetration.[897] HE and **gasschuss** from German long-range artillery hit the American artillery positions. The deadly combination of **Blaukreuz**, which penetrated the gas mask and forced the intended victim to remove it, in the presence of the lethal **Grünkreuz**, was the standard gas tactic. The volumes of gas released along with HE shells were severe on the labouring artillerymen. Pre-battle aerial coverage from the **FA (A) 298b** confirmed identified dugouts were well constructed and required accurate fire to destroy. The Germans knew the location of thirty-two American batteries thanks to aerial reconnaissance, **Schall-Mess-** and **Licht-Mess-Stellen** [sound ranging and flash spotting]. The

intense hour-and-a-half gas attack accomplished its purpose. The Americans did respond at first with a pretty brisk fire, complicating the final preparations of one of the **Stosstruppkompagnien** on the left flank, causing casualties. However, to the experienced German veterans, the impact of American artillery that day seemed slight.[898] HE and gas soon covered Sibille Trench, Seicheprey, *Bois de Remières*, Beaumont, all Allied battery positions, and the main *boyau* from Beaumont to the front lines. Every part of the 102nd Infantry Regiment's section of the southern Woëvre front received thorough attention.[899] American artillery leadership knew they were duelling with 77mm, 105mm, and 150mm projectiles and gas rounds. Hoffmann and von Stolzmann noted that the American artillery was kept in check, thanks mostly to the **Gasschuss**.[900] To make the barrage even more devastating, **Gaswerfer** were again deployed within **Abschnitt G**, targeting *Bois du Jury* and American positions to the north of Seicheprey. The special batteries of **Gaswerfer** were successful in keeping the gas screen dense. In addition to indigenous **78. R. D.** artillery, **5. Ldw. Div.** and **40. I. D.** assisted with barrage support to the flanks.[901]

EXTRAORDINARY ACCURACY

There was a dramatic loss of Allied communication throughout the battlefield. Lieutenant Strickland recalled telephone lines going out at the first blast of shells. The devastating accuracy of HE rounds on key nodes throughout the southern Woëvre front may well have been helped by spies who had inserted themselves as replacements in the days prior to the attack. The amazing accuracy of the fire reflected the discipline of Hoffmann's preparation over the weeks prior to execution. In many places within the southern Woëvre front, wires were being destroyed as fast as telephone men could repair them. As the barrage unfolded, Colonel Parker noted that the artillery wire was the only one working.[902] The *boyau* that crossed the ridge of Position 1-Bis was wrecked in several places and the telephone wires fastened against the side of the *boyau* were cut in a number of places.[903] Telephone wires were cut between Bouconville and Rambucourt. Colonel Logan had to employ runners to convey the message to General Traub that as of 0345, the 101st Infantry sector was not being shelled. The runners returned to the 101st Infantry PC two hours later.

As the reports trickled in, Colonel Parker learned that *colonel* Bertrand's *162ᵉ régiment d'infanterie*'s Area C on the border of *Bois du Jury* had been hit hard. Bertrand made the decision to suspend counter-artillery preparation and monitor the attack to protect his forces at *Bois du Jury*.[904] To Bertrand's left, Lieutenant Millspaugh's 2nd platoon took cover from the heavy artillery barrage and settled on the forward position of Center A. The German barrage fired on Millspaugh's trench for over three hours, in accordance with the instruction to fire until Seicheprey was vacated. Throughout the day to near midnight, *Bois du Jury* was shelled continually.[905]

SRS near the front line was trapped by the barrage. One 77mm round struck the *abris* near the *SRS*, demolishing one end. Their telephone lines were severed. *SRS* men braved the incoming rounds to investigate the line but discovered reestablishing communication meant stringing new wire. The only telephone communication for a long period was the artillery line between Colonel Parker's 102nd Infantry PC and Colonel Morris Locke's 102nd Field Artillery.[906] The rest of the artillery communications for Locke and his 103rd Field Artillery counterpart, Colonel E. Smith, were cut. During the entire barrage the artillery commanders required runners from battalion PCs to the artillery battery positions, which caused uncertainty and delays of up to 30 minutes. Many runners were killed or wounded almost as soon as they started out.[907] One artillery battalion employed an ambulance to get its runners back and forth.[908] Heroic action at this time became almost commonplace. While the barrage was at its height, Private Joseph C. Parent, Battery C, 102nd Field Artillery, received serious wounds

to the head and leg while repairing telephone lines that reestablished vital communications to his battery.[909] At the same time, Private Harold R. Johnson, Headquarters Company, 102nd Field Artillery, was also seriously wounded while repairing vital telephone lines.[910]

After an hour, General Traub's staff telephoned General Sherburne for an update on the barrage. Sherburne informed them that the enemy was putting down a preparation barrage and Americans were responding with a heavy barrage. Both Colonel Parker and Colonel Logan's PCs were receiving heavy fire. Gas rounds were being fired farther to the rear at Ansauville. Command and control in the American part of the southern Woëvre front was disintegrating. Communication between regimental PCs and the 51st Infantry Brigade was broken. At 0411 artillery headquarters reported lines to infantry were down and asked division headquarters to reestablish communications.[911] General Traub reported that Center H west of Seicheprey was quiet. He mentioned that he was keeping the barrage going despite the fact that he didn't know what was going on. At this time *Général* Passaga authorized Brigadier General Cole, 52nd Infantry Brigade, to release a battalion from the 104th Infantry to Brigadier General Traub's command. At 0430 Major Maybach, G-3, passed the order for 2nd Battalion, 104th Infantry, to prepare to move to the Seicheprey front and await further orders.

SRA reported to *Général* Gérard that his *armée's* artillery reacted vigorously to the barrage and during the counter preparation. Outside of the Seicheprey area, the remaining *VIIIᵉ armée's* southern Woëvre front was encountering very little artillery fire. *SRA* analysis determined the normal registration combined with *avion réglage* did not occur.[912]

"WE GOT THE BUSINESS"

Captain Bartlett, Company A, 101st Engineers, was ordered by Colonel Parker to place his engineers in the 1-Bis trenches next to Beaumont as a precaution against enemy breakthrough.

This was the first time that Bartlett's Engineers had been called on to perform infantry duty. All were willing to join in the fight as infantry, but it revealed the initial chaos. Engineers according to Field Service Regulations were to be so used only in case of extreme emergency. Their skills were the hardest to replace. Using engineers as infantry was perceived as a last resort. Post-war discussion referred to the example of the British, whose engineering efficiency suffered because this combat arm was sacrificed acting outside of its assigned duties. The engineers in 1-Bis were under the constant roar of artillery rounds and great holes were torn in the trench walls, some of which were caved-in so badly that it became a monumental effort for the stretcher bearers to make their way to the rear. [913]

Generalmajor von Stolzmann recognized that the lifeblood of the defensive operations were rear echelons that would quickly reinforce the front lines. He wanted to keep down the enemy artillery's potency as well as target the particularly important enemy position at *Bois du Jury*, to create a barrier against French reinforcements from the *162e régiment d'infanterie* as well as curtail any movements located behind the lines. The main portion of the artillery commenced a heavy systematic fire of destruction directed at the point of the American line which was pierced and also on the west edge of *Bois du Jury*. **MW** formations fired on the breakthrough point. Both artillery and **MW** were to divert the Americans' attention by bombarding the 101st Infantry positions in front of the **Abschnitt G III** and south-west of Richecourt for the first 40 minutes of the barrage. [914] North of Seicheprey, Lieutenant Strickland recalled the incessant slam-bang of shelling kept up for over an hour on all points – which settled down into a steady drum fire with shells dropping every few seconds on given points to prevent troop movements or reinforcement. [915]

After an hour and a half the barrage became more severe – the drum fire continued but larger calibre shells started hitting around the area. German howitzers now targeted trench networks and shelters creating desolation with every strike. No one could move without putting themselves in jeopardy. Company D men north of Seicheprey stayed at their posts but experienced losses in the process. Five were wounded by one blast and were dragged into a nearby dugout where a machine gun was in position. Another six were killed outright when a series of howitzers levelled their trench. [916]

Nearby to the east in *Bois de Remières*, Captain Griswold, Company C, ordered his PC staff officer, Lieutenant Johnson, onto the PC roof to send off flares from a Very pistol. Johnson's flares didn't go high enough so Griswold gave him a short-barreled gun designed to fire flares up above the tree tops. [917] Platoon commanders who, at the first alarm, brought their men together in the prescribed but as yet unfamiliar combat positions saw them get killed or wounded in groups; others who disposed their little forces in the slight shelter of shell holes ran the danger of losing control; direct hits played havoc with both machine guns and field pieces.

Just north of Beaumont, Lieutenant McGlasson's 3rd Platoon, Company D, had just relieved Company M's 4th Platoon occupying Grant trench as part of the thinning out of the front sector to reinforce Position 1-Bis. When the 0300 barrage commenced, McGlasson recalled his "boys" were not worried or nervous: "I was greeted with a grin by a number of them as I went up and down the trench. We began receiving a number of gas shells and everyone put on their masks and kept them on until I gave orders to remove them." [918] Lieutenant Harris, Company F, also held a 1-Bis position with his platoon stood-to in the fire trench. Between 0430 and 0500 the barrage diminished, shifting to cover the section immediately to Harris's right. An indirect fire from German machine guns was laid upon his trench. Harris ordered the men to hug the parapet and to keep a sharp look-out. He counted twenty-four artillery shells falling in his sector. [919]

On the north-east side of Seicheprey near the cemetery, Private Enoch Doble, medic for the 102nd Machine Gun Battalion, was awakened like the rest of his colleagues by the incessant explosions. Lieutenant Walter Tenney, commanding the battery defending Seicheprey, remarked to those wondering what was going on; "The Germans are putting on a barrage on the east side of our positions." Tenney ordered Doble and two others to stay in the dugout. The rest of the battery went above to stand at the machine-gun positions. It was still pitch-black outside. The barrage was slowing down, then it stopped altogether, and in a deathly silence they stood in the dugout entrance as a dark figure approached and spoke: "It's all right, it's Lieutenant Tenney, I think it is all over." Doble recalled: "He had hardly gotten the words out of his mouth when the barrage opened up on our side of the lines. It became more and more intense; the heavy shelling was hitting very close. The earth was shaking violently with every explosion. Then the smell of shell gas filled our nostrils. We knocked off our helmets and my glasses as well, and quickly put on our gas masks."[920]

Seicheprey's respite from the initial barrage was over at 0445. After a minute of peace, artillery and **MW** struck the village with a vengeance and continued incessantly until 0715. The 102nd Machine Gun Company positions covering the right sector commenced fire after receiving a signal. To the east of Seicheprey the barrage created a veritable inferno, striking the forward zones and artillery batteries in Position 2. Company A, 102nd Machine Gun Battalion, operating within the 1-Bis, was pummelled. They burst out of the *abris* at the first barrage and commenced fire. To the west of Seicheprey machine guns commenced fire at 0450. All guns, except four disabled during the firing, continued throughout the duration of the enemy barrage fire. Lieutenant Sanbarn had nothing but praise for the bravery displayed by his machine gunners.[921]

Thanks to the single remaining Ansauville artillery line to Colonel Locke, 102nd Field Artillery commander, Parker learned his regimental counterpart to the west, Colonel Logan, was not being attacked. At 0455, Colonel Parker called *colonel* Bertrand to better understand the extent of the bombardment on *162ᵉ régiment d'infanterie*. Bertrand reported that they were experiencing a violent bombardment

in sector C, the *162ᵉ régiment d'infanterie* sector adjacent to *Bois du Jury*. A barrage of machine guns was now active but his regiment was not being subjected to a very heavy attack. Bertrand commenced preparing a counter-attack to be delivered where liaison with Parker's right existed. Parker commenced his command of the battle through messages sent by runner to the machine guns to lay down indirect barrage. The 102nd Infantry gas alert was sounded.[922]

General Edwards remarked after the war that the German artillery was so accurate that scarcely any of the 2-kilometre stretch to the second line trench was untouched. HE shells, shrapnel and gas shells fell with regular intervals while above the inferno floated the deadly fumes of mustard gas. Seven platoons occupying Sibille Trench between Seicheprey and *Bois de Remières* were "as effectively cut off from all help and assistance as though the ocean divided them from their reserves."[923] Large sections of Sibille Trench were destroyed by the bombardment.

South of Beaumont at Mandres, Ansauville, and the divisional headquarters at Boucq, the relieved battalions from the previous evening did not escape the HE and gas. Their bombardment commenced at 0308 followed shortly by a gas alarm. Position 3 was kept at gas alert for nearly four hours.[924]

The first-aid station was at Beaumont. The doctors and stretcher bearers were "kept on the jump."[925] The first wounded reached the 102nd Field Hospital at 0430 and were evacuated within 10 minutes. The last wounded arrived at 0620. The wheeled-litter bearers had been ordered to follow the infantry back in to pick up all casualties. In his report to the division surgeon at 0730 that morning, Major Paul Waterman, commanding officer of the 101st Sanitary Train, reported that total casualties amounted to twenty-two, fifteen of whom were wounded (two seriously) and three were gassed. "Other cases may be discovered or evacuated later." Little did he know, or could he know, at that early hour, the devastating toll that would be exacted on his own medics by the gas shells that had been fired prior to the raid.

The 104th Ambulance Company was also at Mandres. They set up an advance dressing station that quickly became overwhelmed as casualties arrived from Beaumont and Seicheprey. Working with gas masks on, the men began to treat and evacuate the wounded by ambulance to the 102nd Field Hospital, then at Ménil-la-Tour. It soon became apparent that the operation was a large one. More ambulances and personnel were sent for, including two medical officers each from the 101st and 103rd Field Hospitals, who were dispatched to the 102nd Field Hospital.[926]

Lieutenant Edward Larned's Company I were relieved in Center A position by Company A, and marched south of Beaumont to Mandres, arriving at midnight. Three hours later they came under fire from HE and gas and wore box respirators for the next 3½ hours.[927] At 0630 the 51st Infantry Brigade sent General Traub's aide via motorcycle to inform Sergeant Arthur A. Service, Company L, to proceed immediately to Beaumont for disposition by 102nd Infantry Headquarters. His company had been understrength since they left Chemin-des-Dâmes the month prior. All Company L squads were to open up and march in file because of the heavy shelling. A single round hit Service's squad, killing three instantly.[928]

Lieutenant Boyd, 3rd Platoon, and Lieutenant H. W. Smith, 4th Platoon, of Company M made it to Ansauville after being relieved from the front lines and arrived just as the town was being shelled by both HE and gas. Smith's platoon entered the dugouts where they remained until 0630 wearing their respirators. They returned to Beaumont at 1100 carrying ammunition and supplies to the front lines.[929]

One 26th Division sector did not experience the wrath of the German barrage: the West Grouping rear areas of the southern Woëvre front supporting the 101st Infantry. As Private Wunderlich recalled, "Things were comparatively quiet while we were in Gironville. There was a lot of guerilla warfare going on, with now and then a raid, but there were no major operations."[930]

One of the many soldiers on the receiving end of this barrage, Corporal Charles Boucher, spoke for those in the forward trenches: "We got the business."[931] The 102nd Infantry was taking a horrendous beating. Company D support units experienced serious casualties from the barrage. The meagre shelters became tombs as the explosions buried the occupants. Machine-gun posts identified prior to the barrage were priority artillery targets. What remained in forward outposts were shell-shocked or wounded men. American outposts suffered extensive casualties that broke up the line of defence with little or no communication.

A SECOND VERDUN?

Battery and support positions were thoroughly gassed as well as shelled. The enemy fire continued intensely until 1700 with box barrages laid around Seicheprey and *Bois de Remières* and a rolling barrage across the front for the attacking infantry. After the American batteries had opened with their normal counter-batteries, 102nd Field Artillery leadership called on the 69ᵉ *division d'infanterie* to support, assigning them some of the active batteries of the *Mort-Mare* region to the north of *Bois du Jury*.[932] Parker's executive officer, Lieutenant Dana T. Leavenworth, reported that the positions on the right held by 102nd Infantry were furiously bombarded by HE and gas shells throughout the whole day.[933]

The entire southern Woëvre front artillery supporting the 102nd Infantry was under the most violent bombardment that extended to the farthest reserve positions to the south – lasting for 36 hours. The position was shelled at irregular intervals throughout the day.[934]

The 102nd Field Artillery's 1st Battalion covered the front of sections F-1 and F-2 roughly from Maizerais to Lahayville. The "party" began at 0308 in the morning with their initial barrage hitting targets north of F-1. Twenty minutes later they changed to CPO, firing two rounds per minute from each gun. To the west, 102nd Field Artillery's 2nd Battalion covered the front of sections H-1 to H-2 from Lahayville south-west beyond Richecourt. At 0451, 2nd Battalion transitioned to barrage fire having been firing CPO since 0330. Then at 0527 communications between 102nd Field Artillery Battalion command posts and batteries were cut. When it was reconnected, the telephone did not last very long.

Indirect machine-gun fire covering the northeast corner of *Bois du Jury* to the eastern edge of *Bois de Remières* was provided by Lieutenant Bartram's 2nd Platoon, Company A. His four machine guns were posted on the crest of the hill midway between the Seicheprey Road and *Bois du Jury* and commenced fire a few minutes after the initial German 0300 barrage, after receiving an SOS signal from *Bois du Jury*. Bartram's guns fired until 0415 when activity in that sector ceased. Half an hour later all four guns commenced an indirect barrage.

French observers of the artillery exchange admitted afterwards it resembled the "preparations" of Verdun for intensity and accuracy. Members of *162ᵉ régiment d'infanterie* told their American counterparts later that they thought a second Verdun attack was in progress.[935] The initial barrage at 0300 was heavy on the 103rd Field Artillery's 1st and 3rd Battalions. Captain Barker, 103rd Field Artillery, estimated that no fewer than 2,000 shells fell on or in the close vicinity of the Jones I position of Battery A. The forward position of Battery D and the rear position of Battery E had their parapets blown in and powder exploded.[936] Accurate and directed fire of HE and gas covered the area. They set off the gas alarm and kept firing with masks on.

"WHERE CAN I HELP?"

Major Chaffee's men on the ridge were exposed to the withering fire from the beginning. It appeared the 95mms of Davis Battery were a priority since they were within effective range to create havoc for the **Stosstruppen**. The gun crews were called to their guns under the most violent of barrages. One of the 95mms was already out of commission before the barrage. A second

piece was put out of action almost immediately from a direct hit destroying the gun trail. Battery Davis fired continuously for 5 hours while wearing gas masks in the most uncomfortable conditions. The suffering did not end with the **Gasschuss**. Fifteen out of forty-four Battery Davis men were either killed or wounded that day.[937]

The 95mm gun under the command of Corporal Kenneth W. Lovell was the first 103rd Field Artillery battery to reply to the Germans' initial 0300 barrage. Battery D, 103rd Field Artillery, experienced heavy bombardment at 0300 from 77mm and 150mm guns. Sergeant Joshua K. Broadhead was leading his battery when he was severely wounded with a shell splinter to the back. Broadhead refused to leave, insisting that every man was needed on the guns. He realised his condition was too serious and he was impeding the operation so he left for the dugout. Just as he left, a shell killed him instantly.

"I have ammunition and one gun, where can I help?" – Captain Joseph Carleton Davis.

Chaplain William J. Farrell earned the DSC at Seicheprey. (History of the 103rd Field Artillery)

A few minutes later, an HE shell wounded Lieutenant S. Ayer as he was providing firing data to the gunners. Lieutenant Davis and Lieutenant Renville Wheat scrambled to help Ayer and move him to safety. A shell struck nearby knocking the three to the ground, killing Ayer and severely wounding Wheat. Davis suffered a slight wound, returning to the battery after getting help for Wheat. Private Frank E. Gordon, being held in reserve for Battery E, scrambled outside of his dugout to help his friend Private Roger Wilson who had just been wounded. Gordon picked up Wilson and carried him through a violent barrage. A shell killed them both.[938]

One of the first ambulances to arrive on scene brought Lieutenant William J. Farrell, Regimental Chaplain for both 104th Infantry and 103rd Field Artillery. Farrell was the driving spirit getting ambulances around Dead Man's Curve, working to the point of exhaustion providing treatment and leading the evacuation of the wounded out of the most dangerous point in Position 2. He stayed in the Dead Man's Curve area, sustaining serious wounds

to his arm while helping No. Two section serve their piece. Only after the fire on the ridge had receded did Farrell leave for the hospital. While en route he was observed disregarding his own wound and providing care for the wounded men around him. His veteran colleagues remembered Farrell as the "Fighting Parson ... To him a man's manner of worship was nothing if only he might be permitted to help him over the hard spots ... if one of them needed him, no mud was too deep, no shellfire too heavy to keep him away."[939]

Major Chaffee reflected on the work of his 1st Battalion batteries during this first barrage: "Those men overcame obstacles and went straight on with the fight when everything seemed all shot to Hell. At 'Jones 1' the attack came so close to the howitzer as to be within its minimum range. There were things done during the darkness and light of a dismal day that measure up to the highest standards of devotion to duty." Lieutenant Davis, with all but one of his old French "95s" shot out and half of his men killed or wounded, sent a runner back with the field message, "I have ammunition and one gun, where can I help?"[940]

Wounded, Davis stayed with his gun. Davis' 95mm was the last gun of Battery A. It continued to fire away throughout the day.[941] Major Chaffee reported to General Lassiter what he observed of Battery A's efforts that day:

On the twentieth, after hours of firing, mostly in gas masks, with all telephone lines cut, all guns put out of action except one, one officer and three men killed, and his remaining officer and nine men out of the little command wounded, the Battery commander sent to me by runner, asking for more ammunition ... From what I can learn of that night and day of serving the guns, there were acts of gallantry and devotion that measure up to the highest standards of American artillery. ... All through this little Battalion there was such a response to requests and total disregard for danger as would make you blush with pride. A battalion commander's little part is to walk up and down, up and down among the maps and telephones and plan and plan and try to create resources when one thing after another gives out and to send messengers and linemen and batteries on hazardous work regardless of losses. And we sent them out again and they ate it up.[942]

"WHERE DID HE GET ALL THOSE GUNS?"

For Corporal LaBranche, 102nd Field Artillery, it seemed as if every available enemy gun had been concentrated on their area. Ammunition was expended and resupplied, some of it being destroyed by enemy fire in course of delivery. His journal caught the drama of the moment. "It was our first real test. Here was a real honest-to-goodness battle, with charging infantry, galloping artillery, guns spitting fire and roaring all around, shells falling thickly and shaking the earth, the cough of motorcycle dispatch-riders speeding through the fires of hell and runners wounded, limping along to report and keep up communications. It was war as we had read about, and what a thrill it was to feel one's self a part of it."[943]

That morning the men of 102nd Field Artillery were asking each other, "Where did he get all those guns?" and "Where in the world does he get all the ammunition for them?" In addition to the box barrage the Germans had

in place around Seicheprey, along Beaumont Ridge, and the edge of *Bois du Jury*, the German artillery fire kept falling steadily on advance battery positions, the towns, and sweeping the roads leading up to the front.[944]

Leutnant Thomas's **80.Kompagnie Reserve Pionierezug** left Bouillonville and marched with Grumbrecht's **d-Kompagnie (3./259 Maux, Hans)** and Hellmuth's **c-Kompagnie (2./259)** to *Bois de la Sonnard* at 0030. Thomas's **Zug** proceeded to the regimental **Pioniere** park near St. Baussant at 0220 to collect their explosive charges. The German artillery covering the eastern American area of the southern Woëvre front commenced their barrage. They noticed French artillery conducting counterfire. As they were en route to the departure nest, the American counter-barrage fired gas rounds at 0245. The **Pioniere** proceeded to their departure nest alternately crawling and rushing, arriving at 0350. No losses occurred from artillery fire despite each man being loaded with explosive charges. **Leutnant** Thomas' **Zug** left their nest at 0450 together with **Bataillon Grumbrecht's 4./259 Kompagnie** and commenced their assault.[945]

Hoffmann reported that the enemy's infantry and machine guns were kept in check by short-lived but powerful artillery fire – **MW** being used for the front line – under the cover of which the **Stosstruppen** approached close to the enemy's positions. "The surprise was complete, and was favoured by the foggy weather that prevailed during the attack."[946] **Generalleutnant** Hoffmann concluded: "Despite its short duration, the preparatory fire proved sufficient."

CHAPTER 17

Sturm at the High Water Mark

Offizierstellvertreter [Warrant Officer] Kientz took charge of Freiwilligenkompagnien 7./258 at the front line. 7./258 comprised volunteers that served Leutnant Keun's a-Kompagnie (258./Keun) with the mission to proceed to through Alfa-Wäldchen and Beta-Wäldchen to finally attack the trench networks around Pflaumen-Wäldchen, the oldest battleground in the Seicheprey sector where the *128ᵉ brigade d'infanterie* of the *64ᵉ division d'infanterie* dug the first trenches of *Secteur Lahayville* in October 1914. Kientz proceeded through the wire entanglement. The shock wave from the explosions provided by the large MW firing at the close-by American lines caused his fellow Stosstruppen to fall to the ground. Vizefeldwebel Ettighoffer recalled his chest experiencing a crushing sensation. Then 7./258 saw a rot-grün Doppelrakete [red-green double rocket] fired into the dense mist. It was time for Sturm.[947]

KTK Major Bruns envisioned a four-pronged assault. Four "nests" were set in place with four battalions given specific objectives and a route to cover. Like Einlandung, the Kirschblüte assault was designed to be quick – reaching objectives, destroying trenches, dugouts, pillboxes and annihilating any other resistance before the Americans could figure out what had transpired. To the west, Bataillon Tolle comprising both Res. I. R. 258 Freiwilligenkompagnie and Res. I. R. 259. Res. I. R. Stosstruppen were to head directly

south and diverge within the trench networks around Pfaumen-Wäldchen to the west and American positions south of Seicheprey. The centre thrust was Bataillon Grumbrecht, going right down the north-south Seicheprey-St. Baussant road directly into the south-west entrance to the village. Bataillon Hellmuth to the left of Bataillon Grumbrecht was to strike the eastern flank of Seicheprey and the western side of *Bois de Remières* and occupy Sibille Trench, the main American defensive position within Position 1. Finally, Bataillon Seebohm, under the command of the former Einladung KTK Hauptmann Seebohm, was to strike *Bois de Remières*. This time Seebohm's Stosstruppen were to attack the eastern side of the forest and defend against American reinforcements coming from Beaumont Ridge, or French forces nearby in the eastern *Bois du Jury*.

Conditions were perfect for an assault. The night frost proved perfect for traversing No Man's Land. The fog, which prevailed at daybreak and became denser and denser, blinded the American outposts. The Germans reported that it was impossible to see anything at 100 paces from the village – effectively screening the attack as well as obscuring vital liaison via rocket signals.[948] General Edwards reported three weeks later to Chaumont: "The dense mist was our serious handicap; airplanes could not observe. The enemy reached Seicheprey under their own barrage. Officers tell me that the outlines of a man were indistinct fifty feet away."[949] The dense fog covered the whole area and persisted until about 0800.

Destructive fire shaped the battle as **Sturmtruppen** and **Stosstruppen** moved into their jump-off positions within their assigned nests. Then the barrage shifted. Commencing at 0430, specially detailed batteries began firing and continued until the beginning of the **Stosstrupp** attack. Ten minutes later artillery and **MW** commenced a heavy, systematic fire of destruction directed at the point of the American line to be pierced. Duration of fire by **MW** at the point of penetration was 3 minutes at each "layer" to be annihilated. **Reserve. Pionier Kompagnie. 80** crossed the enemy front line and cut paths through additional wire entanglements protecting the second and third lines. Two **Pionierezuge** carried charges to blow up wire entanglements and concentrated charges to destroy the American dugouts and defence works. A third **Pionierezug** was attached to the battalion attacking *Bois de Remières*.[950] Some passages in the enemy wire entanglements damaged by the annihilating artillery and **MW** fire still required the infantry to blow it up, cut it, or cross it with the aid of portable bridges. It was Hoffmann's contention that wire entanglements were not to be bombarded for the half hour required to open up the passages, since the element of surprise would be forfeited. Hoffmann was pleased and he told **Generalleutnant** Fuchs at **Gruppe Gorz** that the artillery and **MW** had blocked the point of penetration on both flanks and diverted the enemy's attention to **Abschnitt G III**.[951]

Freiwilligenkompagnie 7./258 proceeded to their assault point as the artillery fire dimished. The moon was covered with clouds, while to the east in a former battleground north of Pont-à-Mousson known as **Priesterwald** a red glow hung on the horizon. Montsec's outline was clearly visible to the west. Heavy artillery fire continued from *Bois de Gargantua* to the north and **7./258** could see the devastation in the American front lines that they were to strike. Volleys of flares were loosed and observed by both sides. **7./258**

started to climb on the embankment to the guide lines through the wire entanglements set earlier. Shell craters now had a temporary fill of white lug boards. The guidepath was a carefully constructed lane of white ribbon and straw bundles. The time was now 0430. Artillery rounds screamed overhead.

In preparation for the assault 20 minutes of **MW** hammered northern Seicheprey and the graveyard 20 metres north of the church. **MW** fired into the centre of Seicheprey for 40 minutes. A similar duration of fire battered 1-Bis trenches and the west of Seicheprey. As shells struck Seicheprey, Rau's soldiers ran into their *abris*. A counter-barrage was necessary and Rau took action to alert artillery in Position 2. Rau's *38ᵉ régiment d'infanterie* liaison, *lieutenant* Toulouse, rushed out to the Seicheprey-designated rocket station and attempted to send out a signal calling for barrage. The incoming artillery and **MW** rounds were so heavy that Toulouse couldn't get there. Rau handed Toulouse a rocket and quickly set up an improvised rocket "launcher" made from a sandbag outside his PC. It didn't work. Toulouse lit the rocket but it fell over, burning him on the hand. Rau then took another rocket and rushed to the rocket station. As he ran, an artillery round burst 5 metres away and knocked him down, with fragments and debris hitting his helmet and wounding him in the hand. Rau stopped in a daze. His officers came out of the PC to help. He got up and made it to the rocket station and fired off three in rapid succession that successfully alerted the American artillery to commence with a barrage. Rau now turned to getting his forces ready for an enemy assault, posting sentinels near the PC.

Major Rau reported: "Boche attack at 0500 at Seicheprey. Am holding there."[952] Lieutenant Harry E. Rice, 102nd Field Artillery, was Rau's artillery liaison. Rice ran to the centrally located remains of a building known as the Seicheprey Observatory Tower and fired off a rocket. He observed Germans in Seicheprey at 0530. Since his telephone lines were cut, Rice called for a barrage at that moment using the rocket that signalled "attack underway." From his position in the tower, Rice watched the entire battle unfold.[953]

Major Bowditch's final observation of that time epitomised how the battle was conducted throughout: "No messages from the front line were received for a considerable length of time."[954]

MW fired a short three-minute destructive barrage at the closest targets using bombs armed with delayed action fuses to reduce splintering. **MW** bombs hit the American front lines between **Alfa-Wäldchen** and **Pflaumen-Wäldchen** in the west in a 14-minute barrage to deter any immediate Allied reinforcement. Barrage fire commenced once signals were received from **Stosstruppen**. Another **MW** group fired in front of **Abschnitt G III** for 40 minutes.[955] **Generalleutnant** Hoffmann's close-range artillery conducted the initial barrage and switched to the rolling barrage advancing ahead of the **Stosstruppen**. Keeping reinforcements away from Position 1-Bis and Position 2 south of Seicheprey and at *Bois du Jury* was accomplished by destructive fire of varying strength from Hoffmann's artillery inventory, particularly from his long-range group. Annihilating artillery fire

now covered the entire American sector up to Position 2. Simultaneously with the sudden opening up of **MW** and artillery fire, the infantry approached the points of penetration at 0430 on the whole of the west line. The enemy front lines were crossed a few minutes later without any resistance. The sparsely manned front line had soldiers spread apart who set off fireworks and retreated. No American obstacles slowed down the **Stosstruppen** advance in this part of the battlefield.[956]

Lieutenant Cunningham at 51st Field Artillery headquarters reported at 0447 all quiet in the area as artillery fire shifted from CPO to counter-battery. A minute later Cunningham telephoned 51st Brigade headquarters to inform that the front-line trenches at Seicheprey, *Bois de Remières* and *Bois-Brûlé* were under

FA (A) 298b photographs Seicheprey from the North from 600 feet at the height of the dawn attack. Information provided by the observer: B.FL.298- No1299. – 20.-4.-18.-050V. Seicheprey.H.200m.Br.25m. (History of the One Hundred Second Field Artillery)

heavy bombardment. This was the first notice to General Traub's headquarters that an attack was in progress on trenches around Seicheprey and *Bois de Remières*.[957]

Initial contact was extremely light. Directly north of Seicheprey only four Americans were observed at the first stronghold and to the west at **Alfa-Wäldchen** three soldiers were spotted firing off flares and retreating to the south. No trench obstacles along the front line caused any noticeable delays. One team of four linemen under the command of Corporal Viberts working north of Seicheprey in an outpost called "Philip-P" had been on duty for three weeks, operating the switchboard and repairing the lines. Just prior to the attack they were ordered to remove the switchboard and salvage the wire. It was too late. The outpost was overrun by **Stosstruppen**. One lineman, Private Herbert E. Liming, had to fight his way back through Seicheprey. The others were killed or declared missing.[958]

At the western nest just south of Lahayville, **c-Kompagnie (5./259 Pohl)** advanced unhindered to the American second trench line, just 100 metres from the launch nest. They met their first resistance from the Americans at this point. The second wave's **Freiwilligenkompagnie b-Kompagnie Obermüller Regt. 258** arrived behind **c-Kompagnie** and engaged the Americans in a 25-minute battle, freeing up Pohl's **Stosstruppen** to continue towards their south-west Seicheprey objectives. Machine-gun fire from both sides made the advance difficult. **Leutnant** Obermüller's men advanced on the American dugout and adjacent pillbox complex under the command of Lieutenant Benjamin C. "Bennie" Byrd. The pillbox comprised two large *abris* and three shelters of corrugated iron – from which the Americans fought with every weapon at their disposal. **B-Kompagnie** fought a tenacious adversary. One American *abris* let the **Stosstruppen** advance to a certain point. As the Germans approached an *abris* they were suddenly overwhelmed by a fusillade of fire from the entrance. **Stosstruppen** above one *abris* entrance threw grenades inside which caused

a few Americans to surrender. The Germans quickly became introduced to American baseball skills; their aim with grenades proved deadly. It drove **Leutnant** Obermüller's **Stosstruppen** back. They now resorted to blocking off the trench, surrounding the *abris* entrance and throwing a barrage of grenades. It proved overwhelming for Lieutenant Byrd and his remaining twenty-two men. They came out and surrendered. **Leutnant** Obermüller had his men disperse along Sibille Trench and prepare for counter-attack. Upon close examination of the area, Obermüller's **Stosstruppen** discovered a cache of sixty rifles and destroyed them. Despite the momentary exaltation over the victory, **Hauptmann** Tolle soon learned that his son had become a casualty, shot and killed in the first moments of the assault.[959]

As **c-Kompagnie (5./259 Pohl)** left Obermüller to contend with Lieutenant Byrd's *GC*, **Leutnant** Pohl's **Stosstruppen** continued south and were met with heavy machine-gun fire along the Lahayville-Seicheprey road. In a struggle that lasted 25 minutes they conducted an enveloping movement around the machine-gun nest that resulted in casualties on both sides, including Pohl. **Offizierstellvertreter** Siebrecht, Sergeant Philipp and **Unteroffizier** Neumann took immediate action leading the attack. Breaching the pillbox required a **Granatwerfer** to lob grenades downrange to avoid being hit by the Americans' accurate fire.

A few Americans raised their hands. As the Germans got closer one suddenly threw hand grenades and shot his pistol, wounding Philipp, Neumann, and two other **Stosstruppen**. **Offizierstellvertreter** Siebrecht and his remaining **Stosstruppen** then stormed the defence. One of the four American machine guns captured that day was from this close combat.[960] The remaining **c-Kompagnie** proceeded south and regrouped south-west of Seicheprey with **Bataillon** Tolle's **d-Kompagnie (7./259 Hillemann) Stosstruppen**. The plan was proceeding as **Major** Bruns envisioned.

To the far west of the assault, **a-Kompagnie (258./ Keun)** reached **Alfa-Wäldchen** without meeting resistance. **7./258** advanced through two small wooded areas and crossed into American lines with **MW** bombs impacting just 50 metres ahead of their advance. The first American dugout they overran was empty. The next objective, known as **Beta-Wäldchen**, they also found unoccupied. As Keun's **a-Kompagnie** advanced farther, they were discovered by an American machine-gun nest and took heavy fire from the trench east of **Beta-Wäldchen**. Ettighoffer recalled that the trenches suddenly came alive. They were now confronting a strongly defended position and every traverse had to be fought for. Ettighoffer's **führer**, Kientz directed his **Zug** to divide into three groups and penetrate. Just as they proceeded to execute the plan, Kientz's counterpart, **Offizierstellvertreter** Roos, was shot in the head and died instantly.

It now became close combat between **7./258** and the Americans. They enveloped the American stronghold at this point of the attack and managed to capture six men. Ettighoffer remembered the Americans wore flat steel helmets above their angular, beardless faces. He was struck by the quality of the uniforms the Americans were wearing – particularly their beautiful, long rubber waders – the best apparel for the mud of Seicheprey. **7./258** then discovered a large cache of booty – cans of food, blankets, and other accessories. As much as he wanted to stop, Ettighoffer realised they had to continue the advance to their objective.[961]

Suddenly Ettighoffer and his fellow **Stosstruppen** heard two machine guns firing. Kientz leapt into the closest nest shouting "Hands up, you bloody fools!" Kientz managed to grab the officer in charge, Lieutenant Robert B. McDowell, 102nd Machine Gun Battalion, and simultaneously pulled out his **Dolch** [bayonet] putting it to McDowell's throat. The remaining Americans hesitated and started to raise their hands in surrender. When another machine gun started to fire in the Germans' direction, Kientz threw a grenade that killed the crew. Then the air became thick with American and German grenades exploding around the combatants, creating geysers of sludge. Ettighoffer made a quick body count – ten American corpses there

were most likely were killed during the **MW** barrage. **7./258** casualties so far in the **Erstürmung** were one dead and four slightly wounded.[962]

A few **7./258 Stosstruppen** took charge of Lieutenant McDowell and his remaining men and went back to the German lines. The rest of **7./258** moved on until they came to another large shelter. A **Stosstrupp** rushed the shelter and shoved two grenades into the riser creating a muffled explosion. Kientz went towards the *abris* entrance and ordered the Americans to come out. They responded with pistol shots. Kientz's men threw more grenades into the *abris*. One American near the top of the stairs caught them and threw them back. A **Stosstrupp** shot and killed him. The rest of the *abris* surrendered and came out. Ettighoffer noticed that some of the Americans wore pistols loosely on their belt like a cowboy. Others came out with their hands in the pockets – giving Ettighoffer the impression of schoolboys about to be punished. Kientz then shouted at the assembled prisoners to put their hands up high. The Americans respond slowly. Suddenly an American burst out of the shelter and ran south towards the nearest American line. The startled Germans raised their weapons to fire. The remaining captive Americans started angrily shouting at the Germans – then became exuberant, cheering on their counterpart in the run of his life: "Run Bill!" Bill made it to the next trench and dived in. The Americans erupted into applause – "Hurrah for Bill!" Kientz's **Stosstruppen** had witnessed firsthand what they thought was the Americans' take on this horrific experience – war as a sport. The veteran Germans on the other hand saw themselves as ageing soldiers who had stayed too long at the front. The newly arriving Americans were full of youthful vigour, wanting to continue on in this "game." **7./258** now prepared for defence against a possible counter-attack.[963]

Lieutenant Lockhart's platoon strength was down to eight soldiers. The early morning **MW** barrage on Sub-center H-1 had completely obliterated the trenches, *abris*, and company PC killing five men and wounding sixteen. Communication in Lockhart's area required runners as the telephone wires to the south

Oberstleutnant von Bornstedt's map of Seicheprey. (von Bornstedt, Reserve Infantrie, Regiment 259)

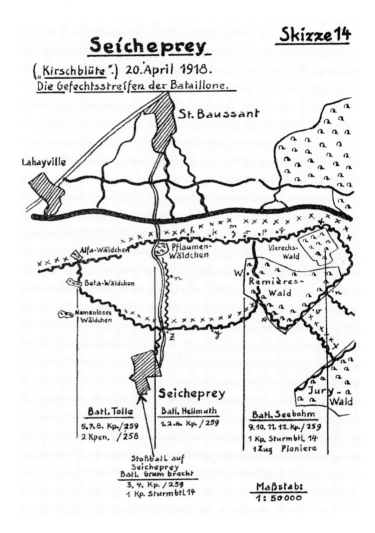

and east were broken. At 0500 Lockhart's *Boyau Nantais* location started receiving rounds from both German and American artillery. Despite the double jeopardy, Lockhart held *Boyau Nantais* using his *Chauchat* automatic riflemen to fire intermittently towards the German wire. The **Stosstruppen** held back and did not advance.[964]

Hauptman Tolle's deep attack **Kompagnie** was **d-Kompagnie (7./259 Hillemann)**. **Leutnant** Hillemann's **Stosstruppen** advanced in orderly fashion despite the foggy conditions and skirmishes underway on the Lahayville-Seicheprey road. Hillemann's lead for the drive was **Unteroffizier** Müller and his **Stosstruppen**. Armed with a number of light machine guns, Müller's men forced their way into a trench full

of Americans next to an observation post southwest of Seicheprey and initiated close combat. Just as the fight commenced, the remaining **Stosstruppen** from **c-Kompagnie** arrived and the two conducted operations against the Americans. They repulsed a minor counterattack from nearby trenches. The **Stosstruppen** were violently resisted by the Americans. One squad of eight American soldiers fought to the last man. **Stosstruppen** moved through the traverses and captured eleven Americans in the area supporting the observation post. The initial attack phase had been completed. Now Tolle's **Stosstruppen** were in place to link up with the newly arriving **Bataillon Hellmuth's a-Kompagnie (6./259 Knop)** coming from the north-east.

Leutnant Knop was a "veteran" of attack on the Americans, having led one of the assaults on *Bois de Remières* during the **Einladung**. Close combat commenced in earnest.[965]

THE FIGHT IN SIBILLE TRENCH

A-Kompagnie (6./259 Knop) advanced along the north-south road, St. Baussant-Seicheprey. They encountered an American *abris* north of Sibille Trench but being the first wave, by-passed them, leaving the third wave to contend with any resistance. Lieutenant Edward A. Kenney, 102nd Machine Gun Battalion, commanded a *GC* that maintained the Hotchkiss machine guns defending the western sector where *Boyau Seicheprey* intersected with Sibille Trench. When the massive **MW** bombardment commenced Kenney ordered his eight men into the *abris* where the **Stosstruppen** found them. At that moment the third wave arrived carrying **Flammenwerfer,** making a convincing argument for surrender. After the battle, Major John D. Murphy, Company B, 102nd Machine Gun Battalion, wrote of the incident that Lieutenant Kenney was "the best officer we had, almost." To the right of Lieutenant Kenney's unit was Captain Freeland, Company D commander and Major Rau's lead in the defence of Sibille Trench. After Knop's **a-Kompagnie Stosstruppen** had captured Kenney, they proceeded east through and above the Sibille Trench network in the fog and cordoned off the defences around Freeland's *GC*. It proved to be a very bloody battle for both sides. **Leutnant** Knop's **Stosstruppen** were grateful when **Bataillon Hellmuth's b-Kompagnie (1./259 Tänzer)** showed up in the assault's second wave. Additional help came as **Bataillon Hellmuth c-Kompagnie (2./259)** serving as reserve for the three waves arrived. Freeland's *GC* fought until every man was killed, wounded or actually overpowered. Captain Freeland was wounded by hand grenade blasts but fought until his wounds proved overwhelming and he was captured.[966] All the **Stosstruppen** realised that they were fighting a determined enemy with tremendous fighting potential when they saw

their **Kompagnie** commander, **Leutnant** Knop, killed by a rifle bullet.[967] Private Alvin C. Lugg – surrounded yet undaunted – broke through the **Stosstruppen** using hand grenades and his bayonet.[968] Sergeant George Nelson fired away with his revolver at a large group of **Stosstruppen** rushing him and was overwhelmed. Corporal James Moody and his *Chauchat* team shot many Germans as they came forward: "We sure piled them up proper, believe me." Prior to succumbing to a head wound he saw four **Stosstruppen** "turning somersaults." Sergeant William Thompson, "scared clear through," shot three Germans and ran for the nearest *abris* avoiding "sure death." Thompson and two other soldiers heard German voices advancing, raising the distinct possibility that "we had but a few minutes to live." They planned to blast away anyone who came to the *abris* door. Instead the **Pioniere** exploded a charge that collapsed the *abris*, knocking Thompson senseless. When he regained consciousness, he discovered he was severely wounded in the leg. Thompson was choking on his own blood. He started digging himself out and after nine hours was able get out of the dugout wreckage and retrieve his comrades as well.[969] Private Charles E. Brundett was surrounded by **Stosstruppen** as they rushed forward. He exhausted his ammunition and fought on with the bayonet. He worked his way back to the support platoon and kept up the fight.[970]

Major Rau was in the dark. TPS messages were sent out by Rau's available signalmen but were not acknowledged. He attempted to use a projector, an electric flare, to maintain communication with Colonel Parker's PC but the mist and poor visibility were too much.[971] The lack of communication became critical. At Beaumont Ridge, Colonel Parker reported to Brigadier General Traub that OP 14, engineers and runners sent out in all directions indicated the barrage on their front was exceedingly heavy up to 0500.[972] Chaumont observers commented that the only means of communication between company commanders and their battalion headquarters were runners and fullerphones. Unfortunately for the soldiers occupying Seicheprey, the fullerphones were quickly out of commission.[973]

So Major Rau depended entirely on his runners. Private Arnon Horton finally got Major Rau's message through and miraculously returned. Runners from the 102nd PC had not arrived.[974] Private C. Peckham was recommended for the Distinguished Service Cross for running messages throughout the day for Major Rau to the 102nd Infantry PC at Beaumont. He only stopped after succumbing to exhaustion.[975] Signal Corps personnel accomplished Herculean tasks trying to reestablish communications. Colonel Parker said of the Signal Corps men under Lieutenant Hannah: "There were no cold feet, there were no yellow streaks in this outfit. Their conduct was simply magnificent."[976]

KIRSCHBLÜTE AM SEICHEPREY

Major Bruns gave **Bataillon Grumbrecht** the honour of assaulting Seicheprey to take possession of the village. The combined **Sturmbataillon.14** and **Res. I. R. Kompagnie** force was to avoid the outlying trenches and annihilate the resistance from within. Aiding **Bataillon Grumbrecht's** assault was **Leutnant** von Ponickau's **Pioniere**. As **Reserve. Pionier Kompagnie. 80** crossed over the third line of trenches they took fire from American snipers. **Unteroffizier** Hober and Friedel immediately turned their squads to the left and attacked the American flank. They took four prisoners, killed three soldiers and captured one Chauchat automatic rifle. **Reserve. Pionier Kompagnie. 80** then opened up two passages in the wire entanglement and continued their advance. At 0500, 10 minutes after commencing the attack, **Leutnant** von Ponickau's **Zug** linked up with **Leutnant** Groote's **Zug** of **a-Kompagnie (4./259 Pfeiffer)**.[977] **Leutnant** Pfeiffer's **Stosstruppen** ran east of the machine guns that proved deadly for **Leutnant** Pohl. Pfeiffer's **Stosstruppen** diverted to the west working with **Leutnant** von Ponickau's **Pioniere** and made it to the north side of Seicheprey. As they went south, they were briefly joined by the elite **Sturmtruppen** of **b-Kompagnie (Sturmbataillon.14)** who ran into fierce resistance at the northern cemetery. **4./259 Pfeiffer** edged around Seicheprey to the west until they came

to the Richecourt road and got into the streets of the southern end of the village at 0530. **Leutnant** von Ponickau ordered his non-commissioned officers to attack the dugouts.[978] **Sturmbataillon.14 b-Kompagnie** advanced toward the church at the north end. Aiding their advance were two light guns. The **b-Kompagnie Sturmtruppen** rushed into Seicheprey on both sides of the church.[979] Thanks to **Leutnant** Knop's **Kompagnie** confronting the Americans at Sibille Trench, **Sturmbataillon.14 c-Kompagnie** rushed unhindered towards the north-east area of Seicheprey near the road to St. Baussant. On the eastern side of Seicheprey, **c-Kompagnie** acknowledged **d-Kompagnie (3./259 Maus, Hans)** as they continued south towards their rendezvous point just east of the village. **Reserve. Pionier Kompagnie. 80, Landwehr II, Leutnant** Maus and **Leutnant** Hans' **3./259** ran towards the vital American machine-gun nest located in *Boyau Seicheprey*. **Leutnant** Thomas, **Reserve. Pionier Kompagnie. 80, Landwehr II**, and **3./259** reached the machine gun next at 0500. **Leutnant** Thomas's **Pioniere** crept up and encircled the machine-gun nest and attacked. They captured five wounded Americans and one Model 07 machine gun.[980] To the German planners, **3./259** were now at the high-water mark of the assault, the point of bifurcation at 295 (see colour section, pp 20–21) where the American machine-gun nest was positioned. **Pioniere** throwing grenades took out the nest.[981] As **Stosstruppen** and **Sturmtruppen** advanced to the south, Sergeant James Walsh, Company A, prepped his men. Soon they were surrounded. The ensuing close combat saw Walsh wounded but his men successfully fought off the attack. Walsh stayed with his unit for several hours until finally relieved.[982]

The **Kirschblüte** die was cast. The time was now 0540. **Sturmbataillon.14 b-Kompagnie** was at the Seicheprey church. **Sturmbataillon.14 c-Kompagnie** was now at the north-east area of Seicheprey near the road to St. Baussant. **Bataillon Grumbrecht's d-Kompagnie (3./259 Maus, Hans)** and **Leutnant** Thomas, **Reserve. Pionier Kompagnie. 80, Landwehr II**, were at 295 and heading north. **Bataillon Grumbrecht's a-Kompagnie (4./259 Pfeiffer)** and **Leutnant** von Ponickau's **Reserve. Pionier Kompagnie. 80 Zug**

German photograph of dead American soldiers at Seicheprey. (*Geshichte der R.I. Regiment 258*)

was on the Richecourt-Seicheprey road and running west. Each **Kompagnie** had their own mission but possessed the independence to decide upon any course of action to overcome the Americans.[983] For the next one-and-a-half hours the Germans and Americans engaged in a desperate struggle amidst the village ruins. The **Kompagnien** were independent, without central command and control, resulting in descriptions of the fighting not being recorded in the post-battle reports.[984] **Sturmbataillon.14** reinforced the **Stosstruppen** advance by providing fire support at the two critical points to prevent the Americans fleeing out of Seicheprey towards Beaumont or reinforcing. As envisioned by **Major** Bruns, Major Rau's forces were trapped, surrounded by **Sturmtruppen** and **Stosstruppen** methodically annihilating any opposition as they proceeded from *abris* to *abris*. After the first wave, the entire fight at Seicheprey became hand-to-hand between each individual **Zug** and *GC*.[985]

Leutnant von Ponickau's **Reserve. Pionier Kompagnie. 80 Zug** reached Seicheprey's northwestern edge while the area was still under barrage causing them to take cover. Together with **Leutnant** Pfeiffer's **4./259 Stosstruppen** they penetrated Seicheprey streets from the west Richecourt-Seicheprey road shortly after 0430,

under fire from all directions. *Lieutenant* Toulouse ventured out into the village. As the first **Bataillon Grumbrecht a-Kompagnie (4./259 Pfeiffer) Stosstruppen** entered Seicheprey and approached Major Rau's PC, they were astonished to see *lieutenant* Toulouse throwing a grenade at them.[986]

Lieutenant Moore ran up the road shouting that the *Boche* were in the town. Three **Sturmbataillon.14 b-Kompagnie Sturmtruppen** were following him and throwing grenades. Moore fired back at the three with his pistols causing them to turn.[987] Color Sergeant Church reported from Major Rau's PC that the **Sturmtruppen** were following very close behind their own barrage, some of them being seen almost at once, less than one hundred yards down the street.[988] Private William B. Bolton ran into the PC after seeing the advancing **Sturmtruppen**. Rau's staff handed Bolton as many papers, maps, and documents as he could safely carry. He left the PC under a barrage and managed to reach Colonel Parker's PC at Beaumont.[989]

Leutnant von Ponickau issued orders to his **Pioniere** to attack the dugouts. Americans in one dugout offered stubborn resistance and refused to come out. Grenades were thrown and then **Pioniere** Rettig attempted to coax the Americans to surrender. They refused and in the process wounded Rettig. **Leutnant** von Ponickau ordered the dugouts destroyed using two charges of 13kg each. The entire *abris* was destroyed. **Reserve. Pionier Kompagnie. 80 Zug** moved on, blowing up an ammunition dump filled with hand grenades and rifle cartridges. Soon cartridges, trench mortar shells, rockets and other combustibles were exploding in every direction. They then proceeded to their final objective – attacking Rau's PC. Machine-gun fire from a nearby ruined house diverted the attack for a few minutes.[990]

Strickland remembered the screams and screeches that made the blood run cold coming from the throats of "half drunken Germans as they hurled their **Handgranaten** at every American that appeared." The fighting was incredibly fierce – rifles used as clubs, pickaxes, trench tools, knives – everything was used. One kitchen was afire where the **Stosstruppen** had shot streams of liquid fire. Carl Jacobs, Company D's mess sergeant and his kitchen police fought off **Flammenwerfer** operators with cleavers and butcher knives. A German with a flamethrower entered the kitchen and a cook threw a pot of water at him, snuffing out the flame. Company D's kitchen force, surrounded and called on to surrender, fought until all were killed or wounded. One German was split through the head to the shoulders by a cleaver blow. Post-war, veterans recalled that one cook killed two of the enemy with his cleaver. About twenty 18th Infantry disciplinary prisoners still clad in blue overalls fought hand-to-hand with the remaining **Stosstruppen** in the broken houses and against the crumbling stone walls. The prisoners hurled chunks of stone and mortar and grabbed picks and shovels to swing. Everyone heard the screams of agony as **Flammenwerfer** operators poured a stream of liquid fire into a pillbox of 102nd machine gunners.[991] Strickland remembered looking up and in the first light of daybreak as the fog dissipated seeing a black German combat aeroplane (**LVG C.V**) drone overhead, almost touching the Seicheprey house tops, signalling with absolute precision to German artillery the location of each little group of American defenders left in Seicheprey.[992]

Later Lieutenant Ingersoll saw someone come into Rau's PC and report that soldiers were retreating. He went outside the PC and saw soldiers coming from all points in the village. Now Rau had a contingent of cooks, signal men and runners to help set up his defensive perimeter.[993] Color Sergeant Church helped Major Rau take the men and quickly set up a line of defence behind sandbags around the battalion PC and within the *boyau* that led towards Beaumont. Church helped arm the stragglers with available ammunition and grenades were issued from the ammunition dump. At the same time Ingersoll took charge of a few men to the east of Rau's PC and posted them behind some sandbags. Rau and his defensive unit saw more men come running up the street followed by about twenty **Stosstruppen**. Rau shouted to the men to jump into the trench running along the Seicheprey *boyau* while the men behind the sandbag pile fired away at the enemy. The PC defence stayed in place for about an hour-and-a-half, then filed down to the first cross street, established a line, and started forward. Rau conducted his own personal reconnaissance within the village. In turn, Lieutenant Ingersoll and Color Sergeant Church took a handful of soldiers and went back into the Seicheprey ruins. Everyone kept up as heavy a rifle fire as possible and the **Stosstruppen** withdrew towards the northern edge of the town.[994] Rau's men reached the northern edge and retired to the trench line. As they moved out, they discovered a dead German officer about 70 metres to the front of the American defenders. Two or three wounded Germans were crawling around on top of the ground. The Americans buried the German officer in a shell hole the following night where he lay.[995]

Rau recalled the time in a letter home that was published after the war: "I had only two companies on the line, attacked by Prussian storm troops and two battalions of reserve infantry. Every man stuck to his post. Our mission was to hold the ground

… We held. They came clear through the town, blew up my first aid station, burned all my kitchen. They captured my doctor and sanitary men the first thing."[996] The American first-aid station was in a large building near the centre of the village and about 50 metres north of the battalion PC, close to where *Boyau Nantais* entered the north-western part of Seicheprey.[997] Lieutenant Burke, medical officer, and all but one of the enlisted personnel in the station were captured. They were busy inside the building tending to casualties when the **Stosstruppen** entered.[998] The Americans figured that the Germans had mistaken the aid station for Rau's battalion command post. The two were the largest remaining structures in the village and were in close proximity on the same street. At the northern end of Seicheprey, Major Rau set up a *Chauchat* automatic rifle to the left of *Boyau Mayonnaise* behind the wall of the building where the *gabions* were in place and continued to fire with it on the cemetery. The Germans later said that an American soldier was firing from the tower.

Corporal Charles T. Blanchard occupied an *abris* with nine Company D men during the bombardment. When it stopped, Blanchard saw

the **Stosstruppen** coming towards them from several directions. The Americans were cornered. They saw at once that it was to be a fight for their lives. The soldiers loaded, cocked and made everything ready. It wasn't long to wait, for they were spotted. Twenty **Stosstruppen** moved in. Blanchard and his fellow soldiers rushed them and fired a volley into their midst, dropping several. The **Stosstruppen** returned fire with a machine gun. The Americans scrambled for cover. With the machine gun providing cover, two **Stosstruppen** with flamethrowers rushed into the room and fired. Corporal Blanchard's mess sergeant was burned by the flame. The building caught fire. More **Stosstruppen** arrived, making the odds three to one in favour of the Germans. Blanchard and his fellow soldiers fixed bayonets and charged. Their audacity worked – the **Stosstruppen** scattered.[999] Private Arthur F. Socia was surrounded. Socia and several soldiers rushed a machine-gun nest set up on the advance. The machine gun was silenced but Socia was the only survivor. He managed to return into Seicheprey crawling from shell hole to shell hole.[1000] Corporal Blanchard saw Private Viberts, an infantry signal man, fight with incredible intensity, killing several Germans. Viberts went through the entire struggle without a scratch, suffering only a tear to his uniform from a bullet. At one moment in the hand-to-hand combat Viberts implored one of his Company D friends not to bayonet a wounded **Stosstrupp**. The German did not appreciate Vibert's charitable impulse, as he attempted to throw a grenade. Viberts' comrade didn't hold back this time and killed him with his bayonet.[1001]

Lieutenant A.P. Thorpe's Battery B, 103rd Field Artillery was positioned directly north of Seicheprey, one of three anti-tank gun units. When the attack commenced, the battery became infantry with each man fighting with

Two recipients of the Distinguished Service Cross for heroic actions at Seicheprey, Colonel John H. Parker and commandant du Boisrouvray. (Strickland, *Connecticut Fights*)

the remnants of Company D, using pistols, hand grenades, machine guns and rifles salvaged from the dead. Thorpe's anti-tankers that survived the onslaught became artillerymen once more and were ordered back to their batteries.[1002]

Captain Stanchfield's machine guns posted around Seicheprey took a serious beating. The initial barrage that led the **Stosstruppen** advance cut off all of Company B and part of Company A. Three of the guns manned by Company B were captured, along with all of their crews. Four of the Company A guns were blown up and destroyed by the barrage. The remaining two guns of Company B were mounted by Stanchfield in pillboxes in Seicheprey.[1003] One gun had been destroyed so the replacement gun unit set up outside the rubble without benefit of shelter. He discovered the guns and crews that occupied the right side of the village and in the trench left of Seicheprey had been captured. One gun emplacement in the orchard to the north side had been hit by a shell, knocking the gun out the emplacement, killing one man and wounding another. The remaining crew managed to remove their gun and established a new field of fire from an intact pillbox.

At dawn's first light Major Rau set out to determine the extent of German occupation outside of Seicheprey. Two combat groups were hastily formed from runners, orderlies, cooks and telephone men defending the wall around Rau's PC. They were sent forward to discover if the Sibille Trench was occupied by the enemy and how far the **Stosstruppen** had fallen back. Major Rau asked his 3rd Battalion counterpart, Captain Clarence Thompson, to organise his fourteen-man patrol and proceed to the west of Seicheprey. Rau also ordered his acting battalion adjutant, Lieutenant Strickland, to lead a ten-man patrol down *Boyau Mayonnaise*. Thompson divided the patrol into two sections. Color Sergeant Church, acting as Battalion Sergeant Major, and Sergeant Smith of Headquarters Company, in charge of signal detachment, both took the extreme left of Captain Thompson's party with several of the battalion liaison men. All through the town and up to within twenty paces of battalion headquarters

they saw dead Germans and Americans. Artillery shells were still falling on the littered streets as the two patrols worked down towards the front lines to gain information.[1004]

Major Rau ordered Lieutenant Moore to take the men who had been pushed out to the left flank. Lieutenant Strickland took his patrol to the right flank to reconnoitre. His patrol also went north and found survivors and casualties from Company D who had engaged in hand-to-hand combat. Strickland recalled: "The men of Connecticut had held the line until annihilated! There they were, dead – in windrows almost, out in front of the fire trenches which by reason of the mud made poor places from which to fight."[1005] Strickland, at great risk to himself, attempted to rescue two men lying nearby with his soldiers providing cover. But they were dead, killed by artillery fire.[1006] Captain Clarence Thompson ordered Color Sergeant Church's platoon to proceed to the west and hold *Boyau Nantais* north-west of Seicheprey with the men he still had. Thompson returned to see Major Rau at 2nd Battalion PC. Church organized a patrol and made for the northern edge of Seicheprey. Throughout this time his bravery and leadership in combat was cited as inspirational. As soon as Church confirmed his area was cleared of **Stosstruppen**, the patrol established a line of defence using *Boyau Nantais* and walls and buildings along the edge of Seicheprey as shelter. Under orders from Lieutenant Strickland, Church then reported to Major Rau that his squad was holding the lower edge of Seicheprey, but had seen nothing of Company C or the remaining soldiers from Company D.[1007] Rau started out through the centre of the town and on arriving near the northern edge saw fifteen to eighteen of the enemy under an open shed. He fired his pistol and the **Stosstruppen** left. In the meantime the line in the rear, without any command from Rau, followed him through the streets and debris. Rau's personal leadership qualities came through. He looked back and found his unit covering his back. The Americans moved to the north side of Seicheprey where they found **Stosstruppen** occupying American trenches. A few well-directed pistol shots from members of the patrols brought some of the "free lancing" German raiders to the ground.[1008]

PRISONERS OF WAR

Private Walter Wolf recalled seeing Seicheprey full of **Sturmtruppen** (from **Sturmbataillon.14 b-Kompagnie**). Five of his comrades went towards Rau's PC to join the remaining Americans in the struggle. Wolf stayed behind to fill his pockets with hand grenades. It proved to be a costly decision for at the exact moment **Sturmtruppen** appeared. Wolf rushed into a dugout and hid behind a wooden partition hoping the enemy would pass him by in the confusion. Unfortunately, he had lit a candle at the entrance of the dugout, which alerted them: "They knew damn well that some bird was hiding there. Quite nonchalantly a few potato mashers came floating in, while I was busy bandaging my wrist. The thin partition saved me. All was quiet again. I peeked out, only to find the nozzle of a liquid fire gun pointed directly at me. Choosing between Scylla and Charybdis, I trotted right out among the boys. This gave them great pleasure. One big fellow going through my pocket with one hand, clapped me on the back with the other, saying 'Don't be afraid.' One thing they did not get, however, my watch, which previous to coming out I had dropped down the neck of my shirt, and it now rested in my trouser leg. This watch I still have. The search completed, I was marched to the rear."[1009]

Battery C, 103rd Field Artillery, under the command of Sergeant Harold "Pa" Tucker manned the front-line anti-tank gun. In their north-east Seicheprey dugout to the right of the ruined church Sergeant Tucker and his "C" battery men – Corporal Lee, Privates Sefton, Sutcliffe, Cardell, Collins, Petochelli, and Goldman – were waiting for the barrage to lift. At the moment that they thought the barrage had stopped Tucker's team rushed outside the dugout right into a horde of soldiers surging through the narrow street next to the church. A momentary glare from star shells revealed German uniforms surrounding them. Battery C's anti-tankers found themselves surrounded and were forced to surrender.[1010]

At the 102nd Machine Gun dugout on the north-east side of the village were Lieutenant Walter Tenney and his medic Private Enoch Doble. In the dim, foggy light at the opening above the back exit of the dugout south of Seine Cemetery, Tenney and Doble could see silhouetted **Sturmtrupp** figures with their unmistakable German helmets approaching fast. Suddenly the firing stopped and Private Doble could hear his corporal yelling: "It's French soldiers." Lieutenant Tenney recognized the mistake and responded, "I'll run to the gun positions." He came out into indirect machine-gun fire and quickly returned. Bullets and flying debris drove the dugout crew away from the entrance down the steps for safety. The dugout was no longer a sanctuary. A grenade exploded close to where they stood. In a rush the soldiers moved all the way down the dugout steps to the bottom. Two more grenades exploded halfway down the stairs. The newly arrived crew of gunners and medics were not familiar with the route to the back exit. They discovered it at the other end of the dugout. The Germans attempted to enter the dugout but Lieutenant Tenney fired a round and they retreated. Both exits were now covered by **Sturmbataillon.14 c-Kompagnie** men. A grenade slid onto the floor beside Tenney and Doble from the back exit. Tenney picked it up to throw it back up the stairs. It exploded in his hand and knocked everyone to the ground.

Doble picked himself up in the smoke, amazed to see Lieutenant Tenney still alive and coherent. He looked around and saw a sergeant slowly standing up. "Are you all right?" Doble called. "I think so," the sergeant answered. Doble picked up Lieutenant Tenney: "I'm done, don't bother with me. Make a run for it to stand at the gun positions with the boys." Doble wiped the blood from Tenney's face, grateful to have something to do when it was certain the next grenade could kill them all. Then they heard a familiar voice at the main exit of the dugout.

"It's all right, it's all right, don't fire." It was the last living member of the gun position – the rest had been killed in the assault. The **Stosstruppen** had cut across the narrow passage to the town. "They [the Germans] are miles in back of us." The **Sturmtruppen** had told him to tell the crew in the dugout to come out or they would blow them out. After a short conference, the remaining Americans came out the front stairway with their hands above the heads. They were met by several **Sturmtruppen** pointing long-muzzled automatics. One of the **Sturmtruppen** without warning fired his automatic straight at Tenney and Doble as they exited. The bullet added another wound to Tenney – this time in the left calf – and tore through Doble's uniform.[1011]

Two **Sturmtruppen** relieved the Americans of their sidearms. They began to go through pockets, taking whatever they found to their liking – a real treasure were the rubber boots the men wore. Doble for some reason was overlooked. A young German sergeant, tall and blonde, pretended to rifle Tenney and Doble's pockets. Doble had $100 in American Express checks, pictures of his parents and his home in Quincy, Massachusetts. The sergeant took nothing at all. Then he said in very good English, "Will you please take care of the lieutenant's wounds, and let me know when you are ready to move?" Doble rebandaged Tenney's shattered hand and again cleaned the blood from his face, thinking Tenney had lost his vision. Doble signalled that they were ready. Doble put his arm around Lieutenant Tenney's waist and the two struggled across No Man's Land.

Top Sergeant Erving "Pete" A. Dresser and Private Ed Clark were assigned to 2nd Battalion Headquarters in the centre of Seicheprey. As the barrage opened up, Clark and fourteen companions were asleep in a small *abris*. They had become adjusted to the "big shells," and realised the barrage was targeting their location. After two hours of barrage there was a moment of quiet. Suddenly, three grenades were thrown inside the *abris*. One landed square on Clark's bed with the other two landing adjacent to

Major George Rau, commander of 1st Battalion, demonstrated exemplary courage throughout the battle. (Strickland, *Connecticut Fights*)

the bed frame. When they exploded, Clark remembered, "They took me along with them and I had my left thumb nearly blown off, my hands filled with shrapnel, also my face and eyes, and a small wound in my right arm and my ears stunned so that I couldn't hear." Clark picked himself up and found he "was a long ways from dead." **Bataillon Grumbrecht d-Kompagnie (3./259 Maus, Hans)** and **Leutnant** Thomas, **Reserve. Pionier Kompagnie. 80, Landwehr II**, engaged in fire with Clark and his comrades; after a few minutes, there came a moment of quiet. Then fifteen grenades flew into the dugout. The resulting explosions killed several soldiers and badly wounded the rest. Clark escaped death but received another wound, this time to his leg. Top Sergeant Dresser and the rest surrendered and came out of the *abris*.[1012]

MEDICAL AID

Post-battle, Colonel Parker paid a glowing tribute to the Sanitary Detachment and recommended for the Distinguished Service Cross the regimental surgeon, Dr Charles W. Comfort. He slipped through the barrage fire and with a detail from the Medical Detachment arrived outside of Seicheprey at about 0800, when the dressing of wounds began. The seriously wounded were evacuated over the top of the trenches. Dr Comfort worked among the wounded in the shelter of the remains of a wall. He administered first aid for thirty-six hours without rest or relief to numerous wounded, in the open, almost constantly under heavy artillery fire, and assisted in their evacuation. Private John R. Cannon was the only surviving member of the medical platoon, the rest were either killed or captured. Cannon, emerging from the aid station, saw a street full of **Stosstruppen** running in his direction. Cannon quickly rolled into a ditch and kept quiet. The men rushed past him and captured Lieutenant Joseph P. Burke and the rest of the medics in the aid station. Later, after working on the wounded all day, Private Cannon was struck by a piece of shrapnel that necessitated the amputation of his leg. On occasion German machine guns were sniping at the party digging out the buried men, even though the Red Cross flag was in plain sight.[1013]

There were examples of humane treatment from both sides. Major Rau found two wounded Americans north of Seicheprey, each with a hot canteen of coffee and a food container placed beside him, both of them neatly bandaged up by the enemy. Sergeant Fred A. Tyrrell, Company F, recalled that some wounded American prisoners were found in the field with their wounds bound up.[1014] Later in the week, a burial party sent out to bury a dead German soldier between the lines was fired on from the German line. The American party held up a wooden cross to be used to mark the grave. The firing stopped and the burial party was allowed to complete its work.[1015]

As **Bataillon Grumbrecht d-Kompagnie** and **Leutnant** Thomas, **Reserve. Pionier Kompagnie. 80,**

Landwehr II converged on the southern limits of Seicheprey, Corporal Robert Conroy's pet Stubby climbed out of the Beaumont trenches close by the 102nd Regiment PC and was injured by artillery shrapnel that struck his left foreleg causing an ugly wound. Everyone around Stubby learned he was hit when he yelped with pain. Stubby limped back to the shelter in the trench where the headquarters company medic dressed and bound the wound. After the battle and for the remainder of his time at Beaumont, Stubby recuperated in the safety of Conroy's *abris*.

RAU DETERMINES GERMAN INTENTIONS

At 0700 a wounded **Stosstrupp** was captured by Major Rau's men fighting at the northern edge of Seicheprey.[1016] The first information as to the magnitude of the raid came from Major Rau, a native of Alsace and fluent in German. He interrogated the man, who later was evacuated to the hospital. The prisoner told Rau that the attack was made by 1,200 stormtroops and two battalions of reserve infantry; one battalion of which was to attack on the French front. Rau learned that the centre of attack was Seicheprey. One thousand or more line troops were in reserve in front and to the flanks of each sub-sector. The raid was to take Seicheprey, to be followed by the seizure of the heights of Beaumont Ridge – to effect a lodgment on the Metz-St. Dizier Road. Then the **Stosstruppen** were to counter-attack fiercely in the hope that they would break through the French-American counter-attack and attain the 1-Bis line, which had been weakened. Then all German forces would sweep through to gain *Bois du Jury* and the St Dizier-Metz Road, holding the ground captured. Major Bowditch in his report to Chaumont stated that "No verification of this story was ever secured."[1017] It was practically an entire fabrication.

Rau's prisoner was subsequently interrogated by *2ᵉ Bureau, 32ᵉ corps d'armée*. What they learned went beyond **Generalmajor** von Stolzmann's plan: to take prisoners and maintain in sector troops the Allies might intend to send to the Somme

Lieutenant Butch Lockhart held the line with eight soldiers throughout the battle. (Strickland, *Connecticut Fights*)

Seicheprey, runners became casualties almost as soon as they started with their messages. Some of them were found later, dead or wounded in shell holes or along the road. Some were never found.[1020] Runners set out at 0410 from Seicheprey and eventually arrived at Colonel Parker's PC at 0633. It was then that Parker learned from Rau, "*Boche* are attacking in force. We are holding yet. Send a barrage <u>Normal</u>. We will hold."[1021] Shortly after, two more messages came from Rau giving details of the fight: "1200 *Boches* attack are still in our front line send barrage quick. Put barrage on our front line trenches they are working toward us. RAU." More information dribbled in from Rau providing Colonel Parker with his first understanding of what was happening. "The enemy put down a very heavy barrage, set kitchen on fire most all dugouts knocked down. 1st Aid station down flat. No doctor. Boche followed barrage by big raid, drove men as far as Battalion P.C. Drove them back here beyond our front line. Am <u>holding</u> large number wounded, some captured have not exact figures, send ambulance or stretcher bearers <u>and doctor</u>. Have taken position farther edge of town still <u>holding</u> still shelling. Started at 0315 attack at about 0430. RAU"[1022] Parker repeated Rau's message to Brigadier General Traub highlighting the fact that the Germans had penetrated Seicheprey but had been driven back to the edge of the town, where Rau was holding. He added that Major Rau wanted a barrage on his front line immediately, had experienced a large number of wounded, and needed ambulances, stretcher bearers and a doctor.[1023]

Rau's intelligence officer, Lieutenant Frederick Oberlin, arrived at Seicheprey around 0800 and continued the interrogation of the three German prisoners, which confirmed Rau's suspicions. It suggested to Rau and those in command that the German attack was intended to remain in place, – an analysis that governed decisions for the next 24 hours.

battlefield; possibly to oblige the Allies to bring reinforcements into the southern Woëvre front; and at the very least, to cause the Allies to use up as much ammunition as possible. The raid's objectives showed Seicheprey village was to be occupied and held until the Allies launched a counter-attack. The estimate of the strength of the German assault was close to the truth, showing 100 men from **Sturmbataillon.14,** the entire **Res. I. R. 259,** and two or three companies from **Res. I. R. 258,** who were to protect the west flank of the attack. **Sturmbataillon.14** was equipped with five or six small model **MW.** Each **Res. I. R. 259 Kompagnie** was likewise equipped with one **Flammenwerfer.** The prisoner heard that the artillery was to be considerably reinforced during the attack – the report commented here, "No details."[1018] The interrogation had to be interrupted because of the condition of the wounded man: "It will be continued later."[1019] It was not. He died two days later from wounds received at Seicheprey.

At this stage of the battle the only successful communication between headquarters and battalion was through runners. That morning at

INDELIBLE MEMORIES

Colonel Parker, Lieutenant Colonel Dowell, and Lieutenant Leavenworth left the 102nd Infantry PC around 0600 and proceeded to the front lines down the hill from Beaumont to see for themselves the extent of combat underway. Parker's sudden departure from his PC left some wondering where he was. The artillery barrage blasted away at his sector. The three officers traversed the main *boyau*, rallying troops to defend the ridge with whatever means possible. Throughout this time, Colonel Parker repeatedly climbed upon the firing step of the trench; a big man, he presented a very visible target to the Germans down the hill. Colonel Parker stood with his back to the barrage despite shell splinters falling about him, and talked calmly to his men. Private Julius T. Fedel, Sanitary Detachment, 101st Engineers, recalled later that Parker called out: "Say fellows, there is nothing happening, you are just as safe here as you would be at home." Fedel said his calm demeanour helped – "if he could do it then so could we."[1024] His decisive and courageous manner greatly buttressed their resolve in a rapidly deteriorating situation. Here Parker earned the first of four Distinguished Service Crosses that he would be awarded over the next five months of the war.

One story suggests that Parker went into the trenches to encourage his men and found a machine gun that had been silenced because its crew had been killed. Two dead Americans lay beside the gun. Parker was quoted as saying, "If these brave boys can stick to their post like that I can do a little." He operated the machine gun until relieved.[1025]

Lieutenant Colonel Dowell went further down the trench line to examine damage to the barbed wire. The troops in place were at the verge of breakdown from the barrage. Dowell spent the time working with the soldiers and calming their nerves.[1026]

During Colonel Parker's temporary absence, four horsemen from the east (an apt number) galloped in under fire at the 102nd Infantry PC. *Colonel* Jules-Alexandre Bertrand and his senior staff from *162ᵉ régiment d'infanterie* wanted to congratulate Parker on the defence they had demonstrated. As Bertrand rode towards Beaumont, German observers reported a cavalry attack in progress and directed artillery at the party. Fortunately, they arrived safely at the PC.[1027] The French quickly exchanged information with the 102nd Infantry staff on the evolving battle. When Parker returned, he discussed with Bertrand the German assault objectives concerning Position 1-Bis and the Beaumont Ridge. German conquest of Beaumont represented a significant gain, providing additional high ground, in addition to Montsec, to better engage the entire *32ᵉ corps d'armée* southern Woëvre front. Standing orders from both *armée* and corps required every man to defend Position 1-Bis at all costs.[1028]

At this time Colonel Parker's French liaison advisor, *commandant* du Boisrouvray, also took action to better understand German intentions and headed into the battle zone during the height of the barrage. His efforts were successful, for his understanding of the situation improved headquarters' awareness of what was transpiring. For this heroic act *commandant* du Boisrouvray was awarded the Distinguished Service Cross. In his post-war work *With the Yankee Division in France*, Frank Sibley paid *commandant* du Boisrouvray the highest compliment: "Major de Boisrouvray was a French officer who represented the best type, the very *beau ideal* of a French officer. His record is written on his breast, where the batterie de cuisine, (kitchenware) as the French call their rows of decorations, is formidable and suggestive of dare-devil fighting. Though a major, he had commanded a regiment, and he was known and adored throughout the French armies."[1029] *Commandant* du Boisrouvray had earned the second highest award for bravery in the US Army.

Major John Gallant was awakened along with the rest of the 102nd Infantry by the early morning artillery barrage at Beaumont. He proceeded to the 102nd Infantry headquarters. Reports were not coming in so Gallant volunteered to go forward and fix the problem. At 0800 Parker sent Gallant to the 1-Bis position just to the north of the 102nd Infantry PC, known as the cave, to organise and relay the reports. When Colonel Parker ordered reinforcement of Seicheprey, Gallant organized the Company B into *GCs* and establish new observation posts from remaining elements.[1030] Somehow in the confusion that morning Colonel Parker credited Major Gallant with retaking Seicheprey. The absence of communication between Seicheprey and Beaumont was the reason. Parker wrongly assumed in his initial report to the 51st Brigade that sending Gallant forward with Company B made the difference. An amended credit for the recapture of Seicheprey went to Major Rau and Captain Thompson in Parker's subsequent report to 51st Brigade.

Battery F, the most exposed of all the American batteries near Dead Man's Curve, fired for 10 hours straight and spent all their HE rounds in the morning barrage. They also lost communication as the battle commenced. The last report they received from their battalion was alarming: "Germans enter Seicheprey – still coming." Battery F men put on rubber boots. They distributed more revolver ammunition. Lieutenant Thompson, battery commander, ordered shrapnel to be cut for 50 metres and the 75mm guns levelled at the Beaumont Ridge. Battery F men did not know if the next man coming over the ridge would be the enemy. One of the men got out his box of cigars from home and passed them around. He didn't want the Germans to get them. Later, after the firing had decreased, Battery F had a good laugh when their magnanimous counterpart regretted his kindness as he had escaped being captured or killed after all.[1031]

At Corporal Ernest LaBranche's Battery E, the possibility of the Germans coming over Beaumont Ridge was equally frightening. Their battery received orders to prepare to retreat. The men were quickly briefed that as the first waves of retreating infantry passed, they were to man certain defences near the battery and await word to move south. The 75mm pieces were to be rendered useless by a welding shell – only to be used in extreme emergency. Both men and the disabling shell were placed at the ready.[1032]

Private Enoch Doble's brother Kendall watched the battle from his position in a trench overlooking Seicheprey from Beaumont Ridge. He told Enoch after the war that the worst and most intense German barrage the 26th Division experienced in the entire war was at Seicheprey that morning. Kendall was in every battle that the 26th Division fought that year.[1033] Private Earl Yeomans' company held the line down the hill from Beaumont. His unit was able to look down into Seicheprey and see the actual hand-to-hand fighting from a distance, but so far away they were powerless to assist. Their mission was to hold the 1-Bis sector.[1034] As Sergeant Fred Tyrrell's patrol reoccupied ground north of Seicheprey one of his soldiers gave him a note found on a sandbag. It read: "Did we make you run Yanks? More are coming."[1035]

Major Bruns' reserve companies followed in the third wave with heavy machine guns, light **MW, Granatwerfer**, medical personnel, stretcher-bearer parties and carriers with ammunition and equipment. The necessary distribution in depth was made immediately after the first wave reached their first objective. Two groups of four light **MW** on flat trajectory gun carriages were assigned to accompany the third wave, taking up positions that supported the **Stosstruppen** by combatting isolated posts of resistance with direct fire. **Hauptmann Tolle e-Kompagnie (Reserve-Kompagnie)** were in the third wave, employing heavy machine guns behind **Kompagnie C** and **Kompagnie D. 8./259 Wegener.** They searched the trenches and then prepared for defence, setting up the heavy machine-guns. Despite their later role, **Leutnant** Wegener's **Kompagnie** suffered the loss of an officer and twenty-two soldiers in the Seicheprey attack.[1036] When the **Stosstruppen** returned from Seicheprey the **MW** assumed positions that produced a protective barrage in front of the newly gained front line. Heavy machine guns were used at *Bois de Remières* and at those points where their fire justified their use in the front line. Heavy machine-guns were in place to support the first waves as well as ward off whatever counter-attack would come. Flank support to the **Kirschblüte**

An aerial photograph of Seicheprey from the south taken after the battle. (NARA)

was provided by **Model 08** machine guns fired through gaps in the Germans' own line or by firing over it, plus two **Sturmbataillon.14** guns from the infantry gun battery. South-west of Lahayville was the west flank for **Kirschblüte**. North of *Bois du Jury* on the east flank was an identical alignment of enfilading fire. **MW** fired on both flanks of the attack for the entire 90 minutes that the attack required.[1037]

What alarmed the Germans reflecting on the battle a week later was that the Americans fought while sitting on walls of houses and in the remains of the church, inflicting losses on **Sturmtruppen** and **Stosstruppen** before being discovered, then disappearing in the rubble to fight again.

American resistance in front of the main line of resistance and in the supporting positions in front of the village of Seicheprey was stubborn. Every man had to be overpowered individually. The light machine guns of the Americans fired up to the last moment. Since the troops occupying the village did not want to come out of their dugouts, but defended the entrances, individual combats, man against man, took place.[1038]

CHAPTER 18

The "Sacrifice Positions" in the *Bois de Remières*

The fighting ability of the individual soldier determined success. Liaison was all shot to pieces, so it was simply a matter of every man for himself. The men seized their weapons and fought hand-to-hand. Isolated machine-gun crews were completely surrounded and, though receiving fire from all quarters, manned their guns and added their support to the hard-pressed infantry. Gunner after gunner was killed at his post, but another was always ready to pull the bleeding body of his comrade clear of the gun and take the dead man's place, though he met the same fate in a moment. A shell landed squarely in one nest and killed the crew. Survivors in the area dug out the gun, mounted it and continued firing.[1039] Combat in *Bois de Remières* was almost totally hand-to-hand.

The heroic actions of Captain Arthur F. Locke, Company M, exemplify the actions of the defenders that day. Captain Locke remained in *Bois de Remières* to orient Captain Griswold and Company C as to the strong points within the forest. Locke's Company M had departed for Ansauville earlier that night. When the barrage commenced, Locke took cover with Company C in a dugout on the eastern end of Sibille Trench. The **Stosstruppen** advanced towards Locke's position. Locke grabbed a Springfield rifle and proceeded to fire clip after clip into their ranks. The **Stosstruppen** then shouted out to Locke to surrender. He refused and continued to fire. As Locke was reloading the fourth clip into the rifle, the **Stosstruppen** rushed in and riddled him with machine-gun bullets.[1040]

KTK Major Bruns and **Hauptmann** Seebohm were north of *Bois de Remières* in their command post monitoring the attack. Their combined **KTK** experience from **Einladung** meant they intimately knew the terrain and obstacles facing their assault troops as they ventured into the woods. Their plan for attacking *Bois de Remières* was like the spokes of a quarter of a wagon wheel, with each spoke representing a **Kompagnie** moving into the south-west sector of the forest. Command and control, key logistic lines and the primary *boyau* connection to *Bois du Jury,* where reinforcements converged, were all there, which made annihilation by **Sturm** a great prize. The effort proved to be costly to both sides.

Bataillon Hellmuth b-Kompagnie (1./259 Tänzer) and **Bataillon Seebohm a-Kompagnie (10./259)** both jumped out of the same nest to the north-west of *Bois de Remières*. Each had ancillary objectives that required one **Zug** to manoeuvre towards the south-west corner. To the east in the fourth major nest for the assault, **Hauptman** Seebohm's **c-Kompagnie (9./259)** served as a second wave and advanced to the north-eastern corner of *Bois de Remières*. Seebohm's **d-Kompagnie (11./259)** went into the centre of *Bois de Remières*. The third **Sturmbataillon** committed to **Kirschblüte, b-Kompagnie (Sturmbataillon.14)**, was to drive to the south-west corner of *Bois de Remières* by way of the southern edge of the forest. Bruns and Seebohm's vision was to have each **Kompagnie** penetrate the forest in a matter of minutes, quickly surrounding and destroying the Americans and with the ultimate objective of reaching the forest's south-west corner. With **Einladung** as a telling memory for **259 Res. I. R.** the operation required an aggressive strike at each stronghold after **MW** had initiated the destruction. Bruns was not going to have **MW** interfere with his **Stosstruppen** as had happened with **Einladung**. Artillery and **MW** were to keep reinforcements at bay in **Kirschblüte**. What their **Sturmtruppen** and **Stosstruppen** did not know was that the Americans remained committed to the French order to fight from a sacrifice position. It was that commitment that made the Seicheprey "affair" a soldier's battle.

Einladung's preliminary use of artillery was replicated. The Germans fired an extensive **Gasschuss** and short destructive barrages on the Americans front lines on the north-east edge of *Bois de Remières*. **MW** then proceeded to fire for 6 minutes at the northern half of the wood, followed by an extended 8-minute barrage on the southern half to annihilate the retreating Americans and repel reinforcements.[1041] One of the first assault units across No Man's Land was **Oberleutnant** Fritz's **Pionier Kompagnie.79** with **Leutnant** Kunze in charge of a **Pionierzug**. The **Pioniere** followed the **MW** destruction of wire entanglements, allowing the **Sturmtruppen** and **Stosstruppen** to move quickly towards their objectives.

Leutnant Tänzer's **b-Kompagnie (1./259 Tänzer)** was not able to report back to **Hauptmann** Hellmuth on combat in progress and alert him to the fact that attempts to establish liaison with **Bataillon** Hellmuth's **a-Kompagnie (6./259 Knop)** were not successful. Tänzer was not aware that **Leutnant** Knop had been shot and his men were struggling at that time in Sibille Trench to the north. Meanwhile, a **Zug** of **Stosstruppen** from **Bataillon Hellmuth b-Kompagnie (1./259 Tänzer)** were the first to enter the north-western edge

of *Bois de Remières* opposite Sergeant William J. Brinley, Corporal Boucher, and the 1st Platoon. They all knew what to expect after the initial heavy barrage had ceased in their area as the dawn came. The first casualty in the platoon discovered in the dawn light was almost completely covered with earth and with blood flowing from the mouth, ears, and eyes. The man ending up choking to death. Boucher's unit did not have enough ammunition on hand, so he ordered his soldiers to hold fire until the **Stosstruppen** hit the barbed wire. It didn't take long. When **b-Kompagnie Stosstruppen** surged into the area, they were pummelled by Boucher's platoon. They advanced in close formation and soon the wire and the ground in front of the Company C unit was covered with German dead and wounded. Those that moved received more rounds. Corporal Boucher saw platoons either side of him being captured and recognized they were surrounded. Soon the casualties mounted. Boucher acquired a wound from an artillery shell blast. He applied an improvised tourniquet from a shoelace and a piece of the trench duckboard and proceeded to hobble along for the rest of the day. Private George H. Cooper, a machine gunner, was hit on the right shoulder early that morning as the **Stosstruppen** rushed and captured him – the only member of the platoon taken prisoner. Corporal Gritzback was in charge of the machine gun squad. Gritzback's gunner, Private Lilley, was shot in the head and died instantly. Gritzback lifted Lilley's body off the gun and took over. Gritzback mowed the **Stosstruppen** down as they advanced. Gritzback took a round just below the brim of his helmet, which glanced off his head and hit one of his men in the face. Corporal Coe got a bullet in the guts and was laid on the parados (the bank behind the trench, designed to give protection from the rear). He kept hollering "Charlie! Oh! Charlie!" (Boucher) "For God's sake, do something for me." Boucher gave him some water from his canteen. He ripped open Gritzback's shirt and discovered a hole in his belly. At that moment a piece of shell hit Gritzback in the neck and decapitated him, so his misery was over. Boucher and his unit decided they were to fight to the death rather than be taken prisoner. Boucher was deteriorating from his wound. Private "Gwatsy" Mendillo tried cheering him up with, "Gee! Charlie! We got them good this [time] and they're running for the woods." Mendillo didn't have a scratch on him. Boucher quickly responded, "For God's sake keep your head down 'Gwatsy'!" Too late. Shrapnel dug through the parapet, opening up Mendillo's chest and he died quickly: "Charlie! They got me."[1042]

B-Kompagnie (1./259 Tänzer) linked up with **Bataillon** Seebohm's **a-Kompagnie (10./259)** and encountered little opposition as they advanced to the south-west corner of the wood. The combined **Kompagnien** from **Bataillon Hellmuth** and **Bataillon Seebohm** arrived at the south-

west edge of the wood where the small-gauge tracks converged with the primary trenches that ran into Sibille Trench. The two companies attacked an array of machine-gun nest s and supporting Company C infantry. The Germans later concluded the Americans had been waiting for them because it proved to be a nasty struggle.[1043] The sector was under the control of Lieutenant Carruth and his 3rd Platoon. A **Zug** of **b-Kompagnie Stosstruppen**, commanded by **Leutnant** von Specht and **Vizefeldwebel** Brüers, advanced into the trench that led into the corner of the forest and inflicted heavy losses on the Americans, taking four prisoners. At the same time they suffered considerable losses. **Vizefeldwebel** Brüers was killed and most of his men were wounded.[1044] The Americans poured machine-gun bullets into the area from a nest

Whiting's painting of an American machine-gun nest at Seicheprey. (Connecticut State Library)

between *Bois de Remières* and *Bois du Jury*.[1045] Despite the convergence of Germans, one Company C GC held the south-east corner of the woods at the end of *Boyau Jury-Remières* throughout the attack.[1046]

Hauptman Seebohm's **c-Kompagnie** advanced to the north-eastern corner of the wood occupied by Lieutenant Koenne's 4th Platoon. While **c-Kompagnie** approached, the Americans in the stronghold set off red signal rockets requesting a barrage. The **Stosstruppen** came across a pillbox crew that was almost annihilated by an **MW** bomb with the first salvo. What few survivors were left were quickly taken prisoner and marched back to the German lines.[1047] **Leutnant** Kunze's **Pionier Kompagnie.79 Zug** blew up several dugouts. They did not have enough concentrated charges to complete the operation, so his **Pionieren** were forced to go back several times to the German lines for resupply.[1048]

To the east at the jump-off point south of *Bois de la Sonnard* **d-Kompagnie (11./259)** faced well emplaced machine-gun nest s that caused many casualties. Artillery helped by destroying two machine-gun nest s and killing the crews. Major Murphy now had two remaining machine guns positioned within *Bois de Remières*.[1049] Soon the **Stosstruppen** were able to overcome the strong points on the eastern flank of the forest, requiring the American survivors to withdraw in the direction of *Bois du Jury* and take up new positions. The **Stosstruppen** from **d-Kompagnie** were held back from their south-west *Bois de Remières* rendezvous with **a-Kompagnie (10./259)** affecting the plan of attack. The third **Kompagnie** of elite **Sturmtruppen** committed, **b-Kompagnie (Sturmbataillon.14)**, reached the south-west *Bois de Remières* objective without much resistance. In their advance **b-Kompagnie** came to the entrance of one dugout and were fired on by Company C soldiers in the trees. Those that were discovered were shot down.[1050] The **Sturmtruppen** established liaison with **a-Kompagnie (10./259)** and **d-Kompagnie (11./259)** at the southern corner and took part in capturing American *abris* that were stubbornly defended. A small detachment of Americans escaping through the *boyau* in the direction of *Bois du Jury* were thought by the Germans to be caught in the dense German barrage fire.[1051]

"IT ISN'T OVER YET"

Captain Daniel Strickland's post-war account quoted an anonymous Company C member: "Our orders were 'no retreat' and we were determined to stay until the last man had been annihilated."[1052]

B-Kompagnie (Sturmbataillon.14) advanced on the PC serving Captain Griswold's Company C. The initial shock of the assault and the resultant destruction made unit integrity impossible to maintain. The destruction of American strong points meant survivors moved on their own to other areas and kept up the fight. Visibility was still poor, owing to fog and smoke. **Sturmtruppen** and **Stosstruppen** threw grenades at every step, machine-guns from both sides were firing and the Americans gauged the volume of fire by the way the twigs were snapping off right and left. At Captain Griswold's PC several attacks were fought off by the soldiers that assembled. Griswold fired away with his automatic, dropping two Germans. He killed three more with a Mills hand grenade. The **Sturmtruppen** captured and disarmed Griswold and he was led by two guards through the forest towards No Man's Land. While en route one of the guards fell into a shell hole. Griswold quickly body blocked the other and scrambled south. He made it through two barrages but suffered a wound from a splinter to his shoulder. Shell shock kept Griswold incapacitated for the next three months.[1053] Griswold was reported in the *Hartford Courant* three days after the battle as having been surrounded and captured three times, as having killed four Germans and escaping after hitting a fourth on the head with his pistol. Thanks to the ongoing chaos from the battle Major Rau did not know what was happening to his Company C until Captain Griswold entered his PC.[1054]

Lieutenant Samuel A. Tyler was from Company L and like his senior, Captain Arthur

Locke, stayed to assist Company C in adjusting to the *Bois de Remières* operations. As the **Sturmtruppen** attacked, Lieutenant Johnson was severely wounded and Lieutenant Tyler took command of the soldiers remaining near the PC, directing them to locations to reinforce the defence. Two **Sturmtruppen** rushed the PC entrance and Tyler shot them both with his pistol. A few minutes later Tyler and a cadre of available soldiers managed to take out a newly established machine-gun position near the PC. Tyler then organized the remaining soldiers into *GCs*. Later that afternoon Tyler received a head wound from debris, but managed to maintain command and hold the position for the next 24 hours until he was finally relieved.[1055]

Corporal James R. Thornley, Company C, was wounded early on in the battle but continued fighting while urging his men to defend their positions. When the **Sturmtruppen** attacked, the fog was so thick to the ground that the defending Americans could not see where the threat lay. Corporal Thornley climbed a lookout post built in a high tree behind the PC and was able to see the **Sturmtruppen** advancing. From this vantage point, the wounded Thornley directed his troops to fire on them.[1056] Private Harry W. Congdon was a runner for Company C. Throughout the day he carried messages through several barrages connecting the remaining Company C elements with updates. He worked until he was exhausted and was carried to a first-aid station.[1057]

Another Company L hero that fought within *Bois de Remières* was Private 1st Class Lionel W. Delesdernier. In the course of the battle Private Delesdernier left the PC to acquire munitions from the ammunition dump. En route he endured intense machine-gun and sniper fire. At one point Private Delesdernier single-handedly prevented the enemy from overrunning the company PC using his pistol and grenades. He passed vital information to rear-echelon units about the status of the company and managed to return to his original firing position to keep fighting.[1058]

North of Company C's PC location other incredible acts of bravery occurred. Private

Edward L. Dion, Company C, completely surrounded by the **Stosstruppen**, fought them off with grenades and rifle fire, finally succeeding in driving them away. Dion then carried a wounded comrade through a rain of shrapnel to a first-aid station and returned to his firing post. Dion continued to help with the wounded under heavy shrapnel fire and remained at his post until the end of the battle.[1059] Sergeant William L. Knox, Company L, also stayed on with Company C after his company was relieved from the front lines that night. Despite the fact that it was not his platoon, he was the senior ranking member so he became de facto leader. When the **Stosstruppen** attacked and surrounded the platoon, Sergeant Knox quickly organized and held ground throughout the entire battle. He was twice wounded by shrapnel and grenades. At one point Sergeant Knox broke through the German positions and established contact with platoons to his right within the forest. Sergeant Knox was an inspiration to the men, leading them to accomplish great feats in the face of vastly superior numbers.[1060] Private Jeremiah Tryon during a heavy artillery barrage climbed out of his trench in the front line and shot a German sniper, who was pouring fire into the trench that he occupied.[1061] Private Patrick Maloney accomplished a dangerous reconnaissance to locate Sergeant Hanson's 2nd Platoon during the height of battle.[1062] Hanson's platoon was put at a severe disadvantage when his two machine guns were destroyed.

Robert D. Brinley, the bugler for Company C, and Private Arthur J. Gagnon arrived at about the same time at the *abris* that provided shelter for the PC members. Brinley remarked to the occupants that he didn't know "if they had jumped or were blown in." A few seconds later Private George F. Stevens from Lieutenant Edward A. Koenne's 4th Platoon stumbled into the *abris* and gasped that the platoon members defending the north-east sector were either killed or captured. Stevens had just run all the way from the 4th Platoon location in his bare feet. About this time fifteen **Stosstruppen** advanced towards the *abris* in a single column. Their leader beckoned the Americans to surrender. The Americans answered with a shower of hand grenades. Acting 1st Sergeant Arvid A.Cederholm, Private Waldo F. Ashley, Private Henry J. Janswick, Private Joseph D. Cahill and Brinley pumped rounds as fast as they could work their bolts. The Americans fought Indian fashion, firing and ducking behind the dugout before the **Stosstruppen** drew a bead. Ashley was an acting company clerk for the PC. He shot two **Stosstruppen** as they came down the trench. "At this stage of the game one of the boys, who couldn't control himself could not get his pants down in time. The platoon had a little laugh over this."[1063] When there was a lull in the action, Sergeant Cederholm came up to Ashley, who was still carrying the few remaining Company C records in a haversack strung over his shoulder and said, "Gosh we were lucky to get out of that alive, wasn't we?" Private Ashley replied, "Yes, but don't say anything, it isn't over yet." Sergeant Cederholm grinned and went on his way around the corner of the trench. A few minutes later the shriek of an incoming artillery shell and explosion rocked the area, killing Sergeant Cederholm along with several others.[1064] Ashley held his ground that day from his position outside the destroyed *abris*. Two days later he was found gazing at the four dead Germans who had tried to break into his area.[1065]

Oberleutnant Fritz and **Pionier Kompagnie.79** encountered numerous strong dugouts that required destruction by means of concentrated charges. Other obstacles were razed using pick-axes and spades. The shelters in the occupied front line were prepared for burning once the Stosstruppen departed. Many hand grenades, much ammunition and all serviceable equipment discovered were destroyed when the men blew up the shelters. His **Pioniere** accomplished their mission in full. Casualties were light. One corporal was missing, presumed dead. Two corporals and three **Pioniere** were wounded. A fourth **Pionier** departed for the hospital with a ruptured eardrum.[1066]

"BEAUTIFUL MACHINE GUN WORK"

The master of American machine guns, Colonel Parker had reason to be proud of what his machine gunners accomplished throughout his sector that day. When his *162e régiment d'infanterie* counterpart, Colonel Bertrand, arrived at the PC, he told Parker that it was "the most beautiful example of machine gun work that he had ever seen in all his life."[1067] Colonel Bertrand described what he has seen at a gully north-west of *Bois du Jury*, two soldiers dead across their gun with many Germans dead from the machine-gun fire and close combat.[1068] Corporal Edward P. Wing and Private 1st Class Bernard T. Fitzsimmons were killed at their post. Their gun was found with the feeder lying across the gun with a feed strip in hand, the pointer seated on the trail with finger on trigger and a ring of Germans in front of the gun, all dead.[1069]

Lieutenant Murphy's Company A covered the north of Seicheprey and flanked *Bois de Remières* on the south and east. Their firing pattern consisted of all machine guns firing simultaneously for 5 minutes followed by alternating fire at 2-minute intervals. Machine guns at the northern end of *Bois de Remières* fired until the guns jammed and went out of action. The guns were then destroyed by the crews. Corporal Edwin Martin and Private 1st Class Ellsworth A. Burnham were quickly surrounded by **Stosstruppen** after their gun was destroyed. The pair managed to make it back to Beaumont through a heavy barrage to get first aid. After receiving medical treatment they both returned to the battle with another gun.[1070] Murphy's remaining four Company A guns were laid to traverse the German front lines and the area covering Sibille Trench from the edge of *Bois du Jury*. Lieutenant Murphy's six machine guns put up heroic resistance. Each gun section fought until their guns gave out. At that point the men destroyed their machine guns, picked up rifles dropped by Company C infantry, and fought their way out. Thousands of rounds of ammunition were poured from the guns for several hours on assigned, yet unseen, targets. The gun crews quietly, yet energetically, went about their duties, firing, loading, and cleaning ammunition. Water was sought in neighbouring shell holes and poured over red-hot gun barrels, while some journeyed to the ammunition dumps.[1071]

At 0515, Captain Stanchfield from his position within *Bois de Remières* could hear the battle underway to the west in Seicheprey. As the **Stosstruppen** followed the **MW** barrage line into the wood, the volume of artillery strikes directed at his machine-gun positions increased. The machine guns were in their own fight for their lives and taking casualties. At Sergeant "Pop" Covery's machine-gun nest , Private Ralph Phinney collapsed when artillery rounds hit the area. Phinney crumpled into the arms of his mates but upon examination they couldn't detect any blood or open wound. Five minutes later, Phinney recovered his composure, climbed back to his post and kept firing until his gun was put out of action. Later examination revealed Phinney had been struck by debris that had lodged deep into his back. Seven hours later, at 1100, Phinney was evacuated to the rear.[1072]

At 0530 Lieutenant Carruth received word that *GCs* to the left of *Bois de Remières* were in combat and needed help. The *Chauchat* automatic rifle team was sent forward. Carruth knew that he did not have enough men to cover the machine guns in his area so he began consolidating his squads. They came across wounded men from initial engagement moving south through the trenches. An hour later more wounded men were moving south. Both Lieutenant Johnson and Lieutenant Tyler covered the retreat in progress. Lieutenant Carruth moved his machine guns from the 3rd Platoon area south towards *Bois du Jury*. Lieutenant Tyler and his men then proceeded to move machine-gun ammunition to the new positions.[1073]

Lieutenant Bartram's machine guns from Company A occupied the ground on Beaumont Ridge. The incessant German artillery barrage destroyed two nests with direct hits. Using indirect fire, Bartram's two remaining guns continued the fight firing incessantly until 0700. The spirit with which Bartram's men conducted themselves was inspirational to other defenders in the area. Each man stuck to his post until the last minute. One gun crew was actually blown out of its emplacement, together with the machine gun and tripod, and survived.[1074] Italian-American Corporal Louis Popolizio recalled: "Lots of the Germans were hanging on the barbed wire in the morning."[1075]

ARTILLERY ON THE MOVE

Throughout the morning the barrage continued with unabated fury. Lethal projectiles – earth, stones, trees, iron, and duckboard fragments – pounded down on helmets and exposed bodies. The shelling was described by one Company C soldier as "blowing holes as large as a cellar excavation for a house."[1076] Artillery changed to the usual box barrages round Seicheprey and *Bois de Remières*, with a rolling barrage across the front for the attacking infantry. The 51st Field Artillery Brigade reported at 0516 that the Germans were putting down a new barrage in front of Sector F-1, which spread to sub-sector F-2.[1077] At 0547 Colonel Parker requested artillery fire to slacken to give the artillery men some breathing space and allow everyone to better understand the situation.[1078]

The 102nd Field Artillery caissons beyond Position 2 were all loaded with shells and proceeded towards the battle area. The various officers, frustrated by inaction, seized this opportunity to enter the fray. Lieutenant Winslow was older than the rest of the officers and had been assigned to administrative duties, much to his disgust. That day he led his column of caissons unflinchingly along the road, which had been blown to pieces by the shells. His drivers were nervous. A shell knocked a big truck completely off the road a few metres ahead of Winslow, causing horses in the column to rear up. Winslow made the decision to let his column gallop their horses. For the soldiers nearby it created an amazing sight, three pairs of horses

A view of Sibille Trench leading into *Bois de Remières*. (Taylor, *New England in France*)

on a caisson flying through the smoke and dust. Sometimes they would stumble but were soon brought to their feet by the drivers. A horse was killed on the lead of one caisson. The driver cut the traces and continued. One officer known as "Lizzie P" led his column through the surge. When horses fell he helped get them moved to the roadside. His men said, "Lizzie had guts," despite the fact that he "had been brought up by a governess." Ford ambulances coming from the front with fresh wounded had to avoid hitting the advancing artillery caissons columns.[1079] The one gun that had been at the "sniping" position had already left for a new location and the three guns that were farther in the rear were also on the road when the shelling commenced. All four guns arrived without mishap and in a very short time commenced operation.[1080]

Early in the morning, Colonel Sherburne, 101st Field Artillery, received word that the Germans had overwhelmed the American front-line trenches and had taken Seicheprey in what appeared to be a major attack. Colonel Sherburne immediately departed for General Edwards's PC at Boucq and received direction

to shift some of his artillery to the east. The 101st Field Artillery's "Flying Battalion" of 75s under Major Richardson were told to prepare to move to Rambucourt as quickly as possible. Battery B covered the 75mm to look like a wagon pulled by a pair of horses. Battery E and Battery F positions were organized on the hill back of Fort Liouville, about 180 metres apart and on the edge of the crested hill that dropped off steeply. The two batteries made a very difficult target for the German counter-battery since rounds ended up in the valley beyond. Short range fire met the cover that the slight crest in front provided. Battery E and Battery F guns for the Flying Battalion had to be lowered piece by piece down the precipitous slope to the road below. Everyone took a hand at the ropes lowering the dismantled guns. Throughout this time they were under fire from a German 150mm battery. The Flying Battalion then loaded onto trucks and quickly moved east to Rambucourt, known by the unit as the "Mud" positions. By the time they set up and were ready for action, the bugle was being sounded at Seicheprey.[1081] Colonel Sherburne then ordered the remaining guns at Fort Liouville distributed partially to fill the vacated Battery E and Battery F positions, to deceive the Germans into thinking his artillery remained in place.[1082]

Although at times the transmission of orders was slow, command was exercised throughout the action by both battalion and regimental commanders. Four 102nd Field Artillery batteries did manage to maintain limited communication thanks to a single wire. It was made possible only by the courage of runners and motorcycle men such as Private Ward M. Parker, who kept the messages moving between battery and command for 26 straight hours in the periods of violent bombardment by HE and gas.[1083]

Lieutenant Cavanaugh's Battery E position 420, a kilometre to the east of Dead Man's Curve, was calmly handling the situation, never for a moment showing anxiety. Cavanaugh depended totally on runners getting through to acquire direction for his artillery fire. Nearby, an ammunition dump behind Beaumont blew up. Cartridges, trench-mortar shells, rockets and other combustibles were exploding in every direction.[1084]

FRENCH FORCES ON THE FLANK

Coordination between French and American PCs at brigade and regiment level was stretched. At 0500, headquarters *32ᵉ corps d'armée* at Toul telephoned Colonel Parker's PC for information and requested they notify *69ᵉ division d'infanterie* on the situation as the 102nd knew it. Ten minutes later *69ᵉ division d'infanterie* was notified via telephone message.[1085] At 0525, *commandant* Gard, *162ᵉ Régiment d'infanterie*'s Area C commander, could not clarify the *Bois du Jury* situation. He was ordered to commence French

reconnaissance of the front lines. At 0615, Gard reported his patrol passed to the right of the railroad in his sector north of Vallon and did not encounter the enemy. They did receive shells from large-calibre guns and MW. French assessment remained patchy owing to a lack of definitive information from American PCs. At 0650, Beaumont got word to *colonel* Bertrand that the Germans had attacked Seicheprey at 0530, followed by a counter-attack that had driven the Germans back to their lines. *Commandant* Gard was then ordered to accomplish reconnaissance of *Boyau Jury-Remières* to confirm the reports and establish liaison with Americans in the area.[1086]

Commandant Gard's men occupied *Boyau Jury-Remières* with Murphy's machine gunners. Two machine guns were initially set up. After an earlier heavy barrage killed two and wounded two other machine gunners, the remaining crews moved the guns east to cover the right flank of *Bois de Remières*. They remained there until relieved later that day. A sixth machine gun was moved to the entrance of *Boyau Jury-Remières* to fire on the wood.[1087]

AVIATION OPERATIONS

At daybreak, 0550, French observers reported a German plane flying over *162ᵉ régiment d'infanterie* lines at a very low height, and heading towards Seicheprey.[1088] **Drachen** were observed in ascendance to the north. Battery C, 102nd Field Artillery, recorded "the planes became very active."[1089] *Colonel* Bertrand reported a decrease of German artillery fire so that aviation assets could determine results.[1090] It was an example of the Germans' extensive planning. German aeroplanes left Les Baraques aerodrome supporting the Stosstruppen attack at commencement. The plan called for one infantry aeroplane, one **Artillerie-Flieger** and three **Schlachtflugzeuge** to arrive. The main duty of the infantry aeroplane was to determine where the front line of battle was and continue to observe and update the commander. The infantry aviator was required to fly over Madine camp and Charey to drop a report to the command centres. After 60 minutes he was to report on the ongoing battle at Seicheprey and then observe how the evacuation proceeded.[1091] The **Artillerie-Flieger** was required to observe both annihilation fire and assist the German counter-battery with observation of American artillery. The aeroplane employed wireless and dropped prepared sketches to **Generalleutnant** Hoffmann at Charey, as well as the receiving station that managed both long- and close-range artillery. The Germans employed **Artillerie-Flieger** with a **Schlachtflieger** escort to circle over the battle zone to observe enemy artillery activity, harass the enemy below and alert commanders and **Stosstruppen** to any signs of a counter-attack. [1092] The Americans in *Bois de Remières* observed a German **Artillerie-Flieger** above the battlefield directing fire. The aeroplane [**LVG C.V**] had two long black streamers and was circling around the battleground looking for targets of opportunity. Any Americans spotted received artillery fire. "It seemed that we were not getting any support from our artillery whatever and no Allied plane to give battle to the Hun plane, which kept signaling our whereabouts."[1093] Another German aeroplane fired machine guns around 0548 at the 1-Bis position "in a very daring manner."[1094] Early in the morning, through the mist and fog, a **FA (A) 298b Halberstadt** or **Hannover C.II** swooped down through the haze, almost touching the Seicheprey rubble and signalling German artillery with information regarding the location of each little group of defenders observed. Meanwhile another **LVG C.V** and **Halberstadt C.II Schlachtflugzeug** wreaked havoc with both machine guns and hand grenades thrown at the fleeing soldiers. At the outpost on Beaumont Ridge that served the sound-ranging unit **DFW C.V, LVG C.V** and **Halberstadt C.II** attacked the building causing the occupants to beat a hasty retreat to their dugout.[1095] Davis Battery near Beaumont was strafed by a **DFW C.V (or LVG C.V)** at an altitude of 50 metres after the first barrage had ceased. The **Schlachtflieger** aircrew was determining the extent of damage to the battery. Everyone that was not firing their 95mm field artillery piece grabbed a rifle and fired back. **Jasta 64**, with Albatros D.Va and Pfalz D.IIIa fighter aeroplanes, flew out of Mars-la-Tour providing aerial cover against any threat posed by 94th Aero Squadron or the region's aerial reconnaissance *escadrilles*. German aviators landed nearby at Bouillonville to telephone updates. **FA (A) 298b** kept in communication with **78. R. D.** throughout the entire operation. **Ballonzug 214 Infanterie Ballon** supplementing the **Schlachtflieger** was observed at Beney. The balloon observer reported to the various headquarters through telephone. **Generalleutnant** Hoffmann's **Ballonzug 123** operated at Jaulny and **Ballonzug 215** was observing from Xammes.[1096]

AN ENEMY'S TRIBUTE

Grenadier Ratey, a member of **Sturmbataillon.14** reflected: "On the defensive, the American is an opponent who must in no way be under-estimated. He does not defend himself in trenches, but in groups and individually in machine-gun nest s, in nests of riflemen and in dugouts. In dugouts he defends himself to the last moment. For instance, into a small dugout two grenades were thrown, machine guns and rifles were fired into it, and still the men did not come out. They surrendered only after the dugout was fired. In spite of the violent artillery fire, a man with a machine gun remained in his nest in a tree. He did not surrender, but had to be shot down. Prisoners had to be handled with great caution. It happened repeatedly that they escaped in an unguarded moment, or that they tried to free themselves by force. During one of such attempts a German officer was shot down by an American. One American, completely surrounded, still tried to defend himself. He had to be knocked down. The American makes frequent use of his trench knife."[1097]

CHAPTER 19

Bugle Call

In Seicheprey a bugle call filled the air, signalling the **Sturmtruppen, Stosstruppen,** and **Pioniere** that it was time to withdraw from the battle area. After the dugouts had been blown up, the order to evacuate the village was issued at 0620 and completed 20 minutes later.[1098] After the evacuation of Seicheprey, **78. R. D**. issued the order to the artillery to withdraw the protective barrage to the newly gained line in the region north of Seicheprey.[1099] As the notes rang out, the Americans could see their enemy withdrawing under the cover of their machine-gun fire, loaded down with their own wounded carried by American prisoners.[1100]

Rau's men were now searching the area for any enemy pockets within the village or to the north. It was later found that they had strung a light field wire along *Boyau Mayonnaise* into the town.[1101] When **Stosstruppen** and **Pioniere** encountered stubborn resistance such as a large dugout at the southern egress from the village (wrongly assumed by the Germans to be a command post), grenades were first thrown through the doors or down the chimney. The **Pioniere** carried larger charges of 13.6kg each that became the final exterminator. In the case of the large *abris* they blew it up with two charges.[1102] Strickland recalled that boxes of HE were set off at *abris* doors and alongside shelters – bringing down tons of mortar and debris on the trapped soldiers within.[1103] In Seicheprey,

the aid station, the dugouts of the men, and the kitchens were wrecked, principally by mobile charges, although shells had fallen in the town.

Broad daylight showed more clearly the ghastly scene. Captain Thompson's twelve-man patrol was reconnoitring the east side of Seicheprey when they commenced fire against **Stosstruppen** occupying Sibille Trench. Rau's other patrol proceeded to the old French cemetery at the north end of the village. The ground was strewn with the dead and dying. Many severely wounded crawled towards the safety of the rubble piles, while German machine-guns swept the terrain. **MW** bombs continued striking the area tearing great holes in the ground and creating even more carnage. Heavy artillery churned up the already pulverised ground.

EVACUATION – 0630

Colonel Parker, with his literary flair, summed up the German artillery command of the battle: "At 0610 a very strong barrage was clamped down on the 1-Bis position from end to end, and held like a vise."[1104] **Generalmajor** von Stolzmann and **Major** Bruns planned that **Stosstruppen** were to hold Seicheprey until the American strongholds were disposed of and all German wounded, dead, prisoners and booty were moved back to German lines. **Erstürmung** on Seicheprey demolished

20 April 1918 – The elite *Sturmtruppen* 14 heading to Pannes after their Seicheprey assault. The *Leutnant* is wearing a captured "Sammy" helmet. (*Deutsche Sturmtruppen*)

several machine-gun nest s, about twenty-nine large dugouts, two ammunition dumps, one gallery, and two viaducts. The returning **Stosstruppen** put themselves at the disposal of **Res. I. R. 259** and reported the status of the evacuation.[1105] After they had assisted in the close combat at the Sibille Trench, **c-Kompagnie** went into Seicheprey to help evacuate the wounded and the dead. The struggle at Seicheprey lasted only 40 minutes, with the **Stosstruppen** withdrawing according to plan.

Leutnant von Ponickau's **Pioniere** withdrew when the bugle sounded. When they had completed their mission, **80. Reserve Pioniere Kompagnie** had blown up thirteen dugouts and an ammunition dump – all charges prepared by the engineers exploded properly. Von Ponickau also took great pride in notifying his seniors that **80. Reserve Pioniere** took twenty-one prisoners from the dugouts.[1106] Major resistance to their assault only came from within a few cellars. The Americans, he recalled, defended their position "desperately." **Unteroffizier** Zikoll's squad was credited with blowing up a cellar containing several Americans but he was severely wounded in the process. **Leutnant** Thomas' **Pioniere** blew

up nine cellars, one dugout, one machine-gun nest and one ammunition dump, capturing thirty prisoners, one machine gun and one automatic rifle.[1107]

When American artillery fire did not abate, **Stosstruppen** battalions commenced to order their **Kompagnien** to withdraw laterally within the trenches and keep to the dugouts, establishing a nest for subsequent operations. **Hauptman Tolle d-Kompagnie (7./259 Hillemann)** and what remained of **Bataillon Hellmuth a-Kompagnie (6./259 Knop)** withdrew to the *boyau* on the St. Baussant–Seicheprey road. **B-Kompagnie (1./259 Tänzer)** stood their ground at the dugout nest at the south-western corner of *Bois de Remières*. **Bataillon Seebohm** companies set up nests near the dugouts and deep trench sections at the south-western and south-eastern edges of *Bois de Remières*.[1108] Heavy machine guns were brought forward to the northern trenches there and at and Sibille Trench. **Bataillon** Hellmuth's **c-Kompagnie (2./259)** as part of the second wave penetrated into the American front line as ordered and encountered little resistance. Together with half of **78. R. D.'s** machine-gun **Kompagnie**, the two units prepared the ground for defence to cover the planned withdrawal and protect the flanks.[1109]

Major Rau and Captain Thompson went north through Seicheprey looking for the enemy. Rau saw Germans standing in a building near the point where *Boyau Seicheprey* left the town. He fired his pistol. Rau wondered if the Germans left because they saw more Americans coming north, or if it was part of their attack plan. The Germans were now at the entrance of the north cemetery sheltered in trenches and dugouts. Rau's troops took up positions along the northern edge of the town's rubble.[1110] His men formed a line on *Boyau Nantais* and along the Seicheprey buildings facing north. They continued firing away at any **Stosstruppen** they saw.

Corporal Blanchard recalled: "By this time the town was pretty well cleaned out and they had retreated over their lines, carrying a great many of their own wounded with them. The rest of the day was hardly more than artillery dueling and so we just stood to and waited for them to show up again. I guess they had enough, for we didn't see them again."[1111]

Hardly a word could get back to headquarters for some time. Not until 0630 did Colonel Parker get definite word that Seicheprey was being attacked. What reports that got through were not hopeful. *Bois de Remières* was lost. Major Rau was merely holding Seicheprey – the Germans had carved out a position between

his two front-line battalions. The French were attacked in *Bois du Jury*. Casualties were being reported as heavy from all sources. American officers had been killed or taken prisoner, as well as many soldiers. Four machine guns had been lost by direct hits from shell fire.[1112]

Generalmajor von Stolzmann's staff telephoned **Gruppe Gorz** with a brief assessment. After a methodical and apparently very effective gas bombardment, the preparatory fire commenced at 0450 by all the artillery and **MW**. Penetration into the enemy position and further progress of the attack was apparently wholly as planned. Seicheprey was taken at 0604. Fighting was still going on at 0645 in the southern part of *Bois de Remières*. A number of captured Americans were under way to the rear. Von Stolzmann did not have an exact number of how many prisoners were taken.[1113]

The bugle call was a welcome respite for many of the veteran **Stosstruppen** and **Pioniere** who fought in Seicheprey that morning. Many were shocked at the tenacity of the enemy. Every dugout appeared to make a last stand. The experience that morning planted an important seed in the minds of all Germans: desperate resistance by the Americans was the result of the fact that they had been told the Germans killed prisoners. So it was either struggles to the death from now on or come up with a way to subdue that spirit.[1114]

Stosstruppen show off their newly acquired booty from Seicheprey – pistols, a "Sammy" helmet and a klaxon gas alarm. (von Bornstedt, *Reserve.Infanterie. Regiment 259*)

BOOBY TRAPS

The Germans left behind large amounts of weapons and explosives. Americans reclaiming their territory found weapons laid out with utmost precision in rows along the parapet. **Sturmbataillon.14** equipment recovered by the French included a very large number of rockets, a number of bags containing grenades, boxes of ammunition, pieces for light machine guns, thirty-two magazines for automatic pistol cartridges, and three phone lines.[1115] Lieutenant Ingersoll discovered the 1st Battalion dumps were booby trapped with explosive. He disarmed the bombs by cutting the wires and removing the ordnance.[1116] In Seicheprey itself, the soldiers found seven mobile charges consisting of 9x10x12-inch wooden boxes with a wooden handle that carried dynamite attached to a coil of wire. When **Pioniere** uncoiled and pulled the wire, the dynamite exploded. Grenades lay around all of the battle area. The discarded weapons and explosives were described as the Germans' "customary damnable collection of tricks." **Handgranaten** were armed with instantaneous fuses. Trench canes, helmets and rifles with wires attached to mines were ready to blow up American reinforcements. Major Rau alerted regimental headquarters of this new threat.[1117] **Pioniere** threw incendiary bombs into all the kitchens and burned them and also into the large dugouts along Sibille Trench. Rau informed the regiment that about twenty-five boxes about the size of the box carried by boot-blacks (16x10x10 inches) were scattered throughout. Each had a handle on top and a coil of wire around the handle with two stick grenades protruding from the end. Rau thought the boxes were filled with dynamite or similar HE. The Germans also left six or seven wrought iron pipes about 2.4 metres long and 5cm in diameter, with a stick grenade driven in one end.[1118]

Subsequent operations were to be alerted to the risk that came with taking German-occupied territory. The Chaumont report gave a basic summary. The German soldier was quite as human as the American soldier –

abandoning ammunition and explosives rather than carrying it back – particularly under stress. The priority for the **Stosstruppen** was returning with their casualties. Rau's men continued to find large stocks of weapons in the main trenches to the north. Along the reverse parapet of Sibille Trench were a very large number of **Handgranaten**, egg grenades and small winged bombs. Rare weapons such as a long gas-pipe torpedo and an incendiary bomb were found. At the point where *Boyau Seicheprey* joined Sibille Trench a strong point had evidently been established because there was a considerable weapons supply as well as a **Granatwerfer**. Steps had been cut in the trench at different places for a bomber or a rifleman to take position. Quite a number of German guns, helmets and pieces of equipment were found in the trenches and the ground nearby.[1119]

HOLDING AT SIBILLE TRENCH

It was now daylight and the fog of the early morning was burning off. Lieutenant Strickland's *GC* started down *Boyau Mayonnaise*, the primary trench that ran north out of Seicheprey. Captain Thompson's *GC* paralleled Strickland with the troops moving along the top of the *boyau*. Thompson told Rau that he assumed his mission was to draw fire so Strickland's patrol could go forward. Both understood what to do next. After they had covered about 100 metres in *Boyau Mayonnaise*, Strickland's patrol entered the western entrance of Sibille Trench. Two of his men started out of the trench and over the edge. As they crawled forward **Stosstruppen** threw grenades but both men managed to escape the blasts unharmed. Strickland's patrol jumped back in the trench just as a German machine gun in the cemetery north of Seicheprey fired at Thompson's patrol. While Captain Thompson and his patrol ran for cover, they knocked over a stick with a white rag tied to it. Apparently, the German machine gun crew had used it to register their fire. Thompson grabbed the stick as he followed his patrol into the trench. Thompson's fourteen soldiers started running down the trench and took up defensive positions.[1120] Color Sergeant Church's patrol was approximately 90 to 140 metres from the rest searching around Sibille Trench. After confirming Germans were still in the area they withdrew to the shelter of the Seicheprey rubble, shell holes, bogs, and partly dug trenches. The German machine gun near the cemetery again fired upon them as they moved back.[1121] The patrols confirmed Germans were still in force at Sibille Trench and had not retreated. Rau and his *GCs* were not capable of conducting an effective counter-attack against the entrenched **Stosstruppen**.[1122] The operations report that day mentioned that only 30 of the 350 men who were in the area within Sibille Trench were able to return to the American sector. As of noon severe fighting was underway in the area.[1123]

Lieutenant Ingersoll sought out Lieutenant Strickland while they were near Sibille Trench. Strickland requested more grenades. Ingersoll assembled a team from some of the cooks turned infantry and they went back into Seicheprey to the dumps that still held ordnance and brought it to the lines. To Ingersoll, based on the quiet of the moment, the fighting seemed to be over. He guessed the time was about 0830 or 0900 – three hours since the first **Stosstruppen** left their assault nest for the **Erstürmung**. Ingersoll heard a groan coming from one of the destroyed *abris*. He commenced digging and kept at it for an hour. At that time more ammunition was required so Ingersoll ceased his rescue and went back to organise more resupply. He then went towards the Beaumont Ridge to contact Company B to request automatic rifle teams to come forward. Company D had none left.[1124]

General Lassiter's 51st Field Artillery Brigade called at 0718 asking for the location in which to drop a barrage for the infantry north of Seicheprey. The answer was Sibille Trench. Captain Stanchfield provided an up-to-date assessment on his machine guns for Major Murphy. Half of his machine guns had been destroyed or captured. Stanchfield reported to Murphy that the Germans now occupied Sibille Trench in large numbers: "Need assistance at once."[1125] Stanchfield's 1st Platoon had suffered heavy casualties and from the limited information that he received it seemed only a matter of time before the survivors were annihilated. Sergeant "Pop" Covery ordered his men to take cover so that they might be ready for direct fire against a German secondary attack once the barrage they were experiencing lifted. Lieutenant Bartram's 2nd Platoon and Lieutenant Morrow's 3rd Platoon now operated from shell holes to avoid the trench that they concluded was well registered as a target for the German artillery.[1126]

REINFORCEMENTS GATHER AT POSITION 1–BIS

Lieutenant McGlasson's 3rd Platoon, Company D, relieved Company M in the Grant Trench, Major Rau sent word at 0730 that all able men were to help carry out the wounded. McGlasson's men cared for the wounded and evacuated them at the first opportunity to field hospitals to the south near Toul. German artillery was still firing on McGlasson's position with HE, shrapnel, and gas. They remained in the trenches through three hours "of the worst hell that can be imagined and which could have easily been seen by the condition of the trench the next morning." While the men occupied the trench, they discovered two 220mm duds.[1127]

Company A engineers endured the heavy artillery barrage but did not directly engage the enemy. They were ordered to hold the 1-Bis sector at all costs. The Germans did not penetrate as far as the 1-Bis line where "A" Company was waiting. The engineers placed several *Chevaux de frise* in the *boyau* while the barrage hammered the area. The engineers also prepared charges for blowing up Colonel Parker's PC and all the valuable records, should the **Stosstruppen** break through and secure Beaumont Ridge. Engineers were ordered later that morning at 0845 to take position in the trench just north of the Seicheprey road. Two engineers occupied a half-dug and partially blown-in trench as an outpost. When one of the engineers entered the main trench he discovered a gas mask and helmet saturated with blood.[1128]

About 0700, after the mist cleared. Major John Gallant, 3rd Battalion commander, and Major Bowditch went to the PC in Beaumont. There was a lull in the bombardment at that time. Colonel Parker ordered Gallant to take command of the line of support. Major Bowditch accompanied him. Gallant proceeded to the dugout serving as the PC for Company B. A few survivors of the Seicheprey battle arrived telling Gallant and Bowditch of their experiences and their assumption that the **Stosstruppen** had departed. Telephone communication with regimental headquarters was re-established at that time and Major Gallant telephoned Colonel Parker updating him on what he had learned from the Seicheprey survivors. Parker instructed Gallant to send twenty men from Company B into Seicheprey and reinforce Company D. Major Gallant proceeded to round up the men in compliance with Colonel Parker's order. Major Bowditch went to Lawrence Trench down the hill from Beaumont to observe both Seicheprey and the right flank, remaining there for some time.[1129]

As planned, all available **MW** commenced a barrage on trenches entering the northern extremity of *Bois du Jury*. The checking fire maintained a fierce intensity during the **Stosstrupp** advance along the eastern edge of *Bois de Remières*.[1130] The German heavy artillery came into play and swept all rear areas blocking roads into this part of the southern Woëvre front.[1131] The Germans reported that some Americans had crept into shell craters west of *Bois de Remières* and were firing on **Stosstruppen** who occupied Sibille Trench.[1132] After completion of the artillery preparation, each American battery observed firing was now targeted by several batteries with **gasschuss** and HE. **Generalleutnant** Hoffmann's long-range group was assigned the counter-battery task. He also designated three heavy batteries from the close-range group to the mission. The remaining heavy artillery were to concentrate on the locations where Americans were taking cover.[1133]

RUNNING THE GAUNTLET

Just before the bombardment commenced, a supply wagon under the charge of Corporal George Rainville, Private Dominick Palosky, and three other drivers, arrived from the new position where they had taken a load of equipment and were preparing to return for another load. The wagon was about half loaded when the battle started and it was impossible for them to move on. Wearing gas masks, the artillery men unhitched their horses and tied them to the wheels.

The men then retired to the captain's dugout, assuming the barrage to be a temporary nuisance. It then became necessary to act, because as soon as it became broad daylight, the wagon on the road became an irresistible target. Corporal Rainville gave orders to the drivers to hitch up and take the gas masks off the horses. The teams galloped down the Paris-Metz highway towards Beaumont. How they ever got down that road, passing Dead Man's Curve and Hell's Half Acre without all being killed was a mystery, since every foot of that road received artillery fire. Corporal Rainville and his men made it, to the wonderment of the soldiers and artillerymen in the area. It was an impressive feat of daring and boldness.[1134]

During the course of the battle, all the batteries ran out of ammunition. One of the officers of Battery C asked for volunteers to drive caissons of ammunition to the positions and especially to Battery G at Dead Man's Curve. Every man in Battery C volunteered and a number were picked out. They loaded the caissons and took off at a gallop. Many received wounds from the artillery explosions. Private Vincente Polito had two horses killed under him trying to get the ammunition delivered. Polito was also wounded with a splinter into the lungs. He cut the dead horses clear of the harness and continued hauling the ammunition to the front lines. Private Dominick Palosky drove his wagon filled with ammunition to the front when a shell hit close by, knocking over the horse he was riding and wounding him in the knee. Soldiers nearby helped the wounded Palosky back on to his saddle and he continued bringing the ammunition to his battery.[1135]

About 0800 the artillery sniping post received orders to abandon their present position and report to a new location. It was a perilous 2-kilometre journey near the Beaumont Ridge. A combination **gasschuss** and HE barrage covered the area. The sniping battery was detained at Beaumont taking shelter from the constant rounds. The **gasschuss** also hit the area they were heading towards. One shell did score a direct hit on the first section gun pit, but no casualties were sustained.[1136]

Another barrage commenced around 0700 in the area of Sibille Trench. An hour later the artillery were told to cease fire, the first since the battle had commenced at 0300. They took up the barrage again after a few minutes rest. The artillerymen had been wearing their gas masks for 5 straight hours in the horrendous conditions. Later that morning more artillery fire was directed at Sibille Trench. With the exception of 8 minutes' rest, most of the American artillery had been firing continuously for 7 hours.[1137]

At 0750, German artillery shells from *Bois de la Sonnard* and the St. Baussant area were reported to Beaumont. The soldiers requested counter-battery reprisal.[1138] 155mm guns carried out gas counter-battery and HE harassment of German trenches and roads until the end of the day, occasionally being shelled by German counter-battery. During the morning they also were strafed by a German **Schlachtflieger**.[1139]

AVIATION NOVITIATE

The infantry communicated with the aviators using various signal devices or canvas panels with specific symbols imparting a particular message. The Germans were well versed in this procedure, while the American infantry and aviators were still learning the trade. At Seicheprey American infantry and aviation failed to communicate.

No ground panels were employed. The absence of credible infantry contact also created considerable uncertainty at Beaumont and at division and brigade headquarters further to the rear, who did not know exactly where the American front lines were during the battle. Post-battle reports pointed out that 1st Battalion, 102nd Infantry, having just arrived the night before, never had the time to get acquainted with this capability in the sector before the German assault commenced.[1140]

The pilots and observers of **FA (A) 298b** had already shown their capabilities in combat and were actively engaged throughout the battle. Meanwhile **Drachen** were operating uncontested along the front supporting infantry and artillery with updates. German aerial observation from **Drachen** was extensive, despite the vagaries of the weather. A total of ten ascents from several points north were reported throughout the day.[1141]

The 94th Aero Squadron commenced a morning patrol with three Nieuport 28s along the front line from St. Mihiel to Pont-à-Mousson three hours after the first barrage commenced. While the Nieuports were taking off and climbing north-west, 51st Field Artillery Brigade reported that seven **FA (A) 298b** aeroplanes were flying low over the front lines of Seicheprey and *Bois de Remières*, firing at the troops with their machine guns. Ten minutes later the Nieuports, flew over Boucq heading north. At 0650, the 51st Brigade learned from a telephone message that the 94th Aero Squadron had scrambled an additional ten aeroplanes to "clear the air;" yet, no combat occurred.[1142] Later that morning, the Germans had sent a **DFW C.V** and **LVG C.V** infantry contact into the area south of Beaumont where the 103rd Field Artillery was operating. Battery A fired machine gun and rifle fire at the two aeroplanes and continued firing their 155mm. They were sighted by two Nieuport 28s (flown by Lieutenant Campbell and Lieutenant Davis) around 0930 and departed the area before the enemy pursuit arrived.[1143] The remainder of the day did not see one aerial combat.

CHAPTER 20

Gefangene und Beute

Kirschblüte had proven successful in capturing prisoners [Gefangene] and acquiring booty [Beute]. The word quickly spread within the German ranks. *Général* Passaga's staff discovered from *2ᵉ Bureau* that a German communiqué had been received by *VIIIᵉ armée* that 5 officers, 185 enlisted men and 25 machine guns had been captured and that they had penetrated 2 kilometres.[1144] It was Passaga's first indication of the extent of losses suffered at Seicheprey.

The first 26th Division senior staff assessment of numbers of prisoners came within a day of the battle. The Commanding General, 26th Division, reported losses as missing, of five officers and 221 enlisted men.[1145] The final confirmed number was 183. Major Rau's exasperation over what had transpired that morning is clear in his report to Colonel Parke around 1450:

Company A, no report
Company B about 40 here
Company C can account for only ten. Rest gone.
Company D can account for about 20. Rest gone.
Company B, 102nd Machine Gun Bn. – 3 guns left-30 men left. 18 liaison men left; 2 sanitary men left, 2 sanitary men gone; 15 snipers gone, 1 left. Dr. Burke gone, interpreter gone, Capt. Freeland gone; Lieut. Byrd gone; Lieut. McDowell gone,

all officers from Co. C gone, except Lieut. A.E. Johnson, who is wounded. Lieut. Stokes wounded. Impossible to get exact data.
GEORGE J. RAU, Major, 102nd Inf.[1146]

As for the listing of officers captured, Rau was unaware that his Company D commander, Captain Freeland, was now wounded and a prisoner. Additionally, the two 102nd Machine Gun Battalion officers, Lieutenant Edward Kenney and Lieutenant Walter Tenney were also being interrogated by the Germans. As a follow up, Captain Stanchfield sent Lieutenant Brouse forward with a squad to find any trace of Lieutenant Tenney in the area of *Boyau Seicheprey* and Sibille Trench. They were unsuccessful. Tenney's exact status remained unknown until *Gazette des Ardennes*, a German propaganda paper distributed in the occupied areas of France and Belgium and in the POW camps from August 1915 to October 1918, published his name. When the Americans later retook Sibille Trench they found Lieutenant Kenney's identification tag on the ground – suggesting the **Stosstruppen** left it to show he had been taken prisoner. [1147]

FIGHT TO THE END

After the Battle of St. Mihiel five months later, a German evaluation of the American fighting soldier read: "He is obviously very much afraid of being taken prisoner. He defends himself violently to the last against this danger and does not surrender. This is probably the result of the propaganda which pictures cruel treatment if he falls into German hands."[1148] The 102nd History commented later that "the Germans considered our men crazy because when surrounded and outnumbered, they refused to surrender and continued fighting regardless of odds until physically overpowered or killed."[1149] Private Louis Ziegra's best friend Harry Marvin spoke for many when he wrote home: "Poor fellow, he is probably breaking rocks or building roads for those miserable, rotten Huns when he would only like one-half a chance to kill them."[1150] Aviator Lieutenant Billy Schauffler recounted one sortie three days after the Seicheprey battle where he almost ended up in Germany: "I had a pretty close call from eating acorn soup for the rest of the war last Saturday."[1151] An exposé regarding the humiliation of prisoners by German captors was front-page news for the first ever edition of the American *Stars and Stripes* on 8 February: "Huns Starve and Ridicule US Captives, A.E.F. Soldiers Compelled to Clean Latrines of Crown Prince. Given Uneatable Bread. Photographed Sandwiched Between Negroes Wearing Tall Hats."[1152]

A prisoner's fate was largely determined at the time of capture. Once the hands went up, it became the victor's decision to render life or death. For most of the war soldiers felt the risks taken by surrendering were greater than the risks incurred by continuing the fight.[1153] Holding prisoners was not without risk for the captors. There were several incidents of Americans breaking away from their German guards and successfully making it back to American lines.

It was a treacherous journey back to the German lines for all concerned. Artillery barrages by both sides struck No Man's Land. Both the 102nd Field Artillery and 103rd Field Artillery bombarded No Man's Land to kill Germans withdrawing from the battleground. The one kilometre distance between the dugout and the German front line seemed a thousand miles.

As incoming rounds blew up around them, the entire party of raiders, prisoners, and wounded flung themselves to the ground for what little protection the churned-up earth could provide. In addition to the threat from rounds and gas, the incredible noise combined with the shock waves of the explosions put everyone into a daze.

RUBBER *BEUTE*

As mentioned by Ettighoffer, rubber waders were a luxury in the swamp-ridden misery of the Seicheprey trenches. For the **Stosstruppen**, they were prized booty. Almost all of the men who wore rubber waders were deprived of them either before the trek across No Man's Land or after reaching the German lines. Some prisoners were forced across No Man's Land in their stocking feet. It became excruciatingly painful as the barbed-wire entanglements cut. Exposure to the chemicals and poisons of battle in the area had long-term consequences as well. Infections required immediate and long-term hospital care and could cause permanent handicap post-war. Private Clifford Milton Markle from the Sanitary Company recalled being stripped of his leather jerkin worn outside his blouse and his French gas mask. Markle stated one American first-aid man was confined in a German hospital for five months as a result of the journey to the German lines and was crippled for life after the war.[1154] Private Walter Wolf of Battery B, 103rd Field Artillery recalled his footwear was ignored. He had the presence of mind to make it as unattractive as possible: "Finding that many of them had lost their shoes to the attacking forces, I walked through all the mud possible to make my own unpresentable. Our trip to the rear was featured by the accurate shelling of our own guns."[1155]

Private Doble for some unknown reason managed to keep his precious rubber waders but was press-ganged as a stretcher bearer. Soon into the crossing a German sergeant came up and stuck a long-muzzled automatic into Doble's ribs and indicated that he was to drop Lieutenant Tenney and get on the front end of a wooden

Seicheprey POWs leave Thiaucourt for the train station that will take them to Chalons for further interrogation and processing. (USAFA McDermott Library Special Collections, SMS 4)

pole, so that a wounded German could be carried back. Doble had a tough time despite his footwear. The wounded German was heavy and Doble stumbled across the uneven terrain.[1156]

INTO THE GERMAN TRENCHES

First impressions were lasting. The prisoners were now objects of curiosity and would be until the Armistice. Both Private Doble and Private Markle remembered reaching the German trenches and seeing the next wave of infantry being readied, equipped in battle gear. Many wore steel-rimmed eyeglasses held to their ears by cords that looked like white American pipecleaner wires. Doble remarked that the German looked at them as if they were "from another planet."[1157] Private Markle was immediately tasked with three other Americans to carry a wounded German back to the rear-trench medical station. Further frisking of the prisoners took place and more booty was acquired. Letters, Bibles or personal trinkets on their persons were either not touched or were returned.[1158]

Most of the duckboards were smashed. Going through the trenches carrying a wounded soldier was difficult no matter what side of No Man's Land you were on. After several mishaps, Doble's foot came out of the boot completely, requiring a long struggle to pull the boot out of the quagmire. Disgusted, the German sergeant got another German to take Doble's end of the

pole. Doble then caught up with Lieutenant Tenney, who was having a hard time tumbling and plunging head first into the pools of mud between the broken duckboards.

The Americans continued along the *boyau* while the German first-aid men walked with pistols aimed at the back of heads. Markle and the others were more successful as stretcher bearers, but it was still precarious. The prisoners arrived at the **Truppenverbandplatz** [regimental aid post] and left their burden, who was subsequently sent to the German rear areas via the narrow-gauge railroad. Upon reaching the German third-line trench, Markle's service as a stretcher bearer ended. A **Flammenwerfer** was hoisted on his already weary back to carry for the next 10 kilometres to Thiaucourt.[1159]

INTERROGATIONS

Prior to taking on the next leg of the journey the prisoners were assembled in a barracks near the third trench line in front of a hillside. Germans came swarming out to look over the first Americans they had ever seen. Doble remembered they felt like monkeys. They still were at risk from American artillery barrages. One by one, the Americans were lined up and taken in for questioning. Lieutenant Tenney in his rapidly weakening state turned to Doble and said, "Well, God knows what we can expect." Doble had two cigarettes left, lit them both and put one in Tenney's mouth. Tenney was called, shook hands with Doble and left him. Doble never saw him again.[1160]

American prisoner recollections conveyed a common theme of inquiry. The Germans needed initial confirmation of the prisoner's unit and background. A priority for April 1918 was the incoming strength of the personnel establishment facing the Germans in the coming months. With only three divisions (1st, 2nd and 26th Division) with front-line experience in the Woëvre region and a fourth (42nd Division) now occupying the front lines at Baccarat east-south-east of Nancy, German intelligence had a fairly accurate idea of their strengths and composition. Other divisions arriving that spring caused greater concern. The only true counter to that growing threat was improving the ability to wage submarine war against the increasing numbers of convoys departing American ports. The actual numbers were overwhelming. More Americans were arriving in France every five weeks than the sum of Germany's annual recruitment. In April 1918 alone, 117,212 American soldiers reached the Continent.[1161]

For the enlisted men waiting their turn, the discussions bordered on gamesmanship – the interogators talking around a subject without giving the impression that the information was of any value. Corporal Thomas Barry recalled: "As soon as they got us they hurried us back of the lines and most of us got questioned, because they didn't have many Americans up to that time. A German would stroll in among us and begin to ask questions. He knew a Hell of a lot more about America than I did; he seemed to know the country well. He would ask us questions, and we would stall. Then he would say: 'O hell, I ain't in the German Secret Service or anything. I was just coming in to see you and ask how everything was back in the good old USA.'"[1162]

German intelligence as usual left nothing to chance. Later, talking genially to captured officers from New Haven and Hartford, they wanted little information; they already knew everything about the 26th Division. They jested about having shelled Brigadier General Traub from

his headquarters. They asked about the health of various company cooks, calling them by their first names, explaining that they often infiltrated their scouts into rear units dressed in American uniforms, and they produced Germans with a working knowledge of New England geography who spoke excellent English.[1163]

Corporal Barry recalled: "We were taken before another guy. He would ask us what regiment we was in, and some fellow might say the 102nd, because they knew that anyhow. Then they would ask: 'What division is that?' The prisoners responded, 'It ain't in any division.' Then the German asked what brigade and where we were from and everything, and we'd tell him we didn't know or some damn lie and refuse. Whereupon the German would snap back, 'Well you fellows are pretty dumb, aren't you?' The German interrogator would then relate about the 51st Infantry Brigade of the 26th Division and where the prisoners came from and when they arrived in France and a lot more."[1164]

Private Doble provided more insight into the intelligence gathering. Two Germans were in the room, one seated at a table, the other on a chair behind him. The interrogator spoke good English and was "quite impressive, with an austere courtesy." After being told to sit down, Doble was asked for his name, occupation, outfit, and where he was from. Doble provided all the information requested. Doble was now introduced to the "good cop, bad cop" line. A single German officer invited him to sit down and pointed to a comfortable chair near him. "Will you have a cigarette?" Doble took the cigarette and received a light. "Well, this is pretty near your first introduction to the trenches," the German interrogator said in a smooth and pleasant sounding voice, "although I know you were on the Chemin des Dames in January and February. Trench warfare is no picnic and perhaps you are lucky to have been taken prisoner and out of it. I've been in Boston, and it is a lovely city. You'll see some beautiful country and cities here in Germany. But let's get down to business. You look like an intelligent American student, quite superior to most of the Americans we've questioned, so I am going to talk to you

On the same road *Sturmbataillon 14* took hours before, American prisoners, many without their shoes, struggle on the road to Thiaucourt. (USAFA McDermott Library Special Collections, SMS 4)

as one intelligent human being to another and hope you'll appreciate my confidence in you. You are a student," he repeated, "you came over on the Antilles, landing at Saint-Nazaire. You have been training near Neufchâteau. We know all about the 26th Division of the United States National Guard." This took Doble aback. The interrogator continued, "You are now my prisoner and you would do well to answer my questions. How many Americans do you think are now in France?" Quickly, Doble answered, "I have no way of knowing, but I would guess there are about two million." The interrogator interrupted "You are lying." Doble responded that he didn't know, but that he was guessing. The interrogator then applied pressure, "Come on, you don't expect me to swallow these lying exaggerations. You better speak the truth for your own good." The Germans now stood over Doble in an act of intimidation. "How many Americans?" they asked again. Again Doble replied, "I can only guess, but perhaps there are over one million but two million would be nearer my guess." The line of questioning from this first interrogation was now over. The interrogator barked, "Get out of here," shoving him into the next room. On concluding the second round of interrogation, the German concluded with a few words that Doble remembered long after the war, "Mr. Doble, I trust we will meet again." He opened the door and Doble left to join the other American enlisted. The officers were now separated and proceeded on a separate journey into captivity.[1165]

TO THIAUCOURT

A 10-kilometre hike to Thiaucourt awaited the captives after their preliminary interrogation. Thiaucourt served as the **Hauptverbandplatz** [main dressing station] for German wounded. The road to Thiaucourt was still within the battle zone. Signs were posted reminding soldiers of the gas danger. It was still morning and artillery from both sides continued to fire into the town and trenchworks. The captives now had a moment to reflect on the events of the past 8 hours. Private Walter Wolf recalled the effort to reach Thiaucourt on foot as long and dreary, taking several hours: "Many of the men were severely wounded, and many without shoes."[1166] Some captives were given pieces of burlap to tie around their feet. The burlap served as the only footwear they would have for months to come. Shortly after the group left the rear echelon trenches, they were photographed to commemorate the success of the operation.[1167] The same photographer had captured a few hours prior the joyous expressions of **Sturmtruppen** from **Sturmbataillon.14** heading on the same road to the Pannes rest area. One junior officer wore a newly captured "Sammy" American helmet.

Markle thought the hike was more arduous than any longer treks with heavy pack undertaken while training prior to Seicheprey. Like Doble, he remembered being observed the entire time. French citizens in tears watched as they passed by. The prisoners arrived at Thiaucourt

A German prisoner. POWs from both sides would become a hugely important part of the story of the affair, not least to the papers back home. (NARA)

by noon. They were herded into a church in the centre of the town, serving as the assembly point for all walking Seicheprey captives.[1168]

Thiaucourt was the first respite that the American captives had since the early morning battle. Approximately 120 prisoners were gathered in the church. A few were questioned by a new set of interrogators. The enlisted were questioned on artillery battery locations – an exercise in redundancy since most sites had been clearly determined over the past four months thanks to extensive use of aerial reconnaissance, other prisoner interrogations, **Schall-Mess-** and **Licht-Mess-Stellen**.

That afternoon a senior German officer came into the church. It was an opportunity for venting anger against a new adversary, one that had kept neutral for most of the conflict and now could turn the tide against a more experienced but rapidly fatiguing army. Markle remembered the German speaking in fluent English: "So you Americans call America a free country, do you? Well, it is not free, but Germany is, and you ought to be glad that you have been captured, as we shall soon demoralise America as we have France, England, and Russia. One thing more, if we ever run across your regiment again we shall give no quarter." The German officer's oration did not shake the morale of the Americans. They were more preoccupied with their physical condition. The senior German's departure set the stage for the most important event of the day: the prisoners received their first sustenance,

a **Blutwurst** slice, black bread and barley soup. It was a memorable meal, tasting good.

Following the meal postcards were distributed which contained the following message, short and to the point: "I am a prisoner of war in Germany." At the bottom left were the three words, "well, sick, wounded." The assembled prisoners crossed out the two not applicable and signed their names bottom right. These cards were supposed to be sent to Washington DC, but the cards never arrived.[1169]

FOR POSTERITY

The remainder of the afternoon was spent under lock and key in the village church.[1170] It was time for a group photograph – one to show the world that the German military was master of the Western Front, especially against Americans new to the "game." The captives were marched to the front of *Succursale* No. 547, a business in Thiaucourt. This was in keeping with German prisoner of war processing. The previous month *10ᵉ division d'infanterie coloniale* prisoners were photographed at the same location. As the German guards arranged the group, a specific kind of front-line experience came into its own. Three 18th Infantry disciplinary prisoners, Private Carlisle Tieman, Private Walter Chimiel, and Private Chester Dorman now had the chance to share their insider knowledge of incarceration with the rest. The three proceeded to turn somersaults in front of the group in an attempt to make everyone laugh.[1171] Approximately seven rows of 117 soldiers were arrayed against the backdrop of the store. The first row sat exposing their stocking feet and newly issued canvas wrapping for shoes. Almost all had their American helmets. A sole *poilu* helmet was observed. In the very centre of the photograph stood a rather large soldier, chest out, with a cocksure grin. That stance defied the uncertainty that was to come. With a flash of the camera Seicheprey became a lasting symbol for all combatants. Pictures were reproduced by the thousands and dropped over the American lines. Doble was lucky. His friend Freddie Schenkelberger recognized him and brought the picture to Doble's brother Kendall, who cabled their parents that Enoch was alive but now a prisoner of war.[1172]

For those in the 103rd Field Artillery, acquiring the photographs was a godsend. Private Paul Danilowicz recovered a photograph released from a **Drachen** that floated into the American sector. It confirmed who had been captured. Sergeant Harold "Pa" Tucker and all of his Battery C crew (Sergeant Tucker, Corporal Lee, Privates Sefton, Sutcliffe, Cardell, Collins, Petochelli, and Goldman) may have become prisoners but "They were alive at least."[1173] Accounting for the missing in action now commenced. It would be several weeks before any official list of prisoners of war was provided to families back in the States.[1174]

The assembled prisoners were now marched to the railroad station at Thiaucourt through more crowds of curious German soldiers of all types – infantry, machine gunners, artillery, aviators, and even **Intendanten** [army supply, or logisticians], who had heard of the capture of the "Amerikaner" and were anxious to catch a glimpse. The weather in the evening was fresh. Most did what was natural, military decorum was forgotten as hands went into pockets. Hardly a remark was passed as they marched along. The series of photographs taken of the march to the train station were also feed for the propaganda mill, both at the front and with German newspapers. The German message was clear –

the Americans in their first significant battle of the war had not only been bloodied but had also suffered a significant loss in prisoners.

The picture's legacy survived to the end of the war and the return of the soldiers to the United States. A former 103rd Infantry captain, Timothy Bonney, was on duty with the 32nd Division near Coblenz and came across a German newspaper with the group photograph emblazoned on the front page. Bonney mailed it to the *Hartford Courant* and it became front-page news for the 9 March 1919 edition. Bonney commented, "It was of great interest to me in that it is a picture of some of those fine men who were with my division during those exciting days at Seicheprey when the 102d put up such a gallant fight against overwhelming odds and veteran troops of the German command ... This is a German picture and shows very clearly the character and makeup of those gallant men that fought the first great engagement of any American troops with the enemy. It was a wonderful fight that these lads put up on that 20th of April, and one that will go down in history. I sincerely hope that some of the home folks back in New England will find the picture welcome."[1175]

Both sides fought an aggressive propaganda campaign and Seicheprey provided more grist. The German-occupied areas of Northern France had to endure the *Gazette des Ardennes*, a French language newspaper. The 1 May 1918 issue featured the names of 183 prisoners – providing Allied intelligence with confirmation of who was captured. In several cases the families of the missing were not informed of their relative's name being on the list, the most accurate account of who was captured on 20 April. This was probably due to the fact that the publishers of the *Gazette des Ardennes* took the opportunity to lead the article with a letter addressed to General Pershing making the point that he was very new to the game – so he might like to know what became of his men. On 25 April three German propaganda balloons descended into Allied territory carrying copies of the *Gazette des Ardennes* with the latest edition describing the Battle of Seicheprey.[1176]

Later that summer the *New York Times* featured "Germans Attempt to Cajole Our Men" through propaganda coming from hot-air balloons floating over the lines, intending to "promote discord among the allies."[1177]

CONFLANS

After an hour on the train the prisoners arrived at Conflans, known by the Allies as the "Pumping Station" for the interrogations that occurred. German officers spent days extracting information from all Allied nationalities: English, French, Italians, Belgians, Cossacks, Russians, Siberians, Romanians, and Serbians. The process was frustrating for the interrogators because the information provided was so diverse that comparing notes only led to confusion. "Why, damn it," exclaimed one German officer to Private Charles Monson after questioning. "We know more about the American Army than you do." Monson replied, "Well, why ask me, then?"[1178]

Seicheprey prisoners now experienced what was to become the standard diet. Their coffee was made from ground acorns (as alluded to by Lieutenant Billy Schauffler), bread was served to each prisoner 10cm square by 3cm. At noon another bowl of soup made from cow-turnips with an occasional bean or minute particle of fish was provided. Work details continued for the afternoon and acorn water soup was served. Six days after Seicheprey, Markle had his first bath in captivity. They left the next day for Germany via Metz. There a large crowd had assembled at the depot. Seeing the prisoners confirmed to the crowd that the United States did have men on the firing line.[1179]

MEDICAL TREATMENT

Lieutenant Walter Tenney's serious medical situation had a positive ending. His eye had been damaged by a fragment from a hand grenade. While in captivity Tenney's vision in that eye was restored by a German surgeon who had practised

medicine in Chicago. Tenney was released following the Armistice in November.[1180]

Private Walter Wolf, Battery B, recalled receiving very good food at first, soup twice a day and a daily issue of black bread. He initially recovered in a German hospital at Germersheim. While in recovery, some of the patients succumbed to dysentery. Wolf's weight fell from 70 to 50kg. He was subsequently moved to a whitewashed warehouse with a few small windows in the roof. In that building Private Wolf received no medical treatment whatsoever: "One either died or got well." Wolf's wounded wrist became infected, with the only treatment being a paper bandage. Only after two months did the medical personnel attend to his wrist, holding him down and digging out the shell fragment with wire cutters.[1181]

Some Seicheprey prisoners achieved something approaching celebrity status while receiving hospital care prior to internment at camps. Captain James Norman Hall, noted post-war co-author of *Mutiny on the Bounty*, was a famous American aviator with the *Lafayette Escadrille*. His subsequent assignment with the US Air Service was spectacular. In March he earned the Distinguished Service Cross for destroying an enemy aeroplane and forcing down two others in the span of 20 minutes. He was subsequently shot down and received treatment at Jarny Hospital. While at Jarny, Hall recorded receiving good medical attention and kindly personal treatment. He met two privates that were captured at Seicheprey. Private William Lilly from Company C was one of the prisoners on the Germans' list. Another named June, whose name was not listed on 102nd rosters, was mentioned as a comrade of Lilly: "Although it was against the hospital rules, the nurses occasionally permitted me to see them for a few minutes." Almost two months later, Hall, Lilly and June were transferred to **Reserve Kreigs-Lazarett No. 2** at Saarbrücken. At the Jarny station the three met ten more 102nd Infantry men who had recovered at the hospital at Conflans. Hall noted: "Their clothing was in a sad condition, covered with dried mud and blood, just as they had taken it off several weeks before. Some of them had lost tunics and caps, and others their boots. These had been taken from them, they told me, by German soldiers. They all said they had been decently treated in hospital and had had enough to eat."[1182] William Lilly was reported after the war to have been at Darmstadt for five weeks, Limburg for three months, and finally at the Opinden Work Camp.[1183]

The family of Private Ed Clark received a welcome letter later that summer that was published in the *Hartford Courant* on 18 August. Private Clark recovered from his Seicheprey wounds at **Festungslazarett III**, in Germersheim of the Rhineland-Palatinate. He asked for any news of those who had died at Seicheprey. He explained that he was still recovering from wounds in his thumb and leg. He concluded with: "No more fighting for me. Just hang around Germany and work until the war is over." [1184]

VON GALLWITZ AND THE SEICHEPREY PRISONERS

Interrogations at the front lines, Thiaucourt, and the Conflans "Pumping Station" were compiled and disseminated to German command headquarters at **Gruppe Gorz, Armeeabteilung C, 5.Armee,** and **Generalstab**. Von Gallwitz recalled reviewing the POW reports. He found some of the NCOs intelligent. One NCO had a German mother and spoke German. Von Gallwitz also observed that "a very bad looking guy" had a German father. The name von Gallwitz mentioned was Thieme. The closest name on the roster of 183 was Carlisle Tieman — one of the three 18th Infantry disciplinary prisoners captured. Von Gallwitz gleaned some interesting insights into the condition of American forces at the time. He discovered that Americans serving at the front lines were sometimes taking desperate measures. Noteworthy was the remark from an American Medical Officer (Lieutenant Burke) that in his battalion (Major Rau's 1st Battalion) inside a few days six cases of self-mutilation had occurred. German commanders learned from the interrogations that the Americans had six

combat divisions in France as of late April. Of the six — 1st Division, 2nd Division, 26th Division, 32ndDivision, 41st Division, and 42nd Division — von Gallwitz commented that two of the divisions were being used at that time as replacements for the active divisions. In reality, the only replacements came from the 41st Division.[1185]

In 1931, von Gallwitz's chief of staff, **Oberst** Keller, commented on the prisoners taken at Seicheprey: "Those Americans taken prisoner gave a good impression; in their new and perfect equipment, young and eager, they afforded us a picture of health and strength which, outwardly, was in strong contrast with that of our own troops and of the Allies, worn out after fighting for years … many of the Americans showed very little insight into the exigencies of warfare. In a very outspoken, indiscreet, friendly sort of way they discussed affairs in and behind the Allied front, thus affording us valuable hints. They had been firmly convinced by unworthy, atrocious propaganda. Even the officers were no exception."[1186]

PRISONER-OF-WAR CAMPS

Maintaining prisoner of war camps became an overwhelming challenge for all combatant nations. Incredible numbers were captured over the course of the war. Prisoners, where possible, became a labour pool. The practice of employing prisoners of war all over the country complicated the organization and routine of the camps. The German military procedure was to have the prisoners assigned to the **kriegsgefangenenlager** [prisoner of war camp] under control of the **Armee-Korps** that captured the soldier. This procedure changed when American prisoners of war were sent to Germany. They were assigned to wherever workers were needed. tHE 150 prisoner of war camps put to work 50 to 75 per cent of the captured men in the camps. Civilian guards were eventually employed to replace military guards sent back to their units. Approximately 3 million prisoners of war required 300,000 German soldiers to oversee them. In the final year of the war such manpower had to be reapplied to a rapidly shrinking front-line force. In the last few months the need for German soldiers became so great that women were used as guards.[1187]

Prisoners were interned with only the clothes they wore – frequently muddy, bloody, and torn. Seicheprey prisoners were no exception. Conrad Hoffman, a Red Cross official, recalled visiting Darmstadt on 4 July 1918 and meeting Private Eugene C. Mielewski, an ailing American prisoner suffering from pneumonia and wearing rags that had been his original uniform and wooden clogs worn from his initial capture on the afternoon of 20 April. After Hoffman's visit, Mielewski's clothing was disinfected and he was assigned to a new camp for Americans known as Rastatt. Hoffman visited Rastatt in September and discovered several prisoners from Darmstadt still convalescing in the infirmary, including Mielewski. He almost died from pneumonia but recovered. Mielewski thanked Hoffman, wearing a big smile, for the books, parcels, underwear, and shoes that he had acquired since the last visit.[1188]

On the July visit Hoffman also contacted the officers' camp at Villingen. Three officers from Seicheprey – Lieutenant (Doctor) Joseph Burke, Lieutenant Benjamin Byrd and Lieutenant Robert McDowell – were initially incarcerated there. Dr Burke subsequently moved to Tuchel, a large **kriegsgefangenenlager** in the north housing both Russians and newly captured Americans. Burke asked for medical books, including a handbook on surgery and a selection of good medical compendiums to aid in his care of prisoners.[1189]

In August the newly established POW camp at Rastatt in southern Germany received American prisoners from all the major camps. By the Armistice, 2,600 American prisoners were at Rastatt. One of the American leaders at Rastatt was Top Sergeant Pete Dresser from 1st Battalion Headquarters. Prior to this Sergeant Dresser had been incarcerated at Darmstadt with Sergeant Louis Ziegra, the soldier who impressed German commanders with his fighting ability.[1190] Countless American POWs sent requests through Hoffman, which "ranged from tea, Quaker Oats … Most important, regular notice of the standing of the American Baseball Leagues."[1191]

Prisoners starved to death without packages and support from their mother country. In April 1918, prisoners of war received approximately 200g per day of dark soggy bread that tasted like sawdust; coffee made from toasted acorns or chestnuts; watery soups; very few vegetables; and practically no meat. Seicheprey prisoners recalled their only solace was the Germans ate the same.[1192] Private Lionel S. Robinson of Company C, wrote to his family from the **kriegsgefangenenlager** at Darmstadt where all non-wounded Seicheprey prisoners were first interned in Germany. His 18 May 1918 letter was subsequently published in the *Hartford Courant* on 1 August: "Say, there are a few things I wish you would send me and if I live to see you again will make it right. I would like to have you send me a box of something to eat … In the box I wish you would send me a little corn meal, can of milk, rice, brown sugar, soup, can of fish, and put in such as I can cook up myself. If you can send it I wish you would, and if you send candy put in chocolate or cocoa. If you put up a box of such things of goods I can cook myself I will make it right, and a little Bull Durham tobacco. Put in all the canned meats and jam you can. I wish I could see you face to face and tell you how I got here. It was in a place I couldn't leave. Well, some day I will tell you all about it, I hope … You can write two letters and four post cards a month. So I will say goodbye. Write soon. Your son, Lionel S. Robinson."[1193] Doble reported that if it had not been for the American Red Cross parcels, he would have starved to death.[1194]

On 11 November, there were 248 American officers and 3,302 enlisted men in the hands of the Germans. By 5 February 1919, all had been released. No American prisoner was condemned to death. One officer and twenty men died while in captivity.[1195] Private Walter Wolf recalled getting back to Battery A, 103rd Field Artillery, shortly after the Armistice. "Then came the great day. Instead of finding myself disgraced for having been a prisoner, all the old men of the battery that were left, greeted me with arms wide open … And now I am back with the Battery again."[1196]

CHAPTER 21

An Attempt at Reinforcement

At 0700 the Germans commenced their next phase of the battle plan. **Res. I. R. 259 Stosstruppen** withdrew behind the line of resistance that now comprised Sibille Trench and established their defensive line against the anticipated counter-attack. **Kirschblüte KTK, Major** Bruns, ordered the remaining **Bataillon Hellmuth a-Kompagnie (6./259 Knop)** and **b-Kompagnie (1./259 Tänzer) Stosstruppen** to conduct operations against a small American pillbox near *Bois de Remières.* The surviving **Stosstruppen** prepared to assault but called off the operation when a heavy barrage struck the area. To the west, **Bataillon Tolle** consolidated forces and aligned their machine guns so that their fire would cross against the expected counter-attack. **Bataillon Seebohm** reported that they had suffered heavy losses from the intense struggle in the forest. They were ordered to return to the German lines. As **Hauptmann** Seebohm's forces moved out, **Leutnant** Grumbrecht's **d-Kompagnie (3./259 Maus, Hans)** and **a-Kompagnie (4./259 Pfeiffer)** became the reserve. **MW** left in position now focussed on potential strongholds. The attached **Sturmbataillon.14** and **Pioniere** were released. **Kirschblüte** was over for them.[1197]

CONFUSION CONTINUES

Brigadier General Traub's testimony spelled out the basics two weeks later: "Early in the morning of April 20th the enemy, after a severe bombardment of the Beaumont zone, launched a heavy attack against sub-centers F-1, F-2 and H-1, which constituted the three sub-centers on the East of my sub-sector, attacking principally *Bois de Remières* in center F-1 and Seicheprey in center F-2."[1198] This was his sector being so heavily attacked and he did what his years of training and experience demanded. His mission was not what had been required in the same area three years prior. The "progression" of *Lieutenant colonel* C. Petitjean's *128ᵉ brigade d'infanterie* mission did not equate to what Traub now had to confront. Traub's mission was to defend in place.[1199]

At 0845, Brigadier General Traub informed Major General Edwards and French commanders that the Germans still occupied Sibille Trench, *Bois de Remières,* and *Bois du Jury. Colonel* Bertrand at Colonel Parker's PC stated that no Germans occupied *Bois du Jury,* since his *162ᵉ régiment d'infanterie* still held the ground.[1200] Discussions at 0900 between Traub and Parker showed further confusion after the Germans had departed. Somehow, as mentioned earlier, Major John Gallant was credited for driving the **Stosstruppen** out of Seicheprey when he in fact had remained within the cave the entire time. The credit to Gallant was even passed on to Chaumont and to Major General Liggett's staff. Traub and Parker were both under the impression that Captain

Griswold was still holding *Bois de Remières* when in fact he had narrowly escaped and had just arrived at Major Rau's PC. Mention of over 300 **Stosstruppen** killed in *Bois de Remières* exaggerated the actual count, a common failing. Two German aeroplanes, it was surmised, had been downed during the battle.[1201]

Major General Edwards that morning made available to Brigadier General Traub a battalion of divisional reserves consisting of four 102nd Infantry companies (I, K, L, and M) at Mandres and Ansauville. Traub ordered the companies to reinforce Colonel Parker at Beaumont and they departed within the hour. Lieutenant Fuessenich's 1st Platoon, Company M, arrived at Mandres about 0945 and reported to battalion headquarters. He was joined by two more Company M platoon leaders, Lieutenant Smith and Lieutenant Boyd, to acquire guidance for their movement forward to reinforce Company C and Company D. Forty-three men were rounded up and the three platoons went north in small *CGs* arriving at Beaumont by 1150.[1202] Adding to the challenge of getting fresh reinforcements to the front line was what Sergeant Arthur A. Service's platoon in Company L had to deal with. As they were getting resupplied before heading back to Beaumont, 40 replacements from the depot arrived. Most had been recently inducted into the army. The replacements soon to be heading into battle could not identify a bandolier of ammunition and had not been schooled in the use of a rifle.[1203]

The fog was lifting from the forward front line after the sun rose. The Germans had been out of

Seicheprey for over an hour. TPS (transmission parameter signalling) low-frequency electromagnetic currents were reestablished between Seicheprey and Beaumont. Lieutenant Harry E. Rice, 102nd Field Artillery, reported at 0800 from the Seicheprey observatory tower that the **Stosstruppen** had commenced another attack. This time Rice called for a barrage using a red signal as well as sending a runner back to Beaumont. His effort succeeded. A barrage passed over 10 minutes later. Two positions of 103rd FA's Battery A and Battery B commenced fire towards the Seicheprey front line.[1204] The Germans observed the Americans had opened a heavy bombardment on their old position opposite *Bois du Jury* at about 0815. This dispersal of fire combined with German counter-battery fire proved advantageous to the German retreat. By 0830 their retreat had begun as planned.[1205]

Lieutenant Rice sent a TPS message at 0830 to lengthen the barrage for safety. He started to receive reports from soldiers rushing back to his position stating that they were taking friendly fire from 75mm artillery. Fortunately, Rice was able to signal the 102nd Field Artillery batteries through Beaumont to readjust. The batteries responded and reports came in that artillery fire was no longer striking American positions.[1206] Rice sent a message to Lieutenant Freeman to keep up harassing fire and to watch the field for attacking parties. He also reported that four of the runners he had sent were either lost or missing. About an hour later at 0920, Lieutenant Rice started receiving reports from the infantry that were confusing. At least he knew they

After the battle, curious soldiers from behind the lines came to see for themselves. This is the arch of the destroyed 12th-century church at Seicheprey. (*Literary Digest*, May 1918)

were still in their trenches.[1207] At 1000 Captain Stanchfield noticed that American artillery began firing short, confirming that artillery fratricide was occurring. This drove his machine gunners back to the south side of the village. Blue on blue continued for eight more hours.[1208]

Lieutenant McGlasson from Company D arrived at the cave down the ridge from the Beaumont PC to report to Major Gallant that "the Boche are out of Seicheprey." Gallant relayed the message to Parker. Major Gallant then sent two officers and ten men from Company B to Major Rau. At 0820, Parker ordered two platoons from Company B presently in Beaumont to immediately counter-attack at Seicheprey. These platoons were the first help that Major Rau received. They cleared the *Boyau Nantais* and the far west sector of Sibille Trench. 101st Engineers under Captain Bartlett were ordered to fill in for Company B and report to Major Gallant. Parker assessed at this time that the Germans' goal was still Beaumont and the 102nd Infantry needed as many reinforcements as possible to "save the situation."[1209]

Colonel Bertrand had remained at Parker's PC and assisted in planning the American counter-attack.[1210] Their assessment based on information cobbled together from runners and the limited connections was basic. French forces were to proceed under Gard's control to *Côte 269.2*, to confirm the Americans were occupying the ground. *Colonel* Bertrand figured that the Germans still occupied *Bois de Remières* and Sibille Trench.[1211]

PRETTY WELL MIXED UP

Lieutenant Oberlin, Lieutenant Strickland and Lieutenant Moore had established an accurate assessment of the **Stosstruppen's** position by 0900. **Stosstruppen** were confirmed holding Sibille Trench in considerable strength.[1212] An effort was made to get word through to the artillery to pound that trench, but the liaison through the runners did not keep pace with the developments on the battlefield. What the artillery knew at this time was the Germans

were still occupying Seicheprey. Their ongoing barrage of the village made life miserable for the Americans still holding on.[1213]

Captain Shanahan sent his first status message on machine-gun posts to Colonel Parker at 0920: "Four machine guns at south-east near Jury woods out of business. Report Boches in Jury Woods to north-east. By direction of French Commandant am sending a reserve platoon to establish liaison."[1214] An hour later Shanahan sent a second message that arrived at the PC around 1135. Lieutenant Tyler was holding his position in *Bois de Remières* with about twenty men. The status of American forces in the woods was grim. All the trenches were caved in. Two machine guns and the remainder of Tyler's men in *Bois de Remières* were believed lost.[1215]

The 102nd Infantry PC reported at 0930, "Infantry reports coming in. Pretty well mixed up. All held in trenches."[1216] At 0935 Colonel Parker received a TPS coded message from his signal man confirming that the front line was wiped out on the eastern side of *Bois de Remières*. Parker became more alarmed as he realised that Position 2's Beaumont–*Bois du Jury* line was in serious danger.[1217]

Lieutenant Joseph W. Rink, 4th Platoon, Company A, was ordered to find what was left of Company C. Rink's platoon arrived in the wood and discovered that Lieutenant Carruth's 3rd Platoon, defending what was left of the southern forest, was in desperate need of ammunition. The two platoons divided up what they had. Rink returned to *Bois du Jury*, met with *commandant* Gard and updated him.[1218] It was indicative of what Company C had been through when Lieutenant Carruth greeted the stragglers coming into his 3rd Platoon area with "Thank God you are safe."[1219]

Parker felt that based on information he had received Position 1-Bis was in danger and reinforcements were necessary. His estimate went to Brigadier General Traub at 0935. Colonel Parker received more information at this time from the now functioning TPS. The time was 0945: "Boches are through Remières Woods; our line just north of Seicheprey between it and cemetery.

Boches are in old trenches and also in Mayonaise." Parker repeated what had been gleaned by Major Rau earlier that morning: "Three wounded Boche prisoners say attack made by 1200 Sturm Truppen, all with knapsacks. Lieut. Albert E. Johnson, C Co. wounded. Shanahan says taking a platoon to Remières to get additional information."[1220] At 0955, after consulting with Bertrand, Colonel Parker ordered Rau to "try to push the enemy back from Seicheprey with all available means, including hand grenades and bayonets. The French on your right are working with Company A through Jury-Remière trench and Jury-Remière C.T. [communication trench/*boyau*] with mission of gaining and holding south-east edge of *Bois de Remières*. See that elevation 269.2, east of Seicheprey, is ours and prevent infiltration of the enemy at that place. Orders for counter-attack are being prepared and will be issued later." Rau learned from Lieutenant Oberlin that he had seventy-five men holding the Seicheprey Trench.

While Colonel Parker was concentrating on how best to support Major Rau, Captain Bissell reported that his men were in the process of moving east from H-2 towards Lockhart's *Boyau Nantais* position and were planning to re-establish American lines by counter-attack on the German right. An hour later, Bissell summarised his situation and indicated that Lieutenant Lockhart was still holding H-1. The remaining uninjured had taken the best position possible and they were resisting as best as they could. Bissell also reported that he had sent two surgeons east along the line and was making telephone contact with the rest of his company at the Beaumont quarry. Five minutes later Captain Bissell's requested ten stretcher bearers for H-2. Captain Bissell's message at 0945 explained the situation west of Seicheprey: "H1 gone; fallen back. Capt. Falstead wounded. H2 o.k. and will continue to hold."

Lieutenant Howard Mathews, 4th Platoon, Company B, and his 3rd Platoon counterpart Lieutenant W.W. Major supported F-1 between Beaumont and Seicheprey. As ordered by Colonel Parker they entered Seicheprey from their positions within *Boyau Seicheprey*. Both platoons were already exhausted, having endured the heavy barrage since 0300. Lieutenant Mathews first sent a detail of ten men forward to help evacuate the wounded. Then both platoons formed *GCs* of six to eight men and proceeded north. Mathews took the first group through to Seicheprey and reported to Major Rau, who directed him to report to Lieutenant Moore holding the first line of defence at the northern edge of Seicheprey. Major's men were ordered to organise a bombing party to clear the Seicheprey front lines of Germans. Mathews dispersed his men along the trenches adjacent to Seicheprey's northern edge. Company B's arrival substantially improved Major Rau's precarious situation. The reinforcements were there to hold ground and not counter-attack.[1221]

Around 1100, Color Sergeant Church received Company B's reinforcements while Seicheprey and the surrounding area was under a heavy barrage. A **Schlachtflieger** flew by and fired on the troops in the village. No casualties were suffered. As Company B proceeded north and took positions at the edge of the village more artillery rounds hit the area. It was American artillery. Lieutenant Major lost two men – his section leader and a corporal – from friendly fire. Major Rau instructed Lieutenant Major to delay any further effort to reinforce the existing remnants of Company D until the American barrage lifted. That occurred 7 hours later. Company B's soldiers stayed on and held the northern edge of Seicheprey for the next 24 hours.[1222]

FRENCH LIAISON

At 1100, *Général* Passaga told his subordinates that he considered the German operation a precursor for a very heavy attack by stronger forces on position 1-Bis. He directed two divisional reserves from the 101st Infantry at Gerard-Sas to move to the northern edge of *Le Faux-Bois-Nauginsard* on position 2.

Général Monroe's *69ᵉ division d'infanterie* patrols did not find Americans holding any part of Sibille Trench.[1223] The division reported their forces were on the eastern edge of *Bois de Remières*, but their exact position was not discernible. Brigadier General Lassiter was horribly uncertain about what was transpiring. He called up his French artillery counterpart at *69ᵉ division d'infanterie* and begged him not to fire any more on the Sibille Trench because he lacked positive confirmation of who actually held it. Lassiter's phone call confused *Général* Monroe because it created the impression that Sibille Trench had been retaken by the Americans. Colonel Morris Locke, 102nd Field Artillery, sent a message at 1036: "Germans have started a barrage on the road from Seicheprey and north of Beaumont. Telephone communications between my headquarters and Beaumont cut, so that can no longer get information from the infantry just what they want us to do. Have stopped firing on Sibille Trench pursuant to instructions from the French. We are now awaiting further orders. Are firing on other targets, but not that."[1224]

That afternoon **Stosstruppen** observed French forces leaving *Bois du Jury* in the direction of the eastern edge of *Bois de Remières*. German machine guns commenced fire.[1225] The *69ᵉ division d'infanterie* telephoned the American commanders stating: "The *69ᵉ division d'infanterie* holds *Jury-Remières*, also a parallel line 300 metres to the rear. Have sent troops to fill up the gap between the south point of the woods at Jury–Remières and Hill 255. Germans were seen going down through *Boyau Mayonnaise* at 1130."[1226]

REINFORCEMENTS FOR 1–BIS

Around 1000, General Pershing's aide, Major James Lawton Collins, was sent to garner more information on Seicheprey. Collins informed Chaumont that the object of the German attack was not immediately apparent at the time – kindling fears that the Germans were set on penetrating Beaumont Ridge to give them excellent observation posts. Collins reminded his seniors that the French plan of defence demanded the ridge be held at all costs.[1227] Until late that evening, German artillery paid noticeable attention to Position 1-Bis. This reinforced Allied thinking that the Germans still intended to capture and hold that position.[1228]

Major Bowditch reported to Colonel Malin Craig that no movement could be observed. Two clouds of smoke were seen in the north of Seicheprey, which Bowditch finally decided were burning houses rather than the smoke of grenades. The American artillery was firing on the first and second trenches north of Seicheprey. The Germans were firing occasionally on the support lines and on Beaumont and Tambucourt road. Both German and American aeroplanes were flying overhead.[1229]

Major Bowditch proceeded with Major Gallant to the Company B command post at the cave as the company and a group of engineers were heading to Seicheprey to reinforce Company D. The Germans from their observation posts at Montsec and from **Drachen** most likely noticed the rise in activity and increased the barrage on Beaumont Ridge. Major Gallant's 3rd Battalion were ordered up to Beaumont. Shortly afterwards Bowditch learned from a verbal report that Company C in *Bois de Remières* had been forced to retire and it was thought the remaining men were on the outskirts of *Bois du Jury*. Company A was sent to reinforce them. Bowditch in discussion with *colonel* Bertrand discovered that French patrols confirmed no Germans in *Bois de Remières*. Bowditch passed Bertrand's information to Colonel Craig.[1230] Elements of Company E that had held the Beaumont Ridge arrived in Seicheprey at 1135. Gallant requested that reinforcements for Seicheprey come to him one squad at a time.[1231]

Company I and Company M reinforcements left their rest area at Mandres, having been ordered back to occupy support positions on Beaumont Ridge. Company I set off at 0900, loaded up with ammunition and other necessities, and arrived back at Beaumont where Colonel Parker directed Lieutenant Edward Larned to take his men into *Boyau Seicheprey* and "hold it to the last man." Two of Larned's men were wounded en route. Lieutenant O'Neill moved his Company I, 2nd Platoon into the *boyau* at 1100 and remained there until 1530, finding whatever shelter they could from the heavy artillery bombardment.[1232] Sergeant Albin Backiel, 3rd Platoon, Company I, had arrived in Mandres the night before after being relieved by Company A; but in Position 2 he didn't escape the incessant artillery fire that included HE and gas rounds. Backiel's men wore their respirators for 3½ hours until the all clear was announced – and then it was back to Beaumont at 0900 with all available ammunition. Sergeant Backiel took his platoon forward to trenches near the south of Seicheprey where they came across the former machine-gun posts that had been destroyed by the **Pioniere**.[1233] There was no shelter except shallow trenches, which were very much battered. Where it was possible, Larned had his men shelter in shell holes and dig themselves further protection. At 1130 all of the Company I men were where Colonel Parker wanted them.[1234]

For the remaining 26th Division regiments occupying front lines to the west, contact with the enemy occurred, albeit not at the same intensity as experienced by the 102nd Infantry. At *Bois-Brûlé* the 103rd Regiment sent a mid-day patrol across the Apremont road, where they were attacked by **5. Ldw. Div.** soldiers: "Our troops overwhelmingly outnumbered but fought to a finish."[1235]

COUNTER-BATTERY AGAINST POSITION 2

German artillery fire commenced on the whole line at mid-morning with concentrated fire on *Bois de Remières*. The morning mist initially helped to mask American battery locations. By noon, the Germans thought they knew every American battery position. Their counter-battery began harassing fire. But the American roving batteries continued to operate. Courageous work by members of Battery F in manoeuvring during the incessant HE and gas fire allowed the guns to continue firing under the worst conditions for 5 hours on open ground.[1236]

The 102nd Field Artillery fire was directed at the Sibille Trench and they kept firing until they exhausted their ammunition. Although a liberal supply had been placed at all gun positions, the sustained rate of fire quickly consumed the stocks. Artillery caissons were ordered to proceed to the dumps at 0930 – a heart-stopping assignment in broad daylight. Despite the risk, only one man and four horses were killed.[1237]

Captain Stuart L. Bullivant's Battery F, 103rd Field Artillery, fired counter-battery against German Battery 3141, a 150mm howitzer. Bullivant's men adjusted fire through the sound-ranging unit. Their attention to this piece resulted in more artillery coming back at them.[1238] Lieutenant Green's battery fired thirty gas shells on Battery 3751 at 0830. Half an hour later the German artillery hit Green's battery location with air bursts, scattering shrapnel around the woods.[1239] Later that afternoon, 1st Aero Squadron conducted *avion réglage* (aerial adjustment of fire) with the 103rd Field Artillery on the same 3751.

The 52nd Infantry Brigade commenced preparation to move units to the front. The 104th Infantry veterans of *Bois-Brûlé* prepared to head east. Major Doane received telephone orders at about 1100 alerting him to be ready to move out, loading his combat wagons with 119 cases of .30-calibre rifle and one case of .45-calibre pistol ammunition.[1240] Despite losses experienced by 102nd Machine Gun Battalion, assistance from the other regiments was not called on. For a while it looked like as if the 101st Machine Gun Battalion might be needed, but it remained in place.[1241]

As the reinforcements trickled into Beaumon, they did their utmost to avoid detection but the continuous artillery fire seemed to follow them. Colonel Parker was ordered to send two companies to the 1-Bis position and hold back any additional reinforcements to ensure 1-Bis was capable of staving off any German attack."[1242]

For the medics in the rear, their workload started to increase at midday. The 26th Division surgeon reported two sick, twelve gassed, forty-two wounded, two shell shocked, and many dead and wounded on the field not yet brought in.[1243]

AERIAL ANNOYANCE

Color Sergeant Church reported that from his forward position north of Seicheprey a "*Boche* aeroplane caused considerable annoyance by firing upon us with a machine gun."[1244] The official **78. R. D.** report stated: "Our own and the enemy's aeroplane activity above the sector of attack was lively throughout."[1245] German aviators flew low without resistance and strafed the American positions. Soldiers occupying shallow trenches suffered.[1246] To the east in *Bois de Remières*, 102nd Machine Gun Battalion member Corporal Arthur Havlin recalled that the German aviators were effective that morning: "The enemy seemed to have uncanny ability in making direct hits on our machine-gun positions and those of the artillery, and even blew several speeding ambulances from the roads. Low-flying German planes, masters of the air, directed fire against moving objects and groups of men most effectively, and at intervals swooped still lower and dropped bombs and darts."[1247] Colonel Parker made it clear to General Traub that aviation was a major concern: "Movement about the sector in groups impossible as long as this German aviator is permitted to continue his operations."[1248]

The 103rd Field Artillery's Battery A received incoming rounds of gas and HE. In the short span of 5 minutes the battery received 208, destroying the kitchen that served both Battery A and Battery F. All battery telephone lines were cut, requiring the use of runners for the entire day. At 1100, the artillerymen of Battery A observed three low-flying aeroplanes (**DFW C.V, LVG C.V, Halberstadt Cl.II**) adjusting artillery fire over the area and playing havoc with their location. Everyone fired what they had at the aeroplanes. The German aviators rose to a higher altitude and continued their artillery adjustment. Later that afternoon more **DFW C.V, LVG C.V,** and **Halberstadt Cl.II planes** flew over the area and it appeared they were focused on Battery A. This time German artillery hit the battery's casement with four rounds. Battery A men assessed the German artillery fire was concentrating on the 1-Bis position where American reinforcements

were being marshalled. They calculated a total of almost 3,000 German artillery shells were fired in their direction that day. Remarkably, only five hits were experienced with no wounded – despite the fact that their gun operated from the rear of the casement that had been hit. At 1300, Battery A was ordered to evacuate. They relocated and continued operations well into the night.[1249]

Lieutenants Sedgwick and Galloway from Balloon Company B/2 ascended from their station at l'Hermitage at 0956. They went to 640 metrest but the visibility was poor in the direction of Seicheprey. Sedgwick and Galloway confirmed the three low-flying aeroplanes over the battlefield making artillery adjustments against 103rd Field Artillery batteries. A **FA (A) 298b DFW C.V** [or **LVG C.V**] appeared from the north at around 1047, forcing Sedgwick and Galloway to descend. **FA (A) 298b** aviators departed the 103rd Field Artillery battery area for another southern Woëvre area, continuing their artillery adjustment. After the threat had gone, the *aérostiers* reascended. Visibility towards Seicheprey was now very poor. Ten minutes later Sedgwick and Galloway were able to report visibility up to 12 kilometres from an altitude of 380 metres. Two fires were reported to the front of the northern part of Seicheprey. Eight minutes later, at 1144, Sedgwick and Galloway reported that German artillery fire was decreasing and the shells were landing to the east of Seicheprey.[1250]

At 0955 1st Aero Squadron directed three Spad XIs 8 kilometres west of Seicheprey at an altitude of 730 metres. The visibility was so poor that they didn't spot any enemy aeroplanes or make observations.[1251] Lieutenant Billy Schauffler recalled: "We had our hands full on that day too, keeping the movements of the Huns under observation and it was rotten flying."[1252]

"OUR GUEST ROLE IS ENDING"

Generalmajor von Stolzmann's **78. R. D.** head-quarters at Thiaucourt submitted their "Noon Report to **Gruppe Gorz**, April 20, 1918" with a bold and confident statement that **Kirschblüte**

had been successful. After a very effective gas bombardment of the enemy's batteries, lasting 1½ hours, and well-directed preparatory fire by artillery and trench mortars, **Res. I. R. 259,.** reinforced by elements of **Res. I. R. 258.**, **Sturmbataillon.14** and **Pioniere**, stormed the enemy's position between **Alfa-Wäldchen** and *Bois de Remières* (inclusive) to a depth of over 1 kilometre. After breaking the enemy's resistance, which was at times stubborn, the objective was reached and held along the whole front of over 2 kilometres. At the time of the report **78. R. D.** confirmed the prisoner count as three officers (including one from the Medical Corps) and 173 men, all of them apparently from the 26th American Division. More prisoners were coming in. Much booty, especially machine guns, was taken, but it was impossible to ascertain the quality. From 0930 on, American artillery fire rose at times to a high pitch of intensity. It was directed especially at coordinate 5991 to the western edge of *Bois de Remières*. In order to avoid needless losses, the Germans occupied the newly captured pillboxes that contained bomb-proof dugouts. The trenches in the area were destroyed and offered neither cover nor shelter. American artillery counter-action was assessed as strong at times but only in the area of *Bois de Remières*. "No counter thrusts on a large scale have thus far taken place. Calm reigns at present on the battlefield. Our own losses do not seem to be very heavy."[1253]

7./258 Stosstruppen spent the afternoon preparing to defend their position against an American counter-attack. They were alerted that **FA (A) 298b** aerial reconnaissance detected troop reinforcements at Toul unloading and possibly heading north – to the **Stosstruppen** it suggested a major effort was being readied by the Allies. **Vizefeldwebel** Ettighoffer expressed amazement that all of this activity was the result of a 600-man **Erstürmung. 7./258** knew they were only to hold the ground until that evening. The machine guns were set up to fire at American lines at Beaumont and Seicheprey. Then it was time. **7./258** slowly withdrew from the battle zone. They had had enough machine-gun and grenade activity for one day. "**Unsere Gastrolle bei Onkel Sam ist beendet.**" [Our guest role with Uncle Sam is ending.] It was now time to celebrate and enjoy food and cigarettes.[1254]

At 1100 (Allied time) **Generalmajor** von Stolzmann's headquarters reported for the first time to **Gruppe Gorz** that a **Res. I. R. 259** battalion under the command of **Leutnant** Grumbrecht had successfully made a bold advance in a southerly direction, taking possession of the whole village of Seicheprey, annihilating its garrison, consisting of about one company, destroying the dugouts there and returning. This was the first time that senior German commanders had been appraised of what had just transpired in **Abschnitt Maas und Mosel**.[1255]

Colonel Parker believed the accomplishments of his soldiers at Seicheprey were outstanding. He proudly recalled the exploits of the true heroes that had led the men through the battle. According to all accounts that Parker acquired from the engagement, the conduct of Major Rau, Captain Thompson, Lieutenant Strickland, Lieutenant Toulouse (liaison from *38ᵉ régiment d'infanterie*) and Color Sergeant Church, was simply beyond all praise. To Parker, these men undoubtedly saved Seicheprey from being taken and held by the enemy.[1256]

At noon, Lieutenant Tyler from the Company C PC at *Bois de Remières* helped the dying Lieutenant Johnson. Tyler asked for volunteers to move Johnson to the rear. Private Jacob Levy from Company G came forward.[1257] Earlier that morning, Private William A. Flynn, from the 102nd Machine Gun Battalion, had fought back against an enemy machine-gun section with his pistol. In the ensuing crossfire Flynn was wounded but managed to withdraw to a French dressing station and had his wound bandaged. Flynn thereupon returned to the battle. Flynn assisted Private Levy in carrying Lieutenant Johnson to the medical field station that had been re-established at Seicheprey. Moving Lieutenant Johnson proved to be an arduous task, but the two were able to deliver him safely to the medics. It was to no avail, for the beloved lieutenant died later of wounds received in that first hour in combat.[1258]

CHAPTER 22

"This is Certainly Hell"

Colonel John Parker claimed that the darkest hour at Seicheprey began at 1300. In his opinion, the most decisive step of the entire Seicheprey battle was about to take place, with the Germans launching a follow-up offensive to take and hold Beaumont Ridge. All the reports he saw reinforced that thinking. Germans were seen at 1130 moving through *Boyau Mayonnaise* toward Seicheprey. There were additional signs that German artillery fire was concentrating on demolition of wire and other defences, creating serious breaches in the main resistance line. Parker's noon hour was spent trying to get the most accurate picture of where the Germans were, what men were left in positions in the sector, and what was necessary to regain ground lost that morning. He heard from Major Rau that Lieutenant Oberlin and his GC were now proceeding through Sibille Trench to learn more of German intentions. Rau asked for artillery support to conduct a barrage on the German front lines.[1259]

Captain Dana T. Gallup, Company C, 102nd Machine Gun Battalion commander, had his machine guns cover the west sector of Seicheprey at Marvoisin, Xivray, and Rambucourt when the **Stosstruppen** approached. Gallup decided Seicheprey should have more protection to avoid being outflanked if the assault broke through. He set up two emplacements with good fields of fire to the east and stood ready to man them with his available crews. In the early afternoon, Gallup received orders from Major Murphy to "place as many guns for harassing fire to cover the flank of [a] counter-attack and play on the enemy trenches north of Seicheprey, as can be safely spared from your own immediate front." Gallup prepared fire data for his total force of five guns: one at Marvoisin, three by the cemetery east of Xivray, and one to the far west of the front.[1260] Lieutenant Humlird operated the three machine guns near Xivray to cover possible German counter-attack approaches from the north and west of Richecourt. By late afternoon, he received word to relocate, since that threat did not materialise.[1261]

Parker's ability to maintain the western part of his sector reached a critical moment at noon. His company commander, Captain Bissell, reported that H-1 still only had Lieutenant Lockhart and seven men in place along *Boyau Nantais*. Bissell urged Parker to allow his men to withdraw: "It is absolutely impossible to stay there with two platoons on the left of H-1. I have drawn back to the Q trench and this leaves our right flank entirely exposed. In my opinion order should be given by someone to withdraw to the 1-Bis line. H-2 is still intact but of course if we should withdraw will leave them open in the rear. We will stay there until orders are received to do different. (signed) Bissell." Colonel Parker replied: "To Bissell, at P.C. Halifax. You stick there until Hell freezes over and then skate on the ice. Parker."[1262]

Lockhart's situation now concerned both regiments of the 51st Brigade. Colonel Logan, 101st Infantry commander, weighed in because 102nd Infantry's attrition not only put at risk Company E's ability to maintain their defence of Position 1-Bis, it also threatened 101st Infantry's ability to operate. Logan telephoned Brigadier General Traub. "H-1 being held by one lieutenant and seven men. It is absolutely impossible to stay there. Two platoons on the left of H have withdrawn back to H. This leaves my right flank exposed. In my opinion orders should be given by someone to withdraw to the 1-Bis line; H-2 still intact but of course should re-withdraw. Will stay here until orders are received to do different. LOGAN."[1263]

Meanwhile, Lieutenant Butch Lockhart attended to his wounded. He sent a runner to Seicheprey updating Major Rau and sent another runner to notify the platoon to the east to guard the right flank. The eight survivors took up positions forward of *Boyau Nantais*, remaining in place until 1200. He had been on the line without rest for over 36 hours. He

Soldiers slogging through the trenches is reminiscent of Lieutenant Van Vechtan's Sound Ranging squad spending a day trying to reach Xivray. (*Pictorial History of the 26th Division United States Army*)

refused to be relieved until he had personally checked up on every member of his platoon.[1264] Lockhart stationed them in various posts while the rest of his men began digging out the entombed soldiers. Private John D. Curry was cited for bravery for holding ground during the heavy barrages. He also saved several wounded men during this time.[1265] It wasn't until late that night that Captain Bissell was able to relieve Lockhart's unit. Upon finally being replaced after his heroic stand with eight soldiers, Lieutenant Lockhart proceeded directly to Beaumont to report to Colonel Parker. Parker was exuberant. Butch Lockhart had a two-day growth of beard, face smeared with powder burns, and clothing muddy from head to heel. Lockhart told Parker: "I have to apologize for my appearance. I have just finished checking up on all the members of my platoon. Eight came out with me when we were relieved, and I found all the rest exactly where I posted them. Not a single one is missing." Parker exclaimed that Lockhart "was one of the finest looking soldiers I have ever seen in all my life at that moment."[1266]

THE GERMANS IN MOTION

German forces finalised their defences for an Allied counter-attack. The artillery was conducting an effective barrage against American positions

throughout the sector. Where they observed gathering of American troops, particularly in the 1-Bis and Position 2 areas, **Generalleutnant** Hoffmann's artillery concentrated their fire.[1267] When **Leutnant** Pfeiffer, **α-Kompagnie (4./259 Pfeiffer)**, learned that the Allies were in the process of marshalling their forces within *Bois du Jury*, he had his **Stosstruppen** consolidate their positions in the south-western edge of *Bois de Remières* to repel any attack. Should the perceived attack not occur, **Leutnant** Pfeiffer's **Stosstruppen** were now in place to serve **Bataillon Seebohm** fighting in *Bois de Remières* as a **Reserve Kompagnie**.[1268]

Général Monroe's *69ᵉ division d'infanterie* reported they now held *Boyau Jury Remières* and were sending troops to fill the gap between the south point of *Bois de Remières* and *côte 255*. At 1225, *commandant* Gard reported to *colonel* Bertrand that the Germans held *Bois de Remières* with a large force.[1269] At the same time Lieutenant Rink reconnoitred *Boyau Jury-Remières* and found Lieutenant Carruth, 3rd Platoon, holding the ground with his forty-man GC. Elements of the surviving machine-gun posts on the left and French units on the right were in place. Germans were observed over 1½ kilometres away to the north. At 1245 Bertrand telephoned Parker from his *162ᵉ régiment d'infanterie* headquarters to inform that his observers saw Germans in St. Baussant and trench Houblons, as well as coming down the *Boyau Carré*. *69ᵉ division d'infanterie's* artillery prepared to commence fire. *Général* Monroe advised Brigadier General Lassiter on the situation and requested American artillery also fire. The Allies proceeded to fire concentrated artillery into the woods to keep the Germans from approaching *Boyau Jury-Remières*. The Germans still retained Sibille Trench and the south-west edge of *Bois de Remières*. Bertrand ended his telephone conversation with Parker by asking, "Just where are the Americans?"[1270]

American reinforcements proceeded north to Seicheprey. Major Rau's infantry held Seicheprey with rifle and bayonet along a wall that ran out beyond the village. They realised another **Stosstrupp** assault meant a last stand.

The exhausted men saw every shadow as the enemy. Lieutenant Howard Mathews reported that at 1300 Company B platoon now occupied the forward edge of the village. A *Chauchat* automatic rifle team covered the *boyau* from the centre of Seicheprey to the Sibille Trench.[1271] Lieutenant Ingersoll met Mathews' *Chauchat* men as they came into the area and posted them in the line. Ingersoll noticed something was amiss. American heavy artillery was now firing dangerously close, sometimes shells bursting within 20 metres of the men, covering them with mud.[1272] Lieutenant Leavenworth from Colonel Parker's PC sent a runner to Major Rau confirming that American artillery was shelling Sibille Trench at 1215.[1273]

After spending the afternoon attempting to observe from the cave entrance, 2nd Lieutenant Middaugh left with the remainder of his Company B platoon and headed into Seicheprey. He was assigned the sector north of Seicheprey and remained in position until the following day. They proceeded under a heavy barrage. After 40 minutes the barrage became harassment fire, making the time in the forward sector more tolerable.[1274]

Individual Company D soldiers started to appear at various places along the front. The company's doughty runner, Private Horton, managed to return to Beaumont with the 1st Battalion orders, maps and other documents. Private Howard Viering crawled out to the front and brought in six of his wounded buddies without assistance, and then collapsed on the ground, mud bespattered and blood drenched. Company D soldiers spent the remainder of the afternoon searching for the remaining wounded but they were not successful.[1275]

REINFORCE POSITION 1-BIS – OR COUNTER-ATTACK

Colonel Parker finally got communication with the village, thanks to Signals repairing the telephone wires as well as providing a basket of pigeons.[1276] Around noon Colonel Parker telephoned General Traub's headquarters and followed up with a pencilled report:

> Enemy attacked on F-1 and F-2 and H-1 with infantry and artillery, 1200 men, according to prisoner; on H-2 and Xivray with artillery only. Our troops overwhelmed by superiority of numbers but fought to the finish. Enemy at Seicheprey, but was driven out by counter-attack by platoon in that town, led by Major Rau and Captain Thompson. Remnants of platoon in F-1 fell back into *Bois du Jury*, one officer and 20 men; remnants of platoon F-2 fell back into Seicheprey; remnants of platoons in H-1 fell back to H-2; H-2 being held. Company B, which occupied center B in 1–Bis position, has been sent forward to reinforce Seicheprey. Its place in center B taken by one platoon of the 101st Engineers. One company of the 3rd Battalion is now going from Mandres to reinforce center B and western half of Center A. One company of the 3rd Battalion from Mandres is going to center B. Two companies from Ansauville are in dugout and in trench in Beaumont and held in reserve. Enemy now occupies the following: Sibille Trench (group seen by patrols); south-west edge of *Bois de Remières*; *boyau* Nantais, as far as its junction with Sibille Trench ; sub-center H-1. We occupy Seicheprey and north of it just north of cemetery, western edge of *Bois Jury*, Marvoisin, and H-2. Patrols have been ordered to western edge of *Bois de Remières*, but no enemy there. Patrols out getting contact with Sibille and Nantais Trenches. Heavy shelling at 1-Bis position, centers A and B, lasted one hour, finishing about 1100. *Boyau* at Seicheprey being heavily shelled. Our artillery was shelling our old front line on centers H-1, F-1 and F-2.[1277]

Colonel Parker was now receiving the divisional reserves that he requested earlier that day. In Parker's estimate his force's ability to continue to hold the line appeared slim.[1278] Company B was ordered forward to reinforce Major Rau at Seicheprey. A platoon of the 101st Engineers was ordered to take their place on the 1-Bis position.[1279] Parker's intent was to launch a counter-attack against the Germans as soon as he could. After the battle Parker provided a more emotive description of events:

> 51st Infantry Brigade headquarters got busy in preparing for a large counter-attack. The French had been insisting all the afternoon that we should counter-attack at once. All night the pressure was exerted to have an immediate counter-attack made to retake F-1 and F-2 regardless of the fact, apparently, that there was up to that time not even sufficient coordination of artillery to protect my small defense at Seicheprey from being shot to pieces in our own town, and notwithstanding the fact that after Rau had driven the *Boche* out and established a line north of Seicheprey he had been compelled to evacuate that line by our own artillery fire. The sector orders turned over to me, absolutely prohibited any attack from 1–Bis or any weakening of 1–Bis to support the line in front. General Traub's orders repeated over the telephone again and again, emphasised in a most emphatic manner that I must not weaken the 1–Bis position by sending anybody from it. Parker had already forwarded all of Company B, in spite of these orders, to Major Rau; and Captain Shanahan, acting under orders, very sound orders from French, had forwarded the remaining platoon of Company C and one platoon of Company A.[1280]

"REPORTS ARE VERY CONFUSING"

Parker wanted to employ the reinforcing companies of the 3rd Battalion from divisional reserve that arrived at midday to conduct a counter-attack from the 1-Bis position on Centers 1 and 2. Major Collins commented to Chaumont that when the companies arrived General Traub, "…with excellent judgement, forbade such counter-attack, as the troops engaged could have been easily put out of the action while descending the open slopes toward

Seicheprey, and the strength on position 1-Bis would have been weakened materially."[1281] Traub stated that no counter-attack should be made without his express permission. Company I and Company K were sent instead to reinforce the line of support. Company L and Company M were held in reserve.[1282]

Major Bowditch sent Colonel Craig his assessment of Seicheprey as of 1400. The headquarters staff were now being kept informed as it happened:

> The lines are practically reestablished now and the whole affair is practically over. No definite reports could be obtained as to losses, beyond the fact that 90 wounded and gassed have passed through Maxey, 68 were wounded, and 1 man killed. Ten machine gun were put out of action in one sector by shell fire. We now hold practically all our lines although it is pretty weak near H.1. We hold Seicheprey firmly and the cemetery north of it. There is nothing in the *Bois de Remières*. Our patrols have been through there. The Boche apparently got what he wanted and has withdrawn. It is possible that there are some Germans in our observation lines. Our artillery is shelling these lines now. Communications were broken the first ten minutes after the bombardment commenced. Reports are very confusing regarding the affair.[1283]

A French description for combat – *une affaire* – had entered the lexicon of American higher headquarters.

ARTILLERY SHAPES THE AFTERNOON BATTLE

Generalleutnant Hoffman's reconnaissance resources were able to confirm that afternoon which American batteries were firing. German counter-battery was thorough – they conducted an energetic bombardment of each individual battery reported. The Germans realised that their counter-battery did not totally silence the American artillery but it did weaken their

firepower throughout the day, particularly that afternoon. The Germans reported that when their artillery opened a heavy counter-bombardment at about 1330, American artillery activity decreased considerably after 1400.[1284] German artillery then shifted their fire against the approach roads coming from Ansauville and Mandres to harass reinforcements and traffic.[1285] **Artillerie-Flieger** observations that afternoon discovered Allied troops assembling in *Bois du Jury*. Their reports resulted in intense annihilation fire. The German believed they had thwarted an Allied attack from *Bois du Jury* with the artillery's concentrated fire.[1286]

American artillery also reported their own deadly fire against German troop assemblies. 51st Field Artillery Brigade artillery massed fire against St. Baussant. The Germans reported back to **Gruppe Gorz** that the trenches in *Bois de Remières*, east of **Alfa-Wäldchen**, as well as the former front American lines, (except north of Sibille Trench) had not suffered much.[1287]

Lieutenant Walter Green, 103rd Field Artillery, reported that his battery commenced fire at 1300 on German batteries 7825 and 5625. The battery shifted at mid-afternoon firing against German batteries 6838 and 6536. Green described his battery receiving counter-battery air burst fire from German 105mm and 150mm in the afternoon until the evening. One casualty that day occurred to Green's battery when an artilleryman dropped a shell and it exploded.[1288]

The 101st Field Artillery were busy firing their 75mm guns from their West Grouping. Corporal Rogers described his battery suffering a direct hit: "I was about two hundred yards away at the telephone shack when the thing happened. There was a heavy explosion followed by cries of 'Stretcher-bearer,' and when I looked across I saw the first section gun pit enveloped in smoke. I joined several men who were running towards the place, and when I got there the sight made me sick to my stomach. A German 150-millimeter shell had exploded between the wheels of the gun, reducing it to junk and turning the gun pit into a shambles ...

There was a wire camouflage net above the pit, and from its meshes hung bits of bloody flesh and rags."[1289]

American artillery fire that did succeed in affecting German planning was in the area of Sibille Trench. The German battalions ordered their **Kompagnien** to find cover within the former American dugouts and establish nests for subsequent advance. **Hauptman Tolle d-Kompagnie (7./259 Hillemann)** and what remained of **Bataillon Hellmuth a-Kompagnie (6./259 Knop)** withdrew to the *boyau* on the St. Baussant–Seicheprey road. There **a-Kompagnie** settled into the dugout nest at the south-western corner of *Bois de Remières*. **Bataillon Seebohm Kompagnien** proceeded to settle into the area along the edge of the forest.[1290] They now had time to prepare for the Allied counter-attack.

Companies occupying 1-Bis trenches suffered nearly as heavily as those in front from the heavy artillery barrage. Major Gallant's 3rd Battalion was ordered forward from Mandres and Ansauville during the afternoon to replace Company B's position on the ridge prior to proceeding into Seicheprey. At the Beaumont-Seicheprey road, Company I went to the right on the 1-Bis position and Company K occupied the trench works to the left. Company L and Company M were retained in reserve at Beaumont. The company of engineers in Beaumont was sent, as infantry, to occupy a part of the 1-Bis position on the left of Center B. Two battalions from General Cole's 104th Infantry were moved from the Auinois rest area to Ménil-la-Tour, and placed at the disposal of General Traub.[1291]

AERIAL OBSERVATION ATTEMPTS

32ᵉ corps d'armée's escadrille Sal.122 Salmson 2 A2 flew five artillery registration sorties over Seicheprey over the course of the day. The aircrews were able to confirm German 105mm artillery batteries (5357, 5463, 5058, 5556) firing at Seicheprey and Beaumont. One Sal.122 aerial photo reconnaissance sortie acquired 36 *clichés*

(13 x 18cm glass plates) from a 26cm camera of *Bois de Remières* and the battle ground north of Seicheprey. 94th Aero Squadron had aeroplanes ready for duty that afternoon but the weather kept them at Ourches.[1292]

The greatest testament to the role of aviation that took place over Seicheprey on 20 April came from Colonel Parker in an afternoon message to General Traub: "Movement about the sector in groups impossible as long as this German aviator is permitted to continue his operations."[1293] **Jasta 64b** never engaged an Allied aviator but did cover the area for the entire duration of the battle. German **Drachen** working from Xammes, Jaulny, and Prény were observed throughout the day.[1294] Xammes had one ascent early that morning for about an hour, at 0600. Jaulny supported **Generalleutnant** Hoffmann with two ascents at 0940 and 1520. Prény had two ascents at 1400 and 1500.[1295]

Betsy the Sniper on Beaumont Ridge claimed success against German aviation that day. The battery heard a German prisoner claim Betsy's continual fire into Lahayville gave them the impression that a battery of 155s was firing, causing extensive casualties. Corporal McGowan, Corporal Plympton, and Corporal Robinson firing machine guns were able to repel an **Artillerie-Flieger** trying to conduct *réglage* on the ridge. Each time **DFW C.V, LVG C.V,** and **Halberstadt Cl.II** aeroplanes approached they received fire from the battery, forcing them to divert to other areas.[1296]

Balloon Company B/2 operations in the afternoon were hampered by decreasing visibility from mist and heavy clouds. The next ascent went to an altitude of 640 metres Lieutenants Sedgwick and Galloway could only see Bernecourt 8 kilometres west of Seicheprey. They persevered for 3 hours and descended at 1605.[1297] That evening Lieutenant Murphy attempted a final ascent. At 730 metres visibility was mediocre at best, observing shells falling nearby at Ansauville. After 2 hours he descended – the last American ascent during the Seicheprey affair. The following day there was poor visibility over the whole southern Woëvre front.

A MARINE AVIATOR OVER SEICHEPREY

A few minutes after the **DFW C.V** and **LVG C.V** planes left the sector, a Spad XI from 1st Aero Squadron flew to Seicheprey via Montsec at 180 metres, gradually increasing altitude to arrive over Seicheprey at an altitude of 460 metres. It was a heroic effort. A telephone call was made from 1st Aero Squadron to the 51st Brigade Headquarters around 1815 after the Spad XI landed. The report was emphatic: "Visibility was excellent and he thinks he would certainly have seen the troops had any been there. There was no troop movement in rear of the German lines that he could see."[1298] The aerial reconnaissance contradicted the previous reporting to General Traub. A third Spad XI flew at 1720 to investigate French ground observation reports that the German were regrouping near Richecourt and Lahayville. That afternoon, 1st Lieutenant Walter "Barney" V. Barneby, 1st Aero Squadron, and the newly arrived Marine aviator Lieutenant Kenneth P. Culbert, flew their only sortie that day over the German first and second lines at 550 metres. Barney Barneby was one of the most experienced pilots in the squadron. Culbert was one of the first Marine aviators to see combat in the First World War. He had graduated from Harvard the previous summer and had been a star of the rowing crew. After officer training, Culbert secured a transfer to the 1st Corps Aviation School at Gondrecourt and was commissioned a Student Naval Aviator on 26 November. Two months later, Culbert was assigned as an aerial observer to *Escadrille* Sop.216 flying Sopwith 1A2s supporting *5e armée* and *38e corps d'armée* operating south of Reims. On 1 April he was transferred to 1st Aero Squadron and was considered by the senior officers in the squadron as being one of the most skillful and daring aerial observers.

The weather was miserable; a hailstorm battered their Spad XI. Lieutenant Barneby and Lieutenant Culbert flew three times over the area but did not confirm any concentration or movement of troops. The 40-minute sortie took them directly to Richecourt where they turned east towards Flirey and entered the airspace over the battlefield. Barneby and Culbert proceeded to give the Germans a dose of their own medicine, firing approximately 100 rounds into the **78. R. D.** first- and second-line trenches. They reported twenty German trucks on the road to Thiaucourt. Their Spad XI flew low and the two aviators fired another 150 rounds at the vehicles. South-east of Essey a battery (9867) was seen firing. Between them 1st Aero Squadron and *escadrille Sal.122* conducted *avion réglage* against seven batteries that afternoon.[1299] Both aviators were awarded the *Croix de Guerre* for operating under heavy fire and in adverse weather conditions.[1300]

Lieutenant Culbert's valour as an aviator continued. On 15 May 1918, while on a mission to photograph enemy **Gaswerfer**, Culbert secured aerial photographs when his pilot descended to 500 metres over the enemy second-line trenches under heavy anti-aircraft and machine-gun fire. Although their plane was severely damaged, they completed their mission and returned with the photographs. The crew both received the Silver Star citation. When the legendary Major Raoul Lufbury of 94th Aero Squadron was killed in May, Lieutenant Culbert wrote to a professor at Harvard:

> General Edwards made a brief address, one of the finest talks I have ever heard any man give, while throughout all the ceremony French and American planes circled the field. In all my life I have never heard taps blown so beautifully as on that afternoon even some of the officers joined the women there in quietly dabbing at their eyes with white handkerchiefs. France and United States had truly assembled to pay a last tribute to one of their soldiers. My only prayer is that somehow through some means I can do as much as he for my country before I too wander west, if in that direction I am to travel.

On the evening of May 22, 1918, while flying near St. Mihiel Lieutenants Barneby and Culbert were hit by an anti-aircraft shell and crashed behind American lines. Barneby was killed instantly and Culbert died later that night.[1301]

A DOUBLE ARTILLERY BARRAGE

Major Rau and his men endured almost 3 hours of friendly fire from American artillery in Position 2:

Report of Major George J. Rau, – 3.00 P.M. 20 April 1918. From 1200 until 1430 today our own artillery has been firing on my own men, wounded a great number, we had them in the front line trenches and the American artillery drove them into Seicheprey. Then the Boche started to shell them. (1445 another beside my P.C.; one on my P.C. and one in rear of my P.C., all American. There are dropping all over town, all the Boche have to do is walk in and take it. We are now between the Boche and American shelling. They have not fired one shot on the old front line or on the German line. It would appear that they are helping the Germans. This is certainly hell. Men are getting wounded right and left, and in our own trenches by our own artillery. If you have any hesitancy in regards what action to take, please direct them to report here. We will hold until the last man is killed, but we cannot hold against two barrages and not a particle of cover. Practically every dugout is demolished. 4 men from Company B wounded. 2 more from Company B wounded; Machine Gun emplacements smashed; only two left. 3 Machine Guns left. 1450 another shell, our own, beside my P.C.[1302]

Around 1400, a Company B platoon on their own initiative wormed their way down into Seicheprey and supplemented Rau's remaining defenders. Their noble gesture met with tragedy. By nightfall, nearly all of the men became casualties due to the American shelling. Twelve soldiers were killed.[1303]

Captain Taylor, Parker's adjutant, quickly pencilled a note to General Traub: "Captain Thompson, in from Seicheprey, reports our heavy guns are continually shooting short into the town, and have caused serious losses. 75s registered correctly."[1304] At 1540 Colonel Parker issued a comprehensive situation report to General Traub. No mention was made of the problems his men were facing from the double artillery barrage in progress.

The Germans also noticed the American artillery targeting areas occupied by their own troops: "The nest of Americans in the trench section between v and t Bois de Remières was very frequently bombarded by American artillery of heavy calibre, either by chance or because enemy aeroplanes were still reporting that trench section was occupied. The crew withdrew from the fire in a southerly direction and was annihilated by machine-gun fire from the south-western edge of Bois de Remières while lying in shell-craters."[1305]

SRA reported that about twenty Germans were observed at 1450 in the trenches near Seicheprey and St. Baussant. Between 1725 and 1735 approximately 160 men were observed near Euvezin and Ravin de Saint-Gibrien. Artillery was fired against all the troops observed. [1306] This reinforced the prevailing thinking that the enemy was concentrating in the trenches in the vicinity of Lahayville (3.2 kilometres north of Seicheprey) to resume the offensive. The 103rd Field Artillery's Battery A and Battery B commenced fire on those locations. Observation posts along the Beaumont Ridge reported trenches smashed and bodies thrown high in the air by the 155mm shells.[1307]

After the battle, Major Rau testified to Lieutenant Colonel Walter S. Grant, tasked to conduct the preliminary investigation into the incident, that the American (or French) barrage fell on his men while they occupied the northern edge of Seicheprey. Then the rounds started to fall even farther back in the town. Rau told Grant that his men experienced fire from 75mm, then 155mm, guns. Lieutenant Rice, 102nd Field Artillery liaison, communicated with the artillery as best he could in order to get them to lengthen their range. Major Rau stated efforts to rectify the problem succeeded later that afternoon.[1308]

Colonel Parker appreciated 101st Infantry's Colonel Logan sending one of his artillery officers to the 102nd to assist coordination.

If the 155mm guns were at fault, it was not acknowledged by the officers. Lieutenant L. E. Hill, Battery D, 103rd Field Artillery, reported that the afternoon was the usual counter-battery work. They received a resupply about noon and fire was resumed at about 1430. Since Battery D only had one gun in action, they could only fire a few rounds that afternoon. The greatest problem Lieutenant Hill was experiencing was with limited telephone communication, which delayed his battery's response.[1309] The fractured communications kept the situation uncertain all the day. Further German activity was expected and feared. The various reports, giving only partial information, made disastrous artillery fire possible. This was especially true during the afternoon, when 155mm guns fired continuously into Seicheprey – despite the fact that the **Stosstruppen** had withdrawn around 0630. Strickland's post-war history captured the pain of the moment: "The bursting of those big shells in the town where our own men held positions, prepared to die in their defense, was sickening. Rockets to lengthen the fire were sent up time and time again, but produced no results. Sybille Trench, filled with Boche, was for a long time absolutely untouched by our artillery."[1310]

AN UNPARDONABLE SIN

The 26th Division had experienced several incidents of fratricide by Allied artillery in their time prior to Seicheprey. While fighting at the Chemin-des-Dâmes, the French assumed responsibility for one. Incidents of fratricide were experienced by 104th Infantry during the battle the week prior at *Bois-Brûlé* on 10 April. 102nd Infantry's Company B stationed in front of Marvoisin reported that rounds from the 155mm battery had killed three men and wounded eight. On the afternoon of 12 April, the artillery PC received several calls from the infantry to lengthen their barrages. At first, it was thought the infantry had mistaken German fire from the left for short fire from their own artillery and the specific location of the short fire was ascertained.

As mentioned during the Apremont battle, a single 103rd Field Artillery howitzer was found with a bulge, which had destroyed its accuracy. The howitzer was promptly removed and the three remaining howitzers of the battery carried the load for the remainder of the battle. Adding to the frustration, when infantry generated a "Lengthened Barrage" signal artillery fire actually got shortened, a distinct reason to distrust one of the most important weapons in the inventory. The 102nd Infantry never felt comfortable with 155mm fire. They did retain perfect confidence in the 75mm batteries, despite Major Rau's comment that 75mm had been a problem that morning. It was a damning indictment that the 102nd Infantry said they only wanted 155mm fire for counter-battery – well beyond their own lines. Sadly, incidents regarding artillery fratricide were reported later at Château-Thierry and finally at Verdun, prior to the Armistice.[1311]

The heavy responsibility rested upon each battery commander. It was an unpardonable sin – nothing destroyed the infantryman's morale quicker than being shot at by his own guns. Some shots would fall short because of variations or carelessness in manufacture; in a barrage, which to be effective had to fall within 200 metres of the front line, there was little margin for error. If a battery commander forgot his wind corrections or simply measured wrong and shot up his own infantry, he would be relieved of his command. It was a constant burden. Everyone in artillery learned that errors were not easily forgiven. In the 101st Field Artillery a lieutenant miscalculated range which resulted in rounds landing way off target. He was relieved of command and spent the next three months with the 101st Infantry as a liaison officer.[1312]

Fratricide due to poor liaison was not unique to the 26th Division. Lieutenant Colonel Robert McCormick's 1st Battalion, 5th Field Artillery, left Ansauville sector and continued to support the 1st Division's infantry. On one occasion McCormick learned his batteries were firing short with shells falling among advancing American infantry. General Summerall called McCormick to the

1st Artillery Brigade and proceeded to berate him for what had happened. It was a far cry from the praise McCormick received the day he had responded without authority to the German **Einladung** raid.[1313] In an incident involving French artillery, the *166ᵉ regiment d'infanterie* published a letter on 17 April 1918 that arrived translated for 26th Division dissemination on 1 May. The letter described barrages frequently being centered on certain portions of the front where they were not called for. In the absence of telephone liaison, the letter insisted that measures be taken so that the signal rocket observers transmitted calls for barrages only to batteries operating on the portion of the front where they could be clearly seen. *166ᵉ régiment d'infanterie* admitted that their own artillery fired short on several occasions, causing losses within their own ranks. Investigations ascertained that the projectiles in question came from batteries of neighbouring *corps d'armée*, who were inaccurately informed as to the constantly varying fronts. Repeatedly, but in vain, the *166ᵉ régiment d'infanterie* commander requested that no fire be carried out in the zone occupied by his unit, unless the objectives had been exactly defined by the division's artillery commander. The letter concluded with stringent regulations to be adopted to avoid a recurrence of such deplorable incidents.[1314] The French were forced to use artillery pieces that were too worn, and there was a huge outcry post-war about the number of French soldiers killed by "errant" rounds. How widespread the problem has been – and how deeply it affects the infantry – is indicated by the present (affectionate) British Army nickname for the Royal Artillery: "Drop Shorts."

Adopting the German attention to artillery accuracy might have helped the Allies. The Pulkowsky method required each artillery piece to be test-fired to determine its peculiar characteristics. The data for each gun was carefully recorded. The ballistic effects from external factors such as wind and atmospheric pressure were recorded. The initial target data was plotted using precise map locations. Obtaining firing data sufficiently accurate to fire

without registration became the norm. These precautions were successfully applied during Operation Michael.[1315]

THE KAISER'S OWN

General Traub and Colonel Parker corresponded over the issue five days after the Seicheprey affair. Parker noted: "In checking up this correction of artillery fire it is important to get the correct conception of the hours because everything depends upon getting the correct conception of the time. The time so bitterly complained of by Major Rau was from 1200 to 1430. Rau's report continued that he would hold until the last, but that he could not hold against two barrages and also the Boche attack."[1316]

Two weeks after the battle, Lieutenant Colonel H. P. Hobbs was tasked with the investigation of the reported fratricide. He added the following addendum to Rau's written correspondence of 20 April: "Note: It should be borne in mind that this message was written under the stress of the battle and that in his official report of the action written on April 26th, Major Rau makes no mention of our own artillery fire on Seicheprey."[1317]

On 7 May, Colonel E. T. Smith forwarded a memo to Brigadier General Lassiter stating "no errors in the computation of firing data" were found. All artillerymen added a factor of safety of 100 metres to "ensure the obtaining of overs on the opening of fire." Smith followed with discussion of the zone of dispersal at the range the 155mm were firing at the time against Germans in Sibille Trench. Two hundred metres from the point of burst had to be added. Replacing ammunition throughout that day meant there was no time to calibrate the lots received. Colonel Smith blamed the dispersal of fire and mixed-powder lots as the chief causes of the fratricide. He concluded: "it is believed that all measures for safety were taken to prevent injury to our own troops."[1318]

Twenty days after the incident, Lieutenant Colonel Hobbs published his findings:

After a careful study of the reports of organization commanders, statements of officers and such other information as I have been able to secure concerning the action at Seicheprey on April 20–21, 1918, I find that a number of shells (undoubtedly 155s) fell in Seicheprey between 12:00 and 16:00, April 20, 1918. This is confirmed by Major George J. Rau, Commanding First Battalion, 102d Infantry, Captain C.C. Stanchfield, 102d Machine Gun Battalion, Second Lieutenant W.W. Major, 102d Infantry, and First Lieutenant P.J. Clark, 103d Field Artillery, all of whom were in Seicheprey during this time. I find that the firing data at the guns, of Batteries A, B, D and E, 103d Field Artillery, that took part in this battle, was carefully checked by responsible and competent officers, and every possible precaution taken to avoid accident or harm to our own infantry.[1319]

Hobbs accepted Smith's reasons for the mishap. The 155mm howitzer's tendency of having dispersal to the rear of the point of impact caused damage as much as 200 metres away and shell fragments were capable of reaching 400 metres. Hobbs stated that a danger zone of up to 600 metres could be created by 155mm ordnance. For Hobbs, uncalibrated artillery rounds were the main cause of the fratricide.[1320]

Hobb's fourth paragraph is almost shocking: "The officers in Seicheprey during the action regret that they had reported this fire on them by our own guns. They express their understanding that such conditions must be expected at times. Neither the human nor the material is perfect, and the infantry are ready and willing to suffer some losses from their own guns rather than lose that most necessary support and assistance from their artillery."[1321] Hobbs concluded: "every precaution was taken by our artillery to support the infantry to the fullest extent possible and at the same time to guard against harm to our infantry. There is nothing to indicate any carelessness or neglect on the part of any one in this matter. Such incidents must be expected and our infantry understand and uncomplainingly accept this necessity and holds its high regard for the most excellent support it has always received from the artillery." In other words, no one was to be held responsible.

Major General Edwards officially commented the next day with no little political acumen: "As to this phase, there is no doubt in my mind that there were a few casualties so sustained … I am pleased by the generous attitude of the infantry who deliberately refuse to complain, denying that they bear any resentment and regretting that I ordered this investigation, stating that they realize that casualties must so obtain in such a battle, and their appreciation of the great aid always given by the artillery which should not be tempered with criticisms of unavoidable losses."[1322] In direct response to Pershing, Edwards made a bold statement: "Liaison is the great difficulty. The one question is 'Where is our infantry?' All our resources are devoted to its solution. General Passaga tells me it has been their greatest difficulty."[1323] No mention was ever made of Traub's artillery advisor, Colonel William M. Cruikshank, being involved in the investigation – suggesting the enquiry was limited in scope.

Among the veterans of the battle, there was a different take. Private Havlin, 102nd Machine Gun Batallion: "Our artillery was not only greatly handicapped by the destructive and accurate enemy fire and the early shortage of ammunition but also by the lack of information as to the infantry's demands and requirements. It has been said that the artillerymen did not learn of the enemy's entering Seicheprey until after the infantrymen had driven them out. The 103rd Artillery were thereafter referred to as the 'Kaiser's own' for firing into the town among the Americans. The fire was so accurately placed on vital targets in the town that there can be no fair conclusion except to place the blame on faulty liaison."[1324]

THE KAISER'S OWN HEAD ACHE

Here's the caption that should have been set years ago. Read this story.—Ed.

I am no writer, never will be but as an ex-perfumer smeller with the 103rd FA, (the smelling refers to the manure piles we slept upon on occasion), I am glad that DOINGS grants me the same rights as those given an ex-General. We artillerymen of the 103rd were a husky, healthy lot. We could take it then—and we can now. I think a lot of the boys were also great soldiers for never by word or deed have we fought back. We fought Jerry but we've tried to take the fun poked at us in good part without rancor. We did NOT win the war. We just did our bit like the rest of you boys, but as I get older I think of the chaps who didn't come back and I rather like the editor's caption on this piece. I wish some one had written it years ago. Way down deep it sort of helps. Thirty thousands of us stuck together all through the jam. When the end came we came home minus our dead. High brow and low brow, the rich and the poor, the pioneer stock and the just-came-over, we loved the other chap for what he was —100% American.

Somehow I like to think that when they call the roll upstairs they'll just add to it, "103rd Field Artillery, Yankee Division." There are 3883 of us left who regardless of the pun that started in fun and happened to outlast the war believe that we had a great bunch in a great outfit in a great division.

We certainly think we were, "The Kaiser's Own Headache."

—HINKY DINKY.

Above: Lieutenant Kenneth P. Culbert, USMC, is the first US Marine aviator decorated for heroism in USMC history. He received the *Croix de Guerre* for a sortie over Seicheprey on April 20. (HUD 3567.219.2 (# 38) Harvard University Archives)

Left: "The Kaiser's Own Head Ache" was published twenty-four years after the sad incident that prompted such painful memories. (*Yankee Doings*)

Below: Members of Company D, 102nd Infantry, assemble prior to mobilizing to the border with Mexico. The next year they were in France. (Connecticut State Library)

CHAPTER 23

"Worst Day I Ever Put In"

By 1500 Colonel Parker was trying to determine if the Germans would repeat their operation in force that night. Holding the 1-Bis position was his priority. He needed to supply the men who had fought for the past 12 hours with food, ammunition and new weapons to replace those lost, damaged or destroyed: "The regiment knows its assignment. It will do its duty."[1326]

That afternoon Colonel Parker provided an assessment for Brigadier General Traub. "H-2 is held complete; H-1 still has a few of Company E holding. F-2 is wiped out. Company D is practically wiped out. F-1 about half Company C wiped out. Possession of one corner of *Bois du Remières* reestablished. One patrol has penetrated to middle of woods without seeing anybody and without being shot at. One whole Company (B) in Seicheprey, most of machine guns in town knocked out. Anti-tank guns placed at disposal of commanding officer by officer in charge of them. Line pushed out to northern edge of town. Attack at present slowed up." Five days later in retrospect Parker wrote that all available information at his disposal had justified his belief that "the Beaumont-Jury Wood line was in serious danger at the point of liaison between [his] regiment and the French on [his] right."[1327]

For Major Rau's 1st Battalion in Seicheprey the afternoon seemed an endless horror. His casualties continued to mount among the handful of men left enduring double barrages

and fire from **Stosstruppen**. Night saw signs of renewed activity by the enemy in the front line. Either another attack was imminent or the Germans were preparing to withdraw. Rau reported his situation as of 1855 and said he required at least one more company equipped with *Chauchat* automatic rifles, ammunition and emergency rations, to arrive as soon after 2045 as possible. Relief poured in with supply trucks and motorcycle sidecars careering through the enemy bombardment to deliver supplies. Colonel Parker's Regimental Supply Officer Captain Connor moved weapons and ammunition from the ordnance depots without requisition. The arrival of the *Chauchat* rifles and ammunition was reassuring. Food came from the 101st Engineer's Company A kitchen detail working continuously for 55 hours, feeding over 700 soldiers.[1328] Parker's enthusiasm over his regiment's response was overt: "A box of Tromblons and grenades was received and has been distributed, brought up through the barrage by the Ordnance people. Splendid! A supply of emergency rations has been brought up through the barrage by the Supply people, and is being distributed. Splendid!"[1329] In his post-battle report to General Traub, Parker was more explicit about what Connor's effort meant: "This was our first actual offer of help from the rear from anybody."[1330]

ENEMY MASSES STREAMING OUT

Traub's staff phoned the 102nd Infantry PC to confirm as of 1655, "Observer at Beaumont has just reported that a number of Germans are in the open east of Richecourt." Fifteen minutes later, 51st Brigade passed on to Major General Edwards, PC at Boucq an update from 102nd Infantry: "Parker just reports that large concentration of Boches along the Richecourt–Lahayville–St. Baussant and *Bois de la Sonnard*. Reports the situation is serious because the 1-Bis line position is so thinly held. Systematically shelling 1-Bis position. About a regiment ... a Boche observation plane giving lots of trouble."[1331]

What the Germans were intending at this time was detailed in the **78. R. D.'s Kirschblüte Abend Bericht** (Evening Report) sent to **Gruppe Gorz** at 1700. German forces occupying American trenches were deterring any possible counter-attack. Patrols continued operating over the captured ground. The trenches in *Bois de Remières* and between **Alfa-Wäldchen** and co-ordinate 5991, as well as the former enemy front lines, except in the vicinity of **Pflaumen-Wäldchen**, had not suffered much damage. **78. R. D.** paid tribute to **FA (A) 298b** for conducting successful artillery adjustment. German artillery was firing on the roads south of Beaumont that were believed to hold reinforcements heading from Toul. One column, about the strength of a company, was dispersed by artillery fire north of Beaumont. Several columns (approximately one battalion) which were reported to be marching from Ansauville north-west to Bernecourt at about 1300 received concentrated and accurate annihilating artillery fire that caused the Americans to retreat – where to could not be ascertained. Finally, Allied trenches at *Bois du Jury* were known to remain occupied at the time of the report and were under fire by the German artillery.[1332]

Generalmajor von Stolzmann's withdrawal schedule was followed. The retreat of all **Stosstruppen** began at 2030 and went as planned, with little interference from the Allies. Positions taken that morning were evacuated by evening.

What made **Kirschblüte** a success beyond the actual combat results was the undetected withdrawal. German dead and wounded were removed throughout the day. The booty from the battle, most of the remaining ammunition, and other weapons not used in the battle were transported to rear areas. Throughout the evening and into the night German artillery fired a heavy bombardment on the Allied positions near *Bois du Jury* and on the heights south and south-east of Seicheprey every 30 to 60 minutes, to screen the evacuation. The reserves manning the flanks remained at their positions until 2130. They did not see any indications of an American advance and departed for their lines. **Model 08** machine guns were to provide a last bastion against an American counter-attack and were to be withdrawn 15 minutes after the last troops headed north to rest locations such as Pannes. The final effort was to be a barrage to deter any Allied counteroffensive. The remaining artillery batteries had stocked gas rounds for this final phase of **Kirschblüte**.[1333]

THE HARDEST HOUR

Colonel Bertrand notified General Traub that his patrols had made contact with Americans in south-west *Bois de Remières* and he required more precise information on American positions. Bertrand knew Americans occupied *Côte 296.2* covering the northern point of *Bois du Jury*, but he wanted exact information on all of *Bois de Remières*. Bertrand's patrols were reporting German machine guns firing from point 248.1. Late that night the Germans conducted a reconnaissance within southern *Bois de Remières* that was met by French forces. Bertrand knew what *commandant* Gard's forces were up to, but not exactly where the Americans were. As late as 0445 the next morning, Bertrand did not have contact with the Americans on his west flank and he felt that wherever they were, they were not in place. A barrage was to be followed by an attack by Bertrand's second battalion, *bataillon Roy*, entering *Bois de Remières* then continuing north to the **Einladung** battleground of *Bois Carré*. When the attack by *bataillon Roy* took place the **Stosstruppen** withdrew, leaving several dead, identified as belonging to **Sturmbataillon.14, Res. I. R. 259,** and an engineer from **80 Res. Pionier Komp.** The **Stosstruppen** were overwhelmed by the French attack, who regained the ground through *Bois de Remières* to *Bois Carré*. On retaking their trenches, French forces discovered a quantity of German weapons.

The 102nd Field Artillery received several calls around 2000 requesting a barrage or CPO.[1334] That evening an American heavy barrage hit German positions opposite *Bois du Jury*. The Germans noticed the American artillery had dispersed their fire. At the same time German counter-battery was homing in on the known American positions. This helped support the **Stosstruppen** retreat from the forward area. **Generalleutnant** Hoffmann assessed that the American artillery that evening had little impact except in the *Bois de la Sonnard* area. Hoffmann's artillery commenced a major barrage at 2015 to pre-empt any Allied counter-attack. They noticed the Allies were not taking advantage of the lull in the battle to prepare their forces to attack the flank positions. A final report mentioned Americans beginning to reoccupy their positions gradually at about 0300.[1335]

The remnants of Company C platoons had been withdrawn from *Bois de Remières* toward the 1-Bis position and into *Bois du Jury*. In Sub-center F-2 there had been a withdrawal of the platoons that had occupied Sibille Trench; the remnants were holding on at Seicheprey. In H-1 the right platoon of Company E was down to one officer and seven men still holding on and in touch with the platoons in H-2. The 1st Battalion of the 102nd Infantry was occupying Center F and had two of its companies back on the 1-Bis position, and the same for the 2nd Battalion of the 102nd Infantry occupying Center H. It had two of its companies back on the 1-Bis position. The companies of Major Gallant's 3rd Battalion were distributed with Company I and Company K and directed to the 1-Bis position.[1336]

That evening around 2000, Company B was in Seicheprey. Company M was ordered into the village as well. When Colonel Parker notified General Traub of the decision, Traub immediately countermanded the order and told Parker not to send any more men to Seicheprey or out of the 1-Bis position. Parker's order to Company M was countermanded before the Company left Beaumont.[1337] What shaped General Traub's thinking was a call from General Lassiter at 1920: "The enemy is putting down a test barrage in rear of Seicheprey in the 1-Bis position. Think it certain that the enemy will make an attack tonight and recommend that steps be taken to meet it."[1338] Company M was in the act of drawing rations but did not actually move to Seicheprey; they held under shelter in accordance with Traub's orders. Company L was also held in the same way and for the same purpose.

Traub instead placed Company L and Company M with 101st Infantry's Company E and Company G at the disposal of Colonel Parker for counter-attack purposes, should the Germans put the 1-Bis position at risk. Major Gallant was put in charge of the defence of the 1-Bis position.[1339] Parker ordered Company E and Company G, 101st Infantry to proceed to *boyau* Seicheprey near Beaumont. There the men could acquire shelter within a trench that was deep and dry with a good duckboard bottom – allowing the men to lie down and be safe from artillery barrage and aeroplane fire. The men also had access to the cave that Major Gallant was operating from within.[1340]

At 2330 Major Rau requested by runner that patrols be sent from Company I and Company K to reconnoitre forward from Seicheprey. Both companies had knowledge of the terrain. Rau also repeated that his request for support had not been realised. Parker stated that he could not explain to Major Rau at that time the reason, since his efforts had been stifled. Parker said that he and Lieutenant Colonel Dowell had thought it over and made the decision not to tell Rau that the reinforcement order had been countermanded. For Parker, this was the hardest hour for him during the entire Seicheprey affair. All his information indicated a probable renewal of the attack by the Boche. Observers reported the advance of the Boche through St. Baussant. Parker did not tell Rau what had transpired over the countermanded order for Company M to proceed into Seicheprey because "the effect of such information on the morale of the little garrison at Seicheprey would be ruinous … I did not see then; I do not see now, how it was possible for them to hold on through the destructive artillery fire to which they were subjected, and still maintain the fighting edge; and I still believe that if that information had been sent its effect would have been very disastrous."[1341]

FALSE SIGNALS

German artillery kept up a severe bombardment, particularly directed along the wire and the trench of the 1-Bis position, extending all the way from *Bois du Jury* to beyond Beaumont to the west. Lassiter's phone call combined with information received that hour from American and French observers reported (General Traub exclaimed later during the ensuing court martial "and it was true") enemy masses streaming out of the Quart-en-Réserve across country into Lahayville, St. Baussant and into *Bois de la Sonnard*. General Traub became convinced – the enemy was streaming across towards *Bois de Remières* and Seicheprey. He directed all artillery, French and American, to concentrate their fire on the enemy masses there with gas and HE shell. It was not known at the time what the result of the Allied barrage would be and what impact it had in averting a second attack in force on the depleted American advanced position.[1342]

A commander's need for the most relevant information and intelligence was emotionally expressed by Brigadier General Traub after the battle in questioning from the general court martial. It displayed his propensity to overextend authority through all echelons:

I'd like to say in connection herewith that I had been trying to get absolutely definite information by patrols to clear up the situation, and now as a last resort I directed again that new patrols be sent out from Seicheprey, practically like this: one to the North-east, one to the North, one to the North-west and one to the West, to get in touch with whatever they found there and report back so I'd know exactly what the situation was out in front. That is the paper by which I directed that those four patrols be sent out immediately, and if they didn't have troops enough in Seicheprey to do that, then to have the patrols sent out right straight from the 1-Bis position and get that information.

That is, you thought without information you felt the situation wasn't clear?

Well, I wasn't without information. I had information all right enough, but it wasn't very late information. I wanted to get the latest thing going.

What was the latest you had?

The latest I had was that our troops were holding Seicheprey and fighting there behind stone walls and ruined buildings.[1343]

General Traub telephoned General Edwards around 2115 with an update: "Parker reports that at 2105 signal went up front F-2, indicating tank attack by enemy. Report repeated to Artillery. Bertrand reports that he is in the south-eastern, southern, and south-western part of Remières Wood, extending from Trench de Jury around to the Trench Sibille. Barrage signal went up from F-1 and F-2 and we have got a barrage down there." Edwards advised Traub that his divisional machine guns were to support with indirect fire if the Germans attacked the 1-Bis position. Edwards also tasked the 104th Infantry to move their Company A to Ménil-la-Tour to replace the Company M reserve battalion that had moved forward.[1344]

REGAINING TERRITORY

Ten hours after the Germans evacuated Seicheprey for Sibille Trench, Major Rau's patrols were able to confirm the true situation of enemy emplacements. All GCs were harassed by snipers as they moved forward. Around 1730, Lieutenant Oberlin, regimental intelligence officer, assiduously gathered information while taking pot shots at the enemy across No Man's Land. Oberlin took two squads from Company I and Company K and advanced up to Seicheprey trench to the original French first-line position. Oberlin's men took possession of Sibille Trench as the night progressed. Once there, he divided his patrols – one to the right to connect with the French and the other to the west to connect with Bissell, confirming whether or not there were any Germans in F-1 and F-2.[1345] While moving east, Oberlin and his unit made contact with a patrol from *commandant* Gard. The unit then proceeded west along the front trenches until it had almost reached H-1, linking up with Bissell's men. Rau and others said Oberlin's accomplishments at this confusing hour were exceptional, as if he had "the strength of ten."[1346] He proved that the line was clear of the enemy.

At about 1700 Lieutenant Rink, Company A, was ordered by *commandant* Gard to take his platoon down the Jury Trench to *Bois de Remières* and if possible to connect with Gard's *poilus*. Rink's GC were led by *poilus* into *Bois de Remières*. As they proceeded into the forest, they drew fire from a German machine gun. Rink and his men crawled back to an American machine-gun post and waited for the volley to cease. When contact was made again with *commandant* Gard, Rink was told to move towards the designated position within the forest and hold the ground.[1347]

Private Chamberlin's view of the experience as a member of the 102nd Machine Gun Battalion was universally held: "Shells all around – Shelled at Dead Man's Curve and field. Was scared good and proper."[1348] Four Company A men seeking shelter with several infantrymen in an artillery observation post near the Seicheprey road were buried by a direct hit. Private "Steine" Wall, with two hospital men, went to their assistance and rescued Private George Merlow, who was buried alive under the debris. The injured Merlow was evacuated. One soldier, Private L.R. King, was sent back badly shocked by the experience. The small group was unable at this time to remove the bodies of Private "Sam" Darling or Private "Bill" Pierce.[1349]

Captain Shanahan reported to Colonel Parker that he was "sending one platoon to trench Jury Remiere between Jury Woods and Remière Woods, to point marked 287.6 on order of *colonel* Bertrand." This was done to cover the French left, and Parker "saw no reason to change it." Shanahan subsequently reported that he had advanced two platoons to *Côte 269.2*. For Parker, Shanahan's move ensured that *Bois du Jury* was secure for the first time since the barrage commenced at 0300. At 1815 Lieutenant Tyler reported that about fifty men of Company C needed ammunition for rifles and automatic rifles, rifle clips, and grenades. The request showed Colonel Parker that his men were still holding the southern edge of *Bois de Remières*.[1350]

The **Stosstruppen** had overestimated Company C's remaining strength. The Americans who remained standing resorted to using rifles and ammunition from dead comrades to ward off last-minute assaults. That afternoon, the hand-to-hand fighting finally ended. The remaining survivors now had to contend with a new threat from the air. The "**Fokkers**" flew low over the woods firing away with machine guns at any Americans they saw. Corporal Boucher and his surviving unit lay still alongside their dead buddies. Just before darkness fell, Boucher heard a noise in a gully that ran into his trench and assumed it was a **Stosstrupp** mop-up patrol. Boucher had a couple of bullets left in the chamber of his forty-five. The noise stopped and a head popped into sight. When Boucher was about to fire, he hesitated and looked again. It was Private George Cooper, the only man taken prisoner earlier that day. Cooper's face was white and distorted. He had about twwenty bullet holes in his body – not one fatal. Boucher grabbed his shoulders and pulled him down into the trench. Cooper made an effort to speak. Boucher told him to keep quiet and conserve his energy. Upon checking his pockets Boucher discovered he had a few malted milk tablets left and forced them into Cooper's mouth, along with the last drops of water from his canteen. Cooper asked Boucher if he had any bullets left in his revolver and begged him, tears rolling out of his eyes, screaming, "Please, for God's sake kill me. Charlie, I just cannot stand the pains any longer." "No, George," Boucher told him, "when night falls, we will crawl under the barbed wire, find the road, and crawl back to our lines." Just then, an aeroplane flew overhead, distracting Boucher. Cooper grabbed the forty-five and was about to squeeze the trigger when Boucher grabbed it away: "And then, night overtook us."[1351]

Corporal Boucher thought his regiment had given up on him and his men, having assumed they were all killed or captured. It was amazing to see his squad straggling south towards Beaumont as darkness came. They used light from flares to help guide them, searching for the church steeple at Mandres which unbeknownst to them had been destroyed by artillery that day. Adding to everyone's misery a barrage of chlorine gas struck their location. Boucher's unit had no protection since their gas masks had been ripped apart by shrapnel. Their uniforms were shredded, covered in mud and blood. Only eight of Boucher's original platoon of over sixty men were uninjured and most of the others were badly wounded.[1352]

In the area between Seicheprey and Bois de Remières, Sergeant Albin Backiel's 3rd Platoon, Company I, was on patrol that evening when the Germans discovered their position and commenced heavy fire. Backiel ordered his platoon into the nearby boyau. He took Sergeant Kline with him to locate shelter for the troops. While traversing the trench a shell exploded, instantly killing Kline. Sergeant Backiel returned to his troops and waited out the barrage. When the barrage stopped Backiel's platoon resumed clearing the trench by sending out two patrols. Backiel sent a runner to Company I's commander and received word to withdraw the platoon to the boyau and prepare for a counter-attack. This was done and 3rd Platoon awaited further orders. They were told to return to their former location and send out patrols. One patrol entered Bois de Remières and was stopped by machine-gun fire so intense that they sought shelter in shell holes for two hours. When a momentary calm returned the patrol continued and saw **Stosstruppen** still holding ground in Bois de Remières. Backiel's other squad heading to Seicheprey reported no Germans in the area. With both patrols Backiel returned to the company. The time was 2250.[1353]

Parker directed his battalions to form strong trench-storming parties to clear Sibille Trench, Boyau Nantais, west of Captain Bissell's PC, and Marvoisin. Bissell was tasked to organise a trench-storming party to work eastward from his position. Major Rau and Captain Thompson were to organise two trench-storming parties – one directed west, the other east to connect with Bissell and 162e régiment d'infanterie units coming from Bois du Remières.[1354]

Lieutenant Harris took ten men from his 4th Platoon of Company F to patrol Boyau Seicheprey and Nantilles Trench, as far as Seicheprey, since the Germans were suspected to be in this trench. He returned at 0100 on 21 April and reported to Major Rau that the trench was clear, although broken in from shellfire. He also reported having found a dead American soldier, buried in debris at the mouth of a dugout 180 metres from town. Harris's men removed the casualty from the trench and finding no identification marks on him and having no stretcher, they left him there. They noticed, however, that the casualty was apparently a machine-gun man and that his pistol and holster were missing. The patrol repeated their mission at 0200. On 21 April an ambush patrol of eight men was placed in the draw between Marvoisin and their former post in H-1. The patrol between H-1 and Seicheprey through the Nantilles Trench and outposts was kept in the front line, as before. No casualties were suffered.[1355]

Before night, Corporal Arthur M. Hubbard from Company C had skirted Bois de Remierès under the heavy barrage to acquire reinforcements for the remaining men in the forest. It took a while, but despite the hazardous conditions, Hubbard acquired additional men and returned.[1356]

NO REST FOR THE ARTILLERY

That evening a French roving battery of 75s from *40ᵉ régiment d'artillerie* under *commandant* Dieudon arrived at the 102nd Field Artillery PC. The battery came from Pont-à-Mousson, 40 kilometres to the east. Mounted on French *camions*, they were a professional force that was responsible and responsive. *Commandant* Dieudon, accompanied by his lieutenants, stepped into the PC, saluted smartly and asked just four questions: "*Les positions? – les missions? – les munitions? – l'échelon?*" The 102nd Field Artillery staff responded. Once *commandant* Dieudon had his answers he and his staff departed immediately, telephoning within the hour that the roving battery was ready to fire. Those present at this particular demonstration of efficiency wondered how much practice it took to reach such a level of competence. Dieudon's 75mm were set up near Hamonville and in a short while were firing away at a fast rate.[1357]

Despite the fratricide that had occurred that day, the 103rd Field Artillery had much to be proud of at Seicheprey. Major E.S. Chafee remembered that to his men, "Barker and Davis are little tin gods hereabouts now." Captain Barker was chief of Battery A. Lieutenant Davis, who earned the Silver Star citation, was invited to lunch with Brigadier General Lassiter. Davis returned from the rendezvous to say that a mere lieutenant was ranked out of food. Chafee recalled: "He sat below the salt and nearly starved, 'but the General is sending out a lot of supplies and equipment for my battery.'" Chafee's tribute to Davis went beyond his personal bravery. "He had taken the odd details of men assigned to him from various units and Battery A of the ancient French 95s and welded it all together into a powerful fighting unit. Davis' skill and determination was laudable. And I may say across the havoc of war he was a very great battery commander."[1358] Davis proved it time and time again. Six days after Seicheprey, Lieutenant Davis further distinguished himself in going to the aid of a wounded soldier under heavy fire while simultaneously keeping his battery in action during a long-term, heavy destructive enemy bombardment. The experience proved deadly for the battery. Half of Davis' detachment were killed or wounded and three guns were put out of action. Despite the horror, Davis personally directed the fire of his remaining gun. Later that summer, while assisting a wounded officer to safety through a shell-swept area, a shell killed the wounded officer and knocked Lieutenant Davis to the ground. A few days later, Lieutenant Joseph C. Davis was killed when an artillery round struck his position.[1359]

SRA analysis for *Général* Gérard revealed the Germans' artillery did not fire west of *Bois-Brûlé*. Most batteries were located at Gargantua, *Mort-Mare* and Vittonville. The *SRA* count of German rounds for the day was 12,000. The artillery consisted of a mixed inventory of 77mm, 105mm and 210mm firing at Position 2 to pre-empt any planned reinforcement. *SRA* totals disclosed 26th Division firing 26,000 75mm rounds. 90mm and 155mm "heavies" fired a total of 3,300 rounds.[1360] The 102nd Field Artillery totals disclosed 13,998 77mm rounds fired in a little over 24 hours, an average of over 500 rounds per gun. It was the maximum one-day expenditure of ammunition by the 102nd Field Artillery in the whole war.[1361]

MEDICS

It was a hectic time for medical personnel. Major Rau's first call for litter bearers and stretchers came back carrying eight wounded and dead. More help was called for.[1362] It was dangerous and exhausting. Litter bearers went all the way into the front lines, and ambulance drivers braved shot and shell driving Ford ambulances over targeted roads. Two were completely destroyed; the driver of one, a member of the 101st Ambulance Company, was killed and his orderly severely wounded.[1363] Ambulances drove through barrages in plain view of German observation into Seicheprey. Six ambulances made the trip in and out successfully. One ambulance was hit and demolished on its way down from Beaumont Ridge. The driver with a broken collarbone went to the Beaumont aid-station to have his "bruised shoulder fixed up in a hurry so he could find another car and get back to Seicheprey." Litter bearers in numbers arrived that afternoon and carried wounded up the battered Seicheprey trench without a single casualty. At Battery F near Dead Man's Curve, ambulances were everywhere, gathering in the wounded and gassed casualties. Down the road at Ansauville, the Red Cross hut was turned into a dressing station. Eight men filled the room within a matter of minutes. As one ambulance filled up, another moved forward to take its place.[1364] Private 1st Class Leo F. McGuire of Section 647 received the Distinguished Service Cross for incredible bravery in performance of his duty as an ambulance driver.

The litter bearers, with a sergeant in charge, moved out from Seicheprey, "leap frog" fashion at intervals of a 90 metres, two each to the wheeled litters stocked with medical supplies. Every 45 metres, one litter group stopped and maintained its position. Major Bowditch reported to Chaumont that a total of ten doctors and seventy helpers were requested. The Chief Surgeon and G-4 surgeon were sent for and the facilities at Toul were readied to take the evacuated wounded. The dressing station was located at *Bois de Rehanne*. From there, an ambulance took the patients to the 102nd Field Hospital at Menil-le-Tour, where records were made and necessary treatment given. Patients were finally delivered to Evacuation Hospital No. 1 at *Caserne de Sébastopol,* north-east of Toul.[1365]

The 102nd Field Hospital issued reports listing casualties. Four officers were wounded and one suffered from gas. Captain Griswold was listed as shell shocked. There were 136 wounded men, thirty-one sick, thirty-four gassed, and twenty-five shell-shocked made 232. During the first day, 254 cases passed through the 102nd Field Hospital alone.[1366] In total, about 650 men were killed, wounded, gassed, or reported missing. When the fighting stopped during early Sunday morning, the Sanitary Train totalled up their own losses. It was an amazing and grim record of the commitment made by the medical corps that day. Fifty-four enlisted men and officers, most of them from the 104th Ambulance Company, had been either killed, wounded, gassed or reported missing.[1367]

Corporal Boucher had carried out the orders to hold the suicide post. "But Oh! God! At what a price!" The survivors literally crawled out of *Bois de Remières* – weak from lack of food and loss of blood. The road was being spattered by rifle fire but it was a welcome sound – "our good old 'Thirty-Thirty' Springfields." With their remaining strength they hollered "For God's sake let up." The Americans came out of their defended positions, scooped Boucher and his wounded in their arms, and carried them to a first-aid station. They received hot drinks, shots in the arms to deaden the pain, and were placed on stretchers to be taken to the 101st Field Hospital. Private George H. Cooper's stretcher was placed next to Corporal Boucher's. They spent a few minutes talking about their shared experiences. Cooper cracked a joke about the time he had borrowed Boucher's rifle when the two were on guard duty along the Mexican Border. They both had a good laugh, then George straightened out and died on the spot.[1368]

The road to the Field Hospital took the wounded through Dead Man's Curve. While waiting to depart Boucher and his men suffered through another gas attack, with klaxons shrieking all along the lines. Boucher was alone on the floor of the ambulance and the driver stopped and asked him if he had a gas mask. Boucher replied, "No but for God's sake put yours on and, I will cover my head with my blanket." Boucher recalled: "Dead Man's Curve was one <u>Hell of a Place</u> but our good old Ford Ambulances plowed through the shell holes and bombardments and didn't let up till we arrived at the One Hundred and Second Field Station where I was given more shots, a cup of hot cocoa, and cigarettes."[1369]

Sergeant Boucher arrived at Toul Field Hospital and was placed under heavy sedation to kill the pain. As his drugs wore off, he realised he was on the operating table. The last words he heard were, "I'm afraid we may be compelled to amputate his leg." This time Boucher was anaesthetised with ether. When Boucher came to he found himself in a large ward:

> I was cussing to beat <u>Hell</u> for I thought I was back up in the <u>Front Lines</u>. I was hollering at my men, 'Give 'em Hell the SOB's!' till I felt the hand of an orderly on my shoulder. He was saying 'Take it easy soldier there are women around.' He was referring to our Army Nurses. I then lay back and calmed down a bit. Then I remember a well built elderly nurse, with gray hair bending over me. And she said, 'Try and be as quiet as you can as you have just had a severe hemorrhage of your wounded leg and, since you've lost so much blood already, when in the trenches, you need every drop of blood you have left.' Then she bent over me and scooped me up in her arms from the blood soaked sheets and put me in another bed, nearby. She gave me a shot and left me to rest.[1370]

AT THE END OF THE DAY

Another heavy barrage hit the front line in *Bois de Remierès* prompting Lieutenant Strickland to surmise another attack was under way.[1371] At midnight Lieutenant Bright, Company A, linked up with Lieutenant Oates, Company A, where both proceeded to dig in and establish liaison between *commandant* Gard's *poilus* and Major Rau's remaining troops at Seicheprey.[1372] As they proceeded into the wood, they encountered Gard's *poilus* preparing for a counter-attack. At first they thought the *poilus* were **Stosstruppen** and nearly commenced fire. Fortunately, the error was discovered in time.[1373]

At Seicheprey Major Rau welcomed *commandant* Gard's liaison, who had arrived at 0030 and provided an update that a counter-attack was being planned for 0440. The liaison shared with Rau that the plan called for six companies in Sibille Trench by 0345. Rau and his men received no other orders regarding this counter-attack. Major Rau stated that the Sibille Trench was lightly occupied and could have been taken easily by his men. From Rau's position the Germans had evacuated Sibille Trench while their artillery fired a barrage into Seicheprey commencing at 2110 and lasting until 2320. For the rest of that night, Rau's men only experienced intermittent machine-gun and artillery fire.[1374] Color Sergeant Church added that the German barrage was accurate. One man was wounded and sent back to the hospital.[1375]

Major George Patton wrote to his wife earlier that day of planned festivities at Chaumont. "The big hospital at G.H.Q. is giving a dance tonight quite shick [chic] with invitations and I am going. It will get me to thinking about something besides Tanks if it is only corns for

Generalmajor von Stolzmann (peering over the head of the officer in front) together with *Major* Bruns, KTK, *Obesrt* von Blanksee and other *Kirschblüte* officers celebrate their success. (von Bornstedt, Reserve. Infanterie.Regiment 259)

Oberleutnant Kimmel and his *Bayerische Flieger-Abteilung (Artillerie) 298* aircrews celebrate their aviation accomplishments with three nurses. (Reinhard Kastner)

all the nurses dance horribly." The next day he wrote, "The dance last night was lots of fun. We danced till one o'clock and the party was still going on when I left."[1376]

Private Chamberlin, 102nd Machine Gun Battalion, wrote in his journal: "April 21. – Rolled in at 2 A.M. Worst day I ever put in – yes! We had five killed, 12 wounded. Sergeant Knapp, Darling, Gordon, Palumbo, and Bill Pierce dead. Quite frequent shelling."[1377] His family learned that he was at Seicheprey and survived without a scratch. Censorship didn't allow a further description but Chamberlin made his point: "I don't know how to express it, save to say we have been through hell, and some did not come back. Nothing we have seen before even suggested it. It is horrible – which is putting it mildly, and I would have to talk to you to adequately express it."[1378]

BRAGGING RIGHTS

At 1700, **7./258** departed for the rear but they remained vulnerable to artillery and sniping. In their final departure, two **Stosstruppen** were wounded by American rifle fire. **7./258** also endured a gas barrage in their final **Kirschblüte** moment. **7./258** discovered and took a few items of booty as they left, including a few American helmets, a pistol, and a crate of American hand grenades. It was time to march the 5 kilometres north to their rest area at Gargantua and boast of their accomplishments with fellow **Stosstruppen**, who were wearing their latest acquired booty from Operation Michael – English trousers and boots.[1379]

CHAPTER 24

Counter-attack?

It had been a long month for the Allies since Operation Michael had commenced. They had fought a revitalised enemy that almost succeeded in a significant breakthrough, one that some say could have won the war. Allied priorities were recapturing lost territory and continuing the momentum to ensure the Germans could never again advance in such a dramatic fashion. Counter-attack was an important topic of conversation among Allied commanders up and down the Western Front. On 19 April, *Général* Foch issued a memorandum that expressed his view of the present German offensive underway in the north:

We cannot afford to lose any ground on the Franco-British front ... Therefore the territory must be defended step by step ... The defensive organisations must constitute two positions at the minimum. The second position is prepared in case the first should be broken into in spite of all resistance. It must be occupied at the critical time by a few light elements, infantry and artillery, specifically designated beforehand, specially equipped and organized for this mission and standing in the immediate vicinity of the position. Counter-attacks especially will check the progress of the enemy and recapture lost ground.

Foch's attention now centred on how counter-attacks were to be accomplished:

On each part of the front the terrain will be the decisive factor in determining the objectives to be assigned to counter-attacks and the scheme of manoeuvre to be employed ... The troops intended for counter-attack must not be simply thrown into the line that is under attack. They usually melt away there as a total loss. To counter-attack to advantage they must be organized as an entity, have their base of departure, their objectives, a specified formation, artillery support and, if the counter-attacks are to be executed with the precision, opportuneness, and coordination from which they derive all their results, they must have been previously planned, prepared, and regulated in the armies, corps, divisions, or regiments. The officers entrusted with their execution (artillery and infantry) must know beforehand the units, point of departure, direction, objectives, so that there is no hesitation whatever in their minds when the time comes.[1380]

In other words, *Général* Foch wanted the Allies to make counter-attack a constant objective for planning while ensuring that vital resources were not wasted. This was applicable throughout the Western Front. Foch's policy did not take hold in time for the Seicheprey affair.

German military tactics viewed the counter-attack as most effective just at the time when advancing troops were beginning to slow up. Counter-attack meant stopping the enemy and regaining lost guns and ground. Unless special orders had been issued by the higher command, German military thinking viewed as successful a counter-attack that held the original lines.[1381] At Seicheprey, while in occupied territory, the Germans immediately set up defensive preparations and energetically prepared to oppose the anticipated counter-attack. Large numbers of machine guns were brought forward. The newly established flanks were protected with additional firepower. German units responsible for this were specifically assigned, so that confusion did not occur during the main attack. German initial interrogations of the captured American prisoners discovered that Americans did not recognise two German fundamental concepts or area definitions of positional war: **Vorfeldzone** (covering or forward zone – designed for ordinary trench warfare) and **Grosskampfzone** (grand fighting or battle zone – for defence against a major attack). German estimates had an Allied counter-attack commencing around 1600 on 20 April based upon ongoing aerial and ground observation showing Allied infantry amassing in *Bois du Jury*. To the east of the 26th Division, **FA (A) 298b** aerial reconnaissance discovered French troops on *camions* coming into the southern Woëvre front. A battalion of **Res. I. R. 259** at Bouillonville was alerted and moved towards the front line. The Germans reported that *Général* Monroe's *69ᵉ division d'infanterie* did attempt a counter-attack from the direction of *Bois du Jury* but this was quickly discovered and repulsed.[1382] As for the Americans' attempt to counter-attack, the Germans determined that what artillery support was in place was not enough. Fears of an immediate counter-attack abated. **Generalmajor** von Stolzmann ordered his **Stosstruppen** evacuated around 2030. Their withdrawal was not interrupted by the enemy.[1383]

GENERAL EDWARDS' DIRECTION

At 1430 *Général* Passaga called on Major General Edwards at Boucq. The discussion was about a counter-attack, the number and distribution of troops to be used, and the cooperation of *Général* Monroe's *69ᵉ division d'infanterie*. *Général* Passaga advised General Edwards that he would be given two reinforcement batteries and the use of a certain number of infantry companies from the corps reserve. *Commandant* Dieudon's roving battery of 75s was one of the reinforcing batteries.[1384]

While *Général* Passaga was discussing options with General Edwards, the *32ᵉ corps d'armée* staff telephoned the 26th Division staff the following:

> April 20, 1918, 2:45 p.m. The situation is not clear, although indications show a withdrawal by the enemy. It is possible that he still holds Sibille Trench and Remières. In these conditions an attack will take place at 1900 with the object of driving the enemy out of our lines and of making prisoners. Two companies of the *69ᵉ division d'infanterie* will attack by the south-east side of Remières Wood in conjunction with the 26th Division, which will attack with six companies, between Boyau Jury-Remières and Center H-1, not inclusive. The colonel commanding the artillery of the *32ᵉ corps d'armée* will arrange for combine artillery action after conference with the two division artillery chiefs. Watches should be perfectly synchronized. The first French Line will not be passed: that is to say, the points 250.4 and 227.5. When the action is over, the disposition in depth will be re-established. It is understood that the attack will take place only in accordance with the information furnished by our patrols. If the enemy has completely evacuated his position it will be re-occupied at nightfall. The artillery in this case will withdraw its fire to the enemy trenches at 1900. The password for French and American forces will be 'America.' PASSAGA *Général* Commanding *32ᵉ corps d'armée*.[1385]

Général Passaga left Boucq at 1515. Having received Passaga's direction, General Edwards' subordinate commanders realised that the 1900 counter-attack was not possible. General Lassiter's 51st Artillery Brigade had exhausted most of the ammunition stocks at hand. At 1630, Lassiter met with his French counterpart at General Edwards' office: "He [Lassiter] stated that, owing to the fact that we only had six batteries of artillery for barrage work for the proposed counter-attack, which at present did not have ammunition, and that the other batteries coming in could not be in time to fire at 1900, he strongly advised that the proposed counter-attack, if artillery was needed, should be postponed until daybreak. This was approved by *Général* Passaga and the time for the daybreak attack was left for General Edwards' decision, the hour decided upon being 0445. The French *colonel* of artillery said that it was understood, and that he would notify the *69ᵉ division d'infanterie*." This decision changing the original order was communicated to both brigade commanders and Liggett's headquarters.[1386]

After the battle General Traub recalled from an infantry perspective that no counter-attack could be made from the 1-Bis position without the direct order of the *corps d'armée* commander. In his instructions to General Traub, *Général* Passaga was said to have requested a counter-attack at 2000 — "8 in the evening, Sir? Yes, 8 in the evening, 20.00." But when *Général* Passaga saw that there was not enough time to carry that out, he then directed that the said counter-attack should take place the following morning at 0445. Traub recalled: "In talking about 'attack' and 'counter-attack', the terms were used in this sense: the enemy had made an attack; he was supposed to be in Sibille Trench; we were going to try and drive him out and drive him back across into his own lines. In that sense the term 'counter-attack' was used — not as an immediate successor to their attack, but as an eventual move to drive him out." Traub's understanding of the situation was based on the report submitted to him by Colonel Parker — "in fact our troops had to withdraw to Seicheprey, where the remnants were fighting behind stone walls and ruined buildings."[1387]

Lieutenant Colonel Duncan Kennedy Major, Jr, the newly arrived 26th Division chief of staff who replaced Lieutenant Colonel Dowell, issued General Edwards' field orders (No. 24 and 24a) ordering a counter-attack at H hour — 0445 on 21 April — by six companies of the 51st Infantry Brigade. The attack was to be in collaboration with two companies of the *69ᵉ division d'infanterie*. The mission was to drive

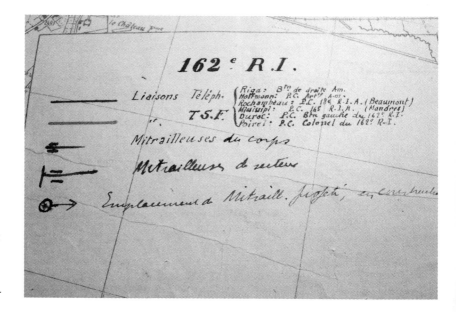

Legend of the French *162ᵉ régiment d'infanterie* machine-gun positions map.

the enemy out and acquire prisoners. Once the attacking force reached the last of the former American lines, disposition in depth was to be re-established. Reoccupation of territory was to be completed by the following evening.[1388]

The seasoned veteran, *colonel* Bertrand, realised that several important goals had to be quickly achieved before any counter-attack. He left his PC and rode over to Beaumont Ridge. His arrival was greatly appreciated by Colonel Parker. Parker's adjutant, Captain Taylor, observed that Bertrand seemed to enjoy skirting danger, making his way through the shelling of enemy sniping batteries, happy to be in action.[1389] First, *colonel* Bertrand needed to know the location of the Germans to be attacked. German machine guns were firing from point 248.1 (north-east *Bois de Remières*) complicating plans to occupy a key portion of the attack area within the forest. Bertrand learned that a German reconnaissance **Zug** re-entered *Bois de Remières* at 2340. Second, where were the Americans? He knew they occupied *Côte 296.2* near *Bois du Jury* based on *commandant* Gard's reporting. Liaison between French and American forces was now urgently required. Bertrand wanted the American officer in charge of the counter-attack (Major Gallant) to make contact with Bertrand's men on the right flank. Bertrand requested that a French patrol be allowed to proceed to Seicheprey. Bertrand then ordered *commandant* Roy to assemble his battalion for the counter-attack. Finally, French artillery were in the process of coordinating their barrage with the Americans to support the counter-attack, striking targets in the *Bois de Remières* centre followed by fire to the north at *Bois Carré*.[1390] Bertrand then departed Parker's PC at Beaumont and went to General Traub's headquarters at l'Hermitage.[1391]

CRUCIAL DELAYS

Général Passaga's staff closely tracked the situation and sent word to General Traub at about 1730 requesting confirmation about whether the Germans were or were not going to attack. General Traub was clear in his own mind that *Général* Passaga was the only one who could order a counter-attack. He reflected later: "That is an order that concerned me simply and didn't concern my subordinates. The way I worded the order to my subordinates was the only thing that concerned them."[1392] At 2230 General Traub telephoned General Edwards to say that he did not approve of an attack the following morning, fearing a German counter-attack on 1-Bis and more casualties. General Edwards relayed Traub's concern to *Général* Monroe's *69ᵉ division d'infanterie* chief of staff – who did not agree with General Traub's recommendation. General Edwards followed up by transmitting the discussion to *Général* Passaga. Passaga asked Edwards what he thought was appropriate. General Edwards said that upon receiving updates from his patrols he felt an attack by three companies was more appropriate. *Général* Passaga replied: "You must attack in the morning, but need only use four companies instead of six; and there would be no artillery preparation before the attack."[1393] General Edwards replied to Traub that orders previously given were to be carried out. General Traub acknowledged men were to reinforce the 1-Bis position and two of the companies were now in position. The other four companies were with Colonel Parker at Beaumont.[1394]

At this critical moment, German wiretappers had fun with the two generals. At the precise moment General Traub was describing his intentions for the counter-attack with General Edwards, both heard voices on the line who introduced themselves as "two crooks" and proceeded to mock Edwards and Traub, saying the Germans were "in the game."[1395]

Recovering from the disruption, at 2300 General Traub ordered two companies from the 101st Infantry to report to Colonel Parker and serve as reserves at the 1-Bis position. Traub then heard from *colonel* Bertrand that the French were patrolling all over *Bois du Jury*.[1396] Colonel Parker gave instructions that as soon as Gallant's 3rd Battalion moved out of the *boyau* from the assembly point at Hill [*Côte*] 275.5

A rest area for German forces as portrayed in *Das Regiment*.

to the line of departure between Seicheprey and *Bois de Remières*, the 101st Infantry was to hold the ground vacated by the 3rd Battalion so as to comply with the standing policy of not weakening the 1-Bis line. Traub issued a message stating patrols were to meet up with the French at *Bois de Remières* and report immediately to him when liaison was established. He then ordered Parker through wireless and courier, "Reports of all patrols to me through you without delay. If you do not feel that Seicheprey is able to send all these patrols send some from your 1-Bis position at point 275.5. The password which will be given to the patrols is 'America.' Patrols must be back by 0230."[1397] Half an hour later Brigadier General Traub ordered Colonel Parker to have Companies I, K, L and M concentrate immediately on the 1-Bis position at *boyau* Seicheprey, so Major Gallant could rendezvous with the troops on his arrival.[1398]

Colonel Parker was remiss in preparing his soldiers for the counter-attack. Company L and Company M were not ready to go forward. Wirecutters were called for but not issued. The soldiers were totally unprepared to deal with the two or three belts of barbed wire that protected the trenches to be covered in the attack. For whatever reason, Parker ignored the timetable for the rendezvous. His soldiers left Beaumont two hours after the scheduled time of 2300. Retracing the journey to the rendezvous point in the post-battle analysis showed the companies had to travel 1,500 metres over ground that was hard going at any time, but especially at night. Parker later admitted in testimony that it was impossible for the battalion members to perform the mission and return by the designated 0230 hrs.[1399]

General Traub had made several errors in his estimate of the situation and the counter-attack plan. He assumed 101st Infantry Company E and Company G would be at Beaumont at 2000. They were not. The two companies did not arrive at the designated point until 0300. Colonel Parker did not move out Company L and Company M promptly for concentration at Hill 275.5, where Major Gallant needed them. This was probably because of the standing zone orders forbidding him from weakening his 1-Bis position. Parker did receive a midnight order from Traub that directed him to concentrate the four available companies (I, K, L and M) for the counter-attack. Parker followed up with his regimental order half an hour later. Brigadier General Traub's delayed order to Parker to mobilise Company L and Company M had consequences. Both companies remained at Beaumont. As mentioned earlier, Company M was acquiring new recruits that had never witnessed combat. Lieutenant Wallace, Company M's newly assigned commander, stated that forty-one replacements were turned over to him on the night of 20 April. He figured he now had about 160 men on paper (the normal strength for the company was 250 soldiers). He knew nothing about the new men but was informed by his fellow officers and NCOs that the replacements had no experience, had never fired a rifle or worn gas masks. Wallace figured he now had an even hundred men.[1400]

At 2315, **78. R. D.** telephoned **Gruppe Gorz** to say that the **Stosstruppen** had evacuated the American positions as planned. Artillery reinforcements were in the process of being withdrawn from the southern Woëvre front and were available to support other divisions as required. The **MW** assigned to **40.I.D.** were also being withdrawn and returned to the division the next day.[1401]

At the same time, Brigadier General Traub was ordering patrols out seeking information as to where the enemy was still in force, particularly in Sibille Trench. He directed Parker to send four patrols from Seicheprey covering the St. Baussant road as far forward as they could get beyond Sibille Trench, north-west and west of point 242.0, and south-west of *Bois de Remières* along road 249.4.[1402]

"I AM DOING YOU A GREAT HONOR"

Major John Gallant was initially notified at 2030 to head to l'Hermitage and report to General Traub. Traub held Gallant responsible for the 1-Bis position that he occupied until his time of departure. It was an arduous 6-kilometre walk over trench lines, up the Beaumont Ridge, down Dead Man's Curve, avoiding any area that drew the attention of Montsec and the incoming artillery. Traub waited quite a while and got a little bit nervous over Gallant not reporting, not knowing by what means he was travelling south. Gallant eventually arrived about 2200 and reported to Traub, apologising for having been so late owing to no transport.

Major Gallant recalled a year later that he was notified by Colonel Parker that General Traub wanted to see him at brigade headquarters around 1800 to discuss the counter-attack. Traub did not ask Gallant what the conditions were at the front. Nor was Gallant shown the *32ᵉ corps d'armée* order, which mentioned the possibility of abandoning the counter-attack plan if the patrols found the Germans were no longer in the American trenches. *Colonel* Bertrand arrived at l'Hermitage while Gallant was working on maps. Gallant asked General Traub for wirecutters, an unusual request that someone in the staff should have dealt with. Traub replied that it was not possible to get any. Gallant had the clerk at l'Hermitage telephone Boucq; wirecutters were then sent from 26th Division headquarters to Beaumont.[1403] In fairness to Major Gallant, the level of detail that Brigadier General Traub was working on throughout this ordeal gave the impression that all requests regarding the counter-attack were to be personally approved at flag level, to include supplies for the men taking part in the operation.

Général Passaga issued revised orders around 2315 to counter-attack with four companies instead of the original requirement for six. This of course necessitated a change in the orders, which Brigadier General Traub accomplished very quickly. Traub explained the changes to Gallant using the map, then had Gallant sit at his desk and carefully read the final order. Traub's artillery advisor was Colonel Cruikshank, a well-known and experienced artilleryman. He then spent a considerable amount of time explaining the barrage line to be executed at H hour.[1404] With time running out, Traub, Bertrand, and Gallant continued to study the wall map describing the known situation in Bois de Remières and figuring out who was liaison and what units were to advance together. Traub learned from that discussion that Bertrand's men had crept around the south-west corner of Bois de Remières and reached the edge of Sibille Trench. Colonel Bertrand said his men had progressed as far as Seicheprey and saw no signs of the enemy. Gallant turned to Bertrand and said, "If there is no enemy found in front of Seicheprey, will the counter-attack take place? There is nothing to do. Why counter-attack?" Colonel Bertrand responded to Gallant that in the absence of the enemy the "thing wouldn't take place." General Traub was pleased because Bertrand's presence meant the counter-attack would have perfect liaison straight through. The whole situation became clear to everyone. Traub did not garner any impression that Gallant would

not execute the counter-attack. With everyone aware of the situation, Colonel Bertrand, like a good soldier, left with his orders and directed his men to proceed through Bois de Remières.[1405] Gallant now spent his time writing his battalion order to execute the counter-attack.

Throughout the time Major Gallant was at l'Hermitage, plans for the counter-attack were made and amended. The order estimated the artillery conducting a barrage lasting half an hour, followed by the advance of the four companies, with the French on the right, at 0430.[1406] Traub considered his orders definitive – providing the right emphasis coming from a higher authority to make the counter-attack. He was also sensitive to the fact that he could not order a counter-attack from the 1-Bis position – an action that required approval from Général Passaga, since it would weaken the 1-Bis position.

Field Orders No. 2 were published by General Traub through his adjutant, Captain William Wade.

1   No further information of the enemy.
2. The 3rd Battalion, 102nd Infantry under Major J.J. Gallant will attack the enemy between 242.4 South West edge of Remières Woods and Center H-1, both exclusive, in conjunction with 2 companies, *162ᵉ régiment d'infanterie* which will attack thru *Bois de Remières*.
3. The attack will be supported by the reinforced Divisional Artillery which will lay down a barrage 300 metres in front of the line of departure at H hour. It will advance at the rate of 100 metres in two minutes beginning at H-2. The barrage will advance to the final barrage line, no point of which will be nearer to our normal objective than 150 metres where it will continue until H-40 minutes.
4. Normal Objective: Our old front line trench (points 250.4 and 227.5) which will not be passed.
5. Line of departure: A line thru point of Southern Salient of *Bois de Remières* and 58.70–32.05. These co-ordinates are the Eastern and Western limits of the line of departure.
6. Troops will be formed up on line of departure at H-1 hour.
7. The attack will be made with three companies in first line and one in reserve.
8. The first line will form in two waves at 50 metres apart.
9. The reserve Company to the left rear will cover the left flank of the front line at a distance of 100 metres therefrom.

10. One half platoon will establish liaison with a half French platoon at 242.4.

11. Upon reaching the normal objective our original dispositions prior to the enemy's present attack this date will be taken up. Observation patrols will remain established to the front.

12. Rifle fire will not be used in *Bois de Remières*. Grenades will be substituted.

13. Liaison will be maintained between the French and American forces. The left of the line of departure of the French will be at 242.4 at H hour.

14. The 1st Aero Squadron and Co. B, Second Balloon Squadron will cooperate in the attack. Reports will be sent to Brigadier General Traub at his present P.C.

15. Watches must be perfectly synchronized between French and American forces, especially Infantry and Artillery.

16. The password for French and American forces will be "America."[1407]

General Traub's plan did not allow enough time. Despite what he had just heard from *colonel* Bertrand, he did not allow sufficient time for his own patrols to learn whether or not the enemy was still occupying ground north of Seicheprey. Traub did not allow for enough time to ensure the movement of Company L and Company M from Beaumont to Hill 275.5 near *Boyau Seicheprey*. Once all units had successfully arrived, additional time was required to effectively concentrate the four companies along the attack line.[1408]

In the flurry of activity, mistakes were being made in judgement and accuracy. Traub instructed Major Gallant that the front of the contemplated attack was 1,000 metres, a distance he himself thought "pretty wide." It was in fact 1,800 metres at the point of departure and 1,450 metres at the point of attack. General Traub called it a typographical error in Paragraph 5 of the field order – a mistake that Traub attributed to the staff officer who drew up the order. Traub assumed his discussion with Gallant sufficed as it concerned the intended line of departure. Gallant's first line was to consist of three companies and form in two waves. The three companies, depleted as they were from the heavy casualties suffered that day, averaged 125 effectives per company – a total of about 375 men and officers. Dividing the total into two

waves and scattering them over a front of 1,000 meters resulted in a wave of men 4.5 metres apart. Adding 800 metres to the actual point of departure now meant Gallant's men were to proceed between nine and ten paces (8 to 9 metres) apart in order to comply with General Traub's order. Those troops were exhausted and frightened, having endured horrendous HE and gas-round fire all day and night and having been deprived of food or drink for the past 36 hours. General Traub also assumed that the companies constituting the 3rd Battalion (I, K, L and M) knew the terrain, since they had been relieved from Center F the previous night. In fact, Company M – the last company to arrive – had, out of its total of 100 men present for duty, forty-one new men (nearly half) who had only joined the day the battle raged. Lieutenant Wallace, the new Company M commander, had only acquired company command following the death of Captain Locke near Sibille Trench in the first hours of the battle.[1409]

Major Brabson was a member of General Edwards' staff supporting Traub. He reported that Gallant arrived visibly nervous and excited, uttering pabulum such as "not many *boches* killed; we lost many prisoners." At this time General Edwards telephoned Traub and asked him point blank if Gallant was in a condition to lead. Traub replied he thought Gallant was OK, despite the fact that Gallant was not familiar with the officers or men assigned him. Edwards hung up with, "All right, I will leave it to you." Edwards then called Brabson and got another update. He followed up with another call to Traub and suggested Parker, Dowell, or Rau lead the attack. Edwards' discomfort continued. He turned to his chief of staff, Lieutenant Colonel Duncan Major. At 0130, Major called Traub's headquarters to arrange a last-minute replacement but it was too late. Gallant had left.[1410]

Major Gallant spent over two hours finalising the counter-attack plan with General Traub. After midnight, Gallant raised no further questions and told Traub that he thoroughly understood the orders. Traub took him into a room where he could give Gallant his last instructions: "I am doing you a great honor, and want you to go into it with all the spirit and soul you have and you will make a success of it" – just as one would any man one were sending off on a mission, patting him on the back.[1411] Gallant replied he would do the best he could. Gallant was asked if he thoroughly understood and if there were any last-minute fears. Gallant responded that he understood and had no further questions. It was 0030. Traub contacted Colonel Parker and told him to get an escort for Gallant when he arrived near the Beaumont PC. Then Traub had his aide provide Gallant motorcycle transport to the ridge. Even with that transportation, it took him several hours to arrive at the counter-attack launch point.[1412]

A HASTY PREPARATION

Lieutenant Boyd, Company M, received an order at 0030 for three patrols to cover ground north of Seicheprey from *Boyau Mayonnaise* and *Bois de Remières* as far forward as the first- line trench. They left at 0045. At 0205 patrols from Company L and Company M arrived in Seicheprey and reported to Major Rau.[1413] General Traub telephoned an order that patrols should be sent out from Seicheprey to *Bois de Remières* to

Members of Davis Battery recover from the battle. Extraordinarily enough, a pet lion cub offers a distraction from the recent horrors experienced. (NARA)

rendezvous with the French, go north on the St. Baussant road, and head north-west of Seicheprey and link up with Captain Bissell's soldiers. These patrols were to report back by 0230, and if their reports indicated complete possession of all the sector, it was Major Gallant's responsibility to transmit the information to Colonel Parker that the counter-attack was not necessary and would not be made. Colonel Parker was to inform General Traub immediately if the patrols brought back a report.[1414]

Traub assumed the patrols could get out and accomplish effective work by 0230 and report what was observed. Had there been any significant changes to the situation, Traub reasoned, he had two hours to make changes. He also did not want to risk any of those patrols being out there beyond Seicheprey when the barrage came down. The patrols returned about 0330. All appeared going well for the planned counter-attack; except the concern voiced by *32e corps d'armée* that the counter-attack should proceed only if patrol reports confirmed the enemy still held portions of the front line. Information was not forthcoming to Colonel Parker's PC. In turn, General Traub ordered at 0200 a final patrol to be split into two parties, with the understanding that vital information be furnished before 0430. This was an unreasonable expectation, even in the best of conditions.[1415]

The hour for the counter-attack was fast approaching. Lieutenant Oberlin's patrols north of Seicheprey along the St Baussant road did not report. Oberlin was aware that liaison with the French had been established by Company A through the Sibille Trench. As the minutes passed, Colonel Parker became concerned that there was no way to reach Lieutenant Oberlin. "Trust to the providence of Almighty God and hope that Lieutenant Oberlin, regimental intelligence officer and his patrols might escape." Likewise Parker did not know whether Lieutenant Lockhart and his remaining men were still holding on in H-2 or whether they had been wiped out. The last report from Captain Bissell stated they were still holding, but various runners relayed different messages.[1416]

Major Gallant's confidence was beginning to wane as General Traub's plan started to unravel. What General Traub understood was necessary and had instructed Major Gallant to execute was to cover a 300-metre distance from the point of concentration on the 1-Bis line to Seicheprey. In fact, the distance was 1,250 metres. Another miscalculation had the distance from Beaumont to Hill 275.5 for the assembly of the companies as 730 metres. In fact, it was twice the distance. In the post-battle review, Colonel Parker eloquently described manoeuvre in the battle zone:

> There is only one way to appreciate distances in that Beaumont zone, and that is to sweat for it. When those distances are multiplied by the conditions of that night, the darkness of a stack of black cats, boyaux shot to hell, the difficulties of getting around were multiplied a hundredfold. Exceedingly difficult. Some places were caved in by shell fire. Other places had chuck holes where you were liable to go through up to your hips. Some places were so knocked about that you had to climb over sections and go part of the way over the top and go down again.[1417]

Major Gallant recalled after the war that he left Beaumont PC at 0245 and went to the 1-Bis position. In contrast, Colonel Parker's record showed him informing Brigadier General Traub that Gallant left the PC at 0218 and headed through *Boyau Beaumont Ravine* to take command of the counter-attack. Every minute counted. Major Gallant did not have much time because he needed to round up what remained of four companies to attack at 0445 H hour.[1418] Company I received their orders around 0230 to concentrate men in the Seicheprey *boyau* for counter-attack. The men displayed the highest devotion to duty – despite being wet, exhausted, and hungry they moved up ready to counter-attack. They had been under constant fire since 0300 the previous day. They awaited orders that never came and held the position until daylight.[1419]

The two reinforcing 101st Infantry companies arrived and proceeded down *boyau Beaumont Quarries* west of the village. Orders were immediately issued to Company L and Company M to proceed to the Seicheprey *boyau* indicated on the map as Hill 275.5 and report to Major Gallant to prepare for the counter-attack. Runners were immediately sent to Company I in the Grant Trench right of Seicheprey road and Company K, left of Seicheprey road, with instructions to prepare to attack.

At 0300, Colonel Parker reviewed the disposition of his forces 24 hours after the first German barrage had begun the battle. To his right, Colonel Bertrand's men were exploring *Bois de Remières*. The southern edge of the woods was held by both the American and the French. At *Côte 269.2* north-east of *Bois du Jury*, Company A was in place. Rau's combat patrols were en route to the original line of American resistance. Lieutenant Oberlin reported on the disposition of the enemy north of Seicheprey. Company I and Company K were holding the 1-Bis front line across Seicheprey road. Company L and Company M in Beaumont were holding, ready to launch the counter-attack. Two companies from 101st Infantry were expected in Beaumont within the hour. At 0400 Parker received two messages from Rau covering his platoons from Company A and Company M. "No orders here to counter-attack. G.T. Rau."[1420]

"YOU BE A WITNESS FOR ME"

Colonel Parker received a written message from Major Gallant that read, "Colonel Parker: It is now 0340 and I have not made connections with Company I, L and M have not arrived. Men of Company L are very weary. Am making all to comply with orders. Gallant." To this message Parker replied, "Take what you have available and make counter-attack at the indicated time with what you can get. An attack must be made."[1421]

Mechanic Kenneth Parkin from Company L had served without a break from the beginning

of American involvement in the war. He was a non-commissioned officer held in high esteem by his soldiers. It was Parkin that led a reconnaissance patrol from Beaumont towards *Bois de Remières* where he made contact with *commandant* Gard's men. He realised that a pending artillery barrage preceding the counter-attack could inadvertently hit the French patrols. Parkin returned to the designated rendezvous point for the counter-attack through a heavy German barrage to inform Major Gallant of the situation. This reinforced Gallant's decision to call off the barrage and in the process possibly prevented French casualties.[1422]

Sergeant Arthur A. Service, Company L, realised while waiting for the counter-attack that another dangerous situation was in the making. Dawn was fast approaching and Service feared Montsec observations would improve German artillery fire on the troops massing. Service left Company L and found Major Gallant just as Parkin's patrol arrived confirming the French occupied *Bois de Remières* near Sibille Trench — the stated objective of the counter-attack. Gallant turned to Service and voiced his concern that the impending barrage would strike the positions now occupied by the French. Since *Bois de Remières* now appeared secured by the French, Gallant realised calling off the attack was now an option. He didn't have much time. Gallant sent one of his officers back to Colonel Parker's PC by the shortest route to call off the barrage and advise the commanders that the planned attack was now unnecessary. At about the same time, Gallant said to Corporal Barcomb, who had been assisting him in a brief but unsuccessful search for Company I, "You be a witness for me." Previously, at regimental headquarters, while on his way to the point of assembly, he had declared that if he couldn't find Companies I and K he would "call off the attack."[1423]

At 0424, a written message was received at Parker's PC via runner from Major Gallant: "Colonel Parker: It is now 4:05 o'clock. Company M has not arrived yet. I have just located Company I. Call off attack. Advise artillery and French on right, also General Traub. Gallant."[1424]

The barrage was set to execute at 0445. It was absolutely impossible to reach Major Gallant. Nothing could be done. It was not even possible at that late hour to advise all the artillery. Colonel Parker jumped to the telephone and got General Traub at 0426, and read the message to him. When Colonel Parker called General Traub telling him that Gallant had called off the counter-attack, Parker heard an audible gasp: "My God, what is that you said?" Parker repeated the message.[1425]

General Edwards learned from a telephone call to General Traub at 0435 that Major Gallant had called off the attack because all his companies had not arrived. General Edwards directed that Sibille Trench be immediately taken, since no Germans were there anyway. In the absence of all the companies at the designated attack point, Edwards wanted strong patrols sent out to get in touch with the enemy and retake lost ground. Edwards directed that the patrols follow the barrage. Edward's modified counter-attack confirmed the Germans had withdrawn. General Edwards also telephoned General Lassiter to go on with the barrage just as though the infantry were present. Steps were taken to reoccupy the American lines.[1426]

The 102nd Field Artillery began the 40-minute rolling barrage at the designated time of 0445. The remaining gun of Davis Battery, all guns of Battery A, and the guns on Battery B, with the exception of the two in the forward position that could not be resupplied with ammunition in time, also commenced barrage fire on enemy strong points and counter-battery for 40 minutes. The 103rd Field Artillery guns were hindered by the lack of ammunition. They reported that they were greatly embarrassed by the majority of their guns being out of action during the middle of the day.[1427] The Germans reported that the artillery mainly targeted *Bois de Remières*. At 0635 the 102nd Field Artillery received notice that the Americans had reoccupied ground lost the previous day. The last rounds of the Seicheprey affair were fired.

Company L was ordered back to Beaumont. Sergeant Service concluded that Gallant should have been commended for his judgement in correctly analysing the situation and acted within his rights as a field officer.[1428]

At 0539, five hours after they had last conversed, General Traub directed that Major Gallant be sent to report to him at once, taking with him his effects, and in status of arrest in violation of the 64th Article of War.[1429]

"GUARD YOURSELF"

Parker sent a runner to Rau at 0445 with the message: "Counter-attack has been called off. Guard yourself. Parker."[1430] Captain Thompson reported from Seicheprey by runner that the supporting company had not yet appeared there. Rau's remaining forces in the village were not aware that reinforcements were not heading to Seicheprey due to the counter-attack.

With the counter-attack cancelled, General Traub directed patrols to link up with the French and occupy Sibille Trench. At 0515, Colonel Parker then ordered Company M to proceed north. Ten minutes later Traub ordered Company L to occupy and hold Sibille Trench as fighting groups. Rau now was aware that the only Germans left were the dead and wounded. The only positive development for Colonel Parker that early morning was that his liaison was working through the Sibille Trench between Major Rau and *commandant* Gard's *poilus* holding *Bois de Remières*. Rau had earlier sent Lieutenant Strickland and Lieutenant Oberlin with patrols to link up and cover the flanks. Thanks to this link up, the French in the forward positions learned what had transpired with the counter-attack. Parker was very pleased. Lieutenant Oberlin's two squads patrolled the front area of Seicheprey and reported to Colonel Parker that the Germans had gone. Oberlin's had cleared up the situation, so far as Parker was concerned. Parker sang Oberlin's praise, stating he distinguished himself from start to finish, not only by a high degree of military intelligence but also by sound judgement and extraordinary courage. Parker told Traub directly, "These officers saw the right thing and did it."[1431] *Colonel* Bertrand reported that his staff received word from the Beaumont PC at 0547 that the attack was not taking place despite the barrage underway. He commenced to reoccupy Sibille Trench, *Bois de Remières,* and *Bois Carré.*[1432] *Commandant* Gard informed the Americans that his patrols confirmed the Germans had vacated the front-line positions in front of *Bois de Remières.*[1433] When Company L and Company M reached Major Rau, he had just been briefed by Lieutenant Oberlin on the situation at Sibille Trench. Rau told the men of Companies L and M to proceed north and man Sibille Trench and to support his remaining men in Seicheprey.[1434] They finally relieved the French later that night. Broken rifles scattered all over the Sibille Trench area confirmed severe hand-to-hand fighting had taken place.[1435]

The weather was miserable. It was cold and wet. No overcoats were available for the men who deployed from Beaumont. At 0544 Captain Marr of the 94th Aero Squadron flew a trial sortie north in fog and rain. The weather ceiling was 400 metres, which worsened to 200 metres. The bad weather continued for the remainder of 21 April. Sorties planned by 1st Aero Squadron and Balloon Company B/2 ascent were cancelled. German aviation was also limited with only two evening sorties flown over the southern Woëvre.[1436]

That morning, Major Rau finally received substantial reinforcements to hold Seicheprey. Company M arrived with 4 officers and about 100 men. Company K arrived soon after. All were directed to Sibille Trench. Sergeant Albin Backiel's men proceeded to Seicheprey before daybreak. They received permission from Major Rau to bed down within the *abris* still remaining.[1437] By the evening of the 21st Colonel Parker was still trying to sort out his available forces. He notified General Traub that "Colonel Bertrand is very insistent that I shall take over *Bois de Remières* tonight and relieve his two companies there. I have only one (Co. 'L') about 100 rifles available.

This reduces me to only the two companies of the 101st Infantry as Sector Reserve ... If you object to my sending Co. 'L' there take it up promptly and stop me. Fix it with the French."[1438] Sergeant Backiel started receiving orders from Captain Thompson, newly enstated commander of 3rd Battalion. Major Gallant, the previous battalion commander, was now under arrest.

"WE LOST THAT GOLDEN MOMENT"

On 23 April, General Edwards told General Liggett that he was very bitter against Gallant. He insisted Gallant was not fit for command and meant to have him tried, which occurred on 7 May. Edwards also expressed dissatisfaction with General Traub in his discussion with Liggett.[1439] Several weeks later Edwards placed the blame: "The action of Major Gallant was the regrettable incident of this battle; not that his disobedience of orders had any bearing on the final success, as it did not ... Major Gallant has been tried and found guilty for this deliberate disobedience of orders. The proceedings have not yet reached me. Therefore nothing more need be said at this time, except that his selection was unfortunate and against my distinct advice."[1440] It was pure Edwards and it worked because he was not relieved from duty like all the other division commanders axed by Pershing. It took another six months before Liggett and Chaumont could bring that about. Colonel John Henry Parker post-war maintained that:

> The psychological moment for such a counter-attack is at the moment of confusion and hand-to-hand in front of you. If you then, at just that moment, throw in an organized force, you win. If you delay until the enemy has time to organize his new position you have lost the golden moment, and only a well-organized attack in superior numbers can hope to win. We lost that golden moment through no fault of ours, nor of General Traub; stern orders from the *corps d'armée* commander prevented it.[1441]

PART 4

MYTHOS

CHAPTER 25

The Press Continues the Battle

On 13 January 1918, General Pershing in discussion with *Général* Petain suggested the press be made aware that American troops were coming into the southern Woëvre front. *Général* Petain counselled caution: better to wait for the 26th Division to come into the sector before announcing the entry of the 1st Division. *Général* Petain revealed that the Germans were wont to test the mettle of a new division by launching a strong raid. It was better to wait and keep the Germans guessing. Pershing adopted *Général* Petain's position.[1442] A few weeks after the 1st Division entered the front lines, General Bullard discussed the process with *Général* Debeney, *Ie armée*, and his divisional commander counterpart to the east, *Général* Monroe, *69e division d'infanterie*. Both offered Bullard their experiences culminating in a simple policy that Bullard accepted – no newspapermen should come into the area.[1443]

The most influential correspondent in the AEF was the newspaperman Frederick Palmer, a personal friend of Pershing from the days they spent together observing first-hand the 1904–1905 Russo-Japanese War.[1444] Palmer became a member of Pershing's staff and assisted in the censorship of media reporting. Captain Patton expressed his thoughts about Palmer to his wife during the first weeks in France: "Maj. Frederick Palmer is a thorn in the flesh. He thinks that the war is run for the newspaper men and he keeps stealing cars from me." (Patton's initial function was to manage the AEF fleet of automobiles.)[1445]

From the outset, war correspondents were regarded "as a necessary evil, a negative rather than a constructive force" by American commanders in France.[1446] Regional correspondent access was determined by General Pershing. He feared the American press being at odds with the Allies, the overtaxing of already crowded cable facilities, the creation of "newspaper heroes", and a possible embarrassment should their Allies see the Americans as publicity-hungry. Playing to the gallery was seen as prejudicial to good order and discipline.[1447]

General Pershing's chief of intelligence, Colonel Dennis Nolan, GHQ AEF G-2, also worked with Palmer in determining the extent to which media could work within division sectors. The policy was revised to allow reporters more freedom of movement to cover 1st Division operations as long as they did not create problems. In his post-war final report Nolan confirmed that the set-up worked. AEF confidence in the press was rewarded by the reporters' adherence to the "facts."[1448]

On the day after **Einladung** the *Chicago Tribune* posted the banner headline: "U.S. MEN WIN GORY FIGHT, German Dead Strew Ground After Repulse". On the West Coast, *The San Francisco Chronicle*'s banner headline was "Yankees Beat First Infantry Assault".

"The Americans stayed in their dugouts until the proper time, when they jumped to the guns and fought like veterans."[1449] A day later, more detail on the raid was provided: "Germans Attack American Front; Driven Back After Trench Battle, Leaving Field Strewn with Dead". Associated Press, reporting in the *Washington Post* stated: "The raid was a complete failure, three German prisoners remaining in American hands. The ground in front of the American trenches was strewn with German dead. The major gas attack on *Bois de Remières* two days prior was described as an attack to give one a taste of gas causing fear among Americans, but the men put on the masks and few were affected." Associated Press reporting published in the *Washington Post* and the *Hartford Courant* mentioned that the "Seventy-eighth reserve division of Hanover" was the unit attacking the Americans. An interesting insight was that the German prisoners had Russian coins in their possession, a suggestion they had arrived from the Eastern Front.[1450] The German response to the **Einladung** raid came from Amsterdam and was published in the *New York Times*: "North-east of Seicheprey our storm troops gained a complete success against the Americans. After a brief, strong prepatory fire our troops here penetrated the enemy's position to a depth of 500 metres. They rapidly broke the American resistance, returning with twelve prisoners and two machine guns. The losses of the Americans were extraordinarily high in the brief preparatory bombardment."[1451]

The exploits of the Yankee Division were also covered by the wire services and major metropolitan dailies that operated news syndicates. The 102nd Infantry actions on the Chemin-des-Dâmes were recounted on 3 March. The subsequent successes of the 104th Infantry at *Bois-Brûlé* were not reported in any major newspaper due to coverage of Operation Georgette against the Allies near Ypres. Field Marshal Haig's dramatic statement "Our Backs to the Wall; Stand to the Death" took precedence on the day the Apremont engagement ended. On page 3 of the *Chicago Tribune* 12 March edition, Apremont was given

a column with the headline, "Yankees Drop Storm Troops in Death Fire, Only Two of 800 reach American lines." The *Hartford Courant* in the back pages gave the troops fighting in *Bois-Brûlé* high praise – every man acted like a hero. The raid's intent to determine what army was in the southern Woëvre front was alluded to; it was reported that the Germans threw a note into the American trench reading "What are you? Canadians or Australians?" The Americans threw back a reply "Come over and find out!"[1452] The ongoing major battles at Ypres and the Somme overshadowed American actions. But it took the Battle of Seicheprey to define the role that the media played regarding American forces at the front line for the remainder of the war.

FRANK P. SIBLEY

The exception to the overall process for media access to the front was the 26th Division. The *Boston Globe* requested that their reporter Frank Sibley be allowed direct access and live with the Yankee Division ("embedded" became the term in the late 20th century) providing "mail special" local-colour exclusive material back to Boston. Unit designations and locations were not to be revealed.[1453] Colonel Nolan in coordination with Palmer approved the *Boston Globe*'s request. In turn, Pershing's chief of staff, Major General Harbord, approved Palmer and Nolan's decision, with the proviso that Sibley's writings should be "instructive and important articles about the American Expeditionary Forces as a whole." Harbord wanted Sibley to do his best work for the army and country, not just New England.[1454]

Secretary of War Baker had concerns over AEF accreditation for newspaper correspondents providing local coverage of units recruited from areas such as New England. He was confronted by the tenacious congressman from Boston, James A. Gallivan, a diehard Yankee Division promoter throughout the war and post-war. Baker advised Gallivan that accreditation had been given to the wire services and major metropolitan dailies that operated news syndicates. Baker told Gallivan that the best source of news was letters from servicemen to their loved ones; a nice sentiment that later created issues for both Baker and Pershing, as such letters often concerned late pay and poor mail service.[1455]

Baker did not prevent Sibley from proceeding. He left with the Yankee Division and served with them throughout the war and their return. Sibley made it clear that his job was to "stick to my trade; to report facts and let opinions form themselves at home; to be wily enough to get past the censors, and yet revealing enough to tell the folks at home what kind of a deal the Division was getting. So I had some victories of my own. Refused accreditation as a correspondent by the Secretary of War, I nevertheless went all the way through without it, against all rules."

Sibley's relationship with the National Guard of New England went back to 1916. He proudly recited his CV in a post-war discussion with the staff of *Yankee Doings*:

I was with the gang during its period of gestation, on the Mexican border in 1916. I was present at its birth in August, 1917, and I named the baby. General Edwards used to receive the reporters daily in his office on Huntington Ave, and one day he told us of the order. Then he said 'You know all these new divisions have names such as the Sunset Division and the Rainbow Division. What shall we call this division, gentlemen?' The other reporters left it to me to speak, because I was the old man among them. And I said 'Call it the Yankee Division, General; we're all Yankees around here.' Edwards looked displeased, and I found out later that he had picked that name himself and was going to pull it on us. By pure chance, I had beat him to it. But YD it was, and I was given the first arm-patch that was made.[1456]

In 1923 a retired Major General Edwards wrote a letter to *Yankee Doings* that provided his take on the naming of the division: "The galley proof of the new division organization was brought over to me by the first Chief of Staff … "What shall I call them?" My first thought

was of the Minute Man … I said, 'Good God, we are Yankees anyhow up here. This will be the 'Yankee Division' and I sat down and drew squares and built a Y inside, and then I made a circular D and tried that, and the next morning I told them it was the Yankee Division and the Battle Hymn of the Yankee Division should be the 'Battle Hymn of the Republic.' That was the first thing I decided on. That was the birth of the YD."[1457]

Sibley was remembered by *commandant* du Boisrouvray as very popular among the men of the 26th Division. Tall, thin, his long nose seen with large sunglasses, wearing a little jacket with a fur collar, Sibley, he recalled, had a beautiful stride. Sibley conveyed optimism and was one for telling anecdotes. "So American" was du Boisrouvray's succinct summation of the man. He also fought every chance he could to make the case for the Yankee Division, especially when matters concerned higher headquarters.[1458]

Sibley's accounts were as accurate as the information he could acquire: "At 0500 the attack came over behind its barrage, following it so closely that some of the attackers became casualties. The leading party consisted of about 1200 **Stosstruppen**, – storming troops specially trained to this work. On their flanks, in support, came a battalion of infantry on each side; a safe estimate of those in the direct attack gives about 2500 men. We learned afterwards that the raid had been rehearsed thoroughly in advance."[1459]

Fundamental to the post-war discussion on Seicheprey was Sibley's description of Yankee Division leadership and staff squabbles with Chaumont. No surprise whose side Frank Sibley took in this argument. *Commandant* du Boisrouvray remembered that when Sibley talked about the antagonists of Chaumont, he had a tendency to refer to them as "lizards". [1460] Sibley wrote "the Division had been severely criticized by General Headquarters because the Yankees lost a large batch of prisoners at Seicheprey. But it happened that General Edwards had nothing to do in this fight except to make suggestions; *Général* Passaga, *corps d'armée* commander, gave orders directly to

"Four heroines of the Battle of Seicheprey": Louise Young, Gladys McIntyre, Ensign Burdick (circled) and Irene McIntyre. (*The Tacoma Times*, May 21 1918)

MAJOR GEORGE J. RAU

CAPTAIN ARTHUR F. LOCKE

CAPTAIN GEORGE C. FREELAND

LIEUTENANT ALBERT JOHNSON

And four heroes. (Strickland, *Connecticut Fights*)

General Traub and Colonel Parker, commanding the 51st Infantry Brigade and the 102nd Regiment."[1461] That theme resonated at the time and continued post-war.

THE FIRST SALVO OF THE AMERICAN PRESS – 21 APRIL

The French released the first official communiqué on the battle in progress at Seicheprey at 0900: "East of ST. MIHIEL, the enemy made this morning a prepared attack on the front of a kilometre towards SEICHEPREY; he gained a footing in some elements of our advanced trenches but our counter-attacks immediately threw him out in part."[1462] Reality was not to be confused with what the public needed to know.

The American press, having waited more than a year for a combat story, feasted on the Seicheprey

fight. A banner headline for the *Washington Post* announced "Huns Pierce American Trenches; Take Seichprey [sic] But are Driven Back." The sub-head announced "1,200 Storm Troops Attack Mile of Front" followed by "Aeros Aid in Assault". The Associated Press reporter revealed that 1,200 German stormtroops, the largest number ever concentrated against the American troops for an offensive operation, were hurled against the American positions. The enemy did succeed in penetrating the front-line trenches and taking the village of Seicheprey. "No Americans Taken." Later updates refuted this. German airmen poured machine-gun fire into the American troops but anti-aircraft batteries came into play and shot down two enemy planes. It was asserted that "The attacking troops carried rations and entrenching tools, indicating that they intended to occupy the American positions for a long period." The AP correspondent viewed the battle from Beaumont Ridge: "Scores of huge shells were seen bursting, throwing up clouds of white smoke in the neighboring hills. The heavy rumbling was heard all day." The drama of the moment was accentuated with the headline, "Men Beg to Fight". "Numbers of men in the rear positions begged their commanders to be sent up to assist the infantrymen bearing the brunt of the attack. The men of all services were eager for an opportunity to fight the enemy in the open."[1463]

The International News Service complemented the lead story with "American Counter Attack Delivered Savagely; Fierce Fighting in Open Areas." This article first mentions German "shock troops" attacking the American infantry. This was an American victory; they had fought back without reinforcements and driven back the enemy after an all-day fight, "marked by exceptional artillery fire and some aerial activity."[1464]

"WAR WITH US IS NO SPORT"

The first introduction of German accounts to the American public came from a *New York Times* article published on 24 April. It said papers received from Berlin the previous day were ablaze with headlines such as "American Positions at Seicheprey Taken" and "Successful Advance on American Line." The *Deutsche Tageszeitung* emphasised the "lesson" of Seicheprey, teaching Americans that "War is Not Sport." The Germans were apparently gloating over American losses. In many ways they paid tribute to the American soldier, something echoed at the highest echelons. "Many Americans were killed by artillery fire in the streets of the village of Seicheprey, their bodies barricading the way of the advancing German troops, who had to drive the Americans from houses, gardens and cellars. But even then Americans continued to fight so tenaciously that they were nearly all killed ... In the woods of Remière, nearby, a similar most sanguinary scene occurred. Here, too, there was bitter fighting, man against man, for the possession of some dugouts ... All reports agree that the Americans made the fiercest possible resistance, notwithstanding that this was probably the first experience which they had had of actual fighting."[1465]

German statements were credible. "Despite their excellent physical condition and yet unbroken vigor, the Americans were not able to withstand the terror of a short artillery preparation, so that our onslaught against their trenches met little resistance."[1466] "North of Beaumont," the *Tageblatt* said, "as well as near Bernecourt, enemy forces were seen advancing at about 2 o'clock in the afternoon, but the German fire broke up their massed formations with heavy losses. At 5 o'clock in the afternoon the enemy trenches at Jury Wood were seen to be full and the German airplanes became active, opening up a machine-gun fire on the American reserves in the rear ... The German batteries then opened fire on the thickly filled trenches at Jury Wood, scattering the American storm troops which were ready to advance. After dark, when the enemy defences and positions were destroyed, we quietly evacuated the positions without the enemy observing it ... The account concludes with the statement that, thanks to the splendid preparation of the whole attack, the German losses were slight, whereas the 'inexperienced

American troops suffered severe losses.'" The *Tageblatt* emphasised that careful preparation was the reason for the attack against American troops on each side of Seicheprey being a complete success. After effective preparation by the artillery and trench mortars, it continued, during which the Americans suffered heavy losses, the Germans stormed the positions on a front of about 2.4 kilometres, and penetrated as much as 2 kilomtres in some places. The fighting near the village is said to have been desperate, and "brave troops were annihilated almost to the last." In the region of *Bois de Remières* there was hand-to-hand combat, and the American losses were "particularly heavy."

The German press put down the "defeat" of the Americans to some extent to the latter's inexperience in warfare. George Wagener wrote in the *Cologne Gazette*, "The Americans have had to learn that war with us is no sport." The *Deutsche Tageszeitung* stated "There is hardly anybody, in Germany who will not say: 'It serves them right.' It is absolutely necessary that the Americans should be taught a lesson concerning the seriousness of war. Our Lower Saxon regiments seem to have done that on April 20 in a manner leaving nothing to be desired. If the Great Headquarters [OHL] reports mention 'extremely heavy losses' we know what that means. We also know what it means when from enemy positions two kilometers and a half long our troops return with only 180 prisoners. The Americans must have had terrible, sanguinary losses. This lesson was badly needed."[1467]

Information acquired from Lieutenant Burke, the doctor captured at Seicheprey, proved a lightning rod for German discussion of the declining morale among the soldiers: "The *Cologne Volkszeitung* alleges that in one battalion alone no less than six soldiers committed suicide in order not to have to go to the front lines." The paper added they shot themselves while cleaning rifles. The *New York Times* sought to head off the suggestion with, "In an effort to minimize the work of the American troops on the Western front the German papers are endeavoring to prove that the morale of the American troops is very bad and that the depression of the soldiers is increasing daily."[1468]

For one American in the Seicheprey battle the comments coming from Berlin contrasted with what he knew. Their official statement of the affair was that it was nothing more than a big raid, in which the withdrawal was just as much a part of the program as was the attack. His reasoning echoed Rau's comment: "The untruthfulness of this statement is shown in the fact that the German troops carried their packs, trench shovels and rations, indicating that they planned to hold any position they might be successful in taking."[1469]

The French media now entered the fray. A dispatch from Paris reported by the *New York Times* denied that shock troops penetrated American and French lines in front of Seicheprey. The fight resulted in the enemy being "energetically forced back to his own lines." It was a "brilliant counter-attack which put them once more in possession of Seicheprey and permitted them to take prisoners ... close co-operation of the two armies once more brought marvelous results which gave us complete success. The ground we previously occupied was completely recaptured, and the enemy, energetically forced back to his own lines, left prisoners in our hands and many dead in front of our barbed wire."[1470]

Four days after the attack the *New York Times* reported the German assertions that Paris reports regarding "the Seicheprey affair" were pure inventions, particularly the Allied details provided to the French wireless service that addressed the reoccupation of trenches by the Americans. The French version was that the Americans successfully recaptured lost ground. The German report stated that the Americans did not regain their positions until about midnight of 21 April when American and French patrols cautiously reconnoitred them. The Germans stated that between 0500 and 0600 the Americans resumed possession of their lost positions. The German reports, now labelled as propaganda, claimed that they never planned to continue the occupation of Seicheprey. The Germans stated that being on low ground, Seicheprey was not in any way suitable for defensive purposes.[1471]

German correspondents at the front who did not witness Seicheprey would continue the battle over perception and reality. Max Osborn in the *Vossiche Zeitung* wrote:

> According to the Americans' own assertions, they hoped to prove the military superiority of American soldiers by surprising raids, by the tenacity of nerve which is the characteristic of a young nation, and by their dexterity in hand-to-hand fighting gained in the practice of many sports. But they have become victims of a complete surprise in the section of the Moselle hills that has been entrusted to them because at that shot each opponent was able to look right into the other's position and observe at long range any offensive preparations. Only a short artillery preparation sufficed to take two and a half kilometres of their position, with scarcely any loss on our part, and in the fight of man to man in and around the village American boxer tricks availed little against our war veterans. If here American troops paid heavily for want of experience, it is only fair to state that lack of ability in conducting operations was responsible if their losses were increased disproportionately when troops were hurried to their aid from the east over exposed roads, right into the German barrage fire, which made it impossible for them to join the battle.[1472]

The *Literary Press* quoted the semi-official Wolff Telegraphic Bureau that the affair was nothing more than a big raid in which the withdrawal was just as much a part of the program as the attack: "Seicheprey was taken by storm and was found full of American dead. Bitter hand-to-hand fighting ensued around dugouts, vantage-points, and cellars, whose occupants were killed almost to the last man ... Severe hand-to-hand fighting also occurred about dugouts in Remières Wood. Here the American casualties were especially heavy ... After dark, when the enemy's defense works and dugouts had been destroyed and blown up, we evacuated the position according to our plans, and unobserved by the enemy. Our losses were slight while those of the untrained Americans were most severe. We captured five officers, one doctor, and 179 men, as well as twenty-five machine guns." [1473]

The 21 April 1918 was not a day for German celebration over Seicheprey. It was overshadowed by the death of **Rittmeister** Manfred von Richthofen, shot down by anti-aircraft fire over the Somme and killed.

DAY 2 – 22 APRIL

The *New York Times* banner headline stated: "3,000 Attacked Americans; Futile German Drive was Much more than a Trench Raid; Launched to Terrify Us; German Prisoners Say it was Meant 'to Teach the Americans a Lesson.'" The press now had a real battle to describe involving Americans on the Western Front:

> Its issue warrants high hopes in the great struggle. The fight for Seicheprey was something more than a raid, even on an important scale, for the cardinal principle of raids is the retirement of the assailants to their own lines as soon as possible after their purpose is achieved, and on this occasion the enemy intended to hold such ground as he could gain. In fact, it appears, according to the statements of prisoners, that the German object was 'to teach the Americans a lesson' that would discourage them from tackling more important operations in the great western battle. If that be the case, the German expectations were singularly disappointed, for the final American and French counter-attack recovered every foot of the ground originally lost and 'our line is integrally re-established.' [1474]

The author of the article provided his analysis. The Germans were aiming for a junction point of the Allied lines with the blow being delivered by special "storm troops" after a short, but heavy, bombardment with gas and HE shells. The article stated that the calibre of the German

divisions in this sector was not first class, based on insight from French experts. None of the elite German divisions were positioned along the whole front from the Oise river to Switzerland. Further analysis described the geographic situation with the Germans occupying the high ground – describing a steep hill (Montsec) some 275 metres in height next to Seicheprey. *Côte 380* was in reality 120 metres high. The attack now had "3,000 men fighting in three columns preceded by picked stormtroops ... Tactics of 'infiltration,' as the French call it – that is, of gradual progress in small groups, supported by quick-firers, along the line of entry thus made in the allied line, with the object of taking our centre in the rear." The counter-attack recovered the village before dawn. "Bitter fighting among the trees" was mentioned. The Germans retreated by Saturday evening. "In view of their defeat, it is not improbable that the Germans will try to represent the affair as a big raid and boast that they withdrew 'according to instructions,' but the troops engaged on both sides know better. For the first time the Germans have met the Americans in serious fighting, and, as the French say, 'they have broken their noses.' It is a good augury for America."

The London *Times* mentioned Seicheprey for the first time on 22 April with "Largest Single Attack on Americans." With each day of the war the public was reminded of the cost. On that day "The War: 4th Year: 262nd Day" was printed after the main column headline. Based on the French communiqués, the British public learned how the Americans were doing: "They lost the village of Seicheprey, but regained it, and inflicted heavy casualties on the enemy." More important for the British reader was news coming from their own frontlines "A Month of Battles" was the column heading. [1475]

DAY 3 – 23 APRIL

The numbers now became headlines: "AMERICANS LOST 200 TO 300, GERMANS 300 TO 400 AT SEICHEPREY;

OUR TROOPS' BRAVE RESISTANCE BALKED ENEMY'S PLAN" *New York Times*. The *Washington Post* flashed the headline, "U.S. Losses 200; Teuton over 400, in Battle, Gen. Pershing Reports; Americans 'Fought to a Finish.'" Albert W. Fox said a report to the War Department on the fighting in and near Seicheprey "would make good reading for the American people." The debate turned on numbers. Casualties were one thing, and now possible large numbers of prisoners of war evolved into an issue that had not been seen since the Civil War 53 years prior. The *New York Times* read: "Brief Report by Pershing; His Estimate of Losses Said to be Based on Incomplete Reports." The subtitles touched the story that was brewing: "Baker Withholds Details. No Contradiction Obtainable of German Story of 183 American Prisoners."

That day a special report in the *New York Times* covered the growing point of contention: "Washington Gives Out no Information About Alleged Capture of 183 Americans; No Explanation Offered; Course is Criticized at Capital – Unchallenged German Claims Likely to Affect Neutrals. Attention turned to Pershing and the War Department." "Not a word is obtainable from any authoritative source in the military administration to indicate whether the German claim is true or false." The article flagged up the lack of verification from both the American military and the War Department. The Wolff Bureau's account that Americans were "mauled" hit a nerve. The *New York Times* narrowed the discussion. The War Department was receiving reports from General Pershing but was declining to furnish any information whatever to the American public. The public was becoming aware of important information being withheld. The *New York Times* began to scold: "No explanation for this attitude is forthcoming, except that when Secretary Baker was in France he agreed with General Pershing that all news of American operations should be furnished to the press by General Pershing's headquarters and not by the War Department."[1476]

Names behind the numbers began to emerge. The *Hartford Courant* published on May 4: "39 Connecticut Men Fall Before Enemy; 13 Killed, 26 Wounded – All Fell On Day of Battle of Seicheprey on April 20." It was the first of many more similar articles published at the local level.[1477]

AEF CONCERNS OVER THE FOURTH ESTATE

One experienced war commentator later claimed that Seicheprey proved the 26th Division "had a plethora of fight spirit and a dearth of fight know-how." Back in the United States, the press theme that Seicheprey was retaken weighed heavily. Many felt that Seicheprey was the first American victory of note. American press dispatches and French communiqués, in the absence of an official GHQ AEF communiqué, stressed the gallantry of American soldiers while German communiqués, reprinted habitually in the American press, emphasised the disproportionate casualties and the relative ease with which Seicheprey fell. Frederick Palmer observed these developments and cautioned General Pershing that there might be more Seichepreys. It was not wise to allow Allies and enemies to continue their attempts to interpret AEF intentions and actions for American public consumption. Seicheprey made Pershing understand that publication of its own daily communiqué or periodic statements released from Chaumont should be initiated. From the War Department on 6 May, General March advised Pershing that Secretary of War Baker had reconsidered and rescinded his earlier order authorising Chaumont alone to release news of the American army in France. Baker now wanted the War Department to release whatever information "the condition of the public mind of America makes desirable." Pershing was directed to provide the War Department with a daily communiqué containing "facts of substantial value" about the activities of his command. Stories from the *Stars and Stripes* should now contain information "of distinct value in keeping up the interest of the people at home in our army abroad." Later in May, the AEF published the first of its daily communiqués.[1478]

The first press dispatches from correspondents with the American Expeditionary Forces said that no Americans were taken prisoner. It is impossible to be more definite in stating what was contained in the dispatch from General Pershing, because the War Department, unlike the War Offices of Great Britain, France and Italy, declined to give out any official information concerning actions in which American troops were engaged. When asked about the German assertion that 183 American soldiers had been captured, Secretary Baker declined to authorise any statement. The press then asked why the War Department did not issue a daily bulletin in regard to military operations affecting American troops. Baker replied that as the American forces were part of the French Army, any statement as to their operations would be covered in the French communiqués. He admitted, however, that the German report that 183 American soldiers had been captured did raise the issue of an American bulletin. The *New York Times* concluded that as things stood, the War Department had information with regard to Seicheprey but declined to make any of it public, although correspondents with the American forces were permitted to cable accounts of the engagements back to the United States.[1479]

Nine years later, *New York Times* reporter Edwin L. James recalled that on the morning of 21 April, "the distinguished gentleman commanding the division, which came from New England [Major General Edwards], sat in a little chateau in the village of Bocq [*sic*] and told a group of gullible correspondents of a German attack on Seicheprey the night before and what a victory the Americans had. The story went back to America." James described denials from Washington being proven wrong when a German aeroplane flew over American lines the following day and dropped mimeographed sheets containing names, outfits, and home addresses of the prisoners of war from Seicheprey. A few days

later another aeroplane flew over and dropped photographs.[1480]

In the absence of an official source the press made the case that German sympathisers in the United States were able to circulate false or exaggerated AEF losses, creating distress among relatives of soldiers. At the same time the press described disinformation coming from odd sources, such as a Liberty Loan orator in a vaudeville theater in New York telling his audience that word had been received from Washington that the 69th New York Regiment (42nd Division) had been virtually wiped out. Such a statement uttered by a man designated to speak in the Liberty Loan drive not only had the potential to create reckless assumptions but also aided German sympathisers. As the *New York Times* pointed out two days after the affair, "With the War Department declining to furnish information as to the engagement at Seicheprey or to say whether it has advices to confirm or deny the German assertion that 183 American prisoners were taken by the enemy, there is no means to counteract indiscreet statements of that character."[1481]

The *Washington Post* pointed out that the French statement was made for the French people and the German statement was made to the German people. Unfortunately, there was no arrangement for an American official statement for the American people. The article asked for an unbiased account of what General Pershing's men did on this occasion. Poignantly, the discussion ended with German accounts of heavy American losses – causing much anxiety in the United States. The article concludes with the author putting words in Pershing's mouth: "This German statement of heavy American losses may, therefore, be taken with more than one grain of salt. Nevertheless it would be more reassuring if the American people had an official statement from General Pershing, perhaps something like this: 'Enemy shock troops pressed our line back 1¾ miles and occupied Seicheprey before we, with the French, counter-attacked, regaining all lost ground. Our casualties not heavy.'"[1482] The *New York Times* summed up their position:

One possible explanation of the present refusal to enlighten the American public as to what occurred at Seicheprey – although the suggestion does not come from any official source – is that the War Department is still without definite information from General Pershing as to the losses suffered in that action. There were indications last night that General Pershing had been unable to check up on the number of American casualties, including prisoners taken by the enemy, and further reports from him were awaited. But not one word would officials say to make it appear that this was the reason for the refusal to answer the German claim that 183 American soldiers had been captured … The understanding obtained here last night from excellent sources that General Pershing had reported that the American losses at Seicheprey were between 200 and 300 and the German losses between 300 and 400, including killed, wounded, and prisoners, brought no definite response today when it was called to the attention of high officials. Instead, some of those in authority spent time in endeavoring to locate the 'leak' through which this information reached the press. It was intimated that the information was incorrect, a statement in marked opposition to the effort to ascertain where the newspapers obtained the information.[1483]

A sub-section to the *New York Times* special report also touched on a strategic issue that had implications for American foreign policy – "Unchallenged German Claims Likely to Affect Neutrals":

Those who criticise the War Department's course say the German claim that a heavy defeat was inflicted on American troops will be spread throughout the neutral countries of Europe to the damage of America's standing as a potential factor in the war … Just now Germany is apparently making a determined attempt to draw Holland into the war on the side of the Central Powers, and the fact that the allegation of an American defeat goes uncontradicted gives strength to the German argument that the Allies and their co-belligerent from across the Atlantic are playing a losing game. Word comes from Holland tonight that the country is being flooded with German newspapers containing accounts of the Seicheprey battle, which represent the American forces as having been wholly defeated. These accounts may find a fertile soil in the minds of people who have been told that the United States was a negligible quantity in the war.

A BARRAGE FIRE OF BABY BONDS

One of the leading American weekly magazines, *The Outlook*, wrote on the Seicheprey battle using the occasion to encourage people to buy more Liberty Bonds. Seicheprey became a rallying cry:

At this writing, April 23, the Third Liberty Bond campaign has eleven more days to run. Americans have eleven more days to show how thoroughly they are determined to back up their brothers and sons who are fighting at the western front to free the world from German slavery. The bravery of our American soldiers needs no advertisement or emphasis. They have just fought their first big battle, the Battle of Seicheprey. Up to this time our troops had been engaged in small raiding parties and in trench warfare … The complete details have not yet been made public by our Government, but it is clear that our soldiers were not only brave but efficient, and their fighting qualities won the complete approval and applause of their allies. It is apparent that the Germans intended to break through to terrify and wipe out the American sector. In this purpose they made a hopeless failure … No matter how many bonds you have bought, go out and buy some more – at least one Baby Bond of $50 in honor of Seicheprey … Let us give the Prussians a barrage fire of Baby Bonds on the last day.[1484]

SALLIES

News from the front lines of the McIntyre sisters, Irene and Gladys, gave the reading public an escape from the grimness. The *New York Times* on 24 April described their exploits with "Mount Vernon Girls Under Fire." Gladys and Irene "during the height of the engagement handed out to the soldiers coffee, chocolate, doughnuts and much good cheer. They went on with their work while the shells were falling all around them, and would not leave until, at last, they were ordered to do so. Now they are called "daughters of the regiment". Irene McIntyre was quoted, 'We want to go back to our boys. They are the finest fellows in the world, not afraid of anything. Any woman would be glad to die to serve them. It is inspiring to hear them talk, for they are filled with enthusiasm and determination to fight to the finish. They say they would like to go home, but not until the victory has been won. When there is a lull in the trenches they come to our village and help us to wash dishes and cook."[1485] The *Hartford Courant* continued the next day relating how the sisters served under fire for 8 hours until a staff officer compelled them to seek safety further back.[1486] The *New York Times* followed up with "The girls of the corps were equipped with gas masks, helmets and revolvers."

SHOTGUNS

Albert W. Fox writing for the *Washington Post* on 23 April under a sub-heading of "Used 'Sawed Off' Guns" described how Americans on several occasions, including the fighting at Seicheprey, were "treating the German shock troops to a most unwelcomed surprise by the use of sawed-off, double barreled shotguns on advancing Teutons with terrific effect." Fox described sprays of buckshot covering a wide area providing a surprise to German shock troops not accustomed to the lethal spray. He mentioned that General Pershing surprised the War Department by asking for 10,000 sawed-off shotguns as used by "the old stage coach drivers on the Western plains."[1487] Both *The Outlook* and *The Literary Digest* made mention of the shotgun at Seicheprey: "They seem to have been effective as weapons of defense, for the correspondents say that the spray of widely scattered buckshot was demoralizing to the advancing German line."[1488]

The Literary Digest got technical: "In this battle, we are told by the *New York Sun*, our boys used a new weapon of the shot-gun type which 'sprays an area nine feet wide and three feet high with balls that will go through two inches of board at one hundred and fifty yards.' This gun is said to be peculiar to the American Army."[1489] The final piece came from *Baseball Magazine*: "The Shotgun Goes to War, *Baseball Magazine* Wins its Fight to Send the Shotgun 'Over the Top' – New 'Trench Gun' Wipes out Huns at Seicheprey." The magazine made it clear that the weapon would "help drive the hordes of Kaiserdom back across the Rhine … Nothing since the introduction of the 'tank' has created so great a sensation among the military men of the world … The gun now being used by Pershing's troops is known as the 'trench gun'." Citing Peter P. Carney, a well-known sporting writer, it noted: "Shotguns are being used effectively in this greatest of all wars. The victory of the American troops at Seicheprey, April 20, was due to the fighting ability of the Americans and the effectiveness of the trench gun … the shotgun would be decidedly more useful than the bayonet, while it would prove less repulsive to our men than the use of 'cold steel.'" An attached bayonet to the single-barrelled shotgun provided an additional benefit: "Also the bayonet is long enough to penetrate beautifully, smoothly and delightfully even a Teutonic waistline." On 8 June the War Department officially announced that 1,000 shotguns were now in depots in France. The 26th Division and 42nd Division each received fifty shotguns to conduct a practical test of the weapon with results provided to the War Department the following month. They were given instructions on proper use to include consideration for future raids.[1490]

The front page of the *New York Tribune*, 21 April 1918.

BRAVADO

Bluster and braggadocio made for exciting reading immediately after the battle. The *New York Times* on 21 April followed by the *Washington Post* on 23 April told the same story, from the

Associated Press: "'Kill the Huns' Our Best Game, Says a Wounded American Lad.'" "'Tell them back home that we are just beginning,' said a lad who was in the thick of the fighting of Saturday at Seicheprey, his back now almost perforated with shrapnel. 'It was fine to see our men go at the

Huns. All of us who thought baseball was the great American game have changed our minds. There is only one game to keep the American flag flying – that is, kill the Huns. I got several before they got me.'" The article ended with the villain of the moment, a wounded German prisoner treated in another ward, who after throwing up his hands to surrender had concealed bombs he had ready to kill use. "A nurse said that he had given more trouble than all the Americans' combined."[1491]

The International News Service managed to elicit more drama from Seicheprey's wounded: "As the Germans tumbled in on us our corporal killed five with his revolver in quick succession. I never saw such a shot." Another was quoted: "We crawled through a trench over some dead Germans ... We crawled through a barrage that reminded me of a story I once read, by Dante, called 'Inferno,' only there was too much racket in this one to be like the one in the book." And a further quote revealed: "Another private who manned a machine gun stationed in what is known as 'Dead Man's Curve' said: 'I tried to keep the road clear and make it safe for our couriers. I finally got mine and here I am. Just let me get another whack at 'em for killing two fellows of our squad, and I'm willing to be planted on the hill with the rows of little wooden crosses.'"[1492]

The reporting helped fan the flames: "One correspondent says that the attacking Germans were 'dope-crazed' and 'like wild men, singing and yelling as they advanced.'"[1493] The Italian newspaper *L'Epoca* of 17 May under "The Bravery of the American Troops" contributed to the feverish outrage by stating: "That evening the ambulance station in Seicheprey was blown up, and the doctor and nurses killed or wounded."[1494]

"HINDENBURG'S TRAVELING CIRCUS"

If there was a tag line that became the lasting legacy of Seicheprey it was the apt description of the **Sturmbataillon.14** and the **Stosstruppen** of **Res. I. R. 258** and **Res. I. R. 259**. The source of the description that survived for all time was never fully revealed. It showed up in newspaper articles

shortly after the affair. Two members of Battery C, 102nd Field Artillery, Lieutenant Sirois and Corporal McGinnis, labelled the attack force in their 1919 book: "Twelve hundred picked German Shock Troops (Hindenburg's Traveling Circus, as we call them) came over the top and advanced towards our lines to teach the Yankees a lesson."[1495] Other histories addressed the German force but varied the numbers. Benwell's history, for example, states: "The German **'Sturmtruppen**,' or Hindenburg's Traveling Circus, as it was called, led the attack. These were a body of picked shock troops, which traveled from place to place, along the German line and delivered raids at regular intervals. After a heavy bombardment they came over, about 400 in number, with about 2,500 more Germans following to consolidate the positions the raiders were expected to take."[1496]

FINAL SIGN OFF

The *Stars and Stripes* in their bi-monthly newspaper for the troops featured an account by Frank Sibley on 26 April: "Hun Attack Smashed by Yankee Defenders". His audience learned that the "fifteen hundred storm troops ... intended to occupy permanently our front line and consolidate it." Without naming names Sibley gave the readers an exciting account on the exploits of several key players, including Captain Griswold and *colonel* Bertrand. Sibley concluded with an account of a sergeant and private buried alive by artillery and managing to dig themselves out from the debris; "Then this pair of unkillables walked to the aid station."[1497]

As for Frank Sibley, he remained a *Boston Globe* reporter until suffering a heart attack in 1934. Sibley worked as an editor from home for the rest of his career. Housebound, with impaired sight, he proclaimed to his 26th Division friends and readership, "I claim still to be happier than any other man I know, and proud to be accounted a friend remembered through a quarter of a century by the gang whose stock greeting was 'Hey, reporter! When are we going home?'"[1498]

CHAPTER 26

Body Count

Winston Churchill wrote in his massive work *The World Crisis* one of the most eloquent statements on positional war. His first chapter on 1915 entitled "The Deadlock in the West" addresses the turmoil and suffering that was being experienced that year – a war that everyone realised in 1915 would not to be ending soon: "By the mistakes of this year the opportunity was lost of confining the conflagration within limits which, though enormous, were not uncontrolled. Thereafter the fire roared on till it burnt itself out." Three years later conflict in the Woëvre continued to strike that awful chord: "Two, and even three, British or French lives were repeatedly paid for the killing of one enemy, and grim calculations were made to prove that in the end the Allies would still have a balance of a few millions to spare." Churchill's views regarding the failure of the military art are relevant to the French policy of "sacrifice positions". Churchill averred that battles were won by slaughter and manoeuvre: "The greater the general, the more he contributes to manoeuvre, the less he demands in slaughter ... The theory which has exalted the '*bataille d'usure*' or 'battle of wearing down' into a foremost position, is contradicted by history and would be repulsed by the greatest captains of the past."[1499] America's effort at the Woëvre became what Churchill called "counting heads at the end."

CHAUMONT CONCERNS OVER CASUALTIES

In a post-war memorandum to the AEF chief of staff, Brigadier General Fox Conner assessed casualty rates suffered by American forces while serving under French and American command. Conner's aggregate showed the 1st Division suffering 900 casualties per day while serving under French commanders. Under American control, the 1st Division suffered only 507 casualties for a twenty-day period. Conner's analysis was intended to show American command was superior in every case cited. Looking at the numbers of casualties for each division per day in the line provides a different perspective. American casualties jumped from 285 per day under French command to 304 per day under American command. This perhaps suggests a command culture that was becoming obsessed with defending the reputation of the leadership at the expense of those who paid the butcher's bill.[1500]

Numbers were easily consumed by Americans. In this, the German dismissal of Americans as seeing combat as a game is credible. The amount of casualties at the Woëvre, particularly in the Seicheprey affair, focused GHQ AEF's attention on the matter. Re-manning was not the problem – the ongoing arrival of thousands of American soldiers in theatre each week made that issue moot. What had to be attended to in the first months on the line was the perception of the public back home. Some commanders actually saw attrition in combat as healthy. Large numbers of casualties seemed to fit with Allied experiences to date and the prevailing view of some high-ranking officers was that they showed the war was being fought "in the right way" by the newcomers. Such was the case with Seicheprey.

The media's voracious appetite for news from the front created a dilemma for American commanders, particularly General Pershing and his chief of staff, Major General Harbord. Casualties required proper notification by authorities. In the French system, it was the responsibility of the mayor of the town where the deceased resided to notify a family of a death. Chaumont became aware of the process when the French press republished lists of American casualties received back from the United States by cable. When the 1st Division suffered losses in *Bois de Remières* from Bruns' gas attack on 26 February, the French press release of the names prompted General Pershing to request the War Department to change their process. Publicising casualties associated with a particular operation informed the enemy about its success. Pershing made it policy not to release casualty lists to correspondents covering American operations. The War Department became responsible for first notifying families.[1501]

Major Bowditch initially reported to Chaumont late on the night of 21 April that "No accurate information with regard to losses could be obtained. At best only a very approximate estimate could be made. The regimental surgeon stated that 150 to 200, all told, had been evacuated through the regimental aid station and the French. This included men from the Engineers and machine gun battalion." Major Bowditch led a three-man team to Beaumont to discuss what happened with 102nd Infantry officers, combatants, and staff. It proved to be a difficult task. He reported to Chaumont that the numbers reeked of overestimate. "Later when we left the regimental P.C. and were at Brigade Headquarters telephone information was received from the

regimental adjutant." Captain Taylor stated there were 287 casualties for the 1st Battalion, 39 killed, 55 wounded, 193 missing. The list of officers to date showed 1 dead, 4 wounded, 5 missing. At the 26th Division headquarters they repeated that the German communiqué claimed 180 men and 5 officers as prisoners. Bowditch also discussed casualties with *commandant* du Boisrouvray. His casualty estimate was between 400 and 450.[1502] Du Boisrouvray reported on 9 May that the Germans "suffered heavy losses." The 102nd Infantry and *162ᵉ régiment d'infanterie* buried a total of 109 Germans. The Germans had three dressing stations. The dressing station near *Bois de Remières* was evacuated on the morning of the attack, where he assessed that 15 Germans were killed, including 2 officers. He estimated that 80 wounded were treated at that station. The station north of Seicheprey handled 70 wounded Germans.[1503]

NUMBERS IN ACTION

Colonel Bertrand reported to *69ᵉ division d'infanterie* seniors on 21 April that "The Battalion commander in SEICHEPREY estimated the number of assailants at about 1,200 men."[1504] General Edwards reported on 23 April that their estimates of the strength of the German attack based on the latest operation assessment was "About 100 men from the 14th Sturm Battalion. Entire regiment of **Res. I. R. 259**. two or three companies of **Res. I. R. 258** used as a west flanking group. Part of their equipment consisted of small **MW** (five or six) for the **Sturmbataillon**, and each **Kompagnie** of the **Res. I. R. 259** was equipped with one **Flammenwerfer**. Intelligence confirmed that **Res. I. R. 259** withdrew from the front on 13 April to train for the operation."[1505] Various reports such as the 26th Division's Operation Report also mentioned 1200 men but that referred to 1,200 **Stosstruppen** in the main attacking party, with a 650-man battalion of German infantry on either flank in support — a total force of 2500 Germans attacking that morning.[1506] French liaison *commandant* du Boisrouvray reported to his seniors the German attack comprised 1

Sturmbataillon (two infantry companies, one machine gun company, and one company of **Minenwerfer**, **Pioniere** and **Flammenwerfer**. The entire **Res. I. R. 259**, two or three companies of the **Res. I. R. 258** were with one battalion of **Res. I. R. 260** in reserve at *Bois de Sonnard*. His estimate had 3,300 German soldiers committed to the attack, of which 1,800 men comprised the key assault force of **Sturmbataillon.14** and two battalions of **Res. I. R. 259**.[1507] Frank Sibley published what were considered the numbers post-war in his book, stating the German force totalled 3,300 men and Major Rau's 1st Battalion force numbered about 350.[1508]

Losses on both sides up to the Seicheprey affair were not catastrophic. **Einladung** showed 41 casualties and missing from the German ranks. The 1st Division's 18th Infantry listed 49 casualties and missing. At *Bois-Brûlé*, GHQ AEF reported the 104th Infantry lost 37 killed and 75 wounded. The report also mentioned 36 **5. Ldw.D.** prisoners captured by the Americans.[1509] **General der Infanterie** Auler reported after the war the German casualties for **Blinddarm** were 32 dead, 161 wounded, and 57 missing.[1510]

On 21 April, **78. R. D.** forwarded a casualty report to **Gruppe Gorz** and higher heaquarters. The summary covered all German combatants. eighty-two men were killed and missing, 263 were wounded, and sixteen men suffered other injuries. The total casualties for the German forces that were accounted for a day after the battle came to 361.[1511] On the American side, General Pershing's aide Major Collins forwarded to Chaumont an accounting of American losses a week after the battle that listed 2 officers, 56 enlisted men killed; 5 officers, 140 enlisted men wounded; and 5 officers and 221 enlisted men missing.[1512]

COLONEL PARKER'S REPORT ON 102ND INFANTRY AND 102ND MACHINE GUN BATTALION

	Officers	Men	Killed	Wounded	Missing
Co. A	7	209	2	10	0
Co. B	4	191	1	19	1
Co. C	5	209	19	34	44
Co. D	4	208	16	40	50
Co. E	5	210	5	20	0
Co. F	5	168	0	1	0
Co. G	8	201	0	2	1
Co. H	8	198	0	2	0
Co. I	5	189	7	30	0
Co. K	9	183	1	3	0
Co. L	8	136	1	4	0
Co. M	5	122	4	10	0
M.G. Co.	7	133	0	0	0
Hdq. Co.	7	294	2	9	4
Supply Co.	4	141	0	0	0
San. Det.	10	41	0	1	8
102nd M.G. Bn			11	22	26
(3 guns captured; 3 destroyed)					
101st Engrs			0	1	0[1513]

APRIL 21, 1918. [GERMAN] CASUALTY REPORT TO GENERAL COMMAND

The following losses have thus far been ascertained:

258th Reserve Inf. Regt.
6 men slightly wounded.
9 men badly wounded, including **Leutnant** Lange.
2 bodies recovered.

259th Reserve Inf. Regt.
102 men slightly wounded, including 2 officers (**Leutnant** Mueller and **Leutnant** Hillemann), who will remain with their units. 42 men badly wounded, including **Leutnant** Gravenhorst, who died later. 35 bodies recovered, including those of **Leutnant** Knoop and **Leutnant** Tapke.
17 men ascertained to be dead, but bodies not recovered.
7 men missing (whereabouts thus far not ascertained).
14 men with other injuries.

14th Assault Battalion
51 men badly or slightly wounded.
13 bodies recovered, including that of **Leutnant** Schmidt.
6 men missing (whereabouts thus far not ascertained).

79th Reserve Engineer Company
2 men slightly wounded.
2 men badly wounded.

80th Reserve Engineer Company
4 men slightly wounded.
3 men badly wounded.

278th Trench-Mortar Company
1 man badly wounded.

260th Trench-Mortar Company
3 men slightly wounded
2 men badly wounded

282nd Trench-Mortar Company
1 man badly wounded (died in meantime).

181st Trench-Mortar Company
1 man slightly wounded.

62nd Reserve Field Art. Regt.
6 men slightly wounded, including **Leutnant** Poppe.
1 man badly wounded.
1 body recovered.

3rd Guard Field Art. Regt.
2 men slightly wounded.

6th Battery, 256th Landwehr Field Art. Regt.
1 man slightly wounded.

6th Battery, 402 Field Art. Regt.
1 man slightly wounded

9th Battery, 8th Landwehr Field Art. Regt.
5 men slightly wounded.
2 men badly wounded.
1 body recovered.

8th Battery, 97th Field Art. Regt.
3 men slightly wounded, including **Leutnant** Luer, and
3 men badly wounded.

2nd Battery, 41st Landwehr Foot Art. Regt.
1 man slightly wounded.
1 man badly wounded.

4th Battery, 41st Landwehr Foot Art. Regt.
1 man slightly wounded

4th Battery, 42nd Landwehr Foot Art. Regt.
4 men slightly wounded
3 men badly wounded
1 man with other injuries (gas).[1514]

SUMMARY

Killed and missing	82 men
Wounded	263 men
Other injuries	16 men
TOTAL	361 men[1515]

"ABSURD RESULTS"

Colonel Bertrand reported *162ᵉ régiment d'infanterie* losses during the fighting on the 20th and the night of 20th to 21st were five dead (one NCO, four *poilu*) and nineteen wounded (one officer, two NCOs, sixteen *poilu*).[1516]

The 102nd Field Hospital gave details at 0600 on the 21st that total casualties they handled came to 257: 147 wounded, 32 sick, 42 suffering from shell shock. The remainder were deaths.[1517] 102nd Field Artillery reported losses at four men killed, one officer and eighteen men wounded, and four men missing. The missing men belonged to the liaison detachment in the front-line trenches and were among those captured.[1518]

On 27 April General Edwards reported through Major Collins to Chaumont two officers and fifty-six enlisted men killed; five officers and 140 enlisted men wounded, and five officers and 221 enlisted men missing for a total of 429 men as of that date.[1519] Two weeks later he revised the numbers to "not greater than 270."[1520] Brigadier General Craig recalled this time. "For two days reports as to losses were made over the telephone by General Edwards who positively denied any losses and claimed absurd results in connection with enemy killed and wounded, and he never did admit losses until I sent him a picture of his prisoners taken with a full list of their names."[1521]

Frank Sibley's body count suggested the numbers reflected a clear win for the Yankee Division: "When it was over, our total casualties were 634; this includes some 130 prisoners, and a large number of wounded in supporting units which were under day-long artillery fire. Our killed were only eighty."[1522]

IDENTIFICATION

Accounting for casualties was never an easy process. Identification tags existed but in catastrophic cases hit by artillery rounds, what remained did not always allow for accurate identification. Private William O'Sullivan, a native of Bristol, Connecticut and fighting with Company D, was a case in point. At the height of the battle O'Sullivan's friend was mortally wounded beyond recognition. O'Sullivan took his blouse off and covered his friend's remains, which resulted in the dead body being identified as William O'Sullivan. The Army officially notified the O'Sullivan family in Bristol by telegram that William was killed in action. The next day after the family learned of O'Sullivan's "death" the *Bristol Press* published the sad news. Ironically, the *Gazette des Ardennes* printed the most accurate list of prisoners and listed "21. William Sullivan". A funeral mass was held for O'Sullivan in Bristol and the family grieved. Meanwhile, O'Sullivan

Todesanzeige for the three officers killed at Seicheprey, posted by Major Bruns, KTK. (*Nachrichten für Staat und Oldenburg*)

was processed as a prisoner of war and spent the remainder of the hostilities in Germany. He was able to send a postcard that June asking for a lockable box, rice, beans, cheese and crackers. An O'Sullivan cousin, Bill Haller, sent the family a letter later that August stating "Bill is not dead" and was a prisoner. Haller clarified that the chaplain processing the accounting of the dead knew every man killed and confirmed that O'Sullivan was not confirmed as a casualty. All correspondence for some reason was delayed and arrived in Bristol in October. At about the same time, the O'Sullivan family also received an official notice from the French government confirming the Germans had released names and William O'Sullivan was included. He returned home to Bristol and lived another 18 years.[1523]

GERMAN CASUALTY ESTIMATES

Based on statements acquired from members of every assault unit, German reporting up to **OHL** stated "the enemy suffered extremely heavy losses. 60-70 bodies were counted in REMIERES Wood alone by parties of the various companies assigned to that task. About 30-40 men were killed in the counter-attacks from the direction of JURY Wood, which were repelled by machine-gun fire, and when the crew that escaped from the American nest at v was dispersed. The number of dugouts blown up or set ablaze by all the assault battalions amounts to from 70 to 80, according to reports from these battalions. A good many of these dugouts were destroyed, together with their crews. After examination of the various reports, the number of enemy dead will likely be estimated at from 200–300."[1524]

The initial estimates of German casualties came from Captain Griswold, Company C. Despite his traumatic experience of being nearly captured and barely escaping through two barrages, Griswold managed to report to Major Rau that his count of Germans killed was 300. Confusing reports based on Griswold's account trickled back to Colonel Parker. General Traub

forwarded the 300 German casualties comment on to Chaumont and had it published in the Operations Report. Captain Griswold was taken to the 102nd Field Hospital and treated. The 26th Division's official summary signed by General Edwards on 23 April attempted to put everything in order. Edwards stated that "our forces lost heavily". In the same breath the report added, "it is believed the enemy suffered very severe losses and paid dearly for the raid." The report cited *colonel* Bertrand as the source of the 300 casualty count in *Bois de Remières*. The missing remains? "All their dead and wounded in this locality were carried away, stretcher bearers carrying white flags continuing this work during the battle." Other pieces of evidence were thrown in: "One of our officers going over the ground on the 22nd reports having seen nine dead bodies, one an officer. Rows of helmets, probably indicating where rows of German dead had been laid preparatory to carrying away, were found in and near *Bois de Remières*."[1525]

The 26th Division provided a methodology to estimate German casualties: "From the fact that the counted German dead buried by the Americans was reported to be about 45 and that if we consider the ratio of dead to wounded as 1 to 9, it would give us as German casualties about 450. It must be remembered, however, that the Germans carried off presumably more of their dead, which might make these figures larger, although it is believed that the ratio of 1 to 9 is too large."[1526] Reports received by Traub said over forty German corpses were buried. Colonel Parker reported that many German dead were buried by his men. Sixteen German dead were reported cared for in *Bois de Remières* by the French. Nine more German dead were found by patrols out in front of Seicheprey near the old first line. Major Rau reported that his men at Seicheprey buried thirty of the enemy and during the last night before the 2nd Battalion was relieved, nine more bodies were discovered by Lieutenant Moore. The replacements were to bury those casualties.[1527] Major Collins from Chaumont reported over forty-one buried by the Americans. Collins also reported that two of

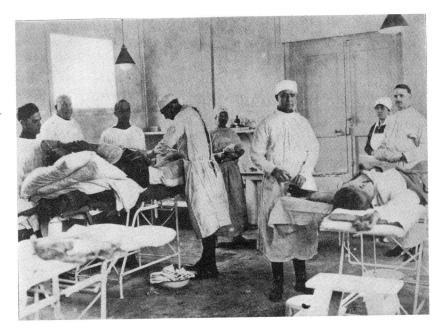

After the battle; surgeons at work at Evacuation Hospital No. 1 post-Seicheprey. (*Pictorial History of the 26th Division United States Army*)

the three wounded prisoners captured during the Seicheprey attack died.[1528]

Eight years after the affair, **Oberstleutnant** von Bornstedt's **Res I. R. 259** history said two of their officers and fifty soldiers were killed in the immediate battle. One officer subsequently died from wounds and forty-two men were severely wounded. One officer and 101 soldiers were lightly wounded. Six men received other types of injury. Total casualties for **Res. I. R. 259** at Seicheprey were four officers and 198 soldiers.[1529]

CONFIRMATION THROUGH INTELLIGENCE

General Edwards in his 11 May report informed Chaumont: "A prisoner captured yesterday states that the German high command admitted to their own troops in a communiqué that the German losses, killed and missing, were six hundred."[1530] The *VIIIe armée 2e Bureau* provided highlights from an interrogation of a deserter from **Res. I. R. 260** captured on 9 May near Flirey. The prisoner described the **Res. I. R. 259** raid on Seicheprey and *Bois de Remières*, claiming German losses were high.

He personally counted about 260 wounded. At one aid station the numbers of dead came to 13 men and 2 officers – similar losses were seen at the other aid stations.[1531] This apparently significant debrief was immediately forwarded to *Général* Passaga and Major General Edwards. The net losses of the **78. R. D.** at Seicheprey were now 600 casualties (killed, missing or wounded). It was a number that everyone could remember and became the benchmark for all subsequent discussions and assessments. Americans after the war cited German newspapers as the source and the number was subsequently claimed by the Allies, including Pershing in his post-war memoirs.[1532]

BRISTOL, CONNECTICUT

When Company C and Company D survivors were finally relieved and recovering well behind the front lines from the horror of the previous days, Colonel Parker arrived. He walked from one to the other putting his arms around them and crying like a child over those he had lost. Parker then rose up in anger, "his bulky frame quivering and his heavy voice roaring like a bull, he damned the Germans to the lowest circle of hell and swore he'd avenge his men with his own bare hands before the war was over."[1533]

Parker kept vigil for his Connecticut soldiers in the decades that followed. Speaking about the experience he went to those towns that had suffered the greatest losses at Seicheprey. In 1920 while speaking at Bristol he mentioned that the men of Company C and Company D "were picked for sacrifice." He told the rapt audience in attendance:

I had orders to post two companies in place against terrific odds, each man to fight to his death in place, and not to send reinforcements without permission from the division headquarters … We were outnumbered five to one, by specially trained soldiers, 3500 of the flower of the German shock troops that did not know defeat. We have evidence that they had been in training three weeks for this test. They were supported by the heaviest artillery that could be massed. The fate of an empire was at stake. A drive of five kilometers would break the French and British line of communication, and Paris would be doomed. The end was in sight for civilization. Upon Connecticut men fell the duty to hold that line.[1534]

There were approximately sixty-five men from Bristol in the 102nd Infantry ranks. On 20 April 1918, the Bristol contingent lost eight soldiers at Seicheprey and eighteen wounded. Six of the eight killed were in Company D with Major Rau fighting from F-1 (Seicheprey). Five Bristol residents – Top Sergeant Erving "Pete" A. Dresser, Sergeant George Nelson, Private William O'Sullivan, Private Joseph Lagasse, and Private Claude J. Nelson – were prisoners of war. Bristol never forgot. A memorial was constructed on the town mall and the American Legion named their post Seicheprey.[1535]

BURIAL

On 23 April the Germans conducted a service at the cemetery west of the village of Bouillonville. The place held the remains of hundreds of German soldiers killed in **Abschnitt zwischen Maas und Mosel** since the first campaigns of 1914.

Ich hatt' einen Kameraden; a service for the German casualties of Seicheprey. (*Geschichte des Reserve-Infanterie-Regiment Nr. 258*)

forty-one casualties from the battle were buried at Bouillonville that day. All but one of the graves contained two bodies. **Leutnant** August Tabke from Oldenburg shared a grave with **Vizefeldwebel** Emil Winkelmann.

On 21 April a large detail comprising members of the 102nd Infantry Band dug graves for the men who had lost their lives at Seicheprey the day before. The bodies were placed in wooden boxes and laid side by side in one long grave, just east of the French cemetery. A total of eighty-three graves were dug, with a wooden cross at the head of each and an identification tag bearing the inscription: "102nd Infantry."[1536] "Of all the work that a man may be called upon there is nothing so repulsive or gruesome as that of burying one's own friend and especially on a battlefield where the shelter half acted as coffin and the graves held seven heroes in one hole, yet the boys of the 102nd Band performed this duty with courage and fortitude, which called for the high praises from the Commanding Officers."[1537] Names of sixty-four of the eighty-three soldiers buried were transcribed by Captain W. P. S. Keating of the Medical Corps and forwarded to the *Hartford Courant* a year later. Keating call this the "sacrifice division" casualty list.[1538] The remains were later moved to Thiaucourt cemetery.

THE BUTCHER'S BILL TO COME

Casualties became numbers in a report; but four years of statistics on the Woëvre Front did not convey the emotion of the experience, nor the tragedy.

Fratricide was perhaps the most damning incident. "As to this phase, there is no doubt in my mind that there were a few casualties so sustained. I am comforted in my regret of this incident by the reports which I have on file of several French divisions that have gone to rest after suffering casualties in the great offensive in the north, and they are replete with criticisms of themselves as to several casualties sustained in a similar manner by friendly guns ... casualties

must so obtain in such a battle, and their appreciation of the great aid always given by the artillery ... should not be tempered with criticisms or unavoidable losses."[1539] Edwards' words were a direct steal from those of his investigating officer Lieutenant Colonel Hobbs quoted earlier: "I am pleased by the generous attitude of the infantry who deliberately refuse to complain, denying that they bear any resentment and regretting that I ordered this investigation, stating that they realize that casualties must so obtain in such a battle, and their appreciation of the great aid always given by the artillery which should not be tempered with criticisms of unavoidable losses."[1540]

Over the remaining time the 26th Division fought on the Western Front, one of every two men became a casualty. The division ranked fifth in the number of casualties of all American divisions in the war. Total casualties were 13,664 with 1,587 killed in action, 694 dead from wounds received in battle, and 11,383 wounded. In New England, Massachusetts had 10,984 total casualties, with Connecticut next with 5,262 casualties. New York, Illinois, Ohio and Pennsylvania had more casualties than Massachusetts.[1541]

Major General Edwards was relieved of command on 24 October. He was replaced by Brigadier General Frank E. Bamford, who had previously served within the 1st Division. Chaumont had succeeded in its quest to rid itself of this meddlesome general. Three days prior to the relief Brigadier General Harold B. Fiske, Assistant Chief of Staff G-5, had dinner with Bamford and told him he was to be given command of the division. Fiske noted:

> In my opinion it was probably the poorest American division in France ... The enlisted personnel of the division has been excellent. Its officer personnel has been poor. The spirit of the division as a whole has been poor. The mental attitude of the officers, with notable exceptions, has always seemed to be that too much was being required of the men, and that it was the business of their officers to shield the

Sergeant Benedict Driscoll visits the grave of his brother Private Timothy Driscoll, one of several casualties from Bristol, Connecticut. (Bristol Historical Society)

men from the exactions of higher authority. This attitude I charge chiefly to the former division commander, General Edwards, and next to the militia and local politics with which the officer body seemed to be infested.[1542]

General Bamford left Fiske with a mission. Bamford relieved Brigadier General Cole, 52nd Infantry Brigade; Colonel Logan, 101st Infantry; and Colonel Hume, 103rd Infantry, owing to "inertia". The reporter Frank Sibley had an opportunity in a later interview to ask Bamford what exactly he meant by that term. "The quality of a division is determined by its leaders, by its commander and by its colonels. What is needed in a division like this [26th Division] is colonels who are drivers. Drivers will make a division do things. Look at the 1st Division. That Division has had 33,000 men pass through it; it has had 33,000 losses. That shows accomplishment. It is too bad that this division [26th] is not one of the elite divisions of the army." Sibley had to ask, "Do you mean that a division's excellence is measured by its losses?" Bamford replied, "Well, you can't make an omelette without breaking eggs."[1543]

Leadership at all higher echelons accepted that casualties were a fact of life in positional war and they had to live with it. Four years later it took a special session of the Senate Armed Services Committee to approve the promotion to colonel in the post-war army of General Edwards' former chief of staff, Duncan Major. Brigadier General Cole, 52nd Infantry Brigade commander, remembered Major's callousness when he spoke in a public forum: "The efficiency of this regiment or any regiment is measured by its casualties. There are plenty of replacements."[1544]

CHAPTER 27

After-Action Reporting

Erster Oberquartiermeister General der Infanterie Erich Ludendorff recognized the significance of the Seicheprey engagement from the reports received. In his two-volume memoirs published in 1924, he mentioned the affair: "The Americans fought well; but our success had nevertheless been easy."[1545] German staff spent time assessing their newest enemy. **Kirschblüte** provided **OHL** with empirical information. The Germans saw the Americans conforming to French positional war standards.[1546]

In the days that followed it was apparent that **Res. I. R. 259** was badly shaken by **Kirschblüte**. They were surprised by the tenacity of the American resistance. **Generalmajor** von Stolzmann held an inquiry. His soldiers concluded that they had faced very tough resistance. The Americans had fought desperately in defence, often to the death, and had made good use of their weapons and positions.[1547] A few days later a deserter from the **Res. I. R. 260** reported that **Res. I. R. 258** was ordered to execute a follow-up raid between 23 and 24 April. Soldiers refused to leave their positions, suggesting a growing discontent in **Res. I. R. 258**, despite the success of the previous days. Soldiers were serving at the front without relief and morale was in decline.[1548]

Official German military post-battle accounts covering **Kirschblüte** were positive overall. The attack was successful based on an accounting of prisoners and arms captured.[1549]

The independence that **Kirschblüte** offered the attacking **Kompagnien** was assessed in the following days as not conducive to effective command and control. German command reports said the fighting in Seicheprey was chaotic. **Kompagnien** were badly mixed up. The command commented that "no description of the fighting of the individual companies can therefore be given." It was the reporting by **Oberst Freiherr** von Ledebur, chief of staff to **Generalleutnant** Fuchs' **Armeeabteilung C** that generated the most balanced and detailed assessment of American efforts during **Kirschblüte**. At the beginning of the German attack, at 0450, only two small outposts were observed in the forward enemy trenches. The men in the outposts fired off their pyrotechnics and fled to stronger centres of resistance. Initial encounters were slight. Then they found themselves in close combat with Americans stubbornly defending themselves. One counter-attack near Sibille Trench along the Seicheprey–St. Baussant road was repulsed. To the east a machine-gun nest covering the south-west *Bois de Remières* held out for several hours despite **Sturmtruppen** and **Stosstruppen** attempting a double envelopment. Resistance was eradicated thanks to artillery. Americans fighting from trees elicited comment as well. As for combat in Seicheprey, von Lebedur highlighted the intense struggle from house to house and the *abris* within. As a member of the

Generalstab, von Ledebur's report resonated with all that higher headquarters indicated what was to be expected in future battles with American soldiers. His final words in capitals served as admonition: NOT ONE AMERICAN SURRENDERED WITHOUT A FIGHT.[1550] This observation was echoed later by the Kauffman assessment from the **Generalstab**. "Although we know from experience that troops participating in a battle are apt to overestimate the combat value of their opponents, there can be no doubt that the 1st Battalion of the 102nd American Infantry Regiment defended itself stubbornly in close combat at Seicheprey."[1551] The men impressed the Germans with their physical stature; but soldierly bearing was very lax according to German standards.

The performance of GHQ AEF was also considered. Seicheprey obviously did not compare with major offensives fought since the war began, so the jury was still out. But the Germans saw GHQ AEF as lacking practical experience, yet to be put through the ultimate test of a major offensive such as Ypres, Verdun, or the Somme.[1552] They did think American leadership in the battles fought at the Woëvre had been found wanting. In the fighting around Seicheprey no influence of the command on artillery or infantry action was noticed. There was no planned employment of reserves for counter-attacks or coordinated artillery fire on the points of penetration.[1553] The Germans assessed junior officers at company level as lacking battle experience, but they were credited as courageous and setting a good example for their men.

The Germans judged the American soldier as "good", hardened and showing courage and calmness during the fight. However, in comparison to the experienced French *armée*, American discipline was not so good. Again, the prevailing view that Americans looked upon the war as a sort of sport was mentioned. The individual American fighting man lacked actual war experience, however he quickly became accustomed to conditions, so that within a year's time the enemy could figure on a good

force of "stationary fighters." Should a mobile battleground open up, the stationary fighters would be at a disadvantage because they lacked experience. Finally, the Germans were impressed with the quality and serviceability of the American equipment.[1554] One post-war record did accuse the Americans of using dum–dum bullets.[1555]

A more sobering and it must be argued more accurate assessment of this time was given by Ettighoffer in his post-war book *Gespenster am Toten Mann*. Years of combat had seen changes in the German **Armee** that had created fissures within the fighting ranks. His comments most likely addressed the decline of **Res. I. R. 258** and **78. D. R.**:

> During our excursions we recognise the unfair distribution of the troops: a thin line fights at the front, and in the rear they lie in large numbers in the staging villages, far away from the fire, people in the trains, at staffs and in any offices. For each frontline soldier there are at least three, if not more rear echelon troops who talk about the greatest heroic acts and how long they were in the frontline. Their uniforms are still smooth, hardly worn off, not soiled, those boots even shined. They walk with canes and wear high collars. Their faces are soft. They are scared of aircraft and spend many a night in the 'Hero' basements next to their accommodation, many a moon-lit night. The field soldiers are easy to recognise by their walk and weather-hard brown faces and by the threadbare uniforms. Had we had nevertheless all these strapping boys and the rear echelon pigs in the front line, how fast would we be out of the war and have won. No, it is always the same tired people, who get only few days rest in half destroyed villages, always the same regiments, always the same officers and crews.[1556]

Ettighoffer and his comrades would fight mostly Americans for the remainder of the war. The memory of the sacrifice posts resonated for many. What impressed the Germans was the indisputable bravery of individuals. Combat groups were killed, fighting to the last man, at their posts. Surrounded, there was many a soldier who, summoned to surrender, fought with broken rifle, and when overpowered, still struggled with his captors. For every prisoner taken, the Germans paid in good measure.

AN ASSESSMENT OF ARTILLERY

According to **Generalstab** assessment, the American batteries were held in check thanks almost entirely to the initial heavy **gasschuss** involving **Gaswerfer**. American artillery acted very cautiously, not interfering with the German withdrawal that commenced at 0730. It was around 0915 before the reinforcing batteries started firing from rear positions. In the course of the afternoon, however, the Germans succeeded in weakening the firepower of these batteries too. From then on, when the Americans finally reoccupied their former positions early the next morning, this was accomplished under the protection of heavy artillery fire.[1557]

Generalleutnant Hoffmann saw the solution to overcoming American resistance was through better **MW** targeting of pillboxes. Better targeting meant a major reduction of **Stosstrupp** losses. A total of 64 batteries, including those of the adjacent divisions, and 108 **MW** were engaged in **Kirschblüte**. Nine close-range group batteries were not used, in order that their full fighting power should be preserved for the preparatory fire on the positions to be stormed. Thirty-nine batteries were engaged in the preparation of the point of penetration. The number of batteries used was sufficient, although Hoffmann considered that a greater number of heavy high-trajectory guns, especially **Minenwerfer**, would have been desirable.[1558]

The volume of artillery rounds fired on 20 April was staggering. **Generalleutnant** Hoffmann confirmed German artillery fired a total of 22,000 gas shells and 42,000 HE shells. His heavy batteries fired 6,000 HE shells. *VIII* *armée* SRA reporting to *Général* Gérard said the Germans fired a total of 59,169 rounds, mainly

at 26th Division and *69ᵉ division d'infanterie* over the two days. Reporting for the first 24 hours did not cover American "consumption" of artillery. *69ᵉ division d'infanterie* artillery fired 2,230 77mm rounds, 1,071 90mm rounds, 356 95mm rounds, 1,114 120mm rounds and 523 155mm rounds during the first day. The next day's SRA report showed 26,000 75mm, 1,700 90mm, and 1,600 155mm rounds fired by 26th Division.[1559] The 51st Field Artillery Brigade reported that the approximately 25,000 rounds fired between 20 and 21 April was far in excess of its normal allowance![1560]

HEADQUARTERS RESPONDS

Général Passaga issued various instructions to the 102nd Infantry sector of operations about improving defensive positions. *Abris* in the advance lines were not to be improved. Men at those positions were to use what limited shelter there was and be relieved every 24 hours. Within *Bois de Remières* more barbed wire was strung and more pillboxes were constructed. The 1-Bis positions were repaired with more telephone lines inserted. Operations now imposed new procedures simulating occupancy at the front lines. Flares and bursts of fire were a nightly event. Additional attempts at deception included lighting fires within the old dugouts and generating smoke to feign occupancy. As for Seicheprey, the trenches were never fully repaired.[1561]

In the afternoon of 21 April, General Traub was deep in discussion with General Edwards on how the battle was fought. "When we were issuing orders over the telephone incidents took place that would be hair-raising to you as they were to me, of which I did not want to worry you at the time; that will account for some of my remarks to you. When Grizzley Bear [Brigadier General Traub's headquarters] was talking to my people someone would cut in on the other wire, mention my name and mention your name and tell who they were and give contrary orders and let you know they were in on the situation, and they knew all our code words for places. The 'S.O.B.s' are listening right in and hear me talk, and you can expect any moment to have a chap break in and say 'yes' and that is the situation of our wires."[1562] (Again, it must be stressed there is no witness corroboration from the German accounts; but the **Ahrendtstationen** were certainly active and effective.)

Lieutenant Colonel Grant working for Colonel Conner critcized Major Rau for setting up an ineffectual communications network between his PC, Sibille Trench, and *Bois de Remières*. Grant provided four reasons for Rau's failed liaison. Rau did not place a high enough priority on communication. His men postponed sending information until they thought they had something to send and his battalion did not practise various methods of communication on a daily basis. Finally, the trenches in the area were the ultimate spoiler. Grant made it clear: "The condition of the trenches is extremely bad ... A runner cannot make fast time in such trenches."[1563]

Major Bowditch completed his initial assessment of the Seicheprey affair for Colonel Malin Craig on the night of 21 April. It was a repeat of his observations earlier that week for Colonel Conner regarding what had transpired at *Bois-Brûlé*. Bowditch made it clear in his memorandum to Craig that he had tried to be objective: "I have not attempted to criticize. The lessons or rather impressions of this affair are the same as in the other affair – poor liaison – discipline not too good – junior officers not taking enough command. Col. Kerth I think would advise going slow about sending a regiment of 32nd Division to the 26th for instruction."[1564]

Bowditch considered that all of the information he was getting regarding plans, casualties, and booty had to be taken as hearsay until corroborated. Colonel Parker made his assessment of his regiment's status that day, despite having been actively fighting and leading forces for the previous 30 hours. Three of his companies (B, C and D), at present had no fighting value and four more (E, K, L, M and I)

had little. His lines on the right of Seicheprey held by 1st (Rau) and 3rd (Thompson) battalions were very weak. The 3rd Battalion, despite being relieved by the 1st Battalion on the night of 19/20 April, was depleted, having been active for the past 72 hours. A combination of being understrength for the mission at Chemin-des-Dâmes the previous month and deployment for three straight weeks at Seicheprey had taken its toll. Like the 1st Division's, the 26th Division's sector was constantly being shelled. His troops were "utterly worn out" requiring the regiment to be relieved immediately. Bowditch was of like mind. He left Beaumont to impress upon 26th Division seniors the current state of the 102nd Infantry. While en route to General Edwards' PC at Boucq, Bowditch stopped by l'Hermitage and discussed the situation with Traub's staff. Bowditch concluded his comments after his discussion with General Edwards with, "*mucho aere caliente*."[1565]

The 102nd Infantry was relieved on the night of April 23/24 by a battalion of the 101st Infantry. The 1st Battalion, 102nd Infantry went to Rambucourt for rest, remaining there as part of the Divisional Reserve. The Company C and Company D survivors were marched to the rear and lived for several days in the old engineer camp at *Bois de Rehanne* while the rest of the regiment was being relieved.[1566]

CLEARING UP AND LOOKING TO THE FUTURE

Once the Americans regained their trenches, they came across items left by the Germans that had been carried by the third wave to prepare against counter-attack. Equipment included two **Granatwerfer**, grenades of all types, 125 trench-mortar bombs, one water-cooled machine gun, two or three light machine gun barrels, ammunition, rifles, bayonets, gas masks, belts, and overcoats.[1567] *Colonel* Bertrand's men recovered a large number of rockets, a number of bags containing greanades, boxes of ammunition, pieces for light machine guns, thirty-two magazines for automatic pistol cartridges, and three phone lines.[1568] The French considered this haul meant the Germans had been in disarray and had departed hastily to avoid the American counter-attack.[1569]

102nd Infantry's 3rd Battalion now occupied the battleground. Colonel Parker insisted to *Général* Passaga and General Edwards that despite the losses of the previous days, though his regiment were physically exhausted they were not down in spirit. He praised in particular Major Rau and Captain Thompson. In Parker's eyes both were cool, modest officers, disclaiming all credit for any success in repelling the raid and asserting that whatever was done had been done by the men. Lieutenant Colonel Grant let Chaumont seniors know that morale was good despite the losses. The men were smiling, cheerful, and while they did not appear to be especially energetic in gathering together the scattered rifles and other odds and ends about the trenches, so far as spirit went they appeared to be ready for another fight.[1570]

German statements that twenty-five heavy machine guns were captured by the raid were dismissed by Chaumont, since the order of battle for the southern Woëvre front did not contain that number. In the vicinity of Seicheprey and *Bois de Remières*, there were only twelve Hotchkiss machine guns, and there were evidently fewer than that number between Seicheprey and H-1. The claims most likely included *Chauchat* automatic rifles, which were classified by the Germans as light machine guns.[1571]

Edwards took Colonel Parker's assessment of the 102nd Infantry's strength to heart and requested of Passaga and General Liggett, I Army Corps, that the regiment be withdrawn or change sectors with the 101st Infantry. To Liggett, Edwards made it clear that the Beaumont sector had been smashed and *Bois-Brûlé* sector required new trenches. A lot of work was required to keep the sector "as an American one ... In fact, there is a good month's work for a whole division on the assumption that the sector would be '*trés tranquil*'." Edwards

suggested having the 32nd Division come forward with a regiment to work with the 26th Division for "quicker assimilation of the experience offered." Edwards' suggestion was not acted upon. The 2nd Battalion, 101st Infantry did relieve the 1st Battalion, 102nd Infantry, on the morning of 24 April.

Major Stackpole went to Boucq on 23 April and paid a courtesy call on General Edwards and his staff. Edwards, Major Hyatt, and Stackpole had a chance to review. Stackpole's journal described General Edwards giving a rather incoherent account of the Seicheprey affair, dwelling on details of minor consequence, and using the expression, "This is how we won the fight." The discussion was pure Edwards – bombastic, full of contradictory input, and quick to focus on a visceral image of the moment. Edwards explained to Stackpole the discussion he had had with *Général* Passaga over the counter-attack that Major Gallant halted. He quickly shifted to Gallant's failure, despite a splendid rolling barrage that drove the Germans out of their occupied American trenches. Edwards demurred, saying that the attack was unnecessary and might have been disastrous. The absence of German bodies was due to casualties being returned by comrades and prisoners.[1572]

Major General Edwards brought up the subject of spies with Major General Liggett. It clearly was an issue that disturbed him greatly. He told Liggett that spies were operating in large numbers through all the villages. Edwards suspected local French natives and told Liggett that *Général* Passaga did not permit him to take measures against the civilians. Stackpole observed that Edwards had ordered sentries "to shoot at any light appearing at night, etc."[1573] The experience at Seicheprey had spooked Edwards – his ability to communicate via secure means had been seriously compromised.

Stackpole managed to ascertain something about the chaos of the battle. Major Hyatt and General Edwards' Harvard-educated aide, Captain Nate Simpkins, had more to share but discretion prevailed. He parroted back to Liggett that "runners were the only effective means of liaison;

General Pershing awards the Distinguished Service Cross to 26th Division recipients in July 1918. (*Pictorial History of the 26th Division United States Army*)

that some outfits had been without ammunition for two hours; that twenty-five machine guns were unaccounted for; that some units had been all cut up; that no one knew even then the extent of American losses, and there was nothing but conjecture as to *Boche* casualties." Stackpole entered into his journal, "They were all over the place."[1574]

The day after the Seicheprey affair Colonel Fiske of GHQ AEF G-5 called General Liggett's office and had a conversation with Stackpole. They discussed how divisions now in the trenches might be put through a schedule of training in open warfare while still holding their respective sectors. Stackpole called this a "pedantic idea".[1575] G-5 continued to press for their initiative. On 25 April Chaumont sent all AEF divisions including the 26th Division headquarters memorandum No. 952-G-5, specifying that training in open warfare was to be emphasised. General Pershing directed officers in the line to participate in a progressive series of carefully framed terrain exercises involving bodies of troops from patrols to divisions to learn the arts of open warfare. Exercises were to be habitually prepared, conducted, and umpired by a superior commander. If the tactical situation permitted, all available officers were to participate in one terrain exercise and troops in one manoeuvre each week. General Liggett was tasked by Chaumont to supervise the training and recommend modifications. The policy was

signed by Colonel Benjamin Alvord, Pershing's adjutant-general. Like Traub, Alvord had been an instructor of languages (French) at the Military Academy. There was no record of the 26th Division response to the G-5's initiative posted so soon after the Seicheprey affair.

26TH DIVISION CHIEF OF STAFF

Quickly becoming adjusted to the pace at General Edwards headquarters was Colonel Duncan K. Major, the newly arrived 26th Division Chief of Staff. He had a challenging position, directly supporting Major General Edwards on division issues and being discreet about contact with Chaumont. Colonel Major's time with the 26th Division was testy and remained controversial four years later in the US Senate hearing over his promotion to Colonel. *Commandant* du Boisrouvray had a balanced view of the man. Duncan Major was intelligent, energetic, correct, distant and endowed with a great capacity for work. He served Edwards very well as a staff officer but had a talent for alienating everyone. National Guard officers (militia) did not appreciate his aristocratic demeanour. *Commandant* du Boisrouvray's relationship with Colonel Major was "correct." On one occasion Major took great delight in stating two sub-sectors of a battle zone were named Connecticut and

Massachusetts and then watching his French Allies try painfully to attempt pronunciation.[1576] Frank Sibley did not share du Boisrouvray's view: "After the Seicheprey affair, he [Major] went to the staff college to lecture and said publicly that the Division had messed the Seicheprey business. It was not true, in any fair sense; if it had been true, to criticize his own division was not loyal."[1577] Lawrence Stallings summed up the feelings Edwards' men had for Colonel Major. "Not one of the Yankees gave a damn what he said until he criticized the 'faulty dispositions' of their 'beloved leader' —which was the way they referred to their own West Pointer, General Edwards. Then, if the colonel had cared to strip the silver eagles from his shoulder straps behind the latrine, 26,500 men would have stood in line to fight him."[1578]

Parker mentioned his beef with Major in his memoirs: "When we were discussing the Battle of Seicheprey at Division Headquarters, after it was all over, the Chief of Staff [Duncan Major] mentioned an alleged request from me by phone during the battle to have American Artillery Fire laid down on my own main position at the exact hour when the Germans had massed at San [St,] Baussant to finish their job by carrying the Beaumont Ridge. Of course, I never made such a demand; and only the fact that there was a stenographer at my elbow every moment of the battle, taking down in stenographic notes every word I uttered, cleared me of the allegation of sending this false message."[1579] Colonel Parker's memoirs included the following, which was to be edited out before publication: "A Helava situation, say I, when an American Commander in battle must take such precautions as that to protect himself against treachery at the superior offices of his own command; but I knew the Chief of Staff of that Division, knew he was no friend of mine, no friend of General Edwards, and did take the precaution. Damned good thing I did."

A TOAST

On 22 April *commandant* du Boisrouvray received a visit from *Général* Ragueneau, Chief of French Military Mission to the American Army. The two French officers proceeded to Beaumont to meet with Colonel Parker. It was 0700 when they arrived. Du Boisrouvray described Colonel Parker as always very friendly to the French but, when receiving a distinguished guest, he was "*magnifique!*" Parker procured a bottle of Burgundy and had it served in his shelter and poured three glasses. *Général* Ragueneau, pretending to adjust his glasses, whispered to du Boisrouvray, "I never drink, especially at this hour!" Du Boisrouvray replied under his breath, "It does not matter, but do not refuse!" Colonel Parker raised his glass and toasted in a loud voice, '*A la santé de Mademoiselle Saint-Paul, colonel honoraire du 102ᵉ R. I. U. S.*' [To the health of Mademoiselle St. Paul, Honorary Colonel of the 102nd Infantry.] *Général* Ragueneau then whispered, "What is he saying?" Again du Boisrouvray quietly replied, "I will explain but keep drinking." They swallowed another glass of wine, hearing Parker telling stories of the prowess of his 102nd Infantry. Upon departure, Parker straightened his tall frame, puffed out his chest, and said slowly, "I have already issued an order for the next battle!" Adjusting his glasses one last time, a worried *Général* Ragueneau asked, "What is he saying?" A quick translation allowed both to smile and depart, enchanted. In the automobile, *Général* Ragueneau broke his long silence with, "What a guy!" [1580]

FRENCH LIAISON RETHOUGHT

Seicheprey generated another look at the role of French liaison with American divisions. A policy note arrived at the headquarters of both *VIIIᵉ armée* and *32ᵉ corps d'armée* on 24 April. The new policy wanted the *division d'infanterie United States* (*DIUS*) to become more responsive to French command, going beyond their role as advisors to the Americans. This change was delicate since the French liaison up until that time did not possess any authority over the Americans. The relationship required discretion. French commanders were not to push for direct control or supervision. The policy stipulated that the officers of the Liaison Mission were to be at the disposal of the *corps d'armée* commanders to inform them about the *DIUS*. The French *généraux* wanted to share their extensive experience and felt their knowledge still mattered. It was hoped that through the Liaison Mission such tactical input could be accepted.[1581] In many ways the timing of the memorandum suggested a criticism of what had occurred at Seicheprey. It was to remind the Americans that they still were novices and allowing liaisons to have more authority meant giving them a greater role in future decision-making during an operation or battle.

As for the 26th Division liaison, because of the quality of the officer, the relationship that had developed between the French and Americans was sound. *Commandant* du Boisrouvray was called to Boucq in May to meet with General Edwards. *Général* Augustin Gérard was there. Gérard turned to Edwards and asked point blank: "And your officers of the French mission? They are here. I hope you make them work!"[1582] *Commandant* du Boisrouvray worked very well – his heroism at Seicheprey being recognized by his American counterparts was testament to that.

GÉNÉRAL RAGUENEAU PRESENTS AN OPTION

A week after *Général* Ragueneau and Colonel Parker enjoyed that memorable breakfast, the French Military Mission startled the American senior staff at Chaumont with a written request. *Général* Ragueneau sent a 1 May memorandum to Colonel Conner, addressing a verbal understanding reached that morning between the French and Americans. The French command wanted the *127ᵉ division infanterie* to entrain on 4 May and relieve the 26th Division around 8 May. The 26th Division was to regroup to the zone of Lafauche south of Toul with the objective of taking part in active operations after a period of instruction under conditions that the French had yet to define. *Général armée de*

l'Est was generating orders to *Général* Augustin Gérard's *VIIIᵉ armée* to commence planning the relief, echeloning and duration of movements. The 26th Division was to depart and head to the new sector by road march. *Chef d'état-major* Dutilleul had the honour of requesting the Americans to organise all details for executing the 26th Division's move directly with *VIIIᵉ armée*. Colonel Conner pencilled a note on the memorandum: "This was not accepted by us and statement in first paragraph is incorrect. F.C."[1583]

The French proposal was delivered to both Major General Edwards' 26th Division headquarters at Boucq and Conner at Chaumont. The French wanted to concentrate the 26th Division in the *IVᵉ armée* area to acquire open warfare training. "We constantly work toward creating an American sector. By virtue of work done, material installed, and hospital and supply facilities created, the present 26th Division sector has gradually been organized to conform to American necessities. In carrying out the work developing the southern Woëvre front as an American sector, a considerable number of army troops had been assigned to work in close connection with the sector." Conner's summary was a declaration of independence on French soil. Americans held the ground. Replacing that sector with a French division contradicted Chaumont's intentions to fully establish a front with an American Army. He recommended that the French be informed that GHQ AEF desired to have the available French division relieve either the French-brigaded 2nd Division or 42nd Division. Conner made it clear that the 42nd Division was in better condition, especially in command and staff, than the 26th Division. In his view, the 42nd Division should have been sent to the battlefront before the 26th Division. At this time GHQ AEF did not desire the 26th Division be relieved by any division. In a final regular over militia shot, Conner concluded GHQ AEF G-5 concurred with the substance of his proposed memorandum and remarked that the 2nd Division was at least 20 per cent superior to the National Guard 42nd Division.[1584] The French proposal was not addressed again.

A DRESSING DOWN AND SELF-DEFENCE

General Pershing provided his official position on Seicheprey ten days after the battle. It was a blistering attack and he singled out 26th Division leadership for failure to take charge and for taking the wrong approach to *Général* Gérard's tactical command regarding "islands in the stream." This showed poor command and control, a woeful application of intelligence, and a blind application of forces in what appeared to be a misinterpretation of an Allies' policy. Pershing directly castigated his division commanders. He shared some of the blame by stating that some of the defects were "traceable to defects in our methods of instruction." First and foremost was the failure of command and control, in the contemporary parlance, "liaison". Operations and training within the AEF now required liaison to be a priority. Major General James G. Harbord, Pershing's Chief of Staff at Chaumont, periodically received reports on how liaison was faring within the divisions. Pershing directly confronted the policy of *Général* Gérard: "The front lines are too strongly occupied. This is, at this stage of the war, a serious oversight on the part of the higher command. These lines need only to be held lightly at any time, but more especially at night and during the fog." Sacrifice units were no longer the defence that Americans were to use from then on. Lack of preparedness for a surprise attack was inexcusable and not to be tolerated in Pershing's command. He did offer to reconfigure the outposts with telephone or sound communications to better alert the other echelons of an attack in progress. Pershing's comments were supposed to ring in the ears of all his division commanders. He singled out Edwards for his lack of thoroughness: "As I have pointed out a number of times to various division commanders. Including the Commanding General of the 26th Division …"[1585]

Brigadier General Traub sent Edwards his "Report of Action, 20th–21st April 1918" the day after the Pershing rebuke, presenting his view on what happened in Center F and sub-centers F-1 and F-2. He cited his troops'

determined resistance. He said liaison was kept up with the artillery, despite what Chaumont observers noted and Pershing later affirmed. His response to information from Parker that ground observers and French counterparts reported "swarms of the enemy streaming through Richecourt, Lahayville, St. Baussent, and *Bois de le Sonnard*" was important. He said the artillery reacted, firing in the areas where German reinforcements were massing.[1586] Traub knew the Germans were good at deceiving the Americans. "As the enemy knows our barrage signal he may try and divert our barrage to some other point by sending up his false signals, as has happened before. Should the French call for barrage as specified above, the greatest care must be exercised not to divert any portion of that barrage to some other point or portion of our front unless action by enemy makes such call for barrage on our own part imperative."[1587]

Edwards' official report to General Liggett on 11 May "set forth the facts." It was pure Edwards, flooded with reports from as many subordinates he could find that had "any participation in this battle." He reminded Liggett that he was working for two different bosses: "The work of this division in this battle has been commended by General Passaga, the French Corps Commander; by Colonel Bertrand, General Girard [*sic*] of the 8th Army and by General de Ragneau [sic], head of the French mission at Chaumont; all of whom have made official calls at these headquarters and expressed their congratulations and commendation of the conduct of the battle and of the troops involved, as did also Generals Mauchard and Munroe." Edwards' sought to neutralise the fratricide account with assertions that the problem was not solely his division's. The French had done it elsewhere.

Major General Harbord recalled later that General Pershing had intended minor disciplinary action against key members of the 26th Division. However, *Général* Passaga's timely response to the battle with a liberal distribution of *Croix de Guerre* took the wind out of Chaumont's sails. General Pershing subsequently informed his senior Allied counterparts officially that henceforth, "No decoration of either Nation [France or Great Britain] will be awarded an organization, nor an officer or soldier of the other Nation, without the prior assent in each case of the General Headquarters of the Forces of the Nation to which said organization, officer or soldier belongs."[1588] The ceremony at Boucq for the heroes of *Bois-Brûlé* was the last honorific of its type before the new policy took effect. (The fallout from this directive affected the 369th.)

LACK OF AGGRESSION

On 16 May 1918, Brigadier General Traub through his adjutant, Major William W. Wade, forwarded a memorandum to the 101st Infantry and 102nd Infantry:

It is imperative that in order to identify the enemy troops opposite us prisoners must be taken, and patrols must penetrate the enemy's lines until the troops opposite us are encountered. The condition of the enemy's wire is well known to us and in future the only mission for patrols will be to take prisoners. Patrols must be more aggressive and in the future patrols will not be considered as having accomplished their mission unless prisoners are taken. We have been in this sector forty five days and not one prisoner has been made except the wounded left at Seicheprey. This is a deplorable state of affairs and shows lack of aggressiveness and spirit on the part of the officers and men taking part, and casts reflection on the Division and this Brigade.[1589]

Lack of aggressiveness within the ranks was not really an issue, as was clearly demonstrated a few days later. A German artillery barrage had struck 101st Infantry companies at Bernecourt. The men were mainly Irish from South Boston. The next night the Germans unleashed a **Gasschuss** from **Gaswerfer** that hit hard. Orders came down for a reprisal raid. The group known as the "Milk Battalion" responded. Members of the 2nd Balloon Company watched as volunteers from the Milk Battalion marched north to the German lines carrying rifles on one shoulder and shillelagh clubs with barbed wire wrapped around the heavy end on the other. The balloon ground crew remembered it was one of the funniest sights they ever saw. The fight that followed was not funny. No prisoners were taken, despite General Traub's directive. The Milk Battalion survivors making it back to Bernecourt lines said that the score was now even. The Germans retaliated in kind through their artillery. The next day they fired a barrage lasting for several hours against Bernecourt.[1590] The 26th Division's tough Boston Irishmen felt right at home. One officer asked his sergeant about "the number of Huns" engaged in a previous assault. The sergeant replied: "Oh, not too many this morning. I'd say about three saloonsful."[1591]

RECOGNITION

One of Clarence Edwards' greatest qualities was his strident effort to gain recognition for the men under his command. His 104th Infantry had been acclaimed the week before at *Bois-Brûlé*. Following Seicheprey, Edwards was equally active in getting correspondence on his soldiers processed for battle honours. After responding to Chaumont's assessments on the affair, Edwards had General Orders No. 40 published on 13 May to congratulate sixty-two members of the 102nd Infantry, from Lieutenant Colonel Cassius M. Dowell down to thirty-five privates of four companies. It was typical of Edwards and it endeared him to his troops for the remainder of the war and decades thereafter.[1592] What was not known by many was that Edwards came to Colonel Parker's PC on 22 April, insisting on going to the extreme front line of observation. Edwards was ready to personally go into No Man's Land and conduct his own reconnaissance of the most active part of the line. Parker was so touched by Edwards' bravery that he wanted to forward a request to higher headquarters that he be considered for a Distinguished Service Cross. Parker, instead, in light of the difference in rank between the two, reminded General Edwards that he was not allowed to expose himself to any danger of capture.[1593]

A few days later, Parker strutted through Beaumont with his orderly Lieutenant Carl Lockwood, talking with everyone, saluting smartly, and exuberant over his men's courage and bravery. "Well," he said, "I guess they will cease knocking the militia now … The 102nd is the greatest thing in the world." As he passed another man he said: "They thought we had lost 300 men, captured and missing, but they have got the figure down to 150." And to the next he said: "My boys, I worship and idolize you and I'd give my soul for you."[1594] Sergeant Edman from Company D caught Parker's infectious confidence and pride and wrote in a letter: "When you read the news about what the Americans did April 20, you will know what regiment it was, the smiling 102nd! D. Company is keeping its old record and making it better every chance it gets."[1595]

Those who manned machine guns that day received the highest praise from their battalion commander, Major Murphy: "the conduct of all men bear[s] out the best traditions of machine gunners."[1596] Colonel Parker put his verbal comments into writing, describing the 102nd Machine Gun Battalion's as the most effective machine-gun fire accomplished in the war.[1597] "They were ordered to hold to the death. They inherited positions that were impossible to improve upon and which had to be held. They accomplished their mission in a manner that brought the highest praise possible from our French neighbors, with terrible loss to themselves. Their conduct is beyond praise, it was heroic, it was sublime. We shall try to improve the selection of positions for the right company of this sector and we may hope to put in better machine gun service, but so long as gallantry marks American arms we may never hope to have a finer example of devotion to duty and self-sacrifice in carrying an order to the bitter end than that given by Captain Stanchfield's company and Lieutenant Sanborn's company of the 102nd M.G. Battalion."[1598]

The exploits of several 18th Infantry disciplinary prisoners inherited by the 102nd Infantry contributed to the folklore. Nine lived through the battle resulting in their pardon and reinstatement as soldiers. The Yankee Division adopted them for the remainder of their time in service.[1599] Private John C. Ryan was recognized by the 26th Division for his actions in fighting the **Stosstruppen** at Seicheprey. Special Orders No. 86 stated: "The example set by this man in the combat against greatly superior numbers attracted the favorable notice of every officer and member of the 102nd Infantry in Seicheprey at the time." Private Harold DeWitt, Private Robert Maher, Private Ambrose C. McKenzie, Private George Wicker, and Private William H. Cameron were also recognized for gallantry at Seicheprey, released from confinement, restored to duty, and assigned to Company D, 102nd Infantry. The remaining prisoners were either wounded, absent without leave (AWOL), or missing. Three disciplinary prisoners were captured by the Germans and their names posted on the *Gazette des Ardennes* list.[1600]

Général Passaga presented some veterans of the Seicheprey battle with the *Croix de Guerre*. Corporal James T. Bird, Private William B. Bolton, Private Ernest Firth, and Private Alvin C. Lugg were recipients. Corporal Bird had been surrounded by **Stosstruppen** for three hours. He then helped his lieutenant carry the wounded back despite being injured. Bird wrote: "Yes, it's some medal. I'll tell you. Some French General pinned them on our blouse, shook hands with all the boys and wished us the best of luck."[1601]

After Seicheprey 26th Division senior officers visited various hospitals. One colonel came to the cot of one soldier, who responded in a very reserved manner. The colonel asked what was wrong. The soldier replied he had no money to spend because he was still paying off a court-martial fine. "Who fined you?" the colonel queried. "You did." The young soldier had been among a group that had swapped uniforms with some *poilus* and, looking ridiculous, had tried to get past the sentries guarding a whorehouse door.[1602]

CHAPTER 28

The Seicheprey Legacy

The 19 April was not a good day for President Woodrow Wilson. While inspecting a British tank on display in Washington, DC, he mistakenly grabbed a pipe connected to a running engine that was extremely hot, severely burning his hand. Wilson immediately returned to the White House for medical attention. It took several weeks to heal. His appointments and discussions did not include Seicheprey or the conduct of American forces at the front during this time.[1603]

British Prime Minister Lloyd George responded to the news in a letter to a friend: "The American leadership in the combats up to now has been found wanting. In the fighting around Seicheprey no influence of the command on artillery or infantry action was noticed. There was no planned employment of reserves for counter-attacks or coordinated artillery fire on the points of penetration." This minor episode strengthened Allied doubts about the readiness of the AEF. Lloyd George observed: "This kind of result ... is bound to occur on an enormous scale if a large amateur United States Army is built up without the guidance of more experienced General Officers."[1604] Lloyd George was annoyed about where the Americans were deploying their forces. The Royal Navy was committed to bringing the convoys of Americans safely to Europe. He felt the Americans should be shouldering the burden to the north as well. It was not until the Americans demonstrated their multi-division offensive capability at the Second Marne that Allied anxiety faded. The American Army confirmed to sceptical Allies that they were entirely competent to defeat the Germans on 18 July.

Reaction by the Supreme Allied Commander and commanders-in-chief on the day of the Seicheprey affair was not mentioned. *Général* Foch was fully engaged with the major operations to the north. What discussion there was revolved around American divisions reinforcing depleted British and French divisions at Ypres and the Somme. Field Marshal Haig happened to have dinner with General Pershing on the evening of 20 April. The talk covered the British "scheme for incorporating American infantry in our divisions." The ongoing battle at Seicheprey was not mentioned in Haig's diary. The strategic issues around sharing British artillery with American manpower drove the conversation that night. There was now an understanding that American troops on arrival behind the British front were to be allocated to British cadre divisions. Haig recorded that "Pershing expressed himself as being quite pleased with our proposals."[1605]

UNITED STATES V. JOHN J. GALLANT, MAJOR, USR

Major Gallant was placed under arrest on 21 April for violation of the 64th Article of War, having received a lawful command from his superior officer, Brigadier General Peter E. Traub. Gallant went through trial by general court-martial at Headquarters 26th Division on 10–11 May. The court-martial was convened at General Edwards' Headquarters (codename Quebec) at Boucq. Twelve field grade officers and one junior officer Assistant Judge Advocate were assigned. Major Gallant appeared before the court with his assigned counsel, Captain Emerson G. Taylor, Adjutant to the 102nd Infantry.[1606]

The case was made that on 20 April 1918 the enemy had occupied certain ground, running westward from *Bois de Remières*, in the Beaumont sector. An attack referred to by witnesses in the trial as a counter-attack, by American infantry, in conjunction with French infantry, was ordered. Major Gallant, the accused, was placed in command of the American infantry. Pursuant to instruction to communicate to him he reported to his brigade commander, General Traub, at his headquarters, at about 2200 on 20 April, and there received from him Field Order No. 2, 51st Infantry, Brigade, dated 20 April 1918. The order was thoroughly explained to Major Gallant by General Traub in a conference lasting about two hours. In the course of that conference Major Gallant was no doubt informed "that H hour would be at 0445, 21 April 1918." At about 0050, 21 April, Major Gallant, after stating that he understood the order and had no questions to ask, left brigade headquarters in a motor sidecar to carry out the order. His instructions were "to get right strength to Hill 275.5", the point of assembly of his command, four companies, I, K, L and M, 102nd Infantry, and organize his command. Major Gallant should have reached Hill 275.5 in at most two hours – or not later than 0230. It does not appear that he went there at all. He stopped instead about 115 metres short of Hill 275.5, at the command post of Company K, where Company L reported to him at about 0300, and Company M at 0408. While at the Company K command post he sent out a runner to look for Company I. That company had concentrated at the assembly point between 0230 and 0300. "It thus appeared

that an admittedly competent order from his commander, definite and unconditional in terms, was not obeyed by Major Gallant, and further that the disobedience was more than a failure to obey – was in effect a countermand by him of the order of his military superior."[1607]

Major Gallant did not take the stand himself. His defence was derived from cross-examination of the government's witnesses and from the argument of his counsel. Captain Taylor tried to make the case that General Traub's order was ill-advised, could not have been prepared and issued with a full knowledge of existing conditions, and was impossible to successfully execute. It was argued on his behalf that there was confusion and lack of coordination in the assembling of the battalion, owing to difficulties of travel and communication, and that reconnaissance patrols which had been sent out to locate the enemy had not reported. Major Gallant was without information as to the location and strength of the forces he was to attack. The court decided that the defence issued a plea of confession and avoidance.[1608]

The defence said that to carry out the attack by the battalion, given the confusion of orders at various echelons and the current strength of the battalion was an impossibility. Gallant had to pull the companies together as best he could in a very short period of time. To carry out his orders meant a superhuman effort. He had no report in from his reconnaissance patrols, he was given no information of the enemy, and he was given no information as to liaison with the French to the right. Gallant did not know who was on his left. The state of the trenches and *boyaux* and the runners and all on that night, after a day of strain and bombardment, was something the brigade could not fully understand. Gallant made an honest effort to carry out the brigade commander's order, but the helter skelter way in which he tried to implement the order was a recipe for failure. Gallant, a witness testified, was "trying to do too many things at once." Gallant had been under steady fire and strain for many, many hours. He had been hurried about from one duty to the other, he was out on the 1-Bis position, he was pulled to brigade headquarters, hurried back again, and he was given this mission at a headlong pace. Finally, the defence made the case that as an "old soldier," having the years of experience that he had, he understood the execution of an order. Calling on drill regulations that allow for making a decision when the senior does not have all the facts, the defence made the case that Gallant took responsibility to annul the order knowing full well what the consequences were. Gallant's first remark having called off the attack was "This means a court-martial."[1609]

Major Gallant entered a plea of not guilty to the charge and the specification. The court found him guilty as charged and sentenced him "to be dismissed [from] the service and to be confined at hard labor at such place as the reviewing authority may direct for three (3) years." The subsequent reviewing authority on 18 May 1918 approved the sentence and designated the United States Disciplinary Barracks at Fort Leavenworth, Kansas, as the place of confinement. Major General Edwards published "Action," approving Gallant's removal to Fort Leavenworth. The record of the trial was forwarded to General Pershing as Commander-in-Chief, under provisions of the 48th Article of War. General Pershing's office on 9 July confirmed the sentence providing for dismissal from the service, but held in abeyance the order directing the execution of the sentence pending review of the record.[1610] General court-martial order No. 100, American Expeditionary Forces, was published by command of General Pershing, dismissing Major Gallant from the service as of 29 July 1918.

Brigadier General Traub had to explain his actions during the Seicheprey battle. He was found at fault for the way that he handled the planning for the counter-attack, as well as his ability to conduct the operation. This did not block his eventual selection to command the 35th Division and promotion to Major General.

Later that summer, during the ongoing Second Marne offensive, Major General Liggett called on Edwards on 24 July at *Grande Rue Farm*.

Liggett told Edwards that some of his colonels were to be transferred. Edwards remarked that he was sending in a letter making recommendations for the relief of Colonel John Parker and Lieutenant Colonel Foote (104th Infantry). General Liggett asked Edwards about the other regiment commanders, Colonel Logan (101st Infantry) and Colonel Hume (103rd): "Edwards said Logan was very popular and willing and Hume was the only Regular colonel he had." Edwards and Liggett then had a private talk that Liggett relayed afterwards to Major Stackpole. Liggett told Edwards that the trouble with him was that he never obeyed his [Liggett's] orders or made his officers obey theirs – intruding his own judgement or allowing officers to exercise their ideas, when only one thing was called for – exact obedience. Liggett reminded Edwards that he had himself insisted on a court-martial for Major Gallant, who had failed to carry out an order at Seicheprey.[1611] It was one of the last recorded observations that Stackpole made in his journal regarding Major General Edwards – colouring assessments of Edwards' ability to command in the eyes of historians forever.

A TROUBLESOME (AVIATION) MATTER

The initial US aerial photographic effort was abysmal. Almost all of the sorties attempted were either cancelled by weather or suffered aeroplane motor problems. What sorties were generated did not yield any coverage of value. Only ten plates were acquired in a period of two weeks and were of no value in alerting the American forces to German intentions. Captain Emerson Taylor mentioned in his post-war history of the 26th Division that "The air service was of little use to the American artillery at Seicheprey. Other means of information were insufficient to meet the emergency."[1612] Assessments on American aviation support to the 26th Division showed little or no interaction between the two leading up to Seicheprey. The official history stated:

Except in the one case of the attack on Seicheprey, no opportunities offered for contact patrols. This one attempt – the first made – proved unsuccessful, partly owing to lack of experience in this work, but chiefly owing to the lack of training of the infantry in showing their panels. In particular, although exercises were carried out with the 26th American Division, it was not thoroughly appreciated by all how vitally important, during active operations, is liaison between ground troops and airplanes. This was to prove a very troublesome matter in the later days, and had its importance been realized earlier, more vigorous steps might have been taken to secure this liaison.[1613]

The aviators made it clear that their ability to support rested with the division they were serving: "No definite training program with the troops was laid down by the division commander. By individual arrangement between artillery commanders and observers of the group panel, exercises for the instruction of radio and panel details of artillery battalions were frequently undertaken and carried to a successful issue." This was not just a problem with the 26th Division. Attempts to train inbound divisions to the concept of infantry and *avion réglage* met with indifference. For the aviators, their limited experience did not replicate the environment at the front lines.[1614]

Post-war histories from the United States Air Service clarified their abilities at this time. The 1st Aero Squadron was the only active 1st Corps Observation Group aero squadron during the time of the Seicheprey battle. Their official history was matter of fact:

Work was light. One squadron, operating at high tension, would have been sufficient for the accomplishment of all missions required by the tactical situation. Numerous artillery adjustments, neither very important nor very arduous, were successfully carried out by the group … The 1st Aero Squadron effected successful photographic missions at frequent intervals … It is noteworthy that the work

of the group was seldom hampered by the presence of enemy pursuit aircraft. Practically no experience in combat was gained. On the other hand, the enemy antiaircraft fire in the sector was exceedingly dense, active and accurate. Pilots of the group were adept at evading antiaircraft fire after a month on the southern Woëvre front.[1615]

The 1st Observation Group did feel that their constant watch along the lines made preparations for a large-scale enemy attack more difficult. Balloon observation was not given credit in this report. Detection of increased enemy transport, artillery, dumps, and cantonments was virtually certain. The experience laid down basic principles of observation that were important for the campaigns fought that summer and autumn.

Continued aviation support of *32ᵉ corps d'armée* after Seicheprey included *Escadrille de corps d'armée à TOUL Sal.122*, and *Escadrille AR41* supporting *40ᵉ division d'infanterie* and *69ᵉ division d'infanterie*.[1616] Like the 26th Division, the 1st Corps Observation Group remained under the tactical control of the *32ᵉ corps d'armée* and administrative control of the I American Army Corps. The 1st Corps Observation Group now comprised three aero squadrons: 1st Aero Squadron flying Spad XIs, 12th Aero Squadron flying AR 2s, and 88th Aero Squadron flying Sopwith 1 A2s. With the exception of 1st Aero Squadron, observation pilots had never served on the front prior to Seicheprey. The observers, on the other hand, had almost all served with French *escadrilles*. Their experience proved invaluable in forming the group.

General Pershing's aide, Major Collins, summed up the entire issue of failed aviation liaison:

There is no doubt that the liaison service in this division as well as in all our divisions, is poor, because not enough attention is paid in quiet times to concentrated drills with all the means of communication available. A system of communication between observation planes and the infantry would also have materially aided in clearing up the situation with respect to the location of our front line, but Major Rau's battalion had not been in the trenches for eight hours when the attack on them took place, and no such system had been practiced.[1617]

Post-war reports by aviators did not dodge the issue: "It is true that liaison, as it later came to be understood, was here practically non-existent. No close personal understanding based on good general tactical principles between staff and Air Service ever existed. The activities of the Air Service were unfamiliar to the staff. The activities of the staff and the units it controlled were unfamiliar to the Air Service. The situation at the time demanded no such intimacy between Air Service and line as later became indispensable. Lacking the incentive of urgency neither staff nor Air Service realised the gap that remained to be bridged. The later operations of the group at Château-Thierry were handicapped by lack of liaison experience."[1618]

American balloon observation required more experience to become an important asset to artillery and infantry operations. A program of liaison between *aérostiers* and infantry regiments was established to allow observers to better understand the needs of infantry and explain to the services what the balloons could offer. It was a start; but post-war reports did not show major progress. The AEF did not have sufficient numbers of balloon companies to provide dedicated coverage at infantry training areas. Liaison deficiencies generated over the year between *aérostiers* and aviation pilots never got rectified. Both served artillery adjustment but leadership never took the next step to fully define the mission. The French made it routine for aviation resources to confer on the next day's mission assignments. American aviation did not. Conferences occurring during the 26th Division's time at the southern Woëvre front only addressed how best to attack a balloon, how to evade an attack, and how efficient anti-aircraft fire was. The mission for artillery adjustment was never effectively addressed. Once military campaigns became more mobile, such liaison lost priority and was soon forgotten.

Prior to leaving the Woëvre, the 26th Division and 1st Observation Group conducted a training exercise that had effective displays of panels and Bengal lights that aerial observers were able to locate, even within the woods. The infantry was reminded to watch constantly for aerial observers and maintain communication. In turn, the aeroplane was reminded to better announce itself to the infantry through its identification signal light. Radio contact was recommended but required constant practice.[1619] It was telling that almost a month after the exercise, Colonel Craig sent General Edwards a memorandum entitled "Infantry-Aeroplane liaison" tactfully

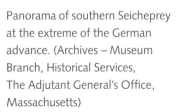
Panorama of southern Seicheprey at the extreme of the German advance. (Archives – Museum Branch, Historical Services, The Adjutant General's Office, Massachusetts)

pointing out that "The Commanding General directs me to invite your attention to the necessity of insuring the efficiency of the liaison between infantry and aeroplanes, especially under the conditions obtaining in this sector … Responsibility for organizing this instruction and seeing that it is actively pursued until it functions efficiently rests with the division commander."[1620]

One particular drawback of aviation operations in the southern Woëvre region was identified by America's leading ace, Captain Eddie Rickenbacker, in his post-war memoir. He pointed out that the high ground of Montsec dominated aviation's role. From the observation posts the Germans maintained constant surveillance of the airfields south of the front lines at Seicheprey:

> Not a machine could leave our field at Toul without being seen by these watchers atop Montsec! No wonder their many photographing machines escaped us! Many and many a time we had hurried out to the lines in answer to an alert, only to find that it was a false alarm. Now we understood why we lost them. The Germans had seen our coming, and by signaling their machines had given them warning in time to evade us. They retired and landed and waited until we had returned home, then they calmly proceeded with their interrupted work![1621]

In February 1919 Major General Mason Patrick, Chief of United States Air Service, forwarded a volume on the subject of the operations of the Air Service on the front to Brigadier General Fox Conner. It was a volume that Patrick admitted he had not personally edited prior to forwarding but he was sending it anyway to complete G-3 files of operations. The history recalled that the southern Woëvre front served as a place for breaking in pursuit as well as observation squadrons. "No close personnel understanding based on good general tactical principles between Staff and Air Service ever existed. The activities of the Staff and the units it controlled were unfamiliar to Air Service."[1622] From a command point of view, the work of American observation in the southern Woëvre front might have been considered inadequate but what was gleaned laid the foundation for a brand new arm of the American military. By the time American aviation met its next test at Château-Thierry, it was confident enough to support operations at corps level. The professionalism and courage demonstrated by the two initial aviation units at Toul, 1st Aero Squadron and 94th Aero Squadron, at the major American offensives of St. Mihiel and Meuse-Argonne, helped define aviation's role twenty years later in the Second World War.[1623]

"LITTLE VERDUN" – COMBATANTS ASSESS THE AFFAIR

The French soldiers nicknamed Seicheprey "Little Verdun".[1624] The *162ᵉ régiment d'infanterie* logbook noted the horrendous barrage. Some expressed concern that it had ominous implications for the state of the fighting force. After the battle, Private Wunderlich, 101st Engineers, began to hear from the fellows who were in it speak of what they had done, each one telling how many Germans he had accounted for.[1625] Private Wunderlich later wrote: "Throughout the day and night the battle raged, but the Hun, with his forty years of preparation and training, was mastered by the Yank who 'didn't know how to fight,' and the dawn of a new day found the Americans in undisputed possession. They had lost heavily but they had made the Germans pay a dearer price."[1626]

Such sentiment was not initially shared by the British soldier. Some of the Tommies fighting in Belgium that summer, when they first heard about Seicheprey, decided that "the Americans were not going to do much."[1627]

Vizefeldwebel Paul Ettighoffer was in reflective mood when he concluded, "**Erdrücken werden heute vielleicht noch nicht, aber morgen**" [Today (we) might not be crushed, but tomorrow].[1628] Later that summer **Generalmajor** von Stolzmann's **78. R. D.** faced the Americans again at Second Marne. Success at Seicheprey came at a price. Coming from the voices of the attacking Yanks came the cry "**Rache für Seichprey!** [Revenge for Seicheprey!]"[1629] Ettighoffer's war ended when the French took his position and he became a prisoner of war.

Lieutenant Strickland continued to lead his men until the Second Marne when he was wounded by a shell fragment in the right forearm. He was taken prisoner and spent the rest of the war in a Posen, Germany, hospital. He managed to escape ten days before the Armistice and fled via a circuitous route through Warsaw to Vienna and Treviso, Italy. As for Seicheprey, Strickland first gave credit to the enemy – it was "a wonderfully planned piece of artillery

work by the Germans. Not a trench, *boyau*, road or village but was pounded until daylight with a constant deluge of shells which made it impossible for troops or even messengers to pass through alive." But then again, "The Germans may have claimed Seicheprey as a victory, but their losses were unexpected. The Connecticut boys defended their trenches and gave the German General Staff a sample of what was to be expected from America ... It was the first full fight of any size for American troops, and while not a battle in the full sense of the word, was certainly a desperate resistance, and of great consequence to the morale of both sides."[1630]

The 102nd Adjutant to Colonel Parker, Captain Emerson Taylor, described Seicheprey from both strategic and tactical viewpoints: "The German estimate of American troops in France was wrong. They appeared to have no idea of what actually was being accomplished in the matter of building and transporting an army. The German press might sneer as it would about the effort of the United States to assist her Allies; the men 'up front' knew that their new adversaries were dangerous in a stand-up fight ... The first considerable engagement fought alone by American troops in France, the contest took on an unexpected value in stimulating interest in America over subscriptions to the third popular loan for the expenses of the war, full accounts of the valor of the New England troops being sent home at once, through official channels." For Taylor:

> The moral advantage rested with the Americans. They suffered, they lost prisoners; but the losses they inflicted on the enemy were exceeding heavy ... The mission of the American troops – to fight to the death in place without reinforcement – was performed ... The enemy was driven out of Seicheprey and Remières Wood by bloody, hand-to-hand fighting. A **Sturmbataillon**, backed by other troops of long experience, yielded before the courage, tenacity, and fighting spirit of some despised New England militia. The Yankee infantry recovered its organization and fought

Major John J. Gallant, a different kind of casualty of Seicheprey, for a decision made on the battlefield on the morning of 21 April 1918. This is the only known photograph of him, attached to his passport application to go to war. (Boston Public Library)

Replacements for the depleted regiments started showing up. Private Havlin of the 102nd Machine Gun Battalion recalled: "Our first replacements were assigned to the company – nineteen of them. Of course, our first question was: 'Were you invited to this war or just horned in?' The majority came from New York City; so we had to learn a new accent."[1634]

"A NASTY, GRUELING FIGHT"

successfully to a stand up finish ... The troops came out of Seicheprey bruised and bleeding; but their heads were held high.[1631]

Frank Sibley reflected: "After the Battle of Seicheprey a deep calm fell on the sector. The Germans seemed to have decided that the American troops whose mettle they had been trying out were worth letting alone. Every time they had gone against the Yankee Division they had been repulsed with larger losses than those they inflicted. It is true, too, that at this time the Germans were preparing the great second Marne offensive and were quite content to leave other sectors quiet."[1632]

Rumours re-emerged as operations settled down along the southern Woëvre front. The capture of Montsec resurfaced as the main topic of the day. When Corporal LaBranche saw extra batteries concentrating in the area, he was sure that it was only a matter of time before the 26th Division was sitting on Montsec, looking ahead for more hills to conquer. There was also a rumour that Montsec was not to be overrun but blown to pieces instead. The sappers were already laying mines under Montsec, it was said.[1633]

Despite the soldier's battle that occurred at Seicheprey, General Pershing's main affection remained with the 1st Division. He greatly appreciated how they relocated to the Picardy region, established operations, and commenced successful planning to attack and hold Cantigny. The battle was the first American offensive in the war. Cantigny clearly demonstrated to the British and French that the American army could fight and win on the Western Front. It demonstrated the Americans' ability to hold the ground against a concerted German counter-attack. American military prestige and morale was at risk when the 1st Division launched the offensive at Cantigny. The Germans recognized this and launched repeated and intense counter-attacks. Pershing proudly reported to General March and General Baker in Washington that the division's attack had been "well planned and splendidly executed ... It is my firm conviction that our troops are the best in Europe and our staffs are the equals of any." It was a tribute to the 1st Division staff, particularly Lieutenant Colonel George C. Marshall.[1635] One veteran turned historian concluded, "Cantigny like Seicheprey was a nasty, grueling fight. April 20 and May 28 both were milestones in the national history."[1636]

CHAPTER 29

The Woëvre is Restored

After the third German offensive General Pershing talked with *Général* Pétain at Chantilly on 19 May about the possibility of the American Army taking complete charge of the southern Woëvre front, should circumstances allow. Pershing called the area occupied by the 26th Division the nucleus of the sector. His plan was to have American divisions occupy the Woëvre as they became available – occupying the right and left of the sector defended by the 26th Division. When four divisions were on the front line with two more in reserve, the French were to turn over the responsibility for defending the southern Woëvre front to the Americans.

Pershing and Pétain further agreed that if the fluctuations of the conflict should make it necessary to take American divisions from the newly established American sector, the GQG would replace the American divisions with French divisions under the American command. *Général* Pétain took the next step. He gave orders for *Groupe d'armées de l'Est* to make a complete study of the sector in question to determine necessary communications, establishments, and local services for a transfer to the Americans.

Nothing further was done. The 26th Division pulled out and was replaced by the 82nd Division. Everyone's attention was diverted to the battle taking place at Château-Thierry – a threat to Paris. The next major campaign was the Second Marne campaign. Pershing sought an interview with *Général* Foch on 14 July to outline his reasons for an American sector. Pershing insisted that it was necessary to look further into the future and consider the early establishment of a permanent American sector to better conform his divisions as they arrived in theatre. Pershing pointed to the Toul-Nancy region as the logical American sector. *Général* Foch's response was agreement in principle. Foch stated moreover that the cause of the Allies would be better served by an American Army under its own chief such as Pershing than by an American Army with its units dispersed. Château-Thierry was the appropriate location for temporary assignment of American divisions at that time. However, Foch felt a permanent American sector was best considered after 1 October.[1637]

CHANGES IN THE SECTOR

The **78. R. D.** was relieved in the Woëvre around 11 May 1918 by the **8. Bavarian R. D.**, a division rated first class by Allied intelligence and experienced in fighting mountain warfare. **8. Bavarian R. D.** occupied **Abschnitt G** for two months.[1638] Later that summer, **Generalmajor** von Stolzmann's **78. R. D.** moved west of Dammard in the Ourcq region. After two weeks of heavy fighting the **78. R. D.** ceased to be an operational division. On 20 July it was withdrawn and the three regiments became replacements for remaining line divisions. **Major** Bruns' **Res. I. R. 259** saw his three battalions reassigned to the **2. Guard. I. D.**[1639]

On 19 May the 26th Division was notified that it was to vacate the western sector of St Agnant that the 104th Infantry successfully defended the previous month and occupy the battleground that the *162ᵉ régiment d'infanterie* had defended under *colonel* Bertrand. The new 26th Division sector moved 3½ kilometres to the east to a point 1½ kilometres north-west of Flirey. At the western sector area, replacing the 104th Infantry, was a Senegalese regiment from the *34ᵉ division d'infanterie*. **General der Infanterie** Auler's **5. Ldw. Div.** now faced a totally different enemy.[1640]

Colonel Frank Hume's 103rd Infantry occupied the eastern flank of the *34ᵉ division d'infanterie* when the **5. Ldw. Div.** executed **Brotausgabe** [bread ration] on 16 June 1918 to the west of Seicheprey at Xivray. Prior to the raid, German patrols discovered the front-line American trenches at Xivray were empty. **Brotausgabe** involved 300 **Stosstruppen** from **5. Ldw. Div.** and 80 men each from **Sturmtruppen 14** and **Pionier Komp. 16**. The assault was rehearsed for three days with three columns using **Flammenwerfer**, **MP-18** light machine guns and **Model 08** heavy machine guns. At 0315 the Germans unleashed a barrage similar to Seicheprey, slamming the forward positions and villages to the rear. HE and **gasschuss** targeted all American battery positions covering the sector. Again, the elite **Sturmbataillon.14** led the way, attacking Xivray from the west. The second column bypassed Xivray and proceeded to encircle from the south, while a third column attacked from the east. **Brotausgabe** did not go well for the Germans. When the operation commenced, the Americans quickly evacuated back to the 1-Bis position and counter-attacked, which resulted in twelve German prisoners for the loss of a single American. The 26th Division had learned important lessons from Seicheprey.[1641] **5. Ldw. Div.** remained in *Bois-Brûlé* area until September 1918. The division never showed initiative or capacity for offensive

operations like the one of 10 April at Apremont. During the St. Mihiel offensive in September, **5. Ldw. Div.** lost heavily in prisoners, among whom was the entire staff of the **65. Ldw.R. 3. Bataillon**. The **5. Ldw. Div.** retreated and took up positions at the **Michelstellung** holding that sector until the Armistice.[1642]

THE 26TH DIVISION LEAVES THE WOËVRE

On 11 June, Colonel Conner sent General Liggett the AEF GHQ directive that the 82nd Division was to commence relief of the 26th Division on 14 June.[1643] Between 24 and 28 June, *154ᵉ division d'infanterie* and the 82nd Division accomplished the task. The 26th Division left the southern Woëvre front on 1 July for Toul, then proceeded west to assist the ongoing battle being fought by the 2nd Division at Belleau Wood. The 26th Division supported the American counteroffensive at Château-Thierry, were at Belleau Wood where the Marines fought, and then participated in the Second Marne offensive.[1644]

It was characteristic of *Général* Passaga to praise the forces that had served so valiantly under his command. As he had recognized the 1st Division when they departed that April, Passaga did likewise for the 26th Division. He issued a general order:

> At the moment when the 26th Division of the United States is leaving the *32ᵉ corps d'armée*, I salute its colours and thank it for the splendid services it has rendered here to the common cause. Under the distinguished command of their chief, General Edwards, the high spirited soldiers of the Yankee Division have taught the enemy some bitter lessons, at *Bois-Brûlé*, at Seicheprey, at Xivray-Marvoisin; they have taught him to realize the staunch vigour of the sons of the great Republic fighting for the World's Freedom. My heartiest good wishes will accompany the Yankee Division always in its future combats.[1645]

CHANGES IN COMMAND

With the move to the west, additional leadership changes were implemented for the 26th Division. Major General Edwards retained command but his 51st Brigade commander, Brigadier General Traub, left to take command of the 35th Division composed of National Guard soldiers mainly from Kansas and Missouri. Brigadier General Shelton left the 104th Infantry and assumed Traub's command. With the assumption of division command, Traub was promoted to Major General. The following months of combat culminating in the Meuse-Argonne offensive that October did not go well for the 35th Division. Major casualties were experienced in the opening days of the offensive, resulting in the 35th Division being withdrawn from the front. As at Seicheprey, General Traub's communication with subordinate commanders was not effective – echoing his experience with Colonel Parker. Traub failed to trust their judgement. After the Armistice Traub was relieved of command, returning home with a replacement division of no consequence or distinguished record.[1646]

Colonel Parker proved his courage several times during the summer of 1918, earning three more DSCs. During the Second Marne offensive, Parker steadied his men through an intense artillery barrage prior to their assuming the front line. As the artillery rounds struck the

The cover of the 78. Reserve Division's *Das Regiment* that included the Ettighoffer article has a backward swastika: a protest or a typesetting error? The German counterpart to Stubby takes centre stage. (*Das Regiment*)

area, the soldiers scrambled to what limited cover was available. Colonel Parker was observed riding his horse through the lines calmly talking to his men and kept them ready to proceed to attack. Parker's final DSC was awarded on 10 November, the last full day of combat in the First World War. It was recognition for his actions at Seicheprey.

Sergeant Tyrrell wrote of Colonel Parker decades later: "Colonel John H. Parker, commanding the 102d Inf. was a very good leader under any circumstances. I served him as acting Regimental Sergeant Major for four months and admired him for his ability during battle and at all times."[1647] Such was the feeling of many other 102nd Infantry veterans. In his last official letter to the regiment dated 8 August, Parker, in compliance with General Orders No. 65, 26th Division, 31 July 1918, relinquished command. For Parker, departure was in many ways traumatic. He listed the engagements fought together, including Chavignon, Seicheprey, and Remières Woods. Of Seicheprey he said: "Under the force of attack of picked storm troops you held your ground at Seicheprey or retook by hand-to-hand fighting every inch the enemy had gained in his first rush. When your turn came to attack, no troops were ever more furious in the assault or more relentless in the pursuit. The honor of having commanded this regiment in these actions is one that never can be taken away and pride in your success is only equaled by appreciation of the soldierly qualities you have always displayed … Our trails part here."[1648]

82ND DIVISION

The 82nd Division soldiers were the first National Army troops that the 26th Division had seen.[1649] The National Army consisted of soldiers conscripted from all classes. Under the command of Major General William P. Burnham it comprised mainly North Carolina, South Carolina, and Florida draftees. The National Army appointed regular officers to command the regiments, brigades and divisions. The lower ranks were filled by young officers from training camps. The Allies assessed the National Army divisions in December before they arrived in theatre as of better quality in many ways than their National Guard counterparts. The 82nd Division continued the relationship that the 1st and 26th Divisions had previously established by remaining under administrative control of Major General Liggett's I Corps. *Général* Gérard's *VIIIᵉ armée* and *Général* Passaga's *32ᵉ corps d'armée* remained the tactical command. The 82nd Division moved to the Woëvre front, where they became affiliated with the *154ᵉ division d'infanterie*. Their line of responsibility now covered Limey and Flirey to the east. Seicheprey remained central to the defence. Through its continual occupation by American forces that summer it became known as the "Old Home Sector."[1650] *Général* Gérard's policy "to hold positions to the last and under all conditions unless withdrawn by order of the Army Commander" was still in effect and remained when the 89th Division assumed control of the sector.[1651]

89TH DIVISION

On 4 August the 89th Division under the command of Major General William M. Wright assumed control from the 82nd Division and established divisional headquarters at Lucey.[1652] The relief of the 82nd Division by the 89th Division was distinct, for it was the first American division ever permitted to enter the line as a unit and without having been previously brigaded with French or British troops.[1653] The Germans fired one of the largest barrages of mustard gas against the departing 82nd Division serving as guides for the arriving 89th Division on 7–8 August. The area of concentration was *Bois du Jury*, *Bois de la Hazelle*, and areas near Flirey. Approximately 820 casualties resulted from the **gasschuss** – and the inexperience of the men under it. *Général* Passaga issued an order directing that "ground shelled with a 'lasting gas' must be evacuated immediately and reoccupied no sooner than eight days later unless thorough decontamination can be performed." *Groupes de combat* were now required to plan for alternative positions to hold ground, dependent on wind direction at the time of attack.[1654]

ST. MIHIEL OFFENSIVE

On 20 August, the higher command of the southern Woëvre front passed from the French to the American Army. Pershing's divisions no longer came under the tactical control of *Général* Gérard and *Général* Passaga. It was not an entirely clean break. On 29 August, Pershing and his staff settled into the advanced headquarters for the St. Mihiel offensive at Ligny-en-Barrois. They received a visit from *Général* Gérard and his staff. *Général* Douchy, Gérard's *chef d'etat-major* for *VIIIᵉ armée* presented General Pershing with two

huge volumes containing a total of 300 pages of plans for Woëvre region offensive and defensive operations. Pershing was tactful and did not mention to *Général* Gérard's staff that his plan for St. Mihiel was already prepared. His guidance had six pages covering offensive operations and eight pages for defence! Pershing mentioned this "to show the difference between planning for trench warfare, to which the French were inclined, and open warfare, which we expected to conduct."[1655] The *VIIIᵉ armée* model was not followed. The southern Woëvre front now

Generalstab map showing the Allied advance at Seicheprey to the Michel *Stellung*. (*As They Saw Us; Foch, Ludendorff and Other Leaders Write Our War History*)

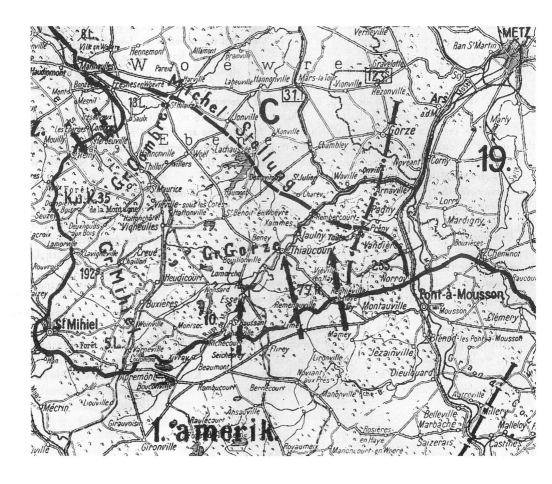

was officially under American control in mind and spirit.

German forces occupying **Abschnitt zwischen Maas und Mosel** in the Woëvre that summer were depleted. Seven divisions comprising three **Landwehr**, one Austro–Hungarian and one reserve division (that had just arrived from Russia) provided the main forces. The reserve division had just experienced a mass desertion by 800 Lorrainers that summer, practically putting the division out of action. **Armeeabteilung C** staffs in consultation with the division commanders suggested the newly arrived reserve division be replaced by a more reliable division but ended up deciding to keep the divisions in place because the situation was so dire. **Generalleutant** Fuchs' headquarters entertained the idea of conducting a major surprise attack on American forces to upset preparations, but his remaining divisions were too weak.[1656] The *34ᵉ division d'infanterie* now fought **5. Ldw.D.** on the Montsec battleground. **Abschnitt G** in Richecourt, Lahayville, and St. Baussant was covered for the final German occupation by **10. I.D.**, a former first-class division that had suffered major losses in the Second Marne, and **77. R.D.**, veterans of the Russian front.[1657]

German wiretapping paid dividends at St. Mihiel. Chaumont coded messages were easily deciphered once intercepted. **Armeeabteilung C** learned the disposition of American troops staging in the Woëvre region for the upcoming offensive. The information included the number and names of the divisions, followed by the actual H-Hour for the attack – intelligence that allowed German forces to commence their withdrawal before the full attack was executed. Allied armies launched a major offensive against an already retreating enemy.[1658] Montsec, the formidable fortress holding 5,000 German troops throughout the war, was deserted prior to the offensive and was taken without a fight. Later, a reporter remarked, "But how pathetically the inane hill looks today compared with what Mont Sec meant in 1918." French troops proceeded through Apremont and Woinville and took Montsec with the first American veterans of the Woëvre, the 1st Division covering their right flank.

Chaumont finally had the opportunity to establish an American command in the Woëvre after the Second Marne. The 26th Division was placed at the northern end of the St. Mihiel Salient and successfully drove south towards Vigneulles when the offensive commenced. The 1st Division returned to the Woëvre under the command of Major General Joseph Dickman's IV Corps, occupying the western sector limits that the 6th Infantry and 26th Infantry first held that winter. The 1st Division advanced north and linked up with the 26th Division, cutting off the remaining German forces within the salient.

The 42nd Division was next, positioned due north of Seicheprey facing St. Baussant and occupying *Bois de Remières* and *Bois du Jury*. The last American unit to fight from *Bois de Remières* was the 165th Infantry under the command of Lieutenant Colonel "Wild Bill" Donovan. The regimental chaplain, Father Duffy, described the forest as "a most miserable spot." His New York National Guard regiment had the distinction of launching the offensive. At the jump off Donovan shouted to his men, "Get forward, there, what the hell do you think this is, a wake?" When they broke through St. Baussant thanks to Lieutenant Colonel Patton's tanks, Donovan and thirty of his men jumped into the Rupt de Mad and made it across under fire from the Germans. The Germans were eager to surrender.[1659] Finally, IV Corps' 89th Division surrounded *Bois de Mort-Mare*, the bane of the *5ᵉ compagnie du 63ᵉ régiment d'infanterie*. *Bois de Mort-Mare* was still considered impregnable in 1918. When the St. Mihiel offensive commenced, Major General Wright, 89th Division commander, opted to send his infantry around each flank and mop up *Bois de Mort-Mare* from the rear.[1660] With the successful completion of the American offensive, *Bois de Mort-Mare* ceased to be a symbol of successful German resistance on the southern Woëvre front line.

Lieutenant Colonel George Patton spent 1918 honing the skills and taking the novice Tank Corps into battle. Patton's 1st Tank Brigade received their baptism of fire at St. Mihiel when *Renault* tanks of his *char d'assaut* assembled and moved across the Rupt de Mad near Xivray.

The 1st Tank Brigade was assigned to support the 1st Division and 42nd Division in the core of the IV Corps sector. French *Schneider* tanks from *IV Groupement* were placed under Pattons' command. He merged the *Schneiders* with the *Renault* tanks of his 327th Tank Battalion and had them move north through the eastern edge of *Bois de Remières*. Patton's 327th Tank Battalion of Renaults supported the 1st Division moving north-west of Seicheprey at Xivray-Marvoisin. The 1st Division had worked with armour at Cantigny and were familiar with the manoeuvres. The 42nd Division had no previous experience working with tanks, so Patton spent more time preparing that front. On 11 September the tanks moved into final positions. His diary for September 12 reads:[1661] "At 5 the show started at 5:30 could see tanks beyond Xivray [327th Tank Battalion] having a hard time. Moved at 7 to Seicheprey. Saw some prisoners & wounded … got some shelling … at 9:30 took Pannes at 10:40 attacked Beney got shot at by m.g. & had to recall tank as … [infantry] would not go in."[1662] Patton had proved his worth. His tanks had successfully supported the first day's advance and secured Pannes, the **Stosstruppen** rest area. One thing he learned from this first day of battle was to ensure their was enough gasoline to continue the advance. Patton remembered that lesson when he fought the Battle of the Bulge 26 years later.

Generalleutnant Fuchs praised his **Armeeabteilung C** divisions on 14 September for the successful withdrawal, creating the optimum force structure to counter-attack. He took time to thank his soldiers, especially the **Landwehr** for their leadership and bravery at this time and throughout the war. A few days later the Kaiser personally awarded the **Eisernen Kreuz I** [iron cross 1st class] to fifteen **5. Ldw. D.** soldiers for their action on 12 September. [1663] It was the Kaiser's last honour for his Woëvre veterans.

A DISCREET ASSESSMENT

Allied intercessions on the role and purpose of the American Army at the Western Front either stimulated or muddled thinking on how to adapt to modern warfare. General Dennis Nolan, Pershing's G-2, said the British were "very anxious that they would make us understand how serious all these things were. The French had the same solicitude but they were less tactful in expressing it … Their attitude was more 'Well, this is the way it is; you can take it or leave it.' The British attitude was 'this is the way it is: for God's sake take it, take our word for it.'"[1664]

A candid Allied interpretation of American operations at St. Mihiel was assembled by the British liaison to Chaumont and discreetly hidden from American eyes with a classification of SECRET. "Notes on American Offensive Operations" had a further caveat – "From information received from French sources":

The date originally fixed for the attack had to be postponed for ten days owing to the American preparations being belated. The attack was carried out by the American 1st Army, under the command of General Pershing, consisting of eight American divisions on the southern flank of the salient, one French and one American Division [26th Division] on the Northern flank, between these two attacks there were three French Divisions, while opposed to them were 7 German and 2 [pencilled correction – This should be 1] Austrian Divisions. The French lent a large amount of artillery, aeroplanes, tanks, Staff Officers, etc. and helped in the preliminary organization. The attack took place under exceptionally favourable conditions on the 12th, as it caught the enemy halfway through his arrangements for evacuating, which should have been completed on the 15th. The bombardment did not cut the wire and the Americans had to stamp it down or cut it by hand. Fortunately there was practically no resistance, as is shown by the fact that the total killed was under 200, whilst one French Division took 2,500 prisoners and had only 4 men killed. It was hoped that the two enemy Divisions in the point of the salient would have been cut off, but they got away by a new road through the forest apparently without any great difficulty. The American attack [1st Division] from the South reached the neighbourhood of Vigneulles just about the same time as the Northern attack [26th Division] was approaching it, and the two appear to have engaged each other, both reporting that they could not get on, on account of intense machine-gun fire. After the initial attack the Germans appear to have got clear away, owing to the great confusion existing in the American lines on the communications leading to the front, and though it was reported that there was great confusion also behind the German lines, no effort could be made to exploit the success. Generally speaking, the set-piece part of the operations was satisfactorily organized and carried out, particularly the approach march and the concentration of the guns, but the army was immobilized after the first twelve hours by inexperience in re-organising under battle conditions. A serious feature, also, was that a large amount of rolling stock was locked up behind the American Army, and although urgently required elsewhere, it could not be extricated. But perhaps the most unfortunate part of an otherwise successful operation was that it confirmed the American High Command in an exaggerated estimate of the efficiency of the American military machine, and of their ability to control it – This has been dearly paid for since.[1665]

Commentary on the ongoing Meuse-Argonne battle, the largest battle fought by American forces since Gettysburg, were horribly reminiscent of the liaison problems experienced at the Woëvre earlier that spring with 1st Division and 26th Division:

On the first day the Americans advanced about 11 kilometers, but did not maintain all their ground. The following days were characterized by confusion everywhere. The American idea of road control appeared to be that someone on the spot would rise to the occasion and straighten things out. In actual practice this led to one unit's transport trying to jockey that of every other unit … Liaison from rear to front appeared to be unsatisfactory, and panicky reports kept coming in, such as might be expected in the case of raw troops, as indeed these were. Liaison between divisions was also insufficient, and one division frequently did not know where those on its flank were. All this time Army Headquarters were making frenzied endeavors to get the troops forward, but the knowledge and grip of the situation necessary to organize attacks in these conditions were not possessed by the staff … The net result of all this was that from 27th September to 18th October the Army only gained another 5 kilometres, whilst wastage from wounds, sickness and straggling was very severe. On one occasion a division [35th Division under the command of Major General Traub] moving up in support had 5,000 casualties from enemy artillery without firing a shot.[1666]

The conclusion was damning, but hugely debatable: "The general impression is that, in spite of the gallantry and spirit of the individual, and owing to inexperience, particularly in the higher ranks, American divisions employed in large blocks under their own command, suffer wastage out of all proportion to results achieved, and generally do not pull more than a small fraction of their weight. It is felt that in insisting on the premature formation of large American Armies, General Pershing has not interpreted the altruistic wishes of the American Nation, and that he has incurred a grave responsibility both as regards unnecessary loss of life amongst his troops, and in the failure of the operations."[1667]

GERMAN COMMAND POST-SEICHEPREY

The final years of the German commanders and seniors were obscured by the tumult of the inter-war years and the rise of the **Nationalsozialistische** movement. **Generalleutnant** Hoffmann, artillery commander, lived until 1934, primarily remembered in the records that survived as former commander of **29. Feldartillerie-Brigade**. **Generalmajor** Paulus von Stolzmann departed **Abschnitt G zwischen Mass und Moselle** in May. In the last German offensive of the war in June 1918, von Stolzmann led the **78. R. D.** with Bruns still commanding **Res. I. R. 259** against French and American forces under **7. Armee** at Soissons. The German attack failed and the **78. R. D.** suffered great losses, requiring the remaining troops to serve as replacements for other divisions on the line. **Res. I. R. 258** soldiers were subordinated to the **185. I. D.** and became part of the **I. R. 65, I. R. 161** and **Res. I. R. 28**.[1668] On 15 June 1918 von Stolzmann was promoted to **Generalleutnant** and became commander of **16. I. D.**, a Rhenish division. Under the command of **17. Armee**, the **16. I. D.** fought their last battles in the area of Dury and Villiers-lez-Cagnicourt. They were pushed back from the **Siegfriedstellung**. The division was moved to support the **6. Armee** in the north at the **Hermannstellung**. His last battle was at Antwerp–Maas. After the Armistice von Stolzmann led **16. I. D.** back to Germany where he assumed new responsibilities as a senior officer in the new German republic. On 9 May 1919, he was transferred to the **XI Armeekorps** and became leader of **National Guard Brigade 11**

followed by command of Defence area IV in the Dresden region. Von Stolzmann achieved a final promotion to **General der Infanterie** and retired on 15 June 1921. Von Stolzmann dedicated his remaining years to supporting the veterans organization known as the **Stahlhelm** Movement. He contributed a few articles to *Das Regiment*, the **78. R. D.**'s veterans magazine. When he died in August 1930, **General der Infanterie** von Stolzmann was mourned by the soldiers that he led.[1669]

Major Frederick Bruns commanded **Res. I. R. 259** until its termination in August, when he was reassigned to **I.R. 138**. Bruns received a personally autographed picture of Kaiser Wilhelm for repeated distinguished service in the face of the enemy. Bruns was awarded the *Pour le Mérite* as a Colonel, on November 16 1918, just before war's end. As for accounts of recognized heroism by **KTK Major** Bruns' **Stosstruppen**, no

Members of the former *Reserve Infanterie Regiment 258* lay a wreath in memory of the *78. Reserve Division*, Hannover, 23 September 1933. (*Geschichte des Reserve-Infanterie-Regiments Nr. 258*)

known record survived. Despite the accolades mentioned in the reports to higher headquarters, there are no records that **Leutnant Grumbrecht** or any of the other **Kirschblüte** combatants receiving an award. If the percentage of Iron Crosses from **Einladung** recommended by **Hauptman** Seebohm applied to **Kirschblüte**, approximately 440 **Sturmtruppen** and **Stosstruppen** would have been awarded the Iron Cross 2nd Class. With the **Res. I.R. 259** demise, Bruns was reassigned to **42. I.D. 3** (Lower Alsace) **I.R. 138** on 16 August and remained in that unit until the Armistice. In the major French offensive in the Champagne region, Bruns personally led his regiment into the most advanced line of defence. They suffered major losses against the French attack, but Bruns formed a final unit of resistance and attacked, stopping the French momentum with a barrage of grenades. **Generalmajor** Buchholtz recommended Bruns for the *Pour le Mérite* for this battle. On 6 November, **Oberstleutnant** Bruns received the highest award for his bravery and leadership in executing the successful counter-attack. After the Armistice **Oberstleutnant** Bruns returned to Germany with **I.R. 138** and demobilized the unit. He became a commander of a newly formed infantry regiment of the **Friekorps Faupel (Goerlitz)** in March 1919. In that capacity he led an assault on Dachau and fought in München. He remained an active member of the **Stahlhelm** organization and later the **SA Reserve**.[1670]

THE WOËVRE RETURNS TO FRENCH CONTROL

At the end of the St. Mihiel offensive the 89th Division held the new front line for the southern Woëvre front. On 1 October, 89th Division relieved the 42nd Division and linked up with the *39ᵉ division d'infanterie*. The 89th Division's sector continued to expand along the Woëvre when they relieved the 78th Division, occupying ground east of Flirey. Three days later, the 89th Division minus the artillery was relieved by the 37th Division, a depot division that remained in

position on the Woëvre until 16 October 1918. On that day France's *131ᵉ division d'infanterie* relieved them and the Woëvre returned to total French control for the remainder of the war.[1671]

POST-ARMISTICE – *VIIIᴱ ARMÉE* ASSUMES A NEW MISSION

Général Gérard and his *VIIIᵉ armée* received a new mission at the Armistice. He was ordered to proceed with *VIIIᵉ armée* to occupy the Rhineland Palatinate. His counterpart, *Général* Charles Emmanuel Marie Mangin, commanded the *Xᵉ armée* with their headquarters at Mainz. Their *armée* group commander, *Général* Emile Fayolle, deferred any political involvement with German citizens to Mangin and Gérard. The issue was annexation of the Rhineland – a very sensitive topic for the occupying powers, the defeated nation of Germany, and the citizens of the region.[1672] Gérard managed to incense the German government, who accused him of violating the terms of the Armistice agreement to promote and support revolution and separation of the Palatinate from Bavaria and Germany. In May 1919, the German government demanded Gérard be relieved of his command immediately. Clemenceau scolded rather than fired the two generals – avoiding a domestic furor within France. Needless to say, the issue complicated relations not only with an unstable post-Kaiser German government, but with the Allied military leadership occupying German territory as a whole. After almost a year, Clemenceau finally relieved Gérard and Mangin and established a permanent *Armée du Rhin* under the command of *Général* Jean Marie Degoutte. As the summer heated up, so did the anger of those in the occupied areas. Clemenceau summed up the controversy for President Wilson and Prime Minister Lloyd George: "The marshal [*Maréchal* Foch] has placed at Mainz and Köln [it was actually Landau] two generals of whom one, Mangin, is a good soldier but a bad politician, while the other, Gérard, is a mediocre soldier and an execrable politician."[1673]

CHAPTER 30

To the Victors the Historical Record

On 30 May members of the 26th Division held a memorial service at Ménil-la-Tour. Every 102nd Field Artillery battery had members attending the ceremony, led by the regimental band to the graves. General Traub was present with a few French officers. As the American flag was raised, the French officers advanced and placed the French tricolour next to it. General Traub placed a flag upon every grave – a total of 200 in all. Traub then spoke. He said he was not there to talk about patriotism, that virtue was evident from the surroundings and the men in attendance. Sacrifice and courage were mentioned. Then General Traub requested the soldiers to turn west in the direction of the United States and salute. The soldiers responded, tears welling in their eyes. The ceremony ended with the playing of the French and American national anthems. For the members of the 102nd Field Artillery, one detail was never forgotten. As General Traub went from grave to grave decorating them with flags, a muffled sob came from the ranks. He was approaching Private Dell Warner's grave. Warner was a medic for the battery. Someone whispered, "The General is decorating Dell's grave now." The soldiers looked aside and saw Warner's younger brother in the ranks, tears rolling down his cheeks and trying to maintain composure. Warner was killed on the day of the Seicheprey battle. Flowers for the graves were purchased by the soldiers or gathered from the nearby fields. The soldiers had gone into the fields and collected enough flowers to fill the company truck bed.[1674]

A SPIRITUAL BONDING

The American correspondent Heywood Broun of the *New York Tribune* saw the battle as symbolic, or a synecdoche: "Seicheprey, the first big American battle, had every element of the World War in little. Before the loss of the village … the troops defending it had fought from ambush and in the open, had fought with gas and liquid fire, with grenades, rifles, and machine-guns. In the inferno the new troops were giving proof of valor that was to come out later and be scattered broadcast, as a measure of what America would bring. In and out of the streets of Seicheprey, in its little public square, from the yards of its houses, hundreds of American soldiers were fighting for their lives. France lay behind them, trusting to be saved."[1675]

United States Ambassador to France, Hugh C. Wallace, gave an oration at the grave of the unknown soldier at the *Arc de Triomphe* on 29 May 1921: "Soldier of France! I speak to you, for you still have ears to hear. We praise you, but we can do you but little honor, for you are above and beyond all earthly tribute. Your resting-place, a hallowed tomb for you, is for us a shrine … The spirit which took you into battle was the spirit of France. The courage and devotion which led you on to the supreme sacrifice of life for home and country are at once a precious memory and an example to be followed by all who shall come after you. France will not perish while that memory lasts."[1676] *L'Action Française* responded to Wallace's words with: "Such sentiments show us the height which French prestige and thought have attained in the world; they solemnly attest the pure idealism, the generous humanism which inspire the guiding spirit of the young American civilization. They honour France, to whom they are addressed, as much as they honour America, whose soul they reveal."[1677]

A PULITZER PRIZE AND AN ADVERSARY'S SUMMARY

The two leading First World War commanders both mentioned Seicheprey in their works. General Pershing told his story in the Pulitzer Prize-winning two-volume history published in 1931. As it concerned Seicheprey, there was no credit given to the German military's masterful planning nor blame directed at his command. Instead, General Pershing succinctly covered in twelve sentences what he considered relevant for the reading public:

On the night of April 20th-21st, the Germans made a raid on the 26th Division in the vicinity of Seicheprey. The attack covered a two-mile front extending west from the *Bois de Remières*. It came during a heavy fog and was a complete surprise to our troops, who were considerably outnumbered. The fighting in Seicheprey was violent, causing heavy losses on both sides. The town was taken by the enemy. The success of the raid may be attributed largely to the destruction by the German artillery of the divisional system of communications, which naturally resulted in some confusion in the division. Although cooperation among the units was difficult under the circumstances, it was finally established and the original front

was reoccupied the following day. In this affair we lost 1 officer, 80 enlisted men, killed; 11 officers, 176 enlisted men wounded; 3 officers, 211 enlisted men, gassed; and 5 officers, 182 enlisted men, missing and prisoners. The losses of the enemy killed and wounded were reported as even greater.[1678]

As mentioned earlier, the counsel provided by Lieutenant Colonel George Marshall on 24 November 1930 regarding the draft was telling:

Criticism of the 26th Division is a delicate affair. There is this to be said on the side of the division: A raid was usually, almost invariably, a surprise – by the very nature of the operation. Most raids, I guess about 80%, succeeded for this reason, the local garrison having a small chance against the overwhelming assault, and under the heavy concentration of artillery fire. Furthermore, and especially, Seichprey [sic] was one of the most vulnerable spots on the western front. (I labored personally with its defense for several months.) I suggest you pass this affair by without adverse comment. Nothing is gained by the criticism, mild as it is, and the solid animosity of an entire region will certainly be awakened. The game is not worth the candle.[1679]

General Pershing's primary German adversary for most of the war, **General der Artillerie** von Gallwitz, summed up the attack in his memoirs, repeating what he had been told by the **78. R. D**. command. He echoed Hoffmann's assessment that the American artillery counter-barrage was weak. However, the 1st Battalion, 102nd Infantry Regiment was mentioned for its close combat ferocity, despite having completed relief just two hours prior. Von Gallwitz listed the "spoils" from the attack as 5 officers, 178 men, 10 heavy and 15 light machine guns. He referred to the information gleaned from prisoners of war. He was very interested in the 26th Division prisoner roll call and how they identified themselves: 78 as Americans; 8 German; 22 Irish; 7 Swedes; 22 French; 4 Russian; 14 English; 2 Scots; 13

Private Cyril Finnegan and Lieutenant Theodore Finnegan; a Seicheprey veteran ponders his past while his son – a combat veteran of the Pacific Theatre – looks to the future. (Finnegan)

Italians; 1 Dane; 9 Poles; and 1 Swiss.[1680] The numbers of different "ethnic" groups in just one regiment was disturbing. A massive flood of soldiers was arriving to continue the battle against what was left of the Germans, a diverse entourage that included German descendants, and all enemies of Germany.

THE APOLOGISTS

Reporters, veterans, and friends of the Yankee Division published their own accounts of the exploits. Most mixed high drama with propagandistic flair. The stories had a common purpose – ensure the history was positive for a venerable fighting force with a tradition that went back to the earliest days of the nation. T. Howard Kelly was a leading figure, publishing his book, *Hey Buddy*, and producing a movie that featured a cameo by Major General Edwards. He wrote a fierce defence of Edwards that caught the attention of Pershing, who placed it in his personal file on the man. As it concerned Seicheprey, Kelly's writing inserted every excuse possible to soften any negativity:

Shortly after this Battle of Seicheprey it was widely rumored that G.H.Q. had severely criticized us for losing about 130 prisoners.

The Germans made this attack in such superior numbers and under superior strategical military conditions that it was impossible for us not to have lost prisoners. Edwards had protested the 'sacrifice' plan. The Corps Commander exercised direct authority over the brigade commander, and Edwards could not rush reinforcements into the fight. Our total casualties were 634 including prisoners taken, and eighty men killed, because many men were killed and wounded in battery positions and other parts of the front by enemy artillery … Our estimate of the German losses was placed at about 1200 to 1500. We buried 165 Germans … The sum total of Seicheprey was that the Germans evidently came over to stay in parts of our own lines … Officers tell me that there are German reports, in the War Department archives, that literally admit we licked the Germans to a frazzle at Seicheprey.[1681]

Three histories appeared shortly after the war ended that displayed varied degrees of accuracy and passion: from Benwell, Sibley, and Taylor.[1682] Harry Benwell wrote what he thought the veterans wanted to remember. It was "a tribute to the men of the Division and to its great leader, Clarence Ransome Edwards." Detail was subsumed in speculation. "The Boches were favored by a heavy fog, and were upon the

New Englanders before they realized what had happened. Company C of the 102d Infantry was surprised, and practically the whole unit was captured. Many desperate combats took place in the mist." Bertrand was the great heroic figure: "It was at this time that Colonel Bertrand, commanding a French regiment, led his troops in a counter-attack on Fleury, mounted on a horse." Benwell allowed General Edwards ample space to tell his story of Seicheprey:

> Early in the morning, 4 o'clock, the most violent bombardment on all the rear areas, on Seicheprey, Rombacaur and on the connecting trenches, took place … Thirteen hundred shock troops came down between Seicheprey and Ramschelle, and another 1,500 came around from Remier, starting for Seicheprey, and the artillery just smothered us … The Germans swept down into the middle of the town. They overran our machine guns, and they had big clubs; they carried 5-kilogram nitroglycerine boxes, and they all had trench knives … They outgunned us by 4 or 5 to 1, and they kept up this artillery concentration for over thirty-six hours. It was as much as your life was worth to go anywhere. I would not let them go to pick up our dead. We buried 164. The Boches worked thirty-six hours with twenty-six pairs of litter bearers taking away their wounded. We carefully examined prisoners, and everybody else after that, and there is no doubt that their casualties amounted to 1,200. We lost very nearly 150 prisoners. We had gassed or slightly wounded about 600, and the permanent losses were about 200 … We found the Boche coming down the Laiville trench, and we put all the Twenty-sixth artillery on that trench, as well as the 69th, and we massacred them.[1683]

Major Emerson Gifford Taylor, known by his feloow officers as the "millionaire adjutant", published his evaluation of the 26th Division in 1920, *New England in France, 1917–1919*. Taylor referred to the inherent defects of the National Guard system, as well as the particular weakness of the Guard in 1917 owing to the recent numerous withdrawals resulting from the experiences on the Mexican border and the attractions of the Reserve Officers Corps. But the disadvantages were more than counterbalanced by the volunteer spirit of both the old members and new recruits, the stimulus of local patriotism, and the sympathy existing between officers and men. He also admitted that the guardsmen were slow in acquiring discipline and efficiency, but the Yankee Division had a legitimate cause for complaint thanks to its treatment by the War Department, the higher authorities of the American Expeditionary Force, and many individual officers of the Regular Army. It took a leader like Major General Edwards to counter this. The National Guard suffered a temporary suspension of recruitment and replacement of militia regimental commanders by regulars. In France, the coolness towards the National Guard continued. For the Yankee Division, it spurred the members to prove themselves as good or better than regular troops. Finally, Taylor made the case that the 26th Division suffered considerable inconvenience from Chaumont, who neglected to return healed wounded veterans to their units and were tardy in sending replacements, which destroyed the solidarity and weakened the unit's fighting strength. The practice of limiting promotions to one-third of the vacancies caused by battle casualties and filling of all others by replacements caused many men who had proved their worth to be deprived of well-earned rewards and brought into the division some utterly incompetent officers.[1684]

GENERAL EDWARDS TELLS HIS STORY

General Edwards' account of Seicheprey was a paean to the fallen. Their efforts were not in vain. His veterans still saw him as their leader, even unto death. Edwards teamed up with Augustin Maher in 1919 to tell his side. Filled with lofty terminology and exhortations, General Edwards pushed the limits of credibility. It was intended for one audience – his soldiers. It must be compared to the actual report that he signed off on 23 April 1918. While at his headquarters at Boucq, he issued the "Report of Enemy Raid on Troops of the 26th Division at Seicheprey, April 20/21, 1918". Edwards claimed the German rationale for attacking Seicheprey was to challenge the 26th Division's ability to hold the southern Woëvre front area that previously had been thinly held by one-and-a-half French divisions.[1685]

Edwards inflated his numbers "Out of Richecourt, the nearest town on the north-west held by the Germans, filed eighteen hundred German shock troops, picked from the forces in the north for the purpose of teaching the Yankee his first lesson in the World War. To the north-east, through Bois de Remières, came fifteen hundred more of the same picked troops. The two forces aimed for the ends of the Sibille Trench, and as they came through the German wire they picked up the German forces in the Hun trenches ... shortly after 4 o'clock the seven platoons of Connecticut guardsmen were surrounded on all sides by over 3,500 German troops."[1686]

Excitement builds with his description of the fight in the Seicheprey village: "The German picked shock troops and the boys from Connecticut met in the center of the town. Rifles were abandoned except to be used as clubs, while hand grenades and bombs and knives did their deadly work in a hand-to-hand encounter ... No man who was in that fight in the town of Seicheprey any more than he who was in the Sibille Trench will ever forget that hour which made Seicheprey famous. The Germans remained in the town of Seicheprey not more than fifteen minutes on that black morning of April 20."[1687] Edwards kept the excitement going to the very last paragraph:

They intended to crucify us. They wanted to put the iron into our souls and show us that we couldn't fight in this war in which they had been so long triumphant. And I want to say right now, and I want the people of Connecticut to appreciate it, for I am mightly glad that they are interested in their boys, that no regiment in the

American Expeditionary Force in France has a better record than the 102nd Infantry, which was made up of the old Connecticut National Guard. The Battle of Seicheprey was the first effort of the Huns to try out the American troops ... the Huns had not had a chance to test the metal of the American fighter ... The Americans were mad ... There were reports that some of the boys in the Sibille Trench and some of the prisoners had been mutilated by the Germans. They wanted revenge and they wanted it quick ... The American forces crossed the intervening mile and a quarter space and were upon the Germans occupying the old American trench. They took sweet revenge for the morning before, but the Germans didn't wait to be exterminated, as they would have been, for they fled out of the trench and across No Man's Land and beyond their own wire ... But I will say this, and I say it without fear of contradiction, that no regiment in the whole American Expeditionary Force had a better record than the 102d.[1688]

EMOTIONS RIDING HIGH

After the war, several commanders on both sides wrote their memoirs to supplement their pension, or to "set the record straight." On the German side, Hindenburg, Ludendorff and Gallwitz wrote what remains today the most important work for our understanding of the German **OHL** and senior commands on the Western Front. General Pershing's work is considered by many to be the most definitive assessment of America's accomplishments in the war. Other American generals first published memoirs through popular periodicals and then as books. Lieutenant General Robert Bullard first published an article through William Randolph Hearst's newspapers entitled "Story of the World War", and followed it with *Personalities and Reminiscences of the War* describing his experience with the 1st Division and subsequent commands. His shots directed at Major General Edwards resurrected animosity on both sides. He devoted an entire chapter to them, "Relief From the Quiet Sector." Seven years after the Armistice, the media reintroduced the spat between Bullard and Edwards. Bullard used a sneering understatement: "During our occupation of this sector we had the good luck always to repel his efforts successfully and even severely but the American Twenty-sixth Division that relieved our own here suffered a serious mishap."[1689] Bullard flagged up his own magnanimity and contrasted it with his antagonist's complaints to higher authority:

> Everybody was generous and helpful to our relief, the 26th ("Yankee") Division, of New England, commanded by General Clarence Edwards, which, however, was so fault-finding and officially critical of our shortcomings, made such bad reports of us to our common military superiors that for long afterward we were kept explaining, fighting our own people behind while we fought the enemy in front. We welcomed the 26th Division everywhere, fed them in some places (in person I saw to the rationing of one battalion or regiment whose commander vehemently declared that it was "starving"), provided them with ammunition and equipped them with many essential articles that they had not. They may have appreciated all of this – I don't know – but I do know that they did not fail to note and report us for all faults and shortcomings that we had committed and many that we had not committed.[1690]

Edward's apologist T. Howard Kelly, a sergeant who proudly served in the Yankee Division, fired back in his article, "Why General Edwards Was Sent Home."[1691] The Yankee Division Veterans Association monthly newsletter published their own piece on the Bullard versus Edwards story, going to Edwards for his thoughts on the matter. Edwards responded with lofty discretion: "I cannot find it in my heart at this time to say anything, even to repel an unjust attack upon the Twenty-sixth Division, which might bring discord among comrades who fought a great fight together in a great and triumphant cause

… I shall take for my guide the counsel of Ecclesiastics, 'Strive for the truth unto death and the Lord God shall fight for thee.' For your information I am glad to be able to assure you that I never at any time made any report to any authority in criticism of the First Division."[1692]

Lieutenant General Hunter Liggett's thoughts on the 1st Division and 26th Division in the Toul sector were expressed in *Commanding an American Army,* ghostwritten by his aide Major Stackpole, followed three years later by *A.E.F.: Ten Years Ago in France,* courtesy of Wesley W. Stout and the *Saturday Evening Post.*[1693] *Bois-Brûlé* and Apremont were not mentioned and Seicheprey was portrayed as "a defeat".[1694] Veterans wrote asking the general to account for statements that were incorrect on the timing of the division's arrival in theatre, for the lack of training at the front when the 26th Division was serving with the French at Chemin-des-Dâmes, and the absence of any mention of Apremont. The response to Seicheprey being labelled a defeat prompted a passionate reminder that this wasn't a fair fight: "These Yanks, though practically surrounded and hemmed in on a small piece of ground, put up as game and as desperate a fight as did any American unit on any part of the front during the remainder of the war. They never lost an inch of ground unless they were killed or taken prisoners. They held their sector for twenty-eight hours under the severest of fire, and that is no small accomplishment in itself." The author John H. Smith, formally of the 101st Infantry, concluded by pointing out that Liggett did not mention the 26th Division's successful drive to Vigneulles in the St. Mihiel offensive, securing the area before the 1st Division. Smith's final comment to his former commander summed up the sentiment of many a 26th Division veteran: "Thanking you for your attention and trusting that you will adjust your somewhat inaccurate article and present it to the American people whom the Guard did just as much to protect as did the regulars."[1695]

Perhaps the most emotional response was from the monthly "Diablo" column of *Yankee Doings* entitled "They're At It Again":

The military wizards upon whose shoulders rested the enormous task of winning the late war are still telling the world how rotten some of us were and patting a few on the back. The latest "Higher Up" to sock the old YD is this Liggett bird. He seems to take the same inane delight in whacking the devil out of us as did Bullard not so long ago … he [Pershing] must have told his "dog robbers" to lambast the old YD every chance they got, because every time one of these Generals is approached with an offer from a magazine to dig up some dirt, they promptly sock the YD. Liggett says we had no discipline, no liaison in the rumpus at Belleau Woods; suppose he expected us to keep a perfect line such as he was accustomed to viewing back in the states on evening parade … You regulars will always feel antagonistic toward our Grand Old Man [Edwards], but he proves himself a far better man and soldier than you by keeping his mouth shut, and letting his friends defend him as best they can. Your day is done, your star has set, and by your own pen you have cast to the winds all affection thousands of ex-soldiers who served under you might have had. Silence is the gold of wisdom.[1696]

Liggett amended his subsequent published book to describe **Einladung** briefly, without reference to who fought at that time or where, and followed up in the next paragraph by describing Seicheprey: "Our first skirmish was a check. On the enemy's part, it really was only a large-scale raid for information purposes. We avenged it in the first ten minutes of the St. Mihiel drive five months later." Again, no mention was ever made of *Bois-Brûlé* and Apremont.[1697]

A TACTICAL COMMANDER REVIEWS HIS TROOPS

In 1927, *Général* Passaga had the opportunity to come to the United States to visit New England and Washington DC and become reacquainted with soldiers that served under his tactical command in 1918. He was feted at dinners

and memorials. At Fort Devens, Massachusetts, the 26th Division and the 104th Infantry gave a review for their Corps Commander. The moment epitomised the general, a stern veteran with a compassion that complemented that of his division commanders, particularly General Edwards. He awarded the *Croix de Guerre* to two soldiers who were still recovering from battle wounds suffered at *Bois-Brûlé* on 12 April 1918. Nine years later, Lieutenant Corbin and Sergeant Dickerman were officially awarded their medals on the fields of Massachusetts.

SERVICE TO THE NATION

Irene McIntyre spent 256 days along the southern Woëvre front exposed to enemy artillery. She worked with the 26th Division and 82nd Division at Raulecourt before the St. Mihiel drive. Both Irene and Gladys went to Vacqueville and supported the 77th Division and 37th Division. Gladys had to leave the front as a result of an appendicitis. In the second week of the Meuse-Argonne offensive Irene was back with the 1st Division assisting surgeons with triage support. She was twice gassed – earning two personal citations in US Army orders. "Under fire of high explosives and gas, she established and conducted huts that were noted for their good cheer and hospitality. Her courage and devotion to her voluntary work were a splendid inspiration to the troops." Irene saw more of the war at close quarters than any other American woman. Her support to the American forces was so well respected that she was recommended for the Distinguished Service Cross, requiring an act of Congress. It did not happen.[1698]

During the war Irene met Lieutenant Robert E. Walbridge, Supply Officer to the 103rd Machine Gun Battalion, 26th Division. It was a casual acquaintance. In 1920, Irene was invited to an Armistice Day celebration at Peterborough, New Hampshire. Dressed in the faded uniform that she wore during her year at the front, she came to the speaker's platform and met Walbridge for the first time since the war.

Général Passaga is finally able to award the *Croix de Guerre* in 1928 to Sgt Dickerman, the trench-mortar hero at Apremont. (*Yankee Doings*)

Their friendship turned into romance and marriage a year later. Irene settled in Robert's home in Peterborough. Her commitment to veterans became inspirational as the President of the Ladies Auxiliary of the American Legion throughout the 1920s.[1699]

STUBBY'S LEGEND CONTINUES

Today Seicheprey is almost synonymous with Stubby, the dog wounded near the 102nd Infantry PC. Stubby accompanied Corporal Robert Conroy through all four major campaigns fought by the 102nd Regiment. Stubby earned one wound stripe and three service stripes at the front. The media splashed his image whenever they could. In later life Stubby was met by three American presidents: Wilson, Harding, and Coolidge. On July 6, 1921, General Pershing decorated Stubby as a wounded hero of the First World War, and he became a symbol not only of the Yankee Division but of the American soldier. When Robert Conroy attended Georgetown University, he managed to persuade the school to adopt Stubby as their official mascot. When Stubby passed away, Conroy donated the remains of one of the most beloved mascots ever to serve with the military, along with Conroy's own archives, to the Smithsonian Institution.[1700]

A FLAIR FOR THE DRAMATIC

Seicheprey accounts were buried under the impressive exploits of the following campaigns at Cantigny, Château-Thierry, Second Marne, St. Mihiel and Meuse-Argonne. Jack Pearl, a Second World War veteran of the North Africa, Sicily, and Italian campaigns, turned to television scripts and wrote an exciting account of the A.E.F. in France. His version of the Seicheprey battle reveals a creative imagination:

On April 21, under cover of a devastating artillery barrage, 5,000 determined Germans advanced on the strategic village. They cut through Remières Wood, the strongest flanking defensive position to the west of Seicheprey, hit the other flank and isolated the Connecticut Battalion inside the town, then launched a sledge-hammer blow squarely on the "button" of Major Rau's Yankee outfit. With German shells whistling through the bare rafters of the demolished HQ, Rau's staff was badly rattled. Rau sensed that his outfit would soon fall apart unless he could think of something to fire its spirit. Rising to the occasion, as only a great commander can, he leaned back in his chair, propped up his feet on a littered desk, and stuck a big black cigar in his mouth. "Boys," he said lightly, "now we got 'em right where we want 'em. The poor slobs have got us surrounded." That did the trick. A loud war whoop went up from the officers, and the Connecticut Battalion was in business again. No group of men ever were more magnificent than were Rau's men that day. The Germans must have believed they were facing a regiment rather than a battalion.

Every man in the outfit became an infantryman – cooks, clerks, medics, and even an assortment of prisoners from a local US post stockade with the big white PW initials stenciled on their prison jackets ... They [the Germans] were ambushed singly and collectively from thickets, low-hanging tree branches, and from behind rocks. One cook, who had been a butcher in civilian life, wielded two meat cleavers with fiendish abandon. He split two German skulls "as neatly as I used to split a hog's head," and beheaded a third with a roundhouse slash ... the 26th Division was in Seicheprey to stay.[1701]

CONNECTICUT REMEMBERS

In 1968, the fiftieth anniversary of Seicheprey, the state of Connecticut held a simple ceremony. It was a bad time for memorialising past battles. The United States was immersed in the Vietnam War and 1968 was the nadir, with the Tet offensive just concluding. On 20 April, the commemoration proceeded with Governor John Dempsey presiding: "Though they had the advantage of a fierce artillery barrage before their assault, and although they battled tenaciously, the proud Sturmtruppen were thrown back, their mission a failure. The Battle of Seicheprey proved once and for all to France and to Britain that the United States troops were fighting men of the finest quality, and that the United States would prove to be the ally that was needed to bring the First World War to a victorious conclusion. Those who fought at Seicheprey fifty years ago today, may always be proud of their performance, as Connecticut always will be proud of them."[1702]

POSTHUMOUS EXONERATION

Major John J. Gallant was dismissed from the US Army and did not serve his conviction at Fort Leavenworth. He returned to the United States a broken man with a dishonourable discharge. In February 1919, he wrote to General Edwards requesting his help in getting his case overturned.

Edwards' resentment appeared to have waned: "I do not know what to say to your letter. I gave orders that you should have any counsel that you wanted in the whole division or any other place and detailed the man that you chose. I read over your proceedings several times. You were so silent on many of the issues that it seemed to be an acquiescence." Edwards told Gallant to write to General Samuel T. Ansell in Washington DC to commence proceedings for an appeal.[1703] He did so:

> General Edwards suggests that I try and get my case before you. I was tried in France for disobedience of orders and sentenced to dismissal from the service. Trial and everything connected therewith was an injustice. I have appealed to the President. The papers are probably with the Adjutant General. Will you kindly advise me if I am not entitled to another trial (Par 21 M.C.M.)? Is it not possible to have an investigation made. There are a number of important witnesses whose names I do not know. Several important witnesses desired by me were not called. The name of one appeared during the trial. My counsel was apparently trying to save others from blame. Several of the facts on which I depend to prove my allegations have not been stated by me as I do not at the present time care to give those who oppose me any information. Very respectfully, John J. Gallant. (Ex-Major USR).[1704]

Gallant's plea was rejected. Frank Sibley took up his cause and let Gallant state his position in his book as an appendix. Gallant's writing did not generate much response; his dishonourable discharge was retained. The multi-lingual Gallant found employment with the Nicholson File Company of Providence, R.I., as their travelling foreign representative. In 1933 while serving in India he was stricken with a disease that crippled him and resulted in his death two years later at the age of 59.[1705]

Veterans of the 3rd Battalion, 102nd Infantry, were shocked while attending a 1932 reunion to learn that Major Gallant had been tried and court martialled. No one had known. They thought he had been transferred to another unit. Gallant had ceased all communication with them. 102nd Infantry veterans attempted to appeal but were informed the case was closed.[1706] The case against Major John Gallant was nevertheless taken up by Sergeant Arthur A. Service and Sergeant Frederick Clinton of Company L. It took them nearly 40 years struggling with government red tape and indifference to prevail. They argued that the confused situation before the planned counter-attack was largely due to the determination of General Traub to bypass Colonel Parker and attempt to direct the action from his 51st Brigade headquarters far to the rear. Sergeant Service pointed out that telephone communications were broken and liaison by runner was slow. The basic order from the *32ᵉ corps d'armée* for the counter-attack was conditional upon the reports of patrols concerning the location of the enemy. The 51st Brigade rewrote the attack order making the operation mandatory – ignoring any findings from reconnoitring patrols. Although the intended attack was proven unnecessary and if undertaken would have resulted in heavy casualties to the French troops, the Brigade commander [Traub] brought charges against Major Gallant on the grounds that the *corps d'armée* order's conditionality "concerned simply me and didn't concern my subordinates. The way I worded the order to my subordinates was the only thing that concerned them."[1707]

Sergeant Service and Sergeant Clinton remembered being ordered to counter-attack in *Bois de Remières* despite knowing that French troops were holding the ground. Clinton recalled: "If we had moved on Remières we would have barraged the French and attacked them from behind. It would have been a calamity and led to an international incident." Working with Congressman Monagan of Connecticut, the case was effectively reintroduced. The judgement, on 30 June 1972, reads:

It appears that the evidence only supports beyond a reasonable doubt a failure to obey

rather than a willful disobedience of a lawful command from his superior officer … The modifications of the sentence to no punishment is not intended to affect the findings of guilty, as modified. All rights, privileges, and property of which the accused has been deprived by virtue of that portion of the findings of guilty and that portion of the sentence so set aside will be restored. George, S. Prugh, Major General, USA, The Judge Advocate General.[1708]

CHIEFS OF STAFF

Four soldiers that played major roles during the 1st Division's time at Seicheprey led the US Army later in life as Chief of Staff. Colonel John L. Hines served as Chief of Staff at the rank of Major General from September 1924 to November 1926. Brigadier General Summerall, 1st Artillery Brigade commander, followed Major General Hines and served as Chief of Staff from November 1926 to November 1930. Colonel Malin Craig ended his career as Chief of Staff from October 1935 to August 1939. On his last day as Chief of Staff he said, "I'm going out to California and practice keeping my mouth shut."[1709] His successor, Lieutenant Colonel George Marshall, was promoted from BG and Deputy Chief of Staff to become Chief of Staff in 1939 at the critical moment as war in Europe commenced for a second time in the 20th century.

THE FINEST SOLDIER

George Marshall persevered for the next twenty years waiting for promotion to general rank – a goal that remained elusive despite a stellar record and accomplishments that were recognized by General Pershing and fellow seniors as the best. He epitomised the excellence of instruction at Fort Leavenworth, the schooling ground of the army elite prior to the war. His time at the Woëvre confirmed his ability to apply operational experience to masterful planning,

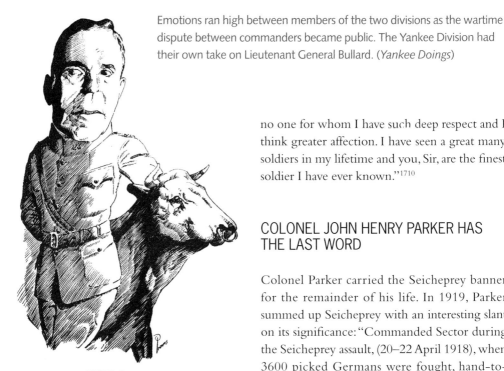

Emotions ran high between members of the two divisions as the wartime dispute between commanders became public. The Yankee Division had their own take on Lieutenant General Bullard. (*Yankee Doings*)

BULLard

culminating in Meuse-Argonne. Marshall's appointment as Chief of Staff was more than fortunate. He provided the US Army with the leadership that ensured the mature application of American army military might, making a critical difference in the Allies' winning the war. Marshall retired on 18 November 1945, returning to public service as President Harry Truman's Secretary of State. Perhaps the most eloquent tribute to this legendary figure came from Henry Stimson, Secretary of War under President William Howard Taft (at which time he was a personal friend of General Edwards) and later to President Franklin D. Roosevelt. Stimson had been integral in reforming the US Army into a division-organization prior to the First World War and was one of the greatest war secretaries in the nation's history while serving Roosevelt. At noon on Victory in Europe (VE) day, Secretary Stimson assembled a select group of generals and senior officials to his office, where he concluded his praise of General Marshall with: "It is rare in late life to make new friends; at my age it is a slow process but there is

no one for whom I have such deep respect and I think greater affection. I have seen a great many soldiers in my lifetime and you, Sir, are the finest soldier I have ever known."[1710]

COLONEL JOHN HENRY PARKER HAS THE LAST WORD

Colonel Parker carried the Seicheprey banner for the remainder of his life. In 1919, Parker summed up Seicheprey with an interesting slant on its significance: "Commanded Sector during the Seicheprey assault, (20–22 April 1918), when 3600 picked Germans were fought, hand-to-hand, 36 hours by one battalion and a half, and were finally driven back with loss of about half of their effectives. This attack was coincident with the heavy German drive on Amiens; and it was the news of the American success at Seicheprey that stiffened up the British line and saved Amiens."[1711]

A few months later, *Infantry Journal* published a review (in the February 1920) edition of *The American Army in the European Conflict*, a book by *colonel* De Chambrun and *capitaine* De Merenches. Colonel Parker immediately responded to both the review and the book in a 3,000-word letter to the editor:

This excellent review presents a very fine appreciation of the tribute by these two distinguished French Officers to the American Army, and as a book review is an admirable piece of work. It appears, however, that the reviewer might have possibly written that part of his review bearing upon the Seicheprey Raid in a different tone if his knowledge on that subject had been equal to his literary skill. As the Commanding Officer of the regiment that withstood the German Raid at Seicheprey, it seems to me that the time has come that a halt should be called to the criticisms based upon incomplete information, calculated to discredit a performance of American troops worthy to be classed with the best on record in this or any other war. Without raising the question as to the accuracy of the number stated by the reviewer as missing, because I have not on hand the exact data, and if the question is raised the data should be exact and official, it is desired to call attention to the fact that whether or not a loss of prisoners to the enemy is discreditable depends upon the circumstances of the loss and upon the mission of the troops that suffered the loss.[1712]

Parker refought the affair with all his vigour. His passion and eloquence went on the speaking trail throughout the state of Connecticut.

In 1937, Brigadier General (retired) John H. Parker was still fighting the good fight as the Spanish Civil War raged and the military power of Germany grew:

The Germans did take some prisoners at Seicheprey. They almost annihilated that front line battalion, but it (and our regimental company of machine guns) stopped them so dead that they never even reached our main line of resistance, the 1-Bis position. The box barrage they put around Seicheprey and Remeires [sic] Woods was so dense that a field mouse could not pass through it without having its tail cut off. Into the area thus protected they poured picked men, ten to one at the points of contact, and carried away the wounded who were capable of being transported … But the German attack at Seicheprey was broken up by our "Isles de Resistance," which were never completely carried by the enemy; and then

that 102nd Infantry machine gun company, the only machine guns I had been permitted to locate myself on the terrain, took the swine under continuous long range, overhead fire, swept their new trenches from end to end continuously hour after hour, and when our Observation Posts detected the massed German Troops at San Bausant [sic], just clamped down on them at long range, by map, a devastating machine-gun fire that flesh and blood could not withstand. It was not the correct moment for a counter-attack of that sort; it was exactly the wrong moment. If I could have thrown forward an equal force while the struggle was still going on in Seicheprey and Remières Woods, hand-to-hand, such a counter-attack would have had every prospect of success. But my orders strictly prohibited any such counter-attack. I risked initiative by ordering reinforcements forward;

Pershing and Marshall; two close friends for the rest of their lives, they shared the foundation of the modern US Army. (Marshall, *Memoirs*)

the order was peremptorily countermanded by General Traub, and I was vehemently told to bring back those who had started, and to stay, myself, at my PC unless special permission was given for me to leave it … Acts of gallantry innumerable; not one single instance ever came to my knowledge of anything else. Even the incident of Major John B. [sic] Gallant seems to me, in retrospect, to have been an exhibition of that supreme moral courage which dares to disobey an order in the belief that such disobedience is justified by the situation. It was at least proved that such an advance as Gallant was ordered to lead was wholly unnecessary, for a few patrols were able to cover the whole area Gallant was to have covered, without the loss of a man, whereas if Gallant had obeyed his orders by moving a whole battalion openly forward the losses would have been terrific when the Germans clamped down their box barrage around the battalion, as they would have done without a doubt.[1713]

So for Parker, Gallant is very far from being a coward; he saved lives. Parker concluded his memoir draft with another reference to morality: "One memory stands out. The Germans shot up our ambulances seeking to remove the wounded at Seicheprey. When the big gas concentration was sent over into *Bois de la Sonnard*, about June 11th, and caught a big concentration of Germans there, we suspended fire on that part of their lines until they had a chance to remove their injured men. We watched them for two days from our Observation Posts, and never fired a shot to impede them. Just a small difference in the ethics of the military profession….The 'Hun' never did make war except by 'frightfulness.' They don't understand any other way. So much for Seicheprey."

CONCLUSION

It was an exhilarating time for the US Army in early 1918, with enthusiastic soldiers in Regular Army and National Guard divisions arriving on the continent and launching into "The National Business" of warfare. New weapons of war were introduced and some had great potential, such as aviation's transformation of the third dimension, providing both aerial reconnaissance and aerial bombardment. Only the missions of airlift and airborne had yet to be created. Ironically, Dr Emil Reymond, one of the first to see the potential of airlift for casualties, was killed in the opening weeks of battle flying aerial observation over the Woëvre. Those first months of 1918 closed a vast gulf of understanding between the Allies. French commanders, emotionally scarred from having seen vast numbers of their countrymen and colonials slaughtered by new weapons and techniques, became godfather to the US Army. Some were innovative. Most fell back on their own experiences and the mantra of "they shall not pass." With this rigid doctrine in place, the French tutors brought Americans into the front lines piecemeal from late 1917 until June 1918. The exception was the deployment of the 1st Division followed by the 26th Division into the Woëvre. With that deployment the American army assumed a new 20th-century role – not imperialist but one in the spirit of cooperation – holding ground that was not theirs to possess. That spirit defined the United States for the remainder of the First World War, the Second World War, and the entire Cold War.

The Woëvre taught the US Army that the modern combat environment put everyone within range at serious risk. The new arsenal transformed the US Army and the brigade of US Marines that comprised half of the 2nd Division. All combatants came to terms with the incessant destruction by artillery, machine guns and sniper. Artillery shells with a variety of warheads formed the entire landscape of trench, revetment, and *abris*. Chemicals – a new weapon of mass destruction – created more casualties and fatalities and added to the feeling of helplessness, of stalemate.

INTELLIGENCE COLLECTION

America's introduction to the modern battlefield was further complicated by the German ability to monitor electronic communication, to the point of distorting command's perception of reality – an ideal objective of modern day Information War. Major Theodore Roosevelt Jr.'s candid admission of how the 1st Division dealt with wiretapping – talking faster over the phone line – shows how new the communication challenge was. The wireless intercept, combined with the Germans' ability to penetrate American lines almost at will and integrate themselves into American positions, seriously undermined operations. There is no telling how many Germans assigned to the task of interception had spent time in the United States and could understand whatever was said. As previously mentioned, there is no surviving data that details who penetrated the phone lines and set up false arrangements, or broke those lines when the operation required "decapitation" of the command element.

The 1st Division makes no mention of the Germans successfully intercepting the division's communications. The mocking of Edwards and Traub about "learning the game" that the Germans interjected on the American line as they spoke harmed the German effort in the remaining months of the war, as it made Americans take the responsibility of learning the daily code more seriously.

Erroneous intelligence played a role in shaping the affair. Brigadier General Traub made the decision to reinforce against an attack of forces streaming down from Richecourt and St. Baussant. Observation posts surmised an attack was being readied. Aerial reconnaissance did not confirm.

COMMAND AND STAFF

The Byzantine machinations of the Chaumont staff during this time did nothing to enchance the fighting potential of the American soldier as he faced the most arduous of challenges. The bias demonstrated by Pershing's staff bordered on harassment. The problem of liaison, be it between Allies, divisions on the line, or throughout the division itself, was not solved by the time of the Armistice. Chaumont should have led the effort in concert with the French to establish a culture of security that addressed wiretapping, spies, and secure communications throughout all operations in the battle zone. Attention to artillery disasters caused either by faulty weapons or procedures that led to fratricide should have involved recognized US Army artillery experts such as General Traub's advisor Colonel Cruikshank, to lead the

investigation and establish procedures for the entire AEF. Chaumont was the appropriate level to address the problems with the French-made 155mm field artillery piece, which appeared to be the main culprit. The command culture's insistence on monitoring ongoing division and staff decisions bordered on incompetence. A "hands off" process was called for to reinforce a division's confidence. As it was, the two-way lack of trust made Major General Edwards forward reports that were too guarded and had too little substance. Chaumont also failed to establish an appropriate protocol with *Général* Gérard, *VIIIe armée* staff at this time. The result was a botched relief between 1st Division and the 26th Division, one that created animosity for the remainder of the war between leadership and staffs. It reflected a dysfunctional relationship for commanders such as Edwards dealing with an administrative commander, General Liggett, who was simultaneously answering to his tactical commander *Général* Gérard. Finally, the fatal policy of "sacrifice positions" deserved immediate attention by Chaumont, which it did not get at Seicheprey and *Bois de Remières*, with dire outcomes. (As some kind of defence of Chaumont, everything was new to them: Joffre once said that the price of training a general officer was 25,000 casualties.)

Almost all of the commanders of the US Army knew each other. It was a small community of the elite, mainly groomed at West Point, and followed a similar path of assignments in the West, skirmishes in China, and the long-standing guerrilla war in the Philippines, where the future leaders played polo together. Several senior officers remembered Malin Craig as a little boy at a Western army post. America's adjustment to positional war should have been eased by such a culture. Everyone of course had the same objective of ensuring America's military role on the Western Front was a success; but Pershing's command staffs became obsessed with establishing dominance. Lieutenant Colonel Marshall complained about it. General Summerall described one staff member as sadistic. The ongoing hostility between 26th Division and Chaumont has never been forgotten by the veterans. In retrospect, it would have better served the US Army to replace commanders at the start with someone who reflected the attitude of the general staff. Pershing could have exploited Edwards' political acumen and sent him back to Washington with Major General Peyton March while the 26th Division was brigaded with the French at Chemin-des-Dâmes. A cadre of senior officers came to equate a division's fighting ability to the numbers of casualties sustained.

The Seicheprey affair could have been a subject of intense pride in the light of the heroism clearly demonstrated by soldiers placed in "sacrifice positions". Likewise, the Americans at *Bois-Brûlé* and Apremont the week before deserved similar acclaim. National Guard divisions proved themselves the equal of the Regular forces over the course of the war. But the fighting was clouded by the in-fighting. Chaumont should have been concentrating on the problems of wiretapping and infiltration (the uniform is not a passport) which would not only have been of great utility but also have demonstrated to the Allies that the Americans were rapidly assimilating the requirements of a modern battlefield. The next engagement at Cantigny continued to demonstrate American military potential and subsequent heroics at Belleau Wood and the Second Marne proved the depth of America's commitment. Serving American soldiers and marines became the equals of their seasoned Allied counterparts.

FRENCH LESSONS

French tactical command played a major and positive role in preparing American commanders and their divisions. The Americans had the human resources but knowledge of how to effectively work the line required time in place – a luxury that did not exist with the Allies as the changing dynamic of the war shifted permanently to the West after the Treaty of Brest-Litovsk. French *armées* held 80 per cent of the Western Front and it was logical that American forces learn the ropes while making

a contribution to the total defence supporting French divisions in a quiet region like the Woëvre. It became quickly apparent that French forces should assume tactical control of America's divisions in combat. The senior staffs knew the ground, the adversary, and held to principles that worked for positional war. It was to the Americans' lasting credit that despite their desire to be independent from any foreign military, they adhered to the French military's tactical control while retaining administrative control. This worked. It matured America's knowledge of the military art, applying a recognized baseline of French methods, including *groupe de combat*, *avion réglage*, and *aérostier* operations. All required a commitment to French standards and doctrine – one that paid off in the long run because Americans made it work within the context of their own independent culture.

Central to this important and overlooked period was the role played by *Général* Fénelon François Germain Passaga, *32ᵉ corps d'armée* commander. His stature was acknowledged by the American forces, as was his compassion in recognising American accomplishments in the Woëvre. Major General Bullard as the first division commander to serve under Passaga set the standard for communicating with a foreign boss – deferential and respectful. Bullard's successor, Major General Edwards, was equally deferential and quick to sieze any opportunity to praise his division, with Passaga's endorsement or personal attendance. Passaga expressed his concern when the 104th Infantry became engaged in the fighting at *Bois-Brûlé*. After arriving and seeing how the battle was successfully being fought, he departed with a confidence that allowed the 26th Division to continue the fight on their own terms. A few weeks later Passaga would personally award 117 *Croix de Guerre*.

AERIAL FORCE DEMONSTRATES ITS POTENTIAL

American aviation became a relevant part of the American combined arms over the southern

Woëvre front line. It was an ideal setting for grooming squadrons to better understand mission requirements in positional war. The two squadrons, 1st and 94th Aero Squadrons, became integral to the American presence on the line, supporting the 26th Division with aerial reconnaissance and pursuit. Both missions became proficient in the coming weeks, allowing the Americans to proceed to the next fight at Château-Thierry with a greater ability to support the divisions and engaging a more experienced German aviation threat. It was illuminating to see 1st Aero Squadron fly into the battle airspace and give it back in kind to the Germans – who clearly understood what their aviators needed to better support infantry on the line. The 94th Aero Squadron benefitted greatly from time in the Toul sector. Combat was limited but as the first American victories over their airfield demonstrated, American pilots had the ability to apply skills gleaned from French instruction. Confidence gained from time serving in an assigned sector allowed pursuit aviation to better understand how to support surface operations. This matured aviation's potential – and it became legendary in the remaining months of 1918.

APRIL 1915 AND APRIL 1918

In retrospect, the failed offensive of 19 April 1915 by the *5ᵉ compagnie du 63ᵉ régiment d'infanterie* to recapture the last 200 metres of trenches at *Bois de Mort-Mare* provides a stark symbol of the early war on the Woëvre. The *5ᵉ compagnie* attacked entrenched German lines with only forty men, who were annihilated by artillery. The added dreadful retribution by French command, including the contribution of *Général* Joffre at the very top, against those arbitrarily selected for punishment added to the sad litany of the

war's victims. The executed were also casualties. The four *poilus* from *5ᵉ compagnie du 63ᵉ régiment d'infanterie* (*Soldat* François Fontanaud, *Caporal* Antoine Morange, *Soldat* Félix François Louis Baudy, and *Soldat* Henri-Jean Présbot) were executed at a desperate time for France. Almost three years to the very day of the executions, on the same Woëvre front 3 kilometres away, a similar decision not to execute a counter-attack led to the court martial of Major Gallant. April 1918 was not April 1915. The feeling of desperation and impending doom of 1915 was clearly not clouding the thoughts of American forces in 1918. Both decisions were eventually overturned.

A STRATEGIC VIEW OF THE WOËVRE EXPERIENCE

The Woëvre was the longest-held section of the line for the Americans in the entire war. It brought the US Army into the modern age and demonstrated a deep commitment by all echelons to uphold the mission, even accepting the foreign concept of sacrifice positions. It also demonstrated that the American soldier could endure some of the worst conditions of any battlefield of the war. The Woëvre was the beginning of the role America's military took for the remainder of the century and to the present day. The US Army came of age those first months of 1918 to become the combat force necessary to continue the fight at Château-Thierry, Second Marne, and the return to St. Mihiel. It was a military force that readily served on foreign lands without expectation of retaining ground gained. For Europe, such commitment defined America's military response to the Second World War – a dedication that created one of the greatest military alliances in history – the North Atlantic Treaty Organization (NATO).

CHERRY BLOSSOM BATTLE PLAN

Divisionsbefehl Nr. 3, 18.April. 18[1714]

78th Reserve Division Section Ia. No. 929. Secret.
Subject: Cherry Blossom.
Extracts only to be distributed below Regimental Infantry and Artillery Staffs.
Strictly secret.
Divisional Order No. 3.
Order to attack.

1. The Division will attack the enemy's positions between ALFA Wood and REMIERES Wood (both inclusive), as well as the village of SEICHEPREY, in the early morning of y day from the region of LAHAYVILLE – western edge of SONNARD Wood, and will hold the position gained (excepting the village of SEICHEPREY) until further orders.

2. Object: Permanent damage to the enemy through losses, capture of prisoners and booty, as well as destruction of his positions and the strong point, SEICHEPREY, before evacuation.

3. Commander of Operations: Major General von Stolzmann.

   Commander of Infantry Attack: Colonel von Blankensee, Commander of the 78th Reserve Infantry Brigade.
   Artillery Commander: Lt. General Hoffmann. Generalleutnant und Artl. Kdr.
   Commander of Assault Troops: Major Bruns, 259th Reserve Infantry Regiment.
   Troops:
   a) **Infantry**: 259th Reserve Infantry Regiment; 3 companies of 258th Reserve Infantry Regiment; 2 assault companies and 1 machine-gun company of 14th Assault Battalion, wth flame projectors.
   b) **Artillery**: 22 Field Gun Batteries; 18 light Field Howitzer Batteries; 13 heavy Field Howitzer Batteries; 5 ten-centimeter batteries; 1 Infantry Gun Battery.
   c) **Minenwerfer**: 18 heavy Minenwerfer; 36 medium Minenwerfer; 60 light Minenwerfer.
   d) **Engineers**: 3 engineer platoons.
   e) Divisional Intelligence equipment as required.
   f) **Air Forces**: reinforced 298th Air Detachment (LES BARAQUES) reinforced 64th Pursuit Flight Squad, (MARS la TOUR), 123rd, 214th and 215th Balloon Sections.

Mission:

a) **Infantry**: Objects of attack are the enemy positions on the line ALFA Wood –p-q-w-y- (coordinate No 5991) -t-v- trench fork 200 metres south of m (co-ordinate No 5992) –south-western and south-eastern edge of REMIÈRES Wood. This line will be held until further notice.

One battalion with two engineer platoons and flame projectors will advance beyond this line to SEICHEPREY without stopping and will take possession of that village provisionally.

The assembling of the assault troops and the auxiliary weapons placed at their disposal will take place during the night of y-day in or directly behind our own front line between LAHAYVILLE and red point i 2 (coordinate No. 5993).

The attack is to take place in three waves. Simultaneous with the sudden beginning of the destructive fire and the back and diverting barrage of the artillery and Minenwerfer at x A.M., these will work their way forward to the departure trench. The assault troops will break into the foremost enemy lines in three waves close behind each other at the last shot of the Minenwerfer on the point of penetration. See attached sketch for general direction of assault.

The strong first wave will penetrate the first enemy lines without stopping and take possession of the line designated as the objective of the assault, which is to be cleared, occupied and prepared for defense. A large number of light machine guns and several heavy machine guns on portable carriages will be brought up immediately with a view to utilising possibilities for enfilading fire.

The Battalion sent against SEICHEPREY will advance beyond the point of attack without stopping and, with two of its companies advancing on SEICHEPREY from the north, two from the east and one from the west, will take possession of the village. Two strong assault detachments with light machine guns, hastening in advance of the assault companies, will be detailed to get a foothold at the south-east and south-west corners of the village and, on the one hand, to facilitate the advance of the companies by fire support at those points and, on the other, to prevent the escape of the enemy towards the south or counter-attacks from a southerly direction.

SEICHEPREY will be held until the enemy garrison has been disposed of, all the wounded, as well as our own dead, prisoners and booty have been taken to the rear and the fortifications and shelters have been destroyed. After completion of this task, the Battalion will return behind our lines to place itself at the disposal of the Regiment and will report the evacuation by all the means of communication available.

It will be the task of the weaker second wave to break up the first enemy lines and clean them up. The reserve companies will follow in the third wave with heavy machine guns, light Minenwerfer, grenade throwers, medical personnel, stretcher-bearer parties and carrying parties with ammunition and equipment. The necessary distribution in depth will be made immediately after the first wave has reached the first object of attack.

Heavy machine guns will be used in the first line generally only at REMIÈRES wood, or, in exceptional cases, at those points where a particularly favourable fire effect would justify their use in the front line. The bulk of the machine guns model 08 will be put into action further back at such points where, by firing through gaps in our own line, or by firing over it, they can be utilised for supporting the attack and for warding off enemy counter-attacks.

A large number of machine guns 08 will be put into action south-west of LAHAYVILLE and in the vicinity of Fort Gideon (coordinate No. 5994) in order to block the attack by enfilading fire from each side, to hold the enemy flanking positions in check and to repel enemy counter-attacks. Attention is directed particularly to the repelling of enemy infantry aviators by means of machine guns model 08 designated for that purpose.

The battalions of the 258th and 259th Reserve Infantry Regiments, at present occupying the old positions, will remain in them as emergency garrisons. They will hold themselves in increased readiness one hour before x o'clock on y-day.

b) **Artillery**: The enemy batteries will be bombarded with gas shells by the long-range artillery, supported by the close-range group, in the night before the attack. The bombardment will be opened by surprise. It will be the duty of the long-range artillery after x o'clock to keep down the enemy artillery and particularly important enemy position at JURY Wood, to operate against enemy reinforcements and movements that have been recognized in the terrain behind the lines and, together with Minenwerfer, to divert the attention of the enemy by bombarding the enemy positions in front of G III left and south-west of RICHECOURT from x to x + 40.

The attack on the rear enemy positions, REMIÈRES Wood and SEICHEPREY will start abruptly at x o'clock after preparation by the close-range artillery, which will accompany it by a rolling barrage advancing ahead of the assault troops. "Blue cross" gas shells will not be used in bombarding SEICHEPREY. While SEICHEPREY is being destroyed by our assault troops, the positions south of SEICHEPREY and at JURY Wood will be held in constant check by destructive fire of varying strength, the latter ones by the long-range group. Upon request of the infantry by means of the signal for barrage fire (yellow light balls), a protective barrage will be maintained around SEICHEPREY and in front of the newly gained positions north-east and north-west of the village.

After the evacuation of SEICHEPREY, the Division will issue an order to the artillery to withdraw the protective barrage to the newly gained line in the region north of SEICHEPREY.

In the distribution of the fire, the dugouts in REMIÈRES Wood, north of SEICHEPREY, as well as the village itself and the enemy trenches which, from aeroplane photographs, have been observed to be particularly well constructed, will be laid under very heavy fire from heavy artillery. The village of SEICHEPREY, in particular, will be laid under concentrated destructive fire before the assault begins. In case of favourable wind, an endeavour will be made to cover the enemy positions at JURY Wood and the strong points north of SEICHEPREY with fog clouds.

Batteries in readiness to engage fleeting targets will be assigned to special tasks during the attack. The duration of the fire on the individual objectives may be seen from the attached diagram.

The infantry gun battery of the 14th Assault Battalion will be put into action for the immediate support of the assault column. Two guns each will be put into action at Fort LESSNER (co-ordinate No. 5994) and south-west of LAHAYVILLE, in order to render immediate support to the infantry's advance and, in case of enemy flanking thrusts, to enfilade these effectively themselves. Two more guns will accompany the infantry assault columns, following directly behind them.

c) **Minenwerfer**: The Minenwerfer operating in the sector of the attack will fire a short destructive barrage on the enemy's front lines between ALFA Wood and the region east of Plum-Tree Wood, as well as on the northern edge of REMIÈRES Wood. The duration of the fire on the individual objectives may be seen from the attached diagram. In order to reduce the effects of splintering, only mines with delayed action will be used.

Two groups of Minenwerfer, each composed of four light Minenwerfer on flat trajectory gun carriages, will be assigned to accompany the third wave. Upon reaching the front enemy line, they will take up position there and first support the infantry attack by combating isolated posts of resistance with direct fire. After the return of the Battalion from SEICHEPREY, they will hold themselves in readiness to throw a protective barrage before the newly gained line.

The Minenwerfer operating outside of the sector of the attack will throw a protective and checking barrage on the trenches at –r-n- (coordinate No. 5990) and –o- (coordinate No. 5991), as well as on the positions –o-1- (coordinate No. 5994) and the northern extremity of JURY Wood. All the available Minenwerfer will be put into action for this purpose. The checking fire on JURY Wood is of particular importance and must be kept up at the greatest intensity during the advance of the assault troops along the eastern edge of REMIÈRES Wood. If the wind is favourable, smoke bombs will be used at this point.

The duration of fire on these objectives will be provisionally 1½ hours, but will be reopened later, as the situation requires, upon signals for barrage fire.

Another group of Minenwerfer will deliver diverting fire in front of Sector G III left, duration of fire 40 minutes.

d) **Engineers**: A platoon of engineers will be attached to the Assault Battalion detailed to attack REMIERES Wood, and two platoons to the Battalion advancing on SEICHEPREY. They will be provided with charges in chain-form for blowing up wire entanglements, and with concentrated charges for the destruction of dugouts and defense works.

The dugouts behind the line to be held, the use of which appears necessary and desirable during the defense of the line, will be temporarily exempted from destruction in as far as the fighting permits. The Brigade will make general arrangements pertaining hereto before the assault in as far as they can be determined from the map and aeroplane photographs.

e) **Intelligence Equipment**: The employment of Intelligence equipment is regulated by the special instructions attached hereto.

f) **Air Forces**: The following will start from LES BARAQUES aerodrome at x o'clock and reach the point of attack by the shortest course:

1 infantry aeroplane, 1 artillery aeroplane and three battle aeroplanes.

The infantry aviator will drop a report at x + 40 minutes near MADINE Camp and CHAREY as to whether the objective of the attack has been reached, at x + 60 minutes on the situation of the attack on SEICHEPREY, and later, on the complete evacuation of that village.

The artillery aviator will observe the fall of our annihilating and protective fire, as well as the enemy artillery activity, and will report thereon by wireless or by dropping prepared sketches to the Artillery Commander at CHAREY or the receiving station of the long and close-range group.

The battle aeroplanes will take part in the fighting by means of machine-gun fire.

An artillery patrol aeroplane with an escorting aeroplane will circle over the captured positions during the entire day, their duties being constantly to observe the enemy artillery activity and the rear, and to recognise enemy counter-attacks betimes. The Commander of the reinforced 298th Aviation Detachment will regulate details.

The reinforced 64th Pursuit Flight Squad will be in readiness at its aerodrome at MARS-la-TOUR from x o'clock on, to start at any time when demanded against enemy aeroplanes putting in an appearance.

An advanced landing ground has been established in the vicinity of BOUILLONVILLE. A telephone line will be laid thence to the Brigade telephone exchange at MADINE Camp. A liaison officer from the 298 Aviation Detachment will be detailed at Divisional Headquarters throughout the entire operation.

The 214th Balloon Section, with balloon bed near BENEY, is detailed as infantry balloon. The 123rd Balloon Section, balloon bed near JAULNY, and the 215th, balloon bed ner XAMMES, are placed under the Artillery Commander.

6. Army Medical Service: will be regulated by special orders.

7. The Infantry Brigade will make special arrangements for the bringing back of prisoners and booty and the supply of infantry ammunition, close-range equipment and material. THIAUCOURT will be the collecting station for prisoners.

Time will be communicated by the Division by telephone as follows:

First communication, April 18, between 12.15 P.M. and 12.30 P.M.
Second communication, April 19, between 12.15 P.M. and 12.30 P.M.
Third communication, April 19, between 6.30 P.M. and 7.00 P.M.
Fourth communication, April 19, between 10.00 P.M. and 10.30 P.M.
Communication will be made by orderly officer to:
78th Reserve Infantry Brigade,
Artillery Commander, 78th Division,
Engineer Commander, 378th Battalion,
Divisional Signal Commander, 478th Division (at the same time Infantry Balloon),
298 Aviation Detachment.
These departments will be responsible for proper forwarding to subordinate troops.

9. The Divisional Staff will remain at Divisional Headquarters during the Cherry Blossom operation.

SIGNED VON STOLZMANN

NOTES

1 'Seicheprey Rises from War's Ruins to a Better Life,' *Hartford Courant*, 20 July 1922.

2 *De Flirey à Apremont - Le bois de Mortmare (2),* http://jmpicquart.pagesperso-orange.fr/Flirey2.htm; accessed 23 July 2012.

3 *Armée de Lorraine* comprised *67ᵉ division d'infanterie, 65ᵉ division d'infanterie,* and *75ᵉ division d'infanterie reserve.* Joseph Joffre, *The Personal Memoirs of Joffre, Field Marshal of the French Army* (New York and London: Harper & Brothers Publishers, 1932), I, 166 (translated by Colonel T. Bentley Mott).

4 Douglas Wilson Johnson, *Topography and Strategy in the War* (New York: Oxford University Press, 1921), 370–371.

5 *GQG* can be equated to the Joint Chiefs of Staff with leadership under the command of a single general. John Mosier, *The Myth of the Great War* (New York: Perennial, 2002), 105.

6 Hugh M. Cole, *The Lorraine Campaign* (Washington DC: GPO, 1950) 25–27.

7 Russell Gordon Carter, *The 101st Field Artillery, A.E.F., 1917–1919* (Boston: Houghton Mifflin Company, 1940), 82.

8 Joffre, I, 94–95.

9 Michael S. Neiberg, *Dance of the Furies* (Boston: Harvard University Press, 2011), 174; Rémy Cazals and André Loez, *Dans le tranchées de 1914–1918* (Pau: Cairn, 2008), 24–25.

10 President Raymond Poincaré quoted in Barbara W. Tuchman, *The Guns of August* (New York: The MacMillan Company, 1962), 262.

11 "L" was used at the Woëvre. Douglas Porch, *The French Secret Services* (New York: Farrar, Straus and Giroux, 1995), 74.

12 *De Flirey à Apremont – Le bois de Mortmare (2).*

13 Hanns Möller: *Die Geschichte der Ritter des Ordens pour le mérite im Weltkrieg 1914–1918;* Abschnitt; *General der Infanterie von Strantz;* Hermann Cron, *Imperial German Army 1914–18: Organisation, Structure, Orders-of-Battle* [first published: 1937]. Solihull, West Midlands, UK: Helion & Co., 2002, 84.

14 *Battles in the Woëvre.*

15 Joffre, I, 285.

16 Mosier, 107.

17 *Die Schlacten und Gefecte des Grossen Krieges 1914–1918* (Berlin: Verlag von Hermann Sact, 1919, 46)

18 Arthur C. Havlin, *The History of Company A, 102d. Machine Gun Battalion, Twenty-Sixth Division, A.E.F.* (privately printed, 1928), 64.

19 "Military Geography of the Western Front, Headquarters A.E.F.," December 4, 1917, *United States Army in the World War, 1917–1919,* ii (Washington DC: GPO, 1989), 91 (henceforth referred to as *US Army in the World War*).

20 *De Flirey à Apremont – Le bois de Mortmare (2).*

21 *Général* Fénelon Passaga, *The Cavalry of Verdun, The Americans around Verdun* (Paris: Charles-Lavauzelle, 1927), 25 (translated by Captain J.L.E. Cuny and Major A.G. Kenchington).

22 Mosier, 107–108.

23 *Propositions au sujet de l'occupation du nouveau secteur affecté á la 128ᵉ brigade, 13 Octobre 1914,* SHD 14 N 1552.; *Le bois de Mortmare (2).*

24 *Die Schlacten und Gefecte des Grossen Krieges 1914–1918,* (Berlin: Verlag von Hermann Sact, 1919), 46.

25 *Le bois de Mortmare (2).*

26 *Propositions au sujet de l'occupation du nouveau secteur affecté à la 128ᵉ brigade.*

27 Cornelis De Witt Willcox, Colonel, *A French-English Military Technical Dictionary* (Washington, DC: GPO, 1917, 564.).

28 Lieutenant Colonel C. Petitjean, *31ᵉ corps d'armée Ordre, Mandres aux 4 Tours le 26 Octobre 1914*, SHD 14 N 1552.

29 *Propositions au sujet de l'occupation du nouveau secteur affecté à la 128ᵉ brigade.*

30 Society of the First Division, *History of the First Division During the World War 1917–1919* (Philadelphia, PA: The John C. Winston Company, 1922), 43.

31 Edward D. Sirois, Lieutenant, and William McGinnis, Corporal, *Smashing Through "The World War" With Fighting Battery C. 102nd F.A. "Yankee Division" 1917 – 1918 – 1919* (Salem, MA: The Meek Press, 1919), 47.

32 Raymond Wunderlich, Private, *From Trench and Dugout* (Stockton, CA: Private printing, 1919), 43.

33 Joffre, II, 343.

34 Joffre, II, 338.

35 Note: The four corps and cavalry corps comprised *Iᵉ corps d'armée, 2ᵉ corps d'armée, 12ᵉ corps d'armée, 17ᵉ corps d'armée,* and *Iᵉ corps de cavalerie.* Joffre, II, 344–345; *Le bois de Mortmare (2).*

36 Joffre, II, 345.

37 Robert A. Doughty, *Pyrrhic Victory, French Strategy and Operations in the Great War* (Cambridge, MA: Harvard University Press, 2005), 143–147.

38 Joffre, II, 346.

39 Mosier, 147–148.

40 Roger Monclin, *Les Damnés de la Guerre, Les Crimes de la Justice Militaire* (Paris: Mignolet & Storz, 1935), 51 (translated by Monique Duval). There is some doubt as to the accuracy of the story.

41 Généeal Delétoille commanded *31ᵉ corps d'armée* from 8 September 1914 – 1 January 1917. Henry Andraud, *Quand on fusillait les innocents* (Paris : Éditions Gallimard, 1935).

42 Monclin, 51.

43 *De Flirey à Apremont – Le bois de Mortmare (2); Flirey le drame;* Monclin, 53, 61.

44 Henry Sheahan, *A Volunteer Poilu* (Boston: Houghton Mifflin Company, 1916), 108–110.

45 *Battles in the Woëvre.*

46 General Pershing quoted in Donald Smythe, *Pershing, General of the Armies* (Bloomington, IN: Indiana University Press, 1986), 23–24.

47 "Relations with Allied Governments and Armies," General Headquarters, A.E.F., June 30, 1919, *US Army in the World War*, xii, 72.

48 Wunderlich, 28.

49 Millett's work is the definitive biographical reference on Lieutenant General Bullard and the time the 1st Division spent at the Woëvre. Major Hugh A. Drum diary quoted in Allan R. Millett, *The General, Robert L. Bullard and Officership in the United States Army 1881–1925* (Westport, CT: Greenwood Press, 1975), 342.

50 "Occupation Files," Box 786, RG 120, NARA.

51 William L. Langer, in James H. Hallas, *Doughboy War, The American Expeditionary Force in World War I* (Boulder, CO: Lynne Rienner Publishers, 2000), 9.

52 Edward M. Coffman, *The War to End All Wars, The American Military Experience in World War I* (Madison, WI: The University of Wisconsin Press, 1986), 144.

53 Colonel Shelton in James H. Fifield, *The Regiment, A History of the 104th U.S. Infantry, A.E.F. 1917–1919* (privately printed, 1946), 141.

54 William L. Langer, quoted from the 2nd edition of *With "E" of the First Gas* entitled *Gas and Flame in World War I* in Hallas, *Doughboy War*, 9.

55 "Notes of a Conference held at Paris on November 25, 1917," *US Army in the World War*, II, p. 81.

56 Wilhelm F. Flicke, *War Secrets in the Ether*, I (Laguna Hills, CA: Agean Park Press, 1977), 35–36; Porch, 86.

57 "German estimate of American Forces, No. 1873," Box 790, 26th Division, RG 120, NARA.

58 George Mozley, Private, *Our Miracle Battery* (Privately printed, 1920), 12.

59 Clemenceau became Prime Minister in November 1917. Forrest C. Pogue, ed. *George C. Marshall: interviews and reminiscences for Forrest C. Pogue.* Lexington, VA: George C. Marshall Research Foundation, 1991, 237.

60 "Notes of a Conference held at Paris on November 25, 1917," *US Army in the World War*, II, 81.

61 Historical Section Army War College, *The Genesis of American First Army* (Washington, DC: Government Printing Office, 1929), 10–11.

62 "Relations with Allied Governments and Armies," 71.

63 Martin Blumenson, *The Patton Papers 1885–1940* (Boston: Houghton Mifflin Company, 1972), 431.

64 Pétain was in reality a Lieutenant General equivalent. Blumenson, 433.

65 French Military Mission Archives (Vincennes) quote from French liaison officer in Millett, 347.

66 Pershing quote in Richard W. Kedzior, *Evoluation and Endurance, The U.S. Army Division in the Twentieth Century* (Santa Monica, CA: RAND, 2000), 9–10.

67 "Notes of a Conference held at Paris."

68 Colonel "Gatling Gun" Parker, *Memories of the Service*, Draft, 10 May 1937. West Point Archives.

69 The Selective Service Act of 1917 was signed into law 18 May 1917 and transformed an institution that had existed well before the American Revolution. The National Archives (TNA) WO 106/490, "Summary of French Note on the American Army. State of American Army on 1st January, 1918."

70 The Generalstab estimated the United States had fielded 5 divisions of fighting strength (144,000 men) by the end of March 1918. "German Assessment of American Army, No. 1873," Box 790, 26th Division, RG 120, NARA; H. von Kuhl, General der Infantrie, *Der deutsche Generalstab in Vorbereitung und Durchführung des Weltkrieges* (Berlin, Verlag von Ernst Siegfried Mittler und Sohn, 1920).

71 Victor Keller, Colonel, "A German Reply to Gen. Pershing's War Story," *New York Times*, May 2, 1931.

72 John B. Wilson, *Maneuver and Firepower, The Evolution of Divisions and Separate Brigades* (Washington DC: Center of Military History United States Army, 1998), 47–48; "Relations with Allied Governments and Armies," 72; Historical Section Army War College, 10.

73 Historical Section Army War College, 6.

74 I.B. Holley, Jr., *General John M. Palmer, Citizen Soldiers, and the Army of a Democracy* (Westport, CT: Greenwood Press, 1982), 302.

75 Historical Section Army War College, 6.

76 Adding an engineer regiment, a signal battalion, and supply and medical units increased the strength of American square divisions to a nominal 28,061 soldiers. Wilson, 52–53; Michael D. Doubler, *I am the Guard, A History of the Army National Guard, 1636–2000* (Washington DC: Department of the Army Pamphlet No. 130–1, 2001), 172; Weigley, 385–386.

77 War Department. *Order of Battle of the United States Land Forces in the World War; Zone of the Interior*. Vol. 3, part 1 (Washington DC: GPO, 1949), 281.

78 The National Guard from New England region was known as the 6th Division prior to 1917. Doubler, 172–173.

79 French Military Mission Archives (Vincennes) quote from French liaison officer in Millett, 347.

80 "Relations with Allied Governments and Armies," 88.

81 Smythe, 27; Historical Section Army War College, 5; Society of the First Division, 42.

82 "Sector for the American Expeditionary Forces Recommended," November 24, 1917, in *US Army in the World War*, II, 80.

83 Later in the war General Pershing offered four regiments (369th Infantry, 370th Infantry, 371st Infantry, 372nd Infantry) containing black soldiers to be placed under French command. Pétain quoted in Historical Section Army War College, 12.

84 John J. Pershing, *My Experiences in the World War* (New York: Frederick A. Stokes Company, 1931), I, 299.

85 "Relations with Allied Governments and Armies," 79.

86 Foch was promoted to *Maréchal* in August 1918. "Relations with Allied Governments and Armies," 88.

87 "Air Service, AEF Balloon Notes, AEF No. 1, December 3, 1917," *Gorrell Report*, Series F, RG 120, NARA.

88 "Personal and Secret Instruction on the Conduct of Defence in the Sector of the 32nd A.C.," 32nd Army Corps Headquarters, Feb. 7th, 1918, Box 43, 1st Division, RG 120, NARA.

89 Jere Clemens King, *Foch versus Clemenceau, France and German Dismemberment, 1918–1919* (Cambridge, MA: Harvard University Press, 1960), 31.

90 "Air Service, AEF Balloon Notes, AEF No. 1, December 3, 1917," *Gorrell Report*.

91 Passaga, 144.

92 "Relations with Allied Governments and Armies," 79.

93 Pogue, *Marshall interviews and reminiscences*, 240.

94 A fifth division, the 41st, was designated as depot, serving as a manpower pool for the four active divisions. Blumenson, 484; Historical Section Army War College, 9, 12.

95 Major General James G. Harbord, "New Chief of Staff, U.S. Army," *The New York National Guardsman*, December, 1935, 3.

96 Historical Section Army War College, 12; "Air Service, AEF Balloon Notes, AEF No. 1, December 3, 1917," *Gorrell Report*, Series F.

97 Bullard's positive impressions of Summerall were given in his memoirs. Summerall became 1st Division commander in the latter half of 1918. Timothy K. Nenninger, ed. *The Way of Duty, Honor, Country, The Memoir of Charles Pelot Summerall* (Lexington, KY: University Press of Kentucky, 2010), 113; General Robert Bullard, *Personalities and Reminiscences of the War* (Garden City, NY: Doubleday and Company, 1925), 110.

98 "Personal and Secret Instruction on the Conduct of Defence."

99 Christian O.E. Millotat, Oberst I.G., *Understanding the Prussian-German General Staff System* (Carlisle Barracks, PA: Strategic Studies Institute, March 20, 1992), 37.

100 Millotat, 42–43.

101 Millotat, 20.

102 *German Army Handbook April 1918* (London: Arms and Armour Press, 1977), 39.

103 *German Army Handbook*, 40.

104 Max von Gallwitz, General der Artillerie, *Erleben im Westen, 1916–1918* (Berlin: Verlag von E.S. Mittler & Sohn, 1932), 94.

105 *Translations of War Diaries of German Units Opposed to the Second Division (Regular)* quoted in James H. Hallas, *Squandered Victory, The American First Army at St. Mihiel* (Westport, CT: Praeger, 1995), 41.

106 Von Gallwitz, 285; Herwig and Heyman, 160.

107 Generalmajor Paulus von Stolzmann, Möller, 382–383.

108 *VIIIeme Armée Bulletin, April 23, 1918, Summary of Information*, No. 32, May 2, 1918, SHD.

109 The German term for a sector was simple. The unit was between two distinct geographical features. In the Woëvre region it was zwischen Maas und Mosel [between the Maas and Moselle rivers]. Gunther Von Bornstedt, *Reserve. Infanterie. Regiment 259* (Oldenburg, Berlin: Verlag von Gerhard Stalling, 1926), 170–171.

110 Günter Wegner, *Stellenbesetzung Der Deutschen Heere, 1815–1939*, 4 vol. (Osnabruck, GE: Biblio Verlag, 1990), i, 512.

111 *Capitaine* Seligmann was the son of the great art dealer and afterwards ran art stores on Rue Royale in Paris and Fifth Avenue in New York. Pogue, *Marshall interviews and reminiscences,* 233, 237.

112 Jacques Rouvier, Captain, *Present-Day Warfare, How an Army Trains and Fights* (New York: Charles Scribner's Sons, 1918), 173.

113 Aalain du Boisrouvray, "Avec la 26ᵉ D.I. Americaine," *Revue des Deux Mondes* (Paris: 15 Septembre 1933, 334–365), 345.

114 French Military Mission Archives (Vincennes) quote from French liaison officer in Millett, 347.

115 du Boisrouvray, 339.

116 Blumenson, 535.

117 Office of Chief of Staff, Executive Division, Intelligence Branch, "American Participation in the War, French Attitude," *Weekly Intelligence Summary*, March 30, 1918.

118 "Organisation," Brigadier General Peter E. Traub, 20 February 1918, Box 32, 26th Division, RG 120, NARA.

119 "[The British] are our allies: the American is a pal. You understand?" Englander, 58.

120 Willcox, 564.

121 "Tactical History of Air Service," Gorrell Report, Series D, 1.

122 Terrence J. Finnegan, *Shooting the Front: Allied Aerial Reconnaissance in the First World War*, 2nd Edition (Stroud, Gloucestershire, UK: The History Press, 2011), 132.

123 Harold E. Porter, *Aerial Observation* (New York: Harper & Brothers Publishers, 1921), 190.

124 "Manual for Trench Artillery," *United States Army (Provisional) Part I Trench Artillery*, March 1918, 23–24.

125 "Personal and Secret Instruction on the Conduct of Defence."

126 *Boyau de communication* was commonly expressed as just *boyau*. Colonel Oliver Lyman Spaulding and Colonel John Womack Wright, *The Second Division American Expeditionary Force in France 1917–1919*, reprint (Nashville, TN: The Battery Press, 1989), 17.

127 *Notes on the Interpretation of Aeroplane Photographs*, March 1917 (S.S. 550), 9.

128 "Instructions for the Employment of Machine Guns in the Attack," February 1918, British G.H.Q., April 6, 1918, *Summary of Information, No. 15, April 15, 1918*, SHD 16 N 1090.

129 Wunderlich, 28.

130 *Notes on the Interpretation of Aeroplane Photographs*, March 1917 (S.S. 550), 9.

131 Timothy K. Nenninger, "Unsystematic as a Mode of Command": Commanders and the Process of Command in the American Expeditionary Forces, 1917–1918," *The Journal of Military History* 64 (July 2000), 739–768, 764.

132 Litter bearing through trenches entwined with telephone wires became an art winding through the obstacles. *History of the 102nd, United States Infantry, 26th Division*, Box 44, 102nd Infantry, RG 120, NARA.

133 Lieutenant C.W.H. Smith quoted in Chamberlin, 45–46.

134 "Memo on Definition of Positions & Management of Works." 1st Army: 32nd A.C. Hqrs. February 7th, 1918, 1; "Personal and Secret Instruction on the Conduct of Defence."

135 "*Patrol and Control of No Man's Land*." Arthur Conger Papers, Box 2. USAMHI, Carlisle, PA.

136 *History of the 102nd, United States Infantry*.

137 Theodore Roosevelt, Lieutenant Colonel, *Average Americans* (New York: G.P. Putnam's Sons, 1919), 108.

138 Robert H. Ferrell, Ed., *In the Company of Generals, The World War I Diary of Pierpont L. Stackpole* (Columbia, MO: University of Missouri Press, 2009), 15–16.

139 "Memo on Definition of Positions."

140 *History of the 102nd, United States Infantry*.

141 Lieutenant Colonel W.S. Grant, Memorandum for Assistant Chief of Staff, G-3, Subject: "Report on 26th Division Affair of April 20th," 24 April 1918, Box 14, Edwards Papers, MHS, 9.

142 *History of the 102nd, United States Infantry*.

143 Grant, "Report on 26th Division affair of April 20th."; Frank P. Sibley, *With the Yankee Division in France* (Boston: Little, Brown, and Company, 1919), 138.

144 *History of the 102nd, United States Infantry.*

145 Frank P. Sibley, *With the Yankee Division in France* (Boston: Little, Brown and Company, 1919), 138.

146 Emerson Gifford Taylor, *New England in France, 1917–1919* (Boston: Houghton Mifflin Company, 1920), 101–102.

147 "Memo on Definition of Positions. February 7th, 1918, Staff: 3rd Bureau N 470 Bie 8/3, "Personal and Secret Instruction on the Conduct of Defence."1st Division, RG 120, NARA.

148 "Personal and Secret Instruction on the Conduct of Defence."

149 *Being the Narrative of Battery A of the 101st Field Artillery* (Cambridge, MA: The Brattle Press, 1919), 84.

150 *History of the 102nd, United States Infantry*; Assistant Chief of Staff 24 Apr 18 Memorandum, Massachusetts Historical Society papers, 9; Johnson, 325, 370–372.

151 Wunderlich, 40. (Wunderlich lost his leg at Belleau Wood in July 1918. See p. 179).

152 Lieutenant Colonel Bevans and Lieutenant Colonel Frederick Jones quoted in Michael E. Shay, *A Grateful Heart, The History of a World War I Field Hospital* (Westport, CT: Greenwood Press, 2002), 56.

153 Wunderlich, 32.

154 Cushing and Stone, 14–15.

155 *History of the 102nd, United States Infantry.*; Assistant Chief of Staff 24 Apr 18 Memorandum, Massachusetts Historical Society papers, 9; Johnson, 325, 370–372.

156 Wunderlich, 42.

157 Edward A. Schafer, Response to Military History Institute questionnaire.

158 Wunderlich, 40.

159 "History of Fifty-First Field Artillery Brigade", RG 120, Box 57. This history does not mention the Seicheprey battle despite the brigade's role there.

160 *History of Battery B, One Hundred Third Field Artillery Twenty-Sixth Division* (Providence, RI: E.L. Freeman Company, 1922), 52; W.F. Kernan and Henry T. Samson, *History of the 103rd Field Artillery (Twenty-Sixth Division, A.E.F.) World War 1917–1919* (Providence, RI: Remington Printing Co., 1919), 36–37; *Being the Narrative of Battery A*, 84, 88–89.

161 Sirois and McGinnis, 48.

162 M.A. De Wolfe Howe *Memoirs of the Harvard Dead in the War Against Germany*, *iii* (Cambridge: Harvard University Press, 1922), 155.

163 Oberstleutnant Friedrich Bruns, Möller, 164–165.

164 Stephen Bull, *German Assault Troops of the First World War, Stosstrupptaktik The First Stormtroopers* (Stroud, Gloucestershire, UK: Spellmount, 2007), 124–127.

165 *Capitaine* Andre Laffargue, "The Attack in Trench Warfare"; July 1916, *Infantry Journal*, vol. 13 (1).

166 Bull, 40.

167 *Der Angriff im Stellungskrieg* was "Part 14 (Provisional)" of the "Manual of Position Warfare for All Arms." Amendments were added on 26 January and 27 July. Bull, 43.

168 Stefan Westmann quoted in Bull, 92–93.

169 Bull, 121.

170 "Arméebefehl, Arméeabteilung C, Armée-Oberkommando, 22.2.17. [sic]," *78. Reserve. Division Files*, RG 165, NARA, 22. (RG 165 NARA subsequent reference is *78.R.D. Files*); "Army Order, 22-2-17, [sic]" *World War Records, First Division A.E.F. Regular. German Documents*, Vol. 1, (Washington, DC: War College, 1930), (henceforth referred to as *First Division Records, German Documents*).

171 78. R.D. War Diaries leave the impression that Sturm-Kompagnie, Sturmkompen, and Kompagnie were one and the same. Likewise, Stoss and Sturm get applied to the same unit and combat group. "Regimentsbefehl," Res. I. R. 259, 18.2.1918., *78.R. D. Files*, 15; "Regimental Order, 18-2-18," *First Division Records, German Documents.*

172 "Combat drill," *Summary of Information, March 6, 1918, No. 145*, SHD 14 N 1409.

173 Timothy T. Lupfer, *The Dynamics of Doctrine: The Changes in German Tactical Doctrine During the First World War* (Fort Leavenworth, KS: Combat Studies Institute, 1981), 27.

174 "Attack Tactics of the Enemy in Recent Raids," *Summary of Information*, SHD 14 N 1409; "Program of Instruction of German Raiding." 26th Division, RG 120, NARA.; "German Raid of Night of November 2-3 1917," "Instructions for the Employment of Machine Guns." Box 47, 1st Division, RG 120, NARA.

175 "Regimentsbefehl," Res. I. R. 259, 18.2.1918, 78.R.D. Files; "Regimental Order, 18-2-18," *First Division Records, German Documents*; Von Gallwitz, 71.

176 "Instructions for the Employment of Machine Guns."

177 "Cherry Blossom. Divisional Order No. 3, April 18, 1918." *Extracts from the War Files, Staff of 78th Reserve Division. April 20, 1918.* 4–5, Box 160, RG 165, NARA. (Henceforth referred to *Extracts, April 20, 1918, 78.R.D. Files.*)

178 "Attack Tactics of the Enemy in Recent Raids"; "Organization of an Assault Battalion," *Summary of Information, March 16, 1918, No. 158,* SHD 16 N 1090.

179 "Program of Instruction of German Raiding"; "German Raid of Night of November 2–3 1917"; "Attack Tactics of the Enemy in Recent Raids."

180 Philip J. Haythornthwaite, *The World War One Source Book* (London: Arms and Armour Press, 1996), 202.

181 "Flame Projector," *Summary of Information, No. 161,* March 22, 1918, SHD 16 N 1090.

182 Martin Samuels, *Command or Control? Command, Training and Tactics in the British and German Armies, 1888–1918* (London: Frank Cass, 1995), 92.

183 Ludendorff, C.G.S. of the Field Army, Ia-48580. 30 March 1918, in *Summary of Information,* SHD 16 N 1090; "Note on the Use of Trench Mortars in Offensive Combat," *Summary of Information,* SHD 16 N 1090; "German Trench Mortars," *Summary of Information, No. 80,* June 19, 1918, SHD 16 N 1090; Rouvier, 7.

184 Gudmundsson, *On Artillery,* 73–74; 82–83.

185 Supplement to part 15 of the Manual of Position Warfare for all Arms, 1 February 1918 in "Mortars."

186 Rouvier, 49.

187 Twelve **1916 Schwere MW** were assigned to German forces opposite the 26th Division in April 1918. "Manual for Trench Artillery," *Part I,* 46–49; *German Army Handbook,* 103.

188 "German Trench Mortars."; "Manual for Trench Artillery" 49–50; *German Army Handbook,* 104.

189 "German Trench Mortars."; "Manual for Trench Artillery," 49–50; *German Army Handbook,* 104.

190 36 1916 Med MW were assigned to German forces opposite the 26th Division in April 1918. Summary of Information, No. 80, June 19, 1918, SHD 14 N; "Manual for Trench Artillery," 50–51; *German Army Handbook,* 104.

191 60 Neue Lichte MW were assigned to German forces opposite the 26th Division in April 1918. "Manual for Trench Artillery," 53–54; "German Trench Mortars."; *German Army Handbook,* 105.

192 "Manual for Trench Artillery," 9; *Handbook of the M. L. Stokes 3-Inch Trench Mortar Equipments,* (London: H.M. Stationery Office, 1920), 2.

193 "Manual for Trench Artillery," 9.

194 Bull, 124–127; Lupfer, 41.

195 "Attack Tactics of the Enemy in Recent Raids."

196 "Organization of an Assault Battalion."

197 "Program of Instruction of German Raiding."; "German Raid of Night of November 2-3 1917."; "German Tactics – wire cutting by Bangalore torpedoes," *Summary of Information, No. 152, March 13, 1918,* SHD 16 N 1090.

198 Note: Instruction for Infantry Combat – French Bulletin, 2 January 1918 – extract from a document published by German Army Headquarters 7-Ia. No. 59, August 1917 in "Instructions for Infantry Combat," *Summary of Information, No. 91, January 11, 1918,* SHD 16 N 1090.

199 Bruce I. Gudmundsson, *Stormtroop Tactics, Innovation in the German Army, 1914–1918* (Westport, CT: Praeger, 1989), 67–68.

200 "Instructions for the Employment of Machine Guns."

201 "Attack Tactics of the Enemy in Recent Raids."

202 "A Few Observations with Regard to Operations in Open Country on the Somme Front," VIIIth Army, 32nd Army Corps, H.Q. May 14, 1918, Box 41, 26th Division, RG 120, NARA.

203 "German Infantry Tactics," Summary of Information, March 16, 1918, No. 155, SHD 14N 1409.

204 "Instructions for Infantry Combat."

205 "German Infantry Tactics," Summary of Information, March 16, 1918, No. 155, SHD 14N; "Program of Instruction of German Raiding."; "German Raid of Night of November 2-3 1917"; "Instructions for Infantry Combat."

206 Bull, 131.

207 Bull, 124–127.

208 Bull, 131.

209 Horatio Rogers, *The Diary of an Artillery Scout* (North Andover, MA: Privately printed, 1975), 62.

210 O.O. Ellis and E.B. Garey, *The Plattsburg Manual – A Handbook for Military Training* (New York: The Century Co. 1917), 183.

211 "Balloon Notes," *Gorrell Report,* Series F.

212 Rouvier, 55.

213 "Einladung Vorarbeiten," Br. Gef. St., 17.II.18. *78.R.D. Files;* "Vorschlag uber artilleristische Unterstutzung fur Unternehmen gegen Remiers-Wald," 17.2.18, *78.R.D. Files, 14;* "Suggested Artillery Support for the Raid against Remières Wood,"17-2-18, *First Division Records, German Documents.*

214 "Suggested Artillery Support for the Raid."

215 "Einladung Vorarbeiten."

216 "Artillerie-Befehl," 23.2.18 *78.R.D. Files,*

28; "Artillery Order," 23-2-18, *First Division Records, German Documents.*

217 G-2, 2nd Army, 'Effectiveness of Different Weapons,' Box 10, 2nd Army, RG 120, NARA; Terence Zuber, *Ardennes 1914, The Battle of the Frontiers* (Stroud, Gloucestershire, UK: Tempus, 2007), 44.

218 Bull, 124–127.

219 Finnegan, 49, 132–133; Fred Ambrose McKenna, Ed., *Battery –A – 103rd Field Artillery in France* (Providence, RI: Livermore and Knight Co. 1919), 134; "Air Service Information," Balloon School, Gorrell Report, Series F.

220 *One Hundred Second Field Artillery*, 35.

221 Rogers, 68–69.

222 Washburn, 93–94.

223 Ernest E. LaBranche, Corporal, *An American Battery in France* (Worcester, MA: Belisle Printing & Publishing Co., 1923), 143.

224 *One Hundred Second Field Artillery*, 36–37.

225 Rouvier, 9; Gudmundsson, *On Artillery*, 71.

226 Gudmundsson, *On Artillery*, 38.

227 LaBranche, 143.

228 "Organization of a Rolling Barrage in the XVIIIth German Army," *Supplement to the French G. Q. G. Bulletin, April 12, 1918, No. 155,* SHD 15 N 1090.

229 Rolling barrage corresponded to the number 5 used in the artillery fire orders. "Organization of a Rolling Barrage."

230 "Organization of a Rolling Barrage."

231 *Tactical Use of Machine Guns, Supplement to Machine Gun Drill Regulations (Provisional 1917),* Prepared at General Headquarters American Expeditionary Forces, France, July 1918, 9, Box 40, 26th Division, RG 120, NARA.

232 Rogers, 114.

233 Sirois and McGinnis, 48–49.

234 Rogers, 143.

235 101st Battery A interview in Karen Macnutt, *Hail & Farewell, A Salute to the 26th Yankee Division,* Boston: Macnutt Art Trust Production, 1995.

236 *Tactical Use of Machine Guns*, 9–10.

237 Based on *Service des renseignements de l'artillerie (SRA)* Report used in Woëvre Sector – March – May 1918. "Comparison de l'Activité des Deux Artilleries," *Bulletin de Renseignements,* SHD 22 N 1756.

238 Carter, 34–35.

239 Rogers, 141; Doughty, 117–118.

240 Doughty.

241 McKenna, 124–125; *History of Battery B,* 53.

242 McKenna, 133; Kernan and Samson, *History of the 103rd Field Artillery,* 201–203; Haythornthwaite.

243 Two batteries fired against 1st Division on 1 March 1918. *German Army Handbook,* 70–72; Herbert Jäger, *German Artillery of World War One* (Ramsbury, Marlborough, Wiltshire, UK: Crowood Press, 2001), 117.

244 Three F.K. 16 batteries were in place against the 1st Division on 1 March 1918 and the 26th Division in April 1918. *German Army Handbook;* Jäger, 117.

245 3 batteries of l.F.H.16 were in place against the 1st Division on 1 March 1918. 18 batteries of l.F.H.16 were in place against the 26th Division in April 1918. *German Army Handbook.;* "Abschrift." 78.Reserve-Division Abt.Ia Nr. 310 op. 3.3.18., *78.R.D. Files;* "Divisionsbefehl, 22.2.18" *78.R.D. Files;* "Division Order, 22-2-18," *First Division Records, German Documents.*

246 1 battery of 10cm Kanone 04 fired against the 1st Division on 1 March 1918. 5 batteries of 10cm Kanone 04 were in place against the 26th Division in April 1918. "Abschrift. 78.Reserve-Division Abt.Ia Nr. 310," 3.3.18., *78.R.D. Files,* 69; "Concerning Raid on the 1-3-18," *First Division Records, German Documents German Army Handbook;* Jäger, 17.

247 4 batteries of 10.5 cm Feldhaubitze 98/09 were in place against the 1st Division on 1 March 1918. *German Army Handbook,* 73–75; Jäger, 85.

248 2 batteries of s.F.H.13 were in place against the 1st Division on 1 March 1918. 13 batteries of s.F.H.13 were in place against the 26th Division in April 1918. *German Army Handbook,* 78–79; 15cm. schwere Feld Haubitze 1913, http://www.lovettartillery.com/15cm_schwere_Feld-haubitze_1913.html accessed 8 November 2012

249 3 batteries of 21 cm Mörser 16 were in place against the 1st Division on 1 March 1918. *German Army Handbook,* 81; Jäger, 123.

250 Lieut.-Colonel B. Walcot, "Lecture on Intelligence, For Regimental Officers and Non-commissioned Officers" July 24th, 1916, USAMHI, Arthur L. Conger Papers, Box 2.

251 Slater Washburn, *One of the YD* (Boston: Houghton Mifflin Company, 1919), 82–83; Rogers, 114; Cushing and Stone, 14.

252 McKenna, 142–143.

253 Sirois and McGinnis, 51.

254 Blumenson, 424.

255 Pogue, *Marshall interviews and reminiscences,* 235.

256 McKenna, 141–143.

257 McKenna, 143–144.

258 "German Trench Mortars"; Bull, 124–127.

259 *German Army Handbook,* 106.

260 Major E. Alexander Powell, *The Army Behind the Army* (New York: Charles Scribner's Sons, 1919), 132–137.

261   1st Lieutenant Dana T. Leavenworth, 102nd
      Infantry, "Memorandum to Company
      Commanders, 8 March 1918," Box, 42, 102nd
      Infantry, RG 120, NARA.

262   Craig S. Herbert, *Eyes of the Army*, (Self-
      Published. 1986), 71.

263   McKenna, 143.

264   "Summary of Information, Wearing of Gask
      Masks, February 27th, 1918," *World War Records,
      First Division A.E.F. Regular, Summaries of
      Intelligence*, Volume IV.

265   "History of Chemical Warfare," 19.

266   *German Army Handbook*, 89.

267   "History of Chemical Warfare," 20.

268   *German Army Handbook*.

269   "History of Chemical Warfare," 21.

270   Gelbkreuz was not fired on American positions
      during *Einladung* or *Kirschblüte* operations.
      German Army Handbook.

271   Cyanogen Chloride – An Overview,
      CYANOGENCHLORIDEforweb_000
      accessed 11 November 2012.

272   Haythornthwaite, 91.

273   *German Army Handbook*.

274   Ernst Harold Baynes, *Animal Heroes of the Great
      War* (New York: The Macmillan Company,
      1925), 26.

275   Onorio Moretti, Captain, *Notes on Training
      Field Artillery Details*, (New Haven, CT: Yale
      University Press, 1917), 196–198.

276   *History of the 102nd, United States Infantry*.

277   *History of Battery B*, 130.

278   Rogers, 89.

279   Wunderlich, 34.

280   McKenna, 110.

281   Capitaine Jean de Lennoy de Bissy quoted in
      Finnegan, 15.

282   John W. Hyatt, "Memorandum: For All
      Intelligence Officers, February 25, 1918," Box
      12, 26 Division, RG 120, NARA.

283   Porter, 195–196.

284   "Aerial Photography for Pilots," NASM,
      A30.2/2.

285   Study and Use of Aerial Photographs, 15
      January 1918, sec. II, 6, Box 819, RG 120,
      NARA; Hardy, "Interpretation of Aerial
      Photography," 3, NASM, A30.2/28; Porter, 197;
      Hahn, 22.

286   John W. Hyatt, "Memorandum: For All
      Intelligence Officers, February 25, 1918," Box
      12, 26 Division, Box 12, RG 120, NARA.

287   "Role of a Regimental Intelligence Officer",
      Box 12, 26th Division, RG 120, NARA.

288   Finnegan, Terrence J., "Military Intelligence at
      the Front, 1914–1918," *Studies in Intelligence*, Vol.
      53 (4) December 2009, 173–176.

289   Walcot, "Lecture on Intelligence."

290   Lieutenant Biddle, "Report on the collection,
      analysis and distribution of German documents
      captured at the front," Conger Papers,
      USAMHI, Carlisle, PA.

291   Lieutenant McKay, "Report on a mission
      to the French Second Bureau. Soldbuchen,"
      February 24th 1918. Conger Papers, Box 2.
      USAMHI, Carlisle, PA.

292   1st Lieutenant Colman D. Frank, "Report
      of a Visit to VIIIth. Army Headquarters to
      attend the Interrogatory of Prisoners Taken
      in the Coup de Main on the Lorraine Sector,
      February 20, 1918." Conger Papers, USAMHI,
      Carlisle, PA.

293   Sergeant Jesse R. Hinman, *Ranging in France
      with Flash and Sound* (Portland, OR: Press of
      Dunham Printing Co., 1919), 30.

294   Town File – Sectors 1-5 A.E.F. General Head-
      quarters G-2-A-3, Box 5576, RG 120,
      NARA.

295   Town File – Sectors 1-5 A.E.F.

296   George C. Marshall, *Memoirs of My Services in
      the World War, 1917–1918* (Boston: Houghton
      Mifflin Co., 1976), 61–62.

297   "Role of a Regimental Intelligence Officer,"
      Box 12, 26th Division, RG 120, NARA.

298   Town File – Sectors 1-5 A.E.F.

299   POW Report – Interrogation of Prisoners of
      the 56th Regiment (14th Division), taken 8
      January 1918, north of Seicheprey.

300   Town File – Sectors 1-5 A.E.F.

301   Major J.E. Hahn, *The Intelligence Service within
      the Canadian Corps* (Toronto: The Macmillan
      Company of Canada), 188.

302   Walcot, "Lecture on Intelligence."

303   Earl Yeomans, private, quoted in Martin Marix
      Evans, ed., *American Voices of World War I,
      Primary Source Documents 1917–1920* (Chicago:
      Fitzroy Dearborn Publishers, 2001), 56.

304   McKenna, 154.

305   Kernan and Samson, *History of the 103rd Field
      Artillery,* 35–36.

306   Wunderlich, 29.

307   McKenna, 155.

308   Town File – Sectors 1-5 A.E.F.

309   Newhall quoted in James Carl Nelson, *Five
      Lieutenants* (New York: St. Martin's Press, 2012),
      186.

310   Town File – Sectors 1-5 A.E.F.

311   Town File – Sectors 1-5 A.E.F.

312   "Notes on the French System of Intelligence,"
      5–6, TNA, PRO: WO 198/983.

313   *Study and Use of Aerial Photographs*, 15 January
      1918, sec. I, 26–27, Box 819, RG 120, NARA.

314   "Services of Captain Chapelon," Headquarters First Field Artillery Brigade, February 19, 1918, SHD 19N 1474.

315   John R. Innes, *Flash Spotters and Sound Rangers: How They Lived, Worked and Fought in the Great War* (London: George Allen & Unwin, Ltd., 1935), 132.

316   SRS stood for Sound Ranging Sections in American units. Joseph Goldstein in Bernard Edelman, *Centenarians, The Story of the 20th Century by the Americans Who Lived It* (New York: Farrar, Straus and Giroux, 1999), 246.

317   Flash spotting was also referred to as light spotting. Carter, 92–93.

318   "Balloon Notes," *Gorrell Report*, Series F.

319   Hinman, 44.

320   Town File – Sectors 1-5 A.E.F.

321   "Summary of Information for Divisional Headquarters, No 153, GHQAEF, Second Section, General Staff March 14, 1918." SHD 16N 1090.

322   "Summary of Information for Divisional Headquarters, No. 154.

323   Hyatt, "Memorandum."

324   G-2-C Topography, 7–8, Nolan Papers, in Finnegan, 175.

325   Bull, 131.

326   Author discussions with Helmut Jäger and Dieter Gröschel. Summary of Air Information, Air Intelligence Bulletin, May 1918.

327   Author discussions with Helmut Jäger and Dieter Gröschel; Cron, 184–185.

328   *SRA, Bulletin de Renseignements, N 169, du 20 au 21 Avril, 1918, de 1600 à 1600*, SHD 22 N 1756; Les escadrilles de l'aeronautique militaire francaise, Paris, 284–285. SAL 122 was assigned to the sector in March supporting *Ire armée* and *Général* Passaga's *32e corps d'armée* flying out of Saizerais and Toul. SAL 47 flew Salmson 2A2, Spad XVI, Caudron G6 and Letord aerial reconnaissance out of Belrain until late March. They left for Mesnil-St Georges in late March supporting the Allied counter-attack against Operation Michael and returned to Belrain in early April.

329   *Les escadrilles de l'aeronautique militaire française*, Paris, 247–248; *Compte-Rendu des operations de la journée*, SHD 22 N 1672.

330   American aviators forced to fly AR 1's stated the "large, cumbersome, dupperdessin controlled ships were a great joke." "88th Aero Squadron history." *Gorrell Report*, Series E.; Compte Rendu, 8 Armée Aéronautique, 12 Avril 1918, SHD 22 N 1672.

331   Les escadrilles de l'aéronautique militaire

332   Millett, 344.

333   "The First Corps Observation Group in the Toul Sector, Tactical History of the Air Service," *Gorrell Report*, Series D, 5.

334   *Operation Projetée par les U.S., Février 1918.* SHD 14 N 1474.

335   "First Corps Observation Group in the Toul Sector," 2.

336   *One Hundred Second Field Artillery*, 31.

337   "First Corps Observation Group in the Toul Sector," 5–6.

338   "First Corps Observation Group in the Toul Sector," 3.

339   *Projet d'Occupation du Secteur de Royaumeix, 6 Janvier 1918*, SHD 14 N 1474; "History of Balloons, First Army," *Gorrell Report*, Series F, 114.

340   Commandant Mandin, "Tactical Employment of the Balloon," *Gorrell Report*, Series F.

341   "Air Service Information," Balloon School, *Gorrell Report*, Series F.

342   "Balloon History," *Gorrell Report*, Series F.

343   William A. Morgan, "Invasion on the Ether: Radio Intelligence at the Battle of St. Mihiel, September 1918," *Military Affairs*, 51, Issue 2 (April 1987), 57–61.

344   Walcot, "Lecture on Intelligence."

345   Kahn, 313.

346   , 32.

347   Kahn, 314; Porch, 84–85.

348   "Confidential Order No. 1. France, February 16, 1918", Box 5, 26th Division, RG 120, NARA.

349   1st Division Intelligence Section, Memorandum No. 10. "Telephone conversations." *World War Records, First Division A.E.F. Regular, Summaries of Intelligence, Vol. IV.*

350   Theodore Roosevelt, Jr., 114–116.

351   *History of Battery B*, 145.

352   Carter, 98.

353   Cushing and Stone, 79.

354   Herbert, 122.

355   "Service Memorandum," *VIIIe armée*, 15 April 1918, Box 13, 26th Division, RG 120, NARA.

356   Strickland, 123–126; *History of the 102nd, United States Infantry*; Taylor, 132–133; Cushing and Stone, 79; Stallings, 52.

357   "Tagesbericht, "2.3.18., *78.R.D. Files*, 62; "Report of the Day Covering the developments of the 1-3-18, 2-3-18," *First Division Records, German Documents*.

358   1st Division report, Box 44, 1st Division, RG 120, NARA.

359 Strickland, 124.

360 "Memorandum for the Armies, General Headquarters of the Armies of the North & North-east Staff – 3rd Bureau, No. 13685, G.H.Q. April 13, 1918, RG 120," Box 42, 26th Division, Box 42 RG 120, NARA.

361 "Report of Private Rogers and Taylor," Box 19, 26th Division, RG 120, NARA.

362 Sirois and McGinnis, 47–48.

363 *History of the 102nd, United States Infantry.*

364 Fifield, 119.

365 Rogers, 117.

366 Washburn, 86.

367 Wunderlich, 38.

368 *History of the 102nd, United States Infantry.*

369 Wunderlich, 40.

370 *History of the One Hundred Second Field Artillery July, 1917 – April, 1919* (Boston: Private, 1927), 28; Marshall, 63.

371 *Die Schlachten und Gefechte des Grossen Krieges 1914–1918*, 208.

372 Wunderlich, 40.

373 To a present day enthusiast, Montsec resembles J.R.R. Tolkien's Eye of Mordor. *Narrative of Battery A of the 101st Field Artillery*, 84; Marshall, 63; Cushing and Stone, 70–71; Sirois and McGinnis, 47; Millett, 341–342; *Narrative of Battery A of the 101st Field Artillery*, 84.

374 *Narrative of Battery A of the 101st Field Artillery*, 86–87.

375 Earl Yeomans, Private, quoted in Martin Marix Evans, ed., *American Voices of World War I, Primary Source Documents 1917–1920* (Chicago: Fitzroy Dearborn Publishers, 2001), 56.

376 McKenna, 202.

377 1st Division sources contained in the comprehensive 25-volume *World War Records, First Division A.E.F. Regular* do not mention any wireless interecepts on the division while in Ansauville sector. Arthur C. Havlin, 75.

378 French Foreign Legion. Bullard, 136; Society of the First Division, 52.

379 All the commander's listed became general officers. Summerall became 1st Division commander in the latter half of 1918. Nenninger, *The Way of Duty, Honor, Country*, 113.

380 *1st Division Infanterie Américaine* [*DIA*] was the French name for the 1st Division. *Instruction Particulière N 20 pour le General Commandant la Iʳᵉ armée, 7 Janvier 1918*, SHD 14 N 1474.

381 Society of the First Division, 46.

382 Millett, 343.

383 Robert Lee Bullard diary, 5–10 February 1918, Bullard Papers, Library of Congress.

384 Major General Bullard Instruction No. 1 in Society of the First Division, 43.

385 Cochrane, *The 1st Division at Ansauville*, 16.

386 Bullard diary, 10 February 1918.

387 Nenninger, *The Way of Duty, Honor, Country*, 118–119.

388 Marshall, 66–67.

389 Larry I. Bland, ed., *The Papers of George Catlett Marshall, Volume I* (Baltimore, MD: The Johns Hopkins University Press, 1981), 129.

390 Marshall, 61.

391 Nenninger, *The Way of Duty, Honor, Country*, 117.

392 Blumenson, 485.

393 Marshall, 61.

394 TNA WO 106/466, 18 February 1918 letter, Brigadier-General C.M. Wagstaff, Headquarters American Expeditionary Force.

395 Ervin was awarded the DSC and Silver Star later in the war. He was a Senator during the Watergate crisis of 1974. Ervin quoted in Nelson, 192–195.

396 In World War 2, Brigadier General Theodore Roosevelt, Jr. led the 4th Division on D-Day (6 June 1944). His heroism that day was posthumously rewarded with the Medal of Honor. Theodore Roosevelt, Sr. was awarded the Medal of Honor posthumously in 2001. Pershing, i, 91.

397 Kermit Roosevelt, *War in the Garden of Eden* (NY: Charles Scribners, 1919), 25.

398 Alexander Gardiner, "The Girl Who Wore O.D." *The American Legion Magazine*, April 1928, 58.

399 "Girl Twice Under Fire." *New York Times*, 23 April 1918.

400 Gardiner, 58.

401 Brigadier General John H. Sherburne, *The Rambling Reminiscences of an Old Timer* (Boston: privately printed. 1961), 47.

402 Captain Alban B. Butler, General Summeral's aide, prepared a cartoon daily which was mimeographed with news of the war and sent to the trenches and battery positions every night. Post-war, several of Butler's cartoons were captured in *Happy Days*. Cochrane, *The 1st Division at Ansauville*, 16; "History of Chemical Warfare," 22.

403 Cochrane, *The 1st Division at Ansauville*, 2.

404 Bullard, 193–194; Cochrane, *The 1st Division at Ansauville*, 1.

405 Cochrane, *The 1st Division at Ansauville*, 13.

406 Marshall loved telling this story and Bullard put it in his memoir without naming Marshall. Nenninger, *The Way of Duty, Honor, Country*, 117; Bullard, 161.

407 *SRA, Bulletin de Renseigements N 90, 2 Février au 3 Février 1918*, SHD 22 N 1756.

408   Cochrane, *The 1st Division at Ansauville*, 16.

409   *SRA, Bulletin de Renseignments N 90, 4 Février au 5 Février 1918*, SHD 22 N 1756.

410   Cochrane, *The 1st Division at Ansauville*, 18.

411   "History of Chemical Warfare," 22.

412   *Projet d'Occupation du Secteur de Royaumeix.*

413   Balloon Company B/2 subsequently conducted operations in the Toul Sector. *1ere Armée Etat-Major 3eme Bureau Au Q.G.A., le 24 Février 1918*, SHD 14 N 1474.

414   Cochrane, *The 1st Division at Ansauville*, 18.

415   Auler, 62.

416   Cron, 390.

417   "Einladung Vorarbeiten."

418   Bull, 88.

419   A similar raid was planned for the Chemin-des-Dâmes sector, presently held by the French with the 26th Division in training. It was also executed on 1 March 1918. "Einladung Vorarbeiten."

420   Cochrane, *The 1st Division at Ansauville*, 20.

421   Samuels, 176.

422   "Regimentsbefehl."

423   "Divisionbefehl, 22.2.18," *78.R.D. Files*, 26.

424   "Artillerie Befehl, 23.2 18," *78.R.D. Files*, 28.

425   "Artillerie-Tagesbefehl Nr.7, 25.2.1918.," *78.R.D. Files*, 47; "Artillery Order of the Day No. 7, 25-2-18," *First Division Records, German Documents*.

426   "Voranschlag fur Beteilfgung der Minenwerfer am Unternehmen vor G.II" 17.2.1918. *78.R.D.* 17.; "Initial proposals for the participation of the Minenwerfer in the raid in front of G.II.," *First Division Records, German Documents*; "Vorschlag uber artilleristische Unterstutzung fur Unternehmen gegen Remiers-Wald."

427   "Artillerie-Befehl, 27.2.18," *78.R.D. Files*, 53; "Artillery Order, 22-2-18 [sic]," *First Division Records, German Documents*.

428   "Arméeabteilung C, Armée-Oberkommando, 22.2.17 [sic]," *78.R.D. Files*.

429   "Brigade-Befehl," 25.II.18, *78.R.D. Files*, 37; "Brigade Order, 25-II-18.," *First Division Records, German Documents*.

430   Lieutenant Colonel R. H. Griffiths, "Trench Mortar Gas Shell Barrage," February 26, 1918, Box 43, 18th Infantry, RG 120, NARA.

431   War Diary Files 335-351, 26–2, *78.R.D. Files*, 1.

432   Cochrane, *The 1st Division at Ansauville*, 19.

433   "History of Chemical Warfare," 25; Cochrane, *The 1st Division at Ansauville*, 24.

434   The men were assigned to the trench mortar battery and Company K. Cochrane, *The 1st Division at Ansauville*, 24; Charles E. Heller, *Chemical Warfare in World War I: The American Experience, 1917–1918* (Fort Leavenworth, KS: Leavenworth Papers, September 1984), 74–75.

435   Lieutenant Colonel R.H. Griffiths, "Supplementary Report on Trench-Mortar Bombardment in Center F," February 26, 1918, February 27th, 1918, Box 43, 18th Infantry, RG 120, 18th Infantry; Cochrane, *The 1st Division at Ansauville*, 25.

436   Heller.

437   Cochrane, *The 1st Division at Ansauville*, 20.

438   War Files 352–363, 27–2, *78.R.D. Files*, 1; Cochrane, *The 1st Division at Ansauville*, 22.

439   *SRA, Bulletin de Renseignements, N 117, 27 au 28 Février 1918, 12 H à 12 H*, SHD 22 N 1756; *Compte-Rendu des Evenements, N 117, Du 27 au 28 Février 1918, De 12 H à 12 H.*, SHD 22 N 1756.

440   Cochrane, *The 1st Division at Ansauville*, 26.

441   "Service Memorandum," *VIIIᵉ armée*, 15 April 1918," 103rd Infantry, RG 120, NARA.

442   Cochrane, *The 1st Division at Ansauville*, 26.

443   General Leonard Wood quoted in Millett, 344.

444   SHD 14 N 1474.

445   "Defense of Ansauville Sector", in Bland, *The Papers of George Catlett Marshall, Vol.I*, 130.

446   Millett, 345.

447   Pogue, *Marshall Interviews and Reminiscences*, 237; Marshall, 69.

448   Pogue, *Education of a General*, 160. Pogue interviewed both Marshall in 1957 and Seligman in 1962 on the incident. He also interviewed Major Charles S. Coulter in 1960. Both divisional and regimental intelligence sections claim credit for the warning. Bullard to CG, 32nd French Corps, 2 March 1918; Pogue, *Marshall Interviews and Reminiscences*; Marshall, 67–68.

449   Colonel Frank Parker, Narative [sic] report of raid made on Subsectors, #F 1 and #F 2, Center "F" March 1st. 1918. March 1st. 1918. Box 48, 18th Infantry, RG 120, NARA.

450   "Bataillons-Befehl, 28.2.1918," *78.R.D. Files*, 112–113; "Battalion Order, 28–2-1918," *First Division Records, German Documents*.

451   Nenninger, *The Way of Duty, Honor, Country*, 106.

452   "Artillery Plan," February 24, 1918. SHD 14 N 1474.

453   TNA WO 106/466, February 26th 1918 letter, Brigadier-General C.M. Wagstaff, Headquarters American Expeditionary Force; "Report of patrol," February 23, 1918, Box 39, 26th Division, RG 120, NARA.

454   0640 – German time on this date was an hour later than Allied time (as in the Second World War). Hauptmann von Bulow mentioned the count of 720 MW rounds in his next-day report to the Generalstab. Hauptmann von Bulow, "Tagesbericht uber den Verlauf des

1.3.18, 2.3.18" *78.R.D. Files*, 63; Report of the Day, Covering the developments of the 1 3-18, *First Division Records, German Documents*; "Ortskommandantur, 1.Marz 1918," *78.R.D. Files, 67*; "District Commander, March 1, 1918, *First Division Records, German Documents*.

455 Hauptmann von Bulow "Tagesbericht uber den Verlauf des 1.3.18, 2.3.18."

456 "Bericht uber das Unternehmen "Einladung" am 1 Marz 1918. 1.Marz 1918," *78.R.D. Files*, 66; Hauptmann von Bulow "Tagesbericht uber den Verlauf des 1.3.18, 2.3.18." *78.R.D. Files*, 63.

457 The Stosstruppen were mainly from Brunswick. "Gefechtsbericht uber das Unternehmen, 'Einladung' am 1.3.1918," *78.R.D. Files*, 63–65.

458 "Gefechtsbericht uber die Tatigkeit der 2.Sturm-Kompagnien bein Unternehmen 'Einladung' am 1.3.18.," *78.R.D. Files*, 113–114.

459 Spanish aavalry was originally a Dutch wooden obstacle with spikes and jagged edges used to deter Spanish cavalry forces. "Ortskommandantur, 1.Marz 1918"; "Bericht uber das Unternehmen "Einladung" am 1 Marz 1918. 1.Marz 1918," *78.R.D. Files*, 66.

460 "Gefechtsbericht uber das Unternehmen 'Einladung' am 1.3.1918," 63–65; Dem Regiment Gefechtsbericht uber das Unternehmen "Einladung" am 1.3.18.," *78.R.D. Files*, 119–122.

461 Commanding General First Division (Bullard) to Passaga, 32nd Corps d'Armée, March 2, 1918, "Enemy raid on Center F, March 1st," SHD 19N 1474; Lieutenant Colonel Griffiths, "Narative [*sic*] report of raid."

462 Breach A – 86.32; Breach B – 88.32; Breach C – 88.30. GHQ AEF Second Section, General Staff, 2 March 1918, "Supplement to Summary of Information for Divisional Headquarters" "German Raid, Bois De Remières, 1 March 1918." SHD 19N 1474; Lieutenant Colonel Griffiths, Narative [*sic*] report of raid.

463 Lieutenant Greene was awarded the Distinguished Service Cross for this action. Lieutenant A.B. Butler, "Journal of Operations," 1 March.

464 "Gefechtsbericht uber das Unternehmen "Einlaudung" am 1.3.1918, *78.R.D. Files*, 63–65.

465 Lieutenant Markoe was a recipient of both the Distinguished Service Cross and Silver Star citation. Sergeant William Norton, and Sergeant Patrick Walsh were recipients of the Distinguished Service Cross.

466 Breach A – 86.32; Breach B – 88.32; Breach

C – 88.30. GHQ AEF Second Section, General Staff, 2 March 1918, "Supplement to Summary of Information for Divisional Headquarters" "German Raid, Bois De Remières, March 1, 1918." SHD 19N 1474.

467 "Abschrift, 3.3.18." *78.R.D. Files*, 69–72.

468 Lieutenant Colonel Griffiths, Narative [*sic*] report of raid.

469 General Summerall reported to General Bullard that Major Downer first heard firing at 0538 and commenced fire at 0542. Post-battle assessment by Generalmajor von Stolzmann concluded the American artillery first responded seven minutes after Einladung commenced. Major Downer received the Silver Star citation. "Enemy raid on Center F, March 1st."

470 "Dem Regiment Gefechtsbericht uber das Unternehmen "Einladung" am 1.3.18.," *78.R.D. Files*, 119–122.

471 Major Robert McCormick was a former Illinois National Guard cavalry officer who was assigned to the 1st Division as a field artillery battery commander. He is best known as the publisher of the *Chicago Tribune*. McCormick's home in Wheaton, Illinois, was named "Cantigny Farm" and was maintained as a museum for the 1st Division. Major McCormick quoted in Richard Norton Smith, *The Colonel, The Life and Legend of Robert R. McCormick 1880–1955* (New York: Houghton Mifflin Company, 1997), 199; Lieutenant A.B. Butler, "Journal of Operations," March 1st.

472 *Compte-Rendu des Événements, N 118, du 28 Février à 1 Mars 1918*, SHD 22 N 1756; Nenninger, *The Way of Duty, Honor, Country*, 119.

473 Private Hugh Weatherman was a posthumous recipient of the Distinguished Service Cross.

474 Captain von Holtzendorf and Private Smiley received the Silver Star for bravery under fire. Lieutenant A.B. Butler, "Journal of Operations," March 1st; "Enemy raid on Center F, March 1st."

475 *Compte-Rendu des Événements N 118*.

476 Captain von Holzendorf and Private Smiley received the Silver Star certificate for bravery under fire. Lieutenant A.B. Butler, "Journal of Operations," March 1st; "Enemy raid on Center F, March 1st."

477 "Abschrift, 3.3.18.," *78.R.D. Files*, 69–72.

478 *Compte-Rendu des Événements, N 119, 1 au 2 Mars 1918, de 1600 à 1600*, SHD 22N 1756.

479 Frhr. Von Puttkammer, "'Abschrift,'" Sturmbataillon 14, Einladung, 4.3.1918," *78.R.D. Files*, 74.

480   "Bericht uber das Unternehmen "Einladung"
      am 1 Marz 1918, *78.R.D. Files*, 66.

481   Leutnant Solaro quoted in Johannes Ostendorf,
      *Gedenkblätter der Stadtgemeinde Lohne. 1. Folge:
      Weltkrieg 1914 – 1918* (Oldenburg, GE:
      Heimatverein, 1957), 21.

482   "Enemy raid on Center F," March 1st."

483   The 1st Division experience was not applied
      on 20 April 1918. "Enemy raid on Center F,"
      March 1st."

484   "Gefechtsbericht uber das Unternehmen
      "Einladung" am 1.3.1918," 63–65.

485   "Gefechtsbericht uber das Unternehmen
      "Einladung" am 1.3.1918," 63–65.

486   Hauptmann von Bulow "Tagesbericht uber
      den Verlauf des 1.3.18., 2.3.18.," 62–63.

487   "Abschrift. 78.Reserve-Division, 3.3.18."
      78.R.D. Files, 69–72.

488   "Dem Regiment Gefechtsbericht uber
      das Unternehmen "Einladung" am
      1.3.18.," *78.R.D. Files,* 119–122.

489   "'Abschrift,' 3.3.18., *78.R.D. Files*, 69–72.

490   "Generalkommando XXXVIII Reserve
      Korps, 1.3.18," *78.R.D. Files*, 62; "Abschrift.
      78.Reserve-Division, 3.3.18." *78.R.D. Files*,
      69–72; Hauptmann von Bulow "Tagesbericht
      uber den Verlauf des 1.3.18., 2.3.18.," 62–63.

491   "Generalkommando XXXVIII Reserve Korps,
      1.3.18."

492   "Enemy raid on Center F," March 1st."

493   Lieutenant John H. David from the Citadel
      [class of 1914] was another officer casualty.
      "Eadie a Football Star," *The Sun*, March 4, 1918.

494   "Ortskommandantur" 1.Marz 1918," *78.R.D.
      Files*.

495   *Compte-Rendu des Événements*, N 118, du 28
      Février à 1 Mars 1918, SHD 22 N 1756.

496   "Station Coburg, Abteilung 478, aufgenommen
      an 2.3.1918, Fernspruch aus den Felde," *78.
      R.D. Files*, 68.

497   Tuchel became infamous for the vast numbers
      of deaths from disease. In post-war Poland,
      thousands of Russians died. "Camp at
      Darmstadt," RG 120, NARA.

498   "Abschrift. 78.Reserve-Division, 3.3.18."
      78.R.D. Files, 69–72; "Bericht uber das
      Unternehmen "Einladung" am 1 Marz 1918.
      1.Marz 1918," *78.R.D. Files,* 66.

499   Pionier Kompagnie.79 was identified in 1st
      Division Intelligence Report as the unit that
      the wounded Germans were from. Reserve-
      Inf.Brigade Abt.Ia Nr. 70 op. 2.3.1918, 78.R.D.
      Files.

500   "Enemy raid on Center F," March 1st;
      Lieutenant Alban.B. Butler, "Journal of
      Operations," March 1st.

501   Society of the First Division, 56–57.

502   Lieutenant A. B. Butler, "Journal of
      Operations," March 1st.

503   Society of the First Division, 56–57.

504   The great offensive was Operation Michael.
      GHQ AEF Second Section, General Staff,
      2 March 1918, "German Raid, Bois De
      Remières, March 1, 1918," *Supplement
      to Summary of Information for Divisional
      Headquarters, No. 141*, SHD 16 N 1090.

505   Smith, 199.

506   Pogue, *Marshall Interviews and Reminiscences,*
      238.

507   Pogue, *Marshall Interviews and Reminiscences,*
      238–239.

508   Marshall, 57.

509   'The American fist' was a favorite Passaga term.
      "Commendation," March 2, 1918, *US Army in
      the World War*, iii, 479.

510   General Marshall cited the time as the
      following morning – most likely a slip. General
      Pershing's diary entry shows the meeting
      as Sunday 3 March 1918. Pogue, *Marshall
      Interviews and Reminiscences,* 238–239; Pershing,
      i, 337; *The Washington Times*, March 5, 1918.

511   Pershing, I, 337.

512   Pershing, I, 340.

513   *History of the 102nd, United States Infantry*;
      "German Raid upon Elements of 102nd
      Infantry," March 1, 1918, *US Army in the World
      War*, iii, 603–604.

514   "German Raid upon Elements of 102nd
      Infantry;" *History of the 102nd, United States
      Infantry*.

515   Bishop, Olsen, Sanderson, and Brown were
      awarded Distinguished Service Crosses. 2nd
      Lieutenant Ralph L. Bishop, Report of Action,
      2 March 1918," Box 41, 102nd Infantry, RG
      120, NARA; "Raid on 102nd Infantry."

516   *History of the 102nd, United States Infantry.*

517   Colonel Parker letter to General J.G. Harbord,
      March 16, 1918, quoted in Doubler, 184.

518   Wunderlich, 35.

519   Lieutenant Thomas W. Ryan Memoirs, 16.

520   Marshall, 70–71; Lieutenant Thomas W. Ryan
      pocket diary typescript, 5.

521   Lieutenant Thomas W. Ryan Memoirs, 16–19.

522   Lieutenant Thomas W. Ryan Memoirs, 19;
      General Bullard report to Général Passaga,
      March 5, 1918, "Report on failure of raids
      planned for March 3d-4th," Box 44, 1st
      Division, RG 120, NARA.

523   General Bullard report to Général Passaga."

524   Major Patton accompanied General Pershing.
      When Patton started to make for a forward
      observation post to watch the show, Pershing

thundered, "Where in hell are you going?" A resentful Patton stayed and watched from the safety of the brigade PC. Lieutenant Thomas W. Ryan Memoirs.

525 Nenninger, *The Way of Duty, Honor, Country,* 116–117.

526 Compte-Rendu, N 119, du 1er au 2 Mars 1918. SHD 22 N 1756; Von Stolzmann, Generalmajor u. Div.Kommandeur. "Monat Marz 1918. 2.3. K.A. 397–407c.," *78.R.D. Files,* 2.; *SRA, Bulletin de Renseignements, No 120, Du 2 au 3 Mars 1918, 12 H a 12 H.,* SHD 22 N 1756.

527 Von Stolzmann, Generalmajor u. Div. Kommandeur. "Monat Marz 1918. 3.3. K.A. 408–424," *78.R.D. Files,* 2–3.

528 Von Stolzmann, Generalmajor u. Div. Kommandeur. "Monat Marz 1918. 4.3. K.A. 425–441," *78.R.D. Files,* 3.

529 *SRA, Bulletin de Renseignments, Du 4 au 5 Mars 1918, De 12 H a 12 H.,* SHD 22 N 1756.

530 Von Stolzmann, Generalmajor u. Div. Kommandeur. "Monat Marz 1918. 7.3. K.A. 468–482," *78.R.D. Files,* 3.

531 Cochrane, *The 1st Division at Ansauville,* 31.

532 Cochrane, *The 1st Division at Ansauville.*

533 Von Stolzmann, Generalmajor u. Div. Kommandeur. "Monat Marz 1918. 8.3. K.A. 483–497," *78.R.D. Files,* 3.

534 *SRA, Bulletin de Renseignments, Du 7 au 8 Mars 1918, De 12 H à 12 H.,* SHD 22 N 1756; Cochrane, *The 1st Division at Ansauville.*

535 Cochrane, *The 1st Division at Ansauville.*

536 Von Stolzmann, Generalmajor u. Div. Kommandeur. "Monat Marz 1918. 8.3. K.A. 483–497," *78.R.D. Files,* 3.

537 Marshall, 64.

538 *Le 9 Mars 1918, Le Capitaine Tuczkiewicz du 34 Bataillon du Genie au Chef de Bataillon Commandant le 2éme Groupe Z.* SHD 25 N 726.

539 *Ordre particulier du Capitaine Coutton Commandant la Compagnie, G.A.E. Ire Armée 2e Groupe Z, 21 Mars 1918,* SHD 25 N 726.

540 *Le 9 Mars 1918, Le Capitaine Tuczkiewicz du 34 Bataillon du Genie au Chef de Bataillon Commandant le 2éme Groupe Z.*

541 Von Stolzmann, Generalmajor u. Div. Kommandeur. "Monat Marz 1918. 9.3. K.A. 498–513," *78.R.D. Files,* 3.

542 Marshall, 66–67.

543 Von Stolzmann, Generalmajor u. Div. Kommandeur. "Monat Marz 1918. 10.3. K.A. 514–426," *78.R.D. Files,* 3; Cochrane, *The 1st Division at Ansauville,* 32.

544 Cochrane, *The 1st Division at Ansauville,* 33.

545 "Intelligence Report," First Division, Summary of events, March 10–11. *World War Records First Division A.E.F. Summaries of Intelligence.*

546 *SRA, Bulletin de Renseignements 10 à 11 Mar 1918,* SHD 22 N 1756.

547 Hauptmann von Bulow, "Tagesbericht uber den Verlauf des 11.III.1918," 12. Marz 1918, *78.R.D. Files,* 84–86.

548 78.Res.Inf.Brig. "Vorlaufige Meldung" [Preliminary Message], 11.III.18, *78.R.D. Files,* 81; Mittagsmeldung vom 11.III.18 an Genkdo.38.Res.Korps, *78.R.D. Files,* 82; *SRA, Bulletin de Renseignements 11 au 12 Mars 1918,* SHD 22 N 1756.

549 G-2 report in Cochrane, *The 1st Division at Ansauville,* 34–35.

550 G-2 report in Cochrane, *The 1st Division at Ansauville.*

551 Cochrane, *The 1st Division at Ansauville,* 36.

552 Hinman, 35–36.

553 Headquarters First Division, "Commanding General to Commanding General, 32d Army Corps, Special Operations Report. March 12, 1918," SHD 14 N 1474.

554 Society of the First Division, 59.

555 Headquarters First Division, Commanding General to Commanding General, 32d Army Corps. Special Operations Report. March 12, 1918. SHD 14 N 1474.

556 "Meldung (Zusatz), 11.3.18." *78.R.D. Files,* 82.

557 "Mittagsmeldung vom 11.III.18 an Genkdo.38.Res.Korps," *78.R.D. Files,* 82.

558 "Abendmeldung von 11.3.18," *78.R.D. Files,* 83.

559 Marshall, 72–73.

560 "Raid on Enemy," March 11, 1918, *US Army in the World War,* iii, 481.

561 Headquarters First Division, Commanding General to Commanding General, 32d Army Corps. Special Operations Report. March 12, 1918. SHD 14 N 1474.

562 Marshall, 73.

563 Cochrane, *The 1st Division at Ansauville,* 34.

564 March 12, 1918, Commanding General, 1st F.A. Brigade, A.E.F. to Commanding General, 1st Division, A.E.F. Subject: Report Upon Operations of 1st F.A. Brigade During Raids, Executed March 11. World War Records First Division A.E.F. Operations Reports, Volume XIV.

565 Lieutenant Colonel (rank at the time of the award) Downer received both the Distinguished Service Cross and Silver Star citation for his heroic action.

566 Cochrane, *The 1st Division at Ansauville,* 32.

567   Archie Roosevelt spent the rest of the war
       recuperating from the wounds. In World
       War II he commanded troops in the Pacific
       and suffered wounds to the same leg. Hq. 1st
       Division, General Orders No. 13, March 16,
       1918, *Military Times Hall of Valor*; Eleanor Butler
       Roosevelt, *Day Before Yesterday* (Garden City,
       NY: Doubleday & Company, Inc. 1959), 95.

568   Cochrane, *The 1st Division at Ansauville*, 35.

569   Hauptmann von Bulow, "Tagesbericht uber den
       Verlauf des 11.III.1918," *78.R.D. Files*, 84–86.

570   Headquarters First Division, Commanding
       General to Commanding General, 32nd Army
       Corps. Special Operations Report. March 12,
       1918. SHD 14 N 1474.

571   Von Stolzmann, Generalmajor u. Div.
       Kommandeur. "Monat Marz 1918. 12.3–15.3
       K.A. 550–597," *78.R.D. Files*, 5–6.

572   Cochrane, *The 1st Division at Ansauville,* 33.

573   First Division Intelligence Report, March
       20–21. World War Records First Division A.E.F.
       Summaries of Intelligence.

574   Von Stolzmann, Generalmajor u. Div.
       Kommandeur. "Monat Marz 1918. 16.3. K.A.
       598–617," *78.R.D. Files*, 6.

575   Hinman, 37–38.

576   "History of Chemical Warfare," 26.

577   Cochrane, *The 1st Division at Ansauville*, 33.

578   Blumenson, 499.

579   Newton Baker quoted in Millett, 346.

580   David T. Zabecki, *Steel Wind, Colonel Georg
       Bruchmüller and the Birth of Modern Artillery*
       (Westport, CT: Praeger, 1994), 47.

581   J.B.A. Bailey, *Field Artillery and Firepower* (Oxford:
       The Military Press, 1989), 143–144; Marshall,
       61–62.

582   Zabecki, *Steel Wind,* 48.

583   "German Attack on March 21, 1918," 23 March
       1918, *US Army in the World War*, ii, 249.

584   Robert B. Bruce, *A Fraternity of Arms, America &
       France in the Great War* (Lawrence, KS: University
       Press of Kansas, 2003), 191.

585   Millett, 354.

586   Ferrell, *In the Company of Generals,* 43.

587   Ferrell, *In the Company of Generals,* 45.

588   "Request for Extension of 1st Division," March
       23, 1918, *US Army in the World War*, iii, 482.

589   "1st Division to Relieve 10th Colonial
       Division," March 28, 1918, *US Army in the World
       War*, iii, 483.

590   "Relief of 1st Division by 26th Division," March
       29, 1918, *US Army in the World War*, iii, 608–609.

591   "Orders to Hold Ground at All Costs," March
       27, 1918, *US Army in the World War*, ii. 260.

592   Theodore Roosevelt, 112–113; Lieutenant
       Holmes and Sergeant Murphy were both

       awarded the Distinguished Service Cross
       and Silver Star Citation. *Military Times
       Hall of Valor.*

593   *War Diaries, 3rd M.G. Battalion, World War
       Records First Division A.E.F., Regular*, vol.
       17, Date 22 March 1918; Cochrane, *The 1st
       Division at Ansauville,* 40–41.

594   Von Stolzmann, Generalmajor u. Div.
       Kommandeur. "Monat Marz 1918. 22.3. K.A.
       686–708," *78.R.D. Files*, 7–8.

595   Von Stolzmann, Generalmajor u. Div.
       Kommandeur. "Monat Marz 1918. 24.3. K.A.
       718–748," *78.R.D. Files*, 8; *Histories of Two
       Hundred and Fifty-One Divisions of the German
       Army*, 444.

596   Mark E. Grotelueschen, *The AEF Way of
       War* (Cambridge and New York: Cambridge
       University Press, 2007), 69.

597   Von Stolzmann, Generalmajor u. Div.
       Kommandeur. "Monat Marz 1918. 7.3. K.A.
       776–787," *78.R.D. Files*, 9.

598   Ferrell, *In the Company of Generals,* 45.

599   Cochrane, *The 1st Division at Ansauville*, 42.

600   Cochrane, *The 1st Division at Ansauville*, 45–46.

601   Von Stolzmann, Generalmajor u. Div.
       Kommandeur. "Monat Marz 1918. 31.3,"
       78.R.D. Files, 10.

602   Private Edward Armstrong letter quoted in De
       Wolfe Howe, 197–203.

603   De Wolfe Howe, 161.

604   Lieutenant Redwood was a recipient of the
       Distinguished Service Cross and *Croix de
       Guerre* for this heroic mission and subsequently
       an oak leaf cluster for his actions at Cantigny.
       De Wolfe, 159; Nelson, 197–203.

605   *8 Armée 2' Bureau, "Interrogatoire de 4 prisonniers
       de la 1 Cie du 259 Res, 2 Avril 1918"*, SHD
       19N 1411.

606   1st Division, 2nd Division, 26th Division, 42nd
       Division. Ferrell, *In the Company of Generals,*
       48–49.

607   Kernan and Samson, 35.

608   General Malin Craig did not leave papers.
       What little record is left at USMA is almost all
       newspaper clippings.

609   Benwell's history says that Edwards always pre-
       ceded his troops into a new sector and made
       a personal reconnaissance of the front being
       assigned. Benwell, 49. "Confidential Memor-
       andum," Brigadier General Malin Craig to
       General Hugh A. Drum, December 8, 1920,
       USAMHI, Drum Papers.

610   Ferrell, *In the Company of Generals*, 13–14.

611   Office of the Chief Surgeon, Headquarters
       26th Division, March 9, 1918, Box 31, 26th
       Division, RG 120, NARA.

612   Ferrell, *In the Company of Generals*, 34–35.

613   Ferrell, *In the Company of Generals*, 47.

614   "Instructions for Training with French," I Army Corps, A.E.F., March 9, 1918, U.S. Army, iii, 499–500.

615   *Military Times Hall of Valor*.

616   Taylor, 92.

617   Mirecourt HQ was also at Chaumont. "Probable Relief of 1st Division," March 29, 1918, *US Army in the World War*, iii, 485.

618   "Relief of 1st Division," March 30, 1918, *US Army in the World War*, iii, 485.

619   Havlin, 63.

620   General Traub File. "Report by I.G. to C. in C. of tactical inspection of 26th Div." Box 8, RG 200, NARA.

621   "Summary History of the 26th Division, IV In La Reine (Boucq) Sector *Bois-Brûlé* Seicheprey Xivray Humbert Plantation, 2, Box 6, 26th Division, RG 120, NARA.

622   Taylor, 103.

623   Général Passaga 4 April 1918, History of the First Division, 65.

624   Général de Maud'Huy order in "Facts about 104th U.S. Infantry, Twenty-Sixth Division."

625   Remarks by Captain Crochet, French Army, Memorandum for Brigade Commanders, 10 January 1918. World War Records First Division A.E.F. Training First Division, Vol. XX.

626   James F. McGrath, Former Rgt. Sgt. Major, "The Real Story," *Yankee Doings*, vol. 6 (8) August 1925, 5.

627   Craig report in Millett, 355–356.

628   Millett, 356.

629   Nenninger, *The Way of Duty, Honor, Country,* 120.

630   Ferrell, *In the Company of Generals*, 49.

631   "Confidential Memorandum," USAMHI, Drum Papers.

632   Taylor, 104–105.

633   Taylor, 104.

634   Headquarters 26th Division, Memorandum for all Organization Commanders, March 25, 1918, in Sibley, Appendix C.

635   Taylor, 103.

636   Charles E. Merrill, ed., "*Excerpts from the Personal Memoirs of Charles Leo Boucher,"* (np: Edited Transcription, 2002), 23–24.

637   The Yankee Division soldiers were awestruck at the meeting with the former President's son, in Seicheprey of all places. Strickland, 117.

638   Maj. Gen. Joseph Dorst Patch, *A Soldier's War* (Corpus Christi, TX: Mission Press, 1964), 21.

639   Joseph Edgar Chamberlin, *The Only Thing for a Man to Do, The Story of Raymond Chamberlin*, (Boston: Privately printed, 1921), 44.

640   Enoch H. Doble, "Eyewitness to the Great War," in *The World Wars Remembered* (Dublin, NH: Yankee, Inc., 1979), 21.

641   Chamberlin, 45.

642   Brigadier General Traub testimony in "Proceedings of a general court-martial which convened at "Quebec", Headquarters 26th Division, AEF, France, pursuant to the following order: SPECIAL ORDERS No. 123. France, May 5, 1918, 6, RG 153, NARA. (Henceforth cited as Traub testimony in "Proceedings of a general court-martial.") 6.

643   Fifth District – Misamis Province – June 15, 1905, *Report of the Philippine Commission 1906*, 36.

644   Gallant was wounded in battle at Tientsin, China during the Boxer Rebellion. *History of the 102nd, United States Infantry*; Strickland, 116–117.

645   Carter, 79–81.

646   Carter, 81.

647   Nenninger, *The Way of Duty, Honor, Country,* 119–120; Taylor, 102.

648   Carter, 78–79; History of Fifty-First Field Artillery Brigade, RG 120, Box 57.

649   Charles L. Furber, "The Artillery at Apremont," *Yankee Doings*, Vol. 5 (4) April 1924, 7.

650   Major Harry L. Doane, "The First Victory of American Arms" *Yankee Doings*, Vol. 3 (3) April 1922, 13.

651   Carter, 86.

652   Washburn, 86–90.

653   Sirois and McGinnis, 46.

654   Sirois and McGinnis, 45–46; Earl Yeomans, Private, quoted in Martin Marix Evans, ed., *American Voices of World War I, Primary Source Documents 1917–1920* (Chicago: Fitzroy Dearborn Publishers, 2001), 56.

655   McKenna, 35–36; Kernan and Samson, *103rd Field Artillery*, 36.

656   *History of Battery B*, 50–52.

657   Washburn, 81.

658   Washburn, 84–85.

659   Kernan and Samson, *103rd Field Artillery*, 36.

660   *Narrative of Battery A of the 101st Field Artillery*, 89–90.

661   Walter Wolf cited in *History of Battery B,* 112; *Narrative of Battery A of the 101st Field Artillery*, 107.

662   Everitte S. Chaffee, Major, *The Egotistical Account of an Enjoyable War* (The Adams Company, 1951), 24–25.

663   Bullard, 175.

664   "Change of Division Headquarters," April 11, 1918, *US Army in the World War*, iii, 489.

665 Millett, 355.

666 Marshall, 76.

667 War Department, *Order of Battle of the United States Land Forces in the World War American Expeditionary Forces* (Washington DC: GPO, 1931), 9.

668 Bullard, 181.

669 Pershing, I, 392.

670 Pershing, I, 393.

671 Pershing, I, 394–395.

672 Millett, 356.

673 Von Stolzmann, Generalmajor u. Div. Kommandeur. "Monat Marz 1918. 30.3. K.A. 818.829," *78.R.D. Files*, 10.

674 Summary of Intelligence, April 2nd - April 3rd (noon to noon), Box 8, 26th Division, RG 120, NARA.

675 A December 1918 inspection of the 35th Division gave Pershing the justification he needed to send Major General Traub home early without his division. "Report of Inspection of 26th Division," 27 February 1918, *US Army in the World War*, iii, 600–601.

676 Colonel "Gatling Gun" Parker, Memories of the Service, Draft, 10 May 1937. 221. West Point Archives.

677 *Order of Battle, Zone of the Interior*, 225.

678 *Order of Battle, Zone of the Interior*, 43.

679 Marshall interview, April 5, 1957, in Forrest C. Pogue, *George C. Marshall: Education of a General, 1880–1939* (New York: The Viking Press, 1963), 146.

680 Von Gallwitz, 309.

681 General der Infanterie Hofmann, "Telephone Message," *78.R.D. Files*.

682 Dr. Stepkes and Major L. Menzel, *Geschichte des Reserve-Infanterie-Regiments Nr. 258* (Selbstverlag, Stammgruppe Koln des Gesamtverbandes ehem. 258er, 1935), 192–194.

683 Oberstleunant Elsner, "Meldung, 5. April 1918," *78.R.D. Files*, 101–102; Stepkes and Menzel, 192.

684 Summary of Intelligence, April 4th-April 6th (noon to noon), Box 8, 26th Division, RG 120, NARA.

685 Private 1st Class Lane received the Distinguished Service Cross for his heroic action. Harry R. Stringer, ed. by. *Heroes All!* (Washington, DC: Fassett Publishing Co., 1919), 233.

686 Major George J. Rau, "Report of casualties, Company B, on the morning of April 10, 1918, at about 6:30 o'clock," Box 45, 26th Division, NARA.

687 *History of the One Hundred Second Field Artillery July, 1917 – April, 1919* (Boston: privately printed, 1927), 38–39.

688 *One Hundred Second Field Artillery*, 33–34.

689 Evangeline Booth and Grace Livingston Hill, *The War Romance of the Salvation Army* (Philadelphia and London: J.B. Lippincott Company, 1919), 145–146.

690 Private 1st Class Cyril Finnegan letters, April 24, 1918. Author's collection.

691 Joseph Chamberlin, *The Only Thing for a Man to Do, The Story of Raymond Chamberlin* (Boston: privately printed, 1921), 45.

692 Booth and Hill, 141; Gardiner, 32.

693 Booth and Hill, 145–146.

694 Wunderlich, 52.

695 Corporal Skelsky in Francis M. Coan, "A Few Men in the Great War: The Experiences of the Soldiers of Company D (Bristol), 1st Connecticut National Guard Regiment, March 1917-April 1918," Thesis, Central Connecticut State University, April 1990, Coan, 45.

696 Betsy served the 103rd Field Artillery to the Armistice firing approximately 8,500 rounds. McKenna, 137–138.

697 Doble, 21; *History of the 102nd, United States Infantry*, 11.

698 Fred Tyrrell Papers, 102nd Regiment files, USAMHI.

699 Taylor, 106.

700 Doble, 21–22; Enoch H. Doble, "Seicheprey Revisited," *Yankee Doings*, Vol. 8 (8) September 1927.

701 Chaffee, 24–25.

702 Washburn, 92–93.

703 Wunderlich, 42.

704 Carter, 86.

705 Washburn, 46.

706 Rogers, 106.

707 "Address of Major General James G. Harbord at Memorial Service for General Edwards on April 5th," *Yankee Doings*, vol. 12 (4), April 1931.

708 General Edwards letter to Général Passaga, 6 April 1918, Box 22, 26th Division, RG 120, NARA.

709 du Boisrouvray, 348.

710 Herbert, 95.

711 Elsie Janis, *The Big Show, My Six Months with the American Expeditionary Forces* (New York: Cosmopolitan Book Corporation, 1919), 63.

712 Wunderlich, 25.

713 du Boisrouvray, 341–342 [translated by Monique Duval].

714 C. R. Edwards, "Rest and Sanitization for tired troops coming into the Corps Reserve," 18th May 1918, Box 26, 26th Division, RG 120, NARA.

715 "Confidential Memorandum," Drum Papers.

716 Samuel Johnson Woolf, *Drawn from Life* (New York and London: Whittlesey House, 1932), 42–45; William Allen White, *A Puritan in Babylon, The Story of Calvin Coolidge* (New York: Capricon Books, 1938), 142.

717 Sherburne, *The Rambling Reminiscences of an Old Timer*, 39.

718 Pershing note in F. Warren Pershing papers, Smythe, 215.

719 "Address of Major General James G. Harbord at Memorial Service for General Edwards on April 5th".

720 Gatling Gun evolved into Machine Gun. Parker Obituary, *New York Times*, 1942.

721 Walter Barlow Stevens, *Centennial history of Missouri: (the center state) one hundred years in the Union, Vol. 2* (St. Louis, Chicago: S.J. Clarke Pub. Co., 1921), 892.

722 Bullard letter cited in draft "Action Front! A Saga of the Service," Parker files, USMA.

723 Colonel "Gatling Gun" Parker, Memories of the Service, Draft, 10 May 1937. 211. West Point Archives.

724 Major General J. Franklin Bell quoted in Edward M. Coffman, *The Regulars, The American Army 1898–1941* (Cambridge, MA: The Belknap Press, 2004), 161–162.

725 Parker Obituary, *New York Times*, October 14, 1942.

726 Quoted in Rainey, "Ambivalent Warfare," 38, 45, note 21 in Grotelueschen, 38.

727 Colonel John H. Parker, "Raid April 20–21st on Beaumont Zone," 25 April 1918, Box 44, 102nd Infantry, RG 120, NARA.

728 Blumenson, 460.

729 Walter Barlow Stevens, Centennial history of Missouri: (the center state, 1921, Volume 2. 892.

730 Draft "Action Front! A Saga of the Service," Parker files, USMA, 15.

731 Colonel "Gatling Gun" Parker, Memories of the Service, Draft, 10 May 1937. 216. West Point Archives.

732 Draft "Action Front! A Saga of the Service," Parker files, USMA.

733 Colonel "Gatling Gun" Parker, Memories of the Service, Draft, 10 May 1937. 221–222. West Point Archives.

734 du Boisrouvray, 349.

735 du Boisrouvray, 350–351.

736 du Boisrouvray, 352.

737 Draft "Action Front! A Saga of the Service," Parker files, USMA.

738 Fifield, 103–104.

739 Colonel B.F. Cheatham, *Historical Data 104th U.S. Infantry, draft files*, 11.; Doane, "The First Victory of American Arms."; Albertine, 115.

740 Albertine, 113–114.

741 Auler, 63–65.

742 Auler, 65–66.

743 6 April is General der Infanterie Auler's date of the raid. Auler, 66–67; *Summary of Intelligence, April 6th–April 7th (noon to noon)*, Box 8, 26th Division, RG 120, NARA.

744 French thinking also favoured the use of small columns in single file over deployed lines. It was advocated as the normal formation for small units. *VIIIᵉ Armée Bulletin, April 23, 1918*, "German Raid West of Apremont, April 12, 1918," *Summary of Information, No. 32, May 2, 1918*, SHD 16 N 1090; Doane, "The First Victory of American Arms," 14.

745 Doane, "The First Victory of American Arms."

746 *SRA, Bulletin de Renseignements N 158 9 au 10 Avril 1918 1600 à 1600*, SHD 22 N 1756; Fifield, 113; Cushing and Stone, 76.

747 Doane, "The First Victory of American Arms," 13.

748 Furber, 7; Cheatham, 12.

749 Carter, 87–88.

750 Cheatham.

751 *Military Times Hall of Valor.*

752 Doane, "The First Victory of American Arms," 13.

753 Private Edwin H. Hobbs, Battery D, received the Silver Star citation for his efforts this day. Furber, 8.

754 Carter, 88.

755 Corporal LaBranche later received the French Croix de Guerre with silver star in recognition of his rescue of soldiers from a gas-filled dugout that had caved in. (31 October 1918). LaBranche, 109.

756 Doane, "The First Victory of American Arms," 14.

757 "German Raid West of Apremont, April 12, 1918"; Auler, 67.

758 "Counter-attack by 104th Infantry in Bois-Brule," April 13, 1918, *US Army in the World War*, iii, 609–610.

759 LaBranche, 109.

760 Auler, 67.

761 Cheatham; *Le Crapauillot* (Lewiston, ME: privately printed, 1919), 71.

762 Sergeant John A. Dickerman was awarded the Silver Star citation and the *Croix de Guerre* for his heroism that day. Dickerman spent two years recuperating at Walter Reed Hospital in Washington. He married Marion Schaefer, a caregiver at the hospital. Albertine, 117, 122; Stallings's account referred to Dickerson. Stallings, 51; "John A. Dickerman," *New York Times*, June 20, 1930.

763   Furber; Carter, 89–90.

764   *SRA, Bulletin de Renseignements N 160, 11 au 12 Avril 1918 de 16 heures à 16 heures,* SHD 22 N 1756.

765   Carter, 89–90.

766   "German Raid West of Apremont, April 12, 1918."

767   This was an intermediate decoration between Iron Cross 1st Class and the Pour le Mérite. Leutnant Hoerning from Ldw. I. R. 25 also was a recipient from this battle. Auler, 69.

768   *2. Ulanen. Regiment. Nr. 16* was a lancer regiment brought to the front lines. Cheatham, 13.

769   Carter, 89–90.

770   Fifield, 124.

771   Fifield, 137.

772   "German Raid West of Apremont, April 12, 1918."

773   Doane, "The First Victory of American Arms," 15.

774   Phillips was promoted to captain after Apremont. Later that summer he was promoted to major. He was killed while leading his battalion in the Château Thierry offensive. Fifield, 137.

775   LaBranche, 109.

776   Doane, "The First Victory of American Arms," 16.

777   Furber.

778   Doane, "The First Victory of American Arms."

779   Hill was awarded the Distinguished Service Cross and *Croix de Guerre* for *Bois-Brûlé.* Fifield, 135–136.

780   Albertine, 123; Fifield, 117–118.

781   Reverend Father DeValles was a Knights of Columbus chaplain who technically was not a US Army chaplain but was allowed to serve at the front under the auspices of that religious order. Fifield, 138.

782   *SRA, Bulletin de Renseignements N 162, 13 au 14 Avril 1918 de 16 heures à 16 heures,* SHD 22 N 1756.

783   LaBranche, 110–111.

784   Herbert, 97.

785   The 2nd Division was brigaded with the French at this time. "German Raid," 2d Division, A.E.F., April 14, 1918; U.S. Army, iii, 512–513.

786   Casualty counts differed with reports. See Chapter 26. Doane, "The First Victory of American Arms"; Albertine, 124.

787   Colonel Craig letter in Cheatham, 17.

788   "Service Memorandum," *VIIIe armée,* 15 April 1918.

789   "Operations Report."

790   This source cites 36 German prisoners, not 42. "German Attack on Bois-Brûlé," April 16, 1918. *US Army in the World War,* iii, 611–612.

791   *Histories of Two Hundred and Fifty-One Divisions of the German Army,* 118–119.

792   "German Attack on Bois-Brule."

793   Havlin, 67.

794   "German Raid West of Apremont, April 12, 1918."

795   Furber, 7.

796   Passaga order, No. 1870–3 General Orders No. 124 in Cushing and Stone, 75.

797   Passaga, 144–145.

798   The *Cour de Guerre,* or cord of war, is a regimental decoration as distinguished from the *Croix de Guerre,* or cross of war, which is conferred upon individuals. The *Cour de Guerre* consisted of a green ribbon, dotted with red, which was buttoned under the flap on the left shoulder and brought down in front under the arm. An act of Congress had to be passed to permit the acceptance of foreign decorations. Havlin, 67.

799   "I award you the *Croix de Guerre,* with the *corps de l'armée's* citation." Kelly, 122.

800   Generalmajor von Stolzmann memo to Gorz Group, April 9, 1918, *Extracts, April 20, 1918, 78.R.D. Files,* 2.

801   Generalleutnant Hoffmann Report, April 10, 1918, *Extracts, April 20, 1918, 78.R.D. Files,* 3.

802   Generalleutnant Hoffmann memo to Gorz Group, April 14, 1918, *Extracts, April 20, 1918, 78.R.D. Files,* 4–5.

803   "Divisionsbefehl Nr. 3, 18. April. 18", Box 159, RG 165, NARA; "Divisional Order No. 3, April 18, 1918," Box 159, RG 165.

804   *"Interrogatoire sommaire d'un prisonnier blessé du 259 R. (capture le 20 Avril à Seicheprey), le 25 Avril 1918,"* SHD 19 N 1411.

805   Vigneulles was occupied by the 26th Division in September during the St. Mihiel offensive. Havlin, 74–75.

806   Draft "Action Front! A Saga of the Service," Parker files, USMA, 13.

807   *Grand Quartier General des Armées du Nord et du Nord Est, NOTE N 21.556, 24 Avril 1918,* SHD 16 N 1695, (translation by Monique Duval).

808   "Personal and Secret Instruction on the Conduct of Defence."

809   Sibley, 138.

810   Box 25, 26th Division, RG 120, NARA.

811   Lieutenant Colonel Dowell was a 1924 recipient of the Distinguished Service Medal for his accomplishments in the war. Sibley, 131.

812   Traub's 13 April 1918 memorandum was not located in the research. Based on the available

French documentation regarding sacrifice positions and subsequent Traub correspondence with Parker, the policy was consistent throughout this period – hold the ground at all cost. "Strength of outposts," Colonel Parker memo to General Traub, Box 43, 102nd Infantry papers, RG 120, NARA.

813   Parker memoirs, Parker file, USMA, 205.

814   To the last man was being promulgated by both British and French at this time – having suffered under Operations Michael and Georgette. Draft "Action Front! A Saga of the Service," Parker files, USMA, 13.

815   Draft "Action Front! A Saga of the Service," Parker files, USMA, 13–14.

816   VIIth Army [sic], 32nd Army Corps Staff – 3rd Bureau, No. 1956/3, April 17, 1918, Memorandum for Division, Box 42, 26th Division, RG 120, NARA.

817   Field Order, Headquarters 102nd U.S. Infantry, A.E.F. 17 April 1918, To: Commanding Officer, Co. L, 102nd U.S. Infantry, Box 42, 102nd Infantry, RG 120, NARA.

818   Headquarters 51st Infantry Brigade, "Subject: Changes in location of troops and new contruction. April 18, 1918." USAMHI.

819   Box 25, 26th Division, RG 120, NARA.

820   Grant, "Report on 26th Division affair of April 20th."; 102nd United States Infantry, Box 211, 12; Major George J. Rau, "Report of Action Morning of April 20th, 1918," Box 44, 102nd Infantry, RG 120, NARA.

821   Rau, "Report of Action Morning of April 20th, 1918."

822   LaBranche, 112.

823   Strickland's version includes the detail that one of the officers was supposd to be a full colonel who aroused suspicion when someone noticed his eagles were pinned upside down. Strickland, 124; History of the 102ndUnited States Infantry, 11.

824   Author's discussion with Wells Ziegra. History of the 102nd, United States Infantry, 11–12; Private Harry Marvin letter cited in Deep River, Connecticut, June 7, 1918; P. C. Ettighoffer, Gespenster am Toten Mann (Köln: Gilde, Verlag GMBH, 1931), 223, Translation by Jan Milles.

825   Stepkes and Menzel, 190.

826   Stepkes and Menzel's history of the Res. I. R. 258 and Captain Strickland's book cover the incident at the bridge. Vizefeldwebel Ettighoffer's writing for some reason describes an attack on an observation post that no other record substantiates. Stepkes and Menzel, 190; Strickland, 132–133; History of the 102nd, United States Infantry; Ettighoffer, 223; Official History 51st Infantry Brigade in Cushing and Stone, 72.

827   Sergeant Ziegra was the 183rd name on the list of prisoners in the Gazette des Ardennes. Von Gallwitz, 316; Washington Times-Herald, December 3, 1922.

828   VIIIth Army, 32nd Army Corps Staff – 3rd Bureau, No. 1956/3, April 17, 1918, Memorandum for Division, Box 42, 26th Division, RG 120, NARA.

829   Thanks to the efforts of the Ziegra family, Louis Ziegra was posthumously awarded the Purple Heart. Ziegra was promoted to Sergeant on 9 April 1919. History of the 102nd, United States Infantry, 12.

830   General Summerall made that a priority for the remainder his active service but was not successful. Nenninger, The Way of Duty, Honor, Country, 115.

831   "First Corps Observation Group in the Toul Sector," 2.

832   "88th Aero Squadron History," Gorrell Report, Series E.

833   "History of Photographic Section #1, Air Service, U.S.A. 1918," 1–2, Gorrell Report, Section G, RG 120, NARA; William G. "Billy" Schauffler, Edited by Stanley Walsh, Over the Front, Vol 23, No. 2, Summer 2008, 97.

834   1st Corps Observation Group in the Toul Sector, 1–2.

835   Montsec observations also contributed to the aviator's warning network. 8 Armée 2 Bureau, 15 Avril 1918, Interrogatoire d'un des aviateurs de la Jagdstaffel 64; G.H.Q. A.E.F. SERIAL Second Section, General Staff No. 2. April 19, 1918 Summary of Air Information Air Intelligence Bulletin.

836   An American observer assigned to a French aerial bombardment escadrille claimed the first kill by an American combatant in February 1918. Author discussion with Ted Hamady; Theodore Hamady, The Nieuport 28, America's First Fighter (Atglen, PA: Schiffer Military History, 2008), 10–14; 8 Armée 2 Bureau, 15 Avril 1918, Interrogatoire d'un des aviateurs de la Jagdstaffel 64; "Tactical History of the Air Service," Gorrell Report, Series D, 1–2.

837   Hamady, 14–17.

838   Author discussion with Ted Hamady; Lieutenant Winslow in Hamady, 17.

839   Ferrell, In the Company of Generals, 50.

840   Herbert, 92.

841   Herbert, 85.

842   "Diary of Company "B" 2d Balloon Company," Gorrell Report, Series F.

843   SRA, Bulletin de Renseignements N 167, 18 au 19 Avril 1918, de 1600 à 1600, SHD 22 N 1756.

844 "Notes on Anti-Aircraft Guns" (Washington DC: GPO, 1917), 5.

845 Washburn, 102–103.

846 LaBranche, 111.

847 LaBranche, 112.

848 S.O.S. was the subject of ridicule by the combatants. The author's grandfather said that S.O.S. were the first Americans at the Armistice to acquire as much booty as possible. Unidentified diary in Strickland, 138.

849 *History of the 102nd, United States Infantry*, 9.

850 Company C troops were mainly from Middletown, Bristol, and New Haven. Company D were mostly from Bristol and New Haven. Strickland, 133–134; *History of the 102nd, United States Infantry*, 12.

851 Henry Berry, "For Some Old Soldiers, France was Yesterday," *New York Times*, 30 April, 1978.

852 Merrill, 23–29.

853 Lieutenant Koenne was listed as 4th Platoon commander. Sergeant Charles Hanson was listed as 2nd Platoon commander. Merrill goes to great lengths to substantiate Boucher's assignment as 1st Platoon commander for the Seicheprey affair. Both Sibley and Strickland mention Sergeant William A. Brinley as the commander. The author will cite both as helping to lead 1st Platoon that day. Merrill, 25–27.

854 Griswold addressed Boucher as sergeant since he held the senior rank in Company C's 1st Platoon at that moment. Boucher was to acquire his third stripe officially in August. Merrill, 25–27.

855 Corporal Charles Leo Boucher earned a Silver Star for his heroism this day. It was awarded almost thirty years later on 11 December 1947. Merrill, 29.

856 Cushing and Stone, 76.

857 Major Murphy, April 27, 1918, RG 120, 102nd Infantry, Box 55.

858 Lieutenant Sanbarn, 25 April 1918, RG 120, 102nd Infantry, Box 55.

859 Parker, "Raid April 20–21st on Beaumont Zone."

860 Grant, "Report on 26th Division affair of April 20th."

861 Lieutenant Boyd, 3rd Platoon, Comapny M.

862 2nd Lieutenant C.R. Middaugh; Parker, "Raid April 20–21st on Beaumont Zone."

863 "Colonel Parker to Brigadier General Traub memorandum."

864 Kernan and Samson, *103rd Field Artillery*, 38.

865 Major Edward Bowditch, Jr. 20 April 1918 letter to Colonel Craig in Pershing file on Major General Clarence Edwards, Box 8, RG 200, NARA.

866 Sirois and McGinnis, 50–51.

867 VIII Armée, *Compte-Rendu des Opérations Aériennes, 19 Avril 1918*, SHD 22N 1758; "Headquarters First Army A.E.F. Office of Chief, Air Service. Report of Operations for April 29, 1918."

868 VIII Armée, *Compte-Rendu des Opérations Aériennes, 19 Avril 1918*; SRA, *Bulletin de Renseignements N 167, 18 au 19 Avril 1918, de 1600 à 1600*, SHD 22N 1756.

869 Herbert, 103.

870 "Diary of Company "B" 2d Balloon Company," *Gorrell Report*, Series F; Herbert, 103.

871 Parker memoirs, USMA, Parker File, 201–202; Nenninger, *The Way of Duty, Honor, Country*, 118–119.

872 "78th Reserve Division Divisional Order No. 4, April 19, 1918," Box 159, RG 165, NARA.

873 Artillery Commander No. 78, "Report on our Operation, April 20, 1918," 38, Box 160, RG 165, NARA.

874 79th Reserve Engineer Company. Report on Cherry Blossom, April 20, 1918. 32.

875 Ettighoffer, 225.

876 Operations Report from Noon April 19th to Noon April 20th. Box 23, 26th Division, RG 120, NARA.

877 "Telephone message," Box 19, 102nd Infantry, RG 120, NARA (henceforth referred to as "Telephone Message," Box 19).

878 Colonel Edward Logan is remembered by the citizens of Massachusetts by the Boston airport named after him. Captain Stanchfield, Report of operations of April 20–21, April 26th 1918, Box 55, 102nd Infantry, RG 120, NARA.

879 Washburn, 96.

880 There is some doubt as to when the German barrage actually started. German plans and reporting stick to 0300. American reports vary from 0300 to 0316. The latter was in Colonel John H. Parker's report. Strickland, 134; Sirois and McGinnis, 52.

881 Sirois and McGinnis, 52.

882 Lieutenant Sanbarn, April 25, 1918, RG 120, 102nd Infantry Files, Box 55.

883 Grant, "Report on 26th Division affair of April 20th."

884 Parker, "Raid April 20–21st on Beaumont Zone."

885 Rau memo, "Report of Action, Morning of April 20th, 1918."

886 The German signal for barrage was yellow light balls.

887 Private Cassie was awarded the *Croix de Guerre* with gilt star by *32ᵉ corps d'armée*. Robert Cassie, personnel card, Massachusetts National Guard Museum & Archives.

888 Wolf cited in *History of Battery B,* 112.

889 "Bowditch letter to Colonel Craig"; Taylor, 123.

890 *History of the 101st United States Engineers,* 153.

891 "Telephone message," Box 19.

892 Captain Stanchfield, Report of Operations of April 20–21, April 26th 1918, RG 120, 102nd Infantry, Box 55.

893 Eittighoffer, 225–226.

894 Carter, 93–94.

895 Wunderlich, 40.

896 Chaffee, 29–30.

897 Hoffmann, "Report on our Operation, April 20, 1918," 78.R.D. Files.

898 78 Reserve Division. Divisional Headquarters. Section Ia No. 1049 op. April 27, 1918, Box 160, 15.

899 Sibley, 140.

900 Hoffmann, "Report on our Operation, April 20, 1918," April 23, 1918, 35–40, *Extracts, April 20, 1918, 78.R.D. Files.*

901 Hoffmann, "Report on our Operation, April 20, 1918," 36.

902 Parker, "Raid April 20–21st on Beaumont Zone."

903 Grant, "Report on 26th Division affair of April 20th."

904 "*Rapport du Colonel Bertrand, Commandant le 162e Régiment d'Infanterie et le Sous-Secteur de la HAZELLE, sur les combats des 20 et 21 Avril 1918,*" SHD 24 N 1730.

905 The German term for this sector fire was "von x bix zur Räumung von Seicheprey." Lieutenant Millspaugh, 26 April 1918.

906 "Bowditch letter to Colonel Craig."

907 Colonel E.T. Smith, Report of the Action, April 20th – April 21st, April 27, 1918. Box 62, 103rd Field Artillery, RG 120, NARA; Kernan and Samson, 103rd Field Artillery, 42–43.

908 Sibley, 140–141.

909 Private Parent was awarded the Distinguished Service Cross and Croix de Guerre with gold star. Stringer, 306.

910 Private Johnson received the Distinguished Service Cross. Stringer, 211–212.

911 G-3, GHQ, AEF: 26th Division: Operation Reports, 26th Division, A.E.F., Boucq, Meurthe-et Moselle, April 23, 1918. "Report of Enemy Raid on Troops of the 26th Division at Seicheprey, April 20/21, 1918" in *U.S. Army History,* 3, 613; "Telephone message," Box 19.

912 *SRA, Bulletin de Renseignements N 168, 19 au*

913 *20 Avril 1918, de 1600 à 1600,* SHD 22N 1756.

913 *History of the 101st United States Engineers,* 153–154.

914 "Divisionsbefehl Nr. 3, 18.April.18"; "Divisional Order No. 3, April 18, 1918."

915 Strickland, 134

916 Lieutenant McGlasson, 3rd Platoon Company D, Report, Box 53, 102nd Infantry, RG 120, NARA.

917 Strickland citing Company C source, 138.

918 Lieutenant McGlasson, 3rd Platoon Co. D, Box 53, 102nd Infantry, RG 120, NARA.

919 Lieutenant R.K. Harris, Fourth Platoon Company F, Box 53, 102nd Infantry, RG 120, NARA.

920 Doble, 22–23.

921 Lieutenant Sanbarn, April 25, 1918, RG 120, Box 55.

922 "Bowditch letter to Colonel Craig"; Taylor, 123.

923 Mustard gas was not used in this battle. Augustin F. Maher, *When Connecticut Stopped the Hun, Battle of Seicheprey April 20–21, 1918* (New Haven, CT: Press of S. Z. Field, 1919), 1.

924 Lieutenant Boyd, 3rd Platoon, Company M.

925 Wunderlich, 40.

926 Shay, *A Grateful Heart,* 60–61.

927 Lieutenant Edwards Larned. Company I. 26 April 1918, Box 53, 102nd Infantry, RG 120, NARA.

928 Statement of activity of Company L 102nd U.S. Infantry during the period of April 19-20-21, 1918. *Application for Relief from General Courts-Martial Findings United States vs John J. Gallant, A.E.F. France #100 May 10–11, 1918,* RG 153, NARA (Henceforth referred to as *United States v. John J. Gallant*).

929 Lieutenant H.W. Smith, 4th Platoon, Company M; Lieutenant Fuessenich; Lieutenant Boyd, 3rd Platoon, Company M.

930 Wunderlich, 31.

931 Merrill, 29.

932 Colonel E.T. Smith, Report of the Action, April 20th – April 21st, April 27, 1918. 103rd Field Artillery, Box 62, 26th Division, RG 120, NARA; Kernan and Samson, *103rd Field Artillery,* 42–43.

933 1st Lieutenant Leavenworth report.

934 1st Lieutenant J.C. Davis, 103 *Field Artillery.* 95mm battery, "Action of this organization on April 20th and 21st 1918," Box 62, 26th Division, RG 120, NARA.

935 Kernan and Samson, *103rd Field Artillery,* 39; Havlin, 77.

936 Kernan and Samson, *103rd Field Artillery,* 38–39.

937 McKenna, 124.

938 Sergeant Broadhead was posthumously awarded the Distinguished Service Cross. Corporal Gordon was posthumously awarded the Distinguished Service Cross and *Croix de Guerre*. McKenna, 126; *History of Battery B*, 55–56; Kernan and Samson, *103rd Field Artillery*, 39. *Heroes All!* Washington, DC: Fassett Publishing Co., 1919, 166.

939 1st Lieutenant Chaplain Farrell was awarded the Distinguished Service Cross, Silver Star citation, and *Croix de Guerre* for his actions. Kernan and Samson, *103rd Field Artillery*, 40; *History of Battery B*, 56.

940 Chaffee, 29–30.

941 Kernan and Samson, *103rd Field Artillery*, 39–40.

942 Général Passaga awarded the *Croix de Guerre* to Lieutenant Davis, Chaplain Farrell, and Sergeant Broadhead (posthumously) on 7 June 1918. Chaffee, 29–30.

943 LaBranche, 112–113.

944 *One Hundred Second Field Artillery*, 42.

945 Thomas Platoon. Report of Engineer Platoon on Cherry Blossom Operation, April 24, 1918, 31–32, RG 165, NARA.

946 Hoffmann. "Report on our Operation, April 20, 1918," *Extracts, April 20, 1918, 78.R.D. Files*, 35–40.

947 Ettighoffer, 228; Von Bornstedt, 179–180; Petitjean, *31ᵉ corps d'armée Ordre*.

948 *Extracts, April 20, 1918, 78.R.D. Files*, 15; *History of the 102nd, United States Infantry, 26th Division*, 12–13; Taylor, 124; Sibley, 144.

949 "Major General Clarence Edwards memorandum," Box 25, 26th Division, RG 120, NARA.

950 Von Ponickau Platoon. "Report of Engineer Platoon on Cherry Blossom Operation," *Extracts, April 20, 1918, 78.R.D. Files*, 30–31.

951 Artillery Commander No. 78, "Report on our Operation," 36.

952 "Colonel Parker Memo to Brigadier General Traub."

953 "Telephone Log," Box 42, 26th Division, RG 120, NARA; Rice message, Box 19, 26th Division, RG 120, NARA.

954 "Bowditch letter to Colonel Craig."

955 Hoffmann, "Report on our Operation, April 20, 1918, *Extracts, April 20, 1918, 78.R.D. Files*, 35–40.

956 Hoffmann, "Report on our Operation, April 20, 1918.

957 "Telephone message," Box 19; G-3, GHQ, AEF: 26th Div.: Operation Reports, 26th Division, A.E.F., Boucq, Meurthe-et Moselle, April 23, 1918. *Report of Enemy Raid on Troops of the 26th Division at Seicheprey, April 20/21, 1918* in *U.S. Army History*, 3, 613.

958 Private Liming received the *Croix de Guerre*. Corporal Blanchard quoted in Hills, 15.

959 Von Bornstedt, 179.

960 *Extracts, April 20, 1918, 78.R.D. Files*, 17.

961 *Extracts, April 20, 1918, 78.R.D. Files*, 18; Ettighoffer, 229–230.

962 Ettighoffer, 229–230.

963 Ettighoffer, 230–231; *Extracts, April 20, 1918, 78.R.D. Files*.

964 *History of the 102nd, United States Infantry*, 13.

965 Von Bornstedt, 180; *Extracts, April 20, 1918, 78.R.D. Files*, 16.

966 Strickland states Captain Freeland died of wounds. He was the highest-ranking officer captured that day. Subsequent newspaper accounts still listed him as alive. *History of the 102nd, United States Infantry*, 13.

967 Von Bornstedt, 179–180; *Extracts, April 20, 1918, 78.R.D. Files*, 17–18.

968 In addition to the *Croix de Guerrre*, Private Lugg was awarded the Silver Star citation. His recognition was overlooked over the decades. On 24 April 1966, Private Lugg was recognized in New Haven, CT. Strickland, 136.

969 Coan, 49–50.

970 Private Brundett was awarded the Distinguished Service Cross. Stringer, 76.

971 Grant, "Report on 26th Division affair of April 20th."

972 "Colonel Parker Memo to Brigadier General Traub."

973 The Fullerphone was a portable direct-current line Morse telegraph, devised as a secure signalling set for positional warfare. Grant, "Report on 26th Division affair of April 20th.".

974 Strickland, 143.

975 Strickland, 134.

976 Three were awarded Silver Star citations for heroism. "Colonel Parker Memo to Brigadier General Traub."

977 Von Ponickau Platoon. "Report of Engineer Platoon on Cherry Blossom Operation," *Extracts, April 20, 1918, 78.R.D. Files*, 30; Von Bornstedt, 181–182.

978 *Extracts, April 20, 1918, 78.R.D. Files*, 19–20; Von Bornstedt, 183–184; Report of Engineer Platoon on Cherry Blossom Operation, 30.

979 *Extracts, April 20, 1918, 78.R.D. Files*.

980 Thomas Platoon. Report of Engineer Platoon on Cherry Blossom Operation, *Extracts, April 20, 1918, 78.R.D. Files*, 32.

981 *Extracts, April 20, 1918, 78.R.D. Files*.

982 Sergeant Walsh was awarded the Distinguished Service Cross for his actions that day. Stringer, 404.

983 "Kauffman assessment. Outline of Mil. Intell. Org. of Deputy General Staff in Berlin III B" in Dennis Nolan papers, USAMHI.

984 *Extracts, April 20, 1918, 78.R.D. Files,* 21.

985 *History of the 102nd, United States Infantry,* 12–13; Taylor, 124; Sibley, 144.

986 du Boisrouvray, 353; Von Ponickau Platoon. "Report of Engineer Platoon on Cherry Blossom Operation," 30–31.

987 Rau, "Report of Action Morning of April 20th 1918."; Conn. Vets Remember Seicheprey, James S. Jackson, *Hartford Courant,* April 17, 1927.

988 Church, 25 April 1918.

989 Strickland, 137.

990 Von Ponickau Platoon, "Report of Engineer Platoon on Cherry Blossom Operation," 30–31.

991 Strickland, 136; du Boisrouvray, 353; 102nd History; Edwards, 5–6; Berry, "For Some Old Soldiers, France was Yesterday."; Fred Tyrrell Papers, 102nd Infantry files, USAMHI; Stallings, 53.

992 Strickland, 136.

993 Lieutenant Ingersoll Report, Box 55, 102nd Infantry, RG 120, NARA.

994 Rau, "Report of Action Morning of April 20th 1918."

995 Reports of dead German officers did not match the casualties that Res.I.R. 259 forwarded to Gruppe Gorz. Leutnant Schmidt's (Sturmtruppen.14) and Leutnant Tabke's bodies were recovered and buried by the Germans the next day. Rau, "Report of Action Morning of April 20th 1918."

996 Conn. Vets Remember Seicheprey, James S. Jackson, *Hartford Courant,* April 17, 1927.

997 Grant, "Report on 26th Division affair of April 20th."

998 *History of the 102nd, United States Infantry,* 12–13; Taylor, 124; Sibley, 144.

999 Corporal Charles T. Blanchard quoted in Hills, 14–15; *Hartford Courant,* August 18, 1918 in Michael E. Shay, *The Yankee Division in the First World War, In the Highest Tradition* (College Station, TX: Texas A&M University Press, 2008), 81–82; Coan, 50.

1000 Private Socia was a recipient of a Silver Star citation. Strickland, 136.

1001 Corporal Charles T. Blanchard quoted in Hills, 15.

1002 *History of Battery B,* 56; Kernan and Samson, *103rd Field Artillery,* 39.

1003 Major Murphy, April 27, 1918, Box 55, 102nd Infantry, RG 120, NARA.

1004 Rau, "Report of Action Morning of April 20th 1918"; Church, 25 April 1918; Strickland, 134–135.

1005 Strickland, 135; Coffman, *The War to End All Wars,* 149.

1006 Strickland, 135.

1007 Color Sergeant Church received a Silver Star citation for this operation. Church, 25 April 1918.

1008 Strickland, 135–136.

1009 Wolf cited in *History of Battery B,* 113; *History of Battery B,* 56.

1010 Henry T. Samson and George C. Hull, *The War Story of C Battery, One Hundred and Third U.S. Field Artillery* (Providence, RI: The Plimpton Press, 1920), 64; Kernan and Samson, *103rd Field Artillery,* 41.

1011 Doble, 23–24.

1012 "Bomb Landed in His Bed but Lad Escaped Death", *Hartford Courant,* August 18, 1918.

1013 Later in the war, Dr Comfort was awarded a bronze oak leaf for his Distinguished Service Cross for administering first-aid to the wounded under violent artillery and machine-gun fire on the front line. Parker, "Raid April 20–21st on Beaumont Zone."; Strickland, 142–143; Sibley, 143.

1014 Fred Tyrrell, Army Service Experiences Questionnaire, USAMHI.

1015 Parker, "Raid April 20–21st on Beaumont Zone."

1016 "Telephone Log," Box 42.

1017 "Bowditch letter to Colonel Craig."

1018 Headquarters 26th Division, G-2, (translation of 32nd Army Corps, 2nd Bureau, "Report of the Interrogatory of a Wounded Prisoner of the 259th Reserve." Box 12, 26th Division, RG 120, NARA; "Telephone Log," Box 42.

1019 Report of the Interrogatory of a Wounded Prisoner of the 259th Reserve."

1020 Taylor, 123; LaBranche, 114.

1021 "Colonel Parker Memo to Brigadier General Traub."

1022 Field Messages, 20 April 1918. Box 19, 102nd Regiment, RG 120, NARA.

1023 "Colonel Parker Memo to Brigadier General Traub."

1024 Private Julius T. Fedel quoted in Macnutt, 1995.

1025 Hinman, 57.

1026 Dowell received the Silver Star citation. "Recommendation for the Award of the D.S.C." [draft], Box 15, Edwards Papers, MHS.

1027 Sibley, 148.

1028 Collins, "Raid on Seicheprey."

1029 Sibley, 91.

1030 John Gallant, Appendix A in Sibley, 357–358.

1031 Mozley, 27.

1032 LaBranche, 113–114.

1033 Doble, 24.

1034 Unknown author, Earl Yeomans papers, 102nd Infantry, USAMHI.

1035 Fred Tyrrell Papers, 102nd Regiment files, USAMHI.

1036 Von Bornstedt, 179–180; *Extracts, April 20, 1918, 78.R.D. Files.*

1037 *Extracts, April 20, 1918, 78.R.D. Files,* 27.

1038 Outline of Military Intelligence Organization of Deputy General Staff in Berlin III. Dennis E. Nolan Papers, USAMHI.

1039 Cushing and Stone, 77.

1040 Collins, "Raid on Seicheprey."; Strickland, 147; Sibley, 144; Berry, "For Some Old Soldiers, France was Yesterday."

1041 *Extracts, April 20, 1918, 78.R.D. Files,* 19; Von Bornstedt, 181.

1042 Corporal Gritzback was posthumously awarded the Silver Star citation for his heroic actions. Merrill, 30–31.

1043 *Extracts, April 20, 1918, 78.R.D. Files,* 19; Von Bornstedt, 181.

1044 *Extracts, April 20, 1918, 78.R.D. Files;* Von Bornstedt, 181–183.

1045 Lieutenant Murphy, Company B 102 Machine Gun Batallion 1st Platoon, 4-26–18, RG 120, 102 Regiment, Box 55; Lieutenant Murphy, Company B 102 Machine Gun Batallion 1st Platoon, 4-26–18, Box 55, 102nd Regiment, RG 120, NARA; Major Murphy, April 27, 1918, Box 55, 102nd Regiment, RG 120, NARA; Strickland, 140.

1046 *History of the 102nd, United States Infantry,* 13.

1047 The 78. R.D. war files state c-Kompagnie met with "relatively little resistance." American accounts on the north-east sector of *Bois de Remières* had 4th Platoon "all killed or captured." *Extracts, April 20, 1918, 78.R.D. Files;* Von Bornstedt, 183–184; Strickland, 138.

1048 79th Reserve Engineer Company. Report on Cherry Blossom, April 20, 1918. 32.

1049 Sergeant Covery; Havlin, 71–72.

1050 *Extracts, April 20, 1918, 78.R.D. Files,* 23–24; Von Bornstedt, 183–184.

1051 *Extracts, April 20, 1918, 78.R.D. Files,* 23; Von Bornstedt, 184.

1052 Company C source quoted in Strickland, 141.

1053 "Children Alone Honor Capt. Alfred Griswold, Hero of Seicheprey," *Hartford Courant,* 23 February 1919, 8.

1054 "Capt. Griswold Kills Four Germans in Seicheprey Fight", *Hartford Courant,* April 23, 1918.

1055 Tyler was recommended for the Distinguished Service Cross. Strickland, 141.

1056 Corporal Thornley received the Distinguished Service Cross. Stringer, 390.

1057 Private Congdon was awarded the Silver Star citation and *Croix de Guerre* with Gold Star. On 10 November 1918, he was killed north of Verdun. The American Legion Post No. 11 in Bridgeport, CT is named after him. State of Connecticut Military Service Record.

1058 Private Delesdernier received the Distinguished Service Cross. *Military Times Hall of Valor;* Arthur C. Havlin, 70–71.

1059 Private Dion was awarded the Distinguished Service Cross.. Strickland 139–141; Sibley, 158.

1060 Sergeant Knox was awarded the Distinguished Service Cross. *Military Times Hall of Valor.*

1061 Private Tryon was awarded the Distinguished Service Cross. Stringer, 394.

1062 Private Patrick Maloney was awarded the Silver Star citation. Strickland 140.

1063 Ashley and Stevens were recommended for a Distinguished Service Cross. Company C source cited by Strickland, 138–139.

1064 Company C source cited in Strickland, 141.

1065 Private Ashley was awarded the Silver Star citation; Berry, "For Some Old Soldiers, France was Yesterday."

1066 79th Reserve Engineer Company. Report on Cherry Blossom, April 20, 1918. 32.

1067 "Telephone Log," Box 42.

1068 Sibley, 148.

1069 Parker, "Raid April 20–21st on Beaumont Zone."; Maher, 6–7; Taylor, 126.

1070 Captain Stanchfield, Report of Operations of April 20–21, April 26th 1918, Box 55, 102nd Regiment, RG 120, NARA; Captain Stanchfield Report, May 21, 1918, Men in Seicheprey engagement, Box 55, 102nd Regiment, RG 120, NARA.

1071 Havlin, 70.

1072 Sergeant Covery, First Platoon, 102nd Machine Gun Bn, Report action 20th-21st April 1918. Box 55, 102nd Regiment, RG 120, NARA; Havlin, 71

1073 Sibley, 154–155.

1074 Lieutenant Bartram, Report on activity of April 20–21, 1918, for the 2nd Platoon Company A. Box 55, 102nd Regiment, RG 120, NARA.

1075 Christopher M. Sterba, *Good Americans, Italian and Jewish Immigrants During the First World War* (Oxford: Oxford University Press, 2003), 179.

1076 Ashley and Stevens were recommended for a Distinguished Service Cross. Company C source cited by Strickland, 138–139.

1077 "Telephone message," Box 19.

1078 "Colonel Parker Memo to Brigadier General Traub."

1079 LaBranche, 113.

1080 Sirois and McGinnis, 53.

1081 Carter, 94.

1082 *Narrative of Battery A of the 101st Field Artillery*, 93–94; Carter, 94.

1083 *One Hundred Second Field Artillery,* 42; Private Ward M. Parker was awarded the French *Croix de Guerre* with gilt star. Private Ward M. Parker, personnel record, Massachusetts National Guard Museum & Archives.

1084 Strickland, 136–137.

1085 "Telephone message," Box 19.

1086 "*Rapport du Colonel Bertrand, 20 et 21 Avril 1918.*"

1087 Lieutenant Murphy, Company B 102 Machine Gun Batallion 1st Platoon, 4-26–18, RG 120, 102 Regiment, Box 55; Lieutenant Murphy, Co.mpany B 102 Machine Gun Batallion 1st Platoon, 4-26–18, Box 55, 102nd Infantry, RG 120, NARA; Major Murphy, April 27, 1918, Box 55, 102nd Infantry, RG 120, NARA; Strickland, 140.

1088 "*Rapport du Colonel Bertrand, 20 et 21 Avril 1918.*"

1089 Sirois and McGinnis, 53.

1090 "Colonel Parker Memo to Brigadier General Traub."

1091 *Extracts, April 20, 1918, 78.R.D. Files*; "Manual of Position Warfare for all Arms. Part 6. Communication between Infantry and Aeroplanes or captive balloons." Translation of a German document in "The Means of Communication between Aeroplanes and the Ground" (Washington, DC: GPO, 1917), 29.

1092 *Extracts, April 20, 1918, 78.R.D. Files.*

1093 Company C source quoted in Strickland, 140.

1094 "Colonel Parker Memo to Brigadier General Traub."; *History of the 102nd, United States Infantry,* 12.

1095 Strickland, 136; Hinman, 60.

1096 *Extracts, April 20, 1918, 78.R.D. Files.*

1097 Outline of Mil. Intell. Org. of Deputy General Staff in Berlin III B. Dennis E. Nolan Papers, USAMHI.

1098 *Extracts, April 20, 1918, 78.R.D. Files*, 22.

1099 *Extracts, April 20, 1918, 78.R.D. Files.*

1100 Strickland, 136.

1101 Grant, "Report on 26th Division affair of April 20th."

1102 *Extracts, April 20, 1918, 78.R.D. Files.*

1103 Strickland, 136.

1104 "Colonel Parker Memo to Brigadier General Traub."

1105 *Extracts, April 20, 1918, 78.R.D. Files.*

1106 Von Ponickau Platoon. "Report of Engineer Platoon on Cherry Blossom Operation," 30–31.

1107 Thomas Platoon. Report of Engineer Platoon on Cherry Blossom Operation, 32.

1108 *Extracts, April 20, 1918, 78.R.D. Files.*

1109 Von Bornstedt, 181; *Extracts, April 20, 1918, 78.R.D. Files;* "Kauffman assessment."

1110 Grant, "Report on 26th Division affair of April 20th."

1111 Corporal Blanchard quoted in Hills, 14–15.

1112 Taylor, 126.

1113 "Telephone message to Gorz Group, 8.05 A.M., April 20th," *Extracts, April 20, 1918, 78.R.D. Files*, 6.

1114 "Kauffman assessment."

1115 "*Rapport du Colonel Bertrand, 20 et 21 Avril 1918.*"

1116 "Lt Ingersoll Report."

1117 Strickland, 136–137.

1118 Rau, "Report of Action Morning of April 20th 1918."

1119 Grant, "Report on 26th Division affair of April 20th."

1120 Rau, "Report of Action Morning of April 20th 1918"; Church, 25 April 1918.

1121 Church, 25 April 1918.

1122 Rau, "Report of Action Morning of April 20th 1918."; Church 25 April 1918.

1123 "Operations Report from Noon April 19th to Noon April 20th, Box 23, 26th Division, RG 120, NARA.

1124 "Lt Ingersoll report."

1125 "Telephone message," Box 19; Message for Chief of Staff, 1st Corps, and G-3, G.H.Q. April 20, 1918, Box 19, RG 120, NARA.

1126 Havlin, 72.

1127 Lieutenant McGlasson, 3rd Platoon Company D, Box 53, 102nd Infantry, RG 120, NARA.

1128 *History of the 101st United States Engineers*, 154.

1129 "Bowditch letter to Colonel Craig."

1130 Hoffmann. "Report on our Operation," *Extracts, April 20, 1918, 78.R.D. Files*, 35–40.

1131 Sirois and McGinnis, 54.

1132 "Telephone message to Gorz Group, 10.00 P.M., April 20th," *Extracts, April 20, 1918, 78.R.D. Files*, 9.

1133 Hoffmann. "Report on our Operation," *Extracts, April 20, 1918, 78.R.D. Files*, 35–40.

1134 Sirois and McGinnis, 53.

1135 Sirois and McGinnis, 55. Private Polito and Private Palosky were awarded the Silver Star citation and *Crois de Guerre*. Personnel record, Massachusetts National Guard Museum & Archives; Sibley, 158.

1136 Sirois and McGinnis, 54.

1137 *One Hundred Second Field Artillery,* 42–43.

1138 Field Messages, 20 April 1918. Box 19, 26th Division, RG 120, NARA.

1139 Lieutenant Hill report cited in Kernan and Samson, *103rd Field Artillery,* 45–46.

1140 Grant, "Report on 26th Division affair of April 20th."; "Tactical Aviation History," Gorrell Report, Series D; Mauer, ed. by "The First Corps Observation Group in the Toul Sector," *The U.S. Air Service in World War I,* Vol. 1, (Washington DC: GPO, 1978), 182.

1141 *SRA, Bulletin de Renseignements N 168, 19 au 20 Avril 1918, de 1600 à 1600,* SHD 22 N 1756.

1142 The telephone message was not substantiated by the 94th Aero Squadron log – there was no record of any flights by the squadron at this time. "Telephone message," Box 19.

1143 Box 23, RG 120, NARA; Kernan and Samson, *103rd Field Artillery,* 43–45.

1144 G-3, GHQ, AEF: 26th Div.: Operation Reports, 26th Division, A.E.F., Boucq, Meurthe-et-Moselle, April 23, 1918. *Report of Enemy Raid on Troops of the 26th Division at Seicheprey, April 20/21, 1918* in *U.S. Army History,* 3, 615.

1145 Collins, "Raid on Seicheprey."

1146 Lieutenant Colonel H. Hobbs memo of 6 May mentions Captain Ireland gone, Lieutenant McDaw gone. "Colonel Parker Memo to Brigadier General Traub."

1147 "Report of operations of April 20–21, Captain C.C. Stanchfield, Box 55, 102 Machine Gun Batallion, RG 120, NARA; "Telephone message," Box 19.

1148 Annex to II Corps Summary American E.F. NO 16. Translation of German Document Captured on Corps Front. 17/10/18, Intelligence Officer, G.H.Q. 24/9/18. Extract, XIX Army "The Americans in Battle," quoted in Martin Marix Evans, ed. by, *American Voices of World War I, Primary Source Documents 1917–1920* (Chicago: Fitzroy Dearborn Publishers, 2001), 221.

1149 *History of the 102nd, United States Infantry,* 13.

1150 Marvin letter, Deep River, Connecticut.

1151 *First Over the Front,* 116.

1152 *Stars and Stripes,* 8 February 1918, Vol. 1 No. 1, 1.

1153 Niall Ferguson, *The Pity of War* (New York: Basic Books, 1999), 368.

1154 Clifford Milton Markle, *A Yankee Prisoner in Hunland* (New Haven, CT: Yale University Press, 1920), 7–8.

1155 Wolf cited in *History of Battery B,* 113.

1156 Doble, 23–24.

1157 Doble, 24–25.

1158 Clifford Milton Markle, *A Yankee Prisoner in Hunland* (New Haven, CT: Yale University Press, 1920), 7–8.

1159 Markle, 8–9

1160 Lieutenant Tenney survived the remainder of the war as a prisoner. Doble, 25.

1161 James G. Harbord, Major General. *America in the World War* (Boston: Houghton Mifflin Company, 1933), 74–75.

1162 "Prisoners Taken at Seicheprey Back," *Boston Daily Globe,* 8 January 1919.

1163 Stallings, 52. Though it is difficult to find corroborative evidence.

1164 "Prisoners Taken at Seicheprey Back."

1165 Doble, 26.

1166 Wolf cited in *History of Battery B,* 113.; "Prisoners Taken at Seicheprey Back," *Boston Daily Globe,* 8 January 1919.

1167 Doble recalled: "When I was at first home in Quincy, Massachusetts, and answered the mailman's morning ring, I saw in the *Stars and Stripes* that he gave me, a photo to be given to the first A.E.F. soldier to identify correctly who it was. I immediately recognized the scene: the Germans on horseback in front and to the rear of us; the boys marching with burlap on their feet and legs … I figured out where I should be and there I was, with mustache, helmet, and the only rubber boots there that had not been taken by the Bavarian sergeant." Doble, 26–27.

1168 Clifford Milton Markle, *A Yankee Prisoner in Hunland* (New Haven, CT: Yale University Press, 1920), 8–9.

1169 Markle, 9–10.

1170 Wolf cited in *History of Battery B,* 113–114.

1171 The comic actions of the three 18th Infantry prisoners was not appreciated by the rest. Doble, 26.

1172 Doble, 26.

1173 Kernan and Samson, *103rd Field Artillery,* 41–42.

1174 Doble.

1175 "Soldiers of the 26th Division Who Were Made Prisoners April 20, at the Battle of Seicheprey," March 9, 1919, *Hartford Courant.*

1176 "Réplique Aux Américains," *Gazette des Ardennes,* N. 617, 1 Mai 1918; "Americans Meet Attack of Foe Side by Side with French Allies Fighting in Defense of Amiens," *Washington Post,* April 25, 1918.

1177 Edwin L. James, "Germans Attempt to Cajole Our Men," *New York Times,* July 7, 1918.

1178 Prisoners Taken at Seicheprey Back, *Boston Daily Globe,* 8 January, 1919.

1179 Markle was killed in May 1943 in an automobile accident in Tunisia while serving as field director of the American Red Cross. Markle, 12–13.

1180 Cushing and Stone, 78–79.

1181 Wolf cited in *History of Battery B*, 112–114.

1182 James Norman Hall comments in *Over the Front*, 17/2, 170.

1183 William J. Lilly's father McIntyre Lilly served in Company G and was wounded in the battle. "Connecticut Boys German Prisoners Reach London," *Hartford Courant*, 30 November 1918.

1184 "Bomb Landed in His Bed but Lad Escaped Death," *Hartford Courant*, August 18, 1918.

1185 Von Gallwitz, 316–318.

1186 Keller, "A German Reply to Gen. Pershing's War Story."

1187 Conrad Hoffman, *In the Prison Camps of Germany* (New York: Association Press, 1920), 65–66; Carl P. Dennet, *Prisoners of the Great War* (Boston and New York, Houghton Mifflin Company, 1919), 38–39.

1188 Hoffmann, 164.

1189 Hoffmann, 154.

1190 Sergeant Ziegra never discussed his war experiences with his family. In part, his reticence was due to his perceived negative connotations of being of German ancestry. He was posthumeously awarded a Purple Heart for 15 April 1918. Author discussions with Ziegra family.

1191 Boston Red Sox won the World Series that year. Hoffman, 152; 165.

1192 Dennet, 19.

1193 "Robinson Writing of German Prison," *Hartford Courant*, Aug 1, 1918.

1194 "Seicheprey Hero Returns to New York," *Hartford Courant*, 12 February 1919.

1195 *Order of Battle Zone of the Interior*, 91.

1196 Wolf cited in *History of Battery B*, 116.

1197 78 R.D., "Cherry Blossom" Operation Final Report, April 27, 1918, 78.R.D. Files, 24; Von Bornstedt, 184–185.

1198 Traub testimony in "Proceedings of a general court-martial," 4.

1199 Willcox, 564.

1200 "*Rapport du Colonel Bertrand, 20 et 21 Avril 1918.*"

1201 *Jasta 64* or *FA (A) 298b* records did not mention any losses on 20 April. "Telephone message," Box 19; Report also contained in Message for Chief of Staff, 1st Corps, and G-3, G.H.Q. April 20, 1918; "Telephone Log," Box 42.

1202 "Telephone Log," Box 42.

1203 Statement of activity of Company L 102nd U.S. Infantry during the period of April 19-20–21, 1918. *United States v. John J. Gallant.*

1204 *History of Battery B*, 55-56; Harry R. Stringer, ed. by. *Heroes All!* Washington DC: Fassett Publishing Co., 1919, 72; Kernan and Samson, *103rd Field Artillery*, 39–40.

1205 "Cherry Blossom" Operation Final Report, April 27, 1918, 78.R.D. Files.

1206 Lieutenant Green report cited in Kernan and Samson, *103rd Field Artillery*, 46–47.

1207 Rice message, Box 19, 26th Division, RG 120, NARA; "Telephone Log," Box 42.

1208 Captain Stanchfield, Report of Operations of April 20–21, April 26th 1918, Box 55, 102nd Regiment, RG 120, NARA.

1209 "Colonel Parker Memo to Brigadier General Traub."

1210 Office of the Acting Judge Advocate General for the American Expeditionary Forces in Europe. GHQ, AEF, July 24, 1918. *United States v. John J. Gallant.*

1211 "*Rapport du Colonel Bertrand, 20 et 21 Avril 1918.*"

1212 *History of the 102nd, United States Infantry*, 13.

1213 Sibley, 145.

1214 "Telephone message," Box 19.

1215 "Colonel Parker Memo to Brigadier General Traub."

1216 "Telephone Log," Box 42.

1217 "Colonel Parker Memo to Brigadier General Traub memorandum."

1218 Lieutenant Rink, April 26, 1918.

1219 Strickland, 141.

1220 "Telephone message," Box 19.

1221 *History of the 102nd, United States Infantry*, 13–14.

1222 2nd Lieutenant Howard Mathews; 2nd Lt W.W. Major, Comapny B 102nd Inf. April 26, 1918. Subject: Action of 3rd platoon Company B, in operation of April 20–21, Box 44, 102nd Infantry, RG 120, NARA; Color Sergeant Church, 25 April 1918, Box 44, 102nd Infantry, RG 120, NARA.

1223 "Telephone Log," Box 42.

1224 "Telephone message," Box 19; "Message for Chief of Staff, 1st Corps, and G-3, G.H.Q. April 20, 1918," Box 19, 26th Division, RG 120, NARA.

1225 78 R.D., "Cherry Blossom" Operation Final Report, April 27, 1918, 78.R.D. Files.

1226 "Telephone message," Box 19; "Message for Chief of Staff, 1st Corps, and G-3, G.H.Q. April 20, 1918"; G-3, GHQ, AEF: 26th Div.: Operation Reports, 26th Division, A.E.F., Boucq, Meurthe-et Moselle, April 23, 1918. *Report of Enemy Raid on Troops of the 26th Division at Seicheprey, April 20/21, 1918, U.S. Army History*, iii, 614–615.

1227   Collins, "Raid on Seicheprey."

1228   Sibley, 145; Havlin, 72–73.

1229   "Bowditch letter to Colonel Craig."

1230   "Bowditch letter to Colonel Craig."

1231   "Colonel Parker Memo to Brigadier General Traub memorandum."

1232   Lieutenant E.G. O'Neill, Second Platoon, Co. I. April 26, 1918. "Operations April 20, and 21st, 1918," Box 53, RG 120, NARA.

1233   Sergeant Albin W. Backiel, Co. I, Commanding 3rd Platoon, Box 53, 102nd Infantry, RG 120, NARA.

1234   Lieutenant Edwards Larned. Company I. 26 April 1918, Box 53, 102nd Infantry, RG 120, NARA.

1235   Box 23, 26th Division, RG 120, NARA.

1236   *One Hundred Second Field Artillery,* 37; Andrew William Thompson, personnel card, Massachusetts National Guard Museum & Archives.

1237   *One Hundred Second Field Artillery,* 43.

1238   Captain Bullivant report cited in Kernan and Samson, *103rd Field Artillery,* 47–48.

1239   Lieutenant Green report cited in Kernan and Samson, *103rd Field Artillery,* 46–47.

1240   Major Harry L. Doane, 104th Infantry, "Report of how Battalion was affected by attack Apr. 20–21, 26 April 1918," Box 53, 104th Infantry, RG 120, NARA.

1241   Philip S. Wainwright, 1st Lieutenant., *History of the 101st Machine Gun Battalion* (Hartford, CT: The 101st Machine Gun Battalion Association, 1922), 34.

1242   "Telephone message; Message for Chief of Staff, 1st Corps, and G-3, G.H.Q." April 20, 1918," Box 19, 26th Division, RG 120, NARA.

1243   Telephone message, Message for Chief of Staff, 1st Corps, and G-3, G.H.Q."

1244   Church, 25 April 1918.

1245   "Evening Report to Gorz Group, April 20, 1918," *Extracts, April 20, 1918, 78.R.D. Files,* 8.

1246   Von Bornstedt, 185.

1247   Havlin, 72–73.

1248   Parker 15.40 report to Traub.

1249   "C.O. Btry A 103rd F.A., Report per Bulletin #95 on operations of April 20–21, 1918," Box 62, 26th Division, RG 120, NARA.

1250   "Headquarters First Army A.E.F. Office of Chief, Air Service. Report of Operations for April 20, 1918," *Gorrell Report,* Series D; "Diary of Company "B" 2d Balloon Company," *Gorrell Report,* Series F.

1251   Headquarters First Army Corps A.E.F. Office of Chief, Air Service, Report of Operations for April 20, 1918.

1252   "William G. "Billy" Schauffler," 109; *First Over the Front, Lt. William G. Schauffler, Jr.,* 120.

1253   Noon Report to Gruppe Gorz, April 20, 1918, 78.R.D. Files.

1254   Ettighoffer, 235–236.

1255   Despite the glowing report on *Leutnant* Grumbrecht no document remains that tells of the honours provided to all recognized *Kirschblüte* combatants. The criteria for receiving *Pour le Mérite* apparently was not met by this battle. "Noon Report to Gorz Group, April 20, 1918, 78.R.D. Files.

1256   Parker, "Raid April 20–21st on Beaumont Zone."

1257   Private Jacob Levy was awarded the Silver Star citation. Strickland, 140.

1258   Captain Stanchfield Report, May 21, 1918, Men in Seicheprey engagement, Box 55, 102nd Machine Gun, RG 120, NARA.

1259   "Colonel Parker Memo to Brigadier General Traub"; "Telephone message," Box 26.

1260   Captain Gallup. Box 55, 102nd Machine Gun Batallion, RG 120, NARA.

1261   Lieutenant Humlird, Report of 1st Platoon Company C, Box 55, 102nd Infantry, RG 120, NARA.

1262   "Colonel Parker Memo to Brigadier General Traub."

1263   "Telephone message," Box 19.

1264   Lieutenant A.W. Shriver, Company E, 2nd Platoon, "Report of action April 20 – 21," Box 53, 102nd Infantry, RG 120, NARA; Strickland, 145.

1265   Private Curry was awarded the Silver Star citation and *Croix de Guerre.* State of Connecticut Military Service Record.

1266   Lockhart was awarded the Silver Star citation for his heroic actions and leadership. Parker, "Raid April 20–21st on Beaumont Zone"; Strickland, 145; Taylor, 126.

1267   Von Bornstedt, 185.

1268   "Cherry Blossom" Operation Final Report, April 27, 1918, 78.R.D. Files.

1269   "*Rapport du Colonel Bertrand, 20 et 21 Avril 1918.*"

1270   "Colonel Parker Memo to Brigadier General Traub"; "Telephone Log," Box 42; "Telephone message," Box 19; Message for Chief of Staff, 1st Corps, and G-3, G.H.Q. April 20, 1918, Box 19, 26th Division, RG 120, NARA.

1271   2nd Lieutenant Howard Mathews.

1272   "Lieutenant Ingersoll report."

1273   "Colonel Parker Memo to Brigadier General Traub."

1274   2nd Lieutenant C.R. Middaugh.

1275 Strickland, 143.

1276 "Colonel Parker Memo to Brigadier General Traub."

1277 "Telephone message," Box 19; Message for Chief of Staff, 1st Corps, and G-3, G.H.Q. April 20, 1918, Box 19, 26th Division, RG 120, NARA; Field Message 2 26–32.16, Box 19, 26th Division, RG 120, NARA.

1278 Taylor, 126.

1279 Collins, "Raid on Seicheprey."

1280 "Colonel Parker Memo to Brigadier General Traub."

1281 Collins, "Raid on Seicheprey."

1282 "Bowditch letter to Colonel Craig."

1283 Craig report on Edwards, Pershing file.

1284 78 R.D., "Cherry Blossom" Operation Final Report, April 27, 1918, 78.R.D. Files.

1285 Evening report to Gruppe Gorz, April 20, 1918, 78.R.D. Files.

1286 78 R.D., "Cherry Blossom" Operation Final Report, April 27, 1918, 78.R.D. Files.

1287 Evening report to Gruppe Gorz, April 20, 1918, 78.R.D. Files.

1288 Lieutenant Green report cited in Kernan and Samson, 103rd Field Artillery, 46–47.

1289 Horatio Roger, The Diary of an Artillery Scout (North Andover, MA: privately printed, 1975), 117–118.

1290 78 R.D., "Cherry Blossom" Operation Final Report, April 27, 1918, 78.R.D. Files.

1291 History of the 102nd, United States Infantry, 14; "Colonel Parker Memo to Brigadier General Traub"; Sibley, 145.

1292 VIII Armée, Compte-Rendu des Operations Aeriennes et des Renseignements, 20 Avril 1918.

1293 Parker 15.40 report to Traub.

1294 SRA, Bulletin de Renseignements N 169.

1295 VIII Armée, Compte-Rendu des Opérations Aériennes et des Renseignements, 20 Avril 1918.

1296 McKenna, 138–139.

1297 "Headquarters First Army A.E.F. Office of Chief, Air Service. Report of Opérations for April 20, 1918,"; "Diary of Company B 2d Balloon Company."

1298 "Telephone message," Box 19; "Headquarters First Army A.E.F. Office of Chief, Air Service. Report of Operations for April 20, 1918."

1299 VIII Armée, Compte-Rendu des Opérations Aériennes et des Renseignements, 20 Avril 1918.

1300 Lieutenant Bright, 26 April 1918.; "American Squadron is Flying Near Toul", New York Times, 24 May 1918.

1301 M. A. De Wolfe Howe, Memoirs of the Harvard Dead in the War against Germany, Vol. 3 (Cambridge: Harvard UP, 1922), 96–97.

1302 Lieutenant Colonel Hobbs memo of 6 May mentions Captain Ireland gone, Lieutenant McDaw gone. "Colonel Parker Memo to Brigadier General Traub"; Rau in Box 25, 102nd Infantry, RG 120, NARA.

1303 Strickland recorded that the first incident of friendly fire experienced by the 102nd Infantry occurred during a raid when the soldiers were crossing a canal using rafts. Strickland concluded with "Thus ended the first offensive action of the 102nd Regiment in the World War." Strickland, 143.

1304 Message received at 15:50. Captain Taylor note to Commanding General 51st Brigade Box 19, 26th Division, RG 120, NARA.

1305 78 R.D., "Cherry Blossom" Operation Final Report, April 27, 1918, 78.R.D. Files.

1306 SRA, Bulletin de Renseignements N 169.

1307 Kernan and Samson, 103rd Field Artillery, 40.

1308 Grant, "Report on 26th Division affair of April 20th."

1309 History of Battery B, 55–56; Lieutenant Davis report cited in Kernan and Samson, 103rd Field Artillery, 45–50; 1st Lieutenant J.C. Davis, 103rd Field Artillery 95mm battery, Action of this organization on April 20th and 21st 1918," Box 62, 26th Division, RG 120, NARA.

1310 Strickland, 146.

1311 History of the 102nd, United States Infantry, 11; Furber, 8.

1312 Rogers, 120.

1313 Smith, 199.

1314 166th Infantry Division, April 17, 1918, "Liaisons," Box 19, 26th Division, RG 120, NARA.

1315 Lupfer, 47.

1316 "Colonel Parker Memo to Brigadier General Traub memorandum."

1317 Report of Operations (Seicheprey 20–21 April 1918) Memo of H. P. Hobbs, Lieutenant Colonel, Infantry Division Inspector Box 25, 26th Division, RG 120, NARA.

1318 C.O. 103rd Field Artillery, A.E.F., May 7, 1918 – To Comdg. Gen. 51st Brigade, A.E.F., Box 45, 26th Infantry, RG 120, NARA.

1319 Hobbs memo in Box 25, 26th Division, RG 120, NARA.

1320 Hobbs memo, Box 25.

1321 Lieutenant Colonel H.P. Hobbs, 10 May 1918, Division Inspector, 26th Division, American E.F. Memorandum, NARA RG 120, Box 25.

1322 Edwards letter, 11 May 1918, Box 25, 26th Division, RG 120, NARA.

1323 Edwards memo to Commanding General 1st Army Corps, American E.F., "Report on an attack, April 20–21, 1918, Seicheprey –

Remières Wood," Box 25, 26th Division, RG 120, NARA.

1324 Havlin, 76.

1325 The paragraph will be substituted by the actual article from the periodical. 'The Kaiser's Own Head Ache," *Yankee Doings*, Vol. 22 (2), February 1941, 9.

1326 Parker 15.40 report to Traub, 20 April 1918.

1327 "Colonel Parker Memo to Brigadier General Traub."

1328 *History of the 101st United States Engineers*, 154–155.

1329 Colonel John H. Parker Memorandum for General Traub, 2200 hours, 20 April 1918, Box 42, 102nd Infantry, RG 120, NARA.

1330 "Colonel Parker Memo to Brigadier General Traub."

1331 Phone message from Grizzly Bear, 16:00 O'clock, Box 19, 26th Division, RG 120, NARA.

1332 Evening Report to Gruppe Gorz, April 20, 1918, 78.R.D. Files.

1333 78 Reserve Division, April 19, 1918, Section Ia No. 963 Operations. Strictly Secret Subject: Cherry Blossom. Divisional Order No. 5, Evacuation of Positions Taken, 78.R.D. Files.

1334 *One Hundred Second Field Artillery*, 43–44.

1335 78 R.D., "Cherry Blossom" Operation Final Report, April 27, 1918, 78.R.D. Files.

1336 Traub testimony in "Proceedings of a general court-martial."

1337 "Colonel Parker Memo to Brigadier General Traub"; Lieutenant Fuessenich.

1338 "Telephone message," Box 19.

1339 Traub testimony in "Proceedings of a general court-martial."

1340 Colonel John H. Parker, "Memorandum for General Traub, 2200 hours, 20 April 1918," Box 42, 26th Division, RG 120, NARA.

1341 "Colonel Parker Memo to Brigadier General Traub memorandum."

1342 Traub testimony in "Proceedings of a general court-martial," 4–5.

1343 Traub testimony in "Proceedings of a general court-martial," 12.

1344 "Telephone message," Box 19.

1345 "Colonel Parker Memo to Brigadier General Traub."

1346 Grant, "Report on 26th Division affair of April 20th."

1347 Lieutenant Rink, April 26, 1918.

1348 Chamberlin, 47–48.

1349 Havlin, 73.

1350 "Colonel Parker Memo to Brigadier General Traub."

1351 Merrill, 30–31.

1352 Merrill, 31–33.

1353 Sergeant Albin W. Backiel, Company I, 102nd, Commanding 3rd Platoon, Box 53, 102nd Infantry, RG 120, NARA.

1354 Parker 15.40 report to Traub, 20 April 1918.

1355 Lieutenant R.K. Harris, 4th Platoon Company F, Box 53, 102nd Infantry, RG 120, NARA RG 120.

1356 Hubbard received the Silver Star citation. Merrill, 31.

1357 *One Hundred Second Field Artillery*, 34. LaBranche, 114.

1358 Chaffee, 30–31.

1359 Captain Joseph C. Davis was killed with six of his men while in command of Battery E on 30 July 1918. He received the Distinguished Service Cross posthumously. *Military Times Hall of Valor*.

1360 *SRA, Bulletin de Renseignements N 169.*

1361 *One Hundred Second Field Artillery*, 44.

1362 *United States v. John J. Gallant.*

1363 Shay, *A Grateful Heart*, 60.

1364 Mozley, 27.

1365 Shay, *A Grateful Heart*, 61.

1366 Message Center, Box 26, 26th Division, RG 120, NARA.

1367 Shay, *A Grateful Heart*, 60.

1368 Private Cooper was posthumously awarded the Silver Star citation for his heroic actions that day. Merrill, 33.

1369 Merrill, 33.

1370 Merrill, 33–34.

1371 Strickland, 144.

1372 Lieutenant Bright, April 26, 1918.

1373 Lieutenant Oates, April 26, 1918.

1374 Rau, "Report of Action Morning of April 20th 1918."

1375 Church, 25 April 1918.

1376 Blumenson, 521.

1377 Chamberlin, 48.

1378 Chamberlin, 51.

1379 Ettighoffer, 237–238.

1380 *Général Foch* was promoted to *Maréchel* in August 1918. "Defense Against the German Calais Offensive," April 19, 1918, *US Army in the World War*, ii, 332.

1381 "German Counter-attacks," *Summary of Information*, No. 18, April 18, 1918, SHD 16 N 1090.

1382 German reports do not corroborate *Général* Monroe's *69e division d'infanterie* ongoing planning with the 26th Division at this time. Frh. von Ledebur, Colonel, Chief of Staff of Army Headquarters "C", report in Dennis Nolan Papers, USAMHI.

1383 "Attack on Seicheprey on April 20, 1918, Service Report. Attention Historical Section. 20 January 1922." Box 786, Occupation, RG 120, NARA; Kauffman assessment. Outline of Mil. Intell. Org. of Deputy General Staff in Berlin III B. In Dennis Nolan papers, USAMHI; Samuels, 181.

1384 G-3, GHQ, AEF: 26th Division: Operation Reports, 26th Division, A.E.F., Boucq, Meurthe-et Moselle, April 23, 1918. "Report of Enemy Raid on Troops of the 26th Division at Seicheprey, April 20/21, 1918" in *U.S. Army History*, 3, 615; "Telephone message," Box 19.

1385 "Telephone message," Box 19; General Traub, after-action report, 27 April 1918; Major Collins Memo, 1–2.

1386 G-3, GHQ, AEF: 26th Division: Operation Reports, 26th Division, A.E.F., Boucq, Meurthe-et Moselle, April 23, 1918. *Report of Enemy Raid on Troops of the 26th Division at Seicheprey, April 20/21, 1918* in *U.S. Army History*, 3, 615; "Telephone message," Box 19.; "Telephone Log," Box 42; Major Collins Memo.

1387 Traub testimony in "Proceedings of a general court-martial," 11.

1388 "Field Orders 24, Field Orders 24a. 26 Division, 20th April 18, 1500," Box 13, 26th Division, RG 120, NARA.

1389 Taylor, 127–128.

1390 *"Rapport du Colonel Bertrand, 20 et 21 Avril 1918."*

1391 Traub testimony in "Proceedings of a general court-martial," 16.

1392 Traub testimony in "Proceedings of a general court-martial," 14.

1393 Telephone memorandum, Box 19, 26th Division, RG 120, NARA; G-3, GHQ, AEF: 26th Division: Operation Reports, 26th Division, A.E.F., Boucq, Meurthe-et Moselle, April 23, 1918. *Report of Enemy Raid on Troops of the 26th Division at Seicheprey, April 20/21, 1918* in *U.S. Army History*, 3, 615.

1394 G-3, GHQ, AEF: 26th Division: Operation Reports, 26th Division, A.E.F., Boucq, Meurthe-et Moselle, April 23, 1918. *Report of Enemy Raid on Troops of the 26th Division at Seicheprey, April 20/21, 1918* in *U.S. Army History*, 3, 615–616.

1395 "Report of Action, 20th – 21st April, 1918," General Traub, in Strickland, 148–150.

1396 "Colonel Parker Memo to Brigadier General Traub."

1397 Traub testimony in "Proceedings of a general court-martial," 12; *United States v. John J. Gallant*.

1398 Traub testimony in "Proceedings of a general court-martial," 6.

1399 *United States v. John J. Gallant*.

1400 *United States v. John J. Gallant*.

1401 78 R.D., "Cherry Blossom" Operation Final Report, April 27, 1918, 78. R.D. War Diary.

1402 Traub testimony in "Proceedings of a general court-martial," 12.

1403 John Gallant, Appendix A in Sibley, 358.

1404 Traub testimony in "Proceedings of a general court-martial," 5.

1405 Traub testimony in "Proceedings of a general court-martial," 14.

1406 Taylor, 129.

1407 *United States v. John J. Gallant*.

1408 *United States v. John J. Gallant*.

1409 *United States v. John J. Gallant*.

1410 "Telephone Memorandum," Box 19, 26th Division, RG 120, NARA.

1411 Traub testimony in "Proceedings of a general court-martial," 15–16.

1412 Traub testimony in "Proceedings of a general court-martial," 6.

1413 Major Rau stated Company M arrived at 0700, 21 April. Lieutenant Boyd, Company M.

1414 "Colonel Parker Memo to Brigadier General Traub."

1415 Taylor, 129.

1416 "Colonel Parker Memo to Brigadier General Traub."

1417 Colonel Parker testimony in *United States v. John J. Gallant*.

1418 John Gallant, Appendix A in Sibley, 359–360.

1419 Lieutenant E.G. O'Neill, Second Platoon, Comapny I, Box 53, 102nd Infantry, RG 120, NARA; Lieutenant Edwards Larned. Company I. 26 April 1918, Box 53, 102nd Infantry, RG 120, NARA.

1420 "Colonel Parker Memo to Brigadier General Traub."

1421 "Colonel Parker Memo to Brigadier General Traub"; Traub testimony in "Proceedings of a general court-martial," 15–16.

1422 Memo Arthur A. Service on Kenneth E. Parkin (deceased), RG 153, NARA.

1423 Statement of activity of Company L 102nd U.S. Infantry during the period of April 19-20–21, 1918. *United States v. John J. Gallant*.

1424 "Colonel Parker Memo to Brigadier General Traub"; Traub testimony in "Proceedings of a general court-martial," 15–16.

1425 *United States v. John J. Gallant*.

1426 G-3, GHQ, AEF: 26th Division: Operation Reports, 26th Division, A.E.F., Boucq, Meurthe-et Moselle, April 23, 1918. *Report of Enemy Raid on Troops of the 26th Division at Seicheprey, April 20/21, 1918* in *U.S. Army History*, 3, 616.

1427 Box 23, 102nd Infantry, RG 120, NARA.

1428 "Statement of activity of Company L 102nd U.S. Infantry during the period of April 19-20–21, 1918." *United States v. John J. Gallant.*

1429 Traub

report, 27 April, 2; Parker, "Raid April 20–21st on Beaumont Zone."

1430 "Colonel Parker Memo to Brigadier General Traub."

1431 Parker, "Raid April 20–21st on Beaumont Zone."

1432 *Rapport du Colonel Bertrand, 20 et 21 Avril 1918.* SHD 24 N 1730.

1433 Lieutenant Bright, April 26, 1918.

1434 Parker, "Raid April 20–21st on Beaumont Zone."

1435 Box 23, 102nd Infantry, RG 120, NARA.

1436 *SRA, Bulletin de Renseignements N 170, 21 au 22 Avril 1918,* SHD 22 N 1756.

1437 Rau, "Report of Action Morning of April 20th, 1918"; Sergeant Albin W. Backiel, Company I, 3rd Platoon, Box 53, 102nd Infantry, RG 120, NARA.

1438 Field Message, Colonel Parker to Général Traub, 21 April 1918, Box 19, 26th Division, RG 120, NARA.

1439 Ferrell, *In the Company of Generals,* 51.

1440 Edwards, 11th May 1918 memo, in Box 25, 26th Division, RG 120, NARA.

1441 Colonel "Gatling Gun" Parker, "Memories of the Service, Draft, 10 May 1937," 213. USMA Archives.

1442 "Summary of Conversation of January 11 between General Petain and General Pershing," 13 January 1918, *US Army in the World War,* ii, 155–157.

1443 Ferrell, *In the Company of Generals,* 29.

1444 Nathan A. Haverstock, *Fifty Years at the Front, The Life of War Correspondent Frederick Palmer* (Washington, London: Brassey's, Inc. 1996), 133–134.

1445 Blumenson, 409.

1446 Haverstock, 197–198.

1447 Michael Harold Clark, *The Personal War of John J. Pershing.* MA Thesis, University of Wisconsin, 1973, 33.

1448 Clark, 265.

1449 "Yankees Beat First Infantry Assault," *San Francisco Chronicle,* March 1, 1918, 1.

1450 *Washington Post,* March 2, 1918, 1; *Hartford Courant,* March 2, 1918, 1.

1451 "Berlin Claims Success Against Our Troops," *New York Times,* March 4, 1918, 4.

1452 "American Troops Show Bravery," *The Hartford Courant,* April 19, 1918, 22.

1453 Clark, 76.

1454 Clark, 77.

1455 Gallivan post-war described the Regular Army seniors who took issue with General Edwards as mostly "petted favorites who would run away from a baked apple." Clark, 32–33.

1456 Frank Sibley, "Reminiscence," *Yankee Doings,* Vol. 24 (3) March 1943, 4.

1457 "A Little Tip from Dad," *Yankee Doings,* Vol. 4 (9) October 1923, 4.

1458 du Boisrouvray, 362.

1459 Sibley, 141.

1460 du Boisrouvray, 362.

1461 Sibley, 139.

1462 Official Communiqués, April 20, 1918, Summary of Information, SHD 14 N.

1463 "Huns Pierce American Trenches," *Washington Post,* April 21, 1918; "Greatest Attack Yet on American Lines", *Hartford Courant,* April 21, 1918.

1464 "American Counter Attack Delivered Savagely; Fierce Fighting in Open Areas", *Washington Post,* April 21, 1918, 3.

1465 "Germans Exulting in 'Lesson' To Us," *New York Times,* April 24, 1918.

1466 "Berlin Papers Still Slight Our Troops," *New York Times,* April 24, 1918.

1467 "Germans Exulting in 'Lesson' To Us," *New York Times,* April 24, 1918.

1468 *New York Times,* April 24, 1918; "The American Victory at Seicheprey," *The Literary Digest,* May 4, 1918.

1469 Hinman, 58.

1470 "Forced Germans Back. French note denies that they Retired Voluntarily from Seicheprey," *New York Times,* April 24, 1918.

1471 "Berlin Papers Still Slight Our Troops," *New York Times,* April 24, 1918.

1472 Max Osborn, *Vossiche Zeitung* in "Berlin Papers Still Slight Our Troops," *New York Times,* April 24, 1918.

1473 Wolfe Telegraphic Bureau quoted in "The American Victory at Seicheprey," *The Literary Digest,* 4 May 1918.

1474 *New York Times,* April 22, 1918, 1.

1475 "A Month of Battles," *The Times,* April 22, 1918, 8.

1476 "Holds Up All News Sent by Pershing," *New York Times,* April 24, 1918.

1477 "39 Connecticut Men Fall Before Enemy," *Harford Courant,* May 4, 1918.

1478 Clark, 129–130.

1479 *New York Times,* 22 April 1918.

1480 Edwin L. James, "Mont Sec Remains as War Scarred It," *New York Times,* September 23, 1927.

1481 *New York Times,* 22 April 1918.

1482 Albert W. Fox, *Washington Post,* April 22, 1918, 1.

1483 *New York Times*, April 24, 1918.

1484 "Buy Liberty Bonds," *The Outlook*, May 1, 1918, 5–6.

1485 "Foe's Guns Active Against Our Lines," *New York Times*, 24 April 1918.

1486 "American Girls Brave Under Fire, McIntyre Sisters Heroines of Seicheprey Battle," *Hartford Courant*, 25 April 1918.

1487 "Used 'Sawed Off' Guns", *Washington Post*, April 23, 1918, 1.

1488 "Buy Liberty Bonds," *The Outlook*, May 1, 1918, 5–6; "The American Victory at Seicheprey," *The Literary Digest*, May 4, 1918.

1489 *The Literary Digest*, May 4, 1918.

1490 Shotguns referenced here were the M1897 "trench gun" manufactured by Winchester Arms. Bruce N. Canfield, *U.S. Infantry Weapons of the First World War* (Lincoln, RI: Andrew Mowbray Publishers, 2000), 293.

1491 *New York Times*, April 21, 1918; *Washington Post*, April 23, 1918, 1.

1492 *Washington Post*, April 23, 1918, 4.

1493 *The Literary Digest*, May 4, 1918.

1494 *L'Epoca*, May 17, 1918 in Strickland, 151.

1495 Sirois and McGinnis, 54.

1496 Benwell, 71–72.

1497 *Stars and Stripes*, April 26, 1918, Vol. 1, No. 12. 1.

1498 Sibley, "Reminiscence."

1499 Winston S. Churchill, *The World Crisis, 1915* (New York: Charles Scribner's Sons, 1929), 1–5.

1500 Douglas V. Johnson II, "Training the 1st Division for World War I," *Cantigny at Seventy-Five, A Professional Discussion, May 28–29, 1993* (Chicago, IL: Robert R. McCormick Tribune Foundation, 1993), 71.

1501 James G. Harbord, *The American Army in France, 1917–1919* (Boston: Little, Brown, and Company, 1936), 222; Pershing, i, 341.

1502 Captain Mitchell and Lieutenant Rostrand comprised the other members of the team. "Bowditch letter to Colonel Craig."

1503 Box 25, 26th Division, RG 120, NARA.

1504 "*Rapport du Colonel Bertrand, 20 et 21 Avril 1918*."

1505 G-3, GHQ, AEF: 26th Division: Operation Reports, 26th Division, A.E.F., Boucq, Meurthe-et-Moselle, April 23, 1918. *Report of Enemy Raid on Troops of the 26th Division at Seicheprey, April 20/21, 1918* in *U.S. Army History*, 3, 616–617.

1506 "Operations Report from Noon April 19th to Noon April 20th," Box 23, 26th Division, RG 120, NARA; *History of the 102nd, United States Infantry*, 12–13.

1507 Box 25, 26th Division, RG 120, NARA.

1508 Sibley, 139.

1509 GHQ AEF accounts on *Bois-Brûlé* differed. 104th Infantry reported an even 200 casualties. "German Attack on Bois- Brûlé," 612.

1510 Auler, 69.

1511 *Extracts, April 20, 1918, 78.R.D. Files*, 14.

1512 Collins, "Raid on Seicheprey."

1513 Lieutenant Sanbarn reported on 25 April that the 102nd Machine Gun Batallion casualties were five killed, eleven wounded, and four machine guns put out of action. Parker, "Raid April 20–21st on Beaumont Zone."; Lieutenant Sanbarn, 25 April 1918, Box 55, 102nd Infantry, RG 120, NARA.

1514 "German Report, 12-14", Box 160, RG 165, NARA.

1515 "German Report, 12–14."

1516 *Colonel Bertrand, 20 et 21 Avril 1918*. SHD 14 N.

1517 Box 26, 26th Division, RG 120, NARA.

1518 *One Hundred Second Field Artillery*, 44.

1519 Collins, "Raid on Seicheprey."

1520 Edwards Memo, 11 May 1918, Box 25, 26th Division, RG 120, NARA.

1521 "Confidential Memorandum," USAMHI, Drum Papers.

1522 Sibley, 139.

1523 "Cold words from McCain ancestor," http://bristolnews.blogspot.com/2008/04/cold-words-from-mccain-ancestor.html, accessed 20 June 2013.

1524 78. Reserve Division, 27–28.

1525 G-3, GHQ, AEF: 26th Division: Operation Reports, 26th Division, A.E.F., Boucq, Meurthe-et-Moselle, April 23, 1918. *Report of Enemy Raid on Troops of the 26th Division at Seicheprey, April 20/21, 1918* in *U.S. Army History*, 3, 616–617.

1526 Grant, "Report on 26th Division affair of April 20th."

1527 Rau, "Report of Action Morning of April 20th 1918."

1528 Collins, "Raid on Seicheprey."

1529 Von Bornstedt, 187.

1530 Edwards in 11 May 1918 memo.

1531 *8 Armée 2ᵉ Bureau, 6 Mai 1918, Interrogatoire d'un deserteur du 260 Rég. (78 D.R.)*, SHD 19 N 1411.

1532 *8 Armée 2ᵉ Bureau, 11 Mai 1918, Compte rendu d'interrogatoire sommaire d'un prisonnier du 260 R*, SHD 19N 1411.

1533 Strickland, 147.

1534 Colonel Parker quoted in "C and D Companies Picked for Slaughter," *Hartford Courant*, 22 April 1920.

1535   Coan says about 20 to 25 Bristol soldiers were captured. Coan, 52; "41 More New England Men in Casualty List", *Boston Globe*, 13 May 1918; "Surprises Family; Finds Mother Dead, Bristol Soldier First Prisoner Home-Escaped from Camp," *Hartford Courant*, 3 January 1919.

1536   Hinman, 64.

1537   Emerson G. Taylor, "A Brief History of the 102nd Regiment Band."

1538   "Sends Corrected List of Soldiers of the 102d Who Fell at Seicheprey," June 1, 1918, 1.

1539   Edwards 11 May, 1918, Memo, Division Commander, TO: Commanding General, 1st Army Corps, American E.F., Subject: Report on an attack, April 20–21, 1918, Seicheprey – Remières Wood. Box 25, 26th Division, RG 120, NARA.

1540   "Edwards letter, 11 May 1918," Box 25, 26th Division, RG 120, NARA.

1541   *Yankee Doings*, 8 (January 1927).

1542   Compare Fiske's sentiment with Major General Edwards' letter to the troops regarding "Rest and Sanitization for tired troops coming into the Corps Reserve," 18 May 1918. Brigadier General H. B. Fiske, "'Conversation with General Bamford relative 26th Division,' Memorandum for the Inspector General, 4 January 1919," Box 11, RG 200, NARA.

1543   Sibley, 323–324.

1544   Colonel Parker later referred to Major in a post-war note to Major General Edwards as "the south end of a horse travelling due north." "Nomination of Lieutenant Colonel Duncan K. Major, Jr. to be a Colonel," Congressional Testimony, April 22, 1922, 30.

1545   Erich von Ludendorff, *Ludendorff's Own Story, August 1914 – November 1918, The Great War from the Siege of Liege to the Signing of the Armistice as viewed from the Grand Headquarters of the German Army* (New York: Harper & Brothers Publishers, 1919), ii, 243.

1546   Freiherr von Ledebur, "Doc. No. 7., Army Unit "C" Headquarters."

1547   Gregory Martin, "German Strategy and Military Assessments of the American Expeditionary Force (AEF), 1917–18", *War in History*, Vol. 1, (2) July 1994, 181.

1548   8 *Armée 2ᵉ Bureau*, "6 Mai 1918, Interrogatoire d'un deserteur du 260 Reg. (78 D.R.)," SHD 19 N 1411.

1549   "Attack on Seicheprey on April 20, 1918,. Service Report. Attention Historical Section. 20 January 1922." Box 786, RG 120, NARA.

1550   All capital letters were in the report. Freiherr von Ledebur, Colonel, C of S of Army Headquarters "C", Report.

1551   Kauffman assessment. Outline of Mil. Intell. Org. of Deputy General Staff in Berlin III B. In Dennis Nolan papers, USAMHI; Samuels, 181.

1552   "Attack on Seicheprey on April 20, 1918. Service Report. Attention Historical Section." 20 January 1922.

1553   Freiherr von Ledebur, Colonel, C of S of Army Headquarters "C", Report.

1554   "Attack on Seicheprey on April 20, 1918. Service Report. Attention Historical Section."

1555   Von Borstadt, 188.

1556   Ettighoffer, 222. Translation by Jan Milles.

1557   Freiherr von Ledebur, Colonel, C of S of Army Headquarters "C", Report.

1558   Artillery Commander No. 78, "Report on our Operation," 37–39.

1559   *SRA, Bulletin de Renseignements N 169 – N 170, du 20 au 22 Avril 1918 de 16 Heures à 16 Heures*, SHD 22 N 1756.

1560   Taylor, 131; Kernan and Samson, *103rd Field Artillery*, 40–41.

1561   *History of the 102nd, United States Infantry*, 15.

1562   "Telephone Log," Box 42; "Telephone message," Box 19.

1563   Grant, "Report on 26th Division affair of April 20th."

1564   "Bowditch letter to Colonel Craig."

1565   "A lot of hot air." "Bowditch letter to Colonel Craig."

1566   Strickland, 147.

1567   Rau, "Report of Action Morning of April 20th 1918"; Strickland, 146–147. Also captured in *History of the 102nd, United States Infantry*, 14; "Colonel Parker Memo to Brigadier General Traub."

1568   "*Rapport du Colonel Bertrand, 20 et 21 Avril 1918.*"

1569   *Colonel* de Chambrun and *Captaine* de Marenches, *The American Army in the European Conflict* (New York: The MacMillan Co., 1919), 132.

1570   Major Rau was killed that summer by an artillery round. Grant, "Report on 26th Division affair of April 20th."

1571   Grant, "Report on 26th Division affair of April 20th."

1572   Ferrell, *In the Company of Generals*, 51.

1573   Ferrell, *In the Company of Generals*.

1574   Ferrell, *In the Company of Generals*, 52.

1575   "Colonel Fiske, of training section, with him white slave, Major Williams, called…" Apparently, Stackpole had issues with Fiske's treatment of his junior staff. Ferrell, *In the Company of Generals*, 50.

1576   du Boisrouvray, 360–361.

1577   Sibley, 132.

1578 Stallings was a Marine who was seriously wounded and lost his leg. He wrote the classic book on the American experience of the war, *The Doughboys*. Stallings, 55.

1579 Parker memoirs, USMA, Parker File, 201–202.

1580 du Boisrouvray, 353–354.

1581 Translation by Monique Duval. GQG 24 Avril 1918, Note, N 25992, SHD.

1582 *Général* Gérard quote in du Boisrouvray, 342.

1583 "Relief and Regrouping of 26th Division," French Military Mission with American Army, Chaumont, May 1, 1918, *US Army in the World War*, iii, 621–622.

1584 "Recommendations for Changes in Rambucourt Zone," May 3, 1918, *US Army in the World War*, iii, 623–624.

1585 "Comment on Seicheprey Raid," April 30, 1918, *US Army in the World War*, iii, 621.

1586 "Report of Action, 20th – 21st April, 1918," General Traub, in Strickland, 148–150.

1587 Brigadier General Peter E. Traub, Memorandum, May 1, 1918, Box 42, 26th Division, RG 120, NARA.

1588 James G. Harbord, *The American Army in France, 1917–1919* (Boston: Little, Brown, and Company, 1936), 199.

1589 Major William W. Wade May 16, 1918, To C.O. 101st and 102nd Inf. Transmitted. Box 42. 26th Division, RG 120, NARA.

1590 Rogers, 140; Herbert, 105.

1591 Ben B. Fischer (compiled by). *Hände Hoch! Hands Up! An American Hero's Tale of the Great War, The Story of James F. Carty, D.S.C. [Distinguished Service Cross]*, (Privately printed), 23.

1592 General Orders No. 40, 13 May 1918, Strickland, 152–153.

1593 Parker memo, 30 September 1933, Parker files, USMA.

1594 Parker quoted in Hills, *The War History of the 102nd Regiment*, 15.

1595 Sergeant Edman in Coan, 55–56.

1596 Major Murphy, April 27, 1918, Box 55, 26th Division, RG 120, NARA.

1597 Parker memoirs, Parker file, USMA.

1598 Parker, "Raid April 20–21st on Beaumont Zone."

1599 Fred Tyrrell Papers, 102nd Regiment files, USAMHI; Stallings, 53.

1600 102nd Infantry Memos regarding 18th Infantry Disciplinary Prisoners, RG 120, NARA.

1601 Strickland, 136–137; Coan, 53.

1602 Stallings, 55.

1603 Ray Stannard Baker, *Woodrow Wilson, Life and Letters, Armistice, Vol. 8* (New York: Doubleday, Doran & Company, Inc., 1939), 96, 103, 119.

1604 Lloyd George quoted in David F. Trask, *The AEF & Coalition Warmaking 1917–1918* (Lawrence, KS: University Press of Kansas, 1993), 59; Smythe, 108.

1605 TNA WO 256/30, Field Marshal Haig dairy, Saturday 20th April 1918, 55; Historical Section Army War College, 26.

1606 Captain Taylor retired as a colonel and wrote the most complete work on the 26th Division, *New England in France*. *United States v. John J. Gallant*.

1607 *United States v. John J. Gallant*.

1608 *United States v. John J. Gallant*.

1609 *United States v. John J. Gallant*.

1610 *United States v. John J. Gallant*.

1611 Ferrell, *In the Company of Generals*, 110–111.

1612 Taylor, 131.

1613 History incorrectly listed XXXVII. Mauer, 182.

1614 Mauer.

1615 Mauer, 182–183.

1616 French Aviation Reports, SHD.

1617 Collins, "Raid on Seicheprey."

1618 Mauer, 183.

1619 "Critique on Exercises of Aerial Liaison with Infantry Held on 1st June, 1918, by 26th Division and 1st Observation Group," Box 37, 26th Division, RG 120, NARA.

1620 "Infantry-Aeroplane laison." Malin Craig, Chief of Staff, Box 26, 26th Division, RG 120, NARA.

1621 Captain Eddie Rickenbacker, *Fighting the Flying Circus* (New York, Frederick A. Stokes Co., [*c*.1919]; reprint, Chicago: R.R. Donnelley & Sons Company, 1997), 262–263.

1622 "Tactical History of US Air Service," 3.

1623 "Tactical History of Air Service", Gorrell Report," 2.

1624 Mozley, 28.

1625 Wunderlich, 41.

1626 Wunderlich, 40–41.

1627 Edited by Robert H. Ferrell, Joseph Douglas Lawrence, *Fighting Soldier, The AEF in 1918* (Boulder, CO: Colorado Associated University Press, 1985), 50.

1628 Ettighoffer, 212.

1629 Ettighoffer, 237.

1630 Lieutenant Strickland was awarded the *Croix de Guerre* by Passaga. He lost the use of his right hand; and a brother. After the war he attended Yale School of Religion. State of Connecticut Military Service Record; Strickland, 147.

1631 Taylor, 132–133.

1632 Sibley, 160.

1633 LaBranche, 115–116.

1634 Havlin, 82.

1635   "Pershing to March and Baker, June 1, 1918"
       in Bland, *The Papers of George Catlett Marshall,*
       Vol. I, 139.

1636   S.L.A. Marshal, *World War I* (New York:
       American Heritage Press, 1971), 369.

1637   "Relations with Allied Governments and
       Armies."

1638   *Histories of Two Hundred and Fifty-One Divisions
       of the German Army,* 165.

1639   *Histories of Two Hundred and Fifty-One Divisions
       of the German Army,* 536.

1640   "Changes in Boundary," May 26, 1918, *US
       Army in the World War,* iii, 627.

1641   *General der Infanterie* Auler also recorded 13
       men (including one officer) killed, 3 officers
       and 73 men wounded, and one officer and 30
       men lightly wounded. *VIII Armée, 2e Bureau,
       "Interrogatoire de 3 prisonniers de 36 Rgt Lanwehr
       (5 DL) capture devant Xivray, let 16 Juin 1918,"*
       SHD 19 N 1411; Auler, 70–72; *History of
       Battery B,* 57.

1642   *Histories of Two Hundred and Fifty-One Divisions
       of the German Army,* 118–119.

1643   Fox Conner, "Relief of 26th Division," Box 17,
       26th Division, RG 120 NARA.

1644   *Order of Battle of the United States Land Forces in
       the World War American Expeditionary Forces.*

1645   *Général* Passaga General Order, in Sirois and
       McGinnis, 59.

1646   Major General Traub's relief was based on
       medical evaluation of his division's rest area
       after the Armisitice – a failure to maintain
       proper sanitary conditions. Arthur A. Service
       letter to Honorable John S. Monagan, *United
       States v. John J. Gallant.*

1647   Fred Tyrrell Comments to Army Service
       Experiences Questionnaire, USAMHI.

1648   His successor, US Marine Colonel Hiram
       Bearss, had an equally impressive military
       record. Bearss was the recipient of the Medal
       of Honor based on actions against Philippine
       rebels in 1900. Colonel John H. Parker,
       General Orders No. 23, August 8, 1918.

1649   *History of 102nd Field Artillery,* 53.

1650   Harbord, 199.

1651   Rexmond C. Cochrane, *The 89th Division
       Comes Into the Line* (Army Chemical Center,
       MD: U.S. Army Chemical Corps Historical
       Office, 1958), 10.

1652   *History of the 89th Division,* 58.

1653   *History of the 89th Division,* 56.

1654   Cochrane, *The 89th Division Comes Into the
       Line,* 12, 30–31, 41.

1655   Pershing, II, 238.

1656   Keller, "A German Reply to Gen. Pershing's
       War Story."

1657   "Disposition of 89th Division," August 4, 1918,
       US Army in the World War, ii, 728–730.

1658   Yardley, *The American Black Chamber,* 43–45.

1659   Francis P. Duffy, *Father Duffy's Story* (Garden
       City, NY: Garden City Publishing Co., Inc.
       1919), 233, 236; Henry J. Reilly, *Americans All,
       The Rainbow at War* (Columbus, OH: F.J. Heer
       Printing Co., 1936), 563.

1660   *History of the 89th Division,* 60.

1661   Dale E. Wilson, *Treat 'Em Rough! The Birth
       of American Armor, 1917–20* (Novato, CA:
       Presidio Press, 1990), 96–98.

1662   Hallas, *Squandered Victory,* 36; Blumenson, 583.

1663   Auler, 76.

1664   Dennis Nolan quoted in Finnegan, 174.

1665   Brigadier-General C.M. Wagstaff, British
       military liaison to GHQ AEF, was most likely
       the source of this assessment. "Notes on
       American Offensive Operations," TNA WO
       106/528.

1666   The comments are cogent when Colonel
       Conner and Major Bowditch assessed
       the liaison failings by the 104th Infantry
       at Apremont on 10–13 April. "Notes on
       American Offensive Operations."

1667   "Notes on American Offensive Operations."

1668   Stepkes and Menzel, 245.

1669   Generalmajor Paulus von Stolzmann, Möller,
       382–383.

1670   A list of *Kirschblüte* awards was not acquired in
       the post-war records exchange. Oberleutnant
       Friedrich Bruns, *Pour le Mérite,* Möller,
       164–165.

1671   *Order of Battle of the United States Land Forces in
       the World War American Expeditionary Forces.*

1672   King, 30–31; 77–78.

1673   Clemenceau quoted in King, 106.

1674   LaBranche, 118.

1675   Heywood Broun, *Our Army at the Front* (New
       York: Charles Scribner's Sons, 1919), 226.

1676   Beckles Willson, *America's Ambassadors to France
       (1777–1927)* (London: John Murray, 1928),
       423.

1677   *L'Action Française* in Willson, 423–424.

1678   Pershing, II, 16.

1679   George Marshall quoted in The Papers of
       George Catlett Marshall, 366.

1680   Von Gallwitz, 316.

1681   Kelly, 123.

1682   Bland, *The Papers of George Catlett Marshall,* Vol.
       I, 253.

1683   Benwell, 72–74.

1684   A.E.R. Boak, review of *New England in France,
       1917–1919;* in *The American Historical Review,*
       No. 3, April *1921,* 594–595.

1685   Maher, 2–3.

1686 Maher, 2.

1687 Maher, 5.

1688 Maher, 6–8.

1689 Kelly, 122.

1690 Bullard, 174–176; "Bullard vs. Edwards," *Yankee Doings*, Vol. 6 (6) June 1925, 11.

1691 T. Howard Kelly, "Why General Edwards Was Sent Home," *The New McClure's*, November 1928, 122.

1692 "Bullard vs. Edwards."

1693 Hunter Liggett, *Commanding an American Army: Recollections of the World War* (Boston: Houghton Mifflin, 1925); Ferrell, *In the Company of Generals*, 193.

1694 *Saturday Evening Post* carried the story from April to July 1927. The April 30, 1927 and May 7, 1927 editions were the contentious issues for *Yankee Doings* readers. "Veritas" in *Yankee Doings*, 1927, 7.

1695 John H. Smith, "An Open Letter to Gen. Liggett," *Yankee Doings*, Vol. 8 (6) June 1927, 13–14.

1696 Diablo, "They're At It Again," *Yankee Doings*, Vol. 8 (6) June 1927, 17.

1697 Major General Hunter Liggett, *A.E.F., Ten Years Ago in France* (New York: Dodd, Mead and Company, 1928), 67.

1698 Gardiner, 32.

1699 Irene's sister Gladys also married a 26th Division veteran, Lieutenant Russell Harmon of Company C, 104th Infantry; Gardiner, 32–33; "Doughnut Queen YD Bride," *Yankee Doings*, Vol. 2 (6) June 1921.

1700 Stubby the dog was never mentioned anywhere in any 26th Division archive reviewed by the author. All written sources were from the media. Smithsonian Institution, National Museum of American History, Stubby exhibit.

1701 Jack Pearl, *Battleground World War I, The Exciting Saga of the A.E.F. in France* (Derby, CT: Monarch Books, Inc. 1964), 30–31.

1702 Message from Governor John Dempsey, 20 April 1968.

1703 Edwards letter to Major Gallant, 10 February 1919, Box 15, Edwards Collection, MHS.

1704 *United States v. John J. Gallant.*

1705 He was remembered as Lieutenant Colonel Gallant, retired leader of the Philippine Constabulary. "Lt. Col. Gallant Taken By Death After Illness."

1706 Application for Relief from Court-Martial Findings and/or Sentence under the provisions of Title 10, United States Code, Section 869, GCM 1971/1607, *United States v. John J. Gallant.*

1707 Arthur A. Service letter, RG 153, NARA.

1708 Russ Havoured, "WWI 'Coward' Cleared," *Hartford Courant*, August 9, 1972, 1. The entire file never revealed anything about Gallant or his whereabouts after the court-martial. *United States v. John J. Gallant.*

1709 "Craig, Retiring, Aims to Keep Mouth Shut," *New York Times*, June 24, 1939.

1710 Secretary of War Stimson served as a Colonel of Artillery in World War 1. Katherine Tupper Marshall, *Together, Annals of an Army Wife* (New York: Tupper and Love, Inc. 1946), 251.

1711 Colonel John H. Parker career summary, Box 15, Edwards Papers, MHS.

1712 *Infantry Journal*, February 1920. Box 25, 102nd Infantry, RG 120, NARA.

1713 General George Patton's words regarding moral courage are germane: å "Moral courage is the most valuable and usually the most absent characteristic in men." Colonel "Gatling Gun" Parker, Memories of the Service, Draft, 10 May 1937. 213. West Point Archives.

1714 English translation of "Divisionsbefehl Nr. 3, 18. April. 18" is provided in "Divisional Order No. 3, April 18, 1918," Box 159, RG 165, NARA.

BIBLIOGRAPHY

ARCHIVAL AND MANUSCRIPT SOURCES

BOSTON PUBLIC LIBRARY, Boston, MA
COLONEL ROBERT R. McCORMICK RESEARCH CENTER, Wheaton, IL
Lieutenant Thomas W. Ryan Memoirs
CONNECTICUT STATE LIBRARY, Hartford, CT
State Archive Records, Record Group 12, War Records Department
CORNELL UNIVERSITY HISTORICAL ARCHIVES, Ithaca, NY
Edward Bowditch Papers
LIBRARY OF CONGRESS, MANUSCRIPTS DIVISION, Washington DC
Robert Lee Bullard Papers
John J. Pershing Papers
MASSACHUSETTS HISTORICAL SOCIETY, Boston, MA
General Clarence R. Edwards Papers
Thomas and Joann Wallace Collection
Archives – Museum Branch, Historical Services, The Adjutant General's Office, Massachusetts,
    Concord, MA
MUSÉE DE L'AIR ET DE L'ESPACE, Le Bourget, France
Eugène Pépin Papers
NATIONAL AIR AND SPACE MUSEUM, Washington DC
NATIONAL ARCHIVES AND RECORDS ADMINISTRATION, College Park, MD
Record Group 117, Records of the American Battle Monuments Commission
Record Group 120, Records of the American Expeditionary Forces (World War I)
Record Group 153, Records of the Office of the Judge Advocacy General (Army)
Record Group 165, Records of the War Department General and Special Staffs
Record Group 200, National Archives Gift Collection
THE NATIONAL ARCHIVES, London, United Kingdom
War Office Papers (WO)
NIEDERSACHSISCHES STAATSARCHIV, Oldenburg, Germany
SERVICE HISTORIQUE DE LA DÉFENCE (SHD), Vincennes, France
THE SALVATION ARMY NATIONAL ARCHIVES, Alexandria, VA
WEST HAVEN VETERAN'S MUSEUM AND LEARNING CENTER, West Haven, CT
UNITED STATES AIR FORCE ACADEMY (USAFA) LIBRARY, USAFA, CO
UNITED STATES MILITARY ACADEMY (USMA) LIBRARY, West Point, NY
U.S ARMY MILITARY HISTORY INSTITUTE (USAMHI), Carlisle, PA
Frank Sibley Photo Album

CONTEMPORARY PUBLISHED SOURCES

Aerial Observation for Artillery, Based on the French Edition of December 29, 1917. Paris: Imprimerie Nationale, May 1918.

"The American Victory at Seicheprey," *The Literary Digest*, 57 (May 4, 1918).

Andraud, Henry. *Quand on fusillait les innocents*. Paris: Éditions Gallimard, 1935.

Auler, Carl, General der Infanterie. *Die 5. Preusziche Landwehre Division im Weltkriege 1914–1918*. Stuttgart: Belker A.G., 1923.

Being the Narrative of Battery A of the 101st Field Artillery. Cambridge, MA: Brattle Press, 1919.

Baynes, Ernst Harold. *Animal Heroes of the Great War*. New York: Macmillan Company, 1925.

Benwell, Harry A. *History of the Yankee Division*. Boston: The Cornhill Company, 1919.

du Boisrouvray, Alain. "Avec la 26e D.I. Americaine," *Revue des Deux Mondes*. Paris: 15 Septembre 1933.

Bonney, Frank E., Major. "Operations of the 35th Division in the First Phase of the Meuse Argonne," *The Infantry School, Advanced Officers' Course. 1922–1923*.

Booth, Evangeline and Grace Livingston Hill. *The War Romance of the Salvation Army*. Philadelphia: J.B. Lippincott Company, 1919.

von Bornstedt, Gunther. *Reserve. Infanterie. Regiment 259*. Berlin: Verlag von Gerhard Stalling, 1926.

Broun, Heywood. *Our Army at the Front*. New York: Charles Scribner's Sons, 1919.

Bullard, Robert L., Major General. *Personalities and Reminiscences of the War*. Garden City, NY: Doubleday, Page and Company, 1925.

Bulletin of the Aerial Photography Department in the Field. Washington DC: GPO, 1918.

Butler, Alban B., Captain. *"Happy days!" A humorous narrative in drawings of the progress of American arms, 1917–1919*. Washington DC: Society of the First Division, A.E.F., 1928.

"Buy Liberty Bonds," *The Outlook*, Vol. 118 (18) May 1, 1918.

Chamberlin, Joseph Edgar. *The Only Thing for a Man to Do, The Story of Raymond Chamberlin*. Boston: privately printed, 1921.

de Chambrun, Colonel, and Captain de Marenches. *The American Army in the European Conflict*. New York: The MacMillan Co., 1919.

Cheatham, B.F., Colonel. *Historical Data 104th U.S. Infantry, AEF*. N.p.: 1919.

Chef des Generalstabs des Feldheere. *Der Angriff im Stellungskrieg, 'Part 14 (Provisional) of the Manual of Position Warfare for All Arms.'* 1 January 1918.

Cole, Ralph D. and W. C. Howells. *The Thirty-Seventh Division in the World War 1917–1918*. Columbus, OH: F. J. Heer Printing Co., 1926.

Cushing, John T., and Arthur F. Stone, ed. *Vermont in the World War*. Burlington, VT: Free Press Printing Company, 1919.

Dennet, Carl P. *Prisoners of the Great War*. Boston: Houghton Mifflin Company, 1919.

Duffy, Francis P. *Father Duffy's Story*. Garden City, NY: Garden City Publishing Co., 1919.

Ellis, O.O., Captain, and Captain E.B. Garey. *The Plattsburg Manual: A Handbook for Military Training*. New York: The Century Co., 1917.

English, George H., Jr. *History of the 89th Division. U.S.A.* Denver, CO: Smith-Brooks Printing Co., 1920.

Foch, Marshal. *The Principles of War*. London: Chapman & Hall Ltd., 1920.

von Gallwitz, Max, General der Artillerie. *Erleben im Westen, 1916–1918*. Berlin: Verlag von E.S. Mittler & Sohn, 1932.

Gardiner, Alexander. "The Girl Who Wore O.D.", *The American Legion Magazine*, 4 (April 1928).

Georgc, Albert E. and Captain Edwin H. Cooper. *Pictorial History of the Twenty-Sixth Division United States Army*. Boston: Ball Publishing Company, 1920.

German Army Handbook April 1918. Reprinted London: Arms and Armour Press, 1977.

Hahn, J.E., Major. *The Intelligence Service Within the Canadian Corps.* Toronto: Macmillan Company of Canada, 1930.

Handbook of the M. L. Stokes 3-Inch Trench Mortar Equipments. London: H.M. Stationery Office, 1920.

Havlin, Arthur C. *The History of Company A, 102d Machine Gun Battalion, Twenty-Sixth Division, A.E.F.* Boston: Harry C. Rodd and Assoc., 1928.

Herbert, Craig S. *Eyes of the Army: A Story about the Observation Balloon Service of World War I,* Lafayette Hill, PA: privately printed, 1986.

Hills, Ratcliffe M. *The War History of The 102d Regiment United States Infan*try. Hartford, CT: privately printed, 1924.

Hinman, Jesse R., Sergeant. *Ranging in France with Flash and Sound.* Portland, OR: Press of Dunham Printing Co., 1919.

Historical Section Army War College. *The Genesis of American First Army.* Washington DC: Government Printing Office, 1929.

Histories of Two Hundred and Fifty-One Divisions of the German Army which Participated in the War, 1914–1918. Washington DC: Government Printing Office, 1920.

History of Battery B, One Hundred Third Field Artillery Twenty-Sixth Division. Providence, RI: E.L. Freeman Co., 1922.

History of the 101st United States Engineers, American Expeditionary Forces 1917–1918–1919. Cambridge, MA: University Press, 1926.

History of the 103rd Infantry, 1917–1919. Boston: H.I. Hymans, 1919.

History of the One Hundred Second Field Artillery July, 1917—April, 1919. Boston: privately printed, 1927.

Hoffman, Conrad. *In the Prison Camps of Germany.* New York: Association Press, 1920.

Howe, M.A. De Wolfe. *Memoirs of the Harvard Dead in the War Against Germany,* Vol. 3 Cambridge, MA: Harvard University Press, 1922.

Instruction sur le Ballon Captif Allonge Type R. Washington DC: Government Printing Office, 1918.

Janis, Elsie. *The Big Show, My Six Months with the American Expeditionary Forces.* New York: Cosmopolitan Book Corporation, 1919.

Joffre, Joseph. *The Personal Memoirs of Joffre, Field Marshal of the French Army.* Vol 1. New York: Harper & Brothers Publishers, 1932.

Johnson, Douglas Wilson. *Battlefields of the World War, Western and Southern Fronts: A Study in Military Geography.* New York: Oxford University Press, 1921.

Kelly, T. Howard. "Why General Edwards Was Sent Home," *The New McClure's,* 61 (November 1928).

Kernan, W.F. and Henry T. Samson. *History of the 103rd Field Artillery (Twenty-Sixth Division, A.E.F.) World War 1917–1919.* Providence, RI: Remington Printing Co., 1919.

von Kuhl, H., General der Infantrie. *Der deutsche Generalstab in Vorbereitung und Durchfuhrung des Weltkrieges.* Berlin, Verlag von Ernst Siegfried Mittler und Sohn, 1920.

LaBranche, Ernest E., Corporal. *An American Battery in France.* Worcester, MA: Belisle Printing & Publishing Co., 1923.

Laffargue, André, Capitaine. "The Attack in Trench Warfare," *Infantry Journal,* 13 (July 1916).

Liggett, Hunter, Major General. *A.E.F., Ten Years Ago in France.* New York: Dodd, Mead and Company, 1928.

———, *Commanding an American Army: Recollections of the World War.* Boston: Houghton Mifflin Co., 1925.

Ludendorff, Erich von, Quartermaster General of the German Army. *Ludendorff's Own Story, August 1914–November 1918: The Great War from the Siege of Liege to the Signing of the Armistice as viewed from the Grand Headquarters of the German Army.* Vol. 2. New York: Harper & Brothers Publishers, 1919.

Maher, Augustin F. *When Connecticut Stopped the Hun, Battle of Seicheprey April 20–21, 1918.* New Haven, CT: Press of S. Z. Field, 1919.

Markle, Clifford M. *A Yankee Prisoner in Hunland.* New Haven, CT: Yale University Press, 1920.

Marshall, George C. *Memoirs of My Services in the World War, 1917–1918.* Boston: Houghton Mifflin Co., 1976.

McCarthy, Robert J. *A History of Troop A Cavalry, Connecticut National Guard, and Its Service in the Great War as Co. D. 102d Machine Gun Battalion.* New Haven, CT: Tuttle, Morehouse and Taylor, Co., 1919.

McKenna, Fred Ambrose, ed. *Battery -A- 103rd Field Artillery in France.* Providence, RI: Livermore and Knight Co., 1919.

The Means of Communication between Aeroplanes and the Ground. Edited at Army War College. Washington DC: Government Printing Office, 1917.

Merrill, Charles E., ed. '*Excerpts from the Personal Memoirs of Charles Leo Boucher.*' N.p. Edited transcription, 2002.

Möller, Hanns. *Die Geschichte der Ritter des Ordens, pour le merite im Weltkrieg 1914–1918.* Berlin: Bernard & Graefe, 1935.

Monclin, Roger. *Les Damnés de la Guerre, Les Crimes de la Justice Militaire.* Paris: Mignolet & Storz, 1935.

Moretti, Onorio, Captain. *Notes on Training Field Artillery Details.* New Haven, CT: Yale University Press, 1917.

Mozley, George, Private. *Our Miracle Battery.* Lowell, MA: Sullivan Brothers Printers, 1920.

Notes on Anti-Aircraft Guns. Compiled at the Army War College from the Latest Available Information. April, 1917. Washington DC: Government Printing Office, 1917.

Office of Chief of Staff, Executive Division, Intelligence Branch. "American Participation in the War, French Attitude," *Weekly Intelligence Summary,* March 30, 1918.

Official History of 82nd Division American Expeditionary Forces. Indianapolis, IN: The Bobbs Merrill Company, 1919.

Parker, John, H., 1st Lieutenant *Gatling Gun Detachment Fifth Army Corps at Santiago, With a Few Unvarnished Truths Concerning that Expedition.* Kansas City, MO: Hudson Kimberly Publishing Co., 1898.

————, Major. *Trained Citizen Soldiery.* Menasha, WI: George Banta Publishing Co. 1916.

Passaga, Fenelon, General. *The Cavalry of Verdun, The Americans around Verdun.* Paris: Charles-Lavauzelle, 1927.

Pétain, Henri Philippe, Marshal of France. *Verdun.* New York: The Dial Press, 1930.

Pershing, John J. *My Experiences in the World War.* 2 vols. New York: Frederick A. Stokes Co., 1931.

Porter, Harold E. *Aerial Observation: The Airplane Observer, the Balloon Observer, and the Army Corps Pilot.* New York: Harper & Brother Publishers, 1921.

Powell, E. Alexander, Major. *The Army Behind the Army.* New York: Charles Scribner's Sons, 1919.

Réau, R.-G. *Les crimes des conseils de guerre.* Paris, 1926.

Reilly, Henry J. *Americans All, The Rainbow at War.* Columbus, OH: F.J. Heer Printing Co., 1936.

Report of the Philippine Commission 1906, Fifth District Misamis Province, 15 June 1905. Washington DC: Government Printing Office, 1906.

Rickenbacker, Eddie, Captain. *Fighting the Flying Circus*. New York: Frederick A. Stokes Co., [*c.*1919];
    reprinted Chicago: R.R. Donnelley & Sons Company, 1997.

Roosevelt, Kermit. *War in the Garden of Eden*. New York: Charles Scribner's Sons, 1919.

Roosevelt, Theodore, Lieutenant Colonel. *Average Americans*, New York: G.P. Putnam's Sons, 1919.

Rouvier, Jacques, Captain. *Present-Day Warfare: How an Army Trains and Fights*. New York: Charles
    Scribner's Sons, 1918.

Samson, Henry T., and George C. Hull. *The War Story of C Battery, One Hundred and Third U.S. Field
    Artillery*. Providence, RI: Plimpton Press, 1920.

Die Schlacten und Gefecte des Grossen Krieges 1914–1918. Berlin: Verlag von Hermann Sact, 1919.

Sheahan, Henry. *A Volunteer Poilu*. Boston: Houghton Mifflin Co., 1916.

A Short History & Photographic Record of the 102nd U.S. Field Artillery – 1917. Cambridge, MA: The
    University Press, 1918.

"The Shotgun Goes to War," *Baseball Magazine*, 21 (July 1918).

Sibley, Frank P. *With the Yankee Division in France*. Boston: Little, Brown, and Company, 1919.

Sirois, Edward D., Lieutenant and Corporal William McGinnis. *Smashing Through "The World War"
    with Fighting Battery C. 102nd F.A. "Yankee Division" 1917–1918–1919*. Salem, MA: The Meek
    Press, 1919.

Society of the First Division. *History of the First Division during the World War 1917–1919*.
    Philadelphia: John C. Winston Co., 1922.

Spaulding, Oliver Lyman, Colonel, and Colonel John Womack Wright. *The Second Division American
    Expeditionary Force in France 1917–1919*. Reprinted Nashville TN: The Battery Press, 1989.

Spencer, E.W. *The History of Gas Attacks Upon the American Expeditionary Forces During the World War,
    Part I*. Edgewood Arsenal, MD: Chemical Warfare Service, 1928.

Stepkes, Dr., and Major L. Menzel. *Geschichte des Reserve-Infanterie-Regiments Nr. 258*. Selbstverlag,
    Stammgruppe Koln des Gesamtverbandes ehem. 258er, 1935.

Strickland, Daniel W. *Connecticut Fights: The Story of the 102nd Regiment*. New Haven, CT:
    Quinnipiack Press, 1930.

Stringer, Harry R., ed. *Heroes All! A Compendium of Names and Official citations of soldiers and citizens
    of the United States and of her allies who were decorated by the American Government for exceptional
    heroism and conspicuous service above and beyond the call of duty in the War with Germany, 1917–1919*.
    Washington, DC: Fassett Publishing Co., 1919.

Study and Utilization of Aerial Photographs. Paris: Imprimerie Nationale, 1918.

Taylor, Emerson Gifford. *New England in France 1917–1919: A History of the Twenty Sixth Division
    U.S.A.* Boston: Houghton Mifflin Co., 1920.

United States Army. Office of Military History. *United States Army in the World War, 1917–1919*. Vol.
    2, *Policies;* Vol. 3, *Training;* Vol. 12. *Reports, Pt. 1.* Washington, DC: Center of Military History,
    reprinted 1989, 1991.

United States Army. American Expeditionary Forces. General Staff. G-2. *Summary of Air Information:
    March, April May, 1918*. Chaumont, France: 1918.

*United States. Senate. Hearing before the Committee on Military Affairs United States Senate, Sixty-seventh
    Congress, Second Session, Relative to the Nomination of Lieut. Col. Duncan K. Major, Jr. to be a Colonel,
    April 25–May 6, 1922*. Washington DC: Government Printing Office, 1922.

United States War Department. *Order of Battle of the United States Land Forces in the World War; Zone of
    the Interior*. Vol. 3, part 1. Washington DC: Government Printing Office, 1949.

————, *Order of Battle of the United States Land Forces in the World War, American Expeditionary Forces,
    Divisions*. Washington DC: Government Printing Office, 1931.

————, "Report of the Director of Military Aeronautics," 3 November 1918. In *Annual Report of
    the Secretary of War for the Fiscal Year 1918*. Washington DC: Government Printing Office, 1918.

Utilization and Role of Artillery Aviators in Trench Warfare. August 1917. Washington DC: Government Printing Office, 1917.

Viereck, George Sylvester. *As They Saw Us; Foch, Ludendorff and Other Leaders Write Our War History.* Garden City, NY: Doubleday, Doran and Co., 1929.

Vocabulary of German Military Terms and Abbreviations (2nd Edition), General Staff (Intelligence), General Headquarters, July 1918. Reprinted London: Imperial War Museum and Nashville, TN: Battery Press, 1995.

Wainwright, Philip S., 1st Lieutenant ed. *History of the 101st Machine Gun Battalion.* Hartford, CT: The 101st Machine Gun Battalion Association, 1922.

Walsh, J.A. *"Le Crapauillot" 101st T. M. B. War Chronicle.* Lewiston, ME: privately printed, 1919.

Washburn, Slater. *One of the YD.* Boston: Houghton Mifflin Co., 1919.

Willcox, Cornelis De Witt. *A French-English Military Technical Dictionary.* Washington DC: Government Printing Office, 1917.

Woolf, Samuel Johnson. *Drawn from Life.* New York: Whittlesey House, 1932.

World War Records, First Division A.E.F. Regular. Vol. 4; Vol. 11; Vol. 14. Washington DC: War College, 1930.

World War Records, First Division A.E.F. Regular. German Documents. Vol. 1. Washington DC: War College, 1930.

Wunderlich, Raymond, Private. *From Trench and Dugout.* Stockton, CA: privately printed, 1919.

Yardley, Herbert O. *The American Black Chamber.* Indianapolis: Bobbs-Merrill Co., 1931.

SECONDARY SOURCES

Albertine, Connell. *The Yankee Doughboy.* Boston: Branden Press, 1968.

Ashworth, Tony. *Trench Warfare 1914–1918, The Live and Let Live System.* London: Pan Books, 2000.

Bailey, J.B.A. *Field Artillery and Firepower.* Oxford, UK: Military Press, 1989.

Baker, Ray Stannard. *Woodrow Wilson, Life and Letters, Armistice.* Vol. 8. New York: Doubleday, Doran & Company, 1939.

Bland, Larry I., ed. *The Papers of George Catlett Marshall,* Vol. I. "The Soldierly Spirit". Baltimore, MD: Johns Hopkins University Press, 1981.

Blumenson, Martin. *The Patton Papers 1885–1940.* Boston: Houghton Mifflin Company, 1972.

Bruce, Robert B. *A Fraternity of Arms: America and France in the Great War.* Lawrence, KS: University Press of Kansas, 2003.

Bull, Stephen. *German Assault Troops of the First World War, Stosstrupptaktik: The First Stormtroopers.* Stroud, Gloucestershire, UK: Spellmount, 2007.

Canfield, Bruce N. *U.S. Infantry Weapons of the First World War.* Lincoln, RI: Andrew Mowbray Publishers, 2000.

Carter, Russell Gordon. *The 101st Field Artillery, A.E.F., 1917–1919.* Boston: Houghton Mifflin Co., 1940.

Cazals, Rémy and André Loez. *Dans le tranchées de 1914–1918.* Pau: Cairn, 2008.

Chaffee, Everitte S., Major. *The Egotistical Account of an Enjoyable War.* Providence, RI: Adams Company, 1951.

Churchill, Winston S. *The World Crisis, 1915.* New York: Charles Scribner's Sons, 1929.

Clark, Michael H. *The Personal War of John J. Pershing.* MA Thesis, University of Wisconsin, 1973.

Coan, Francis M. "A Few Men in the Great War: The Experiences of the Soldiers of Company D (Bristol), 1st Connecticut National Guard Regiment, March 1917–April 1918." Masters Thesis, Southern Connecticut State College, April 1990.

Cochrane, Rexmond C. *The 1st Division at Ansauville.* Aberdeen Proving Grounds, MD: U.S. Army Chemical Corps Historical Office, 1958.

————, *The 89th Division Comes Into the Line.* Aberdeen Proving Grounds, MD: U.S. Army Chemical Corps Historical Office, 1958.

Coffman, Edward M. *The Regulars: The American Army 1898–1941.* Cambridge, MA: Belknap Press, 2004.

————, The *War to End All Wars: The American Military Experience in World War I.* Madison, WI: University of Wisconsin Press, 1986.

Cole, Hugh M. *The Lorraine Campaign.* Washington DC: Government Printing Office, 1950. (*United States Army in World War II*)

Cornebise, Alfred E. *Art From the Trenches: America's Uniformed Artists in World War I.* Madison, WI: University of Wisconsin Press, 1986.

Cron, Hermann. *Imperial German Army 1914–18, Organization, Structure, Orders-of Battle.* (Originally published as *Geschichte des Deutschen Heeres im Weltkriege 1914–1918.* Berlin, 1937). Stroud, Gloucestershire, UK: Helion and Company, 2002.

Davis, Henry Blaine, Jr. *Generals in Khaki.* Raleigh, NC: Pentland Press, 1998.

Doble, Enoch H. "Eyewitness to the Great War," in *The World Wars Remembered.* Dublin, NH: Yankee, 1979.

Doubler, Michael D. *I am the Guard: A History of the Army National Guard, 1636–2000.* Washington DC: Department of the Army, 2001.

Doughty, Robert A. *Pyrrhic Victory: French Strategy and Operations in the Great War.* Cambridge, MA: Harvard University Press, 2005.

Englander, David. "The French Soldier, 1914–18," *French History*, 1 (March 1987).

Edelman, Bernard. *Centenarians, The Story of the 20th Century by the Americans who lived it.* New York: Farrar, Straus and Giroux, 1999.

Ettighoffer, P.C. *Gespenster am Toten Mann.* Köln: Gilde, Verlag GMBH, 1931.

————, *Verdun, Das grosse Gericht.* Gutersloh, Germany: Verlag C. Vertelsmann, 1936.

Evans, Martin Marix, ed. *American Voices of World War I, Primary Source Documents 1917–1920.* Chicago: Fitzroy Dearborn Publishers, 2001.

Ferguson, Niall. *The Pity of War.* New York: Basic Books, 1999.

Ferrell, Robert H., ed. *In the Company of Generals: The World War I Diary of Pierpont L. Stackpole.* Columbia, MO: University of Missouri Press, 2009.

————, ed. Joseph Douglas Lawrence, *Fighting Soldier, The AEF in 1918.* Boulder, CO: Colorado Associated University Press, 1985.

Fifield, James H. *The Regiment: A History of the 104th U.S. Infantry, A.E.F. 1917–1919.* Springfield, MA: 104th Infantry Association, 1946.

Finnegan, Terrence J. "Military Intelligence at the Front, 1914–18," *Studies in Intelligence,* 53 (December 2009).

————, *Shooting the Front, Allied Aerial Reconnaissance in the First World War,* 2nd Edition. Stroud, Gloucestershire, UK: The History Press, 2011.

Fischer, Ben B. *Hände Hoch! Hands Up! An American Hero's Tale of the Great War, The Story of James F. Carty, D.S.C.:* privately printed, 1995.

Flicke, Wilhelm F. *War Secrets in the Ether.* Edited by Sheila Carlisle. 2 volumes. Laguna Hills, CA: Aegean Park Press, 1977.

Gröschel, Dieter H. M. *Geschichte der Königlich Bayerischen Feldfliegerabteilung 3 und Fliegerabteilung 46 Lb. Teil I Geschichte der Feldfliegerabteilung 3. 2005; Teil II Geschichte der K.B. Fliegerabteilung 46.* Charlottesville, VA: private printing, 2008.

Grotelueschen, Mark E. *The AEF Way of War*. Cambridge: Cambridge University Press, 2007.

Gudmundsson, Bruce I. *On Artillery*. Westport, CT: Praeger, 1993.

_____, *Stormtroop Tactics: Innovation in the German Army, 1914–1918*. Westport, CT: Praeger, 1989.

Hallas, James H. *Doughboy War, The American Expeditionary Force in World War I*. Boulder, CO: Lynne Rienner Publishers, 2000.

_____, *Squandered Victory: The American First Army at St. Mihiel*. Westport, CT: Praeger, 1995.

Hamady, Theodore. *The Nieuport 28, America's First Fighter*. Atglen, PA: Schiffer Military History, 2008.

Harbord, James G. *The American Army in France, 1917–1919*. Boston: Little, Brown, and Company, 1936.

Haverstock, Nathan A. *Fifty Years at the Front: The Life of War Correspondent Frederick Palmer*. Washington DC: Brassey's, 1996.

Haythornthwaite, Philip J. *The World War One Source Book*. London: Arms and Armour Press, 1996.

Heller, Charles E. *Chemical Warfare in World War I: The American Experience, 1917–1918*. Fort Leavenworth, KS: Combat Studies Institute, 1984.

Herwig, Holger H., and Neil M. Heyman, *Biographical Dictionary of World War I*. Westport, CT: Greenwood Press, 1982.

Holley, I.B., Jr. *General John M. Palmer, Citizen Soldiers and the Army of a Democracy*. Westport, CT: Greenwood Press, 1982.

Hogg, Ian V. *The Guns 1914–18*. New York: Ballantine Books, 1971.

Innes, John R. *Flash Spotters and Sound Rangers: How They Lived, Worked and Fought in the Great War*. London: George Allen & Unwin, 1997.

Jäger, Helmut *Ekungdung mit der Kamera: Die Entwicklung der Phographie zur Waffe und ihr Einsatz im 1. Weltkrieg*. Munich, Germany: Venorian VKA, 2007.

Jäger, Herbert *German Artillery of World War One*. Ramsbury, Marlborough, Wiltshire, UK: Crowood Press, 2001.

Johnson, Douglas V., II. "Training the 1st Division for World War I," in *Cantigny at Seventy Five, A Professional Discussion, May 28–29, 1993*. Chicago, IL: Robert R. McCormick Tribune Foundation, 1993.

Kahn, David. *The Codebreakers: The Story of Secret Writing*. New York: Macmillan Co., 1967.

Kedzior, Richard W. *Evolution and Endurance: The U.S. Army Division in the Twentieth Century*. Santa Monica, CA: RAND, 2000.

King, Jere Clemens. *Foch versus Clemenceau: France and German Dismemberment, 1918–1919*. Cambridge, MA: Harvard University Press, 1960.

Lupfer, Timothy T. *The Dynamics of Doctrine: The Changes in German Tactical Doctrine During the First World War*. Fort Leavenworth, KS: Combat Studies Institute, 1981.

Macnutt, Karen. *Hail & Farewell: A Salute to the 26th Yankee Division*. Boston: Macnutt Art Trust Production, 1995. [Video]

Marshal, S.L.A. *World War I*. New York: American Heritage Press, 1971.

Marshall, Katherine Tupper. *Together, Annals of an Army Wife*. New York: Tupper and Love, 1946.

Martel, Francis. *Pétain: Verdun to Vichy*. New York: E. P. Dutton & Co., Inc., 1943.

Martin, Gregory. "German Strategy and Military Assessments of the American Expeditionary Force (AEF), 1917–18," *War in History*, Vol. 1 (2) July 1994.

Maurer, Maurer., ed. *The U.S. Air Service in World War I*. Vol. 1. Washington DC: Government Printing Office, 1978.

Michelin Road Atlas France. 9th edition. London: Paul Hamlyn, 1996.

Millett, Allan R. *The General: Robert L. Bullard and Officership in the United States Army, 1881–1925.* Westport, CT: Greenwood Press, 1975.

Millotat, Christian O.E., Oberst i.G. *Understanding the Prussian-German General Staff System.* Carlisle Barracks, PA: Strategic Studies Institute, 1992.

Morgan, William A. "Invasion on the Ether: Radio Intelligence at the Battle of St. Mihiel, September 1918," *Military Affairs,* 51 (April 1987).

Mosier, John. *The Myth of the Great War.* New York: Perennial, 2002.

Moyer, Laurence. *Victory Must Be Ours: Germany in the Great War 1914–1918.* New York: Hippocrene Books, 1995.

Neiberg, Michael S. *Dance of the Furies.* Boston: Harvard University Press, 2011.

Nelson, James Carl. *Five Lieutenants.* New York: St. Martin's Press, 2012.

Nenninger, Timothy K., ed. *The Way of Duty, Honor, Country: The Memoir of Charles Pelot Summerall.* Lexington, KY: University Press of Kentucky, 2010.

_____, "Unsystematic as a Mode of Command: Commanders and the Process of Command in the American Expeditionary Forces, 1917–1918," *The Journal of Military History,* 64 (July 2000).

Occleshaw, Michael. *Armour Against Fate: British Military Intelligence in the First World War.* London: Columbus Books, 1989.

Ostendorf, Johannes. *Gedenkblätter der Stadtgemeinde Lohne. 1. Folge: Weltkrieg 1914–1918.* Oldenburg, Germany: Heimatverein, 1957.

Page, Arthur Wilson. *Our 110 Days' Fighting.* New York: Doubleday, Page & Company, 1920.

Palmer, Alan. *Victory 1918.* New York: Atlantic Monthly Press, 1998.

Patch, Joseph Dorst, Major General. *A Soldier's War.* Corpus Christi, TX: Mission Press, 1964.

Pearl, Jack. *Battleground World War I, The Exciting Saga of the A.E.F. in France.* Derby, CT: Monarch Books, 1964.

Pogue, Forrest C. *George C. Marshall: Education of a General, 1880–1939.* New York: Viking Press, 1963.

_____, ed. *George C. Marshall: Interviews and reminiscences for Forrest C. Pogue.* Lexington, VA: George C. Marshall Research Foundation, 1991.

Porch, Douglas. *The French Secret Services, From the Dreyfus Affair to the Gulf War.* New York: Farrar, Straus and Giroux, 1995.

Rogers, Horatio. *The Diary of an Artillery Scout.* North Andover, MA: privately printed, 1975.

Roosevelt, Eleanor Butler. *Day Before Yesterday;, The Reminiscences of Mrs. Theodore Roosevelt, Jr.* Garden City, NY: Doubleday & Company, 1959.

Samuels, Martin. *Command or Control? Command, Training and Tactics in the British and German Armies, 1888–1918.* London: Frank Cass, 1995.

Shay, Michael E. *A Grateful Heart: The History of a World War I Field Hospital.* Westport, CT: Greenwood Press, 2002.

_____, *Revered Commander Maligned General: The Life of Clarence Ransom Edwards 1859–1931.* Columbia, MO: University of Missouri Press, 2011.

_____, *The Yankee Division in the First World War: In the Highest Tradition.* College Station, TX: Texas A&M University Press, 2008.

Sherburne, John H., Brigadier General. *The Rambling Reminiscences of an Old Timer.* Boston: privately printed, 1961.

Smith, Richard Norton. *The Colonel: The Life and Legend of Robert R. McCormick, 1880–1955.* New York: Houghton Mifflin Co., 1997.

Smythe, Donald. *Pershing, General of the Armies.* Bloomington, IN: Indiana University Press, 1986.

Stallings, Lawrence. *The Doughboys: The Story of the AEF, 1917–1918.* New York: Harper & Row, 1963.

Sterba, Christopher M. *Good Americans: Italian and Jewish Immigrants during the First World War.* Oxford: Oxford University Press, 2003.

Stevens, Walter Barlow. *Centennial history of Missouri (the center state): One Hundred Years in the Union,* Vol. 2. St. Louis: S. J. Clarke Pub. Co., 1921.

Sumner, Ian. *The French Army, 1914–18.* London: Osprey Publishing, 1995.

Trask, David F. *The AEF & Coalition Warmaking, 1917–1918.* Lawrence, KS: University Press of Kansas, 1993.

Tuchman, Barbara W. *The Guns of August.* New York: MacMillan Co., 1962.

Venzon, Anne Cipriano, ed. *The United States in the First World War: An Encyclopedia.* New York: Garland Publishing, 1995.

Walsh, Stanley, ed. *First Over the Front, Lt. William G. Schauffler, Jr.* Bloomington, IN: AuthorHouse, 2011.

_____, "William G. 'Billy' Schauffler." *Over the Front,* 23 (Summer 2008).

War Department. War Plans Division. *"Manual for Trench Artillery," United States Army (Provisional) Part I Trench Artillery,* March 1918. Washington DC: Office of Adjutant General, 1918.

Wegner, Günter. *Stellenbesetzung Der Deutschen Heere, 1815–1939.* Vol. 1. Osnabruck, Germany: Biblio Verlag, 1990.

White, William Allen. *A Puritan in Babylon: The Story of Calvin Coolidge.* New York: Capricon Books, 1938.

Willson, Beckles. *America's Ambassadors to France, 1777–1927.* London: John Murray, 1928.

Wilson, Dale E. *Treat 'Em Rough! The Birth of American Armor, 1917–20.* Novato, CA: Presidio Press, 1990.

Wilson, John B. *Maneuver and Firepower: The Evolution of Divisions and Separate Brigades.* Washington DC: Center of Military History, United States Army, 1998.

Zabecki, David T. *The German 1918 Offensives: A case study in the operational level of war.* London: Routledge, 2006,

_____, *Steel Wind, Colonel Georg Bruchmüller and the Birth of Modern Artillery.* Westport, CT: Praeger, 1994.

Zuber, Terence. *Ardennes 1914: The Battle of the Frontiers.* Stroud, Gloucestershire, UK: Tempus Publishing, 2007.

PERIODICALS AND NEWSPAPERS

Yankee Doings, Yankee Division Veterans Association, Boston, MA

Das Regiment, Geheimes Staatsarchiv Preussischer Kulturebesitz, Berlin, GE

Boston Daily Globe

Braintree Paper

Deep River, Connecticut

The Evening World

Hartford Courant

Nachrichten fur Staat und Land Oldenburg

New York Times

San Francisco Chronicle

Stand To, Western Front Association. 92 [16 September 2011]. Laudan, Sebastian. "Landsknechte v Sportsmen: Operation Kirschblüte Seicheprey, 20 April 1918."

Stars and Stripes
The Sun
Washington Post
Washington Times Herald

PERSONAL ARCHIVES

James Controvich Library
Private 1st Class Cyril V. Finnegan letters, 1917–1918. Author's collection

WEBSITES

Battles in the Woëvre, http://www.1911encyclopedia.org/Battles_In_The_Woëvre.
Canon de 105 mle 1913 Schneider (L13S) Field Gun (1913), http://www.militaryfactory.com/armor/detail.asp?armor_id=467
"Cold words from McCain ancestor," http://bristolnews.blogspot.com/2008/04/cold-words-from-mccain-ancestor.html
Cyanogen Chloride – An Overview, CYANOGENCHLORIDEforweb_000.
15cm. schwere Feld Haubitze 1913, http://www.lovettartillery.com/15cm_schwere_Feldhaubitze_1913.html
De Flirey à Apremont - Le bois de Mortmare (2), http://jmpicquart.pagesperso-orange.fr/Flirey2.htm.
Flirey le drame, http://faurillon.com/Flirey.htm#font
Fold 3, www.fold3.com
Gazette des Ardennes, 1918, http://diglit.ub.uni-heidelberg.de/diglit/feldztggarzarden1918
Granatwerfer 16: the "Bombthrower," http://www.kaiserscross.com/246822.html
Les Américains en 1918, http://www.14–18mag.fr/2013/01/les-americains-en-1918/
Le combat pour Berry Au Bac, Juvincourt et la côte 108, http://chtimiste.com/batailles1418/combats/berryaubac1917.htm
Les fusillés de la Grande Guerre ; http://www.cndp.fr/pour-memoire/les-fusilles-de-la-grande-guerre/la-diversite-des-fusilles-presentation-de-cas-individuels/le-refus-dobeissance.html
Military Times Hall of Valor, http://projects.militarytimes.com/citations-medals-awards/
Nick Forder notes in *Cross and Cockade International*, October 12, 2009, http://www.crossandcockade.com/forum/forum_posts.asp?TID=134#sthash.qb5oI95N.dpbs
The Prussian Machine, http://home.comcast.net/~jcviser/page_9.htm
SHDGR GR 26 N 656 [63rd RI] http://www.memoiredeshommes.sga.defense.gouv.fr/fr/arkotheque/inventaires/ead_ir_consult.php?&ref=SHDGR__GR_26_N_II
Stormtrooper Tactics of World War I, http://johnsmilitaryhistory.com/stormtrooper.html

INDEX

Page references in italics refer to captions. When a term is used frequently, the page references given refer to the most germane definition or information and other entries are indicated as *passim*.

Personnel Index

Page references in italics refer to captions. Translation of ranks to American Army equivalents is contained in square brackets.